Glencoe Spanish 2

¡Buen viaje!

Protase E. Woodford
Conrad J. Schmitt

Glencoe

New York, New York   Columbus, Ohio   Chicago, Illinois   Woodland Hills, California

The McGraw·Hill Companies

Send all inquiries to:
Glencoe/McGraw-Hill
8787 Orion Place
Columbus, OH 43240-4027

ISBN: 978-0-07-879140-6
MHID: 0-07-879140-5

Printed in the United States of America.

3 4 5 6 7 8 9 10   079/055   13 12 11 10 09 08

About the Authors

Conrad J. Schmitt

Conrad J. Schmitt received his B.A. degree magna cum laude from Montclair State College, Upper Montclair, NJ. He received his M.A. from Middlebury College, Middlebury, VT. He did additional graduate work at Seton Hall University and New York University. Mr. Schmitt has taught Spanish and French at the elementary, junior, and senior high school levels, as well as at the undergraduate and graduate levels. In addition, he has traveled extensively throughout Spain, Central and South America, and the Caribbean.

Protase E. Woodford

Protase "Woody" Woodford has taught Spanish at all levels from elementary through graduate school. At Educational Testing Service in Princeton, NJ, he was Director of Test Development, Director of Language Programs, Director of International Testing Programs and Director of the Puerto Rico Office. He has served as a consultant to the United Nations Secretariat, UNESCO, the Organization of American States, the U.S. Office of Education, and many ministries of education in Asia, Latin America, and the Middle East.

For the Parent or Guardian

We are excited that your child has decided to study Spanish. Foreign language study provides many benefits for students in addition to the ability to communicate in another language. Students who study another language improve their first language skills. They become more aware of the world around them and they learn to appreciate diversity.

You can help your child be successful in his or her study of Spanish even if you are not familiar with that language. Encourage your child to talk to you about the places where Spanish is spoken. Engage in conversations about current events in those places. The section of their Glencoe Spanish book called **El mundo hispanohablante** on pages xxi–xxxiii may serve as a reference for you and your child. In addition, you will find information about the geography of the Spanish-speaking world and links to foreign newspapers at **glencoe.com**.

The methodology employed in the Glencoe Spanish books is logical and leads students step by step through their study of the language. Consistent instruction and practice are essential for learning a foreign language. You can help by encouraging your child to review vocabulary each day. As he or she progresses through the text, you will want to use the study tips on pages H16–H31 to help your child learn Spanish. If you have Internet access, encourage your child to practice using the activities, games, and practice quizzes at **glencoe.com**.

¡Buen viaje!

Contenido

Repaso

Capítulo 1 Un viaje en tren

Objetivos

In this chapter you will learn to:

❖ use expressions related to train travel

❖ purchase a train ticket and request information about arrival, departure, etc.

❖ talk about more past events or activities

❖ tell what people say

❖ discuss an interesting train trip in Spain and in Peru

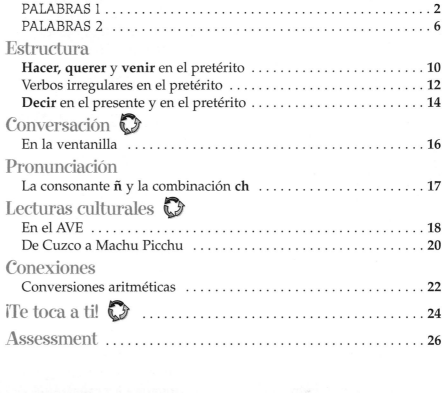

Contenido

Capítulo 2

En el restaurante

Objetivos

In this chapter you will learn to:

❖ order food or a beverage at a restaurant

❖ identify eating utensils and dishes

❖ identify more foods

❖ make a reservation at a restaurant

❖ talk about present and past events

❖ describe some cuisines of the Hispanic world

Capítulo 3 Telecomunicaciones

Objetivos

In this chapter you will learn to:

❖ talk about computers, e-mail, the Internet, faxes, and telephones

❖ talk about past habitual and routine actions

❖ describe people and events in the past

❖ make and receive telephone calls in Spanish

Contenido

Capítulo 4 De tiendas

Objetivos

In this chapter you will learn to:

- ❖ shop for apparel and food in Spanish-speaking countries
- ❖ ask for the quantities and sizes you want
- ❖ find out prices
- ❖ talk about different types of past actions
- ❖ talk in general terms about what is done
- ❖ talk about shopping practices in Spanish-speaking countries

Capítulo 5 Los pasatiempos

Objetivos

In this chapter you will learn to:

❖ talk about popular hobbies and games

❖ talk about activities in the park

❖ give details about location

❖ talk about what will happen in the future

❖ compare objects and people

❖ describe your favorite pastime

❖ talk about pastimes in Spanish-speaking countries

Capítulo 6 En el hotel

Objetivos

In this chapter you will learn to:

❖ **check into and out of a hotel**

❖ **ask for things that you may need while at a hotel**

❖ **talk about future events**

❖ **refer to previously mentioned people or things**

❖ **talk about lodging in the Hispanic world**

Capítulo 7 El vuelo

Objetivos

In this chapter you will learn to:

❖ talk about air travel

❖ discuss the influence of geography on travel in Latin America

❖ talk about things that would happen under certain conditions

❖ talk about air travel in Hispanic countries

Contenido

URGENCIAS →
ALMACENES →
CONSULTAS EXTERNAS ↑
ENTRADA PRINCIPAL ↑

Capítulo 8 Emergencias médicas

Objetivos

In this chapter you will learn to:

❖ talk about accidents and medical problems

❖ talk about hospital stays

❖ discuss things that you and others have done recently

❖ compare things with like characteristics

❖ talk about health care in various areas of the Spanish-speaking world

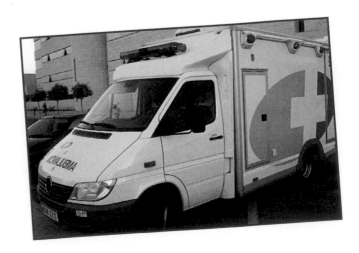

Capítulo 9   Ciudad y campo

Objetivos

In this chapter you will learn to:

- ❖ talk about life in the city
- ❖ talk about life in the country
- ❖ describe things that were happening
- ❖ refer to things that were already mentioned
- ❖ indicate where things are located
- ❖ talk about some cities in the Spanish-speaking world

Contenido

Capítulo 10 La cocina hispana

Objetivos

In this chapter you will learn to:

❖ talk about foods and food preparation

❖ give commands

❖ refer to people and things previously mentioned

❖ prepare some regional specialities

❖ talk about the origin of several foods

Capítulo 11 El coche y la carretera

Objetivos

In this chapter you will learn to:

- ❖ talk about cars and driving
- ❖ give directions on the road
- ❖ tell family and friends what to do and what not to do
- ❖ talk about highways in the Hispanic world

Contenido

Capítulo 12 Los servicios al público

Objetivos

In this chapter you will learn to:

❖ talk about going to the hairdresser/barber shop

❖ talk about having your clothes cleaned

❖ talk about using the services of the post office and bank

❖ talk about things that may or may not happen

❖ express what you would like, wish, or hope others would do

Capítulo 13 ¡Fiestas!

Objetivos

In this chapter you will learn to:

❖ describe and talk about parties and weddings

❖ talk about some holidays

❖ give advice and make recommendations

❖ express doubt, uncertainty, or disbelief

❖ express emotional reactions to what others do

❖ talk about New Year's Eve in the Hispanic world

Contenido

Capítulo 14 · Profesiones y oficios

Objetivos

In this chapter you will learn to:

❖ talk about professions and occupations

❖ interview for a job

❖ state work qualifications

❖ talk about future events

❖ talk about probable events

Literary Companion

Video Companion

Handbook

Guide to Symbols

Throughout **¡Buen viaje!** you will see these symbols, or icons. They will tell you how to best use the particular part of the chapter or activity they accompany. Following is a key to help you understand these symbols.

 Audio link This icon indicates material in the chapter that is recorded on compact disk.

 Recycling This icon indicates sections that review previously introduced material.

 Paired Activity This icon indicates sections that you can practice orally with a partner.

 Group Activity This icon indicates sections that you can practice together in groups.

 Un poco más This icon indicates additional practice activities that review knowledge from each chapter.

 ¡Adelante! This icon indicates the end of new material in each chapter. All remaining material is recombination and review.

 Literary Companion This icon appears in the review lessons to let you know that you are prepared to read the literature selection indicated if you wish.

 Interactive CD-ROM This icon indicates that the material is also on the Interactive CD-ROM.

El mundo hispanohablante

Spanish is the language of more than 350 million people around the world. Spanish had its origin in Spain. It is sometimes fondly called the "language of Cervantes," the author of the world's most famous novel and character, *Don Quijote*. The Spanish **conquistadores** and **exploradores** brought their language to the Americas in the fifteenth and sixteenth centuries. Spanish is the official language of almost all the countries of Central and South America. It is the official language of Mexico and several of the larger islands in the Caribbean. Spanish is also the heritage language of more than forty million people in the United States.

▼ España

▲ México

◄ Perú

▲ Chile

El mundo

OCÉANO ÁRTICO

Mar de Beaufort

Bahía de Baffin

Mar de Bering

Golfo de Alaska

Bahía de Hudson

CANADÁ

Mar del Labrador

AMÉRICA DEL NORTE

ESTADOS UNIDOS

OCÉANO ATLÁNTICO

MÉXICO

Golfo de México

MAR CARIBE

OCÉANO PACÍFICO

VENEZUELA

GUYANA

SURINAM

GUAYANA FRANCESA

COLOMBIA

ECUADOR

AMÉRICA DEL SUR

PERÚ

BRASIL

SAMOA

POLINESIA FRANCESA

BOLIVIA

PARAGUAY

TONGA

URUGUAY

CHILE

ARGENTINA

GOLFO DE MÉXICO

BAHAMAS

CUBA

TURCAS Y CAICOS (R.U.)

OCÉANO ATLÁNTICO

PUERTO RICO (EE.UU.)

ISLAS VÍRGENES (EE.UU. y R.U.)

MÉXICO

HAITÍ

REPÚBLICA DOMINICANA

ANTIGUA Y BARBUDA

BELICE

JAMAICA

SAN CRISTÓBAL-NEVIS

GUADALUPE (FR.)

GUATEMALA

DOMINICA

HONDURAS

MAR CARIBE

MARTINICA (FR.)

SANTA LUCÍA

EL SALVADOR

ARUBA

SAN VICENTE Y GRENADINES

BARBADOS

NICARAGUA

GRANADA

TRINIDAD Y TOBAGO

COSTA RICA

PANAMÁ

OCÉANO PACÍFICO

VENEZUELA

GUYANA

COLOMBIA

SURINAM

GROENLANDIA

Mar de Groenlandia

Mar de Noruega

Mar de Barents

Mar de Kara

Mar de Láptiev

OCÉANO ÁRTICO

ISLANDIA

Mar del Norte

EUROPA

RUSIA

ASIA

Mar de Ojotsk

MELILLA

CEUTA

MARRUECOS

TÚNEZ

MAR MEDITERRÁNEO

TURQUÍA

GEORGIA
ARMENIA

LÍBANO

SIRIA

ISRAEL

JORDANIA

IRAK

AZERBAIJAN

KUWAIT

QATAR
ARABIA
SAUDITA

BAHREIN

EMIRATOS
ÁRABES
UNIDOS

OMÁN

IRÁN

AFGANISTÁN

PAKISTÁN

NEPAL

BHUTAN

KAZAJSTÁN

UZBEKISTÁN

TURKMENISTÁN

KIRGUIZISTÁN

TAYIKISTÁN

MONGOLIA

CHINA

COREA
DEL NORTE

COREA
DEL SUR

Mar del
Japón

JAPÓN

Mar de la
China
oriental

TAIWÁN

OCÉANO
PACÍFICO

SAHARA
OCCIDENTAL

ARGELIA

LIBIA

EGIPTO

CABO
VERDE

MAURITANIA

MALÍ

NÍGER

CHAD

SUDÁN

ERITREA

YEMEN

DJIBOUTI

INDIA

BANGLADESH

MYANMAR

LAOS

TAILANDIA

Golfo
de Bengala

Mar de
la China
meridional

FILIPINAS

MARSHALL

SENEGAL

GAMBIA

GUINEA-
BISSAU

GUINEA

BURKINA
FASO

NIGERIA

GHANA

BENIN

ÁFRICA

REPÚBLICA
CENTROAFRICANA

ETIOPÍA

SRI
LANKA

VIETNAM

CAMBOYA

BRUNEI

MALAYSIA

PALAU

MICRONESIA

SIERRA LEONA

COSTA DE MARFIL

LIBERIA

TOGO

CAMERÚN

UGANDA

SOMALIA

KENYA

MALDIVAS

SINGAPUR

I N D O N E S I A

PAPÚA-
NUEVA
GUINEA

KIRIBATI

NAURÚ

SALOMÓN

SAN TOMÉ E PRÍNCIPE

GUINEA ECUATORIAL

GABÓN

REP. DEL
CONGO

RUANDA

REP. DEM.
DEL CONGO

BURUNDI

TANZANIA

SEYCHELLES

OCÉANO
ÍNDICO

TUVALU

WALLIS Y
FUTUNA

VANUATU

ISLAS
FIJI

ANGOLA

MALAWI

ZAMBIA

MOZAMBIQUE

ISLAS COMORES

MADAGASCAR

MAURICIO

Mar del
Coral

NUEVA
CALEDONIA

OCÉANO
ATLÁNTICO

NAMIBIA

BOTSWANA

ZIMBABWE

REUNIÓN

AUSTRALIA

Mar de
Tasmania

SUDÁFRICA

SWAZILANDIA

LESOTHO

NUEVA
ZELANDIA

ANTÁRTIDA

NORUEGA

FINLANDIA

SUECIA

ESTONIA

RUSIA

IRLANDA

REINO
UNIDO

DINAMARCA

LETONIA

LITUANIA

RUSIA

BELARÚS

PAÍSES
BAJOS

BÉLGICA

ALEMANIA

POLONIA

UCRANIA

LUXEMBURGO

OCÉANO
ATLÁNTICO

FRANCIA

SUIZA

REPÚBLICA
CHECA

ESLOVAQUIA

HUNGRÍA

MOLDOVA

ANDORRA

AUSTRIA

ESLOVENIA

CROACIA

RUMANIA

PORTUGAL

ESPAÑA

MÓNACO

BOSNIA
HERZOGOVINA

YUGOSLAVIA
(Fed. Rep.)

Mar Negro

GEORGIA

ITALIA

BULGARIA

MELILLA

CEUTA

Mar Mediterráneo

ALBANIA

MACEDONIA

TURQUÍA

ÁFRICA

GRECIA

MALTA

CHIPRE

SIRIA

LÍBANO

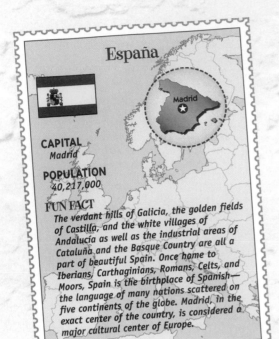

España

CAPITAL
Madrid

POPULATION
40,217,000

FUN FACT
The verdant hills of Galicia, the golden fields of Castilla, and the white villages of Andalucía as well as the industrial areas of Cataluña and the Basque Country are all a part of beautiful Spain. Once home to Iberians, Carthaginians, Romans, Celts, and Moors, Spain is the birthplace of Spanish—the language of many nations scattered on five continents of the globe. Madrid, in the exact center of the country, is considered a major cultural center of Europe.

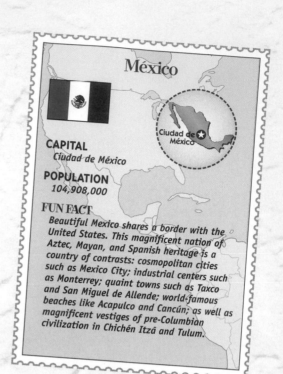

México

CAPITAL
Ciudad de México

POPULATION
104,908,000

FUN FACT
Beautiful Mexico shares a border with the United States. This magnificent nation of Aztec, Mayan, and Spanish heritage is a country of contrasts: cosmopolitan cities such as Mexico City; industrial centers such as Monterrey; quaint towns such as Taxco and San Miguel de Allende; world-famous beaches like Acapulco and Cancún; as well as magnificent vestiges of pre-Columbian civilization in Chichén Itzá and Tulum.

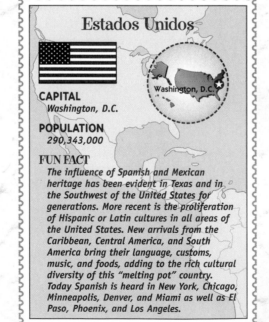

Estados Unidos

CAPITAL
Washington, D.C.

POPULATION
290,343,000

FUN FACT
The influence of Spanish and Mexican heritage has been evident in Texas and in the Southwest of the United States for generations. More recent is the proliferation of Hispanic or Latin cultures in all areas of the United States. New arrivals from the Caribbean, Central America, and South America bring their language, customs, music, and foods, adding to the rich cultural diversity of this "melting pot" country. Today Spanish is heard in New York, Chicago, Minneapolis, Denver, and Miami as well as El Paso, Phoenix, and Los Angeles.

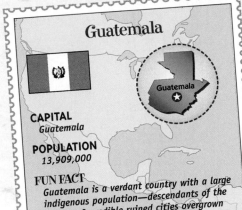

Guatemala

CAPITAL
Guatemala

POPULATION
13,909,000

FUN FACT
Guatemala is a verdant country with a large indigenous population—descendants of the Mayans. Incredible ruined cities overgrown by jungle tell of a civilization that lasted for two thousand years and whose decline has never been definitively explained. Guatemala is considered by many to be one of the most beautiful countries in the world, with its volcanoes, mountains, jungles, and scenic cities and villages, such as Antigua, Panajachel, and Chichicastenango.

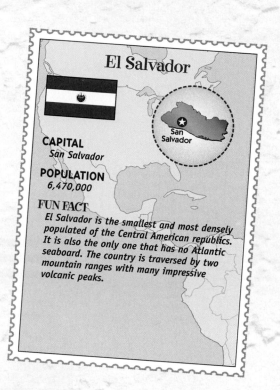

El Salvador

CAPITAL
San Salvador

POPULATION
6,470,000

FUN FACT
El Salvador is the smallest and most densely populated of the Central American republics. It is also the only one that has no Atlantic seaboard. The country is traversed by two mountain ranges with many impressive volcanic peaks.

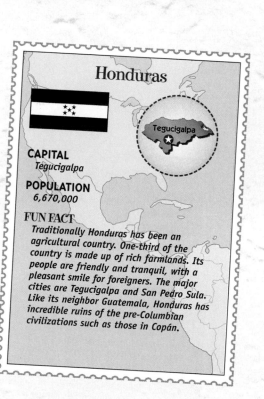

Honduras

CAPITAL
Tegucigalpa

POPULATION
6,670,000

FUN FACT
Traditionally Honduras has been an agricultural country. One-third of the country is made up of rich farmlands. Its people are friendly and tranquil, with a pleasant smile for foreigners. The major cities are Tegucigalpa and San Pedro Sula. Like its neighbor Guatemala, Honduras has incredible ruins of the pre-Columbian civilizations such as those in Copán.

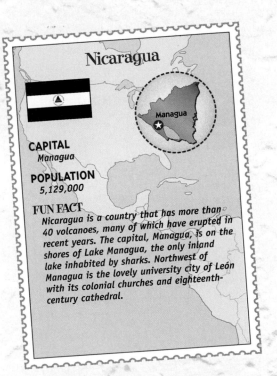

Nicaragua

CAPITAL
Managua

POPULATION
5,129,000

FUN FACT
Nicaragua is a country that has more than 40 volcanoes, many of which have erupted in recent years. The capital, Managua, is on the shores of Lake Managua, the only inland lake inhabited by sharks. Northwest of Managua is the lovely university city of León with its colonial churches and eighteenth-century cathedral.

El mundo hispanohablante

Costa Rica

CAPITAL
San José

POPULATION
3,896,000

FUN FACT
Many consider Costa Rica a very special place. Its residents, Ticos, are polite, peaceful, and extremely friendly. Costa Rica has no army and prides itself on having more teachers than police officers. Costa Rica is a country of sun-drenched beaches on the Pacific, tropical jungles along the Caribbean coast, cosmopolitan cities such as San José, and high mountains in the central valley. Costa Rica is a tourist's paradise as well as home to many expatriates.

Panamá

CAPITAL
Panamá

POPULATION
2,961,000

FUN FACT
Panama is a country of variety—a variety of races, customs, natural wonders, and attractions. It is a country of tropical forests, mountains, beautiful beaches, excellent fishing, picturesque lakes, rivers, two oceans, and—the most incredible engineering feat—the Panama Canal. Panama is also the largest financial center of Latin America. All this in a mere 77,432 square kilometers!

Cuba

CAPITAL
La Habana

POPULATION
11,263,000

FUN FACT
Havana, the capital of Cuba, is known for its gorgeous colonial architecture. This lush island, not far from Florida, is one of the world's greatest producers of sugar cane. Cuba has been ruled by Fidel Castro since 1959 when he overthrew the dictator Fulgencio Batista.

La República Dominicana

CAPITAL
Santo Domingo

POPULATION
8,716,000

FUN FACT
The Dominican Republic shares with Haiti the island of Hispaniola in the greater Antilles. The oldest university in our hemisphere, la Universidad de Santo Domingo, was founded in Santo Domingo. The Dominicans are ardent fans or aficionados of baseball, and this rather small island nation has produced some of the finest major league players.

Puerto Rico

CAPITAL
San Juan

POPULATION
3,886,000

FUN FACT
Puerto Ricans have an endearing term for their beloved island—la isla del encanto—island of enchantment. A commonwealth of the United States, Puerto Rico is a lush, tropical island with beaches along its Atlantic and Caribbean shores and gorgeous mountains with Alpine-like views in its interior. Puerto Rico is the home of the beloved coquí—a little frog that lives only in Puerto Rico and who lets no one see him.

xxvi

Venezuela

Caracas

CAPITAL
Caracas

POPULATION
24,655,000

FUN FACT
Venezuela was the name given to this country by Spanish explorers in 1499, when they came across indigenous villages where people lived on the water and where all commerce was conducted by dugout canoes. The waterways reminded them of Venice, Italy. Caracas is a teeming cosmopolitan city of high-rises surrounded by mountains and tucked in a narrow nine-mile valley. Angel Falls in southern Venezuela is the highest waterfall in the world, reaching a height of 3,212 feet with an unbroken fall of 2,648 feet.

Colombia

Santa Fe de Bogotá

CAPITAL
Bogotá

POPULATION
41,662,000

FUN FACT
Colombia covers over 440,000 square miles of tropical and mountainous terrain. Bogotá is situated in the center of the country in an Andean valley 8,640 feet above sea level. The Caribbean coast in the North boasts many beautiful beaches; the South is covered by jungle, and the southern port of Leticia is on the Amazon River.

Ecuador

Quito

CAPITAL
Quito

POPULATION
13,710,000

FUN FACT
Ecuador takes its name from the equator, which cuts right across the country. Ecuador is the meeting place of the high Andean sierra in the center, the tropical coastal plain to the west, and the Amazon Basin jungle to the east. Snowcapped volcanoes stretch some 400 miles from north to south. The beautiful colonial section of the capital, Quito, is sometimes called "the Florence of the Americas."

Perú

Lima

CAPITAL
Lima

POPULATION
28,410,000

FUN FACT
Peru, like Ecuador, is divided into three geographical areas—a narrow coastal strip of desert along the Pacific, the Andean highlands where nearly half the population lives, and the Amazon jungle to the east. Lima is on the coast, and for almost nine months out of the year it is enshrouded in a fog called la garúa. Peru is famous for its Incan heritage. Nothing can prepare visitors for the awe-inspiring view of the Incan city of Machu Picchu, an imposing architectural complex high in the Andes.

Bolivia

La Paz

CAPITAL
La Paz

POPULATION
8,568,000

FUN FACT
Bolivia is one of two landlocked countries in South America. Mountains dominate the Bolivian landscape. La Paz is the highest city in the world at an altitude of 12,500 feet. Bolivia also has the world's highest navigable lake, Lake Titicaca, which is surrounded by the picturesque villages of the Aymara Indians.

Chile

Santiago

CAPITAL
Santiago

POPULATION
15,665,000

FUN FACT
Chile, a "string bean" country never more than 111 miles wide, stretches 2,666 miles from north to south along the Pacific Coast. The imposing Andes isolate it from Bolivia and Argentina. The northern part of the country is characterized by the super-arid Atacama desert, the South by the spectacular wind-swept glaciers and fjords of Patagonia. Over one-third of the country's population lives in the Santiago area.

Argentina

Buenos Aires

CAPITAL
Buenos Aires

POPULATION
38,741,000

FUN FACT
Argentina is often considered the most European country of South America. Buenos Aires is a beautiful city of parks, boutiques, restaurants, and wide boulevards. Argentina is famous for its beef from the cattle that graze on the huge estancias of the grassy Pampas. Farther south on the Chilean border is the gorgeous lake area with Swiss-like villages around Bariloche. To the south is Patagonia with its rocky countryside where the Welsh still graze sheep.

Paraguay

Asunción

CAPITAL
Asunción

POPULATION
6,037,000

FUN FACT
Paraguay, like Bolivia, is landlocked. Asunción, situated on seven small hills on the east bank of the río Paraguay, is home to one-fifth of the country's total population. Located in the center of South America, this somewhat quaint city is nearly equidistant from the Atlantic and the Andes. The area to the west of the río Paraguay is called the Chaco—a very dry, hot, windy area of grasslands and scrubby forests.

Uruguay

Montevideo

CAPITAL
Montevideo

POPULATION
3,413,000

FUN FACT
Uruguay is the smallest country in South America. Most of the country's terrain is grazing land for sheep and cattle. Montevideo, situated where the río de la Plata empties into the Atlantic, is a rather peaceful city whose suburbs look more like beautiful resorts. The beaches of Uruguay's Atlantic coastline, particularly Punta del Este, attract many people from Brazil and Argentina.

Ceuta and Melilla

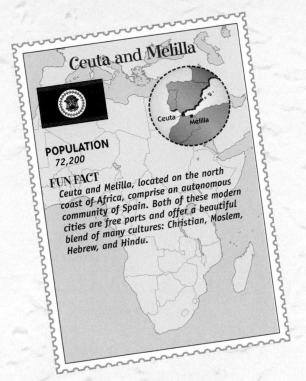

POPULATION
72,200

FUN FACT
Ceuta and Melilla, located on the north coast of Africa, comprise an autonomous community of Spain. Both of these modern cities are free ports and offer a beautiful blend of many cultures: Christian, Moslem, Hebrew, and Hindu.

Guinea Ecuatorial

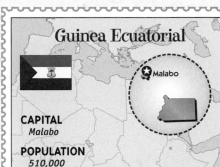

CAPITAL
Malabo

POPULATION
510,000

FUN FACT
The Republic of Equatorial Guinea, on the West Coast of Africa between Gabon and Cameroon, was formerly called Spanish Guinea. The country is made up of some 10,000 square miles on the mainland and several small islands. Its capital, Malabo, is on the island of Bioko. Today two languages are spoken in Equatorial Guinea—Spanish and French.

Las Islas Filipinas

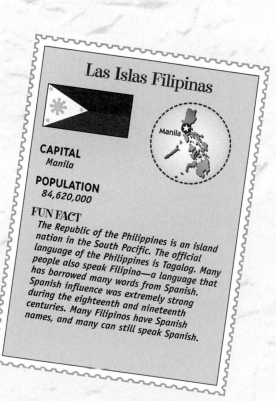

CAPITAL
Manila

POPULATION
84,620,000

FUN FACT
The Republic of the Philippines is an island nation in the South Pacific. The official language of the Philippines is Tagalog. Many people also speak Filipino—a language that has borrowed many words from Spanish. Spanish influence was extremely strong during the eighteenth and nineteenth centuries. Many Filipinos have Spanish names, and many can still speak Spanish.

España

OCÉANO ATLÁNTICO

FRANCIA

MAR CANTÁBRICO

Golfo de Vizcaya

La Coruña
Santiago de Compostela
Oviedo
Santander
San Sebastián
Roncesvalles
ANDORRA

Asturias
Cantabria
Bilbao
País Vasco
LOS PIRINEOS

Galicia
CORDILLERA CANTÁBRICA
Pamplona
Navarra

León
Burgos
Rioja
Río Ebro
Cataluña

Castilla y León
Barcelona

Valladolid
Río Duero
Zaragoza

Salamanca
Segovia
Aragón

Ávila
Madrid
SIERRA DE GUADARRAMA
Río Tajo

Madrid

PORTUGAL
ESPAÑA
Comunidad Valenciana
Menorca

Castilla-la Mancha
Valencia
Islas baleares
Palma

Lisboa
Río Guadiana
Mallorca

Extremadura
Ibiza
Formentera

Alicante
MAR MEDITERRÁNEO

Río Guadalquivir
Murcia
Murcia

Córdoba
Cartagena

Sevilla
Granada

Jerez de la Frontera
Andalucía
SIERRA NEVADA

Málaga
COSTA DEL SOL

Cádiz
Marbella
Estepona

Gibraltar (R.U.)

Estrecho de Gibraltar
Ceuta (Esp.)

Tánger

Melilla (Esp.)

OCÉANO ATLÁNTICO

ARGELIA

MARRUECOS

Islas Canarias

La Palma
Santa Cruz de Tenerife
Lanzarote

Gomera
Las Palmas
Fuerteventura

Tenerife
MARRUECOS

Hierro
Gran Canaria
ÁFRICA

OCÉANO ATLÁNTICO
SAHARA OCCIDENTAL

La América del Sur

MAR CARIBE

OCÉANO ATLÁNTICO

Barranquilla
Cartagena
Maracaibo
Caracas
Lago de Maracaibo
Río Orinoco
VENEZUELA
GUYANA
Medellín
SURINAM
Santa Fe de Bogotá
COLOMBIA
GUAYANA FRANCESA
Cali
Río
Otavalo
Ecuador
Quito
ECUADOR
Río Amazonas
Islas Galápagos (Ecuador)
Guayaquil
Cuenca
PERÚ
BRASIL
El Callao
Lima
C O R D I L L E R A   D E   L O S   A N D E S
Cuzco
Lago Titicaca
BOLIVIA
Brasília
La Paz
Cochabamba
Santa Cruz
Sucre
Trópico de Capricornio
PARAGUAY
CHILE
Asunción
Río Paraná
Vicuña
Córdoba
OCÉANO PACÍFICO
Rosario
URUGUAY
Valparaíso
Buenos Aires
Montevideo
Santiago
La Plata
Río de la Plata
ARGENTINA
Mar del Plata
Puerto Montt
OCÉANO ATLÁNTICO
P A T A G O N I A
Estrecho de Magallanes
Islas Malvinas (R.U.)
Tierra del Fuego
Punta Arenas
Cabo de Hornos

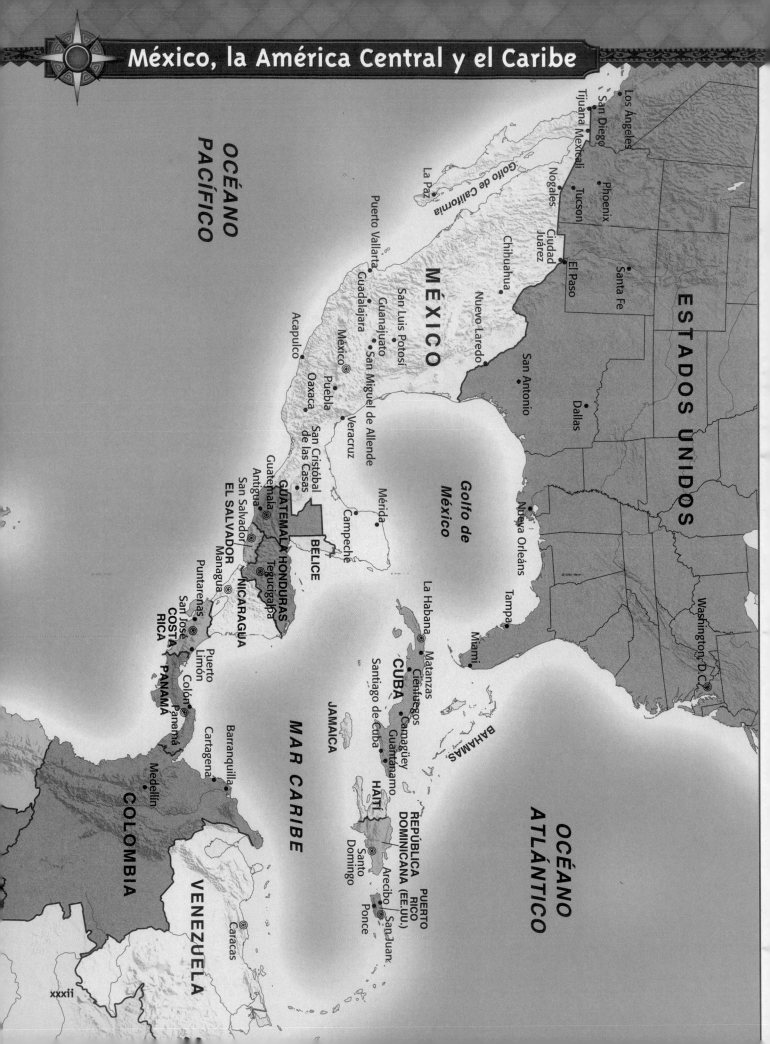

México, la América Central y el Caribe

OCÉANO PACÍFICO

OCÉANO ATLÁNTICO

OCÉANO ATLÁNTICO

MÉXICO

ESTADOS UNIDOS

Golfo de México

Golfo de California

Los Ángeles
Tijuana
San Diego
Mexicali
Nogales
Tucson
Phoenix
Santa Fe
Ciudad Juárez
El Paso
Chihuahua
Nuevo Laredo
San Antonio
Dallas
La Paz
Puerto Vallarta
Guadalajara
San Luis Potosí
Guanajuato
México
San Miguel de Allende
Acapulco
Puebla
Oaxaca
Veracruz
San Cristóbal de las Casas
Mérida
Campeche
Nueva Orleáns
Tampa
Miami
Washington, D.C.

BELICE
Guatemala
Antigua
GUATEMALA
San Salvador
EL SALVADOR
HONDURAS
Tegucigalpa
Managua
NICARAGUA
Puntarenas
San José
COSTA RICA
PANAMÁ
Colón
Panamá
Puerto Limón

La Habana
Matanzas
Cienfuegos
CUBA
Santiago de Cuba
Camagüey
Guantánamo
JAMAICA

BAHAMAS

HAITÍ
REPÚBLICA DOMINICANA
Santo Domingo
Arecibo (EE.UU.)
PUERTO RICO
San Juan
Ponce

MAR CARIBE

Barranquilla
Cartagena
Medellín
COLOMBIA
VENEZUELA
Caracas

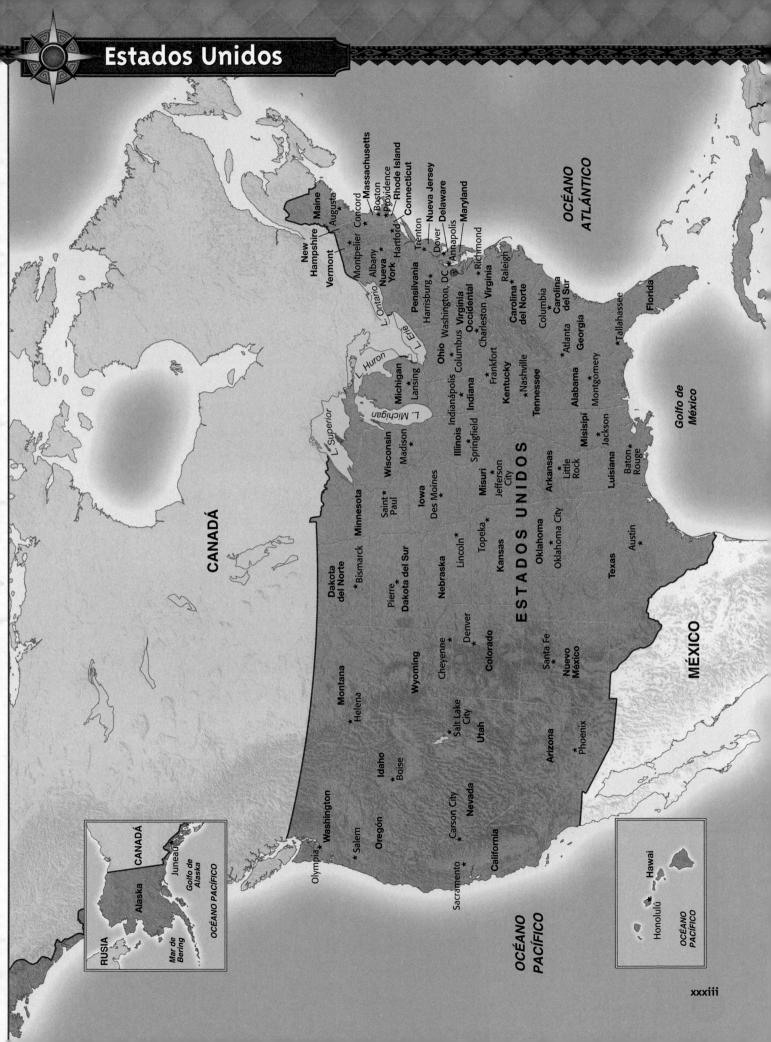

OCÉANO ATLÁNTICO

CANADÁ

OCÉANO PACÍFICO

MÉXICO

Golfo de México

ESTADOS UNIDOS

Maine
Augusta ★
New Hampshire
Vermont
Montpelier
Concord ★
Massachusetts
Boston ★
Providence
Rhode Island
Connecticut
Hartford ★
Albany ★
Nueva York
Nueva Jersey
Trenton ★
Dover ★
Delaware
Maryland
Annapolis ★
Washington, DC
Richmond ★
Virginia
Raleigh ★
Carolina del Norte
Carolina del Sur
Columbia ★
Florida
Tallahassee ★
Pensilvania
Harrisburg ★
Virginia Occidental
Charleston ★
Columbus ★
Ohio
Frankfort ★
Kentucky
Nashville ★
Tennessee
Atlanta ★
Georgia
Alabama
Montgomery ★
Misisipi
Jackson ★
Luisiana
Baton Rouge ★
Indianápolis ★
Indiana
Springfield ★
Illinois
Michigan
Lansing ★
Little Rock ★
Arkansas
Wisconsin
Madison ★
Minnesota
Saint Paul ★
Iowa
Des Moines ★
Misuri
Jefferson City ★
Oklahoma
Oklahoma City ★
Texas
Austin ★
Dakota del Norte
Bismarck ★
Dakota del Sur
Pierre ★
Nebraska
Lincoln ★
Kansas
Topeka ★
Montana
Helena ★
Wyoming
Cheyenne ★
Colorado
Denver ★
Nuevo México
Santa Fe ★
Idaho
Boise ★
Utah
Salt Lake City ★
Arizona
Phoenix ★
Nevada
Carson City ★
Washington
Olympia ★
Oregón
Salem ★
California
Sacramento ★

L. Ontario
L. Erie
L. Huron
L. Michigan
L. Superior

RUSIA
CANADÁ
Alaska
Juneau ★
Golfo de Alaska
Mar de Bering
OCÉANO PACÍFICO

Hawai
Honolulú ★
OCÉANO PACÍFICO

Why Learn Spanish?

The Spanish-Speaking World

Culture Knowing Spanish will open doors to you around the world. As you study the language, you will come to understand and appreciate the way of life, customs, values, and cultures of people from many different areas of the world. Look at the map on pages xxii–xxiii to see where Spanish is spoken, either as a first or second language.

Learning Spanish can be fun and will bring you a sense of accomplishment. You'll be really pleased when you are able to carry on a conversation in Spanish. You will be able to read the literature of Spain and Latin America, keep up with current events in magazines and newspapers from Spain and Latin America, and understand Spanish language films without relying on subtitles.

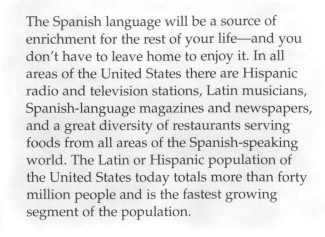

The Spanish language will be a source of enrichment for the rest of your life—and you don't have to leave home to enjoy it. In all areas of the United States there are Hispanic radio and television stations, Latin musicians, Spanish-language magazines and newspapers, and a great diversity of restaurants serving foods from all areas of the Spanish-speaking world. The Latin or Hispanic population of the United States today totals more than forty million people and is the fastest growing segment of the population.

Career Opportunities

Business Your knowledge of Spanish will also be an asset to you in a wide variety of careers. Many companies from Spain and Latin America are multinational and have branches around the world, including the United States. Many U.S. corporations have great exposure in the Spanish-speaking countries. With the growth of the Hispanic population in the U.S., bilingualism is becoming an important asset in many fields including retail, fashion, cosmetics, pharmaceutical, agriculture, automotive, tourism, airlines, technology, finance, and accounting.

You can use your Spanish in all these fields, not only abroad but also in the United States. On the national scene there are innumerable possibilities in medical and hospital services, banking and finance, law, social work, and law enforcement. The opportunities are limitless.

Language Link

Another benefit to learning Spanish is that it will improve your English. Once you know another language, you can make comparisons between the two and gain a greater understanding of how languages function. You'll also come across a number of Spanish words that are used in English. Just a few examples are: **adobe, corral, meseta, rodeo, poncho, canyon, llama, alpaca.** Spanish will also be helpful if you decide to learn yet another language. Once you learn a second language, the learning process for acquiring other languages becomes much easier.

Spanish is a beautiful, rich language spoken on many continents. Whatever your motivation is for choosing to study it, Spanish will expand your horizons and increase your job opportunities. **¡Viva el español! Y ¡buen viaje!**

READING IN A NEW LANGUAGE

Following are skills and strategies that can help you understand what you read in a language you have just begun to learn. *Reading and Succeeding* will help you build skills and strategies that will make it easier to understand what you are reading in your exciting new language.

The strategies you use frequently depend on the purpose of your reading. You do not read a textbook or standardized testing questions the same way you read a novel or a magazine article. You read a textbook for information. You read a novel or magazine article for fun.

In the early stages of second-language learning, your vocabulary is, of course, very limited in comparison to the vast number of words you already know in English. The material presented to you to read in the early stages must accommodate this reality. Your limited knowledge of the language does not have to deter you from enjoying what you are reading. Most of what you read, however, will come from your textbook, since original novels and magazine articles are not written for people who have limited exposure to the language.

As you develop your reading ability in Spanish you will encounter basically two types of readings.

Intensive Readings

These readings are short. They are very controlled, using only language you have already learned. You should find these readings easy and enjoyable. If you find them difficult it means you have not sufficiently learned the material presented in the chapter of the textbook. The vast majority of these informative readings will introduce you to the fascinating cultures of the Spanish-speaking world.

A very important aspect of reading in Spanish is to give you things to "talk about" in the language. The more you read, speak, and use the language, the more proficient you will become. Whenever you finish reading one of the intensive reading selections, you should be able to talk about it; that is, you should be able to retell it in your own words.

Extensive Readings

Since it is unrealistic to assume that you will never encounter new words as you branch out and read material in Spanish, you will also be presented with extensive readings. The goal of these extensive readings is to help you develop the tools and skills you need in order to read at some future date an original novel or magazine article. They do indeed contain some words and structures that are unfamiliar to you. In this *Reading and Succeeding* section, you will learn to develop many skills that will enable you to read such material with relative ease.

- adjust the way you read to fit the type of material you are reading
- identify new words and build your vocabulary
- use specific reading strategies to better understand what you read
- improve your ability to speak by developing strategies that enable you to retell orally what you have read
- use critical thinking strategies to think more deeply about what you read

Identifying New Words and Building Vocabulary

What do you do when you come across a word you do not know as you read? Do you skip the word and keep reading? You might if you are reading for fun. If it hinders your ability to understand, however, you might miss something important. When you come to a word you don't know, try the following strategies to figure out what the word means.

• Reading Aloud

In the early stages of learning a second language a good strategy is to sit by yourself and read the selection aloud. This can help you understand the reading because you once again hear words that you have already practiced orally in class. Hearing them as you read them can help reinforce meaning.

• Identifying Cognates

As you read you will come across many cognates. Cognates are words that look alike in both English and Spanish. Not only do they look alike but they mean the same thing. Recognizing cognates is a great reading strategy. Examples of cognates are:

cómico	nacionalidad	entra	popular	secundaria	clase
cubano	matemática	prepara	video	blusa	televisión

• Identifying Roots and Base Words

The main part of a word is called its root. From a root, many new words can be formed. When you see a new word, identify its root. It can help you pronounce the word and figure out its meaning.

For example, if you know the word **importante,** there is no problem determining the meaning of **importancia.** The verb **importar** becomes a bit more problematic, but with some intelligent guessing you can get its meaning. You know it has something to do with importance so it means *it is important,* and by extension it can even carry the meaning *it matters.*

• Prefixes

A prefix is a word part added to the beginning of a root or base word. Spanish as well as English has prefixes. Prefixes can change, or even reverse, the meaning of a word. For example, the prefixes **in-, im-,** and **des-** mean *not.*

    estable/inestable   **posible/imposible**   **honesto/deshonesto**

Reading and Succeeding

Using Syntax

Like all languages, Spanish has rules for the way words are arranged in sentences. The way a sentence is organized is called its syntax. Spanish syntax, however, is a bit more flexible than English. In a simple English sentence someone or something (its subject) does something (the predicate or verb) to or with another person or thing (the object). This word order can vary in Spanish and does not always follow the subject/verb/object order.

READING PRACTICE

English always states: *John speaks to me.*

Spanish can state: *John to me speaks.*

or *To me speaks John.*

The latter leaves the subject to the end of the sentence and emphasizes that it is John who speaks to me.

Taking into account that Spanish and English syntax vary is one of the many important reasons why, when you read, you should think in Spanish and not try to translate what you are reading into English. Reading in Spanish will then have a natural flow and follow exactly the way you learned it. Trying to translate it into English confuses the matter and serves no purpose.

Using Context Clues

This is a very important reading strategy in a second language. You can often figure out the meaning of an unfamiliar word by looking at it in context (the words and sentences that surround it). Let's look at the following example.

READING PRACTICE

The glump ate it all up and flew away.

You have no idea what a *glump* is. Right? But from the rest of the sentence you can figure out that it's a bird. Why? Because it flew away and you know that birds fly. In this way you guessed at the meaning of an unknown word using context. Although you know it is a bird, you cannot determine the specific meaning such as a robin, a wren, or a sparrow. In many cases it does not matter because that degree of specificity is not necessary for comprehension. Let's look at another example:

The glump ate it all up and phlumped.

In this case you do not know the meaning of two key words in the same sentence—*glump* and *phlumped*. This makes it impossible to guess the meaning and this is what can happen when you try to read something in a second language that is beyond your proficiency level. This makes reading a frustrating experience. For this reason all the readings in your textbook control the language to keep it within your reach. Remember, if you have studied the vocabulary in your book, this will not happen.

Understanding What You Read

Try using some of the following strategies before, during, and after reading to understand and remember what you read.

Previewing

When you preview a piece of writing, you are looking for a general idea of what to expect from it. Before you read, try the following.

- Look at the title and any illustrations that are included.
- Read the headings, subheadings, and anything in bold letters.
- Skim over the passage to see how it is organized. Is it divided into many parts? Is it a long poem or short story?
- Look at the graphics—pictures, maps, or diagrams.
- Set a purpose for your reading. Are you reading to learn something new? Are you reading to find specific information?

Using What You Know

Believe it or not, you already know quite a bit about what you are going to read. Your own knowledge and personal experience can help you create meaning in what you read. There is, however, a big difference in reading the information in your Spanish textbook. You already have some knowledge about what you are reading from a United States oriented base. What you will be reading about takes place in a Spanish-speaking environment and thus you will be adding an exciting new dimension to what you already know. Comparing and contrasting are important critical skills to put to use when reading material about a culture other than your own. This skill will be discussed later.

Visualizing

Creating pictures in your mind about what you are reading—called visualizing—will help you understand and remember what you read. With the assistance of the many accompanying photos, try to visualize the people, streets, cities, homes, etc., you are reading about.

Identifying Sequence

When you discover the logical order of events or ideas, you are identifying sequence. Look for clues and signal words that will help you find how information is organized. Some signal words are **primero, al principio, antes, después, luego, entonces, más tarde, por fin, finalmente.**

Determining the Main Idea

When you look for the main idea of a selection, you look for the most important idea. The examples, reasons, and details that further explain the main idea are called supporting details.

Reviewing

When you review in school, you go over what you learned the day before so that the information is clear in your mind. Reviewing when you read does the same thing. Take time now and then to pause and review what you have read. Think about the main ideas and organize them for yourself so you can recall them later. Filling in study aids such as graphic organizers can help you review.

Monitoring Your Comprehension

As you read, check your understanding by summarizing. Pause from time to time and state the main ideas of what you have just read. Answer the questions: **¿Quién?** *(Who?)* **¿Qué?** *(What?)* **¿Dónde?** *(Where?)* **¿Cuándo?** *(When?)* **¿Cómo?** *(How?)* **¿Por qué?** *(Why?)*. Summarizing tests your comprehension because you state key points in your own words. Remember something you read earlier: reading in Spanish empowers your ability to speak by developing strategies that enable you to retell orally what you have read.

Thinking About Your Reading

Sometimes it is important to think more deeply about what you read so you can get the most out of what the author says. These critical thinking skills will help you go beyond what the words say and understand the meaning of your reading.

Compare and Contrast

To compare and contrast shows the similarities and differences among people, things, and ideas. Your reading experience in Spanish will show you many things that are similar and many others that are different depending upon the culture groups and social mores.

As you go over these culturally oriented readings, try to visualize what you are reading. Then think about the information. Think about what you know about the topic and then determine if the information you are reading is similar, somewhat different, or very different from what you know.

Continue to think about it. In this case you may have to think about it in English. Determine if you find the similarities or the differences interesting. Would you like to experience what you are reading about? Analyzing the information in this way will most certainly help you remember what you have read.

- Signal words and phrases that indicate similarity are **similar, semejante, parecido, igual.**
- Signal words and phrases that indicate differences are **diferente, distinto, al contrario, contrariamente, sin embargo.**

Cause and Effect

Just about everything that happens in life is the cause or the effect of some other event or action. Writers use cause-and-effect structure to explore the reasons for something happening and to examine the results of previous events. This structure helps answer the question that everybody is always asking: Why? Cause-and-effect structure is about explaining things.

- Signal words and phrases are **así, porque, por consiguiente, resulta que.**

Using Reference Materials

In the early stages of second-language learning you will not be able to use certain types of reference materials that are helpful to you in English. For example, you could not look up a word in a Spanish dictionary as you would not be able to understand many of the words used in the definition.

You can, however, make use of the glossary that appears at the end of your textbook. A glossary includes only words that are included in the textbook. Rather than give you a Spanish definition, the glossary gives you the English equivalent of the word. If you have to use the glossary very frequently it indicates to you that you have not studied the vocabulary sufficiently in each of your lessons. A strategy to use before beginning a reading selection in any given lesson is to quickly skim the vocabulary in the **Palabras 1** and **Palabras 2** sections of the lesson.

Enjoy reading as you take **un buen viaje.**

Dear Student,

Foldables are interactive study organizers that you can make yourself. They are a wonderful resource to help you organize and retain information. Foldables have many purposes. You can use them to remember vocabulary words or to organize more in-depth information on any given topic, such as keeping track of what you know about a particular country.

You can write general information, such as titles, vocabulary words, concepts, questions, main ideas, and dates, on the front tabs of your Foldables. You view this general information every time you look at a Foldable. This helps you focus on and remember key points without the distraction of additional text. You can write specific information—supporting ideas, thoughts, answers to questions, research information, empirical data, class notes, observations, and definitions—under the tabs. Think of different ways in which Foldables can be used. Soon you will find that you can make your own Foldables for study guides and projects. Foldables with flaps or tabs create study guides that you can use to check what you know about the general information on the front of tabs. Use Foldables without tabs for projects that require information to be presented for others to view quickly. The more you make and use graphic organizers, the faster you will become able to produce them.

To store your Foldables, turn one-gallon freezer bags into student portfolios which can be collected and stored in the classroom. You can also carry your portfolios in your notebooks if you place strips of two-inch clear tape along one side and punch three holes through the taped edge. Write your name along the top of the plastic portfolio with a permanent marker and cover the writing with two-inch clear tape to keep it from wearing off. Cut the bottom corners off the bag so it won't hold air and will stack and store easily. The following figures illustrate the basic folds that are referred to throughout the following section of this book.

Good luck!

Dinah Zike

Dinah Zike
www.dinah.com

Category Book

Los números Use this *category book* organizer as you learn dates and numbers.

Step 1 **Fold** a sheet of paper (8½" x 11") in half like a *hot dog*.

Step 2 On one side, **cut** every third line. This usually results in ten tabs. Do this with three sheets of paper to make three books.

Step 3 **Write** one Arabic number on the outside of each of the tabs. On the inside write out the respective number. As you learn more numbers, use *category books* to categorize numbers in this way.

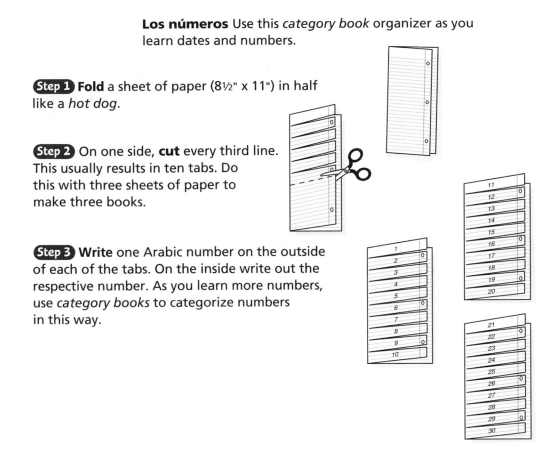

OTHER SUGGESTIONS FOR A *CATEGORY BOOK* FOLDABLE

You may wish to use *category book* foldables to help remember numbers. As you learn numbers, make two *category book* foldables. One will have the numerals on the outside and the numbers written out on the inside. The other will have the numbers written out on the outside and the numerals on the inside. This is a good way for you to practice your numbers on your own. You may also wish to make one foldable containing even numbers and one containing odd numbers.

A *category book* foldable may be useful to you as you are learning terms related to computers, faxes, or telephones. Write the name of the machine in Spanish on the outside of the foldable. On the inside, write instructions for how to use it and terms related to it in Spanish.

A *category book* foldable may be used to help you remember the names of different kinds of stores and markets in the Hispanic world. Use the names of foods and products you already know to describe what is sold in the store on the outside of the foldable. You will write the name of the store or market in Spanish on the inside. Then show your descriptions to a partner and have the partner come up with the name of the store or market in Spanish.

Forward-Backward Book

Las estaciones Use this *forward-backward book* to compare and contrast two seasons of your choice.

Step 1 **Stack** three sheets of paper. On the top sheet, trace a large circle.

Step 2 With the papers still stacked, **cut out** the circles.

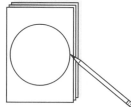

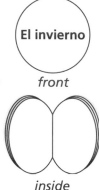

Step 3 **Staple** the paper circles together along the left-hand side to create a circular booklet.

Step 4 **Write** the name of a season on the cover and on the page that opens to the right list the months of the year in that particular season. On the following page draw a picture to illustrate the season.

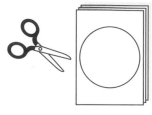

front

inside

Step 5 **Turn the book upside down** and write the name of a season on the cover. On the page that opens to the right list the months of the year in that particular season. On the following page draw a picture to illustrate the season.

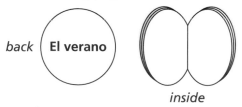

inside

OTHER SUGGESTIONS FOR A *FORWARD-BACKWARD BOOK* FOLDABLE

You may wish to use a *forward-backward book* foldable to organize vocabulary related to the city and the country. Use **la ciudad** as one title and **el campo** as the other. On the inside, list vocabulary words that are related to the category on the right-hand page as well as illustrating a scene on the opposite page. To give information for the second category, turn the book upside down.

It may be helpful to use a *forward-backward book* foldable to organize the food groups. You could use the name of a food group in the target language (meat, vegetables, fruit, etc.) as the title. On the inside, list as many foods in this food group as you can on the right-hand page and illustrate these foods on the opposite page. Give the same information for a second food group by reversing the book.

Pocket Book

La geografía Use this *pocket book* organizer in your ongoing study of all the countries in the Spanish-speaking world.

Step 1 **Fold** a sheet of paper (8½" x 11") in half like a *hamburger.*

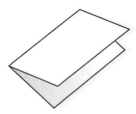

Step 2 **Open** the folded paper and fold one of the long sides up two inches to form a pocket. Refold the *hamburger* fold so that the newly formed pockets are on the inside.

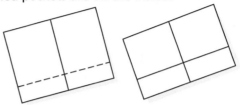

Step 3 **Glue** the outer edges of the two-inch fold with a small amount of glue.

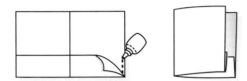

Step 4 **Make a multipaged booklet** by gluing six pockets side-by-side. Glue a cover around the multipaged *pocket book.*

Step 5 **Label** five pockets with the following geographical areas: **Europa, la América del Norte, la América del Sur, la América Central,** and **Islas del Caribe.** Use index cards inside the pockets to record information each time you learn something new about a specific country. Be sure to include the name of the country (in Spanish, of course) and its capital.

OTHER SUGGESTIONS FOR A *POCKET BOOK* FOLDABLE

You may wish to use a *pocket book* foldable to organize masculine and feminine nouns or singular and plural forms. You can make an index card to put in the correct pocket each time you learn a new word.

A *pocket book* foldable may be used to organize information about several subjects. For example, to organize information about traveling, label four pockets with topics such as *the train station, the train, the airport, the airplane* in Spanish. Make cards for all the words and phrases you know that go with each topic.

If you wish to organize what you are learning about important people, works of art, festivals, and other cultural information in countries that speak Spanish, a *pocket book* foldable may be helpful. You can make a card for each person, work of art or event that you study, and you can add cards and even add categories as you continue to learn about cultures that speak Spanish.

Vocabulary Book

Sinónimos y antónimos Use this *vocabulary book* to practice your vocabulary through the use of synonyms and antonyms.

Step 1 **Fold** a sheet of notebook paper in half like a *hot dog.*

Step 2 On one side, **cut** every third line. This usually results in ten tabs. Do this with two sheets of paper to make two books.

Step 3 **Label** the tops of the *vocabulary books* with the word **Sinónimos** on one and **Antónimos** on the other. As you learn new vocabulary in each unit, try to categorize words in this manner. Remember also to think of words you have previously learned to fill in your books.

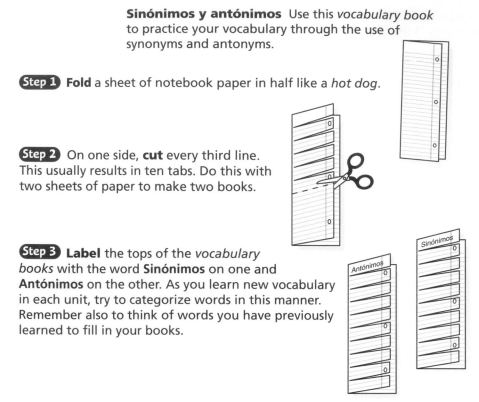

OTHER SUGGESTIONS FOR A *VOCABULARY BOOK* FOLDABLE

You may wish to use a *vocabulary book* foldable to help you remember words related to illness and going to the doctor or hospital. Come up with categories to write on the outside such as *a cold, the flu, at the doctor's office, at the pharmacy, at the hospital,* etc. On the inside, write as many terms and phrases as you can think of which relate to that category.

You can use a *vocabulary book* foldable to help remember any verb conjugation in Spanish. Write the infinitive at the top. If you know several tenses of a verb, you should also write what tense or tenses are being practiced. On the outside of the foldable, write the pronouns, and on the inside, write the corresponding verb form. You can use this as a quick study and review tool for any verb. At a more advanced level, you may wish to write many verbs down the outside and entire conjugations on the inside.

You may wish to use a *vocabulary book* foldable to help organize different kinds of clothing. Come up with categories in Spanish to list on the outside, such as *dressy, casual, men's, women's, both,* etc. On the inside, list as many articles of clothing fitting the category as you can in Spanish.

You can use *vocabulary book* foldables to practice adjective forms. Create two *vocabulary book* foldables, one for singular forms and the other for plural forms. On the singular book, write either masculine or feminine singular adjective forms on the outside and the other forms on the inside. To make this more challenging, write a mix of masculine and feminine forms on the outside, with the corresponding form on the inside. Repeat this process on the second book for the plural forms.

Tab Book

Preguntas Use this *tab book* to practice asking and answering questions.

Step 1 **Fold** a sheet of paper (8½" x 11") like a *hot dog* but fold it so that one side is one inch longer than the other.

Step 2 On the shorter side only, **cut** five equal tabs. On the front of each tab, **write** a question word you have learned. For example, you may wish to write the following.

Step 3 On the bottom edge, **write** any sentence you would like.

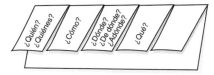

Elena es una alumna en un colegio en Puerto Rico.

Step 4 Under each flap, **write** the word from your sentence that answers the question on the front of the flap.

OTHER SUGGESTIONS FOR A *TAB BOOK* FOLDABLE

You may also use a *tab book* foldable to practice verb conjugations. You would need to make six tabs instead of five. Write a verb and a tense on the bottom edge and write the pronouns on the front of each tab. Under each flap, write the corresponding verb form.

You may wish to use a *tab book* foldable to practice new vocabulary words. Leave extra space on the bottom edge. Choose five or six vocabulary words and write each one on a tab. Under each flap, write a definition or translation of the word. If you can, write an original definition in Spanish. Use the bottom edge to write one or more original sentences using all of the words on the tabs.

You may wish to use the *tab book* to practice the subjunctive. Make a *tab book* foldable with a smaller bottom edge. Use the tabs to write down the different types of expressions requiring the subjunctive. Under each flap, write an original sentence that is an example of that type of expression. You may also make tabs that require the indicative. Label the foldable as being about the subjunctive on the bottom edge.

Miniature Matchbook

Descripciones Use this *miniature matchbook* to help you communicate in an interesting and more descriptive way.

Step 1 **Fold** a sheet of paper (8½" x 11") in half like a *hot dog*.

Step 2 **Cut** the sheet in half along the fold line.

Step 3 **Fold** the two long strips in half like *hot dogs,* leaving one side ½" shorter than the other side.

Step 4 **Fold** the ½" tab over the shorter side on each strip.

Step 5 **Cut** each of the two strips in half forming four halves. Then cut each half into thirds, making twelve miniature matchbooks.

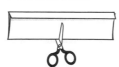

Step 6 **Glue** the twelve small matchbooks inside a *hamburger* fold (three rows of four each).

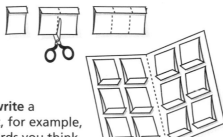

Step 7 On the front of each matchbook, **write** a subject you are going to tell or write about, for example, **la escuela**. Open up the tab and list any words you think you could use to make your discussion more interesting. You can add topics and words as you continue with your study of Spanish. If you glue several sections together, this foldable will "grow."

OTHER SUGGESTIONS FOR A *MINIATURE MATCHBOOK* FOLDABLE

You may use a *miniature matchbook* foldable to test each other on your knowledge of the vocabulary. Work in pairs with each partner making a blank *miniature matchbook* foldable. Each partner writes a topic related to the subjects you have just studied on the front of each matchbook. You may use categories of vocabulary, verbs you have recently learned to conjugate, or the subject of a reading. Your partner then writes as much as he or she can about that topic under the flap. This can alert you if you need to go back and review a topic.

A *miniature matchbook* foldable may help you organize and remember information you have read. After doing a cultural or literary reading, write down a concept presented in the reading on the front of each matchbook. Open up each tab and write down supporting details that support the idea.

Single Picture Frame

Dibujar y escribir Use this *single picture frame* book to help you illustrate the stories you write.

Step 1 **Fold** a sheet of paper (8½" x 11") in half like a *hamburger*.

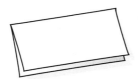

Step 2 **Open** the *hamburger* and gently roll one side of the *hamburger* toward the valley. Try not to crease the roll.

Step 3 **Cut** a rectangle out of the middle of the rolled side of paper, leaving a ½" border and forming a frame.

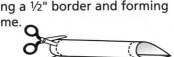

Step 4 **Fold** another sheet of paper (8½" x 11") in half like a *hamburger*.

Step 5 **Apply** glue to the picture frame and place inside the *hamburger* fold.

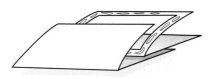

Variation:
- Place a picture behind the frame and glue the edges of the frame to the other side of the *hamburger* fold. This locks the picture in place.
- Cut out only three sides of the rolled rectangle. This forms a window with a cover that opens and closes.

OTHER SUGGESTIONS FOR A *SINGLE PICTURE FRAME* FOLDABLE

You may wish to write about a trip you took in the car using a *single picture frame* foldable. Before you begin, organize what you will say by drawing a map of the route you took on your trip. You can then write about the trip using your drawings as a guide.

Work in small groups. Each student should create a *single picture frame* foldable with a picture glued into it. You may either cut out a magazine picture or draw your own, although it should be fairly complex. Then give your foldable to another member of the group who will write sentences about what is in the picture and what people in the picture are doing. That student will pass it on to a third student who will write sentences about what is not in the picture and what people in the picture are not doing. The foldables can be passed to additional students to see if they can add more sentences.

Minibook

Mi autobiografía Use this *minibook* organizer to write and illustrate your autobiography. Before you begin to write, think about the many things concerning yourself that you have the ability to write about in Spanish. On the left pages, draw the events of your life in chronological order. On the right, write about your drawings.

Step 1 **Fold** a sheet of paper (8½" x 11") in half like a *hot dog*.

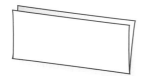

Step 2 **Fold** it in half again like a *hamburger*.

Step 3 Then **fold** in half again, forming eights.

Step 4 **Open** the fold and **cut** the eight sections apart.

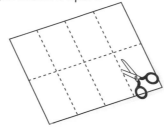

Step 5 **Place** all eight sections in a stack and fold in half like a hamburger.

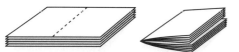

Step 6 **Staple** along the center fold line. **Glue** the front and back sheets into a construction paper cover.

OTHER SUGGESTIONS FOR A *MINIBOOK* FOLDABLE

Work in pairs to practice new verbs and verb forms using a *minibook* foldable. Illustrate different verbs on the left pages. If it is not clear what pronoun is required, you should write the pronoun under the drawing, for instance to differentiate between *we* and *they*. Then trade *minibooks* and write sentences to go with each picture on the right pages, using the new verb and the pronoun illustrated or indicated.

You may also wish to work in small groups and use *minibook* foldables to practice the subjunctive. Each person writes beginnings of sentences that take the subjunctive on the left pages. Then pass your *minibook* to the next group member, who, on the right page, completes each sentence. That student will pass the *minibook* on to a third member, who will write an alternate completion for each sentence under the first one. Repeat this until all group members have written a completion for all sentences.

Paper File Folder

Las emociones Use this *paper file folder* organizer
to keep track of happenings or events that cause
you to feel a certain way.

Step 1 **Fold** four sheets of
paper (8½" x 11") in half like a
hamburger. Leave one side one
inch longer than the other side.

Step 2 On each sheet, **fold**
the one-inch tab over the short side,
forming an envelope-like fold.

Step 3 **Place** the four sheets
side-by-side, then move each
fold so that the tabs are exposed.

Step 4 Moving left to right, **cut**
staggered tabs in each fold, 2⅛"
wide. Fold the tabs upward.

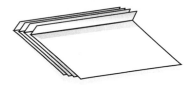

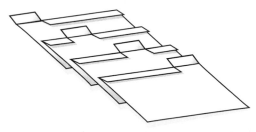

Step 5 **Glue** the ends of the folders together. On each tab,
write an emotion you sometimes feel. Pay attention to when
it is that you feel happy, sad, nervous, etc. Describe the
situation in Spanish and file it in the correct pocket.

OTHER SUGGESTIONS FOR A *PAPER FILE FOLDER* FOLDABLE

You may use a *paper file folder* organizer to keep track of verbs and verb forms. You should
make a folder for each type of regular verb and for each type of irregular verb. Write the
conjugations for some important verbs in each category and file them in the *paper file folder*
organizer. Add new tenses to the existing cards and new verbs as you learn them.

A *paper file folder* organizer can be useful for keeping notes on the cultural information that
you will learn. You may wish to make categories for different types of cultural information and
add index cards to them as you learn new facts and concepts about the target cultures.

Envelope Fold

Un viaje especial Use this *envelope fold* to make a hidden picture or to write secret clues about a city in the Spanish-speaking world you would like to visit.

Step 1 **Fold** a sheet of paper into a *taco*, forming a square. Cut off the leftover piece.

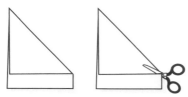

Step 2 **Open** the folded *taco* and refold it the opposite way, forming another *taco* and an X-fold pattern.

Step 3 **Open** the *taco fold* and fold the corners toward the center point of the X, forming a small square.

Step 4 **Trace** this square onto another sheet of paper. Cut and glue it to the inside of the envelope. Pictures can be drawn under the tabs.

Step 5 Use this foldable to **draw** a picture of the city you would like to visit. Or if you prefer, **write** clues about the city and have your classmates raise one tab at a time until they can guess what city the picture represents. Number the tabs in the order in which they are to be opened.

OTHER SUGGESTIONS FOR AN *ENVELOPE FOLD* FOLDABLE

An *envelope fold* can be useful for practicing vocabulary related to airports, trains, hotels, or driving. Draw a scene that depicts many of the vocabulary words. Then write on each of the four flaps the new words that are represented under that flap. You could also give the picture to a partner and have the partner fill in the words.

You may want to use an *envelope fold* to review a selection you have read. Depict a scene from the selection on the paper covered by the tabs. Number the tabs in the order they are to be opened and have a partner open the tabs one at a time to guess what scene is illustrated. The partner should then write a description of the scenes.

Large Sentence Strips

El presente y el pasado   Use these *large sentence strips* to help you compare and contrast activities in the past and in the present.

Step 1 Take two sheets of paper (8½" x 11") and **fold** into *hamburgers*. Cut along the fold lines, making four half sheets. (Use as many half sheets as necessary for additional pages to your book.)

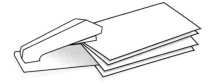

Step 2 Fold each half sheet in half like a *hot dog*.

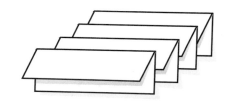

Step 3 Place the folds side-by-side and **staple** them together on the left side.

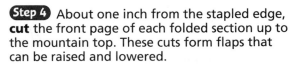

Step 4 About one inch from the stapled edge, **cut** the front page of each folded section up to the mountain top. These cuts form flaps that can be raised and lowered.

Step 5 To make a half-cover, use a sheet of construction paper one inch longer than the book. **Glue** the back of the last sheet to the construction paper strip, leaving one inch on the left side to fold over and cover the original staples. Staple this half-cover in place.

Step 6 With a friend, **write** sentences on the front of the flap, either in the present tense or in the past tense. Then switch your books of sentence strips and write the opposite tense inside under the flaps.

OTHER SUGGESTIONS FOR A *LARGE SENTENCE STRIPS* FOLDABLE

You may work in pairs to use *large sentence strips* to practice using direct and/or indirect object pronouns. On the front of each flap, write full sentences which have direct or indirect objects or both. Then trade sentence strips. You and your partner will each write sentences under the flaps replacing the direct or indirect objects with object pronouns.

Large sentence strips can help you contrast summer and winter activities. On the front of each flap, write sentences about activities that you do in either summer or winter. Under each flap, you should write that in the other season you do not do that activity, and you should tell what you do instead. This may be done as an individual or a partner activity.

You may use *large sentence strips* to practice using verbs that can be used reflexively and nonreflexively. Write a sentence using a reflexive verb on the outside of each flap. Under the flap, write a sentence using the same verb nonreflexively.

Project Board With Tabs

Diversiones favoritas Use this *project board with tabs* to display a visual about your favorite movie or video. Be sure to make it as attractive as possible to help convince others to see it.

Step 1 **Draw** a large illustration, a series of small illustrations, or write on the front of a sheet of paper.

Step 2 **Pinch** and slightly fold the sheet of paper at the point where a tab is desired on the illustrated piece of paper. Cut into the paper on the fold. Cut straight in, then cut up to form an "L." When the paper is unfolded, it will form a tab with the illustration on the front.

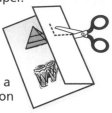

Step 3 After all tabs have been cut, **glue** this front sheet onto a second sheet of paper. Place glue around all four edges and in the middle, away from tabs.

Step 4 **Write** or draw under the tabs. If the project is made as a bulletin board using butcher paper, tape or glue smaller sheets of paper under the tabs.

Think of favorite scenes from a movie or cultural event that you enjoyed and draw them on the front of the tabs. Underneath the tabs write a description of the scene or tell why you liked that part of the movie. It might be fun to not put a title on the project board and just hang it up and let classmates guess the name of the movie you are describing.

OTHER SUGGESTIONS FOR A *PROJECT BOARD WITH TABS* FOLDABLE

A *project board with tabs* may be used to describe games, hobbies, or sports. Illustrate a game or one aspect of that game on the outside of the tab and write a description of your drawing under the tab. You may also wish to illustrate a series of important events in a particular game that you watched or participated in recently. You may wish to work together.

You may describe a visit to a museum or park using a *project board with tabs.* You may wish to sketch your favorite paintings, or write titles and artists, on the outside of the tab and describe them on the inside. To describe a park, you may illustrate what you did at the park or your favorite features of the park.

You may wish to use a *project board with tabs* to practice the future tense. Illustrate what you plan to do in college or in your career on the outside of the tabs. Under each tab, write one or more sentences in the future about your plans.

Sentence Strip Holder

Para practicar más Use this *sentence strip holder* to practice your vocabulary, your verbs, or anything else you might feel you need extra help with.

Step 1 **Fold** a sheet of paper (8½" x 11") in half like a *hamburger*.

Step 2 **Open** the *hamburger* and fold the two outer edges toward the valley. This forms a shutter fold.

Step 3 **Fold** one of the inside edges of the shutter back to the outside fold. This fold forms a floppy L.

Step 4 **Glue** the floppy L tab down to the base so that it forms a strong straight L tab.

Step 5 **Glue** the other shutter side to the front of this L tab. This forms a tent that is the backboard for the flashcards or student work to be displayed.

Step 6 **Fold** the edge of the L up ¼" to ½" to form a lip that will keep the sentence strips from slipping off the holder.

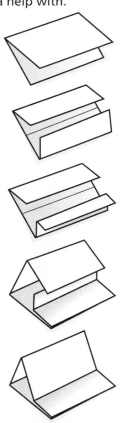

Vocabulary and spelling words can be stored inside the "tent" formed by this fold.

OTHER SUGGESTIONS FOR A *SENTENCE STRIP HOLDER* FOLDABLE

You may wish to practice new or irregular verbs using a *sentence strip holder*. Work in pairs. Make flash cards showing the infinitives of the verbs to practice in Spanish. You should each take half of the cards and take turns setting one verb on the *sentence strip holder*. One partner will then say as many sentences as possible using different forms of that verb, and the other will write down the subject and conjugated verb form (or just the verb form) for each sentence. Partners should check to make sure each verb form is spelled correctly. You can repeat this activity for each verb.

A *sentence strip holder* may be used to practice talking about service activities. Work in small groups and make a flash card with the name of each type of activity, such as going to the bank or to the post office. Each group should make the same number of cards. Put one card at a time on the *sentence strip holder* and spend several minutes writing everything you can about the topic. When you have all finished writing, share what you have written.

Expand your view of the Spanish-speaking world.

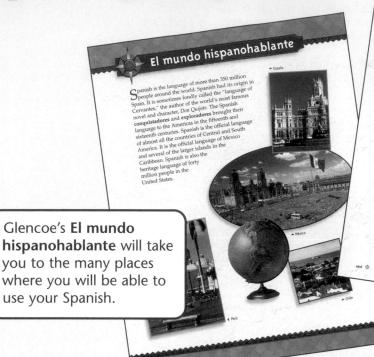

Glencoe's **El mundo hispanohablante** will take you to the many places where you will be able to use your Spanish.

Maps, facts, and figures will serve as a valuable resource for you throughout your journey.

Start your journey into language and culture.

Opening photo provides a cultural backdrop for the chapter.

Objectives let you know what you will be able to do at the end of the chapter.

Fine Art related to the chapter enriches your cultural knowledge and serves as a springboard for discussion.

Continue to explore Spanish language and culture online at **glencoe.com**.

Talk about the chapter theme with your new vocabulary.

Access your book, the practice activities, and the audio recordings on any computer with StudentWorks.

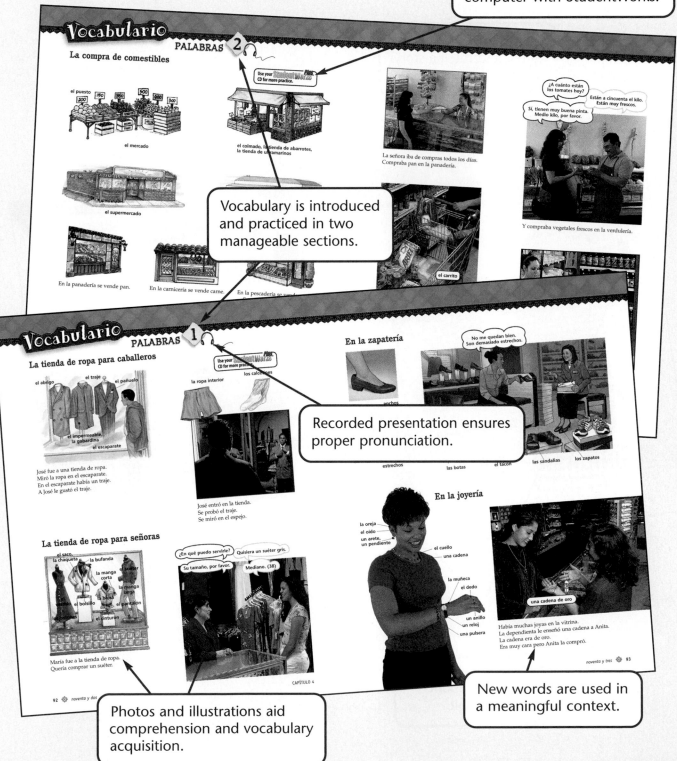

Vocabulary is introduced and practiced in two manageable sections.

Recorded presentation ensures proper pronunciation.

Photos and illustrations aid comprehension and vocabulary acquisition.

New words are used in a meaningful context.

Practice and master new vocabulary.

Historieta enables you to tell and retell a story, using your new words.

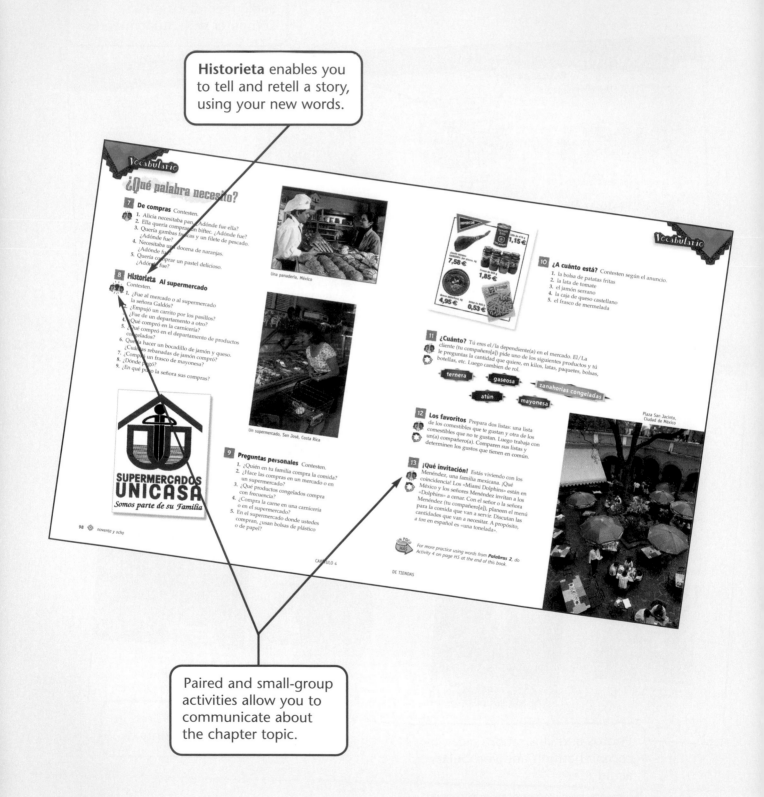

Paired and small-group activities allow you to communicate about the chapter topic.

Learn grammar within the context of the chapter theme.

New structures are presented in simple terms with familiar vocabulary.

Immediate reinforcement shows you how structure works to build meaning.

Practice grammar and vocabulary with fun, online **eGames** at glencoe.com.

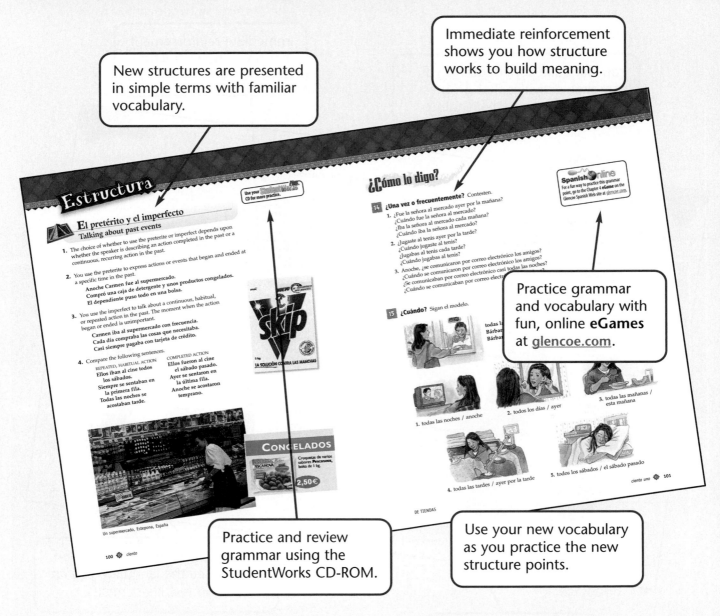

Practice and review grammar using the StudentWorks CD-ROM.

Use your new vocabulary as you practice the new structure points.

Build on what you know.

> Immediate reinforcement shows you how structure works to build meaning.

> You will build confidence as you complete activities that progress from easy to more challenging.

Estructura

16 Historieta Los sábados de Juan Antonio Cambien **Todos los sábados** a **El sábado pasado**. Hagan los cambios necesarios.

Todos los sábados Juan Antonio se levantaba muy temprano. Bajaba a la cocina y él mismo preparaba el desayuno. Después de comer, subía a su cuarto y prendía su computadora. Cuando hacía la conexión a Internet mandaba un correo electrónico a un buen amigo en España. En pocos segundos se comunicaba con su amigo. Los dos escribían de muchas cosas durante horas.

17 Entrevista Vas a entrevistar *(interview)* a un(a) compañero(a). Pregúntale lo que le gustaba hacer cuando era joven y dos cosas que le impresionaron como niño(a). Luego cambien de rol.

18 Tu amigo(a) chileno(a) Estás hablando con un(a) amigo(a) (tu compañero[a]) que antes vivía en Chile. Él o ella te está describiendo «Paseo estación central», donde siempre iba de compras. Te está explicando por qué le gustaba ir de compras allí. Luego explícale donde tú prefieres hacer las compras.

Spanish Online
For more information about Chile, go to Web Explore on the Glencoe Spanish Web site at glencoe.com.

NUESTROS PRECIOS NO TIENEN COMPETENCIA, PORQUE SOMOS FABRICANTES

PASEO
ESTACIÓN CENTRAL
DESCUENTOS PARA TURISTAS

102 ❁ ciento dos

CAPÍTULO 4

Estructura

Dos acciones en una oración
Narrating a sequence of events

1. Often a sentence may have two or more verbs in the past. The verbs may be in the same tense or in different tenses. In the sentence below, both verbs are in the preterite. Both describe simple actions that began and ended at a specific time in the past.

   Laura llegó ayer y Pepe la vio.

2. In the sentence below, the two verbs are in the imperfect because they both describe habitual or continuous actions. The moment when the actions began or ended is unimportant.

   Durante los inviernos, Adela iba a las montañas a esquiar, pero yo trabajaba.

3. In the sentence below, the verb **estudiaba** is in the imperfect; it describes the background—what was going on. The verb in the preterite, **entró**, expresses the action or event that interrupted the ongoing action.

   Yo estudiaba cuando Julia entró.

¿Cómo lo digo?

19 Historieta ¿Qué hacías cuando... ?
Contesten.
1. ¿Estabas en casa cuando sonó el teléfono?
2. ¿Mirabas un video cuando sonó?
3. ¿Contestaste el teléfono cuando sonó?
4. ¿Hablabas por teléfono cuando tu padre volvió a casa?
5. ¿Preguntó tu padre con quién hablabas?
6. ¿Con quién hablabas cuando tu padre entró?

Línea TELECOR
El nuevo servicio de telefonía fija con muchas más ventajas para ti.
40% MENOS
0,021

CENTRO DE INFORMACIÓN UNIVERSITARIA
ALCALÁ

DE TIENDAS

ciento tres ❁ 103

> Realia adds interest to the lesson. You can see the language you are learning in real-life contexts.

> Expand your knowledge about the chapter theme online with **Web Explore**.

Engage classmates in real conversation.

You can watch and participate in the Interactive Conversation on CD-ROM.

Apply newly learned vocabulary and structures to real-life situations.

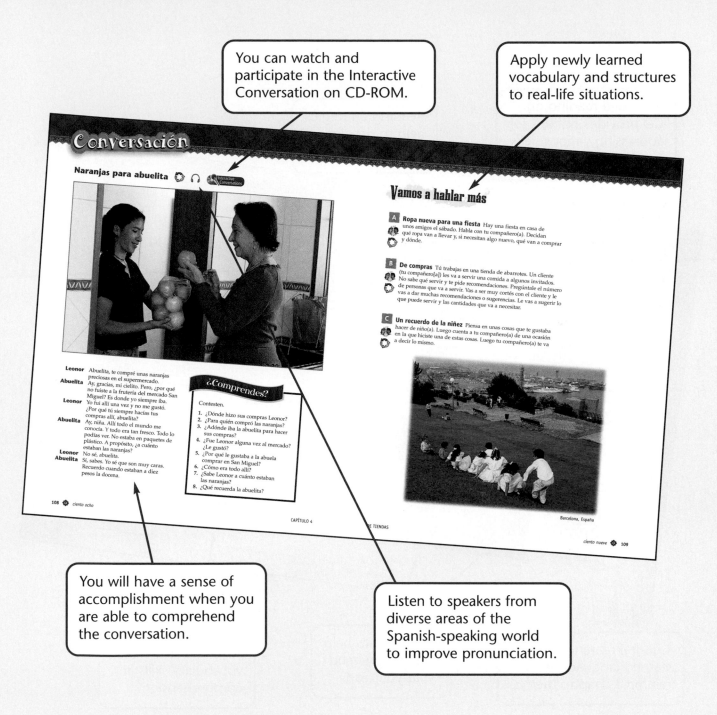

Conversación

Naranjas para abuelita

Leonor Abuelita, te compré unas naranjas preciosas en el supermercado.

Abuelita Ay, gracias, mi cielito. Pero, ¿por qué no fuiste a la frutería del mercado San Miguel? Es donde yo siempre iba.

Leonor Yo fui allí una vez y no me gustó. ¿Por qué tú siempre hacías tus compras allí, abuelita?

Abuelita Ay, niña. Allí todo el mundo me conocía. Y todo era tan fresco. Todo lo podías ver. No estaba en paquetes de plástico. A propósito, ¿a cuánto estaban las naranjas?

Leonor No sé, abuelita.

Abuelita Sí, sabes. Yo sé que son muy caras. Recuerdo cuando estaban a diez pesos la docena.

108 ❁ ciento ocho

CAPÍTULO 4   DE TIENDAS

¿Comprendes?

Contesten.

1. ¿Dónde hizo sus compras Leonor?
2. ¿Para quién compró las naranjas?
3. ¿Adónde iba la abuelita para hacer sus compras?
4. ¿Fue Leonor alguna vez al mercado? ¿Le gustó?
5. ¿Por qué le gustaba a la abuela comprar en San Miguel?
6. ¿Cómo era todo allí?
7. ¿Sabe Leonor a cuánto estaban las naranjas?
8. ¿Qué recuerda la abuelita?

Vamos a hablar más

A **Ropa nueva para una fiesta** Hay una fiesta en casa de unos amigos el sábado. Habla con tu compañero(a). Decidan qué ropa van a llevar y, si necesitan algo nuevo, qué van a comprar y dónde.

B **De compras** Tú trabajas en una tienda de abarrotes. Un cliente (tu compañero[a]) les va a servir una comida a algunos invitados. No sabe qué servir y te pide recomendaciones. Pregúntale el número de personas que va a servir. Vas a ser muy cortés con el cliente y le vas a dar muchas recomendaciones o sugerencias. Le vas a sugerir lo que puede servir y las cantidades que va a necesitar.

C **Un recuerdo de la niñez** Piensa en unas cosas que te gustaba hacer de niño(a). Luego cuenta a tu compañero(a) de una ocasión en la que hiciste una de estas cosas. Luego tu compañero(a) te va a decir lo mismo.

Barcelona, España

ciento nueve ❁ 109

You will have a sense of accomplishment when you are able to comprehend the conversation.

Listen to speakers from diverse areas of the Spanish-speaking world to improve pronunciation.

Heighten your cultural awareness.

Recorded reading on CD provides options for addressing various skills and learning styles.

Reading Strategies help to develop your reading skills.

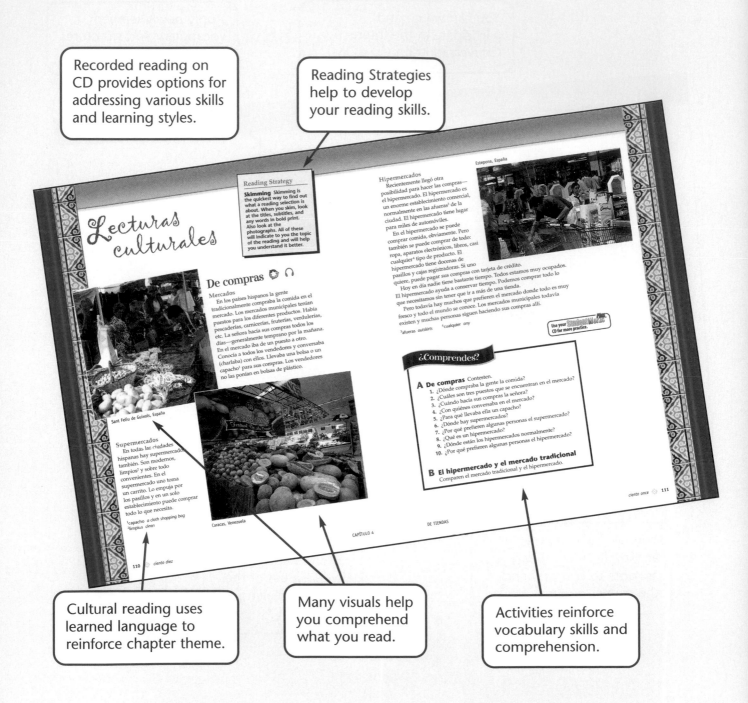

Reading Strategy

Skimming Skimming is the quickest way to find out what a reading selection is about. When you skim, look at the titles, subtitles, and any words in bold print. Also look at the photographs. All of these will indicate to you the topic of the reading and will help you understand it better.

Lecturas culturales

De compras

Mercados

En los países hispanos la gente tradicionalmente compraba la comida en el mercado. Los mercados municipales tenían puestos para los diferentes productos. Había pescaderías, carnicerías, fruterías, verdulerías, etc. La señora hacía sus compras todos los días—generalmente temprano por la mañana. En el mercado iba de un puesto a otro. Conocía a todos los vendedores y conversaba (charlaba) con ellos. Llevaba una bolsa o un capacho¹ para sus compras. Los vendedores no las ponían en bolsas de plástico.

Sant Feliu de Guíxols, España

Supermercados

En todas las ciudades hispanas hay supermercados también. Son modernos, limpios² y sobre todo convenientes. En el supermercado uno toma un carrito. Lo empuja por los pasillos y en un solo establecimiento puede comprar todo lo que necesita.

¹capacho *a cloth shopping bag*
²limpios *clean*

Caracas, Venezuela

Hipermercados

Recientemente llegó otra posibilidad para hacer las compras— el hipermercado. El hipermercado es un enorme establecimiento comercial, normalmente en las afueras³ de la ciudad. El hipermercado tiene lugar para miles de automóviles.

En el hipermercado se puede comprar comida, obviamente. Pero también se puede comprar de todo: ropa, aparatos electrónicos, libros, casi cualquier⁴ tipo de producto. El hipermercado tiene docenas de pasillos y cajas registradoras. Si uno quiere, puede pagar sus compras con tarjeta de crédito.

Hoy en día nadie tiene bastante tiempo. Todos estamos muy ocupados. El hipermercado ayuda a conservar tiempo. Podemos comprar todo lo que necesitamos sin tener que ir a más de una tienda.

Pero todavía hay muchos que prefieren el mercado donde todo es muy fresco y todo el mundo se conoce. Los mercados municipales todavía existen y muchas personas siguen haciendo sus compras allí.

³afueras *outskirts*   ⁴cualquier *any*

Estepona, España

Use your Student Works Plus CD for more practice.

¿Comprendes?

A De compras Contesten.
1. ¿Dónde compraba la gente la comida?
2. ¿Cuáles son tres puestos que se encuentran en el mercado?
3. ¿Cuándo hacía sus compras la señora?
4. ¿Con quiénes conversaba en el mercado?
5. ¿Para qué llevaba ella un capacho?
6. ¿Dónde hay supermercados?
7. ¿Por qué prefieren algunas personas el supermercado?
8. ¿Qué es un hipermercado?
9. ¿Dónde están los hipermercados normalmente?
10. ¿Por qué prefieren algunas personas el hipermercado?

B El hipermercado y el mercado tradicional
Comparen el mercado tradicional y el hipermercado.

CAPÍTULO 4   DE TIENDAS

ciento once   111

110   ciento diez

Cultural reading uses learned language to reinforce chapter theme.

Many visuals help you comprehend what you read.

Activities reinforce vocabulary skills and comprehension.

Enrich your cultural knowledge.

> Optional cultural readings reinforce the chapter theme.

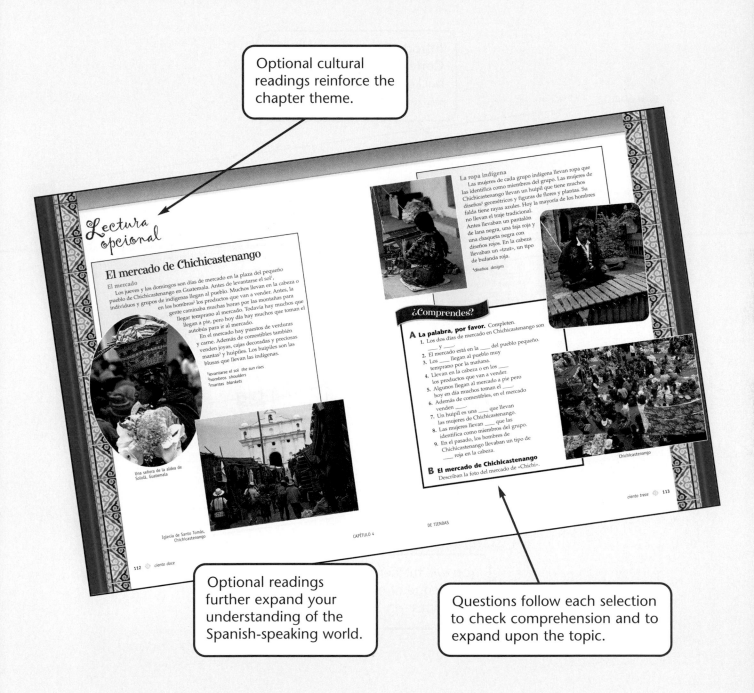

Lectura opcional

El mercado de Chichicastenango

El mercado

Los jueves y los domingos son días de mercado en la plaza del pequeño pueblo de Chichicastenango en Guatemala. Antes de levantarse el sol[1], individuos y grupos de indígenas llegan al pueblo. Muchos llevan en la cabeza o en los hombros[2] los productos que van a vender. Antes, la gente caminaba muchas horas por las montañas para llegar temprano al mercado. Todavía hay muchos que llegan a pie, pero hoy día hay muchos que toman el autobús para ir al mercado.

En el mercado hay puestos de verduras y carne. Además de comestibles también venden joyas, cajas decoradas y preciosas mantas[3] y huipiles. Los huipiles son las blusas que llevan las indígenas.

[1]levantarse el sol the sun rises
[2]hombros shoulders
[3]mantas blankets

Una señora de la aldea de Sololá, Guatemala

Iglesia de Santo Tomás, Chichicastenango

CAPÍTULO 4

La ropa indígena

Las mujeres de cada grupo indígena llevan ropa que las identifica como miembros del grupo. Las mujeres de Chichicastenango llevan un huipil que tiene muchos diseños[4] geométricos y figuras de flores y plantas. Su falda tiene rayas azules. Hoy la mayoría de los hombres no llevan el traje tradicional. Antes llevaban un pantalón de lana negra, una faja roja y una chaqueta negra con diseños rojos. En la cabeza llevaban un «tzut», un tipo de bufanda roja.

[4]diseños designs

¿Comprendes?

A La palabra, por favor. Completen.
1. Los dos días de mercado en Chichicastenango son ____ y ____.
2. El mercado está en la ____ del pueblo pequeño.
3. Los ____ llegan al pueblo muy temprano por la mañana.
4. Llevan en la cabeza o en los ____ los productos que van a vender.
5. Algunos llegan al mercado a pie pero hoy en día muchos toman el ____.
6. Además de comestibles, en el mercado venden ____.
7. Un huipil es una ____ que llevan las mujeres de Chichicastenango.
8. Las mujeres llevan ____ que las identifica como miembros del grupo.
9. En el pasado, los hombres de Chichicastenango llevaban un tipo de ____ roja en la cabeza.

B El mercado de Chichicastenango
Describan la foto del mercado de «Chichi».

Chichicastenango

DE TIENDAS

ciento trece 113

112 ciento doce

> Optional readings further expand your understanding of the Spanish-speaking world.

> Questions follow each selection to check comprehension and to expand upon the topic.

Connect with other disciplines.

> Introduction to the **Conexiones** provides the background for students to understand the reading.

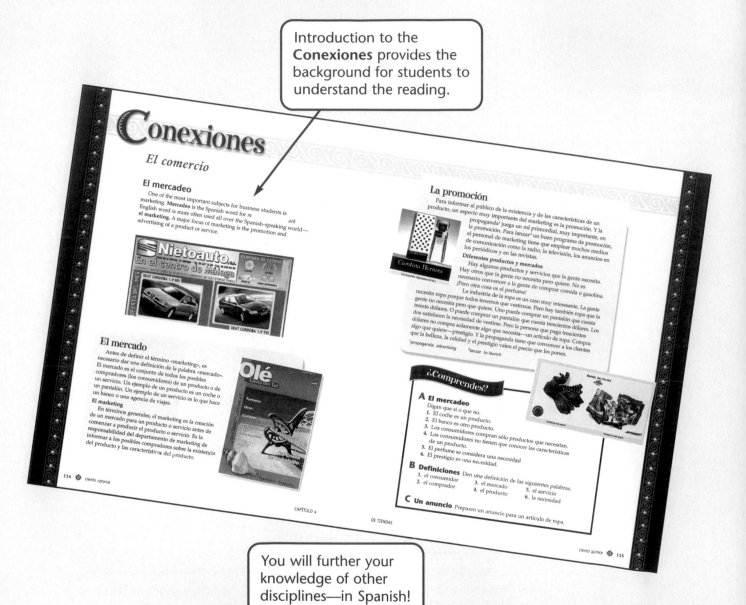

> You will further your knowledge of other disciplines—in Spanish!

It's your turn!
Apply what you have learned.

Use your new skills to communicate in meaningful, open-ended activities.

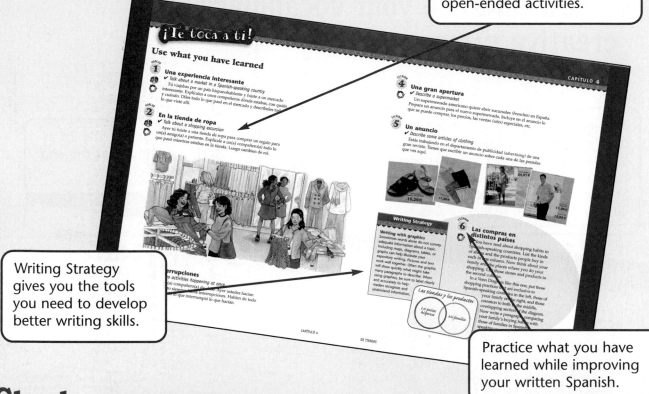

Writing Strategy gives you the tools you need to develop better writing skills.

Practice what you have learned while improving your written Spanish.

Check your progress.

Review what you have learned and prepare for your chapter test.

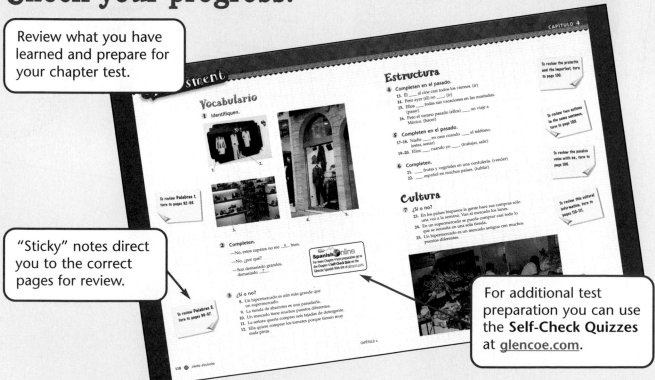

"Sticky" notes direct you to the correct pages for review.

For additional test preparation you can use the **Self-Check Quizzes** at glencoe.com.

Go beyond the text to learn more about culture and language.
Review and use your vocabulary in creative ways.

The illustration provided at the end of each chapter recombines material you have learned to remind you of what you know how to say in Spanish. Use this illustration as a prompt to allow you to demonstrate all you know how to say or write.

You can use the list as a self-check at the end of the chapter.

Vocabulary is categorized to help recall.

¡Hablo como un pro!

Tell all you can about this illustration.

ZARA

CAPÍTULO 4

Vocabulario

Identifying more stores
la zapatería   la joyería

Shopping for clothes and jewelry
mirar en el escaparate   ¿En qué puedo   No me (le) queda(n)
  (la vitrina)   servirle?   bien.
probarse la ropa   Quisiera...

Identifying more clothing
el bolsillo   el suéter   el pañuelo
el saco, la chaqueta   la camisa de mangas   la ropa interior
el abrigo   cortas (largas)   la bufanda
el impermeable, la   el vestido   los botones
  gabardina   el cinturón   las sandalias

Identifying jewelry
las joyas   una cadena   un arete, un pendiente
una pulsera   un anillo   un reloj

Identifying more parts of the body
la muñeca   el dedo
el cuello   la oreja, el oído

Describing clothing and jewelry
mediano(a)   estrecho(a)
ancho(a)   de oro

Identifying more food stores
el colmado, la tienda   el puesto   la panadería   la pastelería
  de abarrotes, la   el supermercado   la carnicería   la verdulería
  tienda de   el hipermercado   la pescadería   la frutería
  ultramarinos

Foods
el pan   el pescado   los pasteles
la carne   los mariscos   las legumbres,
      los vegetales

Shopping for food
hacer las compras, ir   tener buena pinta   la bolsa de plástico   un frasco
  de compras   empujar el carrito   una tajada, una   una caja
¿A cuánto están...?   fresco(a)   rebanada   una docena

las botas
el tacón

VIDEOTUR

Episodio 4

In this video episode, you will join Francisco and Julián on a trip to the supermarket. See page 483 for more information. As you watch, look for gestures the speakers use to help convey their message.

How well do you know your vocabulary?
• Choose any type of store you like to shop in.
• Tell what you like to buy there.

DE TIENDAS

ciento veintiuno   121

Read and learn about the diverse cultures of the Spanish-speaking world with People en español.

> **People en español** articles throughout **¡Buen viaje!** take you to different regions in the world where Spanish is spoken.

> Learn about interesting topics— holidays, foods, entertainment, and famous people—in Spanish you can read!

Enhance your appreciation of literature and culture.

Literary selections present another view of Hispanic culture.

Literary Companion gives you another opportunity to apply your reading skills in Spanish.

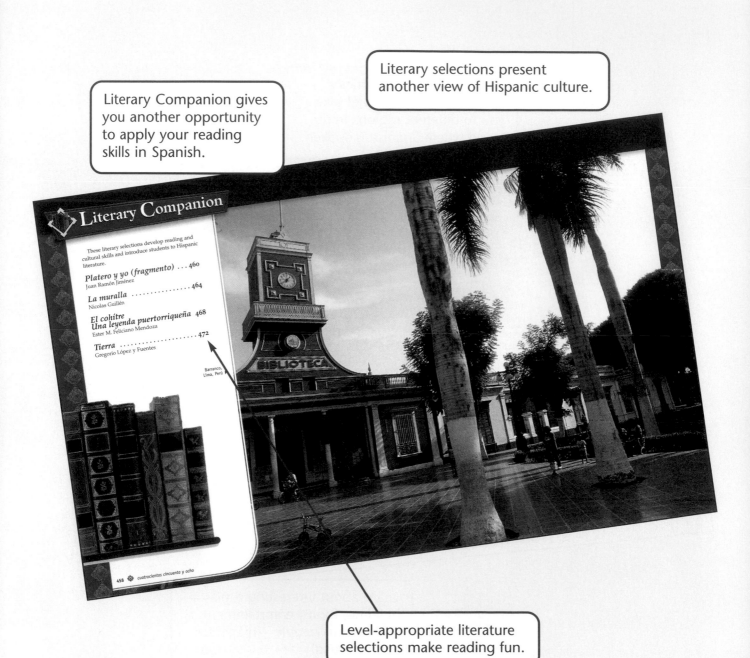

Literary Companion

These literary selections develop reading and cultural skills and introduce students to Hispanic literature.

Barranco, Lima, Perú

BIBLIOTECA

458 cuatrocientos cincuenta y ocho

Level-appropriate literature selections make reading fun.

Go on a tour of the Spanish-speaking world with ¡Viva el mundo hispano!

¡Viva el mundo hispano!, filmed in eight Spanish-speaking countries, lets you experience the diversity of the Spanish-speaking world while reinforcing the language you have learned and improving your listening and viewing skills.

You will love seeing the adventures and mishaps of the ¡Viva el mundo hispano! video characters.

You will visit places where you will hear different accents, dialects, and languages. ¡Viva el mundo hispano! will take you on an exciting tour of the Spanish-speaking world.

Repaso A

Las compras para la escuela

Diego Rivera *Fin del corrido*

Vocabulario

Los alumnos llegan a la escuela a las
   ocho menos cuarto.
Algunos toman el bus escolar.
Otros van a la escuela a pie.

Los alumnos estudian mucho.
Toman apuntes.
Escuchan a la profesora cuando habla.
La profesora enseña.

José está en la papelería.
Necesita materiales escolares.
Compra un cuaderno, un lápiz y
   un bolígrafo.

Teresa está en la tienda de ropa.
Compra una blusa para llevar a la escuela.
Mira la blusa.
Paga en la caja.

1 Historieta En la escuela Contesten.

1. ¿Cómo llegan los alumnos a la escuela? ¿Toman el bus, van en carro o van a pie?
2. ¿A qué hora llegan a la escuela?
3. ¿Con quién hablan los alumnos cuando entran en la sala de clase?
4. ¿Quiénes toman exámenes y quién da los exámenes?
5. ¿Sacan los alumnos notas altas?
6. ¿Prestan ellos atención cuando la profesora habla?

2 Historieta A la papelería Escojan.

1. Alicia necesita materiales escolares. ¿Adónde va ella?
   a. a la cafetería   b. a la tienda de ropa   c. a la papelería
2. ¿Con quién habla Alicia en la papelería?
   a. con el empleado   b. con el profesor   c. con el mesero
3. ¿Qué compra Alicia en la papelería?
   a. un refresco   b. un pantalón corto   c. un cuaderno
4. ¿Dónde paga Alicia?
   a. cien pesos   b. en la caja   c. en el parque
5. ¿En qué lleva ella los materiales escolares?
   a. en una mochila   b. en un cuaderno   c. en una asignatura

3 Historieta En la tienda de ropa
Contesten según se indica.

1. ¿Adónde va Roberto? (a la tienda de ropa)
2. ¿Qué necesita? (una camisa)
3. ¿Busca una camisa verde? (no, roja y azul)
4. ¿Qué talla usa? (38)
5. ¿Compra Roberto una camisa? (sí)
6. ¿Cuánto cuesta? (125 pesos)
7. ¿Dónde paga Roberto? (en la caja)

Use your StudentWorks Plus CD for more practice.

Calle Florida, Buenos Aires, Argentina

Conversación

La apertura de clases

Paco Elena, ¿cómo estás?
Elena Muy bien, Paco. ¿Y tú?
Paco Bien. ¿Adónde vas?
Elena Voy a la papelería. Necesito comprar algunas cosas para la apertura de clases.
Paco Verdad. Septiembre una vez más. ¡Es increíble!

¿Comprendes?

Contesten.

1. ¿Con quién habla Elena?
2. ¿Cómo está Paco?
3. ¿Son amigos Elena y Paco?
4. ¿Adónde va Elena?
5. ¿Qué necesita ella?
6. ¿De qué hablan los dos amigos?

Estructura

Presente de los verbos en -ar

1. Review the forms of the present tense of regular **-ar** verbs.

MIRAR	miro	miras	mira	miramos	*miráis*	miran
TOMAR	tomo	tomas	toma	tomamos	*tomáis*	toman

2. Remember, to make a sentence negative you put **no** before the verb.

No hablamos francés. Hablamos español.

3. Remember to use **tú** when talking to a friend, family member, or person your own age. Use **usted** when speaking to an adult, a person you do not know well, or someone to whom you wish to show respect.

¿Tú estudias español, Roberto?
¿Y usted, señora? ¿Usted también estudia español?

4 **Entrevista** Contesten personalmente.

1. ¿En qué escuela estudias?
2. ¿Cómo llegas a la escuela por la mañana?
3. ¿Cuántos cursos tomas?
4. ¿En qué llevas los materiales escolares?
5. ¿Estudian mucho los alumnos de tu escuela?
6. ¿Sacan ustedes notas buenas?
7. ¿Toman ustedes muchos exámenes?
8. ¿Escuchan ustedes cuando la profesora habla?

Universidad Nacional,
San Andrés, Colombia

5 Historieta En la fiesta Completen.

1. Durante la fiesta todos nosotros _____. (bailar)
2. Felipe _____ el piano. (tocar)
3. Mientras él _____ el piano, Elena y Carlos _____. (tocar, cantar)
4. ¿_____ ustedes refrescos durante la fiesta? (preparar)
5. ¿_____ ustedes fotos durante la fiesta? (tomar)
6. Sí, y todos nosotros _____ las fotografías. (mirar)

Una fiesta en la Ciudad de Guatemala

Los verbos ir, dar, estar

1. Note that the verbs **ir, dar,** and **estar** are the same as regular **-ar** verbs in all forms except **yo.**

ESTAR	**estoy**	estás	está	**estamos**	*estáis*	están
DAR	**doy**	das	da	**damos**	*dais*	dan
IR	**voy**	vas	va	**vamos**	*vais*	van

2. The preposition **a** often follows the verb **ir.** Remember that **a** contracts with **el** to form one word—**al.**

   Voy al café. No voy a la tienda.

6 Historieta Voy a la escuela. Contesten.

1. ¿Vas a la escuela?
2. ¿A qué hora vas a la escuela?
3. ¿Con quién vas a la escuela?
4. ¿Están ustedes en la escuela ahora?
5. ¿Cómo van ustedes a la escuela?

7 Historieta A la tienda de ropa
Completen.

Estepona, España

Yo __1__ (ir) a la tienda de ropa.
Emilio __2__ (ir) también. Él y
yo __3__ (estar) en la tienda. Yo
__4__ (comprar) una camiseta y
él __5__ (comprar) un blue jean.
Nosotros no __6__ (necesitar) mucha
ropa porque __7__ (llevar) uniforme
a la escuela.

Elena y Tomás __8__ (llevar)
uniforme a la escuela también. Ellos __9__ (ir)
a una escuela en las afueras de Lima, en Miraflores.

8 ¿Cuándo? ¿En clase, después de las clases o en la fiesta?
Work with a classmate. He or she will suggest an activity. You will tell
where you and your friends typically take part in the activity.

9 En la tienda de ropa
You are at a clothing store. You need to buy
some things. Your partner will be the sales clerk. Have a conversation
with each other and then reverse roles.

10 Juego ¿Quién es?
Work in small groups. One person tells what
someone in the class is wearing. The others have to guess who it is. If
several people are wearing the same thing, the person giving the clues
will have to give more details.

Repaso B

Amigos y alumnos

Carolina Larrea *Arvores*

Vocabulario

Es María Gorostiza.
Ella es mexicana.
Es rubia y bastante alta.
María es de Guadalajara.
Ella es alumna en el Colegio Hidalgo.

Felipe y Teresa son amigos.
Ellos son alumnos en la misma escuela.
Son alumnos buenos. Son inteligentes.
Y ellos son bastante cómicos.

1 Historieta María Gorostiza

Contesten.

1. ¿De qué nacionalidad es María Gorostiza?
2. ¿De dónde es?
3. ¿Cómo es ella?
4. ¿Es ella alumna?
5. ¿Dónde es alumna María?

2 Historieta Felipe y Teresa

Corrijan las oraciones falsas.

1. Felipe y Teresa son hermanos.
2. Ellos son alumnos en escuelas diferentes.
3. Ellos son alumnos muy malos.
4. No son inteligentes.
5. Son muy serios y tímidos.

Conversación

¿De dónde son?

Julio ¡Hola!
Rosa ¡Hola! ¿Qué tal?
Julio Bien, ¿y tú?
Rosa Bien. Oye, ¿eres un amigo de Teresa Irizarry, ¿no?
Julio Sí, soy Julio Arenal.
Rosa ¿De dónde eres, Julio?
Julio ¿Yo? Soy de San Juan. Y tú eres de Ponce como Teresa, ¿no?
Rosa Sí, soy ponceña.

¿Comprendes?

Contesten.

1. ¿Son puertorriqueños los dos muchachos?
2. ¿De dónde es Julio?
3. ¿Es Julio un amigo de Teresa Irizarry?
4. ¿De dónde son Teresa y Rosa?

1692
PONCE

Ponce, Puerto Rico

AMIGOS Y ALUMNOS

Estructura

 Presente del verbo ser

Review the forms of the irregular verb **ser.**

SER **soy eres es somos** *sois* **son**

Acrílico sobre tela de Tony Capellán. *Arma de doble filo*

Arte dominicano en Puerto Rico

3 **Entrevista** Contesten personalmente.

1. ¿Quién eres?
2. ¿De qué nacionalidad eres?
3. ¿Dónde eres alumno o alumna?
4. ¿Cómo es tu escuela?

4 **Historieta** **El amigo de Andrés**

Completen con **ser.**

Yo __1__ un amigo de Andrés. Andrés __2__ muy simpático. Y él __3__ gracioso. Andrés y yo __4__ dominicanos. __5__ de la República Dominicana.

La capital de la República Dominicana __6__ Santo Domingo. Nosotros __7__ alumnos en un colegio en Santo Domingo. Nosotros __8__ alumnos de inglés. La profesora de inglés __9__ la señorita White. Ella __10__ americana.

Fortaleza de Orzama, Santo Domingo

Sustantivos, artículos y adjetivos

1. Spanish nouns are either masculine or feminine. Most nouns ending in **o** are masculine and most nouns ending in **a** are feminine. The definite articles **el** and **los** accompany masculine nouns; **la** and **las** accompany feminine nouns.

el alumno	los alumnos	la amiga	las amigas
el curso	los cursos	la escuela	las escuelas

2. An adjective must agree with the noun it describes or modifies. Adjectives that end in **o** have four forms.

el amigo sincero	los amigos sinceros
la amiga sincera	las amigas sinceras

3. Adjectives that end in **e** or a consonant have only two forms.

el curso interesante	los cursos interesantes
la asignatura interesante	las asignaturas interesantes
el curso difícil	los cursos difíciles
la asignatura difícil	las asignaturas difíciles

Unas amigas chilenas, Elqui, Chile

AMIGOS Y ALUMNOS

R13

5 **Julia** Describan a la muchacha.

Una muchacha de San Juan,
Puerto Rico

6 **Los amigos** Describan al grupo de amigos.

En la colonia de San Ángel,
Ciudad de México

7 **Mi clase favorita** Describan su clase favorita.

DATOS PERSONALES

NOMBRE Janet A. Sancristóbal Araujo   TELEFONO 9772369
INSTITUTO D. Antonio José d. Sucre AÑO / GRADO 7° SECCION U   MATERIA Historia de Uslo Geografía comercio
DIRECCION HAB. Cumbres de Curumo   TELEFONO 9772110 - 9772369
EN CASO DE EMERGENCIAS LLAMAR AI 9772220   ALERGIAS tiza, polvo.   GRUPO SANGUINEO XXXU

HORARIO						
Hora	Lunes	Martes	Miércoles	Jueves	Viernes	Sábado
7:00 a 8:30	castellano	Inglás	Geografía	Matemática	Historia	nada
castellano	Inglás	Geografía	Matemática	Historia		
8:30 09:00	Recreo	Recreo	Recreo	Recreo	Recreo	
9:00 a 10:30	Inglés	Matemática	e. física	Biología	castellano	
Inglés	Matemática	e. física	Biología	castellano		
10:30 a 12:00	computación	familiar	ciutura	Artes P.	geografía	
computación	ética	castellano	Artes P.	geografía		
11:00 12:15	Recreo	Recreo	Recreo	Recreo	Recreo	
12:15 a	e. familiar	castellano	computación	Biología	Artística	
1:35	e. familiar	castellano	d.P.x	Biología	Artístico	

8 **¡Qué clase tan difícil!** Work in groups of three or four. In each group, rate your courses as **fácil, difícil, regular, aburrido, fantástico.** Tally the results and report the information to the class.

 9 **En Venezuela** You are spending the summer with a family in Venezuela. Tell your Venezuelan "brother" or "sister" (your partner) all you can about your Spanish class and your Spanish teacher. Answer any questions he or she may have. Then reverse roles.

Salto Ángel, Venezuela

 10 **Cursos** You are speaking with an exchange student from Peru (your partner). He or she wants to know about your school, your schedule, and your classes. Tell as much as you can about your school and then ask him or her about school life in Peru.

Una alumna, Lima, Perú

Repaso C

La familia

Leopoldo Romanach *Small Farmers*

Vocabulario

el comedor   la cocina

el cuarto de baño

la sala

los cuartos, las recámaras

Es la familia Ramos.
En la familia Ramos hay cinco personas.
Ellos tienen una casa en San Pedro Sula.
Ellos viven en Honduras.

Su casa tiene siete cuartos.

La familia está en la sala.
La señora Ramos lee un libro.
Su esposo lee el periódico.
José ve la televisión.
Una hermana de José escribe una carta.

En el mercado venden frutas y vegetales.
Venden carne también.
La señora compra un kilo de tomates.
Los tomates están a 50 pesos el kilo.

1 **Historieta** **La familia Ramos** Contesten.

1. ¿Cuántas personas hay en la familia Ramos?
2. ¿Tienen ellos una casa o un apartamento?
3. ¿Dónde viven ellos?
4. ¿Cuántos cuartos tiene su casa?
5. ¿Cuáles son los cuartos de la casa?

San Miguel
de Allende,
México

2 **Expresiones** Pareen.

1. leer
2. escribir
3. vivir
4. aprender
5. vender
6. comer
7. ver
8. ser
9. subir
10. beber

a. mucho en la escuela
b. al quinto piso
c. una novela
d. un alumno bueno y serio
e. una carta con bolígrafo
f. una limonada
g. en una casa particular
h. una emisión deportiva
i. CDs en una tienda
j. carne, ensalada y papas

 3 **Juego** **¿Cuáles son?** Contesten.

1. ¿Cuáles son algunas cosas que comemos?
2. ¿Cuáles son algunas cosas que bebemos?
3. ¿Cuáles son algunas cosas que leemos?
4. ¿Cuáles son algunas cosas que escribimos?

Conversación

¿Dónde viven?

Tomás Elena, ¿tienes una familia grande?
Elena Sí, bastante grande. Somos seis.
Tomás ¿Viven ustedes aquí en la capital?
Elena Sí, vivimos en la calle Mayor.
            Nuestro apartamento está en
            el edificio Bolívar.

¿Comprendes?

Contesten.

1. ¿Con quién habla Tomás?
2. ¿Tiene Elena una familia bastante grande?
3. ¿Cuántas personas hay en su familia?
4. ¿Viven ellos en la capital?
5. ¿En qué calle viven?
6. ¿Dónde tienen un apartamento?

Málaga, España

Estructura

 ## Presente de los verbos en **-er** e **-ir**

1. Review the following forms of regular **-er** and **-ir** verbs.

COMER	como	comes	come	comemos	*coméis*	comen
BEBER	bebo	bebes	bebe	bebemos	*bebéis*	beben
VIVIR	vivo	vives	vive	vivimos	*vivís*	viven
SUBIR	subo	subes	sube	subimos	*subís*	suben

2. Note that the **-er** and **-ir** verbs have the same endings in all forms except **nosotros** (and **vosotros**).

comemos	vivimos
coméis	*vivís*

Lima, Perú

Repaso C

4 **Tú y tus amigos** Contesten.

1. ¿Qué comes cuando vas a un café?
2. ¿Qué bebes cuando estás en un café?
3. ¿Qué aprenden tú y tus amigos en la escuela?
4. ¿Qué leen ustedes en la clase de inglés?
5. ¿Qué escriben ustedes?
6. ¿Comprenden los alumnos cuando la profesora de español habla?
7. ¿Reciben ustedes notas buenas en todas sus asignaturas?

5 **Historieta En un café** Completen.

En el café los clientes __1__ (ver) al mesero. Ellos __2__ (hablar) con el mesero. Los clientes __3__ (leer) el menú y __4__ (decidir) lo que van a tomar. Los meseros __5__ (tomar) la orden y __6__ (escribir) la orden en un cuaderno pequeño o un bloc. Los meseros no __7__ (leer) el menú. Y los clientes no __8__ (escribir) la orden.

Manta, Ecuador

El verbo tener

1. Review the forms of the irregular verb **tener.**

TENER   tengo   tienes   tiene   tenemos   *tenéis*   tienen

2. Note that the expression **tener que** followed by an infinitive means *to have to.*

Tenemos que estudiar y aprender mucho.

6 Historieta Mi familia Contesten.

1. ¿Tienes una familia grande o pequeña?
2. ¿Cuántos hermanos tienes?
3. ¿Cuántos años tienen ellos?
4. ¿Y cuántos años tienes tú?
5. ¿Tienen ustedes un perro o un gato?
6. ¿Tiene tu padre o tu madre un carro?
7. En la escuela, ¿tienes que estudiar mucho?
8. ¿Y tienen que trabajar mucho tus padres?

Barcelona, España

7 Historieta La familia Bravo
Completen con **tener.**

La familia Bravo __1__ un piso o apartamento en Madrid. Su piso __2__ seis cuartos. Está en Salamanca, una zona muy bonita de la ciudad. Muchas calles en la zona Salamanca __3__ los nombres de artistas famosos—la calle Goya, la calle Velázquez.

Hay cuatro personas en la familia Bravo. Teresa __4__ diecisiete años y su hermano __5__ quince años. Ellos __6__ un perro adorable.

Adjetivos posesivos

1. Review the forms of the possessive adjectives **mi, tu,** and **su.** These adjectives have only two forms.

> **¿Dan una fiesta tu hermana y tus primos?**
> **Sí, mi hermana y mis primos dan una fiesta.**
> **Todos sus amigos van a recibir una invitación a su fiesta.**

2. The possessive adjective **nuestro** has four forms.

> **Nuestro primo, nuestra tía, nuestras sobrinas y nuestros abuelos viven todos en Madrid.**

> **¿Te acuerdas?**
>
> In Spain, **vuestro** is the adjective that corresponds to **vosotros:**
> **vuestro piso**
> **vuestra prima**

8 Historieta Mi familia y mi casa Contesten.

1. ¿Dónde está tu casa o tu apartamento?
2. ¿Cuántos cuartos tiene tu casa o tu apartamento?
3. ¿Cuántas personas hay en tu familia?
4. ¿Dónde viven tus abuelos?
5. Y tus primos, ¿dónde viven?

9 Historieta Nuestra casa Completen.

Nosotros vivimos en _____ (name of city or town). __1__ casa está en la calle _____ (name of street). __2__ padres tienen un carro. __3__ carro es bastante nuevo. Yo tengo una bicicleta. __4__ bicicleta está en el garaje con el carro de __5__ padres. Nosotros tenemos un perro. __6__ perro es adorable. __7__ perro está en el jardín. Mi hermano y __8__ amigos siempre juegan en el jardín alrededor de __9__ casa.

10 Apartamentos With a classmate, look at this plan of the fourth floor of an apartment building. A different family lives in each of the two apartments. Give each family a name. Then say as much as you can about each family and their activities. Don't forget to describe their apartment. Be as original as possible.

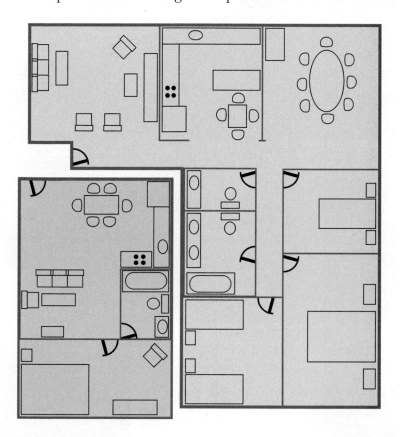

11 En el café Work in groups of three or four. You're all friends from Uruguay. After school you go to a café where you talk about lots of things—school, teachers, friends, home, family, etc. One of you will be the waiter or waitress. You have to interrupt the conversation once in a while to take the orders and serve. Take turns.

Montevideo, Uruguay

Los deportes

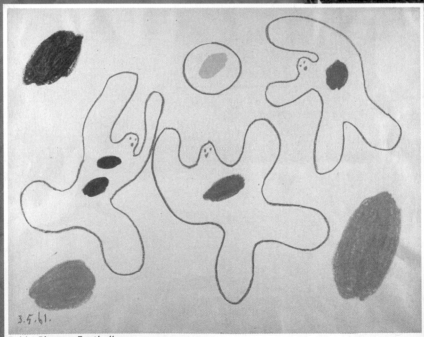

Pablo Picasso *Footballeurs*

3.5.61.

Vocabulario

Los dos equipos juegan (al) fútbol.
Empieza el segundo tiempo.
Los jugadores vuelven al campo de fútbol.
Los dos equipos quieren ganar.

Elena, ¿te gusta el béisbol?

Sí, me gusta. Pero me gusta más el fútbol.

Sí, me gusta mucho. ¿Y a ti?

A mí, no. Me aburre.

Es un partido de béisbol.
El jugador batea la pelota.
Luego corre de una base a otra.

1 Historieta El juego de fútbol

Contesten según se indica.

1. ¿Cuántos tiempos hay en un juego de fútbol? (dos)
2. ¿Cuántos jugadores hay en un equipo de fútbol? (once)
3. ¿Dónde juegan fútbol? (en el campo de fútbol)
4. ¿Quién guarda la portería? (el portero)
5. ¿Qué bloquea? (el balón)
6. ¿Quieren perder los dos equipos? (no, ganar)
7. ¿Pierde un equipo si el tanto queda empatado? (no)

Use your StudentWorks Plus CD for more practice.

2 ¿Qué deporte es? Escojan.

1. El jugador lanza el balón con el pie.
2. Hay cinco jugadores en el equipo.
3. Hay nueve entradas en el partido.
4. El jugador corre de una base a otra.
5. El portero para o bloquea el balón.
6. El jugador tira el balón y encesta.

3 Gustos Contesten.

1. ¿Cuáles son los deportes que a ti te gustan?
2. ¿Cuáles son los comestibles que te gustan?
3. ¿Cuáles son los cursos que te interesan?
4. ¿Cuáles son algunas cosas que no te gustan, que te aburren?

Conversación

Un partido importante

Tadeo Isabel, ¿quieres ir al café Solís con nosotros?

Isabel Gracias, Tadeo, pero no puedo. Quiero ver el partido.

Tadeo ¿De qué partido hablas?

Isabel El Real juega contra el Valencia.

Tadeo ¿Cuál es tu equipo favorito? ¿Cuál te gusta más?

Isabel El Real.

Drake

ATLETICO de MADRID

¡AUPA ATLETI!!

¿Comprendes?

Contesten.

1. ¿Adónde van los amigos de Tadeo?
2. ¿Quiere ir con ellos Isabel?
3. ¿Por qué no puede ir?
4. ¿Qué quiere ver?
5. ¿Qué equipos juegan?
6. ¿Cuál es el equipo favorito de Isabel?

Manuel Martínez
PRESENTADOR DEPORTIVO

CANAL CUATRO
TELEFONOS: 24-1015 - 24-4555
FAX (503) 24-5708
APARTADO POSTAL 444
SAN SALVADOR,
EL SALVADOR, C. A.

Estructura

Verbos de cambio radical

1. Review the following forms of stem-changing verbs. Remember that the **e** changes to **ie** in all forms except **nosotros** (and **vosotros**).

EMPEZAR	empiezo	empiezas	empieza	empezamos	*empezáis*	empiezan
PERDER	pierdo	pierdes	pierde	perdemos	*perdéis*	pierden

2. The following verbs change the **o** to **ue** in all forms except **nosotros** (and **vosotros**).

VOLVER	vuelvo	vuelves	vuelve	volvemos	*volvéis*	vuelven
PODER	puedo	puedes	puede	podemos	*podéis*	pueden

3. The verb **jugar** also has a stem change.

JUGAR	juego	juegas	juega	jugamos	*jugáis*	juegan

4 **Historieta** **Un juego de béisbol** Completen.

El juego de béisbol __1__ (empezar) a las tres y media. Habla Teresa:

—Hoy yo __2__ (querer) ser la pícher.

La verdad es que Teresa __3__ (ser) una pícher muy buena. Ella __4__ (jugar) muy bien. Nosotros __5__ (tener) un equipo bueno. Todos nosotros __6__ (jugar) bien. Nuestro equipo no __7__ (perder) mucho.

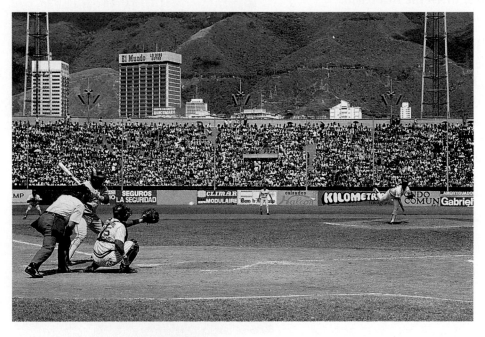

Caracas, Venezuela

5 Historieta Una fiesta Contesten.

1. ¿Quieres ir a la fiesta?
2. ¿Quieren ustedes bailar durante la fiesta?
3. ¿A qué hora empieza la fiesta?
4. ¿Puedes llegar a tiempo?
5. ¿Pueden ustedes tomar el bus a la fiesta?
6. ¿A qué hora vuelven ustedes a casa?

6 Juego Puedo, quiero, prefiero

1. **Puedo…** Tell all that you can do.
2. **Quiero…** Tell all that you want to do.
3. **Quiero pero no puedo…** Tell all that you want to do but for some reason you cannot do.
4. **No quiero porque prefiero…** Tell something you don't want to do because you prefer to do something else.

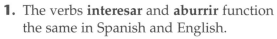

Verbos como aburrir, interesar y gustar

1. The verbs **interesar** and **aburrir** function the same in Spanish and English.

   ¿Te aburre el arte?
   Does art bore you?
   ¿Te aburren los deportes?
   Do sports bore you?
   No, los deportes me interesan.
   No, sports interest me.

2. The verb **gustar** functions the same as **interesar** and **aburrir**. **Gustar** conveys the meaning "to like," but it actually means "to be pleasing to."

   ¿Te gusta el béisbol?
   Sí, me gusta mucho.
   ¿Te gustan los deportes?
   Sí, me gustan.

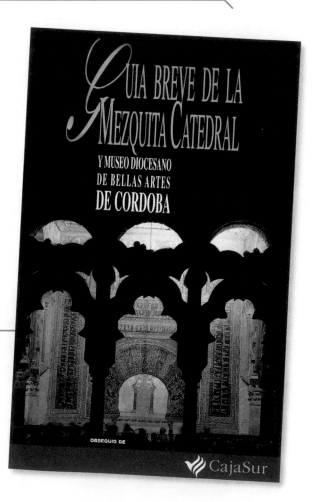

7 **Gustos** Sigan el modelo.

¿A mí? ¿Los tomates? ⟶
Me gustan mucho los tomates.

1. ¿A mí? ¿El pescado?
2. ¿A mí? ¿Los vegetales?
3. ¿A mí? ¿La carne?
4. ¿A mí? ¿El jamón?
5. ¿A mí? ¿Los mariscos?

8 **¿Sí o no?** Contesten.

1. ¿Te interesan o te aburren las matemáticas? ¿Te gustan o no?
2. ¿Te interesa o te aburre la historia? ¿Te gusta o no?
3. ¿Te interesan o te aburren las ciencias? ¿Te gustan o no?
4. ¿Te interesa o te aburre la literatura? ¿Te gusta o no?
5. ¿Te interesa o te aburre la geografía? ¿Te gusta o no?

9 **¿Qué te gusta hacer?** Contesten según los dibujos.

1.

2.

3.

4.

10 **No soy muy aficionado(a).** Work with a classmate. Tell him or her what sport you don't want to play because you don't like it. Tell him or her what you prefer to play. Then ask your classmate questions to find out what sports he or she likes.

11 **Mi equipo favorito** Work with a classmate. Tell him or her about your favorite team. Tell all about the sport and tell why you really like this team in particular. Then ask your classmate about his or her favorite team. Do you by chance have the same favorite team?

12 **Juego** **¿Qué deporte es?** Work with a classmate. Give him or her some information about a sport. He or she has to guess what sport you're talking about. Take turns.

Repaso E

Un viaje
en avión

Francisco Díaz de León *Town of Amecameca with Popocatépetl*

Interna

Spanish Online
To interact with your online edition of
¡**Buen viaje!** go to: <u>glencoe.com</u>.

Vocabulario

Los pasajeros están en el aeropuerto.
La agente de la línea aérea revisa los
    boletos (billetes).
Tiene que mirar los pasaportes también.

Los pasajeros hacen un viaje en avión.
El vuelo 102 con destino a México sale
    de la puerta número diez.
El vuelo está saliendo a tiempo.
No sale con una demora.

Los pasajeros traen bastante equipaje de mano.
Ponen su equipaje de mano debajo del asiento.

1 Historieta En el aeropuerto
Contesten. Inventen una historia.

1. ¿Están en el aeropuerto los pasajeros?
2. ¿Hacen un viaje en avión?
3. ¿Hablan con la agente de la línea aérea?
4. ¿Qué tiene que revisar la agente?
5. ¿Para dónde sale el vuelo?
6. ¿Está saliendo a tiempo o con una demora?
7. ¿Qué traen los pasajeros?
8. ¿Dónde ponen su equipaje de mano?

2 ¿Sí o no? Digan que sí o que no.

1. El avión aterriza cuando sale.
2. El avión despega cuando llega a su destino.
3. Un vuelo internacional es un vuelo que va a un país extranjero.
4. Los agentes de la línea aérea que trabajan en el mostrador en el aeropuerto son los asistentes de vuelo.
5. La tripulación consiste en los empleados que trabajan a bordo del avión.

Aerolínea argentina

Conversación

En el aeropuerto

Felipe Están anunciando la salida de nuestro vuelo, ¿no?

Alejandra Sí, sí. Es nuestro vuelo.

Felipe ¿De qué puerta sale?

Alejandra Sale de la puerta número once.

Felipe ¿Tenemos que pasar por el control de seguridad?

Alejandra Sí, tienen que tomar unos rayos equis de nuestro equipaje de mano.

¿Comprendes?

Corrijan las oraciones.

1. Están anunciando la llegada del vuelo de Felipe y Alejandra.
2. Su vuelo va a salir de la puerta número dos.
3. Ellos tienen que pasar por migración.
4. Tienen que tomar unos rayos equis de sus boletos y pasaportes.

Repaso E

Estructura

 Presente de algunos verbos irregulares

1. Many verbs that are irregular in the present tense are irregular only in the **yo** form. All other forms are regular. Study the following verbs that have a **g** in the **yo** form.

HACER	**hago**
PONER	**pongo**
TRAER	**traigo**
SALIR	**salgo**

2. The verbs **saber** and **conocer** also have an irregular **yo** form.

SABER	**sé**
CONOCER	**conozco**

Saber is used to express knowledge of simple facts. **Conocer** means "to know" in the sense of to be acquainted with someone or something.

> **Yo sé que Madrid está en España.**
> **Yo conozco Madrid.**
> **Yo conozco a Eduardo también.**
> **Yo sé que él es de Madrid.**

Madrid, España

3 **Historieta** **Un viaje imaginario**
Contesten.

1. ¿Haces un viaje a España?
2. ¿Haces el viaje en avión?
3. Antes, ¿haces las maletas?
4. ¿Qué pones en las maletas?
5. ¿Cuándo sales?
6. ¿Sales para el aeropuerto en taxi?
7. ¿A qué hora sale tu vuelo?
8. A bordo del avión, ¿dónde ponen los pasajeros su equipaje de mano?
9. ¿Conoces la ciudad de Madrid?
10. ¿Sabes hablar español?

IBERIA TARJETA DE EMBARQUE

INFORMACION AL PASAJERO						
Vuelo	Destin	Hora Limite	Puerta	Clase	Su asiento	
IB3127	MAD	12.45	15	C		8C

LUNA/GABRIEL

LIS/22APR   C 048

Conserve esta tarjeta hasta su destino

4 **La maleta** Completen con **hacer, poner** o **salir.**

1. Juan ____ su maleta. Él ____ una camisa en la maleta. Él ____ para Málaga.
2. Nosotros ____ nuestra maleta. Nosotros ____ blue jeans en la maleta porque ____ para Cancún en México.
3. ¿Tú ____ tu maleta? ¿Qué ____ en la maleta? ¿Para dónde ____?
4. Mis padres ____ su maleta. Ellos ____ muchas cosas en la maleta. Ellos ____ su maleta porque ____ para Miami.

Málaga, España

El presente progresivo

1. The present progressive tense is used to express an action or activity that is presently going on.

2. To form the present progressive, you use the present tense of the verb **estar** and the present participle. Review the forms of the present participle.

HABLAR **hablando**
COMER **comiendo**
SALIR **saliendo**

¿Qué está haciendo Teresa?
    Teresa está esperando el avión porque está saliendo para México.

Historieta **En el aeropuerto**
Contesten según se indica.

1. ¿Adónde están llegando los pasajeros? (al aeropuerto)
2. ¿Cómo están llegando? (en taxi)
3. ¿Adónde están viajando? (a Colombia)
4. ¿Cómo están haciendo el viaje? (en avión)
5. ¿Dónde están facturando su equipaje? (en el mostrador de la línea aérea)
6. ¿Qué está mirando la agente? (los boletos y los pasaportes)

San Andrés, Colombia

6 **Un boleto para Mérida** Work with a classmate. You want to fly from your hometown to Mérida, México. Call the airline to get a reservation. Your partner will be the reservations agent. Before you call, think about all the information you will need to give or get from the agent: date of departure, time, arrival time in Mérida, flight number, price, etc. Take turns.

7 **Un viaje** You know quite a bit about several Spanish-speaking countries. Work with a classmate. Choose a country you would both like to visit. Discuss how you plan to get there and what you are going to do and see there.

Mérida, México

8 **El aeropuerto** Work with a classmate. Look at the illustration of the many activities taking place at an airport. Tell all about the illustration in your own words.

Repaso F

La rutina y la salud

Gustavo Montoya *La merced*

Vocabulario

Estefanía está bien.
Ella se levanta cada mañana a
las seis y media.

Ella se lava la cara.

Se peina.
Estefanía se mira en el espejo
cuando se peina.

Juan no está bien hoy.
Está enfermo.
Tiene fiebre.
Tiene (una) tos.
Está en cama.

Juan va al consultorio de la médica.
Está en el consultorio.
La médica examina a Juan.

1 Historieta La rutina diaria Contesten.

1. ¿A qué hora se levanta Claudia cada mañana?
2. ¿Ella se desayuna en casa?
3. Después de desayunarse, ¿se cepilla los dientes?
4. ¿Se lava la cara?
5. ¿A qué hora se acuesta ella cada noche?

Use your StudentWorks Plus CD for more practice.

2 La salud Digan que sí o que no.

1. Cuando estamos cansados, queremos dormir.
2. Cuando estamos enfermos, vamos a ver al médico.
3. Tenemos que ir al hospital cuando tenemos un catarro.
4. Tenemos fiebre cuando tenemos la gripe.
5. Estamos contentos y nos sentimos bien cuando tenemos la temperatura elevada.
6. Tenemos que guardar cama cuando tenemos dolor de cabeza.

3 Juego El cuerpo ¿Cuáles son los nombres de todas las partes del cuerpo que sabes en español?

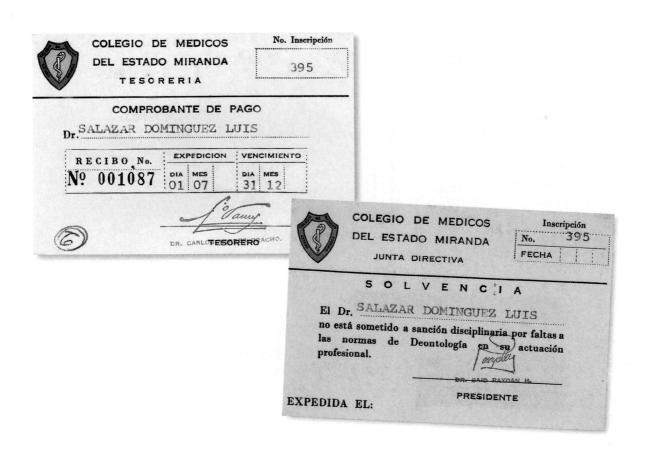

Conversación

¿Cómo estás?

Sandra ¿Cómo estás, Pepe?
Pepe La verdad es que no me siento muy bien.
Sandra ¿Estás enfermo? ¿Qué tienes?
Pepe Tengo dolor de garganta y estoy cansado.
Sandra Pues, sabes donde está la consulta del médico, ¿no?

¿Comprendes?

Contesten.

1. ¿Cómo está Pepe?
2. ¿Cómo se siente él?
3. ¿Qué tiene?
4. ¿Tiene mucha energía?
5. ¿Está cansado?
6. ¿Adónde debe ir?

El dolor de cabeza ¿es muy perro?

DISPRINA va a la cabeza en alivio pronto y efectivo. Y no irrita el estómago.

CONSULTE A SU MÉDICO. NO SE USE EN NIÑOS MENORES DE 14 AÑOS.

DISPRINA se deshace por ti.

sanofi

Estructura

Ser y estar

1. The verbs **ser** and **estar** both mean "to be." **Ser** is used to tell where someone or something is from. It is also used to describe an inherent trait or characteristic.

   Roberto es de Miami.
   Él es inteligente y guapo.

2. **Estar** is used to tell where someone or something is located. It is also used to describe a temporary state or condition.

   Roberto es de Miami pero ahora está en Madrid.
   Madrid está en España.
   Roberto está muy contento en Madrid.

4 **Historieta** **¿En qué clase estás?**
Contesten.

1. ¿Estás en la escuela ahora?
2. ¿Dónde está la escuela?
3. ¿En qué clase estás?
4. ¿Está la profesora en la clase también?
5. ¿Cómo es la profesora?
6. Y, ¿cómo es la clase de español?
7. ¿De dónde es la profesora?
8. Y tú, ¿de dónde eres?
9. ¿Cómo estás hoy?
10. Y la profesora, ¿cómo está?

Alumnos ecuatorianos, Manta, Ecuador

Repaso F

5 **Historieta** **Ángel** Completen con **ser** o **estar.**

Ángel __1__ de Caracas. Él __2__ muy simpático. __3__ gracioso también. Ahora Ángel __4__ en Nueva York. __5__ estudiante en la universidad. Ángel __6__ muy contento en Nueva York.

Nueva York __7__ en el nordeste de Estados Unidos. La Ciudad de Nueva York __8__ muy grande y __9__ muy interesante. A Ángel le gusta mucho Nueva York.

Caracas, Venezuela

Verbos reflexivos

The subject of a reflexive verb both performs and receives the action of the verb. Each subject has its corresponding reflexive pronoun. Review the following forms.

INFINITIVE	levantarse	acostarse
yo	me levanto	me acuesto
tú	te levantas	te acuestas
él, ella, Ud.	se levanta	se acuesta
nosotros(as)	nos levantamos	nos acostamos
vosotros(as)	*os levantáis*	*os acostáis*
ellos, ellas, Uds.	se levantan	se acuestan

6 **¿Y tú?** Contesten personalmente.

1. ¿A qué hora te acuestas?
2. ¿Te duermes enseguida?
3. Y, ¿a qué hora te despiertas?
4. Cuando te despiertas, ¿te levantas enseguida?
5. ¿Te lavas en el cuarto de baño?
6. ¿Te desayunas en casa?
7. Después, ¿te cepillas los dientes?

7 **Su rutina** Describan cada foto.

1. Ellos
   Nosotros
   Ustedes

2. Yo
   Ella
   Tú

8 **Un día típico** Work with a classmate. Compare a typical day in your life with a typical day in your partner's life. Then tell what activities you have in common.

9 **En la consulta del médico**
This is a really busy doctor's office. There is a lot going on at the same time. With a classmate, describe all that you see in the illustration.

Repaso G

El verano y el invierno

Arturo Gordon Vargas *Caserío costero*

Spanish Online
To interact with your online edition of
¡Buen viaje! go to: glencoe.com.

Vocabulario

Raúl pasó el verano en la playa.
Nadó en el mar.

Tomó el sol.
Volvió a casa muy bronceado.

Susana pasó una semana en una
estación de esquí.
Tomó el telesilla para subir la montaña.
Subió en el telesilla.

Ella bajó la pista para expertos.
No bajó la pista para principiantes.

1 **Historieta** En la playa

Contesten.

1. ¿Fue José a la playa?
2. ¿Nadó en el mar?
3. ¿Esquió en el agua?
4. ¿Se sentó en la arena?
5. ¿Tomó el sol?
6. ¿Volvió a casa muy bronceado?

Acapulco, México

Los Andes, Chile

2 **Historieta** En la estación de esquí

Contesten.

1. ¿Fueron a una estación de esquí los amigos?
2. ¿Salieron ellos muy temprano por la mañana?
3. ¿Pasaron el día entero en las pistas?
4. ¿Subieron la montaña en el telesilla?
5. ¿Bajaron la pista para expertos o para principiantes?
6. ¿Volvieron a casa el mismo día?

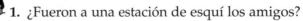

Conversación

¿Qué hicieron los amigos?

José ¿Adónde fuiste ayer, Adriana?
Adriana Fui a casa de Elena.
José ¿Y...?
Adriana Jugamos tenis.
José ¿Tiene Elena una cancha de tenis?
Adriana No, hay canchas en un parque cerca de su casa. Pero Elena tiene una piscina.
José ¿Sí? ¿Nadaron ustedes?
Adriana Sí, nadamos después de jugar tenis.

Fuerte, España

¿Comprendes?

Digan que sí o que no.

1. José fue con Adriana a casa de Elena.
2. La casa de Elena tiene una cancha de tenis.
3. Adriana y Elena jugaron tenis.
4. Jugaron en una cancha en un parque.
5. Nadaron también.
6. Nadaron en una piscina en el parque.

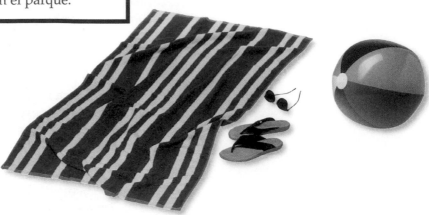

Estructura

 El pretérito

1. Review the forms of the preterite of regular verbs.

INFINITIVE	nadar	comer	subir
yo	nadé	comí	subí
tú	nadaste	comiste	subiste
él, ella, Ud.	nadó	comió	subió
nosotros(as)	nadamos	comimos	subimos
vosotros(as)	*nadasteis*	*comisteis*	*subisteis*
ellos, ellas, Uds.	nadaron	comieron	subieron

2. The forms of the verbs **ir** and **ser** are the same in the preterite. The meaning is made clear by the context of the sentence.

> **fui**   **fuiste**   **fue**   **fuimos**   *fuisteis*   **fueron**

3. The preterite is used to express an event or action that began and ended at a definite time in the past.

> **Ellos pasaron el año pasado en México.**
> **Fueron a Acapulco.**

---

3 **Historieta** **En la escuela** Contesten.

1. ¿Fuiste a la escuela ayer?
2. ¿A qué hora llegaste a la escuela?
3. ¿Hablaste con el/la profesor(a) de español?
4. ¿Tomaste un examen?
5. ¿En qué curso tomaste el examen?
6. ¿Saliste bien en el examen?
7. ¿Comiste en la cafetería de la escuela?
8. ¿A qué hora volviste a casa?

4 Muchas actividades Contesten.

1. ¿Fuiste al cine ayer?
¿Viste una película?
¿Tomaste un refresco en el cine?

2. ¿Salieron ustedes anoche?
¿Fueron a una fiesta?
¿Bailaron y cantaron durante la fiesta?

3. ¿Esquió Sandra?
¿Subió la montaña en el telesilla?
¿Bajó la pista para expertos?

4. ¿Pasaron los amigos el fin de semana en la playa?
¿Te escribieron una tarjeta postal?
¿Nadaron y esquiaron en el agua?

CANAL SUR

8.00	TELETRASTO (Infantil) «LA FAMILIA BIONICA», «EL INSPECTOR GADGET», «TRAS-TO»
9.00	HOSPITAL
10.00	ANDALUCIA NUESTRA
10.30	VECINOS
11.00	LAS MAÑANAS DE CANAL SUR
12.00	CINE MATINAL «LAS PROTEGIDAS»
13.30	SIEMPRE HAY UNA SUEGRA
14.30	EL DIARIO 1
15.00	EL TIEMPO
15.05	PIGMALION
15.30	IMAGINA

Los pronombres de complemento

1. The object pronouns **me**, **te**, and **nos** can be either a direct or an indirect object. Note that the object pronoun precedes the conjugated verb.

Él **me** miró.　　　Él **me** habló por teléfono.
¿**Te** invitó Carlos?　¿**Te** dio una invitación?

2. **Lo, los, la,** and **las** function as direct objects only. They can replace either persons or things.

Pablo compró **el boleto**.　　Pablo **lo** compró.
Pablo compró **los boletos**.　Pablo **los** compró.
Teresa compró **la raqueta**.　Teresa **la** compró.
Teresa compró **las raquetas**.　Teresa **las** compró.
Yo vi **a los muchachos**.　　Yo **los** vi.

3. **Le** and **les** function as indirect objects only.

Yo **le** escribí una carta (a él, a ella, a usted).
Yo **les** escribí una carta (a ellos, a ellas, a ustedes).

R56

REPASO G

5 **Historieta** **A la consulta del médico** Contesten.

1. ¿Fuiste a la consulta del médico?
2. ¿Te habló el médico?
3. ¿Te examinó?
4. ¿Te dio una diagnosis?
5. ¿Te recetó unos antibióticos?

6 **Aquí lo tienes.** Sigan el modelo.

la toalla ⟶
Aquí la tienes.

1. la toalla playera
2. la crema bronceadora
3. el bañador
4. el traje de baño
5. los anteojos de sol
6. los boletos para el telesilla
7. los esquís
8. las raquetas

7 **Historieta** **En el aeropuerto** Completen con **le** o **les**.

La señora Iturria fue al mostrador de la línea aérea. Ella __1__ habló al agente. __2__ habló en español; no __3__ habló en inglés. Ella __4__ dio su boleto y él lo miró. Ella __5__ dio su pasaporte también.

A bordo del avión los asistentes de vuelo __6__ hablaron a los pasajeros. __7__ dieron la bienvenida a bordo y __8__ explicaron las reglas de seguridad.

8 **Las estaciones** Work with a classmate. Tell whether you prefer summer or winter. Explain why you prefer one over the other. Tell what you do during that season. Take turns.

9 **¡A viajar!** Look at these postcards. Work with a classmate. Tell where you prefer to go and why. Take turns.

Costa del Sol

Puerto Marina

Capítulo 1

Un viaje en tren

Objetivos

In this chapter you will learn to:

- ❖ use expressions related to train travel
- ❖ purchase a train ticket and request information about arrival, departure, etc.
- ❖ talk about more past events or activities
- ❖ tell what people say
- ❖ discuss an interesting train trip in Spain and in Peru

Casimiro Castro *Álbum del ferrocarril mexicano*

En la estación de ferrocarril

el tablero de llegadas

el tablero de salidas

el quiosco

la sala de espera

Próximas LLegadas
Regionales y L. Recorrido
H. Proc. Procedencia Vía

13:18	BADAJ/CÁCER	5
13:19	JAEN	
13:46	TOLEDO	4
13:49	CARTAGENA	5
14:15	SANTANDER	5
14:20	ALICANTE	5

Próximas Salidas

Cercanias
Hora Destino Vía

Regionales y L. Recorrido
Hora Destino Vía Tren

Hora	Destino	Vía	Hora	Destino	Vía	Tren
	FUENLABRADA	9	13:10	BARCELONA	5	TALGO
	MOSTOL/SOTO	8	13:33	AVILA	2	REGIO
	PARLA	6	13:50	ALBACETE	5	R EXP
13:05	P PIO/VILLA	7	14:03	SEGOVIA	2	REGTA
13:10	CHAMARTIN	2	14:15	ALICANTE	5	TALGO
13:10	ALCALA	3	14:20	GIJON	5	TALGO
13:13	TRES CANTOS	2	14:25	TOLEDO	4	REGIO
13:16	COSLADA	3	15:03	SEGOVIA	2	REGIO
13:22	GUADALAJARA	3				
13:23	CHAMAR/P PI	2				

MADRID
ALMERIA
GRANADA

el horario

Un billete para Madrid, por favor.

¿En primera o en segunda?

En segunda—de ida y vuelta.

la ventanilla

el billete de ida y vuelta

el billete sencillo

el vagón, el coche

el tren

el mozo, el maletero

la bolsa

el equipaje

la maleta

la vía

el andén

La señora hizo un viaje.
Hizo el viaje en tren.
Tomó el tren porque no quiso ir en carro.
Subió al tren.

El mozo vino con el equipaje.
El mozo puso el equipaje en el tren.
Los mozos ayudaron a los pasajeros
    con su equipaje.

El tren salió del andén número dos.
Algunos amigos estuvieron en el andén.

Vocabulario

¿Qué palabra necesito?

1 Historieta En la estación de ferrocarril

Contesten según se indica.

1. ¿Cómo vino la señora a la estación? (en taxi)
2. ¿Dónde puso sus maletas? (en la maletera del taxi)
3. En la estación, ¿adónde fue? (a la ventanilla)
4. ¿Qué compró? (un billete)
5. ¿Qué tipo de billete compró? (de ida y vuelta)
6. ¿En qué clase? (segunda)
7. ¿Dónde puso su billete? (en su bolsa)
8. ¿Qué consultó? (el horario)
9. ¿Adónde fue? (al andén)
10. ¿De qué andén salió el tren? (del número dos)
11. ¿Por qué hizo la señora el viaje en tren? (no quiso ir en coche)

Atocha, una estación de ferrocarril en Madrid

En la estación de Atocha

2 Historieta Antes de abordar el tren

Escojan.

1. ¿Dónde espera la gente el tren?
   a. en la ventanilla   b. en la sala de espera
   c. en el quiosco
2. ¿Dónde venden o despachan los billetes?
   a. en la ventanilla   b. en el equipaje
   c. en el quiosco
3. ¿Qué venden en el quiosco?
   a. boletos   b. maletas
   c. periódicos y revistas
4. ¿Qué consulta el pasajero para verificar la hora de salida del tren?
   a. la llegada   b. la vía   c. el horario
5. ¿Quién ayuda a los pasajeros con el equipaje?
   a. el mozo   b. el tablero   c. el andén
6. ¿De dónde sale el tren?
   a. de la ventanilla   b. del andén
   c. del tablero

3 **Historieta** **El billete del tren** Contesten según el billete.

1. ¿De qué estación sale el tren?
2. ¿Adónde va el tren?
3. ¿Cuál es la fecha del billete?
4. ¿A qué hora sale el tren?
5. ¿Está el asiento en la sección de fumar o de no fumar?
6. ¿Qué clase de billete es?
7. ¿Con qué pagó el/la pasajero(a)?

4 **RENFE (Red Nacional de Ferrocarriles Españoles)**

You're in Spain and you want to visit one of the cities on the map. A classmate will be the ticket agent. Get yourself a ticket and ask the agent any questions you have about your train trip.

Vocabulario

PALABRAS **2**

En el tren

Use your **StudentWorks** Plus
CD for more practice.

el asiento, la plaza

el revisor

libre

el pasillo

ocupado

el coche-comedor, el coche-cafetería

el coche-cama

la litera

MADRID Puerta de Atocha CADIZ	LLANO	
NUMERO DE TREN	9220	41 (1)
DIAS DE CIRCULACION	LMXJVSD	LMXJVSD
MADRID Puerta de Atocha	10:05	16:05
CIUDAD REAL	11:06	17:06
PUERTOLLANO	11:23	17:23
CORDOBA	12:12	18:11
SEVILLA Santa Justa	13:19	19:26
JEREZ DE LA FRONTERA	14:16	20:23
EL PUERTO DE STA. MARIA	14:27	20:36
SAN FERNANDO DE CADIZ	14:41	20:50
CADIZ	14:55	21:05

El tren salió a tiempo.
No salió tarde.
No salió con retraso
   (con una demora).

bajar(se) del tren

Los pasajeros van a bajar en la próxima
   parada (estación).
Van a transbordar en la próxima parada.

transbordar

¿Qué palabra necesito?

5 **Historieta** **En el tren**
Contesten.

1. Cuando llegó el tren a la estación, ¿subieron los pasajeros a bordo?
2. ¿El tren salió tarde?
3. ¿Con cuántos minutos de demora salió?
4. ¿Vino el revisor?
5. ¿Revisó él los boletos?

Santiago, Chile

Madrid, España

6 **Historieta** **El tren**
Contesten según la foto.

1. ¿Tiene el tren compartimientos?
2. ¿Tiene el coche o vagón un pasillo?
3. ¿Cuántos asientos hay a cada lado del pasillo?
4. ¿Hay asientos libres o están todos ocupados?
5. ¿Está completo el tren?
6. ¿Hay pasajeros de pie en el pasillo?

7 **Historieta** **Un viaje en tren** Completen.

1. Entre Granada y Málaga el tren local hace muchas ____.
2. No hay un tren directo a Benidorm. Es necesario cambiar de tren. Los pasajeros tienen que ____.
3. Los pasajeros que van a Benidorm tienen que ____ en la próxima ____ o ____.
4. ¿Cómo lo sabes? El ____ nos informó que nuestro tren no es directo.

Spanish Online
To plan your own train trip around Spain, go to the Chapter 1 **WebQuest** on the Glencoe Spanish Web site at glencoe.com.

8 ¿Qué tienes que hacer?

Work with a classmate. You are spending a month in Madrid and your Spanish hosts are taking you to San Sebastián. You're trying to pack your bags and their child (your partner) has a lot of questions. Answer his or her questions and try to be patient. The child has never taken a train trip before.

¿Dónde nos sentamos en el tren?

Nos sentamos en un compartimiento.

Madrid

San Sebastián

9 De Santiago a Puerto Montt

You're planning a trip from Santiago de Chile to Puerto Montt. A classmate will be your travel agent. Get as much information as you can about the trip from Santiago to Puerto Montt. It gets rather cold and windy there and it rains a lot. You may want to find out if there are frequent delays. The following are some words and expressions you may want to use with the travel agent: **la demora, la tarifa, reservar, el número de paradas, el horario, el boleto de ida y vuelta, primera (segunda) clase.**

 For more practice using words from Palabras 2, do Activity 1 on page H2 at the end of this book.

Estructura

Hacer, querer y venir en el pretérito
Relating more past actions

Use your **StudentWorks** *Plus*
CD for more practice.

1. The verbs **hacer, querer,** and **venir** are irregular in the preterite. Note that they all have an **i** in the stem and the endings for the **yo, él, ella,** and **usted** forms are different from the endings of regular verbs.

INFINITIVE	hacer	querer	venir
yo	hice	quise	vine
tú	hiciste	quisiste	viniste
él, ella, Ud.	hizo	quiso	vino
nosotros(as)	hicimos	quisimos	vinimos
vosotros(as)	*hicisteis*	*quisisteis*	*vinisteis*
ellos, ellas, Uds.	hicieron	quisieron	vinieron

2. The verb **querer** has several special meanings in the preterite.

Quise ayudar.	*I tried to help.*
No quise ir en carro.	*I refused to go by car.*

SpanishOnline
For more information about travel in Peru and other areas of the Spanish-speaking world, go to **Web Explore** on the Glencoe Spanish Web site at <u>glencoe.com</u>.

¿Cómo lo digo?

10 **Historieta** **¿Cómo viniste?**

Contesten.

1. ¿Viniste a la estación en taxi?
2. ¿Viniste en un taxi público o privado?
3. ¿Hiciste el viaje en tren?
4. ¿Hiciste el viaje en el tren local?
5. ¿Lo hiciste en tren porque no quisiste ir en carro?

Poconchile, Chile

11 **No quisieron.** Completen.

1. —Ellos no __1__ (querer) hacer el viaje.

   —¿No lo __2__ (querer) hacer?

   —No, de ninguna manera.

   —Pues, ¿qué pasó entonces? ¿Lo __3__ (hacer) o no lo __4__ (hacer)?

   —No lo __5__ (hacer).

2. —¿Por qué no __6__ (venir) ustedes esta mañana?

   —Nosotros no __7__ (venir) porque no __8__ (hacer) las reservaciones.

3. —Carlos no __9__ (querer) hacer la cama.

   —Entonces, ¿quién la __10__ (hacer)?

   —Pues, la __11__ (hacer) yo.

   —¡Qué absurdo! ¿Tú la __12__ (hacer) porque él no la __13__ (querer) hacer?

12 **¡Rebelde!** A friend of yours (your classmate) is in trouble with his or her parents because he or she didn't help to get ready for their trip. Find out what your friend didn't do and why. Use the model as a guide.

¿Hiciste la maleta?

No.

¿Por qué no hiciste la maleta?

No hice la maleta porque no quise.

hacer la maleta
reservar un taxi
comprar los billetes
llamar a los parientes
hacer las reservaciones

13 **¿Qué hiciste durante el fin de semana?** With a classmate, take turns asking each other what you and other friends did over the weekend.

Estructura

Verbos irregulares en el pretérito
Describing more past actions

Spanish online
For a fun way to practice this grammar point, go to the Chapter 1 **eGame** on the Glencoe Spanish Web site at glencoe.com.

1. The verbs **estar, andar,** and **tener** are irregular in the preterite. They all have a **u** in the stem. Study the following forms.

INFINITIVE	estar	andar	tener
yo	estuve	anduve	tuve
tú	estuviste	anduviste	tuviste
él, ella, Ud.	estuvo	anduvo	tuvo
nosotros(as)	estuvimos	anduvimos	tuvimos
vosotros(as)	*estuvisteis*	*anduvisteis*	*tuvisteis*
ellos, ellas, Uds.	estuvieron	anduvieron	tuvieron

2. The verb **andar** means *to go,* but not to a specific place. The verb **ir** is used with a specific place.

Fueron a Toledo.
They went to Toledo.

Anduvieron por las plazas pintorescas de Toledo.
They wandered through (walked around) the picturesque squares of Toledo.

Vista de Toledo de El Greco

3. The verbs **poder, poner,** and **saber** are also irregular in the preterite. Like the verbs **estar, andar,** and **tener,** they all have a **u** in the stem. Study the following forms.

INFINITIVE	poder	poner	saber
yo	pude	puse	supe
tú	pudiste	pusiste	supiste
él, ella, Ud.	pudo	puso	supo
nosotros(as)	pudimos	pusimos	supimos
vosotros(as)	*pudisteis*	*pusisteis*	*supisteis*
ellos, ellas, Uds.	pudieron	pusieron	supieron

4. Like **querer,** the verbs **poder** and **saber** have special meanings in the preterite.

Pude parar. *(After trying hard) I managed to stop.*
No pude parar. *(I tried but) I couldn't stop.*
Yo lo supe ayer. *I found it out (learned it) yesterday.*

¿Cómo lo digo?

14 Historieta ¿Dónde está mi tarjeta de identidad estudiantil?
Contesten según se indica.

1. ¿Estuviste ayer en la estación de ferrocarril? (sí)
2. ¿Tuviste que tomar el tren a Toledo? (sí)
3. ¿Pudiste comprar un billete de precio reducido? (no)
4. ¿Tuviste que presentar tu tarjeta de identidad estudiantil? (sí)
5. ¿Dónde la pusiste? (no sé)
6. ¿La perdiste? (sí, creo)
7. ¿Cuándo supiste que la perdiste? (cuando llegué a la estación)

Toledo, España

Estructura

15 Historieta En el mercado
Completen.

El otro día yo __1__ (estar) en el mercado de Chichicastenango, en Guatemala. Ramón __2__ (estar) allí también. Nosotros __3__ (andar) por el mercado pero no __4__ (poder) comprar nada. No es que no __5__ (querer) comprar nada, es que no __6__ (poder) porque __7__ (ir) al mercado sin un quetzal.

Chichicastenango, Guatemala

Decir en el presente y en el pretérito
Telling what people say

1. The verb **decir** (to say) is irregular in the present and preterite tenses. Study the following forms.

	Presente	Pretérito
yo	digo	dije
tú	dices	dijiste
él, ella, Ud.	dice	dijo
nosotros(as)	decimos	dijimos
vosotros(as)	*decís*	*dijisteis*
ellos, ellas, Uds.	dicen	dijeron

¿Cómo lo digo?

16 **¿Qué dices?** Sigan el modelo.

¿Qué dices de la clase de español?

Pues, yo digo que es fantástica. Estoy aprendiendo mucho.

1. ¿Qué dices de la clase de matemáticas?
2. ¿Qué dices de la clase de inglés?
3. ¿Qué dices de la clase de biología?

4. ¿Qué dices de la clase de educación física?
5. ¿Qué dices de la clase de historia?

17 **¿Qué dicen todos?** Completen con la forma apropiada del presente de **decir**.

Yo __1__ que quiero ir en tren pero Elena me __2__ que prefiere tomar el avión. Ella y Tomás también __3__ que no hay mucha diferencia entre la tarifa del avión y la tarifa del tren.

—¿Qué __4__ tú?

—Yo __5__ que es mejor ir en tren.

—Bien. Tú y yo __6__ la misma cosa. Estamos de acuerdo.

18 **¿Qué dijeron todos?** Contesten.

1. ¿Dijiste tú que quieres ir?
2. ¿Dijeron ustedes que es mejor ir en tren?
3. ¿Dije yo que sí?

4. ¿Dijo Elena que ella tiene los boletos?
5. ¿Dijimos la misma cosa?

Andas bien. ¡Adelante!

En la ventanilla

Pasajera	Un billete para Madrid, por favor.
Agente	¿Sencillo o de ida y vuelta?
Pasajera	Sencillo, por favor.
Agente	¿Para cuándo, señorita?
Pasajera	Para hoy.
Agente	¿En qué clase, primera o segunda?
Pasajera	En segunda. ¿Tiene usted una tarifa reducida para estudiantes?
Agente	Sí. ¿Tiene usted su tarjeta de identidad estudiantil?
Pasajera	Sí, aquí la tiene usted.
Agente	Con el descuento son veintidós euros.
Pasajera	¿A qué hora sale el próximo tren?
Agente	Sale a las veinte y diez del andén número ocho.
Pasajera	Gracias.

¿Comprendes?

Contesten.

1. ¿Dónde está la señorita?
2. ¿Adónde va?
3. ¿Qué tipo de billete quiere?
4. ¿Para cuándo lo quiere?
5. ¿En qué clase quiere viajar?
6. ¿Es alumna la señorita?
7. ¿Hay una tarifa reducida para estudiantes?
8. ¿Qué tiene la señorita?
9. ¿Cuánto cuesta el billete con el descuento estudiantil?
10. ¿A qué hora sale el tren?
11. ¿De qué andén sale?

Vamos a hablar más

A **El horario** Look at the train schedule. With a classmate, ask and answer as many questions as you can about it.

B **Vamos a Barcelona.** You and a classmate are spending a semester in Spain. You will be going to Barcelona for a couple of days. One of you is going to fly and the other is going to take the train. Compare your trips: time, cost, and what you have to do the day of departure.

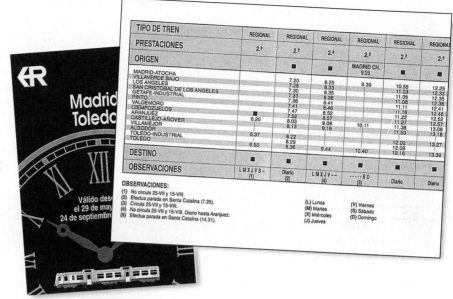

TIPO DE TREN	REGIONAL	REGIONAL	REGIONAL	REGIONAL	REGIONAL	REGIONAL
PRESTACIONES	2.ª	2.ª	2.ª	2.ª	2.ª	2.ª
ORIGEN						
MADRID-ATOCHA		■	■	MADRID CH. 9.25	■	■
VILLAVERDE BAJO		7.20	8.25		10.55	12.25
LOS ANGELES		7.28	8.33	9.39	11.03	12.33
SAN CRISTOBAL DE LOS ANGELES		7.30	8.35		11.05	12.35
GETAFE-INDUSTRIAL		7.33	8.38		11.08	12.38
PINTO		7.36	8.41		11.11	12.41
VALDEMORO		7.41	8.46		11.16	12.46
CIEMPOZUELOS		7.47	8.52		11.22	12.52
ARANJUEZ	6.20	7.52	8.57		11.27	12.57
CASTILLEJO-AÑOVER		8.03	9.08	10.11	11.38	13.08
VILLAMEJOR		8.13	9.18		11.53	13.18
ALGODOR	5.37	8.22				
TOLEDO-INDUSTRIAL		8.29			12.02	13.27
TOLEDO	6.50	8.36	9.44	10.40	12.09	13.39
					12.16	
DESTINO		■		■		
OBSERVACIONES	L M X J V S – (1)	Diario (2)	L M X J V – – (4)	– – – – S D (3)	Diario	Diario

OBSERVACIONES:
(1) No circula 25-VII y 15-VIII.
(2) Efectua parada en Santa Catalina (7.26).
(3) Circula 25-VII y 15-VIII.
(4) No circula 25-VII y 15-VIII. Diario hasta Aranjuez.
(5) Efectua parada en Santa Catalina (14.31).

(L) Lunes   (V) Viernes
(M) Martes   (S) Sábado
(X) Miércoles   (D) Domingo
(J) Jueves

Pronunciación

La consonante ñ y la combinación ch

The **ñ** is a separate letter of the Spanish alphabet. The mark over it is called a **tilde**. Note that it is pronounced similarly to the *ny* in the English word *canyon*. Repeat the following.

señor   otoño   España
señora   pequeño cumpleaños
año

Ch is pronounced much like the *ch* in the English word *church*. Repeat the following.

coche   chaqueta
chocolate muchacho

Repeat the following sentences.

El señor español compra un coche cada año en el otoño.
El muchacho chileno duerme en una cama pequeña en
  el coche-cama.
El muchacho pequeño lleva una chaqueta color chocolate.

Lecturas culturales

En el AVE

José Luis y su hermana, Maripaz, pasan dos días en Sevilla. Vinieron a visitar a sus abuelos. El viaje que hicieron de Madrid, donde viven, fue fantástico. Tomaron el tren y llegaron a Sevilla en sólo dos horas y quince minutos. Salieron de Atocha en Madrid a las 17:00 y bajaron del tren en Sevilla a las 19:15. ¿Es posible recorrer el trayecto[1] Madrid–Sevilla en dos horas quince minutos? Es una distancia de 538 kilómetros. ¡Es increíble!

[1]recorrer el trayecto *cover the route*

Reading Strategy

Interpretation of images Reading passages sometimes use images as a symbol to create an impression. Many times these images are animals. If you are able to identify an image, it is helpful to stop for a moment and think about the qualities and characteristics of the particular symbol the author is using in his or her imagery. Then when you have finished reading, go back and think about how the image and the topic of the reading are alike.

A bordo del AVE

Plaza de España, Sevilla

Sí, es increíble, pero es verdad. El tren español de alta velocidad es uno de los trenes más rápidos del mundo. Viaja a 250 kilómetros por hora. El tren se llama el AVE. ¿Por qué el AVE? Porque el tren vuela como un ave o pájaro.

José Luis y Maripaz tomaron el AVE. Según ellos, el viaje fue fantástico. ¿Por qué? Primero la velocidad. Pero el tren es también muy cómodo[2]. Lleva ocho coches en tres clases. Los pasajeros pueden escuchar música estereofónica o mirar tres canales de video. El tren también dispone de[3] teléfono por si acaso[4] un pasajero quiere o necesita hacer una llamada telefónica.

[2]cómodo *comfortable*
[3]dispone de *has available*
[4]por si acaso *in case*

Torre del Oro, Sevilla

¿Comprendes?

A Una visita a los abuelos
Contesten.
1. ¿Quiénes hicieron un viaje de Madrid a Sevilla?
2. ¿Quiénes vinieron a Sevilla, José Luis y su hermana o sus abuelos?
3. ¿Cómo hicieron el viaje?
4. ¿Qué tal fue el viaje?
5. ¿Cuánto tiempo tardó el viaje?
6. ¿A qué hora salieron de Madrid?
7. ¿A qué hora llegaron a Sevilla?

B Información Busquen la información.
1. uno de los trenes más rápidos del mundo
2. el nombre del tren
3. el número de coches que lleva el tren
4. el número de clases que tiene
5. algunas comodidades que el tren ofrece a los pasajeros

Plaza de España, Sevilla

Lectura opcional

De Cuzco a Machu Picchu

Un viaje muy interesante en tren es el viaje de Cuzco a Machu Picchu en el Perú. Cada día a las siete de la mañana, un tren de vía estrecha[1] sale de la estación de San Pedro en Cuzco y llega a Machu Picchu a las diez y media. Cuzco está a unos 3.500 metros sobre el nivel del mar. El tren tiene que bajar a 2.300 metros para llegar a Machu Picchu. Tiene que bajar 1.200 metros y en el viaje de regreso tiene que subir 1.200 metros.

Pero, ¿quiénes toman el tren para ir a Machu Picchu? Es un tren que lleva a muchos turistas que quieren ir a ver las famosas ruinas de los incas. Machu Picchu es una ciudad entera, totalmente aislada[2] en un pico andino al borde de[3] un cañón. Un dato histórico increíble es que los españoles no

[1]de vía estrecha *narrow gauge*
[2]aislada *isolated*
[3]al borde de *on the edge of*

La Plaza de Armas, Cuzco

El valle del Urubamba, Perú

Machu Picchu

descubrieron a Machu Picchu durante su conquista de Perú. Los historiadores creen que Machu Picchu fue el último refugio de los nobles incas al escaparse[4] de los españoles.

Machu Picchu fue descubierto por Hiram Bingham, el explorador y senador de Estados Unidos, en 1911. ¿Cómo llegó Bingham a Machu Picchu en 1911? ¡A pie! Y aún hoy hay sólo dos maneras de ir a Machu Picchu—a pie o en el tren que sale a las siete de Cuzco.

[4]al escaparse *upon escaping*

¿Comprendes?

¿Sí o no? Digan que sí o que no.
1. Machu Picchu está a una altura más elevada que Cuzco.
2. El tren que va de Machu Picchu a Cuzco tiene que subir 1.200 metros.
3. El viaje de Cuzco a Machu Picchu toma tres horas y media.
4. Hay muy pocos turistas en el tren a Machu Picchu.
5. En Machu Picchu hay ruinas famosas de los incas.
6. Machu Picchu fue una ciudad de los incas.
7. Los españoles descubrieron la ciudad de Machu Picchu durante su conquista de Perú.
8. Hiram Bingham fue un senador de Estados Unidos.
9. Él también fue a Machu Picchu en tren.

Conexiones

Las matemáticas

Conversiones aritméticas

When traveling through many of the Spanish-speaking countries, you will need to make some mathematical conversions. For example, train as well as plane schedules and hours for formal events, radio, and television are given using the twenty-four-hour clock. The metric system rather than the English system is used for weights and measures. Let's take a look at some of the conversions that must be made.

La hora

Cuando lees el horario para el tren o un anuncio para un programa cultural, dan la hora usando las 24 horas. La una (1:00) es la una de la mañana y las doce (12:00) es el mediodía. Las trece (13:00), una hora después del mediodía, es la una de la tarde y las veinticuatro horas (00:00) es la medianoche.

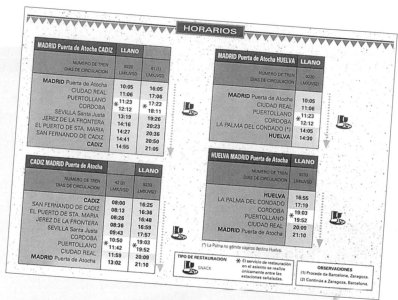

Nuestros amigos José Luis y Maripaz salieron de Madrid a las 17:00 y llegaron a Sevilla a las 19:15. Es decir que salieron de Madrid a las 5:00 de la tarde y llegaron a las 7:15 de la tarde.

El sistema métrico—pesos y medidas[1]

Pesos

Las medidas tradicionales para peso en Estados Unidos son la onza, la libra y la tonelada. En el sistema métrico decimal, las medidas para peso están basadas en el kilogramo, o kilo.

[1]pesos y medidas *weights and measures*

Hay mil gramos en un kilo. El kilo es igual a 2,2 libras. Una libra estadounidense es un poco menos de medio kilo.

Líquidos

Las medidas para líquidos en Estados Unidos son la pinta, el cuarto y el galón. En el sistema métrico es el litro. Un litro contiene un poco más que un cuarto.

Distancia y altura

Para medir la distancia y la altura en Estados Unidos usamos la pulgada, el pie, la yarda y la milla. El sistema métrico usa el metro. El metro es un poco más que una yarda. Un kilómetro (mil metros) es 0,621 millas—un poco más que media milla.

¿Comprendes?

A La hora Read the schedule on page 424 and give the arrival and departure times of the trains using our system of telling time.

Read the schedule on page 424

B El sistema métrico Contesten según las fotografías.
1. ¿Cuánto cuesta un litro de gasolina?
2. ¿Cuál es el límite de velocidad?
3. ¿Cuánto cuesta un litro de leche?
4. ¿Cuánto cuesta un kilo de carne?

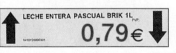

LECHE ENTERA PASCUAL BRIK 1L PVP: 0,79€

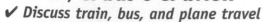

¡Te toca a ti!

Use what you have learned

HABLAR

1 El tren, el bus o el avión
✔ *Discuss train, bus, and plane travel*

Work in groups of three or four. Discuss the advantages **(las ventajas)** and the disadvantages **(las desventajas)** of bus, train, and air travel. In your discussion, include such things as speed, price, location of stations, and anything else you consider important.

HABLAR

2 Y ahora, ¿qué hacemos?
✔ *Discuss what to do if you miss your train*

You and a classmate are on a bus on the way to the Atocha station in Madrid. There's an awful traffic jam **(un tapón, un atasco).** You know you are going to miss your train. Discuss your predicament with one another and figure out what you can do.

La estación de ferrocarril, Málaga

En la estación de ferrocarril
✔ *Talk about activities at a train station*

With a classmate look at the photograph and talk about it.

¡Una experiencia!
✔ *Write about an interesting train trip in Spain*

You took the AVE from Madrid to Sevilla. Write home and tell all about it.

Un viaje excelente

Write about a trip you took to a place you love. The place can be real or imaginary. Describe how and where you went and when. Then describe what the weather is like in that place and what clothing you need there. Continue writing about what you saw and how you got to each place you visited. In your description of the place, try to make your readers understand what it is about the place that you think is so great.

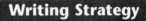

Writing Strategy

Writing a descriptive paragraph Your overall goal in writing a descriptive paragraph is to enable the reader to visualize your scene. To achieve this you must select and organize details that create an impression. Using a greater number of specific nouns and vivid adjectives will make your writing livelier.

Assessment

Vocabulario

1 **Completen.**

1. Elena va de Madrid a Córdoba y va a volver a Madrid. Quiere un billete ____.
2. Los pasajeros esperan el tren en el andén o en la ____.
3. El ____ de llegadas indica a qué hora llegan los trenes a la estación.
4. Venden periódicos y revistas en el ____ en la estación de ferrocarril.
5. Un tren tiene varios vagones o ____.

2 **¿Sí o no?**

6. El revisor trabaja en la estación de ferrocarril.
7. Una litera es un tipo de cama donde puede dormir un pasajero en un tren.
8. El tren que salió a tiempo salió con una demora.
9. Los pasajeros que van de Cuzco a Machu Picchu bajan del tren en Cuzco.

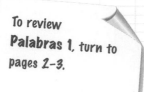

To review **Palabras 1**, turn to pages 2–3.

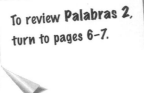

To review **Palabras 2**, turn to pages 6–7.

Spanish Online

For more Chapter 1 test preparation, go to the Chapter 1 **Self-Check Quiz** on the Glencoe Spanish Web site at glencoe.com.

Estructura

3 **Escriban en el pretérito.**

10. Los turistas andan por la plaza principal.
11. Él hace la cama por la mañana.
12. Lo pongo en la maleta.
13. ¿Quién lo sabe?
14. No estamos en la capital.

To review the preterite, turn to pages 10, 12, and 13.

4 **Completen con decir.**

15–16. Yo lo ____ ahora y lo ____ ayer.
17–18. Ellos lo ____ ahora y lo ____ ayer.

To review decir, turn to page 14.

Cultura

5 **Contesten.**

19. ¿Qué es el AVE?
20. ¿A qué ciudad de Andalucía fueron José Luis y su hermana?

To review this cultural information, turn to page 18.

Tell all you can about this illustration.

Vocabulario

Getting around a train station

la estación de
   ferrocarril
la ventanilla
el billete, el boleto sencillo
   de ida y vuelta
la sala de espera
el mozo, el maletero
el equipaje
la maleta
la bolsa

el tablero de llegadas,
   de salidas
el horario
el quiosco
el tren
el andén
la vía
en segunda (clase)
en primera (clase)

How well do you know your vocabulary?

• Choose five words from the vocabulary list.
• Use the words in original sentences to tell a story.

Describing activities at a train station

bajar(se) del tren
subir al tren
transbordar
salir a tiempo
   con retraso, con una demora
ayudar

On board the train

el coche, el vagón
el pasillo
el compartimiento
el asiento, la plaza
   libre
   ocupado(a)
   reservado(a)
completo(a)
el coche-cama
el coche-comedor, el coche-cafetería
la litera
el revisor
la parada
en la próxima parada

VIDEOTUR

Episodio 1

In this video episode, you will join Claudia and Francisco in an unusual train experience. See page 480 for more information.

Capítulo 2

En el restaurante

Objetivos

In this chapter you will learn to:

- ❖ order food or a beverage at a restaurant
- ❖ identify eating utensils and dishes
- ❖ identify more foods
- ❖ make a reservation at a restaurant
- ❖ talk about present and past events
- ❖ describe some cuisines of the Hispanic world

Hernán Miranda *Interiores con mesa*

Spanish Online
To interact with your online edition of
¡Buen viaje! go to: glencoe.com.

En el restaurante

El mesero pone la mesa.

el camarero, el mesero

Tengo hambre.

Tengo hambre y quiero comer.

Tengo sed.

Tengo sed y quiero beber algo.

el vaso

la sal

la pimienta

la taza

el platillo

el plato

la cuchara

la cucharita

el tenedor

el cuchillo

la servilleta

el mantel

La señorita pide el menú.

freír

el cocinero

El cocinero fríe las papas.
Está friendo las papas.

El mesero le sirve la comida.

la tarjeta de crédito

la cuenta

el dinero

la propina

La señorita pide la cuenta.
El servicio no está incluido.
Ella deja una propina.

¿Qué palabra necesito?

Spanish Online

For a fun way to practice this vocabulary, go to the Chapter 2 **eGame** on the Glencoe Spanish Web site at glencoe.com.

1

¿Qué necesitas? Contesten según el modelo.

¿Para tomar leche? —→
Para tomar leche necesito un vaso.

1. ¿Para tomar agua?
2. ¿Para tomar café?
3. ¿Para comer la ensalada?
4. ¿Para comer el postre?
5. ¿Para cortar la carne?

2 **Historieta** **En el restaurante**

Contesten.

1. ¿Cuántas personas hay en la mesa?
2. ¿Tiene hambre María?
3. ¿Pide María el menú?
4. ¿Le trae el menú el mesero?
5. ¿Qué pide María?
6. ¿El mesero le sirve?
7. ¿El mesero le sirve bien?
8. Después de la comida, ¿le pide la cuenta al mesero?
9. ¿Le trae la cuenta el mesero?
10. ¿Paga con su tarjeta de crédito María?
11. ¿María le da (deja) una propina al mesero?
12. Después de la comida, ¿tiene hambre María?

```
                                    155
ALKALDE              CI - B - 28163087
Restaurante
                     24475

Viene de la Fra.     GUEST LKUP    01 M0001
                     CUBIERTO      #0006
N.°                              90   2x
                     PAN             *0
                                     2x
Pasa a la Fra.       TTO.CASA      *300
                     MINERAL/      *810
N.°                  ESPARRAG      *250
                     VERD.JAM      *1650
                     FIL.MIQN      *1350
                     FRITURA       *1800
                     CAFE-INF      *1950
                                     2x
                                   *400
                     SUBTL         *8510
                          %         7.00

                     IMPORTE       *9106
```

3 Palabras relacionadas Pareen las palabras relacionadas.

1. la mesa   a. el servicio
2. la cocina   b. la bebida
3. servir   c. el cocinero
4. freír   d. la comida
5. comer   e. el mesero
6. beber   f. frito

Alcalá de Henares, España

4 Historieta El mesero pone la mesa. Completen.

1. Para comer, los clientes necesitan ___, ___, ___ y ___.
2. Dos condimentos son la ___ y la ___.
3. El mesero cubre la mesa con ___.
4. En la mesa el mesero pone una ___ para cada cliente.
5. El niño pide un ___ de leche y sus padres piden una ___ de café.
6. Ellos tienen ___ y piden una botella de agua mineral.

5 En el restaurante Look at the advertisement for a restaurant in Santiago de Chile. Tell as much as you can about the restaurant based on the information in the advertisement. A classmate will tell whether he or she wants to go to the restaurant and why.

Aquí está Coco

El sabor de los mejores pescados y mariscos del Pacífico Sur, preparados como usted quiera, en un ambiente agradable e informal.

Vocabulario

PALABRAS 2

Más alimentos o comestibles

Use your **StudentWorks Plus** CD for more practice.

la carne

la carne de res, el biftec

la ternera

el cerdo

el cordero

el pescado

los mariscos

los camarones

las almejas

la langosta

la alcachofa

el ajo

la berenjena

el maíz

los guisantes

el arroz

el aceite

La joven pidió un biftec.
El mesero sirvió el biftec.
La comida está rica, deliciosa.

¡Diga!

Quisiera reservar una mesa, por favor.

Sí, señor. ¿Para cuándo?

Para esta noche a las nueve y media.

¿Cuántas personas?

Cuatro.

¿A nombre de quién, por favor?

A nombre de Julio Amaral.

Conforme, señor.

¿Qué palabra necesito?

6 **¿Te gusta(n) o no te gusta(n)?** Contesten según los dibujos.

1.

2.

3.

4.

5.

6.

Barcelona, España

7 **Historieta** **Cenó en el restaurante.**
Contesten.

1. ¿Fue Victoria al restaurante anoche?
2. ¿Quién le sirvió?
3. ¿Pidió Victoria un biftec?
4. ¿Pidió también una ensalada?
5. ¿Le sirvió el mesero una ensalada de lechuga y tomate?
6. ¿Le sirvió una comida deliciosa o una comida mala?

Spanish Online
For more information about varieties of food in the Spanish-speaking world, go to **Web Explore** on the Glencoe Spanish Web site at glencoe.com.

8 ¿Qué te gusta? Contesten personalmente.

1. ¿Te gusta la ensalada?
2. ¿Te gusta la ensalada con aceite y vinagre?
3. ¿Te gusta el biftec?
4. ¿Te gusta el sándwich de jamón y queso?
   ¿Te gusta más con pan tostado?
5. ¿Te gusta la tortilla de queso?
6. ¿Te gustan los huevos con jamón?

9 Una reservación You call a restaurant in Buenos Aires. The headwaiter (a classmate) answers. Make a reservation for yourself and a group of friends.

10 ¿Qué recomienda usted? Here's a menu from a very famous restaurant in Madrid. In fact, it's the oldest restaurant in the city, dating from 1725. There are many items on the menu that you will be able to recognize. A classmate will be the server. Ask what he or she recommends and then order.

C A R T A
I.V.A. 7% INCLUIDO

RESTAURANT
3ª Categoría

ENTRADAS

Jugos de tomate, naranja	2,60
Pimientos asados con bacalao	6,40
Lomo ibérico de bellota	15,00
Jamón ibérico de bellota	16,50
Surtido ibérico de bellota	14,10
Melón con jamón	13,00
Queso (manchego)	5,80
Ensalada riojana	6,20
Ensalada de lechuga y tomate	3,10
ENSALADA BOTIN (con pollo y jamón)	7,90
Ensalada de rape y langostinos	17,00
Ensalada de endivias con perdiz	13,00
Morcilla de Burgos	4,80
Croquetas de pollo y jamón	5,80
Manitas de cochinillo rebozadas	5,20
Salmón ahumado	13,20

SOPAS

Sopa al cuarto de hora (de pescados)	10,60
SOPA DE AJO CON HUEVO	3,80
Caldo de ave	3,20
Gazpacho	5,30

HUEVOS

Revuelto de la casa (morcilla y patatas)	5,50
Huevos revueltos con espárragos trigueros	6,60
Huevos revueltos con salmón ahumado	7,00
Tortilla de gambas	7,00

VERDURAS

Espárragos con mahonesa	8,90
Menestra de verduras salteadas con jamón ibérico	7,80
Alcachofas salteadas con jamón ibérico	5,90
Judías verdes con jamón ibérico	5,90
Setas a la segoviana	6,40
Patatas fritas	2,40
Patatas asadas	2,40

PESCADOS

Angulas (según mercado)	15,70
ALMEJAS BOTIN	24,00
Langostinos con mahonesa	17,00
Gambas al ajillo	18,00
Gambas a la plancha	18,00
Cazuela de pescados	17,40
Rape en salsa	20,00
Merluza al horno o frita	16,00
Lenguado frito, al horno o a la plancha (pieza)	10,00
Calamares fritos	10,10
CHIPIRONES EN SU TINTA (arroz blanco)	

ASADOS Y PARRILLAS

COCHINILLO ASADO	15,40
CORDERO ASADO	16,00
Pollo asado 1/2	6,30
Pollo en cacerola 1/2	8,40
Perdiz estofada (pieza)	16,40
Filete de ternera a la plancha	12,00
Escalope de ternera	12,00
Ternera asada con guisantes	12,00
Solomillo a la plancha	17,00
SOLOMILLO BOTIN (al champiñón)	17,00
"Entrecotte" de cebón a la plancha	16,00

POSTRES

Cuajada	4,30
Tarta helada	4,40
Tarta de la casa (crema y bizcocho)	4,50
Tarta de chocolate	4,70
Tarta de frambuesa	5,30
Pastel ruso (crema de praliné)	5,20
Flan de la casa	2,70
Flan de la casa con nata	4,50
Helado de chocolate o caramelo	3,40
Helado de vainilla con salsa de chocolate	3,50
Surtido de buñuelos	5,70
Hojaldre de crema	4,80
Piña natural al dry-sack	4,00
Fresón con nata	5,10
Sorbete de limón	3,80
Melón	4,20
Bartolillos (sábados y domingos)	4,70

MENU DE LA CASA
(Primavera - Verano)
Precio: 26,00 €
Gazpacho campero
Cochinillo asado
Helado

HORAS DE SERVICIO: ALMUERZO, de 1:00 A 4:00 - CENA, de 8:00 A 12:00
HAY HOJAS DE RECLAMACION
ABIERTO TODOS LOS DIAS

Estructura

Use your StudentWorks Plus CD for more practice.

Verbos con el cambio e → i en el presente
Describing more present activities

1. The verbs **pedir, servir, repetir, freír, seguir** *(to follow)*, and **vestirse** *(to get dressed)* are stem-changing verbs. The **e** of the infinitive stem changes to **i** in all forms of the present tense except the **nosotros** and **vosotros** forms. Study the following forms. Note the spelling of **seguir**.

INFINITIVE	pedir	servir	seguir	vestirse
yo	pido	sirvo	sigo	me visto
tú	pides	sirves	sigues	te vistes
él, ella, Ud.	pide	sirve	sigue	se viste
nosotros(as)	pedimos	servimos	seguimos	nos vestimos
vosotros(as)	*pedís*	*servís*	*seguís*	*os vestís*
ellos, ellas, Uds.	piden	sirven	siguen	se visten

¿Cómo lo digo?

11 **Lo que yo pido** Digan si piden lo siguente o no.

1.

4.

5.

2.

3.

6.

12 Lo que pedimos en el restaurante

Sigan el modelo.

> A Juan le gusta el pescado. ¿Qué pide él?

> Él pide pescado.

Spanish Online
For a fun activity deciding what you would order from a restaurant in Spain, go to the Chapter 2 **WebQuest** on the Glencoe Spanish Web site at glencoe.com.

1. A Teresa le gustan los mariscos. ¿Qué pide ella?
2. A Carlos le gusta el biftec. ¿Qué pide él?
3. A mis amigos les gustan las legumbres. ¿Qué piden ellos?
4. A mis padres les gusta mucho la ensalada. ¿Qué piden ellos?
5. Nos gusta el postre. ¿Qué pedimos?
6. Nos gustan las tortillas. ¿Qué pedimos?
7. ¿Qué pides cuando tienes sed?
8. ¿Qué pides cuando tienes hambre?

13 Historieta Vamos al restaurante. Completen.

Cuando mi amiga y yo __1__ (ir) al restaurante, nosotros __2__ (pedir) casi siempre una hamburguesa. Yo la __3__ (pedir) con lechuga y tomate y ella la __4__ (pedir) con queso. A mi amiga le __5__ (gustar) mucho las papas fritas. Ella __6__ (decir) que le __7__ (gustar) más cuando el cocinero las __8__ (freír) en aceite de oliva.

Marbella, España

14 Entrevista Contesten personalmente.

1. Cuando vas a un restaurante, ¿qué pides?
2. ¿Pides papas? Si no pides papas, ¿pides arroz?
3. ¿Qué más pides con la carne y las papas o el arroz?
4. ¿Quién te sirve en el restaurante?
5. Si te sirve bien, ¿qué le dejas?

15 ¿Por qué no pides... ?

You're in a restaurant with a friend (a classmate). You are hungry and thirsty, but you don't know what to order. Your friend will suggest something. Then you decide.

UN POCO MÁS
*For more practice using words from **Palabras 2** and the verb **pedir**, do Activity 2 on page H3 at the end of this book.*

Estructura

Verbos con el cambio e → i, o → u en el pretérito
Describing more activities in the past

1. The verbs **pedir, repetir, freír, servir,** and **vestirse** have a stem change
in the preterite. The **e** of the infinitive stem changes to **i** in the **él** and
ellos forms.

INFINITIVE	pedir	repetir	vestirse
yo	pedí	repetí	me vestí
tú	pediste	repetiste	te vestiste
él, ella, Ud.	pidió	repitió	se vistió
nosotros(as)	pedimos	repetimos	nos vestimos
vosotros(as)	pedisteis	repetisteis	os vestisteis
ellos, ellas, Uds.	pidieron	repitieron	se vistieron

2. The verbs **preferir, divertirse,** and **dormir** also have a stem change in the
preterite. The **e** in **preferir** and **divertirse** changes to **i** and the **o** in **dormir**
changes to **u** in the **él** and **ellos** forms.

INFINITIVE	preferir	divertirse	dormir
yo	preferí	me divertí	dormí
tú	preferiste	te divertiste	dormiste
él, ella, Ud.	prefirió	se divirtió	durmió
nosotros(as)	preferimos	nos divertimos	dormimos
vosotros(as)	preferisteis	os divertisteis	dormisteis
ellos, ellas, Uds.	prefirieron	se divirtieron	durmieron

¿Cómo lo digo?

16 **Historieta** **Servicio bueno o malo** Contesten según se indica.

1. ¿Qué pediste en el restaurante? (una ensalada)
2. ¿Cómo la pediste? (sin aceite y vinagre)
3. ¿Cuántas veces repetiste «sin aceite y vinagre»? (dos veces)
4. Y, ¿cómo sirvió el mesero la ensalada? (con aceite y vinagre)
5. ¿Qué hiciste? (pedí otra ensalada)
6. ¿Qué pidió tu amigo? (puré de papas)
7. ¿Y qué pasó? (el cocinero frió las papas)
8. ¿Qué sirvió el mesero? (papas fritas)
9. ¿Pidieron ustedes una bebida? (sí)
10. ¿Qué pidieron para beber? (una limonada)
11. ¿Qué sirvió el mesero? (un té)
12. ¿Le dieron ustedes una propina al mesero? (no)

17 **Historieta** Preparando la comida

Completen con el pretérito.

Anoche mi hermano y yo __1__ (preparar) la comida para la familia. Yo __2__ (freír) el pescado. Mi hermano __3__ (freír) las papas. Mamá __4__ (poner) la mesa. Y papá __5__ (servir) la comida. Todos nosotros __6__ (comer) muy bien. A todos nos __7__ (gustar) mucho el pescado. Mi hermano y mi papá __8__ (repetir) el pescado. Luego yo __9__ (servir) el postre, un sorbete. Después de la comida mi hermano tomó una siesta. Él __10__ (dormir) media hora. Yo no __11__ (dormir). No me gusta dormir inmediatamente después de comer.

Valparaíso, Chile

18 **Lo siento mucho.**

You're in a restaurant and you're fed up with the waiter. He hasn't done a thing right. Call over the manager (a classmate) and tell him or her all that happened. He or she will apologize and say something to try to make you happy.

Andas bien. ¡Adelante!

En el restaurante

Teresa	¿Tiene usted una mesa para dos personas?
Mesero	Sí, señorita. Por aquí, por favor.
Teresa	¿Es posible tener un menú en inglés?
Mesero	Sí, ¡cómo no!
Paco	Teresa, no necesito un menú en inglés. Lo puedo leer en español. *(El mesero les da un menú en inglés.)*
Paco	No sé por qué ella me pidió un menú en inglés.
Mesero	No hay problema. Le traigo uno en español.
Paco	Gracias.
Teresa	Pues, Paco, ¿qué vas a pedir?
Paco	Para mí, la especialidad de la casa.
Teresa	Yo también pido la especialidad de la casa.

¿Comprendes?

Contesten.

1. ¿Para cuántas personas quiere la mesa Teresa?
2. ¿Tiene el mesero una mesa libre?
3. ¿Qué tipo de menú pide Teresa?
4. ¿Necesita un menú en inglés Paco?
5. ¿Sabe él por qué ella le pidió un menú en inglés?
6. ¿Qué va a pedir Paco?
7. Y Teresa, ¿qué pide ella?

Vamos a hablar más

A **Fuimos al restaurante.** You and your parents went to a restaurant last night. A classmate will ask you questions about your experience. Answer him or her.

B **Preferencias** Work with a classmate and discuss whether you prefer to eat at home or in a restaurant. Give reasons for your preferences.

Pronunciación

La consonante x

An **x** between two vowels is pronounced much like the English *x* but a bit softer. It's like a **gs: examen → eg-samen.** Repeat the following.

> exacto   examen
> éxito   próximo

When **x** is followed by a consonant, it is often pronounced like an **s.** Repeat the following.

> extremo   explicar   exclamar

Repeat the following sentence.

> **El extranjero exclama que baja en la próxima parada.**

Lecturas culturales

La comida mexicana 🔄 🎧

Es muy difícil decir lo que es la comida hispana porque la comida varía mucho de una región hispana a otra.

Aquí en Estados Unidos la comida mexicana es muy popular. Hay muchos restaurantes mexicanos. Algunos sirven comida típicamente mexicana y otros sirven variaciones que vienen del suroeste de Estados Unidos donde vive mucha gente de ascendencia mexicana.

La base de muchos platos mexicanos es la tortilla. La tortilla es un tipo de panqueque. Puede ser de harina[1], de maíz o de trigo[2]. Con las tortillas, los mexicanos preparan tostadas, tacos, enchiladas, etc. Rellenan[3] las tortillas de pollo, carne de res o frijoles y queso.

[1]harina *flour*
[2]trigo *wheat*
[3]Rellenan *They fill*

Reading Strategy

Thinking while reading
Good readers always think while reading. They think about what the passage might be about after reading the title and looking at the visuals. They predict, create visual images, compare, and check for understanding; they continually think while the author is explaining.

San Miguel de Allende, México

El cultivo del maíz
de Diego Rivera

SECRETARIA DE EDUCACION, CULTURA
Y RECREACION
MUSEO CASA
"DIEGO RIVERA"
GUANAJUATO, GTO.
COOPERACION N$ 5.00

¿Comprendes?

La comida mexicana Contesten.
1. ¿Varía mucho la cocina hispana de una región a otra?
2. ¿Dónde es popular la comida mexicana?
3. ¿De dónde vienen muchas variaciones de la cocina mexicana?
4. ¿Qué sirve de base para muchos platos mexicanos?
5. ¿Qué es una tortilla? ¿De qué puede ser?
6. ¿De qué rellenan las tortillas?

Use your StudentWorks Plus
CD for more practice.

Lectura opcional ①

Málaga, España

La comida española

En España, como en México, hay tortillas también. Pero hay una gran diferencia entre una tortilla mexicana y una tortilla española. La tortilla española no es de maíz. El cocinero español prepara la tortilla con huevos. La tortilla española, que es muy típica, lleva patatas (papas) y cebollas[1].

La cocina española es muy buena y muy variada. Como España es un país que tiene mucha costa, muchos platos españoles llevan marisco y pescado. Y los cocineros preparan muchos platos con aceite de oliva.

[1]cebollas *onions*

Málaga, España

¿Comprendes?

La cocina española Contesten.
1. ¿Cuál es la diferencia entre una tortilla española y una tortilla mexicana?
2. ¿Qué lleva la típica tortilla española?
3. ¿Por qué llevan marisco y pescado muchos platos españoles?
4. ¿Qué usan muchos cocineros españoles para preparar una comida?

Lectura opcional ②

La comida del Caribe

Humacao, Puerto Rico

En el Caribe, en Puerto Rico, Cuba y la República Dominicana, la gente come muchos mariscos y pescado. Es natural porque Puerto Rico, Cuba y la República Dominicana son islas. Pero la carne favorita de la región es el puerco o el lechón[1].

No hay nada más delicioso que un buen lechón asado[2]. Sirven el lechón con arroz, frijoles (habichuelas) y tostones. Para hacer tostones el cocinero corta en rebanadas[3] un plátano, una banana grande, verde y dura. Luego fríe las rebanadas en manteca[4].

[1]lechón *suckling pig*   [3]rebanadas *slices*
[2]asado *roast*   [4]manteca *lard*

¿Comprendes?

¿Lo sabes? Busquen la información.
1. algunos países de la región del Caribe
2. por qué come la gente muchos mariscos y pescado en la región del Caribe
3. una carne favorita de los puertorriqueños, cubanos y dominicanos
4. lo que sirven con el lechón asado
5. lo que son tostones

Conexiones

Las humanidades

El lenguaje

As we already know, Spanish is a language that is spoken in many areas of the world. In spite of the fact that the Spanish-speaking world covers a large area of the globe, it is possible to understand a speaker of Spanish regardless of where he or she is from. Although there are regional differences, these differences do not cause serious comprehension problems.

However, pronunciation does change from area to area. For example, people from San Juan, Puerto Rico; Buenos Aires, Argentina; and Madrid, Spain have pronunciations that are quite different from one another. However, the same is true of English. People from New York, Memphis, and London also have a distinct pronunciation, but they can all understand one another.

The use of certain words also changes from one area to another. This is particularly true in the case of words for foods. Let's look at some regional differences with regard to vocabulary.

Regionalismos

Comestibles

En España son patatas y en todas partes de Latinoamérica son papas.

En casi todas partes es el maíz, pero en México es el maíz o el elote y en Chile es el choclo.

En España son cacahuetes; en muchas partes de Latinoamérica son cacahuates, pero en el Caribe son maní.

En muchas partes es jugo de naranja, pero en Puerto Rico es jugo de china y en España es zumo de naranja.

Las judías verdes tienen muchos nombres. Además de judías verdes son habichuelas tiernas, chauchas, vainitas, ejotes y porotos.

Cosas que no son comestibles

Tomamos el autobús en España, el camión en México y la guagua en el Caribe y en las Islas Canarias.

En España todos duermen en el dormitorio o en la habitación. En México duermen en la recámara y en muchas partes en el cuarto o en el cuarto de dormir.

En España sacas un billete en la ventanilla y en Latinoamérica compras un boleto en la ventanilla o en la boletería.

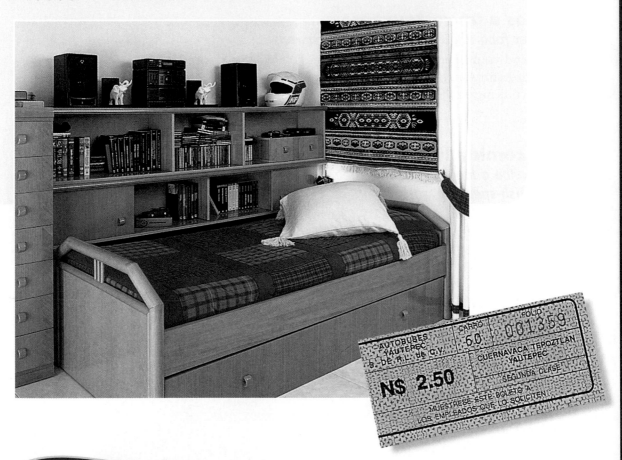

¿Comprendes?

A Hispanohablantes If any of your classmates are heritage speakers of Spanish, ask them to compare the way they say things. Have them share this information with you.

B El inglés There are variations in the use of English words. Discuss the following terms and where they might be heard.

1. bag, sack
2. soda, pop
3. elevator, lift
4. line, queue
5. pram, baby carriage
6. truck, lorry
7. traffic circle, rotary, roundabout
8. subway, underground

¡Te toca a ti!

Use what you have learned

1 Vamos a un restaurante.
✔ *Order food and beverages at a restaurant*

Pretend your Spanish class is at a restaurant. The restaurant serves food from Spain or Latin America. All the waiters and waitresses are Spanish speaking. Order your meal in Spanish and speak together in Spanish during your meal.

2 Una comida hispana
✔ *Describe a meal from some area of the Spanish-speaking world*

Work with a classmate. You have learned about some Hispanic cuisines. Talk about a meal or dish that you want to try **(probar).**

3 La comida
✔ *Talk about categories of food*

Mention a food category, such as meat, seafood, fruit, vegetable. Your partner will give the name of a food that belongs in that category. Take several turns each. Try to use as much as possible of the food vocabulary you've learned.

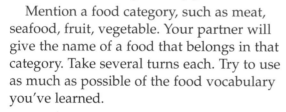

ESCRIBIR

4 El menú

✔ *Plan a menu*

Write out the menu for several meals in Spanish. You can plan meals for **el desayuno, el almuerzo,** and **la cena.**

35° Aniversario

La Estancia

ASADOR CRIOLLO

Lechón al Asador	$ 14,00
Chivito «La Estancia»	$ 16,00
Asado al Asador	$ 11,00

COCINA

Costilla de Cerdo con puré de manzana	$ 10,00
Costilla de Cerdo a la Riojana	$ 12,00
Lomo a la Pimienta con papas a la crema	$ 16,00
Lomo al Champignon	$ 17,00
Milanesa de Lomo	$ 6,50
Milanesa de Lomo a la Napolitana	$ 9,50
Milanesa de Pollo	$ 6,00
Milanesa de Pollo a la Napolitana	$ 9,00
Suprema de Pollo «La Estancia»	$ 10,50
Suprema de Pollo a la Maryland	$ 10,00
1/2 Pollo deshuesado a la Parrilla	$ 10,00

BIFES

Bife de costilla con Lomo con guarnición de papas fritas	$ 8,50
Bife de Chorizo	$ 7,50
Bife especial «La Estancia»	$ 14,50
Bife de Lomo especial «La Estancia».	$ 15,00
Costillas de Cerdo	$ 8,00
Chorizos (c/u)	$ 2,50
Salchicha Criolla (c/u)	$ 3,00
Morcillas (c/u)	$ 2,50
Matambrito Tiernizado	$ 10,00
Bife Aniversario con Lomo	$ 17,00
Mollejas porción	$ 11,00
Longaniza (c/u)	$ 4,00
Riñones porción	$ 5,00
Chinchulines de Ternera porción	$ 5,00
Chinchulines de Cordero porción	$ 9,00
Ubre porción	$ 4,50

Writing Strategy

Writing a letter of complaint When you write a letter of complaint, you must clearly identify the problem and suggest solutions; you should use a businesslike tone. You might be angry when you write a letter of complaint. But to be effective, you must control your emotions since your goal is to get the problem corrected. Your tone of voice is reflected in writing as much as it is in speech; your results will be better if you address the situation calmly and reasonably. In addition, it is important that the letter be addressed to the person who has the most authority.

ESCRIBIR

5 ¡Qué desastre!

Pretend you went to a restaurant where you had a very bad experience. The waiter didn't serve you what you ordered nor the way you ordered it. Write a letter to the management complaining about the food and the service.

Assessment

Vocabulario

Spanish Online

For more Chapter 2 test preparation go to the Chapter 2 **Self-Check Quiz** on the Glencoe Spanish Web site at glencoe.com.

1 Identifiquen.

To review **Palabras 1**, turn to pages 32–33.

1.
2.
3.
4.
5.

2 Identifiquen.

6.   7.   8.

9.   10.

To review **Palabras 2**, turn to pages 36–37.

3 ¿Sí o no? Indiquen si la persona contesta bien.

11. —¿Para cuándo quiere usted la reservación?
    —Para cuatro.
12. —¿A nombre de quién, por favor?
    —Conforme, señor Pereda.

Estructura

4 **Completen con el presente.**

13. El mesero les ____ a los clientes en el restaurante. (servir)
14. Yo siempre ____ la misma cosa, un biftec. (pedir)
15. Ellas ____ elegantemente para ir al restaurante. (vestirse)
16. Nosotros no lo ____. (repetir)
17. El cocinero ____ las papas. (freír)

To review the present of stem-changing verbs, turn to page 40.

5 **Sigan el modelo.**

Él lo pidió. →
Y yo lo pedí, también.

18. Ellos se divirtieron.
    Y yo ____, también.
19. Yo dormí bien.
    Y él ____ bien, también.
20. Tú lo repetiste.
    Y nosotros lo ____, también.
21. Ellos lo prefirieron.
    Y su amigo lo ____, también.
22. Nos vestimos.
    Y ellos ____, también.

To review the preterite of stem-changing verbs, turn to page 42.

Cultura

6 **Contesten.**

23. ¿Cuál es la base de muchas comidas mexicanas?
24. ¿Qué es una tortilla mexicana?
25. ¿De qué rellenan las tortillas para hacer tacos y enchiladas?

To review this cultural information, turn to page 46.

Tell all you can about this illustration.

Getting along at a restaurant

el restaurante
la mesa
el/la mesero(a),
  el/la camarero(a)
el/la cocinero(a)

el menú
la cuenta
la tarjeta de crédito
la propina
el dinero

Identifying a place setting

el vaso
la taza
el platillo
el plato
el tenedor
el cuchillo

la cucharita
la cuchara
el mantel
la servilleta

How well do you know your vocabulary?

- Choose a food category from the list, for example, **la carne.**
- Have classmates choose the names of foods that belong to that category.

Describing some restaurant activities

poner la mesa
pedir
servir
freír

repetir
reservar
tener hambre
tener sed

Identifying more foods

la carne
la carne de res,
  el biftec
la ternera
el cerdo

el cordero
el pescado
los mariscos
los camarones
las almejas

la langosta
el ajo
la berenjena
la alcachofa
el arroz

el maíz
la sal
la pimienta
el aceite
el vinagre

Describing food

rico(a), delicioso(a)

VIDEOTUR

Episodio 2

In this video episode, you will join Vicky and Alberto as they help out at his uncle's restaurant. See page 481 for more information.

Capítulo 3

Telecomunicaciones

Objetivos

In this chapter you will learn to:

❖ talk about computers, e-mail, the Internet, faxes, and telephones
❖ talk about past habitual and routine actions
❖ describe people and events in the past
❖ make and receive telephone calls in Spanish

Ernesto Bertani *Nueva visión*

Spanish online
To interact with your online edition of
¡Buen viaje! go to: glencoe.com.

Vocabulario

La computadora

la computadora, el ordenador

el monitor, la pantalla

la impresora

el disco compacto

el ratón

el teclado

La muchacha prende la máquina.

Ella mete un CD en la ranura.

Ella usa la computadora para hacer las tareas.
Ella entra los datos.

La muchacha no pierde los datos porque los guarda.

Después se comunica con los amigos.
Usa el correo electrónico.

Cuando termina, ella apaga la máquina y saca el CD.

El fax, El facsímil

el facsímil

El señor manda el documento por fax.

Él mete el documento boca arriba.
No lo mete boca abajo.

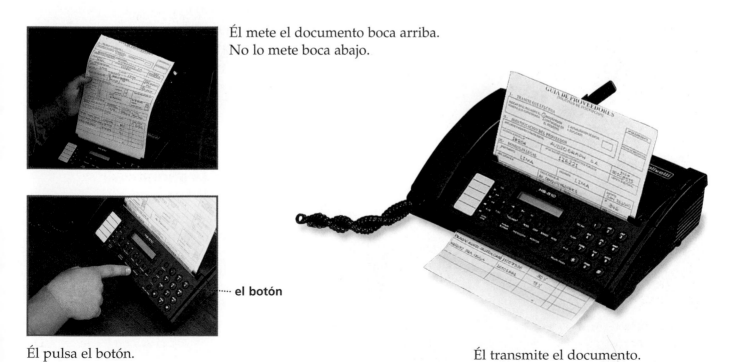

el botón

Él pulsa el botón.

Él transmite el documento.

¿Qué palabra necesito?

1 **¿Usas una computadora?**
Contesten personalmente.

1. ¿Sabes usar una computadora?
2. ¿Cuáles son tres partes de la computadora?
3. El monitor, ¿es de color o blanco y negro?
4. ¿Usas el correo electrónico?
5. ¿Con quién te comunicas por correo electrónico?
6. ¿Haces tus tareas en la computadora?
7. ¿Para qué clase o clases usas la computadora?
8. ¿Usas Internet?
9. ¿Tienes CD-ROM?
10. ¿Cuál es tu juego favorito en la computadora?

Caracas, Venezuela

2 **Los pasos a seguir** Pongan las oraciones en orden lógico.

1. Meto un CD en la ranura.
2. Entro los datos.
3. Prendo la computadora.
4. Saco el CD.
5. Apago la máquina.
6. Guardo los datos.

3 **Historieta** **En la oficina**
Contesten según la foto.

1. ¿Qué quiere hacer la señorita?
2. ¿Usa la señorita la máquina de fax o la computadora?
3. ¿Está prendida la máquina?
4. ¿Cómo mete el documento, boca arriba o boca abajo?
5. ¿Qué pulsa ella?

4 **¿Cómo uso la computadora?** Un(a) alumno(a) de Latinoamérica quiere aprender a usar tu computadora. Explícale. Si él o ella no entiende, te va a hacer unas preguntas. Contéstalas.

5 **¿Cómo mando un fax?** Tú y tu compañero(a) están trabajando en una oficina. Tú sabes usar la máquina de fax, pero tu compañero(a), no. Explícale. Si él o ella no entiende, te va a hacer unas preguntas. Contéstalas.

6 **Programas de software** Con un(a) compañero(a), hablen de cómo pasan el tiempo en la computadora. ¿Juegan mucho o hacen las tareas? Discutan los programas de software que ustedes usan. ¿Son los mismos o no? Luego miren la siguiente pantalla de la computadora. Discutan lo que ven en el monitor. Decidan si consideran útil tal programa.

Spanish Online

For more information about computers and search engines in the Spanish-speaking world, go to **Web Explore** on the Glencoe Spanish Web site at glencoe.com.

Vocabulario

El teléfono

Hola, Paco. Habla María. ¿Dónde estás? ¿Me puedes llamar esta tarde? Gracias.

dejar un mensaje

el contestador automático

el teléfono de botones

Málaga y Melilla

la guía telefónica

la ranura

Telefónica

el auricular

el teléfono celular

el prefijo de país

(34) 952 822-5364

la clave de área

el número de teléfono

el teclado

la tecla

Nota Un **aparato** is usually a device like a telephone or an appliance; **una máquina** is usually something more complex, like a computer.

el teléfono público

Rafael va a hacer una
llamada telefónica.

Él descuelga el auricular.

Él introduce la tarjeta telefónica.
No introduce una moneda.

Él espera el tono.

Cuando oye el tono,
él marca el número.

El teléfono suena.

Cuando yo estaba en Madrid, vivía en
una residencia para estudiantes.

¿Está Alicia?

De Rafael.

Sí, está. ¿De
parte de quién?

Un momento,
por favor.

La hermana de su amiga contesta.

Yo llamaba a mis padres a menudo
  (con frecuencia).
Yo siempre quería hablar mucho. Pero
  las llamadas largas costaban mucho.
Eran muy caras.

Vocabulario

¿Qué palabra necesito?

Lima, Perú

7 Historieta **Una llamada telefónica**
Contesten.

1. ¿El muchacho hace la llamada desde un teléfono público o con un teléfono celular?
2. ¿Es un teléfono celular o de botones?
3. ¿Qué tiene que esperar antes de marcar el número?
4. Si no sabe el número, ¿dónde puede buscar el número?
5. Si no es un número local, ¿qué tiene que marcar primero?
6. Y si es una llamada a un país extranjero, ¿qué tiene que marcar?

8 Aparatos y máquinas Escojan.

1. Las computadoras y los teléfonos públicos tienen ____.
   a. ranuras   **b.** teclas   **c.** monitores
2. Si una persona no está en casa cuando llamas, puedes dejar un mensaje en el ____.
   a. teclado   **b.** auricular   **c.** contestador automático
3. Cuando estás en un coche o cuando no estás cerca de un teléfono público, puedes usar un teléfono ____.
   a. automático   **b.** celular   **c.** electrónico
4. Para usar cualquier máquina eléctrica, primero tienes que ____ la máquina.
   a. prender   **b.** apagar   **c.** marcar
5. Y cuando terminas, tienes que ____ la máquina.
   a. esperar   **b.** meter   **c.** apagar

PARA LLAMAR A MERLÍN
1. Seleccione el código del servicio deseado.
2. Marque el **440-6060**.
3. Tras el mensaje de bienvenida y el "beep" marque en su teléfono las 4 cifras del código seleccionado.

SI NO ESCUCHA EL MENSAJE
4. Marque el 440-6060 y, antes de ingresar el código, marque en su teléfono la tecla datos o, si no tiene, la tecla de asterisco. Luego ingrese el código.
5. Si no tiene ninguna de esas teclas, busque en su aparato una tecla de pulso/tono y póngala en TONO.
6. Si su teléfono es de disco, marque cuidadosamente el código.

Llame a MERLÍN
440-6060

El Comercio
La Verdad en sus manos.

Llame a Merlín al Teléfono **4406060** y marque el código **3539** para ubicar la agencia de publicidad de El Comercio más cercana a su casa y marcando el código **3549** conozca **FONOAVISOS** el nuevo sistema para publicar en El Comercio avisos económicos y destacados por Teléfono.

UN POCO MÁS
*For more practice using words from **Palabras 1** and **Palabras 2**, do Activity 3 on page H4 at the end of this book.*

9 Historieta Linda, la americanita en Madrid

Contesten.

1. ¿Dónde vivía Linda cuando era alumna en Madrid? (en una residencia para estudiantes)
2. ¿Cuándo llamaba a sus padres? (a menudo)
3. ¿Quién siempre contestaba el teléfono? (su madre)
4. ¿Quería hablar mucho Linda? (sí, siempre)
5. ¿Hablaban mucho Linda y su madre? (sí)
6. ¿Costaban mucho las llamadas cortas? (no, largas)
7. ¿Cómo eran las llamadas largas? (caras)

Madrid, España

Puerta del Sol, Madrid

10 Un número equivocado Llamas a un(a) amigo(a) por teléfono, pero otra persona (tu compañero[a]) contesta y dice que tu amigo(a) no vive allí. Dile a la persona el número que marcaste. La persona va a decir que el número es correcto, pero la clave de área, no, y te va a dar la clave de área correcta.

1. (201) 899–6645 Felipe / (301)
2. (513) 371–8302 Andrea / (313)
3. (917) 356–3223 Tomás / (817)
4. (516) 384–1475 Inés / (517)

11 ¿Cómo lo hago? Estás en Madrid y quieres hacer una llamada telefónica. No sabes usar el teléfono público que está en la calle. Le pides ayuda a una persona en la calle (tu compañero[a]). Le preguntas a la persona cómo hacer la llamada. Él o ella te va a explicar lo que tienes que hacer.

Estructura

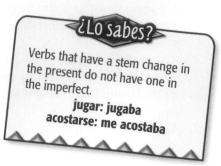

Imperfecto de los verbos en -ar
Talking about habitual past actions

1. In Spanish there are two simple past tenses. The preterite tense, which you have already learned, is used to state an action that began and ended at a specific time in the past. The other simple past tense is the imperfect.

2. The imperfect tense is used to describe a habitual or repeated action in the past. The exact times when the action began and ended are not important. These are the forms of regular -ar verbs in the imperfect.

¿Lo sabes?

Verbs that have a stem change in the present do not have one in the imperfect.
jugar: jugaba
acostarse: me acostaba

INFINITIVE	tomar	llamar	ENDINGS
STEM	tom-	llam-	
yo	tomaba	llamaba	-aba
tú	tomabas	llamabas	-abas
él, ella, Ud.	tomaba	llamaba	-aba
nosotros(as)	tomábamos	llamábamos	-ábamos
vosotros(as)	*tomabais*	*llamabais*	*-abais*
ellos, ellas, Uds.	tomaban	llamaban	-aban

Carlos siempre se levantaba temprano.
Él tomaba el bus escolar a las siete.
El bus llegaba a la escuela a las siete y media.
Algunos muchachos caminaban a la escuela.
Todos los alumnos entraban en clase a las ocho.

San Juan, Puerto Rico

¿Cómo lo digo?

12 Historieta **Carlota iba a la escuela.** Contesten.

1. ¿Carlota se levantaba tarde o temprano todos los días?
2. ¿Carlota caminaba a la escuela o tomaba el bus?
3. ¿A qué hora llegaba a la escuela?
4. ¿Todos los alumnos caminaban a la escuela?
5. ¿A qué hora entraban todos a clase?

13 Historieta **En el primer grado** Contesten.

1. En el primer grado, ¿tú caminabas a la escuela?
2. ¿Cómo se llamaba tu maestro(a) de primer grado?
3. ¿Qué estudiabas en el primer grado?
4. ¿Tomabas el almuerzo en casa o en la escuela?
5. ¿Dónde estaba tu escuela?
6. ¿A qué hora terminaban las clases?
7. ¿Qué te gustaba hacer por la tarde?
8. ¿Con quién jugabas?

14 Historieta **La oficina de Carmen** Completen con el imperfecto.

Todos los veranos Carmen __1__ (trabajar) en una oficina. La oficina __2__ (estar) en la ciudad. Más de treinta personas __3__ (trabajar) allí. Carmen __4__ (tomar) el tren para ir a la ciudad. El tren __5__ (llegar) a las ocho. Carmen __6__ (caminar) de la estación a la oficina. Carmen __7__ (usar) una computadora. Ella __8__ (entrar) datos y los __9__ (revisar). Ella también __10__ (mandar) copias de documentos por fax. A las doce, Carmen y sus amigas __11__ (tomar) el almuerzo. A las cinco, ellas __12__ (terminar) de trabajar. Entonces Carmen __13__ (apagar) las máquinas y __14__ (regresar) a su casa.

Paseo de la Reforma,
la Ciudad de México, México

Estructura

15 **El verano pasado** Mira la lista de palabras. Escoge una y pregúntale a tu compañero(a) si hacía eso con frecuencia durante el verano. Luego cambien de rol. Sigan hasta terminar con la lista.

nadar · comprar helados · tomar el sol · jugar tenis

trabajar · estudiar · viajar · acostarse tarde

levantarse tarde · escuchar discos · mirar la tele

Imperfecto de los verbos en -er e -ir
Talking about habitual past actions

1. The imperfect tense forms of regular **-er** and **-ir** verbs are identical.

INFINITIVE	leer	comer	escribir	vivir	ENDINGS
STEM	le-	com-	escrib-	viv-	
yo	leía	comía	escribía	vivía	-ía
tú	leías	comías	escribías	vivías	-ías
él, ella, Ud.	leía	comía	escribía	vivía	-ía
nosotros(as)	leíamos	comíamos	escribíamos	vivíamos	-íamos
vosotros(as)	leíais	comíais	escribíais	vivíais	-íais
ellos, ellas, Uds.	leían	comían	escribían	vivían	-ían

2. The imperfect of **hay** is **había.**

No había papel en el fax.
No había mensajes en el contestador automático.

¿Te acuerdas?

Remember that verbs that have a stem change in the present do not have one in the imperfect.
querer: **quería**
volver: **volvía**

¿Cómo lo digo?

16 **Cuando yo tenía doce años...** Contesten.

1. Cuando tenías doce años, ¿dónde vivías?
2. ¿A qué escuela asistías?
3. ¿Tenías muchos amigos?
4. ¿Podías hablar español?
5. ¿Sabías usar una computadora?
6. ¿Leías muchos libros?
7. ¿Tenías que estudiar mucho?

17 **¿Qué hacía la gente en la oficina?** Contesten según los dibujos.

1. ¿Qué hacía la señorita Flores?

2. ¿Qué hacían los señores?

3. ¿Qué hacía Eugenio?

4. ¿Qué hacía Teresita?

5. ¿Qué hacían ustedes?

6. ¿Qué hacías tú?

18 **Historieta** **Las amiguitas de Ramona** Completen.

Cuando Ramona __1__ (tener) cuatro años, ella __2__ (vivir) en el campo. Los padres de Ramona __3__ (tener) una hacienda con muchos animales. Ramona __4__ (divertirse) mucho en el campo. Ella __5__ (tener) muchas amiguitas imaginarias. Ella les __6__ (servir) café a sus amiguitas. Las amigas la __7__ (querer) mucho a Ramona. Los padres no __8__ (poder) ver a las amiguitas, pero ellos __9__ (saber) que, para Ramona, las amiguitas sí __10__ (existir). Y Ramona nunca __11__ (aburrirse).

En el campo, Casares, España

Estructura

19 **Entrevista** Prepara una entrevista con tu profesor o profesora de español (tu compañero[a]). Entre otras cosas, tú quieres saber algo de su vida cuando asistía a la escuela secundaria. ¡Usen la imaginación!

Imperfecto de los verbos ser e ir
Talking about habitual past actions

The verbs **ser** and **ir** are irregular in the imperfect tense.

INFINITIVE	ser	ir
yo	era	iba
tú	eras	ibas
él, ella, Ud.	era	iba
nosotros(as)	éramos	íbamos
vosotros(as)	erais	ibais
ellos, ellas, Uds.	eran	iban

¿Lo sabes?

Ver is also considered irregular in the imperfect tense.

veía, veías…

¿Cómo lo digo?

20 **Historieta** **En la primaria**
Contesten.

1. ¿Quiénes eran tus amigos?
2. ¿Adónde iban tus amigos por la tarde?
3. ¿Adónde iban ustedes los sábados?
4. ¿Quién era tu profesor(a) de español?
5. ¿Cómo ibas a la escuela?
6. ¿Quiénes eran tus maestros favoritos?

Estepona, España

21 Historieta Buenos amigos

Completen con la forma correcta de **ser** o **ir**.

Cuando Maribel y Paco __1__ jóvenes, __2__ muy buenos amigos. Ellos __3__ a la escuela juntos. Ellos __4__ a comer juntos. Maribel no __5__ muy buena alumna, pero ella __6__ excelente atleta. Y Paco no __7__ buen atleta, pero __8__ excelente alumno. Maribel __9__ a casa de Paco para hacer la tarea con él. Los dos muchachos __10__ al gimnasio donde Maribel le enseñaba a Paco a hacer los ejercicios. Todo el mundo decía que los dos __11__ a ser buenos amigos para siempre.

Málaga, España

22 Los maestros de cuarto y quinto

 Dile a tu compañero(a) cómo eran tus maestros(as) de cuarto y quinto grado. Tu compañero(a) va a hacer lo mismo. Después digan quiénes eran y cómo eran sus buenos(as) amigos(as) en esos grados.

Una clase de primaria

Estructura

Usos del imperfecto
Describing things in the past

In addition to expressing repeated, habitual actions or events in the past, the imperfect is used to describe persons, places, objects, events, weather, and time in the past.

(handwritten notes in left margin:) la apariencia / la Edad / la condición física / el estado emocional / las actitudes y deseos / el colocación / la Fecha / la hora / el tiempo

APPEARANCE	Victoria era alta y fuerte.
AGE	Tenía dieciséis años.
PHYSICAL CONDITION	Estaba cansada.
EMOTIONAL STATE	Pero estaba muy contenta.
ATTITUDES AND DESIRES	Ella quería ganar el campeonato.
LOCATION	Todos los equipos estaban en la cancha.
DATE	Era el ocho de octubre.
TIME	Eran las cuatro de la tarde.
WEATHER	Hacía bastante frío.

¿Cómo lo digo?

 23 Victoria la victoriosa Contesten.

1. ¿Cómo era Victoria?
2. ¿Tenía veinte años?
3. ¿Estaba enferma o cansada?
4. ¿Estaba triste?
5. ¿Qué quería Victoria?
6. ¿Dónde estaban todos los atletas?
7. ¿Cuál era la fecha?
8. Y, ¿qué hora era?
9. ¿Qué tiempo hacía?

For a fun way to review this grammar point, go to the Chapter 3 **eGame** on the Glencoe Spanish Web site at glencoe.com.

24 Don Quijote y Sancho Panza Contesten.

1. ¿Quién era alto? (Don Quijote)
2. ¿Quién era bajo? (Sancho Panza)
3. ¿Quién tenía un asno? (Sancho Panza)
4. ¿Quién tenía un caballo? (Don Quijote)
5. ¿Quién era idealista? (Don Quijote)
6. ¿Quién era realista? (Sancho Panza)
7. ¿Quién quería viajar? (Don Quijote)
8. ¿Quién quería volver a casa? (Sancho Panza)
9. ¿Quién quería conquistar los males del mundo? (Don Quijote)
10. ¿Quién estaba loco? (Don Quijote)

25 **El año pasado en la escuela** Dile a tu compañero(a) las cosas que tú hacías a menudo en la escuela el año pasado. Tu compañero(a) te va a decir las cosas que él o ella hacía.

26 **Eventos culturales** Tú asististe a uno de los siguientes eventos culturales. Descríbelo en detalle a un(a) compañero(a). Incluye el local, el día, la hora, etc. Di por qué querías asistir. Luego cambien de rol.

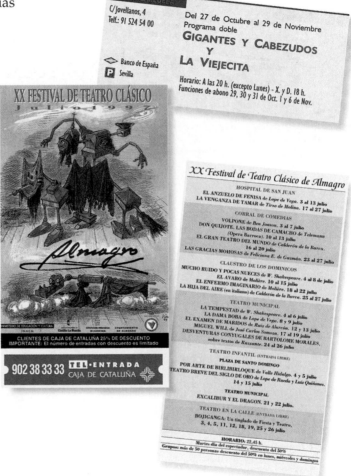

Andas bien. ¡Adelante!

Conversación

Una llamada internacional

Ricardo Operadora, quiero hacer una llamada a Estados Unidos.

Operadora ¿Cómo va a pagar la llamada?

Ricardo Con tarjeta telefónica. ¿La puedo usar?

Operadora Claro que sí, si hay bastante dinero en la tarjeta.

Ricardo Sí, hay bastante. ¿Puedo marcar directamente, o tiene usted que poner la llamada?

Operadora Puede llamar directamente. Sólo tiene que meter la tarjeta en la ranura, marcar el «uno», que es el prefijo de Estados Unidos, y ya está. Usted sabe la clave de área y el número que desea, ¿no?

Ricardo Sí, sí. Ah, si el número está ocupado o si no contestan, no me cuesta nada, ¿verdad?

Operadora Claro que no.

¿Comprendes?

Contesten.

1. ¿A dónde quiere llamar Ricardo?
2. ¿Qué le pregunta la operadora?
3. ¿Qué tiene Ricardo?
4. ¿Hay bastante dinero en la tarjeta?
5. ¿La operadora tiene que poner la llamada?
6. ¿Dónde tiene que meter la tarjeta Ricardo?
7. ¿Por qué tiene que marcar el «uno»?
8. Si nadie contesta, ¿le cuesta algo a Ricardo?

Vamos a hablar más

A **Los abuelos cuando eran jóvenes** Dile a tu compañero(a) todo lo que sabes de tus abuelos cuando ellos eran jóvenes: cómo eran, dónde vivían y trabajaban, qué hacían con tus padres, etc. Tu compañero(a) va a hacer lo mismo.

B **El/La operador(a) internacional** Tú eres el/la operador(a) internacional. Una persona (tu compañero[a]) llama para saber los prefijos de país y las claves de área para las ciudades a donde quiere llamar. Después cambien de rol.

PAÍS	PREFIJO DE PAÍS	CIUDAD	CLAVE DE ÁREA
Chile	56	Valparaíso	32
Ecuador	593	Quito	2
España	34	Sevilla	5
México	52	Acapulco	74
Perú	51	Lima	1
Uruguay	598	Paysandú	722

C **Las cosas que nos gustaban** Habla con tu compañero(a) de las cosas que les gustaba hacer cuando eran pequeños, pero que no les gusta hacer ahora.

D *Juego* **¿Para qué lo/la uso?** With a partner, look at the following photos. One of you will make up a sentence describing something you do with one of the items in the photos. The other will guess which item you need. Take turns. Use the model as a guide.

—**Quiero buscar el número de teléfono de mi tía.**
—**Ah, necesitas la guía telefónica.**

1.
2.
3.
4.
5.

Lecturas culturales

Futura ingeniera

Carmen Tordesillas es estudiante de ingeniería[1] en Madrid. El año que viene va a trabajar para la Compañía de Teléfonos, «la Telefónica». Ella nos habla.

—Cuando yo era niña siempre quería ser ingeniera. Los aparatos electrónicos me fascinaban, especialmente el teléfono. Mi papá me permitía hacer llamadas a casa desde los teléfonos públicos. Era una aventura. Él me levantaba. Me daba unas monedas. Yo las metía en la ranura. Cuando mami contestaba, las monedas caían[2] y empezábamos a hablar. Después de unos minutos sonaba un tono que decía que iba a terminar la conexión. Yo le pedía más monedas a papá. Cuando me daba las monedas, yo estaba contenta; si no, yo protestaba.

Hoy no necesitamos monedas, porque tenemos tarjetas telefónicas y teléfonos celulares que son muy convenientes.

Y van a ver lo que el futuro nos trae. Yo voy a trabajar en «la Telefónica». ¡Voy a crear una revolución en las telecomunicaciones!

[1]ingeniería *engineering*
[2]caían *dropped*

¿Comprendes?

Carmen Tordesillas Contesten.

1. Actualmente, ¿Carmen trabaja o estudia?
2. ¿Dónde quiere Carmen trabajar?
3. ¿Qué quería ser Carmen cuando era pequeña?
4. ¿Qué le interesaba mucho a la pequeña Carmen?
5. ¿Qué le permitía hacer su padre?
6. Cuando alguien contestaba, ¿qué pasaba con las monedas?
7. ¿Por qué le pedía más monedas a su padre?
8. ¿Su padre siempre le daba monedas a Carmen?
9. ¿Por qué no necesitamos monedas para llamar hoy?
10. ¿Qué va a hacer Carmen en el futuro?

Madrid, España

El Palacio Real, Madrid, España

Lectura opcional 1

La tarjeta telefónica— una innovación popularísima

La introducción de la tarjeta telefónica ocurrió en España antes que en Estados Unidos. Allí usan este conveniente método de hacer llamadas con teléfonos públicos. Las tarjetas tienen un microchip que registra la cantidad de dinero para llamadas. Introduces la tarjeta en la ranura del teléfono para hacer la conexión. Las tarjetas son muy convenientes. No tienes que llevar muchas monedas o ir a las tiendas para pedir cambio[1]. Y las compañías ahora tienen otro medio de propaganda. Muchas tarjetas llevan un anuncio[2] comercial. Y algunas compañías regalan tarjetas con sus anuncios a sus buenos clientes. La tarjeta telefónica es un invento muy popular.

[1]cambio *change*   [2]anuncio *advertisement, announcement*

¿Comprendes?

¿Sí o no? Digan que sí o que no.
1. La introducción de la tarjeta telefónica ocurrió primero en Estados Unidos.
2. Usan las tarjetas en los teléfonos públicos.
3. Hay un microchip en las tarjetas telefónicas.
4. Para usar las tarjetas necesitas muchas monedas.
5. Las compañías venden las tarjetas a todos sus clientes.
6. Algunas tarjetas llevan anuncios.

Lectura opcional 2

Quito, Ecuador

La solución a un problema de comunicaciones

En Estados Unidos y en España y las grandes ciudades de Latinoamérica, los teléfonos celulares son muy populares. Los hombres y las mujeres mantienen contacto con la oficina o con los clientes mientras viajan de casa al trabajo y viceversa. Pero en muchos pueblos de Latinoamérica el teléfono celular tiene otro rol.

Hay algunos pueblos y ciudades donde el sistema telefónico está en muy malas condiciones. Las familias tienen que esperar años para la instalación de un teléfono. Donde hay una necesidad, siempre hay una solución. En muchos pueblos y en algunas ciudades, empresarios[1] obtienen[2] teléfonos celulares o aún teléfonos de disco[3] y una conexión con el sistema telefónico. En las calles y las plazas hay mesitas donde un empleado se sienta con un teléfono. Si una persona quiere hacer una llamada, puede usar el teléfono y pagar al empleado. Así el pequeño empresario gana dinero y el público tiene acceso al servicio telefónico.

[1]empresarios *entrepreneurs, businesspeople*
[2]obtienen *obtain*
[3]de disco *rotary*

Plaza de Armas, Trujillo, Perú

¿Comprendes?

A El teléfono celular Contesten.
1. ¿Quiénes usan mucho el teléfono celular?
2. ¿Para qué usan el teléfono celular?
3. ¿Cuál es el problema con el sistema telefónico en algunas partes de Latinoamérica?
4. ¿Qué problema tienen las familias?
5. ¿Dónde puedes ver los teléfonos en partes de Latinoamérica?
6. ¿Qué puede hacer una persona que quiere hacer una llamada?

B La solución a un problema En grupos, expliquen, en sus propias palabras, el uso de un teléfono celular o de disco que describen en la lectura.

Conexiones

La tecnología

La computadora

It's hard to imagine life before the computer and the fax machine. The computer has revolutionized travel, medicine, architecture, the military, banking, and commerce. Hardly a field has been unaffected by computers. Even agriculture and the arts make extensive use of the new technology. The changes have been tremendous. Because the United States has led the way in computer science, much of the vocabulary used worldwide is in English or derived from English. Let's read about some of these changes in technology and the prevalence of English in this field.

Los avances en las telecomunicaciones

Las computadoras de hace treinta años eran enormes. Una computadora antigua, como la original ENIAC de 1946, procesaba menos datos que un PC moderno y llenaba toda una sala. Hoy hay computadoras portátiles que pesan menos de 2 kilos. Lo que ha facilitado el progreso en las computadoras es la «miniaturización». Un solo microchip puede almacenar[1] miles y miles de datos. Los primeros aparatos de transmisión de facsímil también eran muy grandes y las copias que salían en el destino muchas veces no se podían leer.

[1]almacenar *store*

Computadora ENIAC

Laura Ballesteros trabaja en uno de los ministerios del gobierno chileno. Ella es recepcionista. El edificio es del siglo XIX, pero los aparatos que usa Laura son muy modernos. Ella tiene una computadora y un fax. En el colegio Laura estudiaba inglés. Buena idea, porque hay mucho inglés en el vocabulario de la informática[2]. Por ejemplo, tienes que hacer «clic» en un «icono» para tener acceso a un programa de «software». Y un «virus» puede infectar los programas.

Aquí hay otros ejemplos del predominio del inglés en el mundo de las computadoras: monitor, datos, disquete, memoria, documentación, drive, formateo, site de Internet. ¿Sabes lo que son en inglés?

[2]informática *computer science*

Edificio del siglo XIX

Interior del mismo edificio

¿Comprendes?

A ¿Cómo se llama... ? Den la palabra en español.
1. icon
2. access
3. memory
4. program
5. click
6. data

B ¿Qué es? Identifiquen.
1. el proceso de hacer muy pequeño un aparato u otra cosa
2. una copia exacta y precisa
3. la pantalla como la de un televisor en donde proyectan la información de la computadora
4. el disco pequeño para guardar datos que pueden sacar de la computadora
5. el disco grande con mucha memoria dentro de la computadora
6. una computadora muy pequeña que pueden llevar de viaje

¡Te toca a ti!

Use what you have learned

1 ¿Qué pasa?
✔ *Talk about computers, e-mail, faxes, and cell phones*

Con un(a) compañero(a), miren las fotos. Cada uno(a) va a escoger una y explicar lo que pasa.

a.

b.

c.

2 Un mensaje telefónico
✔ *Leave a message on an answering machine*

Tú y tu compañero(a) tienen muchos amigos de habla española. Cada uno(a) de ustedes debe pensar en un mensaje en español para el contestador automático. Comparen sus mensajes y escojan uno para usar en el contestador automático.

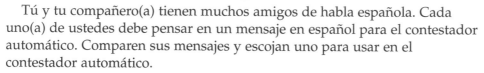

3 Los veranos de mi niñez
✔ *Talk about past habitual actions*

Pregúntale a un(a) compañero(a) de clase lo que hacía en el verano cuando era pequeño(a). Pregúntale adónde iba, con quién, lo que hacía, etc. Luego cambien de papel.

4 Un juego telefónico
✔ *Describe routine actions*

Divide the class into teams by rows. Using the imperfect, the last person in each row will whisper to the person in front of him or her one sentence about what he or she always did in the past. Each person will whisper the same sentence to the next person until the message reaches the front of the row. The first person in each row will say the sentence to the class. The team whose final sentence most clearly resembles the original wins.

5 Recuerdos de mi niñez

✔ *Write about people and events in the past*

Cuando eras niño(a), ¿ibas con frecuencia a visitar a unos primos o amigos? En un párrafo, describe a quién (quiénes) visitabas, cómo eran, qué tipo de casa tenían. Incluye en tu párrafo todo lo que hacían cuando estaban juntos.

Barcelona, España

6 Una historieta o un cuento

✔ *Narrate in the past*

Escribe un cuento utilizando las siguientes categorías como guía.

- Fecha
- Tiempo
- Personajes y lugar (quiénes y dónde)
- Descripción física y emocional de los personajes
- Actitudes
- Deseos
- Actividades usuales

Writing Strategy

Expository writing Expository writing is writing that explains and informs. It helps one understand a topic. Two important expressions to think about while writing an expository piece are "how to" and "why." Use familiar terms in your definitions and descriptions. Be careful not to omit important facts and steps. Be certain not to present steps out of order. These measures will help you present a clear and concise explanation that readers will find interesting and informative.

7 Un trabajo interesante

You had a job this past summer with a service organization in the Hispanic community in your town. You got the job because you speak Spanish. Since you've never worked in an office before, you were excited about learning to use equipment that was all new to you. Send an e-mail to Octavio, your Peruvian key pal, and explain some of the things you did in the office and what equipment you used. Since you know that Octavio has never worked in an office and is not familiar with office machines, be as clear and logical as you can in your explanation.

Assessment

Vocabulario

1 **Escojan.**

1. Antes de empezar a trabajar, es necesario ____ la computadora.
   a. guardar   **b.** meter   **c.** prender
2. La joven mete su CD en ____.
   a. el teclado   **b.** el dato   **c.** la ranura
3. La joven no pierde los datos. Los ____.
   a. guarda   **b.** entra   **c.** saca
4. Ve lo que entra en la computadora en ____.
   a. el ratón   **b.** el teclado   **c.** la pantalla

To review **Palabras 1**, turn to pages 60-61.

2 **Den lo contrario.**

5. prender la máquina
6. meter el CD
7. boca arriba

3 **Identifiquen.**

8.

9.

(34) 952 822-5364

To review **Palabras 2**, turn to pages 64-65.

10.

Spanish Online
For more Chapter 3 test preparation go to the Chapter 3 **Self-Check Quiz** on the Glencoe Spanish Web site at glencoe.com.

4 **Completen.**

11. Él ____ el auricular para hacer una llamada telefónica.

12. Él no introduce una moneda en la ranura. Introduce su ____.

13. Cuando oye el ____, marca el número.

Estructura

5 **Escriban en el imperfecto.**

14. Él habla mucho.

15. Él hace muchas llamadas telefónicas.

16. Tomo fotos de la casa.

17. Yo vivo en la casa.

18. ¿Comes en la cafetería de la escuela?

19. ¿Tomas el desayuno en la escuela?

20. Escribimos muchas cartas a nuestros abuelos.

6 **Completen.**

21–22. Cuando yo ____ muy joven, ____ a la escuela a pie. (ser, ir)

7 **Completen en el pasado.**

23–25. Sancho Panza ____ (ser) el escudero de don Quijote. Don Quijote siempre ____ (querer) conquistar los males del mundo. Los dos ____ (viajar) por toda España.

To review regular -ar, -er, and -ir verbs in the imperfect tense, turn to pages 68 and 71.

To review ser and ir in the imperfect tense, turn to page 72.

To review the imperfect tense, turn to pages 68-75.

Tell all you can about this illustration.

Vocabulario

Describing a computer

la computadora,
  el ordenador
el teclado
el monitor, la pantalla
el disco compacto, el CD
el ratón

la impresora
la ranura
el correo electrónico
el CD-ROM
Internet

Describing computer activities

prender la máquina
meter un CD
entrar los datos

hacer las tareas
guardar
comunicarse

terminar
apagar
sacar

Describing how to send a fax

el facsímil, el fax
el aparato
el documento
boca arriba

boca abajo
mandar, transmitir
meter
pulsar el botón

VIDEOTUR

Episodio 3

In this video episode, you will see Julián try to help Alejandra with a dilemma. See page 482 for more information. As you watch, look for gestures the speakers use to help convey meaning.

Describing a telephone

el teléfono público
la ranura
el auricular
el teléfono de botones
la tecla

el teléfono celular
el contestador automático
dejar un mensaje

Describing telephone numbers

la guía telefónica
el prefijo de país

la clave de área
el número de teléfono

Making a telephone call

hacer una llamada
  telefónica, llamar
descolgar el auricular
introducir la tarjeta
  telefónica
oír el tono

marcar el número
sonar
contestar
¿Está… ?
¿De parte de quién?

How well do you know your vocabulary?

- Choose words to describe your favorite method of communication.
- Write a brief explanation of sending an e-mail or making a telephone call.

Other useful expressions

a menudo

con frecuencia

Capítulo 4

De tiendas

Objetivos

In this chapter you will learn to:

❖ shop for apparel and food in Spanish-speaking countries

❖ ask for the quantities and sizes you want

❖ find out prices

❖ talk about different types of past actions

❖ talk in general terms about what is done

❖ talk about shopping practices in Spanish-speaking countries

Pedro de Vega Muñoz *Market Day, Seville*

Spanish Online
To interact with your online edition of
¡Buen viaje! go to: glencoe.com.

Vocabulario

PALABRAS 1

La tienda de ropa para caballeros

el abrigo
el traje
el pañuelo
el impermeable, la gabardina
el escaparate

Use your StudentWorks Plus CD for more practice.

la ropa interior
los calcetines

José fue a una tienda de ropa.
Miró la ropa en el escaparate.
En el escaparate había un traje.
A José le gustó el traje.

José entró en la tienda.
Se probó el traje.
Se miró en el espejo.

La tienda de ropa para señoras

el saco, la chaqueta
la bufanda
la manga corta
el suéter
la manga larga
la blusa
el vestido
el bolsillo
el pantalón
los botones
el cinturón

¿En qué puedo servirle?   Quisiera un suéter gris.

Su tamaño, por favor.   Mediano. (38)

María fue a la tienda de ropa.
Quería comprar un suéter.

En la zapatería

anchos

estrechos

No me quedan bien.
Son demasiado estrechos.

las botas   el tacón   las sandalias   los zapatos

En la joyería   los tacones

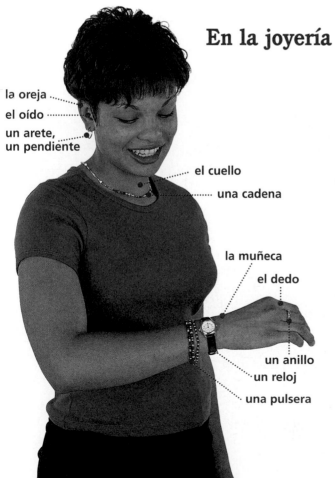

la oreja
el oído
un arete,
un pendiente

el cuello
una cadena

la muñeca
el dedo

un anillo
un reloj
una pulsera

una cadena de oro

Había muchas joyas en la vitrina.
La dependienta le enseñó una cadena a Anita.
La cadena era de oro.
Era muy cara pero Anita la compró.

Vocabulario

¿Qué palabra necesito?

1 **¿Qué es?** Identifiquen.

 1.

2.

 3.

4.

5.

6.

7.

8.

9.

2 **La ropa que llevamos** Escojan.

1. Es el verano y hace calor. Tadeo quiere comprar ____.
   a. un abrigo   **b.** una camisa de mangas largas
   c. una camisa de mangas cortas
2. Llevamos ____ cuando llueve.
   a. una bufanda   **b.** un impermeable   **c.** sandalias
3. ____ tiene botones.
   a. Un calcetín   **b.** Una blusa   **c.** Un pañuelo
4. Llevo ____ cuando voy a la playa.
   a. zapatos   **b.** sandalias   **c.** botas
5. Es necesario llevar ____ con algunos pantalones.
   a. corbata   **b.** calcetines   **c.** cinturón
6. Los zapatos que está llevando Elena tienen un tacón muy ____.
   a. largo   **b.** caro   **c.** alto
7. Isabel no compró los zapatos porque ____.
   a. le quedaban bien   **b.** eran un poco estrechos   **c.** le gustaban
8. Uno puede llevar ____ en el dedo.
   a. una cadena   **b.** un arete   **c.** un anillo
9. Uno lleva una pulsera en ____.
   a. la oreja   **b.** la muñeca   **c.** el cuello

MAJORICA
Joyas y Perlas

Colgante / Pendientes

3 Historieta En la tienda de ropa

Contesten según se indica.

1. ¿Adónde fue Juan? (a la tienda de ropa)
2. ¿Qué vio en el escaparate? (un traje)
3. ¿Le gustó? (sí, mucho)
4. ¿De qué color era? (azul oscuro)
5. ¿Cuántos botones tenía la chaqueta? (tres)
6. ¿Entró Juan en la tienda? (sí)
7. ¿Con quién habló? (el dependiente)
8. ¿Qué le enseñó el dependiente?
   (el traje que vio en el escaparate)
9. ¿Qué hizo Juan? (se probó el traje)
10. ¿Cómo le quedó? (muy bien)

Málaga, España

4 Preguntas personales Contesten.

1. La última ropa que compraste, ¿dónde la compraste?
2. ¿Te atendió un(a) dependiente(a)?
3. ¿Viste el artículo que querías en una vitrina?
4. ¿Qué artículos de ropa te enseñó el/la dependiente(a)?
5. ¿Tenían lo que querías en tu tamaño?
6. ¿Cuánto te costó?

5 Todo nuevo Un(a) amigo(a) te invitó al baile en tu escuela. Vas a la tienda de ropa a comprar algo especial para la ocasión. Habla con el/la dependiente(a) (tu compañero[a]). Describe todo lo que quieres. Él o ella te va a ayudar. Luego cambien de rol.

6 Juego ¿Qué es? Piensa en un artículo de ropa o en algo que ves en una joyería. Descríbelo a tu compañero(a). Él o ella va a adivinar lo que estás describiendo. Luego cambien de rol. Puedes usar el modelo como guía.

Lo llevo en la muñeca y lo uso para saber la hora.

¡Es un reloj!

Vocabulario

PALABRAS 2

La compra de comestibles

Use your **StudentWorks** Plus™
CD for more practice.

el puesto

el mercado

el colmado, la tienda de abarrotes,
la tienda de ultramarinos

el supermercado

el hipermercado

En la panadería se vende pan.

En la carnicería se vende carne.

En la pescadería se vende pescado.
Se venden también mariscos.

En la pastelería se venden pasteles.

En la verdulería se venden
legumbres (vegetales).

En la frutería se venden frutas.

La señora iba de compras todos los días.
Compraba pan en la panadería.

¿A cuánto están los tomates hoy?

Están a cincuenta el kilo. Están muy frescos.

Sí, tienen muy buena pinta. Medio kilo, por favor.

Y compraba vegetales frescos en la verdulería.

el carrito

el pasillo

A veces la señora hacía sus compras en
    el supermercado.
Empujaba el carrito por los pasillos.
Hoy compró:
    seis tajadas (rebanadas) de jamón
    un paquete de guisantes congelados
    seis latas de refrescos
    una botella de agua mineral
    un frasco de mayonesa
    una caja de detergente

En el supermercado la señora siempre
    pagaba en la caja.
La empleada ponía sus compras en
    bolsas de plástico.

¿Qué palabra necesito?

7 De compras Contesten.

1. Alicia necesitaba pan. ¿Adónde fue ella?
2. Ella quería comprar un biftec. ¿Adónde fue?
3. Quería gambas frescas y un filete de pescado. ¿Adónde fue?
4. Necesitaba una docena de naranjas. ¿Adónde fue?
5. Quería comprar un pastel delicioso. ¿Adónde fue?

Una panadería, México

8 Historieta Al supermercado

Contesten.

1. ¿Fue al mercado o al supermercado la señora Galdós?
2. ¿Empujó un carrito por los pasillos?
3. ¿Fue de un departamento a otro?
4. ¿Qué compró en la carnicería?
5. ¿Qué compró en el departamento de productos congelados?
6. Quería hacer un bocadillo de jamón y queso. ¿Cuántas rebanadas de jamón compró?
7. ¿Compró un frasco de mayonesa?
8. ¿Dónde pagó?
9. ¿En qué puso la señora sus compras?

Un supermercado, San José, Costa Rica

SUPERMERCADOS
UNICASA
Somos parte de su Familia

9 Preguntas personales Contesten.

1. ¿Quién en tu familia compra la comida?
2. ¿Hace las compras en un mercado o en un supermercado?
3. ¿Qué productos congelados compra con frecuencia?
4. ¿Compra la carne en una carnicería o en el supermercado?
5. En el supermercado donde ustedes compran, ¿usan bolsas de plástico o de papel?

10 **¿A cuánto está?** Contesten según el anuncio.

1. la bolsa de patatas fritas
2. la lata de tomate
3. el jamón serrano
4. la caja de queso castellano
5. el frasco de mermelada

11 **¿Cuánto?** Tú eres el/la dependiente(a) en el mercado. El/La cliente (tu compañero[a]) pide uno de los siguientes productos y tú le preguntas la cantidad que quiere, en kilos, latas, paquetes, bolsas, botellas, etc. Luego cambien de rol.

ternera

gaseosa

zanahorias congeladas

atún

mayonesa

Plaza San Jacinto,
Ciudad de México

12 **Los favoritos** Prepara dos listas: una lista de los comestibles que te gustan y otra de los comestibles que no te gustan. Luego trabaja con un(a) compañero(a). Comparen sus listas y determinen los gustos que tienen en común.

13 **¡Qué invitación!** Estás viviendo con los Menéndez, una familia mexicana. ¡Qué coincidencia! Los «Miami Dolphins» están en México y los señores Menéndez invitan a los «Dolphins» a cenar. Con el señor o la señora Menéndez (tu compañero[a]), planeen el menú para la comida que van a servir. Discutan las cantidades que van a necesitar. A propósito, *a ton* en español es «una tonelada».

*For more practice using words from **Palabras 2**, do Activity 4 on page H5 at the end of this book.*

Estructura

> Use your **StudentWorks** Plus
> CD for more practice.

El pretérito y el imperfecto
Talking about past events

1. The choice of whether to use the preterite or imperfect depends upon whether the speaker is describing an action completed in the past or a continuous, recurring action in the past.

2. You use the preterite to express actions or events that began and ended at a specific time in the past.

> **Anoche Carmen fue al supermercado.**
> **Compró una caja de detergente y unos productos congelados.**
> **El dependiente puso todo en una bolsa.**

3. You use the imperfect to talk about a continuous, habitual, or repeated action in the past. The moment when the action began or ended is unimportant.

> **Carmen iba al supermercado con frecuencia.**
> **Cada día compraba las cosas que necesitaba.**
> **Casi siempre pagaba con tarjeta de crédito.**

4. Compare the following sentences.

REPEATED, HABITUAL ACTION	COMPLETED ACTION
Ellos iban al cine todos los sábados.	**Ellos fueron al cine el sábado pasado.**
Siempre se sentaban en la primera fila.	**Ayer se sentaron en la última fila.**
Todas las noches se acostaban tarde.	**Anoche se acostaron temprano.**

Un supermercado, Estepona, España

The text on the Skip detergent package reads:

> LEVER
> NUEVO
> SISTEMA DE TRATAMIENTO ANTI-MANCHAS
> **SKIP**
> recomendado para las principales marcas
> 5 kg
> LA SOLUCIÓN CONTRA LAS MANCHAS

The text on the Congelados advertisement reads:

> **CONGELADOS**
> 60 Croquetas de Jamón
> **PESCANOVA**
> Lo bueno sale fuera
> NUEVA Con más trocitos. Hechas al más cremosa
> ENVASE AHORRO
> Croquetas de varios sabores **Pescanova,** bolsa de I kg,
> **2,50 €**

¿Cómo lo digo?

14 **¿Una vez o frecuentemente?** Contesten.

1. ¿Fue la señora al mercado ayer por la mañana?
¿Cuándo fue la señora al mercado?
¿Iba la señora al mercado cada mañana?
¿Cuándo iba la señora al mercado? —

2. ¿Jugaste al tenis ayer por la tarde?
¿Cuándo jugaste al tenis?
¿Jugabas al tenis cada tarde?
¿Cuándo jugabas al tenis?

3. Anoche, ¿se comunicaron por correo electrónico los amigos?
¿Cuándo se comunicaron por correo electrónico los amigos?
¿Se comunicaban por correo electrónico casi todas las noches?
¿Cuándo se comunicaban por correo electrónico los amigos?

15 **¿Cuándo?** Sigan el modelo.

todas las semanas / la semana pasada ⟶
Bárbara, ¿ibas al cine todas las semanas?
Bárbara, ¿fuiste al cine la semana pasada?

1. todas las noches / anoche

2. todos los días / ayer

3. todas las mañanas / esta mañana

4. todas las tardes / ayer por la tarde

5. todos los sábados / el sábado pasado

16 Historieta Los sábados de Juan Antonio Cambien **Todos los sábados** a **El sábado pasado.** Hagan los cambios necesarios.

Todos los sábados Juan Antonio se levantaba muy temprano. Bajaba a la cocina y él mismo preparaba el desayuno. Después de comer, subía a su cuarto y prendía su computadora. Cuando hacía la conexión a Internet mandaba un correo electrónico a un buen amigo en España. En pocos segundos se comunicaba con su amigo. Los dos escribían de muchas cosas durante horas.

17 Entrevista Vas a entrevistar *(interview)* a un(a) compañero(a). Pregúntale lo que le gustaba hacer cuando era joven y dos cosas que le impresionaron como niño(a). Luego cambien de rol.

18 Tu amigo(a) chileno(a) Estás hablando con un(a) amigo(a) (tu compañero[a]) que antes vivía en Chile. Él o ella te está describiendo «Paseo estación central», donde siempre iba de compras. Te está explicando por qué le gustaba ir de compras allí. Luego explícale donde tú prefieres hacer las compras.

Spanish Online
For more information about Chile, go to **Web Explore** on the Glencoe Spanish Web site at glencoe.com.

Dos acciones en una oración
Narrating a sequence of events

1. Often a sentence may have two or more verbs in the past. The verbs may be in the same tense or in different tenses. In the sentence below, both verbs are in the preterite. Both describe simple actions that began and ended at a specific time in the past.

> **Laura llegó ayer y Pepe la vio.**

2. In the sentence below, the two verbs are in the imperfect because they both describe habitual or continuous actions. The moment when the actions began or ended is unimportant.

> **Durante los inviernos, Adela iba a las montañas a esquiar, pero yo trabajaba.**

3. In the sentence below, the verb **estudiaba** is in the imperfect; it describes the background—what was going on. The verb in the preterite, **entró,** expresses the action or event that interrupted the ongoing action.

> **Yo estudiaba cuando Julia entró.**

¿Cómo lo digo?

19 **Historieta** ¿Qué hacías cuando… ?
Contesten.

1. ¿Estabas en casa cuando sonó el teléfono?
2. ¿Mirabas un video cuando sonó?
3. ¿Contestaste el teléfono cuando sonó?
4. ¿Hablabas por teléfono cuando tu padre volvió a casa?
5. ¿Preguntó tu padre con quién hablabas?
6. ¿Con quién hablabas cuando tu padre entró?

CENTRO DE
INFORMACIÓN
UNIVERSITARIA

UNIVERSIDAD DE
ALCALÁ

Plaza de San Diego, s/n.
Teléfono: (91) 885 40 03/06
28801 ALCALÁ DE HENARES
(Madrid)

Línea TELECOR.
El **nuevo** servicio de telefonía fija con **muchas más ventajas** para ti.

TELECOR

Servicios de Telecomunicaciones

HASTA UN
40% MENOS
EN SU FACTURA
TELEFÓNICA

DESDE
0,021e
/minuto*

* Más establecimiento de llamada

Date de alta en nuestra nueva línea, sin ninguna instalación, y en tu próxima factura de teléfono notarás la diferencia.
Podrás hablar más por mucho menos y con los mejores servicios.
Bonos de 500 minutos por sólo 15 Euros al mes.

20 Historieta En la tienda de ropa

Contesten según los dibujos.

1. ¿Adónde fue Susana para hacer sus compras?
2. ¿Qué quería comprar?
3. ¿Qué tomó para subir al segundo piso?
4. Cuando ella llegó a la caja, ¿con quién hablaba la dependienta?
5. Cuando Susana pagaba, ¿quiénes la saludaron?

21 Yo hacía esto cuando eso pasó. Sigan el modelo.

Yo jugaba cuando sonó el teléfono.

jugar · leer · correr · ver · mirar · beber · hablar · sonar · llamar · bailar · comer · subir · servir · llover · pagar

22 Lo que hacía cuando… Habla con un(a) compañero(a). Dile algo que hacías ayer. Tu compañero(a) te va a decir algo que ocurrió e interrumpió lo que hacías. Luego en una sola oración, describe lo que hacías y lo que pasó (ocurrió). ¡Usen la imaginación!

23 Juego Vicente el perezoso Lazy Vicente needs excuses for not turning in his homework. Something always interferes with his studying, reading, writing, etc. Help him out. Give him half a dozen good excuses like: **¡Yo estudiaba cuando el presidente me llamó!** You get the idea. See who can come up with the most original excuse in the class!

Verbos como **querer** y **creer** en el pasado
Expressing feelings in the past

Since most mental processes involve duration or continuance, verbs that deal with mental activities or conditions are most often expressed in the imperfect tense in the past. The most common of these verbs are:

creer	**pensar** *(to think)*
desear	**preferir**
querer	**poder**
tener ganas de *(to feel like)*	**saber**

Él sabía lo que preferíamos.
Yo tenía ganas de salir.
Él creía que yo estaba enfermo.

¿Cómo lo digo?

24 **Yo quería…** Preparen una lista de las cosas que querían hacer.

25 **Yo sabía…** Preparen una lista de las cosas que sabían hacer cuando eran niños(as).

26 **Y yo no podía…** Preparen una lista de las cosas que no podían hacer cuando eran niños(as).

27 **Sabía y podía…** Preparen una lista de las cosas que sabían hacer y que podían hacer.

Caracas, Venezuela

Estructura

La voz pasiva con se
Talking in general terms

1. When we talk about something being done without saying who does it, we use the passive voice in English.

> *Fish is sold at the fish market.*

2. In Spanish, the pronoun **se** is used to express this idea.

> **Se vende pescado en la pescadería.**
> **Se venden papas en la verdulería.**

The verb is singular or plural depending on the subject.

3. You will often see the **se** construction used to express ideas such as:

> *They speak Spanish here.*
> *Spanish is spoken here.*
> *One speaks Spanish here.*
> *People speak Spanish here.*
>
> **Aquí se habla español.**

Una pescadería, Puerto Montt, Chile

Una panadería, Málaga, España

¿Cómo lo digo?

28 **¿Dónde se venden?** Contesten.

1. ¿Se vende pan en la panadería?
2. ¿Se venden suéteres en la tienda de ropa?
3. ¿Se vende carne en la carnicería?
4. ¿Se venden guisantes en la verdulería?
5. ¿Se vende fruta en la frutería?
6. ¿Se venden productos congelados en el supermercado?
7. ¿Se vende pescado en la pescadería?
8. ¿Se venden bolígrafos en la papelería?

29 **¿Qué idioma se habla dónde?** Escojan.

| francés | español | portugués |
| inglés | árabe | alemán |

1. ¿Qué idioma se habla en México?
2. ¿Qué idioma se habla en el Brasil?
3. ¿Qué idioma se habla en Egipto?
4. ¿Qué idioma se habla en Irlanda?
5. ¿Qué idioma se habla en Alemania?
6. ¿Qué idiomas se hablan en Quebec?

Palacio Nacional, Ciudad de México

El Zócalo, la Ciudad de México

30 **El «Hipercor»** Tú estás en un hipermercado y no puedes encontrar las cosas que necesitas. Hablas con un(a) dependiente(a) (tu compañero[a]). Pídele a él o a ella los productos que necesitas. Tu compañero(a) te va a decir dónde se encuentran en la tienda. Luego cambien de rol.

—**Busco el atún.**
—**Ah, sí. El atún se encuentra en el pasillo dos.**

Andas bien. ¡Adelante!

Conversación

Naranjas para abuelita

Leonor   Abuclita, te compré unas naranjas preciosas en el supermercado.

Abuelita   Ay, gracias, mi cielito. Pero, ¿por qué no fuiste a la frutería del mercado San Miguel? Es donde yo siempre iba.

Leonor   Yo fui allí una vez y no me gustó. ¿Por qué tú siempre hacías tus compras allí, abuelita?

Abuelita   Ay, niña. Allí todo el mundo me conocía. Y todo era tan fresco. Todo lo podías ver. No estaba en paquetes de plástico. A propósito, ¿a cuánto estaban las naranjas?

Leonor   No sé, abuelita.

Abuelita   Sí, sabes. Yo sé que son muy caras. Recuerdo cuando estaban a diez pesos la docena.

¿Comprendes?

Contesten.

1. ¿Dónde hizo sus compras Leonor?
2. ¿Para quién compró las naranjas?
3. ¿Adónde iba la abuelita para hacer sus compras?
4. ¿Fue Leonor alguna vez al mercado? ¿Le gustó?
5. ¿Por qué le gustaba a la abuela comprar en San Miguel?
6. ¿Cómo era todo allí?
7. ¿Sabe Leonor a cuánto estaban las naranjas?
8. ¿Qué recuerda la abuelita?

Vamos a hablar más

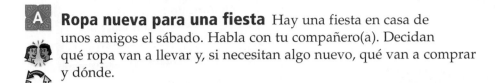

A **Ropa nueva para una fiesta** Hay una fiesta en casa de unos amigos el sábado. Habla con tu compañero(a). Decidan qué ropa van a llevar y, si necesitan algo nuevo, qué van a comprar y dónde.

B **De compras** Tú trabajas en una tienda de abarrotes. Un cliente (tu compañero[a]) les va a servir una comida a algunos invitados. No sabe qué servir y te pide recomendaciones. Pregúntale el número de personas que va a servir. Vas a ser muy cortés con el cliente y le vas a dar muchas recomendaciones o sugerencias. Le vas a sugerir lo que puede servir y las cantidades que va a necesitar.

C **Un recuerdo de la niñez** Piensa en unas cosas que te gustaba hacer de niño(a). Luego cuenta a tu compañero(a) de una ocasión en la que hiciste una de estas cosas. Luego tu compañero(a) te va a decir lo mismo.

Barcelona, España

Lecturas culturales

Reading Strategy

Skimming Skimming is the quickest way to find out what a reading selection is about. When you skim, look at the titles, subtitles, and any words in bold print. Also look at the photographs. All of these will indicate to you the topic of the reading and will help you understand it better.

Sant Feliu de Guixols, España

De compras 🔄 🎧

Mercados

En los países hispanos la gente tradicionalmente compraba la comida en el mercado. Los mercados municipales tenían puestos para los diferentes productos. Había pescaderías, carnicerías, fruterías, verdulerías, etc. La señora hacía sus compras todos los días—generalmente temprano por la mañana. En el mercado iba de un puesto a otro. Conocía a todos los vendedores y conversaba (charlaba) con ellos. Llevaba una bolsa o un capacho[1] para sus compras. Los vendedores no las ponían en bolsas de plástico.

Supermercados

En todas las ciudades hispanas hay supermercados también. Son modernos, limpios[2] y sobre todo convenientes. En el supermercado uno toma un carrito. Lo empuja por los pasillos y en un solo establecimiento puede comprar todo lo que necesita.

[1]capacho *a cloth shopping bag*
[2]limpios *clean*

Caracas, Venezuela

Hipermercados

Estepona, España

Recientemente llegó otra posibilidad para hacer las compras— el hipermercado. El hipermercado es un enorme establecimiento comercial, normalmente en las afueras[3] de la ciudad. El hipermercado tiene lugar para miles de automóviles.

En el hipermercado se puede comprar comida, obviamente. Pero también se puede comprar de todo: ropa, aparatos electrónicos, libros, casi cualquier[4] tipo de producto. El hipermercado tiene docenas de pasillos y cajas registradoras. Si uno quiere, puede pagar sus compras con tarjeta de crédito.

Hoy en día nadie tiene bastante tiempo. Todos estamos muy ocupados. El hipermercado ayuda a conservar tiempo. Podemos comprar todo lo que necesitamos sin tener que ir a más de una tienda.

Pero todavía hay muchos que prefieren el mercado donde todo es muy fresco y todo el mundo se conoce. Los mercados municipales todavía existen y muchas personas siguen haciendo sus compras allí.

[3]afueras *outskirts*   [4]cualquier *any*

Use your StudentWorks Plus CD for more practice.

¿Comprendes?

A De compras Contesten.
1. ¿Dónde compraba la gente la comida?
2. ¿Cuáles son tres puestos que se encuentran en el mercado?
3. ¿Cuándo hacía sus compras la señora?
4. ¿Con quiénes conversaba en el mercado?
5. ¿Para qué llevaba ella un capacho?
6. ¿Dónde hay supermercados?
7. ¿Por qué prefieren algunas personas el supermercado?
8. ¿Qué es un hipermercado?
9. ¿Dónde están los hipermercados normalmente?
10. ¿Por qué prefieren algunas personas el hipermercado?

B El hipermercado y el mercado tradicional
Comparen el mercado tradicional y el hipermercado.

Lectura opcional

El mercado de Chichicastenango

El mercado

Los jueves y los domingos son días de mercado en la plaza del pequeño pueblo de Chichicastenango en Guatemala. Antes de levantarse el sol[1], individuos y grupos de indígenas llegan al pueblo. Muchos llevan en la cabeza o en los hombros[2] los productos que van a vender. Antes, la gente caminaba muchas horas por las montañas para llegar temprano al mercado. Todavía hay muchos que llegan a pie, pero hoy día hay muchos que toman el autobús para ir al mercado.

En el mercado hay puestos de verduras y carne. Además de comestibles también venden joyas, cajas decoradas y preciosas mantas[3] y huipiles. Los huipiles son las blusas que llevan las indígenas.

[1]levantarse el sol *the sun rises*
[2]hombros *shoulders*
[3]mantas *blankets*

Una señora de la aldea de Solalá, Guatemala

Iglesia de Santo Tomás, Chichicastenango

La ropa indígena

Las mujeres de cada grupo indígena llevan ropa que las identifica como miembros del grupo. Las mujeres de Chichicastenango llevan un huipil que tiene muchos diseños[4] geométricos y figuras de flores y plantas. Su falda tiene rayas azules. Hoy la mayoría de los hombres no llevan el traje tradicional. Antes llevaban un pantalón de lana negra, una faja roja y una chaqueta negra con diseños rojos. En la cabeza llevaban un «tzut», un tipo de bufanda roja.

[4]diseños *designs*

¿Comprendes?

A La palabra, por favor. Completen.

1. Los dos días de mercado en Chichicastenango son ____ y ____.
2. El mercado está en la ____ del pueblo pequeño.
3. Los ____ llegan al pueblo muy temprano por la mañana.
4. Llevan en la cabeza o en los ____ los productos que van a vender.
5. Algunos llegan al mercado a pie pero hoy en día muchos toman el ____.
6. Además de comestibles, en el mercado venden ____.
7. Un huipil es una ____ que llevan las mujeres de Chichicastenango.
8. Las mujeres llevan ____ que las identifica como miembros del grupo.
9. En el pasado, los hombres de Chichicastenango llevaban un tipo de ____ roja en la cabeza.

B El mercado de Chichicastenango

Describan la foto del mercado de «Chichi».

Chichicastenango

Conexiones

El comercio

El mercadeo

One of the most important subjects for business students is marketing. **Mercadeo** is the Spanish word for *marketing,* but the English word is more often used all over the Spanish-speaking world— **el marketing.** A major focus of marketing is the promotion and advertising of a product or service.

El mercado

Antes de definir el término «marketing», es necesario dar una definición de la palabra «mercado». El mercado es el conjunto de todos los posibles compradores (los consumidores) de un producto o de un servicio. Un ejemplo de un producto es un coche o un pantalón. Un ejemplo de un servicio es lo que hace un banco o una agencia de viajes.

El marketing

En términos generales, el marketing es la creación de un mercado para un producto o servicio antes de comenzar a producir el producto o servicio. Es la responsabilidad del departamento de marketing de informar a los posibles compradores sobre la existencia del producto y las características del producto.

La promoción

Para informar al público de la existencia y de las características de un producto, un aspecto muy importante del marketing es la promoción. Y la propaganda[1] juega un rol primordial, muy importante, en la promoción. Para lanzar[2] un buen programa de promoción, el personal de marketing tiene que emplear muchos medios de comunicación como la radio, la televisión, los anuncios en los periódicos y en las revistas.

Carolina Herrera

Eau de parfum. Vaporisateur (50 ml.)

Diferentes productos y mercados

Hay algunos productos y servicios que la gente necesita. Hay otros que la gente no necesita pero quiere. No es necesario convencer a la gente de comprar comida o gasolina. ¡Pero otra cosa es el perfume!

La industria de la ropa es un caso muy interesante. La gente necesita ropa porque todos tenemos que vestirnos. Pero hay también ropa que la gente no necesita pero que quiere. Uno puede comprar un pantalón que cuesta treinta dólares. O puede comprar un pantalón que cuesta trescientos dólares. Los dos satisfacen la necesidad de vestirse. Pero la persona que paga trescientos dólares no compra solamente algo que necesita—un artículo de ropa. Compra algo que quiere—prestigio. Y la propaganda tiene que convencer a los clientes que la belleza, la calidad y el prestigio valen el precio que les ponen.

[1]propaganda *advertising*   [2]lanzar *to launch*

HERMÈS. ALL FOR SILK.

HERMÈS
PARIS

NUEVO

Corbata de seda natural   * Pañuelo de seda natural

¿Comprendes?

A El mercadeo
Digan que sí o que no.
1. El coche es un producto.
2. El banco es otro producto.
3. Los consumidores compran sólo productos que necesitan.
4. Los consumidores no tienen que conocer las características de un producto.
5. El perfume se considera una necesidad.
6. El prestigio es una necesidad.

B Definiciones Den una definición de las siguientes palabras.
1. el consumidor   3. el mercado   5. el servicio
2. el comprador   4. el producto   6. la necesidad

C Un anuncio Preparen un anuncio para un artículo de ropa.

¡Te toca a ti!

Use what you have learned

1 Una experiencia interesante

✔ *Talk about a market in a Spanish-speaking country*

Tú viajabas por un país hispanohablante y fuiste a un mercado interesante. Explícales a unos compañeros dónde estabas, con quién y cuándo. Diles todo lo que pasó en el mercado y descríbeles todo lo que viste allí.

2 En la tienda de ropa

✔ *Talk about a shopping excursion*

Ayer tú fuiste a una tienda de ropa para comprar un regalo para un(a) amigo(a) o pariente. Explícale a un(a) compañero(a) todo lo que pasó mientras estabas en la tienda. Luego cambien de rol.

3 Tantas interrupciones

✔ *Talk about two activities happening at once*

Trabaja con un(a) compañero(a) de clase. Ayer ustedes hacían muchas cosas. Pero siempre había interrupciones. Hablen de todo lo que hacían y todo lo que interrumpió lo que hacían.

4 Una gran apertura

✔ *Describe a supermarket*

Un supermercado americano quiere abrir sucursales *(branches)* en España. Prepara un anuncio para el nuevo supermercado. Incluye en el anuncio lo que se puede comprar, los precios, las ventas *(sales)* especiales, etc.

5 Un anuncio

✔ *Describe some articles of clothing*

Estás trabajando en el departamento de publicidad *(advertising)* de una gran revista. Tienes que escribir un anuncio sobre cada una de las prendas que ves aquí.

Writing Strategy

Writing with graphics

Sometimes words alone do not convey adequate information about a topic. Including maps, diagrams, tables, or graphs can help illustrate your expository writing. Pictures and text work well together. Often the graphic will show quickly what might take many paragraphs to describe. When using graphics, be sure to label clearly and accurately to help readers recognize and understand information.

6 Las compras en distintos países

You have read about shopping habits in Spanish-speaking countries. List the kinds of shops and the products people buy in each in one column. Now think about your family and the places where you do your shopping. List those stores and products in the second column.

In a Venn Diagram like this one, put those shopping practices that are exclusive to Spanish-speaking countries in the left, those of your family on the right, and those common to both in the middle, overlapping section of the diagram. Now write a paragraph, comparing your family's buying habits with those of families in Spanish-speaking countries.

Las tiendas y los productos

Los países hispanos / Mi familia

Vocabulario

1 Identifiquen.

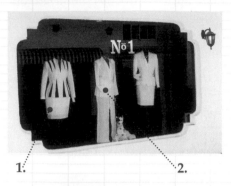

1. _____

2. _____

3. _____

4. _____   5. _____

To review **Palabras 1**, turn to pages 92–93.

2 Completen.

—No, estos zapatos no me __6__ bien.

—No, ¿por qué?

—Son demasiado grandes, demasiado __7__.

Spanish Online
For more Chapter 4 test preparation go to the Chapter 4 **Self-Check Quiz** on the Glencoe Spanish Web site at glencoe.com.

3 ¿Sí o no?

8. Un hipermercado es aún más grande que un supermercado.

9. La tienda de abarrotes es una panadería.

10. Un mercado tiene muchos puestos diferentes.

11. La señora quería comprar seis tajadas de detergente.

12. Ella quiere comprar los tomates porque tienen muy mala pinta.

To review **Palabras 2**, turn to pages 96–97.

Estructura

To review the preterite and the imperfect, turn to page 100.

4 **Completen en el pasado.**

13. Él _____ al cine casi todos los viernes. (ir)
14. Pero ayer (él) no _____. (ir)
15. Ellos _____ todas sus vacaciones en las montañas. (pasar)
16. Pero el verano pasado (ellos) _____ un viaje a México. (hacer)

5 **Completen en el pasado.**

To review two actions in the same sentence, turn to page 103.

17–18. Nadie _____ en casa cuando _____ el teléfono. (estar, sonar)
19–20. Ellos _____ cuando yo _____. (trabajar, salir)

6 **Completen.**

21. _____ frutas y vegetales en una verdulería. (vender)
22. _____ español en muchos países. (hablar)

To review the passive voice with se, turn to page 106.

Cultura

7 **¿Sí o no?**

To review this cultural information, turn to pages 110-111.

23. En los países hispanos la gente hace sus compras sólo una vez a la semana. Van al mercado los lunes.
24. En un supermercado se puede comprar casi todo lo que se necesita en una sola tienda.
25. Un hipermercado es un mercado antiguo con muchos puestos diferentes.

Un mercado,
Málaga, España

Tell all you can about this illustration.

Vocabulario

Identifying more stores

la zapatería   la joyería

Shopping for clothes and jewelry

mirar en el escaparate (la vitrina)

probarse la ropa

¿En qué puedo servirle?

Quisiera…

No me (le) queda(n) bien.

VIDEOTUR

Episodio 4

In this video episode, you will join Francisco and Julián on a trip to the supermarket. See page 483 for more information. As you watch, look for gestures the speakers use to help convey their message.

Identifying more clothing

el bolsillo

el saco, la chaqueta

el abrigo

el impermeable, la gabardina

el suéter

la camisa de mangas cortas (largas)

el vestido

el cinturón

el pañuelo

la ropa interior

la bufanda

los botones

las sandalias

las botas

el tacón

Identifying jewelry

las joyas   una cadena   un arete, un pendiente

una pulsera   un anillo   un reloj

Identifying more parts of the body

la muñeca   el dedo

el cuello   la oreja, el oído

How well do you know your vocabulary?

- Choose any type of store you like to shop in.
- Tell what you like to buy there.

Describing clothing and jewelry

mediano(a)   estrecho(a)

ancho(a)   de oro

Identifying more food stores

el colmado, la tienda de abarrotes, la tienda de ultramarinos

el puesto

el supermercado

el hipermercado

la panadería

la carnicería

la pescadería

la pastelería

la verdulería

la frutería

Foods

el pan

la carne

el pescado

los mariscos

los pasteles

las legumbres, los vegetales

Shopping for food

hacer las compras, ir de compras

¿A cuánto están… ?

tener buena pinta

empujar el carrito

fresco(a)

la bolsa de plástico

una tajada, una rebanada

un frasco

una caja

una docena

Conversación

La Gran Vía, Madrid

¿Cuándo volviste?

Tadeo ¿A qué hora llegaste?

Anita Pues, el tren llegó a tiempo, a las 18:10.

Tadeo ¿Viniste en tren?

Anita Sí, no quería tomar el avión. Tarda mucho tiempo el viaje del aeropuerto al centro.

Tadeo Con el tráfico, no hay duda. ¿Comiste en el tren?

Anita No. Fui a un restaurante cerca de la estación antes de salir. Pedí una tortilla y una ensalada. La tortilla estaba muy buena. Me gustó.

Tadeo ¿Qué hiciste desde que llegaste? Papá quería saber dónde estabas.

Anita ¿Te preguntó dónde estaba? Pues, fui a la Gran Vía. Le compré un regalo para su cumpleaños.

Tadeo Yo le compré un par de zapatos. Y tú, ¿qué le compraste?

Anita Una camisa blanca y azul. Tiene mangas cortas. Creo que le va a quedar muy bien y que le va a gustar.

¿Comprendes?

Anita hizo mucho. Contesten.

1. ¿A qué hora llegó Anita a Madrid?
2. ¿Cómo vino?
3. ¿Por qué no quería tomar el avión?
4. ¿Dónde comió?
5. ¿Qué pidió?
6. ¿Qué tal le gustó?
7. ¿Adónde fue cuando llegó a Madrid?
8. ¿Qué compró?

Estructura

El pretérito

1. Review the following irregular verbs in the preterite.

ESTAR	estuve	PONER	puse	HACER	hice
TENER	tuve	PODER	pude	VENIR	vine
ANDAR	anduve	SABER	supe	QUERER	quise

2. The preceding irregular verbs all take the same endings in the preterite. Review the following.

TENER	tuve	tuviste	tuvo	tuvimos	*tuvisteis*	tuvieron
PONER	puse	pusiste	puso	pusimos	*pusisteis*	pusieron
VENIR	vine	viniste	vino	vinimos	*vinisteis*	vinieron

3. Note that verbs with a **j** in the preterite have the ending **-eron**, not **-ieron**.

dijeron   trajeron

4. Review the verbs with the stem change **e → i** and **o → u** in the preterite.

| SERVIR | serví | serviste | sirvió | servimos | *servisteis* | sirvieron |
| DORMIR | dormí | dormiste | durmió | dormimos | *dormisteis* | durmieron |

Other verbs conjugated like **servir** are **pedir, repetir, freír,** and **seguir**. **Morir** is conjugated like **dormir**.

---

1 Historieta Un viaje en tren Contesten.

1. ¿Hiciste el viaje en tren?
2. ¿Viniste con tu hermano?
3. ¿Estuvieron ustedes mucho tiempo en la estación de ferrocarril?
4. ¿Tuvieron ustedes que hacer cola delante de la ventanilla para comprar sus billetes?
5. ¿Quién hizo las maletas? ¿Tú o tu hermano?
6. ¿Pudieron ustedes llevar las maletas o tuvieron que buscar ayuda?
7. ¿Le pidieron ayuda a un mozo?

El ferrocarril, Chile

2 Historieta En el restaurante

Completen.

El viernes pasado yo __1__ (ir) a un restaurante con mi amiga Julia. Ella __2__ (pedir) la especialidad de la casa. Yo __3__ (pedir) un plato con camarones y langosta. Nosotros dos __4__ (pedir) una ensalada de tomate y lechuga.

La comida estaba deliciosa. Julia __5__ (decir) que le gustaba mucho. Yo le __6__ (repetir) al mesero lo que ella __7__ (decir). El mesero nos __8__ (servir) muy bien.

Yo __9__ (pedir) la cuenta. El mesero la __10__ (traer) y nos __11__ (invitar) a tomar un postre. Yo __12__ (pedir) un helado y Julia __13__ (pedir) flan—un tipo de pudín español.

Lima, Perú

El imperfecto

1. Review the forms of the imperfect tense of regular verbs.

TOMAR	tomaba	tomabas	tomaba	tomábamos	*tomabais*	tomaban
COMER	comía	comías	comía	comíamos	*comíais*	comían
VIVIR	vivía	vivías	vivía	vivíamos	*vivíais*	vivían

2. Review the forms of the irregular verbs **ir** and **ser**.

IR	iba	ibas	iba	íbamos	*ibais*	iban
SER	era	eras	era	éramos	*erais*	eran

¿Te acuerdas?

Ver is also considered irregular.
ver: veía

3. The imperfect tense is used to express an action in the past that is continuous or repeated. The time the action began and ended is not important. The preterite tense is used to express an action that began and ended at a definite time in the past. A sentence will often have both types of past action. The action that was going on is expressed by the imperfect, and the action that intervened or interrupted is expressed by the preterite.

Su hermano iba allí cada año pero Roberto fue solamente una vez.
Él miraba en el escaparate cuando vio a su amigo.

4. The imperfect is used for description in the past.

Él tenía ocho años y era muy inteligente.

3 Cuando yo era niño(a) Contesten personalmente.

1. Cuando tú eras niño(a), ¿dónde vivías?
2. ¿Cuántos cuartos tenía la casa donde vivía tu familia?
3. ¿A qué escuela ibas?
4. ¿A qué hora salías de casa para ir a la escuela?
5. ¿Quién hacía las compras en tu familia?
6. ¿Tenían ustedes una computadora?

4 Historieta Un viaje estupendo Completen.

1. El año pasado mis amigos y yo ____ (hacer) un viaje estupendo.
2. Nosotros ____ (ir) a Guatemala.
3. Yo ____ (tomar) un curso de español en Antigua.
4. Mis amigos ____ (estudiar) el español también.
5. Un día nosotros nos ____ (levantar) temprano y ____ (ir) a Chichicastenango.
6. Nosotros ____ (andar) por el mercado de Chichi.
7. Nosotros ____ (ver) a los indígenas.
8. Las mujeres de Chichicastenango ____ (llevar) una blusa y una falda de colores vivos.
9. En el mercado los indios ____ (vender) los productos que ____ (cultivar) o ____ (hacer) en casa.
10. Con el dinero que ____ (recibir) por las cosas que ____ (vender), ellos ____ (comprar) todas las provisiones que ____ (necesitar).

Antigua, Guatemala

5 Cuando era niño(a) Con un(a) compañero(a), discutan todo lo que hacían con frecuencia cuando eran niños(as) y asistían a la escuela primaria.

6 Un regalo Estás en una tienda de ropa. Tienes que comprar un regalo para un(a) pariente. Conversa con el/la dependiente(a) (tu compañero[a]). Cambien de rol.

7 ¿Usas mucho la computadora? Con un(a) compañero(a), hablen de todo lo que ustedes hacen con la computadora. Luego decidan quién se sirve más de (usa más) la computadora.

Literary Companion
You may wish to read the adaptation of *Platero y yo* by Juan Ramón Jiménez, on pages 460–463. The activities for this reading will help you continue to practice your reading comprehension skills.

Entérate Estados Unidos

Datos interesantes sobre los latinos en Estados Unidos

■ En 1970 el gobierno de Estados Unidos inventó el término "hispanos" para dar un solo nombre a esta diversa población. Muchos "hispanos" prefieren el término "latinos" porque indica el origen de Latinoamérica.

■ Estados Unidos es el 5° país de habla hispana en el mundo, y los latinos son la minoría más numerosa de este país.

■ De mayor a menor, estos son los grupos que viven en Estados Unidos: mexicanos, puertorriqueños, cubanos, dominicanos, salvadoreños, colombianos; el resto son hispanos de orígenes diversos.

■ Muchos mexicanos del suroeste tienen un origen diferente al resto de los hispanos, porque ellos ya vivían ahí cuando Estados Unidos conquistó[1] estos territorios.

■ Los valores[2] culturales más importantes para los hispanos son preservar la lengua española y la unión de la familia.

[1]conquistó: *conquered*

[2]valores: *values*

California, su pasado español

Los colonizadores[1] españoles dejaron su marca más obvia en los numerosos nombres españoles de los diferentes lugares. En la arquitectura también es notable su presencia. Las misiones californianas son un ejemplo del estilo español. Los indígenas construyeron estos bellos edificios de adobe. Hay 21 misiones en todo el estado y hoy día son una gran atracción turística.

Santa Bárbara, fundada en 1786.

[1]colonizadores: *settlers*

Las tiendas latinas

Hay "bodegas" en todos los barrios latinos; son tiendas de comestibles donde la atención personal es muy importante. Como para los latinos es extremadamente importante "verse bien"[1], es una buena idea tener un salón de belleza en sus barrios. Las tiendas donde venden hierbas[2], medicamentos naturales, incienso y velas[3] especiales se llaman botánicas.

[1]"verse bien": *"looking good"*   [2]hierbas: *herbs*   [3]velas: *candles*

SUCESOS

César Chávez

César Chávez es un líder muy respetado entre los chicanos y los trabajadores extranjeros. Latinos en su mayoría, los que recogen[1] las frutas en Estados Unidos hoy reciben un mejor salario gracias al trabajo de Chávez. Un momento importante en su carrera fue en 1970, cuando los rancheros aceptaron pagar más y mejorar las condiciones de trabajo para estas personas. César Chávez murió en 1993.

Sábados Gigantes es uno de los programas más famosos y populares de la televisión hispana. Desde hace 40 años, el chileno "Don Francisco" conduce el programa, un récord que pasó al Libro Guinness de los Récords.

[1]recogen: *pick*

Chef Douglas Rodríguez

El "Mango Gang"

Más y más estadounidenses conocen la diferencia entre una "tortilla" en un restaurante mexicano y en un restaurante español. Pero... ¿quién conoce al "Mango Gang"? Ellos hicieron popular la "Nuevo Latino Cuisine". En Miami, el chef cubanoamericano, Douglas Rodríguez, y sus colegas Norman Van Aken, Robin Haas, Allen Susser y Mark Militello re-inventaron la cocina tradicional latina. Ellos usan frijoles negros y arroz, mangos, aguacates[1], pescado caribeño y los preparan de una manera diferente.

[1]aguacates: *avocados*

La parada puertorriqueña

Calendario de fiestas

5 de mayo En el suroeste, y poco a poco[1] en otras partes de Estados Unidos, se celebra el patrimonio cultural mexicano. En México, la fiesta conmemora la victoria de los mexicanos sobre los invasores franceses.

12 de octubre En 1492 llegaron los españoles a América y hoy se celebra el "Día de la Raza[2]" en esta fecha. Esta fiesta conmemora el patrimonio cultural de todos los latinos en Estados Unidos. Además, el mes de octubre es el "Mes de la Hispanidad".

1° de noviembre "El Día de los Muertos[3]" era una fiesta exclusivamente de los mexicanos al sur de la frontera. Hoy día, más y más mexicanamericanos celebran esta fiesta en Estados Unidos porque les gusta recordar[4] a sus familiares en forma festiva.

6 de junio El segundo domingo del mes de junio se celebra "El día nacional de los puertorriqueños" en la Ciudad de Nueva York. Las estrellas del cine, del deporte y también el alcalde[5] y otras autoridades van a la parada en la Quinta Avenida, donde hay carrozas[6] y mucha música y baile.

[1]poco a poco: *little by little*
[2]raza: *race*
[3]muertos: *dead*
[4]recordar: *to remember*
[5]alcalde: *mayor*
[6]carrozas: *floats*

micocina

Primero, las tortillas y ahora ¡las pupusas!

Esta comida típica salvadoreña se come con la mano y es muy popular entre los latinos de todas partes. Es como una tortilla gorda rellena[1] con carne, queso, frijoles o una combinación de todos estos ingredientes. *(Atención: No es bueno llamar "tortillas" a las pupusas frente a un salvadoreño.)*

Pupusas de frijol con queso
Ingredientes

(Para la masa[2])
2 tazas de harina de maíz
1 taza de agua tibia[3]
1 poco de sal

(Para el relleno)
1 lata de frijoles molidos[4]
250g de queso rallado[5]

Preparación
Mezclar la harina, el agua y la sal para hacer la masa. Formar 12 bolitas medianas. Ahuecar[6] el centro y rellenar con los frijoles y el queso. Luego, aplastar[7] y formar una tortilla gruesa (1/2 pulgada). Freír en aceite caliente y servir con salsa de tomates frescos.

[1]rellena: *filled*
[2]masa: *dough*
[3]tibia: *lukewarm*
[4]molidos: *ground*
[5]rallado: *grated*
[6]ahuecar: *hollow*
[7]aplastar: *flatten*

Pupusas de frijol con queso

¡Acción!

Un latino ganador

Nilo Cruz, el primer Premio Pulitzer latino de teatro

El escritor Nilo Cruz recibió el Premio Pulitzer en el año 2003 por su obra de teatro[1] "Anna in the Tropics". Nilo Cruz nació en Cuba, pero vivió en Miami desde los 10 años. Él estudió en la Universidad de Brown y hoy día es profesor en la Universidad de Yale. "¡Esto es increíble!", dijo al recibir el premio. Sí, es increíble porque Nilo Cruz fue el primer latino ganador[2] de este premio prestigioso.

[1]obra de teatro: *play*   [2]ganador: *winner*

EN EL SET

Blades   Cruz   Pérez   Welch

No solamente el público latino reconoce los nombres de Selma Hayek, Antonio Banderas, Rosie Pérez, Raúl Julia, Rubén Blades, Penélope Cruz y muchos más; también los conoce el público en general en Estados Unidos y en todo el mundo. En el pasado[1], actores como Anthony Quinn, Raquel Welch y José Ferrer también fueron famosos, pero su patrimonio cultural no era el foco de atención. Ahora el éxito de los actores latinos depende de su talento y también de su identidad porque hoy día existe un mercado – hispano y anglosajón – que demanda el sabor latino, una de las expresiones legítimas y modernas del multiculturalismo en Estados Unidos.

[1]en el pasado: *in the past*

Cómo viajar a Latinoamérica sin salir de Estados Unidos

¿Quieres conocer Latinoamérica pero no tienes dinero para viajar? Aquí hay otras alternativas:

■ En Miami tienes **La Pequeña Habana,** el centro de la comunidad cubana en Estados Unidos. Es una zona de 25 calles con muchos restaurantes, botánicas, tiendas de autos y de música. Su calle más famosa es la Calle Ocho. Gracias a sus residentes, este barrio está lleno de vida.

■ En Chicago tienes **Pilsen y La Villita.** Después del Este de Los Ángeles en California, ésta es la comunidad mexicana más grande de Estados Unidos. En la Calle 18 hay restaurantes, panaderías, tiendas de comestibles y agencias sociales. Desde 1987 el Museo de Arte Mexicano ofrece programas de arte y cultura.

De compras en el barrio

■ En Nueva York tienes **El Barrio** donde antes vivían principalmente puertorriqueños, pero desde 1990 también viven allí muchos mexicanos. Es interesante visitar la famosa Marqueta (un mercado) y el Museo del Barrio.

■ En Washington Heights, en la ciudad de Nueva York, residen 3/4 de los dominicanos que viven en Estados Unidos. Por eso, a este barrio lo llaman afectuosamente "**Quisqueya**[1] **Heights**". Caminar por sus calles es como caminar por Santo Domingo. La gente, la música, los restaurantes y las tiendas le dan un tono tropical a este barrio de Manhattan.

[1]Quisqueya: *indigenous name for the island where Haiti and the Dominican Republic are located today*

Marc Anthony

Paulina Rubio

La explosión latina

Esta no es una moda transitoria; tampoco es simplemente el aumento de la población latina. Es la creciente[1] influencia de distintos elementos latinos en la cultura de Estados Unidos. Esto es evidente en la comida, en la moda, en todas las artes y especialmente en la música popular. Los latinos adoptaron rápidamente el estilo pop y hoy día artistas como Shakira, Marc Anthony, Juanes, Cristina Aguilera y Paulina Rubio son conocidos por el público en general. Otra consecuencia de esta explosión es la presencia de los ritmos latinos en la música anglosajona.

[1]creciente: *growing*

Julia Álvarez, una escritora dominicana-americana

"Yo soy una dominicana 'guión[1]' americana", dice esta conocida escritora. "Para mí las cosas más interesantes pasan dentro de ese 'guión'; ahí es donde está la colisión y la combinación de dos mundos." Julia Álvarez nació en Nueva York, pero vivió en la República Dominicana hasta los 10 años de edad. Ella estudió en Nueva York y actualmente es profesora de inglés en Middlebury College. Sus novelas más famosas son: *How the García Girls Lost Their Accent* y *In the Time of the Butterflies*.

[1]guión: *hyphen*

En la tele

George López, un gran comediante

Este nativo de Los Ángeles creció en el valle de San Fernando, en Mission Hills. Él es el co-autor, escritor, productor y actor del programa cómico "George López". A los latinos, a los críticos y también al público en general

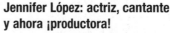

George López

les gusta mucho este programa. George es un artista con muchas habilidades porque también trabaja en el teatro, en el cine y en la radio. Además, ayuda a muchas organizaciones y fundaciones de caridad[1]. Por ejemplo, participa en el programa "Alto a la violencia" del Departamento de Policía de Los Ángeles (LAPD).

Jennifer López: actriz, cantante y ahora ¡productora!

La latina más famosa y mejor pagada de Hollywood decidió trabajar como productora de programas televisivos. "En mi casa yo veía todas las novelas y los programas en español", dice la actriz y cantante. "Quiero narrar la historia de los latinos que viven aquí y

Jennifer López

tienen 'el sueño americano'[2]." Jennifer, como otros artistas, a veces basa su trabajo en sus experiencias personales.

[1]caridad: *charity*
[2]sueño americano: *American Dream*

Capítulo 5

Los pasatiempos

Objetivos

In this chapter you will learn to:

❖ talk about popular hobbies and games
❖ talk about activities in the park
❖ give details about location
❖ talk about what will happen in the future
❖ compare objects and people
❖ describe your favorite pastime
❖ talk about pastimes in Spanish-speaking countries

Gonzalo Cienfuegos *The Enchanted Crystal*

Vocabulario

Los pasatiempos y hobbys

el ajedrez

····· el tablero

el dominó

la ficha

las damas

el crucigrama

los sellos

las monedas

Luisa es coleccionista.
Colecciona sellos y monedas.

Mañana irá al centro.
Comprará unas monedas antiguas.

¿Cómo pasarán el tiempo mañana?

Mañana Ramona jugará al ajedrez con
   un amigo.
Ella es más lista que su rival.
Ramona ganará. Será la campeona.

A Tomás le gustan los crucigramas.
Él llenará un crucigrama.

los juegos de video

la sala de juegos

el futbolín

Vocabulario

¿Qué palabra necesito?

1 **Los pasatiempos** Contesten según los dibujos.

1. ¿A qué juegan las muchachas?

2. ¿Qué hay en el periódico?

3. ¿A qué juegan los señores?

4. ¿A qué juegan los niños?

5. ¿Dónde están los muchachos?

2 **Historieta** **Un juego de ajedrez**
Contesten según se indica.

1. ¿Jugará Tomás a las damas o al ajedrez? (al ajedrez)
2. ¿Con quién jugará? (un amigo)
3. ¿Quién es el jugador más listo? (su amigo)
4. ¿Tomás ganará o perderá el juego? (perderá)
5. ¿Quién será el campeón? (su amigo)

Barcelona, España

3 ¿Qué será? Adivinen.

1. Para completar uno de estos necesitas un lápiz o un bolígrafo.
2. Puedes participar en una carrera de automóviles, una aventura con monstruos, un viaje por las galaxias.
3. Hay juegos que duran horas. Los jugadores piensan mucho antes de mover una pieza.
4. Juegas con un tablero, como el ajedrez, y usas fichas, pero el juego es más fácil que el ajedrez.
5. Es un juego como el fútbol en miniatura. Puedes jugar con un amigo o con tres amigos más.

4 Preguntas personales Contesten.

1. ¿Te gustan los juegos de video? ¿Juegas en casa?
2. ¿Cuáles son los juegos más populares?
3. ¿Tú sabes jugar al ajedrez? ¿Es difícil?
4. ¿Quién es el/la mejor jugador(a) entre tus amigos?
5. ¿Alguien en tu familia llena los crucigramas?
6. ¿A ti te gustan los crucigramas o crees que son aburridos?
7. ¿Eres coleccionista?
8. ¿Qué coleccionas?

Una sala de juegos

5 Juegos de video Con un(a) compañero(a), preparen un cuestionario para determinar:

- cuántos alumnos en tu clase usan juegos de video
- cuántos juegan con los juegos de video en casa y cuántos en salas de juegos
- cuáles son los tres juegos de video más populares

Luego preparen un informe sobre los resultados de su encuesta *(survey)* para la clase.

6 Los gemelos con gustos distintos

Eugenio y Eugenia son gemelos *(twins)*. Ellos tienen la misma apariencia pero no los mismos gustos. Con un(a) compañero(a), hagan el papel de los gemelos. Digan lo que cada uno hace después de las clases y en los fines de semana con su tiempo libre. Usen la imaginación.

El parque

el bote

remar por el lago

el lago

el mono

la jaula

El Zoológico

Refrescos

el (parque) zoológico

el mimo

el payaso

la senda

Mucha gente da un paseo por el parque.
Ellos caminan por las sendas bonitas.

el globo

una piragua

un helado

García Y Molino

Los niños quieren una piragua.
Mamá les comprará una piragua.
Les comprará un globo también.

Mentar

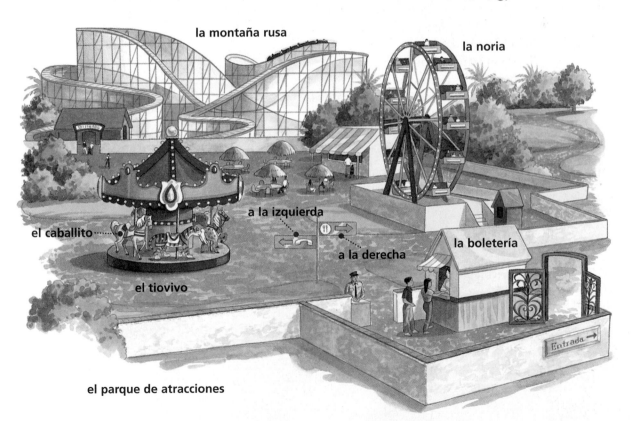

la montaña rusa

la noria

a la izquierda

a la derecha

la boletería

el caballito

el tiovivo

el parque de atracciones

Entrada →

Los jóvenes irán al parque de atracciones.
Están haciendo cola delante de la boletería.
En la cola (fila) Alberto está detrás de
    Alejandra.

Y Alejandra está delante de Alberto.
La entrada al parque está al lado de
    la boletería.

Vocabulario

¿Qué palabra necesito?

7 Historieta Al parque

Contesten.

1. ¿Irán los niños al parque mañana?
2. ¿Visitarán el zoológico?
3. ¿Verán los monos en el zoológico?
4. ¿Se divertirán los niños con los monos?
5. ¿Tomarán los niños una piragua?
6. ¿Les comprarán sus padres un globo?

El Retiro, Madrid

8 Historieta Un día en el parque

Escojan la palabra apropiada.

1. La gente da un paseo por ____ del parque.
   a. las avenidas   **b.** los lagos   **c.** las sendas
2. Algunos ____ por el lago en un bote.
   a. compran   **b.** hacen   **c.** reman
3. Hay muchos animales en el ____.
   a. lago   **b.** zoológico   **c.** parque de atracciones
4. La gente hace cola ____ la boletería.
   a. detrás de   **b.** a la derecha de   **c.** delante de
5. Hay muchas ____ en un parque zoológico.
   a. jaulas   **b.** atracciones   **c.** norias
6. El ____ hace muchos gestos cómicos y extravagantes.
   a. tiovivo   **b.** payaso   **c.** caballito
7. A los niños les gusta tomar ____.
   a. lagos   **b.** atracciones   **c.** piraguas

Spanish Online

For a fun way to review this vocabulary, go to the Chapter 5 **eGame** on the Glencoe Spanish Web site at glencoe.com. For more information about parks and other attractions in Spanish-speaking countries, go to **Web Explore** on the Glencoe Spanish Web site at glencoe.com. You may also want to do the Chapter 5 **WebQuest** activity at this site.

El padre y su hijo se divierten.

9 **¿Dónde está?** Contesten según el plano.

1. ¿Qué hay en el centro del parque?
2. ¿Dónde está la boletería? ¿Delante del lago o al lado del lago?
3. ¿Dónde está la entrada al parque?
4. Y el parque zoológico, ¿dónde está?
5. Estás delante de la boletería. El parque de atracciones, ¿está a tu derecha o a tu izquierda?

10 **En el parque** Con un(a) compañero(a), miren el dibujo. Describan todo lo que ven en el dibujo. Tu compañero(a) te va a hacer preguntas. Contesta a sus preguntas. Entonces tú le puedes hacer preguntas y él o ella contestará.

11 **Haciendo planes** Habla con un(a) compañero(a). Ustedes van a hacer algo el domingo. Tengan una conversación y decidan si van a ir al zoológico, al parque de atracciones o simplemente a un parque cerca de donde ustedes viven. Expliquen por qué prefieren ir adonde van.

UN POCO MÁS

*For more practice using words from **Palabras 2**, do Activity 5 on page H6 at the end of this book.*

Futuro de los verbos regulares
Talking about future events

Use your **StudentWorks** Plus
CD for more practice.

1. The future tense is used to tell what will take place in the future. To form the future tense of regular verbs, you add the future endings to the infinitive. Study the following forms.

INFINITIVE	estudiar	leer	escribir	ENDINGS
STEM	estudiar-	leer-	escribir-	
yo	estudiaré	leeré	escribiré	-é
tú	estudiarás	leerás	escribirás	-ás
él, ella, Ud.	estudiará	leerá	escribirá	-á
nosotros(as)	estudiaremos	leeremos	escribiremos	-emos
vosotros(as)	*estudiaréis*	*leeréis*	*escribiréis*	-éis
ellos, ellas, Uds.	estudiarán	leerán	escribirán	-án

Mañana jugaré al ajedrez.
Tú me verás jugar, ¿no?
Yo seré el campeón.

2. You have already learned the construction **ir a** + *infinitive* to express events that will take place in the near future. In everyday conversation, this construction is actually used more frequently than the future tense.

El año que viene voy a estudiar en Puerto Rico.
Me vas a escribir, ¿no?
Y yo voy a leer todas tus cartas.

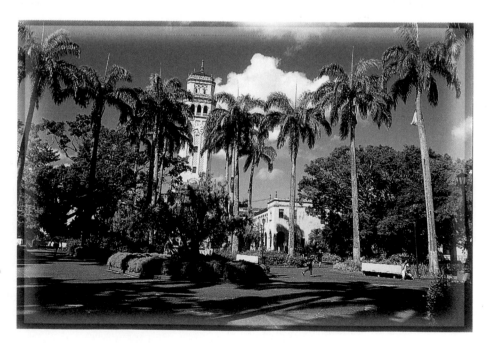

Universidad de Puerto Rico

¿Cómo lo digo?

12 Historieta Daniel viajará a España.
Contesten.

1. ¿Adónde irá Daniel el año que viene?
2. ¿Estudiará en Alcalá de Henares?
3. ¿Asistirá a clases en la universidad?
4. ¿Leerá muchos libros?
5. ¿Su amiga le escribirá con frecuencia?
6. ¿Recibirá las cartas en algunos días?
7. ¿Responderá a las cartas de su amiga?

Universidad de Alcalá, España

13 ¡A divertirse esta noche!
Formen oraciones según el modelo.

los muchachos ⟶
Los muchachos verán la televisión.

1. Raúl

2. el señor Fornos

3. los niños

4. nosotros

5. Leonor

6. los monos

7. tú

8. yo

Estructura

14 Historieta El coleccionista
Sigan el modelo.

> **Mañana voy a ir al centro.** →
> **Mañana iré al centro.**

1. Mañana Carlos va a ir al centro.
2. Yo voy a ir con él.
3. Vamos a visitar los puestos de los coleccionistas.
4. Sé que Carlos va a comprar monedas.
5. Él cree que va a encontrar unas monedas raras.
6. Y yo voy a buscar sellos.
7. Yo sé quien me va a vender los sellos.
8. Y no voy a pagar mucho.

15 Historieta El sábado que viene
Completen con el futuro.

El sábado que viene yo __1__ (viajar) al campo. Allí __2__ (visitar) a mis abuelos. Ellos __3__ (estar) muy contentos. Ellos me __4__ (esperar) en la estación. Entonces me __5__ (llevar) a su casa. Mi tía María Luisa __6__ (preparar) una comida deliciosa. Después de comer todos nosotros __7__ (jugar) al dominó. Abuelita __8__ (ganar) como siempre. Yo __9__ (pasar) dos o tres días con ellos. Yo __10__ (volver) a casa un poco triste. Me gusta mucho visitar a los abuelos.

Una casa de campo, Mucuchíes, Venezuela

16 Ayer no, pero mañana, sí Contesten según el modelo.

> ¿Fuiste a la sala de juegos ayer?
>
> No, pero iré mañana.

1. ¿Fuiste al parque ayer?
2. ¿Viste al payaso ayer?
3. ¿Visitaste el zoológico?
4. ¿Caminaste por las sendas del parque?
5. ¿Te divertiste?

17 **Tengo mucho que hacer.** Prepara una lista de todo lo que piensas hacer mañana. Por ejemplo, **Mañana escribiré una composición para la clase de español.** Puedes escoger algunas palabras de la lista. Entonces compara tu lista con la lista de un(a) compañero(a). ¿Cuáles son las actividades que ustedes dos van a hacer mañana?

estudiar   preparar   comprar   buscar

jugar   trabajar   comer   leer   hablar

volver   escribir   asistir   ir   ver

18 **Mi rutina** Prepara tu rutina para mañana. Luego prepara un informe para la clase. Incluye las siguientes actividades en tu informe: **despertarse, levantarse, prepararse para la escuela, lavarse, vestirse, divertirse, acostarse, dormirse.**

Colegio Santa Teresita, Santurce, Puerto Rico

Estructura

Comparativo y superlativo
Comparing people and things

1. To compare people or things in English, you add *-er* to short adjectives and you use *more* before long adjectives. The word *than* follows.

> *She is taller than her brother.*
> *She is also more intelligent than her brother.*

This construction is called the comparative.

¿Lo sabes?

The comparative is often followed by **nadie.**

> **Él sabe más que nadie.**
> **Tiene más paciencia que nadie.**

2. To form the comparative in Spanish, you put **más** before the adjective or adverb and **que** after it.

> **Ella es más alta que su hermano.**
> **Y también es más inteligente que su hermano.**

3. The superlative is used to describe "the most." To form the superlative in English, you add *-est* to short adjectives and place *most* before long adjectives.

> *She is the nicest person of all.*
> *She is the most intelligent person in the world.*

¿Te acuerdas?

Remember to add **-es** to an adjective that ends in a consonant.

> **mi mejor amigo**
> **mis mejores amigos**

4. In Spanish, the superlative is formed by using the appropriate definite article (**el, la, los, las**) plus **más** with the adjective. The preposition **de** follows the superlative.

> **Ella es la persona más simpática de todas.**
> **Ella es la persona más inteligente del mundo.**

5. The adjectives **bueno** and **malo** have irregular comparative and superlative forms.

> **bueno(a)**   **mejor**   **el/la mejor**
> **malo(a)**   **peor**   **el/la peor**

6. The adjectives **mayor** and **menor** most often refer to age.

> **Yo soy mayor que mi hermana.**
> **Mi hermana es la menor de la familia.**

¿Cómo lo digo?

19 **Compararemos.** Sigan el modelo.

Luis / Pablo / Andrés ⟶
Luis es alto.
Pablo es más alto que Luis.
Andrés es el más alto de todos.

1.  graceful

   Susana / Lola / Anita

3. **cómicos**

   los mimos / los monos / los payasos

2. **ricos** rich

   los Gómez / los García / los Ramos

4. **popular**

   el ajedrez / el futbolín / los juegos de video

20 **¿Cuál es más… ?** Sigan el modelo.

grande   la Ciudad de México / Nueva York ⟶
La Ciudad de México es más grande que
   Nueva York.

1. caro expensive el avión / el tren
2. rápido quick el tren / el bus
3. difícil   el ajedrez / las damas
4. largo long   un kilómetro / un metro
5. pequeña small una habichuela / una papa

21 **¿Y tú?** Contesten.

1. ¿Quién es tu mejor amigo(a)?
2. ¿En qué clase recibes las mejores notas?
3. ¿Quién es el/la mayor de tu familia?
4. ¿Y el/la menor? ¿Quién es?
5. ¿Eres mayor o menor que tu padre?

Ciudad de México

Andas bien. ¡Adelante!

Una diferencia de opinión

Clarita ¿Qué vamos a hacer mañana?
Eugenio No sé. Quizás iremos a casa de Felipe.
Clarita ¿A casa de Felipe? ¿Para qué?
Eugenio Jugaremos ajedrez.
Clarita ¿Jugar ajedrez? Estás loco. A mí no me gusta nada. Es el juego más aburrido…
Eugenio ¡Vale! ¡Vale! Pero te sentarás enfrente de una pantalla de video durante horas.
Clarita Tengo una idea. No jugaremos ajedrez y no miraremos videos. Iremos al cine.

¿Comprendes?

Contesten.

1. ¿Adónde quiere ir mañana Eugenio?
2. Según Eugenio, ¿qué jugarán?
3. ¿Quiere ir Clarita?
4. ¿Le gusta a Clarita jugar ajedrez?
5. ¿Qué dice Clarita del ajedrez?
6. ¿Qué prefiere hacer Clarita?
7. Según Clarita, ¿adónde irán?

Vamos a hablar más

A **Los pasatiempos favoritos** Un(a) estudiante de Colombia (tu compañero[a]) quiere saber cuál es tu pasatiempo favorito. Contéstale y explícale por qué te gusta tanto. Luego cambien de rol.

B **Al parque con tu hermanito(a)** Estás en el parque con tu hermanito(a) de cinco años (un[a] compañero[a]). Él o ella quiere hacer muchas cosas. Tú le dices lo que sí puede hacer y lo que no puede hacer y por qué. Después cambien de rol.

C **¡Qué exagerado!** Vas a crear una persona ficticia. Tu persona ficticia es la más ____ de todos; tiene más ____ que nadie. Al hablar de la persona, exagera todo lo posible. Luego trabaja con unos compañeros. Presenten sus descripciones y decidan quién ha creado la persona más increíble.

D **No, de ninguna manera** Con un(a) compañero(a), miren esta foto. Los dos amigos están hablando de unos planes. Parece que a uno de ellos no le interesa nada el proyecto. Entablen la conversación entre los dos.

Cartagena, Colombia

E **Los videos** Busca un video en español que crees que te interesará. Después de mirarlo, da un resumen de lo que viste. Discute el video con un(a) amigo(a), diciéndole lo que te gustó o no te gustó. Luego compáralo con otro video que has visto en inglés. ¿Encontraste la actuación diferente o parecida. Explica como.

F **Los cantantes** Piensa en los cantantes latinos que conoces. ¿Tienes un(a) favorito(a)? ¿Quién es? Escucha una de sus canciones. ¿Qué tipo de música es? ¿Cuál es el tema de la canción? A tu parecer, ¿hay otro(a) cantante con un estilo semejante? ¿Quién es? ¿Por qué dices que tiene un estilo parecido?

Lecturas culturales

El domingo en el parque 🔄 🎧

Reading Strategy

Being familiar with the genre Be familiar with the kind of passage you are reading—the genre. Examples of genre are novel, short story, essay, and poem. A genre is somewhat predictable. For example, novels, short stories, and other types of prose will all tell a story. A poem will tend to evoke emotion. Knowing the genre will help you to know what to expect in the reading.

Casi todas las ciudades hispanas tienen uno o más parques bonitos. Los parques son un centro de recreo[1] para jóvenes y viejos, especialmente los domingos.

Si vas a un parque como el Retiro en Madrid o Chapultepec en México, verás a los viejos jugando al dominó hora tras hora. Y los niños estarán en fila delante del vendedor de helados o piraguas.

En algunos parques, como Palermo en Buenos Aires, hay un zoológico. El domingo que viene los Rodríguez llevarán a los niños al zoológico. Se divertirán mucho mirando a los cómicos monos. Pero se asustarán[2] un poco al ver los leones y tigres en sus jaulas grandes.

A veces hay también un parque de atracciones. A los niños les gusta subir al tiovivo. Los caballitos suben y bajan al acompañamiento del organillo.

El parque no es sólo para viejos y niños. En el parque verás a muchos jóvenes. Los jóvenes se encuentran y dan un paseo por el parque. Charlan (Hablan) con otros jóvenes que conocen en el parque y hacen nuevos amigos. A veces alquilan (rentan) un bote y reman por el lago del parque.

También veremos en el parque a las personas que demostrarán su arte: caricaturistas que te dibujarán[3] en un momento; fotógrafos que te tomarán una foto; mimos y payasos que te van a hacer reír[4] y vendedores ambulantes vendiendo de todo: globos, dulces, refrescos, camisetas.

[1]recreo *recreation*
[2]se asustarán *they will be frightened*
[3]dibujarán *will draw*
[4]reír *laugh*

Parque de Chapultepec, Ciudad de México

Palermo, Buenos Aires, Argentina

¿Comprendes?

A En el parque Contesten.
1. ¿Quiénes van a los parques en las ciudades hispanas?
2. ¿Cuándo van?
3. ¿Qué juegan los viejos?
4. ¿Qué compran los niños?
5. ¿Qué hay en el zoológico?
6. ¿Qué hay en el parque de atracciones?
7. ¿Qué hacen los jóvenes en el parque?
8. ¿Qué venden los vendedores ambulantes?

B Personajes interesantes Contesten.
1. ¿Qué hacen los caricaturistas?
2. ¿Qué hacen los mimos y los payasos?
3. ¿Qué hacen los fotógrafos?

Buenos Aires, Argentina

C ¿Qué es? Adivinen.
1. un tipo de helado que es en realidad hielo con sirope
2. cualquier lugar adonde va la gente a divertirse
3. un animal bastante gracioso o cómico
4. personas que andan por las calles o parques vendiendo cosas
5. lugar donde exhiben muchos animales
6. dos animales salvajes de la misma familia que el gato

Use your StudentWorks Plus CD for more practice.

Sevilla, España

Lectura opcional ①

Las salas de juegos

El futbolín

Las salas de juegos son muy populares en muchos países hispanos. No son nuevas. Hace muchos años que los jóvenes van a las salas de juegos para jugar al tenis de mesa y al futbolín.

Hoy las salas tienen los más modernos juegos de video. Los jóvenes meten una moneda en la ranura. Pulsan un botón y salen en la pantalla monstruos, guerras intergalácticas y carreras de automóviles. Color, sonido, moción. Para los juegos de video se necesita buena coordinación de ojo y mano y excelentes reflejos[1].

Pero de todos los juegos antiguos y modernos, el juego que les gusta mucho a los jóvenes hispanos es el futbolín. Pueden jugar dos o cuatro y hasta seis muchachos a la vez. El juego es sencillo (fácil). Hay que meter el baloncito en la portería opuesta[2]. Los jugadores humanos mueven los jugadores de madera[3] o plástico para lanzar o bloquear el balón. Un partido entre buenos jugadores puede durar mucho tiempo.

[1]reflejos *reflexes* [2]opuesta *opposite* [3]madera *wood*

¿Comprendes?

A **¿Qué es?** Describan.
1. el juego de video
2. el tenis de mesa
3. el futbolín

Una sala de juegos, Caracas, Venezuela

B **Las salas de juegos** Contesten.
1. ¿Dónde son populares las salas de juegos?
2. ¿A qué jugaban los jóvenes en las salas en el pasado?
3. ¿Qué juegos hay en las salas modernas que no había en las salas antiguas?
4. ¿Dónde salen los monstruos y las guerras intergalácticas?
5. ¿Qué tienes que tener para ser buen jugador de juegos de video?
6. ¿Cuáles son algunas características de los juegos de video?

C **El futbolín** Explica el objetivo del futbolín y cómo se juega.

Lectura opcional 2

Estepona, España

El dominó

El juego es antiguo. Jugaban al dominó en Venecia en el siglo XVIII. Las reglas[1] del juego son las mismas del siglo XVIII. Pero las veintiocho fichas modernas serán de plástico. Las antiguas eran de madera[2], o las más elegantes de marfil[3].

En las plazas de pueblos y ciudades en todo el mundo hispano podemos oír el «cli, cli» de las fichas que los jugadores golpean contra la mesa. Grupos de jugadores pasan horas jugando partida tras partida de dominó. Alrededor de la mesa siempre hay un grupo de «mirones».

Pero, ¿quiénes son los jugadores? Generalmente son señores mayores. Todos los días van a las mismas mesas, a la misma hora, con los mismos compañeros. Los señores son muy serios. Y juegan casi siempre sin expresión en la cara. Para ellos, el dominó es más que un pasatiempo, es un rito[4].

[1]reglas *rules*
[2]madera *wood*
[3]marfil *ivory*
[4]rito *ritual*

¿Comprendes?

A **El dominó** Completen.
1. El dominó es un juego muy ____.
2. En Venecia jugaban al dominó en el siglo ____.
3. Las ____ para jugar al dominó son las mismas del siglo XVIII.
4. Hay ____ fichas en el dominó.
5. Las fichas más elegantes eran de ____.
6. Las fichas modernas generalmente son de ____.
7. Los jugadores ____ las fichas contra la mesa.
8. Los jugadores se sientan a la mesa y los ____ están de pie alrededor de la mesa.
9. Los jugadores generalmente son señores ____.
10. Ellos son muy ____; no tienen ____ en la cara.

B **Los mirones** La lectura habla de «los mirones». ¿Sabes quiénes son?

Conexiones

Las bellas artes

La literatura

The literary genres that we learn about in our English classes are the same ones that students in Spain and Latin America study: the novel, the short story, and poetry. People everywhere enjoy reading for pleasure. It is a very worthwhile pastime during one's leisure hours.

Casa de García Lorca, Granada, España

Los géneros literarios

La literatura les interesa a los jóvenes y a los viejos. Hay personas que pasan horas leyendo novelas, cuentos y poesía.

La novela

La novela es una obra[1] literaria en prosa bastante larga que narra eventos ficticios. La primera novela importante en español es *El Quijote* (1605), obra de Miguel de Cervantes. Hay diferentes tipos de novela. Hay novelas de amor y novelas de aventura. Hoy las novelas policíacas y las novelas de ciencia-ficción son especialmente populares.

El cuento

El cuento, como la novela, es una narración de eventos ficticios. Pero el cuento es mucho más corto que la novela. El cuento, igual que la novela, tiene uno o más protagonistas. El protagonista es el personaje más importante de la obra. El argumento es una narración de lo que pasa o lo que sucede en la novela o en el cuento.

[1]obra *work*

Isabel Allende, novelista chilena

La poesía

El cuento y la novela son obras en prosa. La prosa es el tipo de lenguaje que la gente usa en su habla diaria. La poesía, los poemas, son obras en verso, no en prosa. El poeta usa imágenes, métrica, ritmo y sonidos[2] para crear una reacción emocional en la persona que lee el poema.

A la gente de habla española le gusta mucho la poesía. Muchas veces, en una fiesta familiar, alguien se levanta y recita un poema. Y no es raro encontrar a un dentista o a una profesora que es también poeta.

[2]sonidos *sounds*

¿Comprendes?

A La literatura Contesten.
1. ¿Cuáles son tres géneros literarios?
2. ¿Qué escribió Miguel de Cervantes?
3. ¿Cuáles son cuatro tipos de novela?
4. ¿Cuál es la mayor diferencia entre una novela y un cuento?
5. ¿Qué recitan algunas personas en fiestas familiares?

B ¿Verso o prosa? Digan si es verso o prosa.
1. una poesía   4. un cuento corto
2. un poema lírico   5. un poema épico
3. una novela de ciencia-ficción   6. un artículo de periódico

C Un cuento Vas a escribir un cuento. Para escribir el cuento, haz lo siguiente.

- **Protagonista** El o la protagonista es el personaje más importante del cuento. Le vas a dar un nombre y explicar quién es. Tienes que describir a tu protagonista. Explica cómo es físicamente y da algunos detalles sobre su personalidad.

- **Lugar o ambiente** Tienes que indicar de dónde es el o la protagonista. Indica también dónde tiene lugar la acción de tu cuento. Es necesario dar una descripción del lugar. Puedes describir la casa del protagonista, su pueblo o su ciudad. Incluye todo lo necesario o importante para el desarrollo *(development)* de la acción de tu cuento.

- **Argumento** Di lo que hace el o la protagonista. Escribe todo lo que sucede. Explica a los lectores (a los que leen tu cuento) cómo es la actuación del (de la) protagonista.

- **Desenlace** Explica lo que pasa al final y cómo termina la acción.

¡Te toca a ti!

Use what you have learned

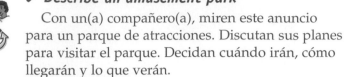

1

El parque de atracciones
✔ *Describe an amusement park*

Con un(a) compañero(a), miren este anuncio para un parque de atracciones. Discutan sus planes para visitar el parque. Decidan cuándo irán, cómo llegarán y lo que verán.

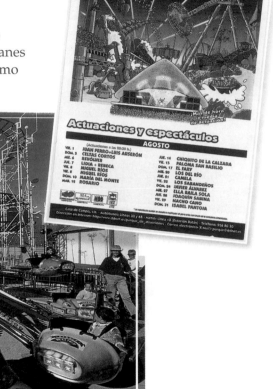

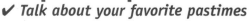

Buenos Aires, Argentina

2

A un restaurante
✔ *Talk about a forthcoming visit to a restaurant*

Vas a estar libre el viernes por la noche. Quieres ir a un restaurante. Llama a un(a) amigo(a) por teléfono para ver si él o ella quiere ir también. Dile a tu amigo(a) a qué restaurante irás, lo que pedirás, si tomarás postre, cuánto costará, etc. Explica a tu amigo(a) como es que conoces el restaurante y por qué te gusta tanto que volverás a comer allí.

3

Mis pasatiempos favoritos
✔ *Talk about your favorite pastimes*

Trabaja con un(a) compañero(a) de clase. Discutan sus pasatiempos favoritos. Decidan si tienen muchos intereses en común.

ESCRIBIR
4 **El programa de actividades escolares**
✔ *Describe extracurricular school activities*

Tú y dos compañeros de la clase de español son miembros de un comité que hace los planes para todas las actividades de su escuela. Escriban una lista de todos los eventos que están planeando para el próximo año escolar.

ESCRIBIR
5 **Los pasatiempos de tu comunidad**
✔ *Describe recreational activities in your community*

Prepara un correo electrónico para una alumna española que viene a tu escuela el semestre que viene. Pregúntale cuáles son los pasatiempos que le interesan; dile también lo que hay en tu comunidad para pasar el tiempo libre.

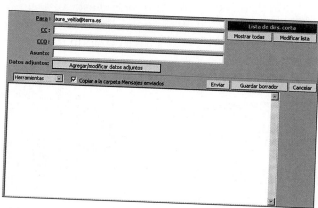

Writing Strategy

Writing about dreams and wishes—the future To imagine the future, it is helpful to look at yourself as you are now. One way to do that is to use clusters to record your likes, interests, feelings, and reactions and how they relate to one another. These connections may help you learn more about yourself and help you see yourself years from now as you begin to think about the future. You can also use clusters to evaluate things as they are now and how you think they will be in the future. Evaluating these changes may help you understand how changes in the world may affect the way your own personal dreams are fulfilled.

ESCRIBIR
6 **Algunas predicciones para el futuro**

You're going to write a composition called **Algunas predicciones para el futuro.** First choose some topics to include in your predictions, such as transportation, family, hobbies and leisure-time activities, communication, education, medicine and hygiene, home, and vacation. If you want you can even predict your own future. Then prepare two lists: one titled **El presente** and the other titled **El futuro.** For each topic describe what it is like now and what you think it will be like in the future. When you finish the two lists, write your composition using the information from the lists.

Assessment

Vocabulario

1 Identifiquen.

1.

2.

3.

4.

To review **Palabras 1**, turn to pages 132-133.

2 Completen.

5. Los jóvenes ____ el bote por el lago.
6. Hay muchos animales en un ____.
7. Los monos y los tigres están en ____.
8. El ____ es muy cómico.
9. La gente camina por las sendas del parque. Ellos dan un ____.

To review **Palabras 2**, turn to pages 136-137.

3 Identifiquen.

10.
11.
12.

Spanish Online

For more Chapter 5 test preparation go to the Chapter 5 **Self-Check Quiz** on the Glencoe Spanish Web site at glencoe.com.

Estructura

4 **Escriban en el futuro.**

13. Ellos estudian para sus exámenes.
14–15. Él lee la novela. No la escribe.
16. Yo contesto la carta.
17. ¿Ves la emisión deportiva en la televisión?
18. Hablamos con él.

To review the future tense, turn to page 140.

5 **Completen.**

19. Elena es muy simpática. Yo creo que ella es ____ simpática ____ todas mis amigas.
20. Él no es muy alto. Pero es ____ alto ____ su hermano. La verdad es que su hermano es muy bajo.
21. Él es un alumno bastante bueno pero no es ____ de la clase.
22. Mi hermana tiene quince años y yo tengo diecisiete. Yo soy ____ mi hermana.

To review the comparative and the superlative, turn to page 144.

Cultura

6 **Contesten.**

23. ¿Qué tienen casi todas las ciudades hispanas?
24. ¿Qué hacen los jóvenes en el parque?
25. ¿Qué venden los vendedores ambulantes?

To review this cultural information, turn to page 148.

¡Hablo como un pro!

Tell all you can about this illustration.

Vocabulario

Talking about pastimes and hobbies

el pasatiempo
el hobby
el ajedrez
el tablero
las damas
el dominó
la ficha
el/la coleccionista

el campeón
la campeona
la sala de juegos
el juego de video
el futbolín
pasar el tiempo
coleccionar sellos (monedas)
llenar un crucigrama

Talking about activities in the park

el parque
el bote
el (parque) zoológico
el mono
la jaula
la boletería
el parque de atracciones
el tiovivo

el caballito
la montaña rusa
la noria
el mimo
el payaso
el globo
el helado
la piragua

How well do you know your vocabulary?

- Choose words to describe a visit to a park.
- Write a brief description of a recent visit to a local park.

Discussing what one does in the park

dar un paseo
caminar por la senda
remar por el lago
hacer cola

Giving location

delante de
detrás de
al lado de
a la derecha
a la izquierda

VIDEOTUR

Episodio 5

In this video episode, you will join Francisco and Alejandra as they spend free time in the park. See page 484 for more information. As you watch, notice gestures the speakers use to help convey their message.

Other useful expressions

listo(a)
la fila
la entrada

Capítulo 6

En el hotel

Objetivos

In this chapter you will learn to:

- ❖ check into and out of a hotel
- ❖ ask for things you may need while at a hotel
- ❖ talk about future events
- ❖ refer to previously mentioned people or things
- ❖ talk about lodging in the Hispanic world

José Agustín Arrieta *View of the Patio*

Spanish Online
To interact with your online edition of
¡Buen viaje! go to: glencoe.com.

HOTEL
RESIDENCIA
LA
CASA
GRANDE

Vocabulario

La llegada al hotel

Use your StudentWorks Plus CD for more practice.

el recepcionista

la recepcionista

el cliente, el huésped

RECEPCION

la recepción

Diego ya reservó un cuarto.
Reservó un cuarto sencillo, no un cuarto doble.

el cuarto, la habitación

la llave

GERENCIA GENERAL

Diego llena la ficha.

PINOS

No. de Registro _____
Fecha __/__/__

Cuarto   Fecha _____
Sencillo
Doble
Nombre _____
Dirección _____
Ciudad _____ Estado _____ Código _____
Cuarto _____
        ( ) Empleo   ( ) Extra
        ( ) Casa
Referencias _____
No. de Licencia __/__ Edad ___ No. Personas ___
Su firma _____

la ficha,
la tarjeta

el ascensor, el elevador

el botones, el mozo

El mozo le subirá el equipaje.
Subirá el equipaje en el ascensor.

El mozo le abrirá la puerta al cliente.
Él le pondrá el equipaje en el cuarto.

La salida del hotel

Diego saldrá del hotel hoy.
Tendrá que abandonar el cuarto antes
del mediodía.

Él pedirá la cuenta y la pagará en la caja.
Pagará su factura con una tarjeta de crédito.

Vocabulario

¿Qué palabra necesito?

1 **¿Qué o quién será?** Identifiquen.

1. ¿Es una llave o una tarjeta de crédito?

2. ¿Es el mozo o el recepcionista?

3. ¿Es la caja o la recepción?

4. ¿Es la ficha o el equipaje?

5. ¿Es el equipaje o la cuenta?

2 **Historieta** **Una visita al hotel**
Contesten.

1. ¿Reservó un cuarto el señor?
2. ¿Tiene él una reservación?
3. ¿Quién lo saludó en la recepción?
4. ¿Qué tendrá que llenar el señor?
5. ¿Quién le subirá el equipaje?
6. ¿Quién le abrirá la puerta?
7. ¿Cuándo tendrá que abandonar el cuarto el señor?
8. ¿Qué pedirá y dónde la pagará?
9. ¿Cómo pagará su cuenta el señor?

Fiesta Inn, Aguascalientes, México

3 **¿Cómo se llama… ?** Identifiquen.

1. la persona que saluda a los clientes y busca la reservación
2. la persona que sube y baja las maletas
3. lo que se usa para abrir la puerta
4. un cuarto para una persona
5. un cuarto para dos personas
6. lo que se puede usar para pagar la cuenta
7. donde uno paga su cuenta

4 Historieta Al hotel

Contesten.

1. Cuando el cliente llega al hotel,
   ¿va primero a la caja?
2. ¿Lleva el mozo el equipaje al cuarto?
3. ¿Hay que llenar una ficha o tarjeta al
   llegar al hotel?
4. Un cuarto sencillo, ¿es para dos personas?
5. ¿Abandona el cuarto el cliente cuando
   llega al hotel?
6. Cuando uno paga la cuenta,
   ¿le da el dinero al botones?

Villa Real, Madrid, España

5 Una reservación

Tu clase de español está pensando en hacer un viaje a España. Todos están muy entusiasmados y todos tienen una tarea para ayudar a planear el viaje. Tú y un(a) compañero(a) tienen la responsabilidad de reservar las habitaciones (los cuartos). Van a llamar al Hotel Regente. Uno(a) de ustedes será el/la alumno(a) y el/la otro(a) será el/la empleado(a) del Hotel Regente. Discutan las fechas, el número de alumnos, el número de habitaciones, las comidas, los precios.

6 El huésped abandona su cuarto.

Eres el/la cajero(a) en el Hotel Regente. Un(a) compañero(a) es un(a) huésped. Está abandonando su cuarto. Preséntale al huésped su factura y explícale los cargos (charges). Tu compañero(a) te hará algunas preguntas sobre los cargos. Después tú le preguntarás cómo quiere pagar la cuenta. Él o ella te dirá.

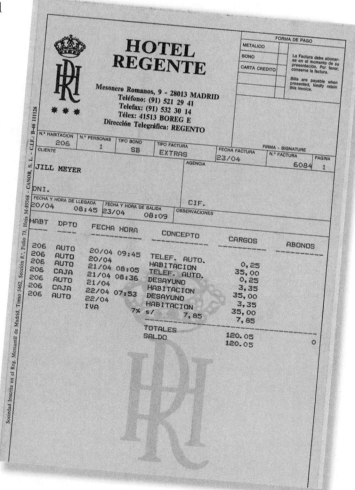

Vocabulario

PALABRAS 2

En el cuarto

Use your StudentWorks Plus CD for more practice.

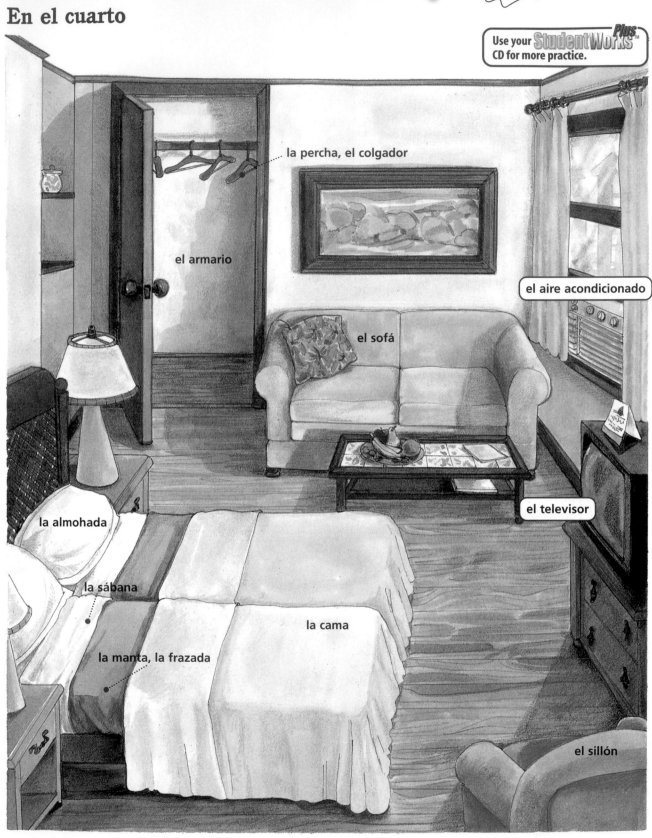

la percha, el colgador

el armario

el aire acondicionado

el sofá

el televisor

la almohada

la sábana

la cama

la manta, la frazada

el sillón

En el baño

la ducha

el jabón

el inodoro, el váter

la toalla

el lavabo

la bañera

La camarera limpiará el cuarto.
Ella hará la cama.

Y cambiará las toallas.

Vocabulario

¿Qué palabra necesito?

7 **¿Qué hará nuestra camarera?**
Expliquen las cosas que hará la camarera según los dibujos.

1.

3.

2.

4.

8 **¿En el baño, en el armario o en el cuarto?**
Digan si las cosas se encuentran en el baño, el armario o el cuarto.

1. la ducha
2. el jabón
3. las sábanas
4. la percha
5. el lavabo

6. las toallas
7. la cama
8. el inodoro
9. el aire acondicionado
10. la manta

¿Lo sabes?

The word **el gancho** means *hook*, but in many areas of the Spanish-speaking world it can also mean *hanger*.

9 **¿Qué necesitarás?** Pareen.

a.

b.

c.

d.

e.

f.

g.

1. Tienes que lavarte las manos.
2. Después de lavarte las manos, tienes que secarlas.
3. Hace mucho frío esta noche.
4. Quieres ver tu programa favorito.

5. Hace calor en el cuarto.
6. Tienes que poner tu chaqueta en el armario.
7. Estás cansado(a) y quieres sentarte.

168 ✦ *ciento sesenta y ocho*

CAPÍTULO 6

10 **Un hotel bueno** Con un(a) compañero(a), discutan lo que les importa cuando se quedan en un hotel. Usen las siguientes expresiones en su discusión.

clase de hotel

tipo de habitación

servicio

cama

precio

baño

aire acondicionado

restaurante

cerca del centro

piscina

gimnasio

desayuno

Hotel El Olivar de San Isidro, Lima, Perú

11 **Un desastre de hotel** Pasaste unas vacaciones en San Juan de Puerto Rico. Lo pasaste muy bien y te gustó todo menos el hotel. ¡Qué horror! Fue un desastre total. Un(a) compañero(a) quiere saber todo lo que pasó. Dile. Usa tu imaginación y exagera todo lo posible. Luego cambien de rol y decidan quién tuvo la experiencia más desastrosa.

*For more practice using words from **Palabras 1** and **2**, do Activity 6 on page H7 at the end of this book.*

Estructura

 Use your **StudentWorks** *Plus* CD for more practice.

Futuro de los verbos irregulares
Expressing more future actions

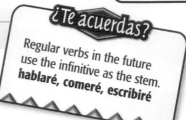
¿Te acuerdas?

Regular verbs in the future use the infinitive as the stem.
hablaré, comeré, escribiré

1. Study the following forms of verbs that have an irregular stem in the future tense. Note that the endings for all irregular verbs are the same as those for the regular verbs.

INFINITIVE	tener	salir	venir	ENDINGS
STEM	tendr-	saldr-	vendr-	
yo	tendré	saldré	vendré	-é
tú	tendrás	saldrás	vendrás	-ás
él, ella, Ud.	tendrá	saldrá	vendrá	-á
nosotros(as)	tendremos	saldremos	vendremos	-emos
vosotros(as)	tendréis	saldréis	vendréis	-éis
ellos, ellas, Uds.	tendrán	saldrán	vendrán	-án

2. Other verbs that follow the same pattern are **poner, saber,** and **poder.**

poner → pondré   saber → sabré   poder → podré

3. The verbs **decir, hacer,** and **querer** also have an irregular future stem.

INFINITIVE	decir	hacer	querer	ENDINGS
STEM	dir-	har-	querr-	
yo	diré	haré	querré	-é
tú	dirás	harás	querrás	-ás
él, ella, Ud.	dirá	hará	querrá	-á
nosotros(as)	diremos	haremos	querremos	-emos
vosotros(as)	diréis	haréis	querréis	-éis
ellos, ellas, Uds.	dirán	harán	querrán	-án

Spanish **online**
For more information about popular vacation spots in the Spanish-speaking world, go to **Web Explore** on the Glencoe Spanish Web site at glencoe.com.

¡Buenas Noches!
Un dulce descanso y
un cálido amanecer
son los deseos de...

HOTELES
KRYSTAL

¿Cómo lo digo?

12 **Historieta** **La huésped llegará mañana.**
Contesten según se indica.

1. ¿Cuándo vendrá la huésped? (mañana)
2. ¿Quién sabrá si tiene una reservación? (el recepcionista)
3. ¿Qué tendrá que llenar la huésped? (una ficha)
4. ¿Quién podrá abrirle la puerta? (el mozo)
5. ¿Dónde le pondrá su equipaje? (en el cuarto)
6. ¿Cuándo saldrá la huésped? (en dos días)

13 **Y mañana, ¿qué?** Contesten según el modelo.

> Teresa no vino hoy.

> No, pero vendrá mañana.

1. Ella no salió de casa a tiempo.
2. Yo no sabía la hora de su llegada.
3. Ella no nos mandó un fax.
4. Nosotros no pudimos ir a buscarla.

14 **Historieta** **Las vacaciones de Ricardo**
Completen.

El invierno que viene Ricardo Valbuena
___1___ (tener) dos semanas de vacaciones. Él y
su familia ___2___ (hacer) un viaje a México. Allí
ellos ___3___ (poder) pasar unos días con sus
parientes. El padre de Ricardo ___4___ (llamar) a
México y les ___5___ (decir) a sus parientes la
hora de su llegada. Todos los parientes de
Ricardo ___6___ (querer) ir al aeropuerto a
recibirlos. Ricardo y sus padres ___7___ (salir) en
el vuelo de las once. El vuelo ___8___ (hacer)
escala en Dallas antes de llegar a México.

Acapulco, México

Estructura

15 **Historieta** **Una reservación**
Completen la conversación con el futuro.

CLIENTE   Buenos días. Soy Elena Sánchez. ¿Quién __1__ (poder)
                 confirmar mi reservación?

RECEPCIONISTA   Pues, yo, señorita. ¿Cuándo __2__ (venir) usted al hotel?

CLIENTE   El jueves. Yo __3__ (saber) la hora exacta más tarde.

RECEPCIONISTA   Un momentito y le __4__ (decir) si tiene reservación. Sí, sí,
                 aquí está. Usted __5__ (venir) el jueves y __6__ (salir) el
                 domingo, ¿verdad?

CLIENTE   Así es. Yo __7__ (tener) que salir a primera hora el domingo.
                 Yo __8__ (querer) transporte al aeropuerto.

RECEPCIONISTA   No hay problema. El conserje le __9__ (hacer) una
                 reservación en la limusina.

CLIENTE   Muchas gracias.

16 **El pronóstico del tiempo para mañana** Completen.

1. Hoy hace calor pero mañana ____ frío.
2. Hoy no tienen que llevar abrigo, pero mañana sí que ____ que
   llevar abrigo.
3. Hoy no pueden esquiar, pero mañana ____ esquiar.
4. Hoy yo no quiero ir a clase, pero mañana ____ ir.
5. Hoy no me pongo el suéter, pero mañana me lo ____.
6. Hoy todo el mundo sale a la calle, pero mañana nadie ____ a la calle.

17 Un trabajo para el verano Este verano trabajarás en un hotel o motel cerca de donde tú vives. El hotel tiene muchos clientes de Latinoamérica. Por eso, el director del hotel (un[a] compañero[a]) te da una entrevista (una interviú) en español. Pregúntale al director todo lo que tendrás que hacer. El modelo les servirá de guía.

> ¿Tendré que venir al hotel temprano?

> Sí, vendrás al hotel temprano.

18 El fin de semana que viene No sabes por qué pero no hay duda que siempre tienes mucho que hacer. Con un(a) compañero(a), hagan planes para el próximo fin de semana. Discutan todo lo que harán. Dividan sus actividades en las siguientes categorías.

pasatiempos

trabajo

obligaciones

estudios

Me lo, te lo, nos lo
Talking about things already stated

1. Many sentences have both a direct and an indirect object pronoun. In these sentences the indirect object pronoun always precedes the direct object pronoun in Spanish. Both pronouns precede the conjugated form of the verb.

Ella **nos** sirvió el helado.	Ella **nos lo** sirvió.
El mozo **me** dio la llave.	El mozo **me la** dio.
Él **me** vendió los libros.	Él **me los** vendió.
Papá **te** hizo las reservaciones.	Papá **te las** hizo.

2. Note that the indirect object **me, te,** or **nos** comes before the direct object **lo, la, los, las.**

¿Cómo lo digo?

19 **El generoso tío Lucas** Contesten según el modelo.

¿Quién te regaló las entradas?

Mi tío Lucas me las regaló.

Nº 036636

VISITA AL ALCÁZAR
Itinerario al dorso

CAJA MADRID

SIGA LA DIRECCION DE LA FLECHA Y LE CONDUCIRÁ A:

PATIO PRINCIPAL: Sala del Arma Blanca, Sala del Arma de
(izquierda)   Fuego, Sala de Maquetas y Planos, Sa-
                    la de Romero Ortiz. Despacho Coronel
                    Moscardó.

SÓTANOS: Aljibes, Horno del pan, Sala del Asedio,
                    Refugios de mujeres y niños, Enfermería,
                    Maternidad, Puerta de carros y Cripta.

GALERÍA PLANTA 1ª: Sala de las Batallas, miniaturas y África
                    S. XIX.

PATIO PRINCIPAL: Sala de África, Sala de Uniformes, Sala de
(derecha)   Órdenes Militares, Sala Documental, SA-
                    LIDA.

1. ¿Quién te regaló la computadora?
2. ¿Quién te regaló los videos?
3. ¿Quién te regaló el balón?
4. ¿Quién te regaló las damas?
5. ¿Quién te regaló los esquís?
6. ¿Quién te regaló el televisor?
7. ¿Quién te regaló las botas?

20 **El mozo del hotel** Contesten con pronombres.

1. ¿Te subió las maletas?
2. ¿Te abrió la puerta?
3. ¿Te dio la llave el mozo?
4. ¿Te prendió el aire acondicionado?

21 **¿Quién te compró todo eso?**
Formen preguntas según el modelo.

Es mi video nuevo.

¿Quién te lo compró?

1. Son mis zapatos nuevos.
2. Es mi equipaje nuevo.
3. Es mi computadora nueva.
4. Son mis revistas nuevas.
5. Es mi bufanda nueva.

22 Doña Flor, la profesora

Contesten con pronombres según el modelo.

Doña Flor nos explicó el sistema. ⟶
Doña Flor nos lo explicó.

1. Doña Flor nos enseñó los poemas.
2. Doña Flor nos explicó la teoría.
3. Doña Flor nos enseñó el vocabulario.
4. Doña Flor nos dio la interpretación.
5. Doña Flor nos explicó las diferencias.

23 No oigo bien. Usen dos pronombres en cada oración.

1. —Carlos me hizo la reservación
   —Perdón, ¿quién ____?
2. —Carlos. Y él me confirmó la
   reservación ayer.
   —Perdón, ¿cuándo ____?
3. —Ayer. Y también me dio las direcciones.
   —Perdón, ¿Carlos ____?
4. —Sí, Carlos. Y me envió las direcciones
   por fax.
   —Perdón, ¿cómo ____?

Hotel Libertador, Trujillo, Perú

Andas bien. ¡Adelante!

Conversación

La llegada al hotel

Recepcionista	Buenas tardes, señor. ¿Tiene usted una reservación?
Cliente	Sí, a nombre de Sorolla, Ramón Sorolla. Un cuarto sencillo para tres noches.
Recepcionista	Aquí está. Usted saldrá el jueves, día doce. Querrá un baño privado, ¿no?
Cliente	Sí, claro.
Recepcionista	Le daré el tres cero dos. Es un cuarto muy bonito. Da al patio. Tendrá que llenar la ficha. ¿Y su pasaporte, por favor?
Cliente	¿A qué hora tendré que abandonar el cuarto el día doce?
Recepcionista	Al mediodía.
Cliente	De acuerdo.
Recepcionista	Aquí tiene usted la llave. Samuel le subirá el equipaje. ¡Samuel!

¿Comprendes?

Contesten.

1. ¿Cómo se llama el cliente?
2. ¿Cuántos días estará en el hotel?
3. ¿Qué día saldrá del hotel?
4. ¿Qué tipo de cuarto reservó?
5. ¿Qué tendrá que llenar el cliente y qué le dará a la recepcionista?
6. ¿A qué hora tendrá que abandonar el cuarto?
7. ¿Quién es Samuel y qué hará él?

Vamos a hablar más

A **Un hotel en Madrid** Tú y tu familia estarán en Madrid este verano. Aquí hay folletos de dos hoteles madrileños que ofrecen muchos servicios a sus clientes. Dile a un(a) compañero(a) en cuál de los dos hoteles quieres quedarte. Explica por qué. Luego tu compañero(a) te dirá su preferencia y te dirá por qué. Discutan por qué se quedarán o no se quedarán en el mismo hotel.

MADRID
HOTEL ORENSE
★★★★

DIRECCION
Pedro Teixeira, 5 (esq. Orense)
28020 Madrid
Tel. (91) 597 15 68
Fax. (91) 597 12 95

CAPACIDAD
• 140 habitaciones todas dobles (incluye 10 suites estilo)

SERVICIOS GENERALES
• Restaurante
• Bar Cafetería
• Comedor privado
• Salón social
• Fax
• Amplio garaje propio
• Desayuno Buffet
• Circuito cerrado de T.V.

SERVICIOS HABITACIONES
• Todas exteriores e insonorizadas
• Teléfono directo
• T.V. color con mando a distancia
• Antena parabólica / Canal +
• Hilo musical
• Radio
• Aire acondicionado
• Climatizador individual
• Cuarto de baño en dos volúmenes
• Secador de pelo
• Caja de seguridad
• Mini-bar
• Room service
• Línea de fax opcional

SITUACION
El Hotel está situado en el corazón de Azca (zona de negocios y centro financiero), junto al Palacio de Congresos, el Paseo de la Castellana y el Estadio Santiago Bernabeu. A 5 minutos de la estación de Chamartín. Acceso directo a la M-40, a 10 minutos del aeropuerto e Ifema.

MADRID
GRAN HOTEL COLON
★★★★

DIRECCION
Pez Volador, 11 (semiesquina con Dr.Ezquerdo)
28007 Madrid
Tel. (91) 573 59 00 / 573 86 00
Fax. (91) 573 08 09
Telex 22984 COLON E

CAPACIDAD
• 380 habitaciones (incluidas suites)

SERVICIOS GENERALES
Restaurante, Bar, Cafetería / Hall, Terraza con jardín, Sauna / Masajes, Peluquería, Rayos uva, Gimnasio panorámico (próxima apertura), Solarium, Agencia de viajes, Alquiler de coches, Garaje privado.

SERVICIOS HABITACIONES
Todas exteriores, Habitaciones con Terraza, Teléfono directo, T.V. color con mando a distancia, Antena parabólica, Radio / Hilo musical, Mini-bar, Caja de seguridad, Aire acondicionado, Servicio de habitaciones.

INSTALACIONES PARA CONFERENCIAS Y REUNIONES
El hotel permite la posibilidad de múltiples transformaciones, debido a que dispone de grandes espacios dedicados a salones. Todo ello contando con retroproyectores de transparencias, traducción simultánea, pantallas, vídeos, T.V., Megafonía y azafatas.

SITUACION
Ubicado en una zona céntrica y residencial, junto al Parque del Retiro. A 5 minutos de la estación de Atocha, del Centro Comercial de Goya y, del Triángulo del Arte. Acceso directo a la M-30 y M-40, (por la nueva prolongación O'Donnell) a 10 minutos del aeropuerto y del Parque Ferial Juan Carlos I.

B **¿Cómo podré hacerlo todo?** Vas a preparar un *skit* muy cómico y divertido con un(a) compañero(a). Uno de ustedes será el ama de llaves *(head housekeeper)* de un hotel y el otro será una camarera nueva. Dentro de poco estarán llegando unos clientes. La pobre camarera no sabe qué hacer. Te hará muchas preguntas. Contesta a sus preguntas. Explícale todo lo que tendrá que hacer y cómo.

Lecturas culturales

Los paradores de España ♻ 🎧

El verano que viene Sandra, Roberto y sus padres harán un viaje a España. Saldrán el 28 de junio. Al llegar a España alquilarán un coche. Viajarán por todas partes del país. Pasarán una semana en el norte y otra en Madrid y sus alrededores. Pasarán la última semana en el sur, en Andalucía.

La señora White, la madre de Sandra y Roberto, está planeando el viaje. Dice que podrán pasar varias noches en algunos paradores.

Hay unos setenta paradores en España. Algunos son muy pequeños como el Parador de Villalba en Lugo, Galicia. Tiene sólo seis habitaciones. Otros son bastante grandes. El Parador de Cádiz tiene 147 habitaciones. Pero lo importante no es el tamaño. Lo más atractivo de los paradores es que son únicos. No son todos iguales. Cada uno tiene su carácter propio.

Algunos paradores son antiguos castillos[1] o monasterios. La madre de Sandra y Roberto dice que hará una reservación en el Parador San Francisco en Granada. Antes era un convento fundado por los Reyes Católicos, Fernando e Isabel. El parador está dentro de las murallas[2] y los jardines de la famosa Alhambra. Pero el Parador San Francisco es tan popular que los White tendrán que reservar una habitación con unos seis meses de anticipación.

[1]castillos *castles*
[2]murallas *walls*

Parador de Cádiz

Parador San Francisco, Granada

Los paradores nacionales son del gobierno[3] español. Los restaurantes de muchos paradores son muy buenos. Sirven platos típicos de las regiones donde se encuentran. Muchos turistas dicen que pasar una noche en un parador es como pasar una noche en un museo—pero un museo con todas las comodidades de un hotel de cuatro estrellas[4]. A ver lo que dirán Sandra, Roberto y sus padres al volver de su viaje a España.

[3]gobierno *government*
[4]estrellas *stars*

Parador de Cardona,
España

¿Comprendes?

A Un viaje a España Contesten.
1. ¿Quiénes harán un viaje a España?
2. ¿Qué día saldrán?
3. ¿Qué alquilarán?
4. ¿Cuánto tiempo pasarán en Madrid y sus alrededores?
5. ¿Quién está planeando el viaje?
6. ¿Dónde podrán pasar algunas noches?
7. ¿Cómo son los paradores?
8. ¿De quién son los paradores?
9. ¿Qué sirven en los restaurantes de los paradores?

B ¿Cómo es? Describan.
1. Describe el Parador de Villalba en Lugo, Galicia.
2. Describe el Parador San Francisco en Granada, Andalucía.

C Lo magnífico de los paradores Expliquen.
1. Lo más atractivo de los paradores es que son únicos.
2. Pasar una noche en un parador es como pasar una noche en un museo—pero un museo con todas las comodidades de un hotel de cuatro estrellas.

Parador San Francisco,
Granada

Use your StudentWorks *Plus*
CD for more practice.

Lectura opcional ①

Los albergues

En España y en algunos países de Latinoamérica hay albergues juveniles. Los albergues ofrecen cuartos limpios y económicos para jóvenes. La mayoría de los jóvenes que se hospedan (pasan la noche) en un albergue son estudiantes. Les gustan mucho los albergues porque no cuestan mucho y allí pueden conocer a otros estudiantes de todas partes del mundo. En los albergues hay casi siempre un salón central donde todos se reúnen para charlar y hacer amigos nuevos.

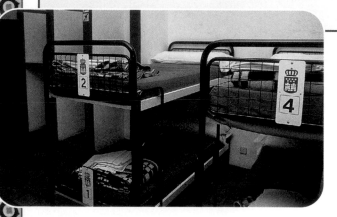

Cuartos en albergues juveniles, España

LOPE DE VEGA

V

★★★

HOSTAL R.

GRAN VIA, 59
28013 MADRID

☎ 247 70 00

¿Comprendes?

A **Los albergues juveniles** Digan que sí o que no.
1. Todos los países latinoamericanos tienen albergues juveniles.
2. Un albergue juvenil es para viejos o ancianos.
3. Los albergues son bastante caros.
4. La mayoría de los jóvenes que se hospedan en un albergue juvenil son estudiantes.

B **Para pensar** Discutan en grupos.
¿Por qué a los estudiantes les gustan mucho los albergues juveniles?

Lectura opcional ②

HOTEL DE LA RECONQUISTA

El Hotel de la Reconquista, construido sobre la traza de un singular edificio del Siglo XVIII, antiguo Hospicio y Hospital del Principado de Asturias, Monumento Nacional, está situado en la zona más céntrica, residencial y comercial de la ciudad de Oviedo.

El Hotel dispone de un total de 142 habitaciones, incluyendo Junior suites y suites, algunas de ellas con preciosas vistas sobre el Patio de la Reina. Todas las habitaciones están perfectamente equipadas con hilo musical y TV vía satélite.

El Hotel le ofrece la oportunidad de disfrutar de la mejor cocina en su Restaurante.

El Hotel ofrece una amplia gama de instalaciones para Reuniones, congresos y Banquetes. Cuenta con una sala de proyecciones, con servicio de traducción simultánea disponible, ocho espléndidas salas de reuniones de 25 a 550 m^2 y encantadores patios para la celebración de todo tipo de conferencias y acontecimientos sociales como congresos, certámenes, exposiciones, banquetes y comidas de empresa con capacidad para albergar hasta 800 personas.

¿Comprendes?

¿Dónde nos dice...?
Busquen la información en el folleto.
1. el nombre del hotel
2. de qué siglo data el edificio
3. dónde está ubicado (situado)
4. el número de habitaciones
5. algunos servicios que ofrece el hotel

Conexiones

La educación física

El ejercicio

Physical fitness is a concern for everyone. Our health depends upon our fitness. Maintaining muscle tone and cardiovascular health and avoiding weight gain are important to our well-being and to our enjoyment of life. Sometimes it's difficult to stay in shape when traveling. For this reason, many hotels in major cities in Spain and Latin America provide exercise rooms or temporary membership to healthclubs for their guests.

El ejercicio

Los hombres y las mujeres que viajan mucho quieren mantenerse en forma. Por eso, muchos hoteles tienen un gimnasio para el uso de sus clientes donde pueden hacer ejercicio. Hay dos tipos de ejercicio, el ejercicio aeróbico o cardiovascular y el ejercicio de fortaleza muscular.

Ejercicios aeróbicos

Los ejercicios aeróbicos como el jogging, el caminar, la natación, el «step» y el «spinning» aumentan temporalmente la respiración. Aumentan también el ritmo del corazón. Hacen más fuertes el corazón y todo el sistema cardiovascular. Algunos ejercicios aeróbicos son muy entretenidos[1] como, por ejemplo, el patinaje lineal[2] y el ciclismo.

[1]entretenidos *entertaining*
[2]patinaje lineal *roller blading*

Ejercicios de fortaleza muscular

Los ejercicios de fortaleza muscular aumentan el tamaño y la fuerza de los músculos como los bíceps y tríceps y los músculos pectorales. Para hacer ejercicios de fortaleza muscular usamos una serie de aparatos—pesas y barras, tubos, ligas y bandas elásticas.

Un buen programa de ejercicios alterna el ejercicio aeróbico con el ejercicio de fortaleza muscular. Es decir, se practica un día aeróbicos y otro día fortaleza. Lo más importante es hacer ejercicio todos los días, aunque por sólo unos veinte minutos. También es importante no hacer demasiado ejercicio. Demasiado ejercicio te puede hacer daño. Tu cuerpo te dice cuando debes descansar[3]. Todo en moderación es siempre una buena idea.

[3]descansar *rest*

los bíceps

los tríceps

los pectorales

¿Comprendes?

A Para mantenerse en forma Completen.

1. Muchas personas que viajan quieren mantenerse en ____.
2. Los hoteles tienen un gimnasio donde los huéspedes pueden hacer ____.
3. Otro nombre para el «ejercicio aeróbico» es «ejercicio ____».
4. El tipo de ejercicio que no es aeróbico es el ejercicio de ____.
5. El ejercicio aeróbico aumenta el ritmo del ____.
6. El ejercicio de fortaleza muscular aumenta el tamaño de los ____.
7. Un programa que ____ el ejercicio aeróbico y el ejercicio de fortaleza muscular es recomendable.
8. Es importante hacer ejercicio ____ pero también es importante ____.
9. Si haces demasiado ejercicio, puedes hacer ____ a tu cuerpo.

B ¿Aeróbico o fortaleza muscular?

Identifiquen el tipo de ejercicio.

1. pesas y barras
2. patinaje lineal
3. «step»
4. bandas elásticas
5. jogging
6. ligas

¡Te toca a ti!

Use what you have learned

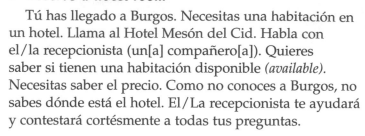

HABLAR
1

Una habitación, por favor.
✔ *Reserve a hotel room*

Tú has llegado a Burgos. Necesitas una habitación en un hotel. Llama al Hotel Mesón del Cid. Habla con el/la recepcionista (un[a] compañero[a]). Quieres saber si tienen una habitación disponible *(available)*. Necesitas saber el precio. Como no conoces a Burgos, no sabes dónde está el hotel. El/La recepcionista te ayudará y contestará cortésmente a todas tus preguntas.

Vista tomada desde la fachada principal de la Catedral

Plaza Santa María, 8
Frente Fachada Principal Catedral
Tels. (947) 20 59 71 - 20 87 15
09003 BURGOS

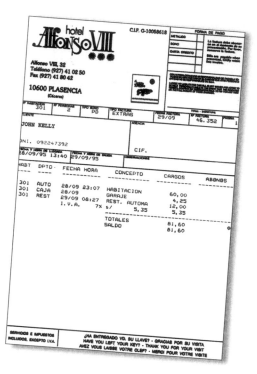

HABLAR
2

La cuenta, por favor.
✔ *Check out of a hotel*

Estás saliendo del Hotel Alfonso VIII. El/La cajero(a) (un[a] compañero[a]) te presenta esta factura. Pero hay un error. Tú no has tenido carro durante tu visita aquí. Tengan una conversación para resolver el problema.

HABLAR
3

La buenaventura
✔ *Tell what will happen in the future*

Trabaja con un(a) compañero(a). Él o ella te hará muchas preguntas porque quiere saber todo lo que le pasará. Tendrás que usar tu imaginación. Después de terminar con las preguntas de tu compañero(a), cambien de rol y tú harás preguntas sobre tu futuro.

184 *ciento ochenta y cuatro*

CAPÍTULO 6

ESCRIBIR 4

Un fax para el hotel Excelsior
✔ *Obtain information about a hotel*

Los padres de uno de tus amigos van a México. Quieren quedarse (hospedarse, alojarse) en el Hotel Excelsior. Saben que tú estás estudiando el español y te piden ayuda. Tú les vas a preparar un fax para el Hotel Excelsior. Para preparar el fax, escribe una lista de toda la información que necesitan los padres de tu amigo. Luego prepara todas las preguntas que tienes que incluir en el fax. Al terminar tus dos listas, prepara la copia final para el fax que vas a enviar.

SpanishOnline

To choose a hotel for your family in a Latin American country of your choice, go to the Chapter 6 **WebQuest** on the Glencoe Spanish Web site at glencoe.com.

ESCRIBIR 5

Un anuncio

A hotel in your community wants to encourage Spanish-speaking guests to stay there. They have asked you to prepare an advertisement describing the hotel and listing its best features. Use the advertisement for the Parador Reyes Católicos in Santiago de Compostela, Galicia, as a guide, but be as original as you can. Be sure your ad reflects services offered by the hotel as well as activities and events in your community.

Writing Strategy

Creating an advertisement
The purpose of an advertisement is to persuade people to buy a product or service. An effective ad will attract attention, arouse interest, and create desire. You can use a striking design to draw readers in. You can use facts and opinions to explain the product's features and to show why readers should be interested in your product—why it is better than the competition. And you can appeal to your readers' reason and emotion to make them want your product.

ciento ochenta y cinco

Vocabulario

1 **Completen.**

1. Diego está viajando sólo. No lo acompaña nadie. Así reservó un cuarto ____.
2. Es necesario tener una ____ para abrir la puerta del cuarto.
3. El ____ subirá el equipaje al cuarto.
4. Diego sale hoy. Tiene que ____ el cuarto antes del mediodía.
5. Diego pedirá la ____ y pagará con su tarjeta de crédito.

To review **Palabras 1**, turn to pages 162-163.

2 **Identifiquen.**

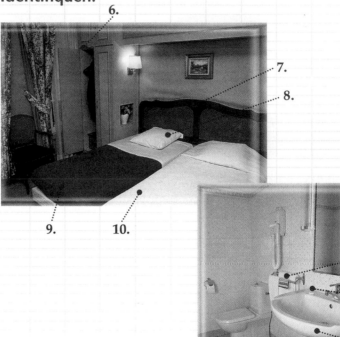

6.
7.
8.
9.
10.
11.
12.
13.

To review **Palabras 2**, turn to pages 166-167.

Estructura

To review the future of irregular verbs, turn to page 170.

3 **Completen con el futuro.**

14. Él ____ que reservar un cuarto. (tener)
15–16. Ellos ____ saber qué día (tú) ____. (querer, salir)
17. Nosotros ____ el viaje en avión. (hacer)
18. Yo ____ ir también. (poder)
19. ¿Tú le ____ cuánto va a costar el hotel? (decir)

4 Contesten con un pronombre.

20. ¿El mozo te abrió la puerta?
21. ¿Abuelita me envió los regalos?
22. ¿Mamá te dio las entradas al zoológico?

To review direct and indirect object pronouns, turn to page 173.

Cultura

5 Completen.

23. Lo más atractivo de los paradores españoles es que ____.
24. Antes, el Parador San Francisco en Granada era ____.
25. Los restaurantes de muchos paradores sirven ____.

To review this cultural information, turn to pages 178–179.

Parador San Francisco, Granada

Tell all you can about this illustration.

Vocabulario

Making a hotel reservation

reservar
la reservación
el cuarto, la habitación

un cuarto sencillo
un cuarto doble

Checking into a hotel

el hotel
la recepción
el/la recepcionista
el/la cliente, el/la huésped
la ficha, la tarjeta

la llave
la puerta
el botones, el mozo
el equipaje
el ascensor, el elevador

Checking out of a hotel

abandonar el cuarto
bajar las maletas
pedir la cuenta
pagar la factura

How well do you know your vocabulary?

- Identify words you would use when reserving a hotel room.
- Describe the type of room you would like to have and how you will pay for it.

Talking about a hotel room

la puerta
la cama
la sábana
la almohada
la manta, la frazada
el televisor

el aire acondicionado
el armario
la percha, el colgador
el sillón
el sofá

Talking about a bathroom

la bañera
la ducha
el inodoro, el váter

el lavabo
el jabón
la toalla

VIDEOTUR

Episodio 6

In this video episode, you will join Francisco on an overnight excursion to a nearby city. See page 485 for more information. As you watch, look for gestures the speakers use to help convey their message.

Talking about cleaning a hotel room

la camarera
limpiar el cuarto

hacer la cama
cambiar las toallas

Capítulo 7

El vuelo

Objetivos

In this chapter you will learn to:

❖ talk about air travel
❖ discuss the influence of geography on travel in Latin America
❖ talk about things that would happen under certain conditions
❖ talk about air travel in Hispanic countries

Susana González-Pagliere *Village with Volcano*

Spanish Online
To interact with your online edition of **¡Buen viaje!** go to: glencoe.com.

Vocabulario

PALABRAS 1

Use your **StudentWorks** Plus CD for more practice.

En el avión

la tripulación

el comandante, el piloto

el copiloto

la cabina de mando, la cabina de vuelo

los asistentes de vuelo

La cabina

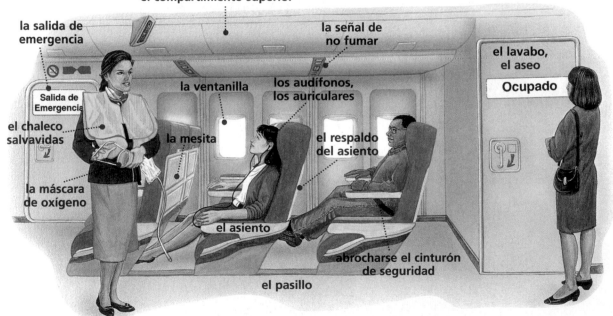

el compartimiento sobre la cabeza, el compartimiento superior

la salida de emergencia

la señal de no fumar

Salida de Emergencia

la ventanilla

los audífonos, los auriculares

el lavabo, el aseo

Ocupado

el chaleco salvavidas

la mesita

el respaldo del asiento

la máscara de oxígeno

el asiento

abrocharse el cinturón de seguridad

el pasillo

La señora iría al lavabo, pero no puede.
Está ocupado.

El asistente de vuelo hizo algunos anuncios.
Dijo que los asistentes de vuelo:

pasarían por la cabina con
   los audífonos;
distribuirían los audífonos;
se los distribuirían a los pasajeros;

servirían bebidas y una
   comida durante el vuelo;

y que en el caso de una emergencia
   las máscaras de oxígeno caerían
   automáticamente.

También dijo que el equipaje
   de mano tendría que caber
   debajo del asiento o en el
   compartimiento superior.

la bandeja

el carrito

Durante el vuelo los asistentes de vuelo
   sirvieron una comida a los pasajeros.

Se la sirvieron de un carrito.
Se la sirvieron en una bandeja.

Vocabulario

¿Qué palabra necesito?

1 **¿Qué es o quién es?** Identifiquen.

1. ¿Es el lavabo o la cabina de mando?

2. ¿Es la máscara de oxígeno o la señal de no fumar?

3. ¿Es el asistente de vuelo o el comandante?

4. ¿Es el chaleco salvavidas o el cinturón de seguridad?

5. ¿Es el pasillo o el compartimiento superior?

6. ¿Es el asiento o la mesita?

2 **Historieta La tripulación** Contesten según se indica.

1. ¿Dónde en el avión está el piloto? (en la cabina de vuelo o en la cabina de mando)
2. ¿Quiénes componen la tripulación? (el piloto o el comandante, el co-piloto y los asistentes de vuelo)
3. ¿Quiénes sirven a los pasajeros durante el vuelo? (los asistentes de vuelo)
4. ¿De qué se responsabilizan los asistentes de vuelo? (de la seguridad de los pasajeros)
5. En el caso de una emergencia, ¿por dónde salen los pasajeros? (por las salidas de emergencia)

3 **A bordo del avión** Pareen.

1. donde uno va para lavarse las manos en el avión
2. donde se pone el equipaje de mano
3. lo que se usa para oír música o ver una película
4. la persona que sirve a los pasajeros en el avión
5. lo que usa el/la asistente de vuelo para servir la comida
6. donde pone el/la asistente de vuelo la comida que le sirve al pasajero

a. el lavabo
b. la bandeja
c. el/la asistente de vuelo
d. la mesita
e. el compartimiento superior
f. los audífonos

4 **Algunas reglas a bordo del avión** Contesten.

1. ¿Qué abrocharías durante el despegue y el aterrizaje?
   a. el cinturón de seguridad
   b. el respaldo del asiento
   c. la máscara de oxígeno

2. Durante el despegue y el aterrizaje, ¿dónde pondrías tu equipaje de mano?
   a. debajo del asiento
   b. en el pasillo
   c. en el lavabo

3. En caso de un cambio en la presión del aire en el avión, ¿qué usarías?
   a. el cinturón de seguridad
   b. los audífonos
   c. la máscara de oxígeno

4. ¿Cómo pondrías el respaldo de tu asiento durante el despegue y el aterrizaje?
   a. en posición vertical
   b. debajo del asiento
   c. en el compartimiento sobre la cabeza

5. En caso de un aterrizaje de emergencia en el mar, ¿qué te pondrías?
   a. el lavabo
   b. la señal de no fumar
   c. el chaleco salvavidas

La aerolínea Avensa

5 **Antes del despegue** Tú eres un(a) asistente de vuelo. Un(a) pasajero(a) (tu compañero[a]) está haciendo su primer viaje en avión. No tiene idea de lo que tiene que hacer. Explícale todo lo que tiene que hacer antes del despegue.

6 **A bordo del avión** Con un(a) compañero(a), mira el dibujo. Juntos describan todo lo que ven en el dibujo. Luego decidan si quieren hacer un viaje en avión. Expliquen por qué.

En el aeropuerto

la avioneta

el helicóptero

el avión de reacción, el jet

la torre de control

la terminal de pasajeros

la pista

el despegue

el aterrizaje

El comandante les habló a los pasajeros.
Les anunció que:
  despegarían a tiempo.
  el avión volaría a una altura de 10.000
    metros.
  sería un vuelo directo; no harían escala.
  sobrevolarían los Andes.
  habría muy poca turbulencia durante
    el vuelo.

Un poco de geografía

la altura, la altitud

la montaña

el pico

la cordillera

el altiplano

la meseta

el lago

el valle

la llanura

Vocabulario

¿Qué palabra necesito?

Caracas, Venezuela

7 Historieta A bordo del avión
Contesten según se indica.

1. ¿De dónde hizo el comandante algunos anuncios? (de la cabina de vuelo)
2. ¿Dijo que despegarían con una demora? (no, a tiempo)
3. ¿Dijo que habría mucha turbulencia durante el vuelo? (no, poca)
4. ¿Dijo que el tiempo de vuelo sería de tres horas? (no, de tres horas y treinta minutos)
5. ¿Dijo que sobrevolarían los Andes? (sí)
6. ¿Qué dijo que podrían ver los pasajeros? (los picos de las montañas)

8 En el aeropuerto Escojan.

1. El avión va a llegar en pocos momentos. Esperamos ____.
   a. el despegue   b. el aterrizaje   c. la salida
2. Los controladores le dan instrucciones al piloto. Se las dan desde la ____.
   a. cabina de mando   b. terminal   c. torre de control
3. Los amigos y parientes de los pasajeros los esperan en la ____.
   a. terminal   b. torre de control   c. pista
4. Otro avión ya va a salir. En pocos minutos veremos ____.
   a. la llegada   b. el despegue   c. el aterrizaje
5. ____ despega y aterriza verticalmente.
   a. La avioneta   b. El avión de reacción   c. El helicóptero

Granada, España

9 **Definiciones** Pareen.

1. parte superior de una montaña
2. extensión de tierra que no tiene altos ni bajos
3. espacio de tierra entre montañas
4. agua que comienza en la tierra y va al mar
5. serie de montañas, una tras otra
6. elevación de tierra que termina en un pico

a. río
b. cordillera
c. pico
d. llanura
e. valle
f. montaña

Los Andes

10 **¿Qué son... ?** Contesten.

1. los Andes, los Apalaches, las Rocosas
2. el Amazonas, el Misisipí, el Nilo
3. Aconcagua, Everest, McKinley
4. Huron, Ontario, Michigan, Erie, Superior

11 **Soy el/la comandante.** Trabaja con un(a) compañero(a). Uno(a) de ustedes es el/la comandante a bordo de un avión de una compañía americana. El vuelo que estás haciendo es el vuelo entre Miami y Guayaquil, Ecuador. Como hay muchos pasajeros a bordo que hablan español, tú vas a hacer algunos anuncios en español. Tu compañero(a) escuchará tus anuncios. Luego cambien de rol y tu compañero(a) será el/la comandante y tú escucharás.

12 **Donde vivimos** Trabaja con un(a) compañero(a). Den una descripción de la geografía de la región donde viven. Pueden usar las siguientes palabras.

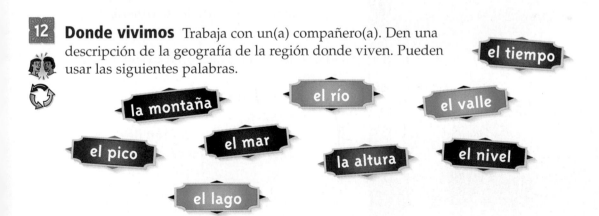

el tiempo

el río

el valle

la montaña

el mar

el nivel

el pico

la altura

el lago

UN POCO MÁS

*For more practice using words from **Palabras 1** and **2**, do Activity 7 on page H8 at the end of this book.*

Estructura

Use your StudentWorks Plus CD for more practice.

Modo potencial o condicional de verbos regulares
Expressing conditions

1. As with the future, the infinitive is used as the stem for the conditional of regular verbs. Study the following forms.

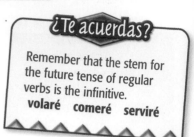

¿Te acuerdas?

Remember that the stem for the future tense of regular verbs is the infinitive.
volaré   comeré   serviré

INFINITIVE	llegar	ver	servir	ENDINGS
STEM	llegar-	ver-	servir-	
yo	llegaría	vería	serviría	-ía
tú	llegarías	verías	servirías	-ías
él, ella, Ud.	llegaría	vería	serviría	-ía
nosotros(as)	llegaríamos	veríamos	serviríamos	-íamos
vosotros(as)	llegaríais	veríais	serviríais	-íais
ellos, ellas, Uds.	llegarían	verían	servirían	-ían

Note that the endings for the conditional are the same as those for the imperfect of **-er** and **-ir** verbs.

La aerolínea LACSA, Costa Rica

2. You use the conditional, as you do in English, to tell what would take place under certain circumstances.

> **El avión despegaría ahora pero no puede porque hace mal tiempo.
> Nosotros viajaríamos a Europa pero no tenemos suficiente dinero.**

3. The conditional is also used to soften requests.

> **¿Me pasaría usted los audífonos, por favor?
> ¿Se abrocharía el cinturón de seguridad, por favor, señor?**

¿Cómo lo digo?

13 Historieta **Imaginándome millonario(a)**
Contesten.

1. ¿Vivirías en la ciudad o en el campo?
2. ¿Viajarías mucho?
3. ¿Adónde irías?
4. ¿Cómo irías?
5. ¿Con quién irías?
6. ¿Comprarías una casa grande?
7. ¿Cómo sería la casa?
8. ¿Trabajarías?

14 Historieta **Las vacaciones del muchacho**
Contesten.

1. ¿Adónde iría el muchacho para las vacaciones?
2. ¿Cómo viajaría?
3. ¿Cuánto pagaría?
4. ¿Dónde nadaría él?
5. ¿A qué jugaría?
6. ¿Qué subiría él?
7. ¿Qué comería?
8. ¿Dónde dormiría?

En una agencia de viajes, España

Lima, Perú

15 **No, no.** Contesten según el modelo.

> Ellos piensan ir. ¿Y tú?

> No, yo no iría.

1. Ellos piensan llamar. ¿Y tú?
2. Yo pienso escribir. ¿Y ustedes?
3. Carolina piensa visitar a sus primos. ¿Y su hermano?
4. Nosotros pensamos ir. ¿Y ustedes?
5. Ellos piensan viajar por avión. ¿Y ustedes?
6. Teresa piensa manejar. ¿Y tú?

16 **Historieta** **Un viaje con unos amigos**
Contesten según se indica.

1. ¿Irían tus amigos a la playa o a las montañas? (a las montañas)
2. ¿Los acompañarías? (sí)
3. ¿Cómo irían ustedes, en tren o en carro? (en carro)
4. ¿Quién manejaría? (Teresa)
5. ¿Cuánto tiempo pasarían ustedes en las montañas? (unos cinco días)
6. ¿Dónde se quedarían ustedes? (en un hotel económico)

Torres del Paine, Chile

Modo potencial de verbos irregulares
Expressing more conditions

The same verbs that are irregular in the future tense are irregular in the conditional. Study the following.

INFINITIVE	FUTURE	CONDITIONAL
TENER	tendré	tendría
PONER	pondré	pondría
SALIR	saldré	saldría
VENIR	vendré	vendría
PODER	podré	podría
SABER	sabré	sabría
HACER	haré	haría
DECIR	diré	diría
QUERER	querré	querría

¿Cómo lo digo?

17 **Historieta** ¿Vendrá tu hermana o no?
Contesten según el modelo.

¿Estará tu hermana?

Dijo que estaría.

1. ¿Vendrá tu hermana?
2. ¿Hará el viaje?
3. ¿Podrá pagar el viaje?
4. ¿Saldrá el viernes?
5. ¿Tendrá bastante tiempo?

mientras
más
quieres
más
tienes

CROWN PACIFIC HUATULCO

SUPER *Vete de Pinta* SIN LIMITE
- Transportación aérea
- Dos noches de alojamiento
- Restaurante de especialidades
- Todas las comidas estilo Buffet
- Snack de medio día, tea time, snack nocturno
- Bebidas nacionales e importadas sin límite
- Propinas *Mini Club para niños
- Deportes acuáticos (no motorizados)
- Shows nocturnos y fiestas (tema diariamente)
- Juegos de mesa
- Traslado aeropuerto-hotel-aeropuerto
- 2 menores comen, beben y duermen gratis 0 a 7 años. Sólo pagan porción aérea

DESDE
1,977
2 NOCHES
DE HOSPEDAJE

Noche adicional $ 438

Ventas y Reservaciones Mexicana
4 4 8 9 8 7 1
o consulta a tu Agente de Viajes

VTP

CROWN PACIFIC
HUATULCO

MEXICANA

* Precio por persona en habitación doble, más IVA, más TUA. Saliendo de la Ciudad de México

Estructura

18 **Uno sí y el otro no** Completen con el condicional.

1. Él sabría la dirección pero su hermano no la ____. *sabría*
2. Yo te lo diría pero ellos nunca te lo ____. *dirían*
3. Nosotros lo haríamos pero ellos no lo ____ nunca.
4. Yo podría ir pero mis amigos no ____.
5. Ustedes lo pondrían en orden pero él no lo ____.
6. Yo tendría que volver pero tú no ____.

19 **Ahora lo hará pero antes no lo haría.**
Completen con el condicional.

1. Carlos podrá pero antes no ____.
2. Los muchachos vendrán pero antes no ____.
3. Tú lo harás pero antes no lo ____.
4. Ustedes saldrán pero antes no ____.
5. Usted me lo dirá pero antes no me lo ____.

20 **Historieta** **A bordo del avión**
Contesten con **sí.**

1. ¿Dijo el comandante que el avión podría despegar a tiempo?
2. ¿Dijo que saldrían dentro de cinco minutos?
3. ¿Dijo el asistente de vuelo que los pasajeros tendrían que poner su equipaje de mano en el compartimiento superior?
4. ¿Dijo que no podríamos fumar cigarrillos durante el vuelo?
5. ¿Dijo que yo podría usar mi computadora durante el vuelo?
6. ¿Dijo el comandante que nos diría la hora exacta de nuestra llegada?
7. ¿Dijo que haríamos escala en Bogotá?

PLAN DE VUELOS Y HORARIOS		
DE LUNES A VIERNES	SALIDA	LLEGADA
Santiago - Bilbao	07:45	09:05
Bilbao - Santiago	09:35	10:55
Santiago - Bilbao	17:15	18:35
Bilbao - Santiago	19:05	20:25
Santiago - Asturias	11:25	12:10
Asturias - Santiago	12:40	13:25
Santiago - Asturias	20:55	21:40
Asturias - Santiago	22:10	22:55
Santiago - Santander	13:55	15:05
Santander - Santiago	15:35	16:45

primair

LA LINEA AEREA QUE PRIMA

21 **Una encuesta** Trabaja con un(a) compañero(a). Van a hacer una encuesta *(survey)*. Esta es la situación. Hay un billete de cien dólares en la calle. Cada uno(a) de ustedes preguntará a cinco compañeros qué harían al encontrar los cien dólares. Luego organicen las respuestas para informar a la clase sobre los resultados.

22 **Lo que haría pero no puedo** ¿No es verdad que hay muchas cosas que te gustaría hacer pero que no puedes porque tienes otras obligaciones? Ten una conversación con un(a) compañero(a). Discutan todo lo que les gustaría hacer pero que no pueden. Expliquen por qué no pueden.

Para volar a Australia y Nueva Zelanda desde Sudamérica, sólo hay que dar media vuelta. No veinte mil.

Sydney • Auckland • Buenos Aires

Ahora, 3 veces por semana con nuestro exclusivo vuelo Transpolar. Con Aerolíneas Argentinas, usted podrá aprovechar el tiempo para pasear por las calles de Auckland o Sidney, y no por los aeropuertos de todo el mundo. Además, sumará puntos para el Programa de Viajeros Frecuentes Aerolíneas Plus y arribará en los horarios ideales para realizar todas las conexiones. Consulte a su Agente de Viajes o llámenos al 340-7777.

Club GOLD

AEROLINEAS ARGENTINAS

Dos complementos con se
Talking about things stated before

1. The indirect object pronouns **le** and **les** change to **se** when used in the same sentence with either **lo, la, los,** or **las.**

> **El asistente de vuelo les sirvió la comida a los pasajeros.**
> **El asistente de vuelo se la sirvió.**
> **El joven le dio los audífonos a su mamá.**
> **El joven se los dio.**

2. Because the pronoun **se** can refer to many different people, it is often clarified with a prepositional phrase.

> **El asistente se la pasó a él (a ella, a usted, a ellos, a ellas, a ustedes).**

> **¿Te acuerdas?**
>
> When there are two object pronouns in the same sentence, the indirect object always precedes the direct object.
>
> **Él me lo dio.**
> **Yo te lo explicaría.**

Estructura

¿Cómo lo digo?

23 Historieta Durante el vuelo
Contesten según el modelo.

> **¿Quién le dio la revista al pasajero?** →
> **El asistente se la dio.**

1. ¿Quién le dio la manta a la señora?
2. ¿Quién le pasó la bandeja a la señorita?
3. ¿Quién le ofreció los audífonos al pasajero?
4. ¿Quién les explicó las reglas de seguridad a los pasajeros?
5. ¿Quién les sirvió la comida a los pasajeros?
6. ¿Quién les anunció la hora de llegada a los viajeros?

Una aerolínea española, Madrid

24 Su abuelita se lo compró. Contesten según el modelo.

> —¿Quién le compró el regalito?
> —Su abuelita se lo compró.

1. ¿Quién le compró la bicicleta?
2. ¿Quién le compró el billete?
3. ¿Quién le compró las entradas?
4. ¿Quién le compró los periódicos?

Plaza de Armas, Cuzco, Perú

25 **A mí, no. A Carlos.** Sigan el modelo.

¿Ramona te daría el regalo?

A mí, no. Se lo daría a Carlos.

1. ¿Tu papá te regalaría las entradas?
2. ¿Te darían la computadora?
3. ¿Tus abuelos te enviarían el dinero?
4. ¿Los muchachos te darían los esquís?
5. ¿Maribel te compraría los periódicos?

26 **Historieta** **Tomás se los llevó.**
Sigan el modelo.

> **Tomás le llevó los vegetales a su mamá.** ⟶
> **Tomás se los llevó a ella.**

1. Tomás le llevó los vegetales a su mamá.
2. Tomás le pidió dinero a su mamá.
3. Su madre le dio el dinero a Tomás.
4. Tomás le dio las legumbres congeladas a su mamá.
5. Tomás le devolvió el cambio a su mamá.

El Corte Inglés, Sevilla

27 **Yo no se lo daría.** Trabaja con un(a) compañero(a). Él o ella te menciona algo que le daría a alguien. Tú le contestas que no se lo darías nunca. Usen el modelo como guía.

> —Yo le daría este disco a Elena.
> —Yo nunca se lo daría a ella.

Andas bien. ¡Adelante!

Conversación

En el avión

Adela No pude oír el anuncio. ¿Qué dijo el asistente de vuelo?

Víctor Que el vuelo sería de tres horas y que llegaríamos a La Paz a tiempo.

Adela ¡Qué bien! La comida está bastante buena, ¿no?

Víctor Sí. No sabía que nos servirían una comida. Es un vuelo bastante corto.

Adela ¿Qué piensas? ¿Habrá una película?

Víctor No. Me dijeron que no podrían presentar una película porque no habría tiempo.

¿Comprendes?

Contesten.

1. ¿Dónde están Adela y Víctor?
2. ¿Adónde van ellos?
3. ¿Qué dijo el asistente de vuelo?
4. ¿Cuánto tiempo dura el vuelo?
5. Según Adela, ¿cómo está la comida?
6. ¿Qué no sabía Víctor?
7. ¿Habrá una película?
8. ¿Por qué le dijeron a Víctor que no podrían presentar una película?

Vamos a hablar más

A ¿Te interesaría el trabajo o no? Trabaja con un(a) compañero(a). Describan el trabajo de los asistentes de vuelo. Después de describir el trabajo, den sus opiniones. ¿Les gustaría ser asistentes de vuelo o no? ¿Les interesaría el trabajo o no? ¿Por qué?

Lima, Perú

B ¡Qué problema! Estás en el aeropuerto de Jorge Chávez en Lima, Perú. Perdiste tu boleto para el vuelo de regreso a Estados Unidos. Explica tu problema al/a la agente (tu compañero[a]). Traten de resolver el problema.

C ¡Por favor! Trabaja con un(a) compañero(a). Uno(a) de ustedes será pasajero(a) y el/la otro(a) será el/la asistente de vuelo. Preparen una conversación basada en lo que ven en cada dibujo.

1.

2.

3.

4.

Lecturas culturales

El aeropuerto que se llama «El Alto»

El aeropuerto El Alto en La Paz, Bolivia, está en una llanura del altiplano andino. Es el aeropuerto comercial más alto del mundo. Está a 13.450 pies o 4.100 metros sobre el nivel del mar[1]. A estas alturas del altiplano hay menos oxígeno en el aire que al nivel del mar. Por esta razón cuando un viajero baja del avión en El Alto, puede tener dificultad en respirar[2]. En el aeropuerto hay botellas de oxígeno para los pasajeros que lo necesitan.

¿Te gustaría hacer un viaje a La Paz algún día? Te aseguro[3] que sería una experiencia maravillosa. Al aterrizar tendrías una vista magnífica de la ciudad de La Paz. La Paz, la capital del país, está a una altura 1.000 pies más abajo del aeropuerto. La ciudad parece estar en un cráter. Y encima de la ciudad el cielo es claro, limpio y muy azul—sobre todo en el invierno.

[1]nivel del mar *sea level*
[2]respirar *breathing*
[3]Te aseguro *I assure you*

Reading Strategy

Distinguishing between fact and opinion When writing, an author will sometimes include his or her opinions among facts. It is important to distinguish between facts and the author's opinions. You must watch for expressions that indicate when an author is expressing an opinion rather than a fact. Some of these expressions in Spanish are: **creo que, prefiero, pienso, en mi opinión.**

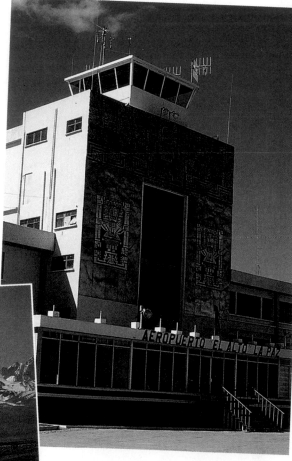

Aeropuerto El Alto

El altiplano, Bolivia

Al terminar tu viaje y salir de La Paz, el avión despegará de una de las pistas más largas del mundo. A esta altura el aire tiene muy poca densidad y no puede sostener el peso[4] del avión. Por consiguiente el avión tiene que alcanzar una gran velocidad antes de poder despegar. Y para poder alcanzar esta velocidad la pista tiene que ser muy larga.

[4]sostener el peso *support the weight*

La Paz, Bolivia

Use your **StudentWorks** *Plus*
CD for more practice.

¿Comprendes?

A Un aeropuerto interesante Contesten.

1. ¿Cómo se llama el aeropuerto que sirve a La Paz, Bolivia?
2. ¿Por qué puede tener un pasajero dificultad en respirar al bajar de un avión en La Paz?
3. ¿Qué tienen en el aeropuerto para su uso?
4. Al aterrizar en El Alto, ¿de qué tendrías una vista magnífica?
5. ¿Cómo es la pista del aeropuerto El Alto?
6. ¿Por qué es tan larga?

B ¿Sí o no? Digan que sí o que no.

1. El aeropuerto El Alto está en la Sierra Nevada.
2. El aeropuerto de La Paz es el aeropuerto comercial más alto del mundo.
3. A esta altura el aire contiene más oxígeno que al nivel del mar.
4. La ciudad de La Paz está a una altura aún más alta que el aeropuerto.
5. En el verano el cielo sobre La Paz es claro, limpio y muy azul.
6. A esta altura el aire no puede sostener el peso del avión si no alcanza una gran velocidad antes de despegar.

Indios quechua

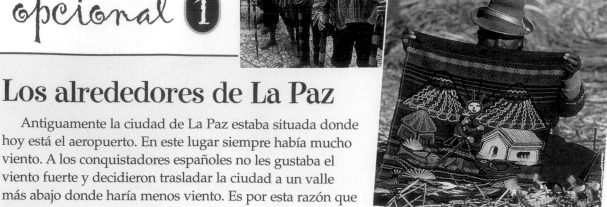

India aymara

Lectura opcional 1

Los alrededores de La Paz

Antiguamente la ciudad de La Paz estaba situada donde hoy está el aeropuerto. En este lugar siempre había mucho viento. A los conquistadores españoles no les gustaba el viento fuerte y decidieron trasladar la ciudad a un valle más abajo donde haría menos viento. Es por esta razón que el aeropuerto está a una altura más elevada que la ciudad. Para ir del aeropuerto a la ciudad el viajero tiene que bajar unos 1.000 pies.

En la carretera que enlaza la ciudad con el aeropuerto se ven muchos anuncios para aerodeslizadores. Estos aerodeslizadores o hidrofoils cruzan el lago Titicaca. El lago Titicaca está entre Bolivia y Perú. Igual que el aeropuerto El Alto es el aeropuerto comercial más alto del mundo, el lago Titicaca es el lago navegable más alto del mundo. Cruzar el lago Titicaca es una experiencia extraordinaria. Al cruzar el lago verías los pueblos de los indios aymara y quechua. Verías también muchas alpacas, llamas, vicuñas y chinchillas. ¿Te interesan los animales y la naturaleza? ¿Sí? Pues, te encantaría un viaje por esta región interesante de la cordillera andina.

El lago Titicaca

Cuzco, Perú

¿Comprendes?

A **Los alrededores de La Paz** Contesten.
1. ¿Qué se ve en la carretera que enlaza la ciudad de La Paz con el aeropuerto?
2. ¿Por qué hay muchos aerodeslizadores?
3. ¿Dónde está el lago Titicaca?
4. ¿Cuál es una característica interesante del lago Titicaca?
5. ¿Quiénes viven a orillas del lago?
6. ¿Cuáles son algunos animales de esta región andina?

B **Análisis** Expliquen.
Expliquen cómo y por qué el aeropuerto está a una altura más elevada que la ciudad de La Paz.

Lectura opcional ②

Emilio Carranza enfrente de su avión Excelsior

Un héroe de la aviación latinoamericana

En 1928 Charles Lindbergh, «El Águila[1] Solitaria», voló de Wáshington a México D.F. en el mismo avión con el que cruzó el Atlántico. Los mexicanos querían responder a tan fino gesto. El 11 de junio de 1928 Emilio Carranza, de 22 años de edad, capitán de las Fuerzas Aéreas Mexicanas y sobrino del ex-presidente Venustiano Carranza, salió de México en su avión Excelsior. Llegó a Wáshington como héroe.

El joven piloto pasó un mes en Estados Unidos. A las 7:05 de la noche del 12 de julio de 1928 despegó del aeropuerto Roosevelt de Nueva York para volver a México. Nunca llegó a México. Cerca de Chatsworth, Nueva Jersey, encontraron los restos del Excelsior y el cuerpo del valiente capitán.

Diez mil soldados y marinos norteamericanos marcharon con el cuerpo del héroe mexicano a la Pennsylvania Station donde un tren lo llevaría a México.

En las escuelas de México hicieron una colecta para levantar un monumento en el lugar de la tragedia. Allí está todavía. Y cada año, en el aniversario de su muerte, militares y representantes de las dos repúblicas dejan flores en honor de Emilio Carranza.

[1]Águila *Eagle*

Venustiano Carranza (a la izquierda)

¿Comprendes?

Dos aviadores Completen.
1. A Charles Lindbergh se le llamaba _____.
2. En 1928 Lindbergh voló de _____ a la Ciudad de México.
3. Emilio Carranza era _____ en las Fuerzas Aéreas Mexicanas.
4. Su tío fue _____.
5. Carranza voló en su avión de _____ a Wáshington.
6. El avión cayó del cielo cerca de _____ en el estado de Nueva Jersey.
7. Los soldados y marinos americanos llevaron su cuerpo a la _____.
8. Los alumnos mexicanos hicieron una colecta para levantar un _____ en Nueva Jersey.
9. Todos los años representantes norteamericanos y mexicanos ponen _____ en el monumento.

Conexiones

Las ciencias naturales

La geografía

Geography, the science, deals with the description, distribution, and interaction of the various physical, biological, and cultural features of the Earth's surface. However, for most people, geography is simply "physical geography" that studies the world's surface, the distribution and description of its land and water areas. The climate and the physical features of a country or region obviously have a great influence on the economy and even on the culture of a people.

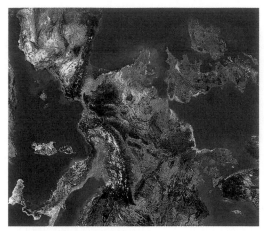

La península ibérica

The geography of Spain has affected its people enormously. The Pyrenees, separating Spain from the rest of Europe—the French have said that "Africa begins at the Pyrenees"—have often insulated Spain from European influence. Spain was a maritime nation in part because of its unique situation as a peninsula with coasts on the Atlantic and the Mediterranean. As you read, you will find out some things you probably did not know about Spain's geography.

La geografía de España

España, con Portugal, forman la península ibérica. La meseta central cubre más de la mitad del país con una altura media de 600 a 800 metros. Una serie de sierras cruza el país de este a oeste. En el extremo norte están los Pirineos, en el centro, no lejos de Madrid, la Sierra de Guadarrama, y continuando hacia el sur, la Sierra Morena y la Sierra Nevada.

Andalucía, España

De todos los países de Europa, sólo Suiza es más montañosa que España. Aunque mucha gente no lo cree, hay importantes estaciones de esquí en la Sierra Nevada y la Sierra de Guadarrama.

La península ibérica se divide en dos, la Iberia seca[1] y la Iberia húmeda. La Iberia húmeda es la región de los Pirineos, el noroeste de España y casi todo Portugal. La mayor parte de España está en la Iberia seca. Por eso, en el verano, si vuelas sobre España, verás un paisaje mayormente árido y pardo[2]. Los ríos, en el verano, llevan poca agua. Los ríos importantes que desembocan[3] en el Atlántico son el Duero, el Tajo, el Guadiana y el Guadalquivir. El río más importante que desemboca en el Mediterráneo es el Ebro. El agua tiene una importancia enorme. Sin agua, no se podría cultivar nada. Y España, hasta años recientes, era un país agrícola, y la agricultura sigue siendo un importante factor económico.

[1]seca *dry*
[2]pardo *brown*
[3]desembocan *empty into*

Sierra Nevada, España

Toledo, España

¿Comprendes?

A Un poco de geografía Completen según la lectura.
1. Los países que constituyen la península ibérica son ____ y ____.
2. Las montañas que están entre Francia y España son los ____.
3. Las sierras importantes van de este a ____.
4. La sierra más cerca de Madrid es la ____.
5. Portugal está en la Iberia húmeda, y la mayor parte de España está en la Iberia ____.
6. Muchos ríos en España desembocan en el ____.
7. Pero el Ebro desemboca en el ____.

B ¿Lo saben? Contesten.
1. Nombra tres ríos importantes de España.
2. Nombra dos sierras donde hay estaciones de esquí.
3. Di lo que uno vería desde un avión volando sobre la meseta central en verano.

Use what you have learned

1 **Yo conozco la América Latina.**

✔ *Describe a Latin American country you would like to visit*

Tú y tu compañero(a) ya saben mucho sobre varios países hispanos. Cada uno(a) de ustedes va a seleccionar el país que te gustaría visitar. Dile a tu compañero(a) por qué te gustaría viajar a ese país. Dile también todo lo que harías allí. Luego cambien de rol.

Patagonia, Argentina

2 **Un viaje estupendo**

✔ *Talk about air travel*

Habla con algunos compañeros sobre un viaje que hiciste en avión. Diles adonde ibas y descríbales todo lo que pasó en el aeropuerto de salida, en el aeropuerto de llegada y a bordo del avión.

3 **¡Un millón de dólares! ¡Increíble!**

✔ *Tell what you would do with a million dollars*

Tú y tu compañero(a) acaban de recibir un millón de dólares. Cada uno(a) de ustedes va a hacer una lista de las cosas que harían con el dinero. Comparen sus listas. Luego decidan quién haría las cosas más interesantes.

ESCRIBIR

4 Un vuelo excelente o terrible

✔ *Write about an airline trip*

Tú acabas de volver de un viaje a Costa Rica. Tu vuelo de regreso fue tan excelente (o terrible) que decides escribir una carta a la línea aérea. Describe el vuelo y diles lo que piensas de la tripulación y los servicios que ofrecen. Da ejemplos de lo que pasó (ocurrió) durante el vuelo.

●Visite San José con conexiones a Guatemala.

Salidas los jueves y lunes 8:20 a.m.

Tels. 724-3330/3444. Consulte a su agente de viajes

Desde $289.00 a San José y $299.00 a Panamá*

*ciertas restricciones aplican

Infórmese sobre nuestro exclusivo servicio de carga a través del

Tel. 723-3160

Con el estilo de... **Lacsa**

Líneas Aéreas de Costa Rica/The Airline of Costa Rica

¡NOS ENCANTA LA GENTE!

Writing Strategy

Identifying sources for a research paper To write a research paper, you must plan, set goals, and gather information. When you find a source, skim it to see whether it has any useful information. If it does, record the publication information on an index card so you can find the source easily when you begin your research. Be sure to use all resources available to you—both print and nonprint. Your school library will be an excellent place to begin looking for sources for your research paper.

Agua Azul, México

ESCRIBIR

5 La geografía del estado de...

You have been asked to write a brief description of the geography of your state for a Spanish-speaking audience. Your school librarian will help you select the most appropriate print resources—encyclopedias, almanacs, and, of course, geography books. The Internet will be an excellent nonprint resource. Log in and go to your state's Web sites. Once you have assembled your resources, scan them for the essential information you will need. Jot down the information you will need for your report. Remember to include references. Prepare a draft of your report in Spanish and ask your Spanish teacher to review it for you. After you have seen your teacher's recommendations, prepare your final version.

Vocabulario

1 Identifiquen.

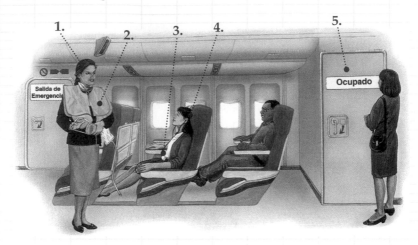

To review **Palabras 1**, turn to pages 192–193.

2 Identifiquen.

To review **Palabras 2**, turn to pages 196–197.

Estructura

3 **Escriban en el condicional.**

    11. Ellos llegan a tiempo.

    12. Yo sirvo la comida.

    13. Vemos una película.

    14. Tú no lo sabes.

    15. ¿Lo pone (él) debajo de su asiento?

To review the conditional, turn to pages 200 and 203.

4 **Contesten con pronombres.**

    16. ¿Quién les serviría la comida a los pasajeros? (los asistentes de vuelo)

    17. ¿Quién le daría el dinero al niño? (su padre)

    18. ¿Quién le compró los boletos? (yo)

To review the use of two object pronouns, turn to page 205.

Cultura

5 **Escriban dos frases sobre el aeropuerto en La Paz, Bolivia.**

    19–20. El aeropuerto en La Paz, Bolivia...

To review this cultural information, turn to pages 210–211.

El altiplano, Bolivia

¡Hablo como un pro!

Tell all you can about this illustration.

Vocabulario

Describing an airplane

el avión de reacción, el jet
la avioneta
el helicóptero
la cabina de mando,
  la cabina de vuelo
la ventanilla
el compartimiento sobre la cabeza,
  el compartimiento superior
la señal de no fumar
la salida de emergencia
el pasillo

el asiento
el respaldo del asiento
el cinturón de seguridad
el chaleco salvavidas
la máscara de oxígeno
el carrito
la mesita
la bandeja
el equipaje de mano
el lavabo, el aseo

Identifying some crew members

la tripulación
el/la comandante, el/la piloto

el/la copiloto
el/la asistente de vuelo

Describing a flight and on-board services

el vuelo
el anuncio
el/la pasajero(a)
el aterrizaje
el despegue
la escala
la altura
la turbulencia
volar
sobrevolar
despegar

aterrizar
anunciar
pasar por la cabina
distribuir audífonos
  (auriculares)
servir bebidas
servir una comida
abrochar
caber
a tiempo
con una demora

How well do you know your vocabulary?

- Choose your words to describe a trip by plane.
- Write a brief description of a trip by plane for someone who is traveling for the first time.

Describing some things at an airport

la pista
la terminal de pasajeros

la torre de control

Talking about geography

la geografía
la altura, la altitud
el pico
la montaña
la cordillera
el altiplano

la meseta
la llanura
el valle
el río
el lago

VIDEOTUR

Episodio 7

In this video episode, you will watch Alberto's friends "help" him get over his fear of flying. See page 486 for more information. As you watch, look for gestures the speakers use to help convey their message.

Repaso

Conversación

En el aeropuerto

Diego ¿De cuántas horas será el vuelo?

Susana Llegaremos a Caracas a las diez. Es un vuelo de cuatro horas.

Diego No sé lo que está pasando. Me parece que no saldremos a tiempo.

Susana Entonces podré hacer un crucigrama más.

Diego A ti te gusta mucho pasar el tiempo llenando tus crucigramas.

Susana ¿Me darías mi maletín?

Diego Te lo doy con mucho placer. ¿Qué quieres? ¿Tus crucigramas?

Susana No. Quiero ver si la confirmación para el hotel está en el maletín.

Diego Yo la tenía pero te la di en el taxi.

Susana Sí, sí. La tengo. Aquí está.

Diego A propósito, ¿cuántas noches vamos a estar en el Hotel Tamanaco?

Susana Cuatro. Es bastante caro el cuarto, ¿sabes?

¿Comprendes?

Antes del vuelo Contesten.

1. ¿Dónde están Diego y Susana?
2. ¿A qué hora llegarán a Caracas?
3. ¿De cuántas horas será el vuelo?
4. ¿Parece que saldrá a tiempo?
5. Si tiene más tiempo, ¿qué podrá hacer Susana?
6. ¿Por qué quería Susana su maletín?
7. ¿Dónde le dio la confirmación Diego?
8. ¿Cuántas noches estarán en el Hotel Tamanaco?

Caracas, Venezuela

Estructura

El futuro y el condicional

1. Review the following forms of the future and conditional of regular verbs.

	FUTURE					
MIRAR	miraré	mirarás	mirará	miraremos	*mirareis*	mirarán
COMER	comeré	comerás	comerá	comeremos	*comereis*	comerán
VIVIR	viviré	vivirás	vivirá	viviremos	*vivireis*	vivirán

	CONDITIONAL					
MIRAR	miraría	mirarías	miraría	miraríamos	*miraríais*	mirarían
COMER	comería	comerías	comería	comeríamos	*comeríais*	comerían
VIVIR	viviría	vivirías	viviría	viviríamos	*viviríais*	vivirían

2. Review the stems for irregular verbs in the future and conditional. The endings for irregular verbs are the same as those for the regular verbs.

INFINITIVE	STEM	FUTURE	CONDITIONAL
TENER	tendr-	tendré	tendría
SALIR	saldr-	saldré	saldría
VENIR	vendr-	vendré	vendría
PONER	pondr-	pondré	pondría
SABER	sabr-	sabré	sabría
PODER	podr-	podré	podría
DECIR	dir-	diré	diría
HACER	har-	haré	haría
QUERER	querr-	querré	querría

Ciudad de México

1 **Historieta** **A México** Contesten.

1. ¿Irá Catalina a México?
2. ¿La acompañarás?
3. ¿Tomarán ustedes el avión?
4. ¿Leerás durante el vuelo o llenarás un crucigrama?
5. ¿Buscarán ustedes un taxi para ir al hotel?

2 Pasatiempos Sigan el modelo.

leer una novela o una revista ⟶
**Nosotros leeríamos una novela
pero él leería una revista.**

1. jugar ajedrez o dominó
2. ir al zoológico o al parque de atracciones
3. comer en casa o en un restaurante
4. coleccionar sellos o monedas antiguas
5. mirar al mimo o al payaso

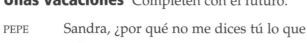

Miraflores, Perú

3 Unas vacaciones Completen con el futuro.

PEPE   Sandra, ¿por qué no me dices tú lo que
    __1__ (hacer) durante tus vacaciones?

SANDRA   No te __2__ (poder) decir nada hasta la semana que viene.

PEPE   ¿No __3__ (saber) hasta entonces?

SANDRA   No, porque yo __4__ (tener) que hablar con Maripaz. Yo sé que
    ella __5__ (querer) hacer algo y yo lo __6__ (hacer) con ella.

PEPE   ¿__7__ (Hacer) ustedes un viaje?

4 Uno sí y el otro no Completen con el condicional.

1. Él sabría el número del vuelo pero su hermano no lo ____.
2. Yo te lo diría pero ellos nunca te lo ____.
3. Nosotros lo haríamos pero ellos no lo ____.
4. Yo podría ir pero tú no ____.
5. Ustedes lo pondrían en orden pero él no lo ____.
6. Yo tendría que volver pero tú no ____.

Los complementos

1. When both a direct and an indirect object pronoun are used in the
same sentence, the indirect object pronoun always precedes the
direct object pronoun.

> **El agente me devolvió el billete.**
> **El agente me lo devolvió.**

2. The indirect object pronouns **le** and **les** change to **se** when used
with the direct object pronouns **lo, la, los,** or **las.** Because **se** can
mean **a él, a ella, a usted, a ellos, a ellas,** or **a ustedes,** the
prepositional phrase is often added for clarity.

> **¿A quién le diste las llaves del cuarto?**
> **Se las di a Teresa.**

5 **A bordo del avión** Contesten según el modelo.

¿Quién te sirvió la comida? ⟶
El asistente de vuelo me la sirvió.

1. ¿Quién te sirvió los refrescos?
2. ¿Quién te dio los audífonos?
3. ¿Quién te buscó la manta?

4. ¿Quién te explicó las reglas de seguridad?
5. ¿Quién te mostró el chaleco salvavidas?

6 **En el hotel** Contesten según el modelo.

¿Quién le dio la tarjeta al cliente? (la recepcionista) ⟶
La recepcionista se la dio.

1. ¿Quién le dio la llave al cliente? (el recepcionista)
2. ¿Quién le abrió la puerta? (el mozo)
3. ¿Quién le subió las maletas? (el mozo)
4. ¿Quién le limpió el cuarto? (la camarera)
5. ¿Quién le cambió las toallas? (la camarera)

Hotel Oro Verde,
Manta, Ecuador

7 **En el hotel** Trabaja con un(a) compañero(a). Están en la recepción de un hotel. Uno(a) de ustedes será el/la recepcionista y el/la otro(a) será el/la cliente. Discutan el precio, el número de noches, el cuarto, etc.

8 **Un vuelo** Trabaja con un(a) compañero(a) de clase. Dentro de poco ustedes van a hacer un viaje juntos. Van a ir en avión. Discutan todo lo que tienen que hacer y todo lo que pasará o sucederá en el aeropuerto y durante el vuelo.

Literary Companion

You may wish to read the adaptation of *La muralla* by Nicolás Guillén, on pages 464–467. The activities for this reading will help you continue to practice your reading comprehension skills.

El renacimiento de una identidad indígena

En 1492, los taínos eran uno de los grupos indígenas más numerosos y tenían la cultura más avanzada de las Antillas Mayores. Cincuenta años después casi no quedaban personas de origen taíno; murieron por las enfermedades que trajeron los españoles a América y por el maltrato[1].

Monolitos y petroglifos taínos en Utuado, Puerto Rico.

Pero la cultura taína fue, y todavía es, un tema importante para los profesores y académicos de las universidades. Los estudios recientes de ADN[2] confirman que hay un alto nivel de material genético taíno en los puertorriqueños. Hoy día existen descendientes directos de los taínos en el Caribe. Por ejemplo, los habitantes de la tribu taína Jatibonicu dicen: "Somos el pueblo original de la isla de Borikén (Puerto Rico), los verdaderos herederos[3] de la cultura taína". Los Jatibonicu tienen un sitio en la Internet. "Tau Ah Taiguey Guaitiao" (¡Hola y buenos días, amigos!).

[1] maltrato: *mistreatment* [2] ADN: *DNA* [3] herederos: *heirs*

Fortaleza San Felipe en Puerto Plata, República Dominicana.

Ciudades coloniales, fortalezas y piratas

La UNESCO declaró a las ciudades de Santo Domingo, La Habana y San Juan Patrimonio Cultural de la Humanidad. Los españoles construyeron estas bellas ciudades a principios del siglo XVI. Aunque cada una tiene su propia personalidad, estas tres joyas caribeñas también tienen muchas cosas en común. La zona histórica de estas ciudades tiene monumentales morros o fortalezas[1] militares, sus iglesias, los edificios de gobierno y las plazas públicas. Santo Domingo es la ciudad colonial más antigua del continente y es también la más "intelectual" de las tres porque ahí se estableció la primera universidad de las Américas.

España construyó esas fortalezas alrededor de las ciudades para proteger los territorios coloniales de sus rivales imperiales y de los piratas. El legendario pirata Francis Drake atacó San Juan varias veces, pero nunca pudo entrar a la ciudad. Roberto Cofresí era menos conocido pero dio muchos dolores de cabeza a los españoles. Era un "Robin Hood" caribeño y como no estaba de acuerdo con el sistema de gobierno español, atacaba los barcos y distribuía el botín[2] entre sus amigos y los pobres de Puerto Rico. En 1825, el capitán norteamericano John Sloat lo capturó.

Francis Drake

[1] morros o fortalezas: *fortresses*
[2] botín: *booty*

Un coleccionista de historia africana

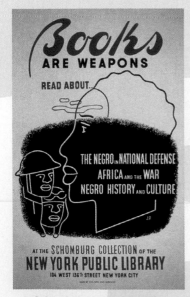

A. Schomburg, puertorriqueño

En Nueva York está la "Colección Schomburg", una de las más completas del mundo. Tiene libros, objetos, artefactos y muchas piezas de arte de origen africano. Y... ¿quién coleccionó todo esto? Un puertorriqueño. Arturo Alfonso Schomburg nació en 1874. Cuando era un niño y después un joven, en su escuela no había libros ni clases sobre la historia de los descendientes de africanos. Así empezó su gran pasión por coleccionar información sobre sus antepasados[1] para combatir el racismo. Su colección mostró al mundo las extraordinarias contribuciones de estas personas a la historia.

[1] antepasados: *ancestors*

¿Restaurante o monumento histórico?

Muy cerca de la Plaza de la Catedral en La Habana Vieja está la "La Bodeguita del Medio". Este restaurante cubano clásico abrió sus puertas después de la Segunda Guerra Mundial[1]. Era una gran atracción para los bohemios, artistas, políticos y escritores. Ellos iban a comer y a conversar con sus amigos para "mejorar" el mundo. Muchas personas famosas tales como Gabriel García Márquez y Ernest Hemingway escribieron sus nombres en las paredes. Hoy día, La Bodeguita del Medio es igualmente popular; miles de turistas visitan el restaurante durante todo el año, porque ahí la comida es muy sabrosa y el ambiente[2]... ¡incomparable!

[1] Segunda Guerra Mundial: *Second World War*

[2] ambiente: *atmosphere*

Calendario de fiestas

Carnaval dominicano

1° de mayo: Día Internacional del Trabajo *(Cuba)*

Esta celebración conmemora a los trabajadores del mundo. Mucha gente va con banderas[1] a la Plaza de la Revolución en La Habana. Allí escuchan los discursos[2] de sus líderes y de otros líderes internacionales.

27 de febrero: Carnaval y Día de la Independencia *(República Dominicana)*

Los dominicanos celebran la Independencia de la dominación del gobierno de Haití (1822–1824) y el fin del carnaval el mismo día. El carnaval es la fiesta más popular en ese país. La gente usa máscaras, se viste con disfraces[3], baila y canta en las calles de las ciudades.

3ra semana de julio, Fiesta de Santiago Apóstol *(Loíza, Puerto Rico)*

En Loíza, Puerto Rico, se celebra la fiesta patronal con una gran parada. La gente se viste con ropa tradicional, baila y canta y hace una parodia de las guerras entre moros y cristianos en España.

[1] banderas: *flags* [2] discursos: *speeches* [3] disfraces: *costumes*

micocina
Un platillo verdaderamente caribeño

Los españoles trajeron a América el arroz y los frijoles. Los caribeños adoptaron rápidamente esta comida y hoy es el plato tradicional de estas tres islas. Este delicioso platillo se llama "arroz moro" en la República Dominicana, "congrí" en Cuba y "arroz con habichuelas" en Puerto Rico. *(El congrí y el arroz moro se preparan con frijoles negros.)*

Arroz con habichuelas[1] *(Puerto Rico)*

Ingredientes
(Para el arroz)
- 2 tazas de arroz blanco
- 3 tazas de agua
- 1 cucharada de aceite
- sal al gusto

(Para las habichuelas)
- 2 cucharaditas de aceite de oliva
- 2 cucharadas de jamón de cocinar, en cubos
- 1 lata de habichuelas coloradas
- 1 lata de salsa de tomate
- 1 paquete de sazón[2]
- 2 cucharadas de sofrito[3]
- 7 aceitunas rellenas con pimiento
- 1 cucharadita de alcaparrado[4]
- 2 papas medianas, en cubos
- 1 taza de agua

Preparación
Hervir las 3 tazas de agua en una olla. Agregar el arroz blanco, el aceite y la sal. Tapar la olla y reducir la temperatura. Cocinar durante 20 minutos. En una sartén con aceite, freír el jamón y el sofrito. Agregar la salsa de tomate, la sazón, las aceitunas y el alcaparrado. Revolver durante 2 minutos. Agregar las habichuelas, las papas, el agua y revolver. Calentar bien la mezcla, tapar la sartén, reducir la temperatura y cocinar durante 20 minutos.

[1] habichuelas: *beans in the Caribbean*

[2] sazón: *seasoning*

[3] sofrito: *mix of lightly fried onions, garlic, and herbs*

[4] alcaparrado: *capers with diced red peppers*

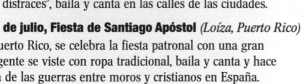

227

¡Acción!

EN EL SET

El Grammy para *Orishas*

La Habana, capital caribeña del Rap

¿Rap en Cuba? ¡Así es! Desde 1995 se celebra en el Anfiteatro Alamar de La Habana un festival de Rap. Ahí participan muchos grupos internacionales. El rap, un estilo musical típico de Nueva York, es popular en Cuba. "Instinto" es el primer grupo de mujeres cubanas "raperas". Pero los más famosos son cuatro cubanos del grupo "Orishas". Ellos viven en Francia y en 2003 recibieron el Grammy por sus composiciones, donde combinan el hip-hop y los ritmos cubanos "para escuchar el 'sonido' de la isla en su música".

En la tele y la radio

Charytín Goyco y el "escándalo[1] del mediodía"

Goyco

Charytín es la presentadora[2] de un programa muy popular: "El escándalo del mediodía". Ella es una persona muy divertida y además tiene otros talentos: es bailarina y cantante. Nació en la República Dominicana y vivió mucho tiempo en Puerto Rico, donde también es famosa. Charytín y su familia viven en Miami desde 1989.

[1] escándalo: *scandal, shock*
[2] presentadora: *host of a TV show*

del Toro

Benicio del Toro es puertorriqueño y a los 13 años llegó a Estados Unidos; estudió actuación[1] en California y después en The Stella Adler Conservatory of Acting en Nueva York. Le gustan los deportes, le gusta leer y también le encanta comer. Pero lo que más le gusta es actuar y en 2001 recibió un Óscar por su rol en *Traffic*. Él va a Puerto Rico cuando puede y si tiene tiempo, participa en campañas de ayuda social.

Rolando

Gloria Rolando es una cineasta[2] cubana de origen africano. Trabajar en el cine no es fácil en Cuba. "Muchas veces empiezo un proyecto sin dinero para completarlo. Pero siempre termino mis películas," dice Gloria. El tema de sus películas es la "diáspora" de los africanos y de los cubanos. Gloria escribió y trabajó como directora en el documental *Los ojos del arco iris*.

Sánchez

Roselyn Sánchez es bailarina, actriz, productora y ahora ¡cantante! "Para mí cantar era un sueño[3]", dice Sánchez. "Borinqueña", su primer CD, es una combinación de ritmos caribeños tradicionales, gospel y elementos del hip-hop y rap. Ella nació en Puerto Rico y sus primeros roles en inglés fueron en la telenovela[4] *As the World Turns* y en la serie de televisión *Fame L.A.* "*Rush Hour II*, mi primera película, me cambió la vida", dice ella con una gran sonrisa.

García

Andy García nació en Cuba, pero vivió en Miami desde los 5 años. Estudió y trabajó como actor en Florida y después en Los Angeles, donde hizo varias series de televisión. Andy es famoso por su rol en *Los Intocables, El Padrino, Parte III* y muchas otras. Le encanta la música de su país y por eso hizo *Cachao… como su ritmo no hay dos*, un film documental[5] sobre el músico cubano Israel "Cachao" López. Andy recibió excelentes críticas por la dirección de este film.

[1] actuación: *acting (theater)*
[2] cineasta: *filmmaker*
[3] sueño: *dream*
[4] telenovela: *soap opera*
[5] documental: *documentary*

República Dominicana

Una isla, un regalo

En su 2º viaje, Cristóbal Colón regaló una isla a un marinero savonés[1] porque éste la vio por primera vez. El nombre original fue Isla Savona pero con el tiempo los dominicanos cambiaron su nombre por **Isla Saona**. Ahora es un Parque Nacional muy atractivo para los turistas por sus playas solitarias, sus aguas cristalinas y por las 13 horas de sol al día. Aquí vive poca gente, pero hay 112 especies de aves[2], muchos otros animales y una vegetación exuberante. Por su clima, su belleza y su paz[3], Isla Saona también hoy es un regalo para todos.

[1] marinero savonés:
seaman from Savona, an Italian city

[2] aves: *birds*

[3] paz: *peace*

SUCESOS

■ **El béisbol, un fenómeno caribeño** El lucrativo deporte del bate y la pelota obtiene del Caribe sus más brillantes estrellas[1]. El béisbol es una antigua tradición en las Antillas Mayores. Hoy muchos peloteros[2] caribeños juegan en las Grandes Ligas de béisbol. Ahora en el béisbol (deporte que antes era fundamentalmente anglosajón), los nombres de Roberto Clemente, Juan Marichal, Bernie Williams y Pedro Martínez forman parte de su historia.

[1] estrellas: *stars*
[2] peloteros: *baseball players*

Bernie Williams

■ **El museo de Ernest Hemingway en La Habana** "Finca La Vigía", al este de La Habana, fue la casa de este famoso escritor. Él vivió 20 años en Cuba (1940–1960). A su casa iba mucha gente famosa y ahí él escribió *El viejo y el mar*. Durante mucho tiempo no era posible visitarla, pero en el 2002 las autoridades cubanas la declararon un museo.

Finca La Vigía

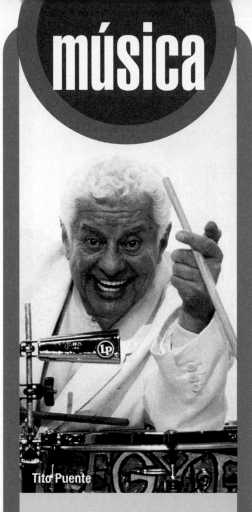

Tito Puente

El jazz latino

Fernando Trueba, un director de cine español, realizó el film "Calle 54" en el 2000. La importante presencia de los músicos caribeños en el Jazz Latino es el tema de este documental "musical". El director muestra a músicos como el percusionista puertorriqueño Tito Puente y a los virtuosos del piano: el dominicano Michele Camilo y el cubano Chucho Valdés. Este film está en muchas tiendas donde alquilan[1] videocintas.

[1] alquilan: *they rent*

Chucho Valdés

Capítulo 8

Emergencias médicas

Objetivos

In this chapter you will learn to:

❖ talk about accidents and medical problems

❖ talk about hospital stays

❖ discuss things that you and others have done recently

❖ compare things with like characteristics

❖ talk about health care in various areas of the Spanish-speaking world

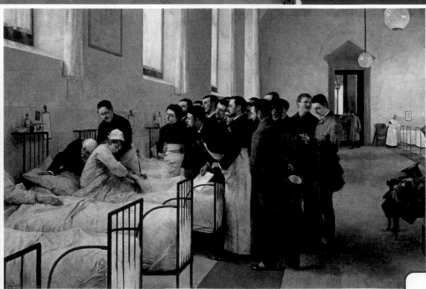

Manuel Jiménez Prieto *Hospital Visit*

Spanish Online

To interact with your online edition of *¡Buen viaje!* go to: glencoe.com.

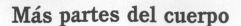

Más partes del cuerpo

Un accidente

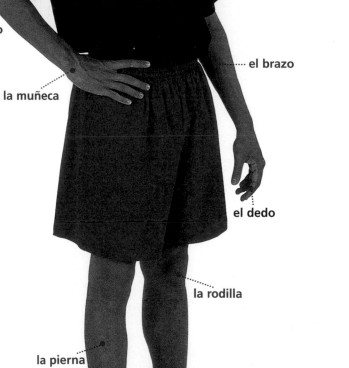

el cuello

el hombro

el pecho

el codo

la muñeca

el brazo

el dedo

la rodilla

la pierna

el tobillo

el pie

hacerse daño, lastimarse

Antonio ha tenido un accidente.
Se cayó de su bicicleta y se hizo daño (se lastimó).
Se rompió el dedo.
Parece que no se ha roto la pierna.

Anita se ha torcido el tobillo.
Tiene el tobillo muy hinchado.
Pero no tiene fractura.

Tomás tiene una herida.
Se ha cortado el dedo.

Una picadura

Una abeja le ha picado a Tere.
Le ha picado en el hombro.
Ella no se siente bien. Le duele mucho.

La cara

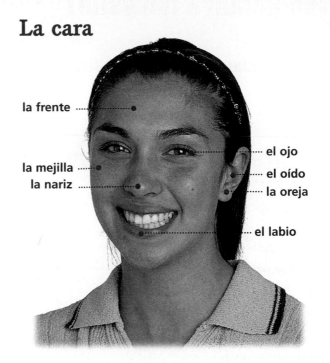

la frente

el ojo
la mejilla
el oído
la nariz
la oreja

el labio

¡A la sala de emergencia!

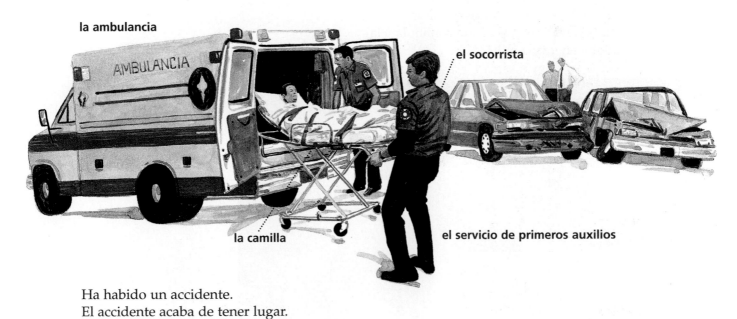

la ambulancia

AMBULANCIA

el socorrista

la camilla

el servicio de primeros auxilios

Ha habido un accidente.
El accidente acaba de tener lugar.
Ha llegado el servicio de primeros auxilios.
Los socorristas han ayudado a la víctima.
La van a llevar al hospital en una ambulancia.

Vocabulario

¿Qué palabra necesito?

1 **Unas heridas** Contesten según los dibujos.

2. ¿Qué se ha torcido Pablo?

3. ¿Qué se ha cortado Elena?

4. ¿Qué se ha cortado Diana?

1. ¿Qué se ha roto Carlos?

2 **Historieta** Un accidente
Contesten con **sí**.

1. ¿Ha habido un accidente?
2. ¿Acaba de tener lugar el accidente?
3. ¿Se ha caído de su bicicleta un niño?
4. ¿Se ha lastimado?
5. ¿Parece que se ha roto la pierna?
6. ¿Ha llegado el servicio de primeros auxilios?
7. ¿Han ayudado los socorristas al niño?
8. ¿Lo van a llevar al hospital en la ambulancia?
9. ¿Lo ponen en una camilla?

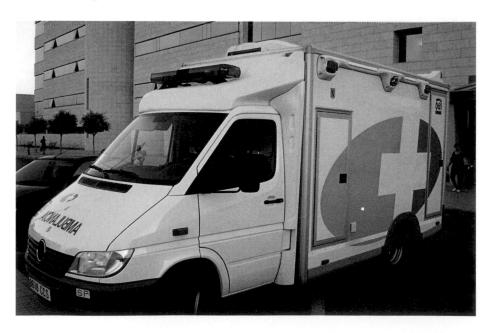

Madrid, España

3 **Historieta** **Una picadura** Contesten.

1. ¿Tiene Anita una picadura?
2. ¿Qué le ha picado?
3. ¿Dónde le ha picado?
4. ¿Le duele mucho la picadura?
5. ¿Tiene Anita alergia a las picaduras?

Granada, España

4 **Partes del cuerpo** Completen.

1. La niña se ha torcido el ____; así no puede andar bien.
2. ____, ____ y ____ son partes del brazo.
3. ____, ____ y ____ son partes de la pierna.
4. Tenemos cinco ____ en cada mano.
5. Vemos con los ____.
6. Y oímos con los ____.

Asturias, España

5 **Un accidente en el extranjero**

Tú y un(a) amigo(a) están viajando por España. Van en bicicleta. Tu amigo se ha caído de la bicicleta y tú crees que se ha roto el brazo. Llega un(a) socorrista (un compañero[a]). Explícale lo que ha pasado y contesta a todas sus preguntas.

6 **Juego** Trabaja con un(a) compañero(a) de clase. Dibujen un monstruo. Luego describan su monstruo a otros miembros de la clase.

En el hospital

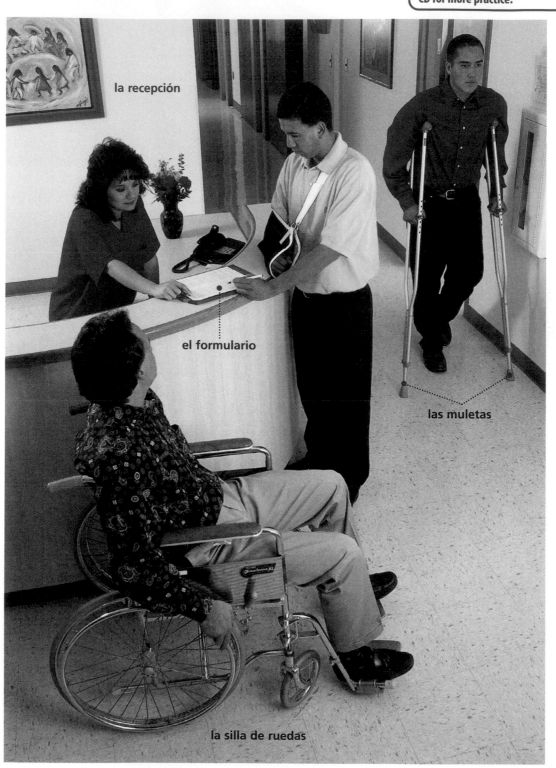

la recepción

el formulario

las muletas

la silla de ruedas

José ha llenado un formulario.
Lo ha llenado en la recepción.

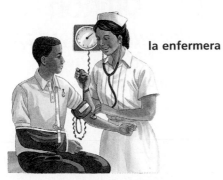

la enfermera

La enfermera le ha tomado
la tensión (presión) arterial.

Le ha tomado el pulso también.

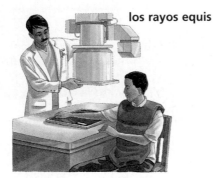

los rayos equis

El técnico le ha tomado una
radiografía.
El joven tiene una fractura.

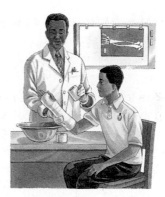

El cirujano ortopédico le ha
reducido el hueso.
Ha puesto el brazo en un yeso.

un vendaje

Paco tiene una herida.
La médica le ha cerrado la herida.
La ha cerrado con unos puntos.
Y le ha puesto un vendaje.

Los dos jóvenes están enfermos.
El uno está tan enfermo como
el otro.
José tiene tantos dolores como Paco.

¿Qué palabra necesito?

7 Historieta El pobre Joselito

Contesten con **sí**.

1. ¿Acaba de tener un accidente Joselito?
2. ¿Le duele mucho la pierna?
3. ¿Lo han puesto en una camilla los socorristas?
4. ¿Lo han llevado a la sala de emergencia del hospital municipal?
5. ¿Le ha tomado una radiografía un técnico?
6. ¿Se ha roto la pierna Joselito?
7. ¿Le ha reducido la fractura el cirujano ortopédico?
8. ¿Tendrá que andar con muletas Joselito?

8 Historieta Andrea va al hospital.

Contesten según se indica.

1. ¿Qué tiene que llenar Andrea cuando llega al hospital? (un formulario)
2. ¿Dónde lo llena? (en la recepción)
3. ¿Qué le toma un enfermero? (la tensión arterial y el pulso)
4. ¿Ha tenido Andrea un accidente? (no)
5. ¿Qué le duele mucho a Andrea? (el estómago)
6. ¿Qué le ha tomado un técnico? (una radiografía)
7. ¿De qué sufre Andrea? (un ataque de apendicitis)

OMRON

Por qué razón debería Ud. controlar su tensión arterial

Me siento bien

Informaciones imprescindibles sobre las causas y los riesgos de las enfermedades de la tensión arterial.
Incluye consejos para tomarse la tensión uno mismo.

Hospital Santrix, Caracas

*For more practice using words from **Palabras 1** and **2**, do Activity 8 on page H9 at the end of this book.*

9 El hospital Digan que sí o que no.

1. Al llegar al hospital, el enfermo o paciente tiene que llenar o completar un formulario.
2. La enfermera le ha tomado la tensión arterial al paciente en la cara.
3. La enfermera le ha tomado el pulso en la muñeca.
4. Los rayos equis son fotografías.
5. El joven ha tenido que andar con muletas porque se ha cortado el dedo.
6. El médico le ha puesto unos puntos porque se cortó la mejilla.
7. Han puesto al herido en una camilla porque lo tienen que llevar al hospital en la ambulancia.
8. Lo han puesto en una silla de ruedas porque no puede caminar.

10 Sinónimos Pareen.

1. la sala de emergencia
2. los rayos equis
3. la tensión arterial
4. los puntos
5. se lastimó

a. la presión arterial
b. la sala de urgencias
c. las suturas
d. se hizo daño
e. la radiografía

Spanish Online
For more information about Ponce and other cities in Puerto Rico, go to **Web Explore** on the Glencoe Spanish Web site at glencoe.com.

11 ¡Socorro! Tú estás en la Calle Sol en Ponce, Puerto Rico. Acaba de ocurrir un accidente de tráfico. No es muy grave, pero las víctimas necesitan ayuda. Desde un teléfono público, llama al 911. Explícale al/a la operador(a) (tu compañero[a]) lo que pasó y contesta a cualquier pregunta.

12 En el hospital Tú eres el/la recepcionista del hospital. Tu compañero(a) es el/la paciente. Tienes que hacerle una serie de preguntas, por ejemplo, su nombre y dirección, el problema médico que tiene, etc. Después cambien de rol.

Ponce, Puerto Rico

Estructura

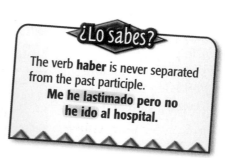

Use your StudentWorks Plus CD for more practice.

El presente perfecto
Talking about recent events

1. The present perfect tense in Spanish is formed by using the present tense of the verb **haber** and the past participle. The past participle of regular verbs is formed by adding **-ado** to the infinitive stem of **-ar** verbs and **-ido** to the infinitive stem of **-er** and **-ir** verbs.

LLAMAR	llamado	COMER	comido	SUFRIR	sufrido
CORTAR	cortado	TENER	tenido	SUBIR	subido

2. The present perfect is called a compound tense because it is made up of two verb forms. They are the present tense of the verb **haber** and the past participle.

INFINITIVE	llegar	comer	salir
yo	he llegado	he comido	he salido
tú	has llegado	has comido	has salido
él, ella, Ud.	ha llegado	ha comido	ha salido
nosotros(as)	hemos llegado	hemos comido	hemos salido
vosotros(as)	*habéis llegado*	*habéis comido*	*habéis salido*
ellos, ellas, Uds.	han llegado	han comido	han salido

3. The present perfect tense is used to describe an action completed very recently in the past. Some time expressions frequently used with the present perfect are:

ya	*already, yet*	**jamás**	*ever, never*
todavía no	*not yet*	**nunca**	*never*

—En tu vida, ¿has tenido un accidente?
—No, nunca he tenido un accidente.
—Todavía no has tenido un accidente. ¡Qué suerte!
 Y yo ya he tenido tres.

¿Lo sabes?

The verb **haber** is never separated from the past participle.
Me he lastimado pero no he ido al hospital.

¿Cómo lo digo?

13 **Historieta** **El accidente** Contesten.

1. ¿Ha tenido un accidente Diego?
2. ¿Se ha caído de la bicicleta?
3. ¿Se ha lastimado?
4. ¿Ha llegado la ambulancia?
5. ¿Lo han atendido los socorristas?
6. ¿Adónde lo han llevado?

Spanish **nline**

For practice identifying and treating medical emergencies, go to the Chapter 8 **WebQuest** on the Glencoe Spanish Web site at glencoe.com.

14 **Sí, ya la he llamado.** Contesten según el modelo.

¿Has llamado a Rita?

Sí, ya la he llamado.

1. ¿Has hablado con ella?
2. ¿Le has preguntado qué le pasó?
3. ¿Le has mandado unas flores?
4. ¿Has buscado sus libros?
5. ¿Los has llevado a su casa?

15 **Historieta** **En el hospital**
Completen con el presente perfecto.

Adela __1__ (llegar) al hospital. Ella __2__ (presentarse) en la recepción y __3__ (llenar) unos formularios. Una abeja le __4__ (picar) en el brazo. Los socorristas la __5__ (llevar) al hospital porque ella __6__ (tener) una reacción a la picadura. La médica la __7__ (examinar) y le __8__ (permitir) volver a casa.

Alergias

La alergia respiratora se produce cuando una persona reacciona al contacto con determinadas sustancias (alergenos), como el polvo, polen, alimentos, algunos medicamentos o la pelusa de animales. Estas reacciones pueden variar, pues es posible que afecten órganos importantes como ojos, nariz, pulmones y piel.

16 **Preguntas personales** Contesten.

1. ¿Has tenido un accidente alguna vez?
2. ¿Te han examinado los socorristas?
3. ¿Te han metido en una ambulancia?
4. ¿Te han llevado al hospital?
5. ¿Has tenido que pasar unos días en el hospital?

17 **Un accidente** Un amigo se ha lastimado y lo han llevado al hospital. Tú llamas por teléfono y hablas con el/la enfermero(a) (tu compañero[a]). Quieres saber lo que le ha pasado a tu amigo, si lo han examinado, etc. Después cambien de rol.

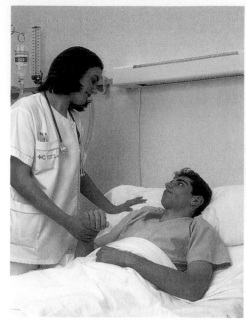

Hospital Costa del Sol, Marbella, España

Los participios irregulares
Talking about recent events

The following verbs have irregular past participles.

DECIR	**dicho**	VOLVER	**vuelto**
HACER	**hecho**	DEVOLVER	**devuelto**
VER	**visto**	MORIR	**muerto**
ESCRIBIR	**escrito**	ABRIR	**abierto**
PONER	**puesto**	CUBRIR	**cubierto**
ROMPER	**roto**		

¿Lo sabes?

Volver means *to return to a place* and **devolver** means *to return something.*

He vuelto a casa.
Le he devuelto sus libros.

¿Cómo lo digo?

18 **Ya lo han hecho.**
Contesten según el modelo.

¿Verlo? →
Pero ya lo han visto.

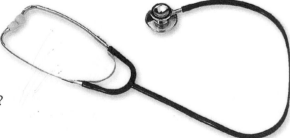

1. ¿Abrirlo?
2. ¿Ponerlo?
3. ¿Devolverlo?
4. ¿Escribirlo?
5. ¿Decirlo?
6. ¿Hacerlo?

 19 **Historieta** **Pobre Antonio** Contesten.

1. ¿Antonio se ha hecho daño?
2. ¿Se ha roto el brazo?
3. ¿Ha ido Antonio a la sala de emergencia?
4. ¿Lo ha visto un médico?
5. ¿Le han puesto un vendaje en el hospital?
6. ¿Ha dicho algo Antonio?
7. ¿Ha vuelto a casa Antonio?

 20 **He estado muy ocupado(a).** Siempre estás muy ocupado(a). Siempre tienes algo que hacer. Trabaja con un(a) compañero(a). Cada uno(a) de ustedes va a preparar una lista de las cosas que ya han hecho hoy. Luego comparen sus listas. Determinen cuáles son las actividades que ustedes dos han hecho. Y decidan quién en realidad ha estado más ocupado(a).

Barcelona, España

 21 **Algún día** Hay tantas cosas que nos gustaría hacer algún día que hasta ahora no hemos hecho. Trabaja con un(a) compañero(a). Hablen de las cosas que quieren hacer algún día pero que hasta ahora no han hecho nunca. Si es posible, expliquen por qué no las han hecho.

Comparación de igualdad
Comparing people and things

1. To compare equal quantities in English you use *as much . . . as* or *as many . . . as.*

> *He has as much money as I.*
> *He has as many problems as I.*

In Spanish you use **tanto… como.** Because **tanto** is an adjective it has to agree with the noun it modifies.

> **Elena tiene tanta energía como yo.**
> **Pero ella no tiene tantos accidentes como yo.**

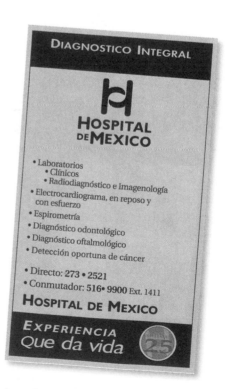

¿Lo sabes?

The subject pronoun always follows a comparison.
Él tiene tanto dinero como yo.
Y yo estudio tanto como tú.
Soy tan inteligente como tú.

2. To compare equal qualities in English you use *as . . . as.*

> *I am as smart as he is.*

In Spanish you use **tan… como** with either the adjective or adverb.

> **Él está tan enfermo como su amigo.**
> **Él se va a curar tan rápido como ella.**

¿Cómo lo digo?

22 **Dos hospitales** Contesten.

1. ¿Tiene el hospital en la ciudad tantas camas como el hospital en las afueras?
2. ¿Tiene el doctor López tanta experiencia como el doctor Salas?
3. ¿Tienen tantos pacientes aquí como en el hospital nuevo?
4. ¿Tiene el hospital nuevo tantas enfermeras como el otro?
5. ¿Tienen tantos técnicos aquí como en el otro?
6. ¿Pagan tanto dinero aquí como en el otro hospital?

DIAGNOSTICO INTEGRAL

HOSPITAL DE MEXICO

- Laboratorios
  - Clínicos
    - Radiodiagnóstico e Imagenología
- Electrocardiograma, en reposo y con esfuerzo
- Espirometría
- Diagnóstico odontológico
- Diagnóstico oftalmológico
- Detección oportuna de cáncer

- Directo: 273 • 2521
- Conmutador: 516• 9900 Ext. 1411

HOSPITAL DE MEXICO

EXPERIENCIA
Que da vida

23 **Historieta** **Los dos son buenos.**
Completen con **tanto… como** o **tan… como.**

1. El Hospital San José es *tan* bueno _____ el Hospital Municipal.
2. Pero el Hospital San José no es _____ grande _____ el Hospital Municipal.
3. Y el Hospital Municipal no tiene _____ enfermeros _____ el Hospital San José.
4. Pero el Hospital San José tiene _____ pacientes _____ el Municipal.
5. La sala de emergencia del San José es _____ moderna _____ la sala de emergencia del Municipal.
6. El Hospital San José está _____ cerca de nuestra casa _____ el Hospital Municipal.

URGENCIAS →

ALMACENES →

↑ CONSULTAS EXTERNAS

↑ ENTRADA PRINCIPAL

Hospital Costa del Sol, Marbella, España

24 **Son muy parecidas.** Trabaja con un(a) compañero(a). Piensen en algunas personas que ustedes conocen que, en su opinión, tienen mucho en común o que tienen las mismas características físicas. Comparen a estas personas.

LAS GEMELAS

Andas bien. ¡Adelante!

Una fractura

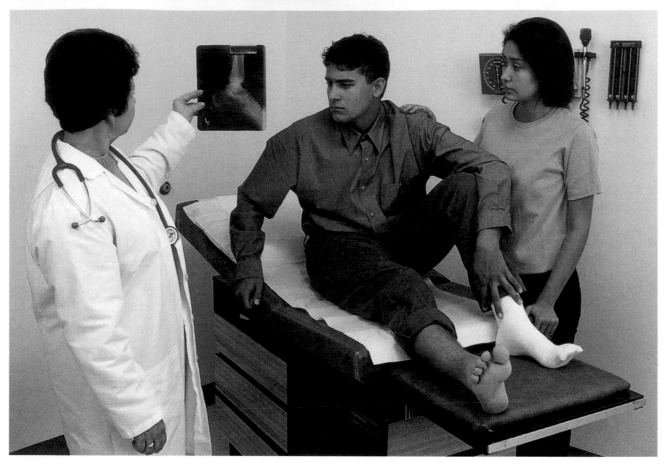

Mónica Pablo, ¿cómo te sientes? ¿Qué te ha pasado?

Pablo Pues, no sé. Me han tomado una radiografía. Pero todavía no me han dado los resultados.

Mónica Aquí viene la médica ahora.

Médica Pablo, tengo la radiografía. Indica que te has roto el tobillo.

Pablo ¿Me he roto el tobillo?

Médica Sí, pero no es una fractura grave. Te voy a poner el tobillo en un yeso y podrás salir del hospital. Voy a volver enseguida y reduciré el hueso.

Pablo ¿Dónde? ¿Aquí? ¿Ahora? Me va a doler mucho, ¿no?

Médica Pablo, no debes estar tan nervioso. ¿La enfermera te ha tomado la tensión arterial?

Pablo Mónica, ¿te quedarás conmigo?

¿Comprendes?

Contesten.

1. ¿Quién ha venido a visitar a Pablo?
2. ¿Qué le ha pasado a Pablo?
3. ¿Le han tomado una radiografía?
4. ¿Sabe Pablo los resultados?
5. ¿Qué le dice la médica a Pablo?
6. ¿Qué va a hacer la médica?
7. ¿Tiene que quedarse en el hospital Pablo?
8. ¿Está nervioso Pablo? ¿Por qué o por qué no?

Vamos a hablar más

A **Estoy nervioso(a).** Tu amigo(a) ha tenido un pequeño accidente. Tú estabas con él/ella cuando ocurrió. Han tenido que llevar a tu amigo(a) al hospital. Y tú tienes que llamar a sus padres para decirles lo que ha pasado. Sabes que los padres tendrán muchas preguntas. Llama a sus padres. Un(a) compañero(a) será el padre o la madre de tu amigo(a).

B **Un examen médico** Tú has recibido una beca *(scholarship)* para estudiar en Madrid. Antes de entrar en la universidad tienes que presentarte para un examen médico. Tu compañero(a) es el/la recepcionista y te va a hacer una serie de preguntas sobre tu salud. Después cambien de rol.

Universidad de Madrid

C **¿Qué te ha pasado?** Tú vas a ser el/la médico(a). Un(a) compañero(a) es el/la paciente. Él/Ella ha tenido un accidente. Hazle preguntas sobre su accidente: dónde, cuándo, cómo ha ocurrido. Pregúntale dónde le duele. Luego dale una diagnosis y explícale el tratamiento—es decir, lo que vas a hacer.

Lecturas culturales

Practicantes 🔄 🎧

Estefanía Reyes es practicante. Ella vive en un pueblo pequeño cerca de Puno en los Andes de Perú. Vamos a ver lo que ha hecho Estefanía esta mañana. Ha estado muy ocupada. Son las once de la mañana y ya ha visto a muchos pacientes.

Le ha tomado la tensión arterial a un señor mayor. Tiene la tensión bastante elevada y Estefanía le ha recomendado una dieta.

Una niña de tres años se ha cortado el pie. Su mamá estaba muy nerviosa. Pero Estefanía le ha puesto cinco puntos para cerrar la herida. Y le ha puesto una inyección contra el tétano.

Ha visto a un señor que tiene dolores abdominales muy fuertes. Le duele tanto el estómago que Estefanía cree que está sufriendo de un ataque de apendicitis. Puede ser algo muy serio. Estefanía lo ha mandado al hospital para ver a un médico.

Pero, ¿qué es Estefanía? Es una practicante. En los países hispanos siempre ha habido practicantes. Son profesionales en el campo de la medicina. El o la practicante es un(a) diplomado(a) en enfermería. Puede poner inyecciones y practicar curas médicas simples y rutinarias. En caso de heridas o enfermedades serias, el practicante manda al paciente a un médico.

En muchos pueblos pequeños de áreas remotas, el practicante es muy importante. A veces es el único profesional médico que tienen los habitantes.

Un pueblo andino, Perú

¿Comprendes?

A Un trabajo interesante Contesten.

1. ¿Qué es Estefanía Reyes?
2. ¿De dónde es?
3. ¿Qué es un(a) practicante?
4. ¿En qué es diplomado(a)?
5. ¿Cuándo manda al paciente a ver al médico el practicante?
6. ¿Por qué es muy importante el practicante en muchas áreas?

B Pacientes Expliquen.

Son las once de la mañana y Estefanía ya ha visto a muchos pacientes. Identifiquen a todos los pacientes que ella ha examinado y describan lo que ha hecho a cada uno.

C Palabras

Empleen las siguientes palabras en una oración.

1. el practicante
2. la tensión arterial
3. le ha puesto puntos
4. el tétano
5. un ataque de apendicitis

SERVICIO DE
A.T.S. / PRACTICANTE
A DOMICILIO

"TODO MADRID"

INYECCIONES
SONDAS
SUEROS
PRESIÓN ARTERIAL
CURAS QUIRÚRGICAS
(ÚLCERAS, HERIDAS, QUEMADURAS...)
SUTURAS
ETC.

Para comunicar su aviso llame al teléfono:
☎ 908 – 72 88 83

(Este teléfono móvil sustituye al anterior servicio de "busca" 450 28 12, abonado nº 3516)

Una zona rural en Bolivia

Lectura opcional 1

EL HOSPITAL BUENA VISTA

La mañana del jueves de esta semana se han abierto por primera vez las puertas del nuevo Hospital Buena Vista. La alcaldesa de la ciudad, doña Emilia Porras Narváez, ha cortado la cinta ceremonial en frente de la entrada principal.

Este modernísimo hospital cuenta con doscientas camas, un quirófano[1] con un equipo técnico muy avanzado, salas de recuperación, una unidad de cuidado intensivo, y departamentos especializados, entre ellos los de cardiología, ginecología, ortopedia, y pediatría. El director del hospital, el doctor Elías Maldonado, ha dicho que la primera responsabilidad del hospital es la salud de la comunidad. Después de la ceremonia de apertura, los invitados fueron a la cafetería del hospital para una recepción.

[1]quirófano *operating room*

¿Comprendes?

A **¿Cómo se dice en inglés... ?** Pareen.
1. la alcaldesa
2. la cinta
3. avanzado
4. cuidado intensivo
5. salas de recuperación

   a. ribbon
   b. advanced
   c. intensive care
   d. recovery rooms
   e. the mayor (female)

B **Especialidades médicas** Contesten.
1. ¿Cuáles son cuatro especialidades médicas que mencionan en el artículo?
2. ¿Cómo se llaman esas cuatro especialidades en inglés?

C **El hospital nuevo** Contesten según el artículo.
1. ¿Cuándo inauguraron el nuevo hospital?
2. ¿Cuántos pacientes pueden dormir en el hospital?
3. ¿Qué hay en el quirófano?
4. ¿Qué ha dicho el doctor Maldonado?
5. ¿Por qué fueron los invitados a la cafetería?

Lectura opcional 2

Problemas médicos de hoy

Al hablar de la salud y la medicina hay tres problemas graves que todos tenemos que confrontar. Son la adicción a las drogas, el abuso del alcohol y el sida.

En todos los países hispanos, igual que en Estados Unidos, verás anuncios que dicen «No a las drogas».

En España y en otros países hispanos hay campañas de castigos[1] rigurosos contra los conductores de automóviles que manejan (conducen) bajo la influencia del alcohol. El número de muertes[2] causadas por accidentes vehiculares excede la tasa[3] de mortalidad de muchas enfermedades.

Se considera el sida la plaga de nuestro siglo. Esta enfermedad contagiosa está matando[4] a miles de personas cada día en todos los continentes del mundo. En todas partes hay programas y campañas para educar a la gente sobre los peligros[5] del uso de las drogas y la promiscuidad sexual, las dos causas principales del sida.

La drogadicción, el alcoholismo y el sida son problemas que todos tenemos que confrontar, resolver y vencer.

[1]castigos *punishments* [4]matando *killing*
[2]muertes *deaths* [5]peligros *dangers*
[3]tasa *rate*

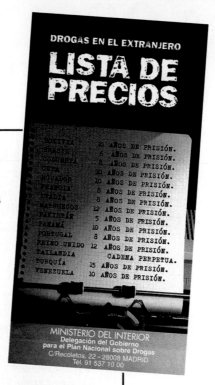

¿Comprendes?

Problemas de hoy

Digan que sí o que no.

1. Actualmente hay tres problemas médicos que son muy graves.
2. El sida es una enfermedad venérea contagiosa.
3. El número de muertes causadas por conductores de automóviles bajo la influencia del alcohol es muy bajo.
4. El sida no existe en muchas partes del mundo.

Conexiones
Las ciencias

La medicina

As you know, many English and Spanish words are cognates. They are similar in form and mean the same thing because both have the same source, usually Latin. Much medical terminology comes directly from Latin. Therefore the number of English/Spanish cognates is particularly great in this field. You will also note a pattern in the endings. The **ía** ending in Spanish is usually *y* in English. The **ólogo(a)** ending is usually *ologist* in English. Let's go over a few of these cognates.

ESPECIALIDADES MÉDICAS	MÉDICOS ESPECIALISTAS
la cardiología	el/la cardiólogo(a)
la ginecología	el/la ginecólogo(a)
la psiquiatría	el/la psiquiatra
la pediatría	el/la pediatra
la oncología	el/la oncólogo(a)
la oftalmología	el/la oftalmólogo(a)
la urología	el/la urólogo(a)
la dermatología	el/la dermatólogo(a)

It shouldn't be too hard to figure out what the names of these specialties and specialists are in English. If you don't know what they are in English, check with your science teacher or the school nurse. Here are a few hints.

la cardiología	*cardiology*
el cardiólogo	*the cardiologist*

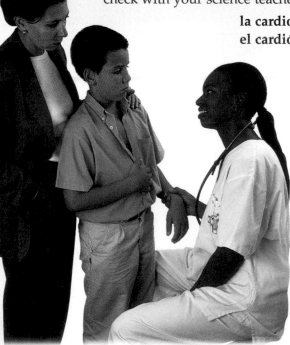

Una pediatra, Estepona, España

Now see whether you can guess the meaning of these diseases or illnesses:

LAS ENFERMEDADES

la tuberculosis   la artritis
el cáncer   la meningitis
la apendicitis   la esquizofrenia
la hepatitis   las úlceras

See whether you can answer these questions.

1. ¿Cómo se llama el especialista que trata las enfermedades de los niños?
2. ¿Quién es el especialista que trata las enfermedades mentales?
3. ¿A qué médico deben ir las personas que sufren de cáncer?
4. Si tienes un problema con los ojos, ¿a qué especialista debes consultar?

Now let's see how much you understand about certain diseases.

1. La esquizofrenia es una enfermedad ____.
   a. de los ojos   **b.** mental   **c.** de niños
2. Esta enfermedad afecta más a las personas viejas. Se les hace difícil usar las manos. La enfermedad es ____.
   a. la artritis   **b.** la tuberculosis   **c.** la hepatitis
3. Si una persona come mariscos contaminados puede sufrir de ____.
   a. apendicitis   **b.** tuberculosis   **c.** hepatitis

Al dejar de fumar su respiración se hace más fácil porque los pulmones están libres de humo y nicotina y los riesgos de desarrollar enfermedades relacionadas con el cigarro disminuyen. Unas de estas enfermedades son cáncer del **pulmón, enfisema, ataque cardíaco** y **embolio cerebral.**

Un cuerpo sano es uno de los beneficios que se gana al dejar de fumar. Se sentirá mejor física y mentalmente, dándole más energía para sí mismo, la familia y amigos.

¡Te toca a ti!

Use what you have learned

1 Servicios médicos de tu comunidad
✔ *Describe medical services*

Hay un(a) estudiante de intercambio en tu escuela (tu compañero[a]). Es de Panamá. Tiene algunas preguntas sobre los servicios médicos que ofrece tu comunidad. Descríbele el hospital local. Si no sabes nada del hospital que sirve a tu comunidad, ve a buscar un folleto sobre el hospital para poder contestar a las preguntas del/de la estudiante de intercambio.

Canal de Panamá

2 Voy a ser intérprete.
✔ *Ask questions about medical problems*

El hospital local tiene un problema. Su intérprete de español ha estado enfermo. Tú vas a ayudar. Vas a trabajar a tiempo parcial en el hospital. Vas a ayudar a los pacientes hispanohablantes. Tu compañero(a) va a ser tu primer(a) paciente. Ayúdale a llenar el formulario en la recepción.

3 Una comedia
✔ *Talk about emergency room procedures and accidents*

Van a divertirse. Trabajando en grupos de cuatro o cinco personas, preparen un «skit». Su «skit» se llama «Un día en la sala de emergencia». No va a ser muy serio. Va a ser muy cómico. Presenten su comedia a la clase.

4 Un formulario
✔ *Fill out a medical form*

En una hoja de papel, escribe la información que te pide el formulario.

HOSPITAL ABC

Apellidos _____ Nombre _____

Dirección _____ Edad _____

Problema médico que tiene _____

_____

_____

Nombres y dirección de padres
u otros parientes _____

Nombre de la compañía
de seguros _____

---

5 Las noticias

Your local Spanish language newspaper has asked you to write a feature story on a person or place in your community. Your parents recently had an accident and had to go to the emergency room. They were transported there by the First Aid Squad in your community. You were extremely pleased with the quality of service, beginning with the paramedics who arrived promptly and administered treatment at the scene. The care your parents received in the emergency room from the staff was equally as good. Write an article about this experience to share with the Spanish-speaking members of your community and to perhaps offer a refreshing perspective to an otherwise unpleasant event.

Writing Strategy

Writing a feature article
When writing a feature article, writers have two challenges: first, they must identify current topics that will be of interest; they must gather the information that will bring the topic to life and give readers the background they need. An important aspect of feature writing is the use of an effective "lead" to describe the opening of the story. This will catch the readers' attention and draw them in.

Assessment

Vocabulario

1 Identifiquen.

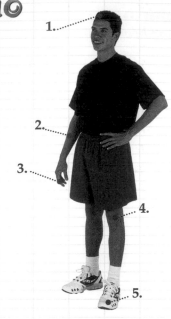

1. ....
2. ....
3. ....
4.
5.

> To review **Palabras 1**, turn to pages 232–233.

2 ¿Sí o no?

6. Cuando alguien se ha torcido el tobillo, tiene una fractura.
7. El servicio de primeros auxilios llega en una camilla al escenario de un accidente.

3 Pareen.

> To review **Palabras 2**, turn to pages 236–237.

a.

b.

c.

d.

e.

Spanish Online

For more Chapter 8 test preparation go to the Chapter 8 **Self-Check Quiz** on the Glencoe Spanish Web site at glencoe.com.

8. ____ Le toma una radiografía.
9. ____ Le toma el pulso.
10. ____ Le pone el brazo en un yeso.
11. ____ Le toma la tensión arterial.
12. ____ Le pone un vendaje.

Estructura

4 **Completen con el presente perfecto.**

13. Ellos _____. (salir)

14–15. Yo no _____ porque no _____ apetito. (comer, tener)

16. Nosotros ya _____ en Puerto Rico. (estar)

17. ¿Tú _____ a tu prima? (llamar)

To review the present perfect, turn to page 240.

5 **Den el participio pasado.**

18. decir

19. ver

20. volver

21. abrir

To review irregular participles, turn to page 242.

6 **Completen.**

22–23. Él es _____ simpático _____ yo pero no tiene _____ paciencia _____ yo.

24. Ella tiene _____ trabajo _____ tú.

To review comparison of equality, turn to page 244.

Cultura

7 **¿Sí o no?**

25. Un(a) practicante es un(a) profesional en el campo de la medicina que hace mucho trabajo que hace el/la médico(a); sobre todo en las áreas rurales donde no hay muchos médicos.

26. Si un(a) paciente está muy enfermo(a), el/la practicante le puede operar.

To review this cultural information, turn to page 248.

Tell all you can about this illustration.

Talking about an accident

tener un accidente	cortarse
hacerse daño, lastimarse	picar
caerse	ocurrir
romperse	tener lugar
torcerse	acabar de

Talking about medical emergencies and a hospital

el servicio de primeros auxilios	la recepción
la ambulancia	la silla de ruedas
la camilla	las muletas
el hospital	la víctima
la sala de emergencia,	llenar el formulario
la sala de urgencias	

Talking about medical professionals

el/la médico(a)	el/la técnico(a)
el/la cirujano(a) ortopédico(a)	el/la socorrista
el/la enfermero(a)	

How well do you know your vocabulary?

- Identify words that describe emergency room procedures.
- Write a few sentences about the steps a doctor takes to treat a medical emergency of your choice.

Talking about medical problems

una fractura	el dolor
una herida	hinchado(a)
una picadura	

Talking about medical care

ayudar	tomar el pulso	poner un vendaje
doler	tomar una radiografía	cerrar la herida
sentirse	tomar unos rayos equis	poner puntos (suturas)
tomar la tensión	reducir el hueso	parecer
(presión) arterial	poner en un yeso	

Identifying parts of the body

el cuerpo	el cuello	la muñeca	la rodilla
el hombro	el pecho	el dedo	el tobillo
el brazo	el codo	la pierna	el pie

Identifying parts of the face

la cara	la mejilla	el labio	el ojo
la frente	la nariz	el oído, la oreja	

VIDEOTUR

Episodio 8

In this video episode, you will watch "daredevil" Vicky. See page 487 for more information. As you watch, look for gestures the speakers use to help convey their message.

Capítulo 9

Ciudad y campo

Objetivos

In this chapter you will learn to:
- talk about life in the city
- talk about life in the country
- describe things that were happening
- refer to things already mentioned
- indicate where things are located
- talk about some cities in the Spanish-speaking world

María Eugenia Terrazas *Inmensidad cordillerana*

Spanish Online
To interact with your online edition of
¡Buen viaje! go to: glencoe.com.

Vocabulario

En la ciudad

el rascacielos

la oficina

En la zona comercial hay
muchas oficinas y tiendas.
Eran las siete y media de la
tarde y mucha gente estaba
saliendo de sus oficinas.

la fábrica

La zona industrial está en las
afueras de la ciudad.
Los obreros estaban
trabajando todo el día en
la fábrica.

el edificio alto

En la zona residencial hay
muchos apartamentos
(departamentos) y
condominios.
Hay pocas casas privadas.

un plano de la ciudad

la plaza

la calle   la avenida, el bulevar

Muchas calles y avenidas desembocan
en la plaza.
Las avenidas son anchas.

Esta calle o callecita angosta es
muy pintoresca.
Está en el barrio viejo de la ciudad.

el semáforo

el cruce

la esquina

los peatones

la acera

Hay un semáforo en la esquina.
Los peatones caminan en la acera.
Cruzan la calle en el cruce de peatones.

La gente estaba esperando en
la parada del bus.

el autobús, la guagua, el camión

La estación del metro

la boca del metro

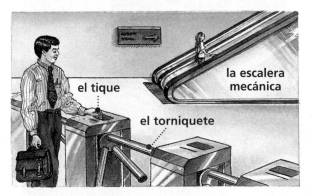

el tique

la escalera
mecánica

el torniquete

La señorita estaba subiendo
la escalera mecánica.
El señor estaba metiendo el tique
en la ranura del torniquete.

¿Qué palabra necesito?

 1 **Historieta** **El señor Salas de Caracas**
Contesten.

1. ¿Estaba viviendo el señor Salas en Caracas?
2. ¿Tenía un apartamento en una zona residencial de la ciudad?
3. ¿Estaba su apartamento en un edificio alto?
4. ¿Trabajaba él en una oficina cerca de la Plaza Simón Bolívar?
5. ¿Estaba su oficina en un rascacielos?
6. ¿Tomaba el señor Salas el metro a su trabajo?
7. ¿Había una boca de metro cerca de su apartamento?
8. ¿Compraba el señor Salas tiques para el metro?

Caracas, Venezuela

2 **El plano de la ciudad**
Contesten según el dibujo.

1. ¿Desembocan muchas calles en la Plaza San Martín?
2. ¿Es ancha o angosta la calle Mina?
3. ¿Hay un semáforo en la esquina de Mina y Luz?
4. ¿Hay una parada de bus en la plaza?
5. ¿Hay muchos coches en la plaza?
6. ¿Hay peatones en la acera?

3 **En la ciudad** Digan que sí o que no.

1. Frecuentemente el barrio viejo de una ciudad es también una zona histórica.
2. Una zona comercial de una ciudad tiene muchas fábricas.
3. La zona industrial siempre se encuentra en el centro mismo de la ciudad.
4. Un obrero trabaja en una oficina.
5. Hay muchas oficinas en la zona comercial de la ciudad.
6. Un rascacielos es un edificio muy alto que tiene muchos apartamentos u oficinas.
7. Los semáforos se encuentran por lo general en una esquina y ayudan a controlar el tráfico.
8. La gente espera el bus en la boca del metro.
9. Los peatones caminan en la calle.
10. Los peatones pueden cruzar la calle en el cruce de peatones.

La Habana, Cuba

4 **El transporte en la ciudad** Contesten.

1. ¿Qué toman los pasajeros para bajar y subir de una estación de metro?
2. ¿Dónde meten los pasajeros el tique antes de abordar el metro?
3. ¿Dónde esperan los pasajeros el bus?
4. ¿Dónde caminan los peatones?
5. ¿Dónde pueden cruzar la calle los peatones?

Santiago, Chile

5   **Una ciudad cercana** Trabaja con un(a) compañero(a). Si ustedes viven en una ciudad, conversen juntos y describan su ciudad. Si no viven en una ciudad, hablen de una ciudad que han visitado cerca de donde viven.

6 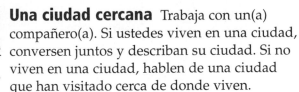 **Opiniones** Trabaja con un(a) compañero(a). Discutan lo que ustedes consideran las ventajas y las desventajas de la vida en una ciudad. ¿Están ustedes de acuerdo o no? ¿Quién preferiría vivir en la ciudad?

Vocabulario

PALABRAS **2**

En el campo

el campesino   una casa de campo   un pueblo pequeño

una finca

el campo

Los campesinos viven en el campo.
Ellos tienen una finca.
Ellos cultivan los campos.

El cultivo de los cereales
es muy importante.

sembrar

la siembra

El campesino va a sembrar cereales.
No está sembrándolos ahora.
Va a sembrarlos en la primavera.

el trigo

la cosecha

cosechar

el maíz

Y va a cosecharlos en el otoño.

el ganado

las vacas

los cerdos

las gallinas

Los agricultores crían animales domésticos.

la pera

el peral

la manzana

el huerto, la huerta

el manzano

los vegetales

Vocabulario

¿Qué palabra necesito?

7 **Historieta** **Los Ayala**
Contesten según se indica.

1. ¿Dónde viven los Ayala?
   (en un pueblo pequeño en el campo)
2. ¿Qué tienen ellos? (una finca)
3. ¿Qué hay en la finca? (campos de cereales)
4. ¿Qué siembran los Ayala? (trigo y maíz)
5. ¿Cuándo siembran? (en la primavera)
6. ¿Cuándo es la cosecha? (en el otoño)
7. ¿Qué crían los Ayala en su finca?
   (animales domésticos)
8. ¿Qué animales tienen? (vacas y cerdos)

Echalar, España

8 **Ya sabemos mucho.** Contesten.

1. ¿Cuáles son todos los vegetales o todas las legumbres
   que ya conoces en español?
2. ¿Cuáles son las frutas que ya conoces en español?
3. ¿Cuáles son los animales que ya conoces en español?
4. ¿Cuáles son las cuatro estaciones del año?

Andalucía, España

9 Cosas del campo Digan que sí o que no.

1. Las vacas nos dan leche.
2. Las gallinas ponen huevos.
3. El tomate es un vegetal.
4. Hay muchas fincas en la ciudad.
5. Los obreros son campesinos.
6. Los campesinos cultivan los campos en una fábrica.
7. El manzano es un árbol y la manzana es la fruta que da el árbol.
8. Una carne que nos da el cerdo es el jamón.
9. Los campesinos viven en una casa de campo.
10. Una huerta produce muchos vegetales.

10 En el campo No importa si vives en el campo o no. A casi todos nosotros nos gusta de vez en cuando pasar un día tranquilo en el campo. Trabaja con un(a) compañero(a). Describan un día fabuloso en el campo. Hablen de lo que ven y lo que hacen.

11 Opiniones Trabaja con un(a) compañero(a). Discutan lo que ustedes consideran las ventajas y las desventajas de la vida en el campo. ¿Están ustedes de acuerdo o no? ¿Quién preferiría vivir en el campo?

Spanish Online
For more information about the country-side of Mexico and other countries in the Spanish-speaking world, go to **Web Explore** on the Glencoe Spanish Web site at glencoe.com.

Oaxaca, México

Sinaloa, México

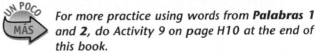

*For more practice using words from **Palabras 1** and **2**, do Activity 9 on page H10 at the end of this book.*

Estructura

 El imperfecto progresivo
Describing what was going on

Use your **StudentWorks** Plus™ CD for more practice.

1. The imperfect progressive is used to describe an action as it was taking place. It is formed by using the imperfect tense of **estar** and the present participle.

> **El obrero estaba trabajando en la fábrica.**
> **Los muchachos estaban comiendo las frutas del huerto.**

¿Te acuerdas?

The present progressive is used to describe events actually taking place.
El obrero está saliendo de la fábrica.
El campesino está cultivando los campos.

2. Most verbs that have a stem change in the preterite have the same stem change in the present participle.

E → I		O → U	
pedir	pidiendo	dormir	durmiendo
servir	sirviendo	morir	muriendo
repetir	repitiendo		
decir	diciendo		

3. The following verbs have a **y** in the present participle.

caer	cayendo	distribuir	distribuyendo
leer	leyendo	construir	construyendo
traer	trayendo	contribuir	contribuyendo
oír	oyendo		

¿Qué palabra necesito?

12 **Historieta** Un día típico en la ciudad
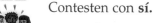
Contesten con **sí**.

1. ¿Estaba circulando mucho tráfico por la ciudad?
2. ¿Estaba dirigiendo el tráfico un policía?
3. ¿Estaban caminando por las aceras muchos peatones?
4. ¿Estaban cruzando las calles?
5. ¿Estaban cruzando las calles en el cruce de peatones?
6. ¿Estaba haciendo cola mucha gente en la parada del bus?
7. ¿Estaba saliendo mucha gente de la boca del metro?
8. ¿Estaba subiendo mucha gente en la escalera mecánica?

Madrid, España

13 **Historieta** Durante el vuelo

Contesten según el modelo.

¿Trabajaban durante el vuelo los asistentes de vuelo?

Sí, estaban trabajando durante el vuelo.

1. ¿Servían refrescos los asistentes de vuelo?
2. ¿Servían una comida?
3. ¿Daban anuncios?
4. ¿Leían las reglas de seguridad?
5. ¿Oían música estereofónica los pasajeros?
6. ¿Leían revistas algunos pasajeros?
7. ¿Dormían otros?

14 **Historieta** El túnel nuevo Completen con el imperfecto progresivo.

Los ingenieros __1__ (construir) el túnel nuevo. El público

__2__ (esperar) la apertura del túnel. Muchos hombres y mujeres

__3__ (trabajar) en su construcción. Este proyecto les __4__ (pagar)

un buen salario. Pero algunas personas __5__ (decir) que no era buena

idea. Ellos __6__ (pensar) en el impacto ecológico del túnel. Pero nadie

__7__ (escuchar) a los ecologistas. El público __8__ (ver) que con el túnel

los viajes al centro serían más cortos.

15 **Ayer a las...** Pregúntale a tu compañero(a) lo que estaba haciendo ayer a la hora indicada. Él o ella te contestará. Luego cambien de rol.

8:00 A.M. · 5:00 A.M. · 6:30 A.M. · 6:30 P.M. · 10:30 A.M.

3:00 P.M. · 8:00 P.M. · 12:00 P.M. · 11:00 P.M. · 4:00 P.M.

16 **Tienes un problema.** Un(a) compañero(a) va a ser tu padre o tu madre. Está muy enfadado(a) *(angry)* porque tú volviste a casa muy tarde anoche. Él o ella tiene muchas preguntas para ti. Tienes que decirle todo lo que estabas haciendo para explicar por qué no podías volver a casa más temprano. Luego cambien de rol.

Estructura

Colocación de los pronombres de complemento
Referring to things already mentioned

1. When the object pronouns are used with the present participle, they may precede the helping verb or they may be attached to the participle.

Estaban comiendo el maíz.	Me estaba mostrando la finca.
Lo estaban comiendo.	Me la estaba mostrando.
Estaban comiéndolo.	Estaba mostrándomela.

2. When the object pronouns are used with the infinitive, they may precede the helping verb that accompanies the infinitive or they may be attached to the infinitive.

Voy a cruzar la calle.	Voy a dar el plano a José.
La voy a cruzar.	Se lo voy a dar.
Voy a cruzarla.	Voy a dárselo.

¿Lo sabes?

To maintain the same stress, a participle carries a written accent when either one or two pronouns are attached to it.

Está sirviéndolo.
Está sirviéndomelo.

¿Lo sabes?

To maintain the same stress, an infinitive carries a written accent only when two pronouns are attached to it.

Quiere darme el plano.
Quiere dármelo.

¿Qué palabra necesito?

17 Historieta En la finca

 Contesten según el modelo.

¿Estaba mostrándote la finca el señor? →
Sí, estaba mostrándomela.
Sí, me la estaba mostrando.

1. ¿Estaba mostrándote la casa de campo el señor?
2. ¿Te estaba describiendo la casa?
3. ¿Estabas admirando la casa?
4. ¿Estabas mirando a los campesinos en la finca?
5. ¿Estaban ellos sembrando los campos?
6. ¿Estaban criando los animales también?

18 Buena higiene Sigan el modelo.

Me voy a lavar el pelo. →
Voy a lavármelo.

1. Me voy a lavar el pelo.
2. Quiero comprarme el nuevo champú en la farmacia.
3. No puedo recordar el nombre del champú.
4. El farmacéutico podrá darme el nombre.
5. Tengo que lavarme el pelo esta noche.

 19 **Historieta** **En el cine** Contesten con pronombres.

1. ¿Quiere ver la película Marisol?
2. ¿Va a ver la película?
3. ¿Está comprando las entradas ahora?
4. ¿Está comprando las entradas en la taquilla del cine?
5. ¿Quiere Marisol ver la película desde la primera fila?
6. Desde la primera fila, ¿puede ver la película bien?

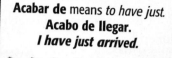

Spanish Online

For a fun way to review this grammar point, go to the Chapter 9 **eGame** on the Glencoe Spanish Web site at glencoe.com.

20 **¿Acabas de hacerlo?** Contesten según el modelo.

¿Acabas de hacer el crucigrama o vas a hacer el crucigrama?

Acabo de hacerlo.

¿Te acuerdas?

Acabar de means *to have just*.
Acabo de llegar.
I have just arrived.

1. ¿Acabas de leer el periódico o vas a leer el periódico?
2. ¿Acabas de escribir la carta o vas a escribir la carta?
3. ¿Acabas de tomar el examen o vas a tomar el examen?
4. ¿Acabas de hacer tus tareas o vas a hacer tus tareas?
5. ¿Acabas de llamar a tu amigo o vas a llamar a tu amigo?

21 **Historieta** **Una carta**

Contesten según se indica.

1. ¿Está escribiendo la carta Elena? (no)
2. ¿Cuándo va a escribírtela? (mañana)
3. ¿Está comprando los sellos ahora? (no)
4. ¿Ya los ha comprado? (sí)
5. ¿Cuándo va a enviarte la carta? (mañana)
6. ¿La vas a abrir enseguida? (sí)
7. ¿Cómo vas a leerla? (con mucho interés)
8. ¿La vas a contestar enseguida? (sí)
9. ¿Vas a enviarle la carta enseguida? (sí)

Estructura

Adjetivos y pronombres demostrativos
Pointing out people or things

1. You use the demonstrative adjectives *this, that, these,* and *those* to point out people or things. In Spanish, the demonstrative adjective, like all adjectives, agrees with the noun it modifies.

2. All forms of **este** indicate someone or something close to the speaker. They mean *this* or *these* in English.

> **Este boleto que tengo aquí es para el metro.**

All forms of **ese** indicate someone or something close to the person being spoken to.

> **Ese boleto que tú tienes allí es para el bus.**

All forms of **aquel** indicate someone or something away from both the speaker and the listener. The forms of both **ese** and **aquel** mean *that* or *those* in English.

> **Aquellos boletos en aquella mesa allá no son usados.**

Note that the adverbs **aquí, allí,** and **allá** indicate relative position—*here, there, over there.*

3. The forms used for the demonstrative pronouns—*this one, that one, these, those*—are the same as those used for demonstrative adjectives.

> **No me gusta este (aquí).**
> **Pero aquellos (allá), sí, me gustan.**

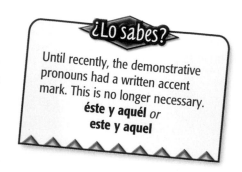

¿Lo sabes?

Until recently, the demonstrative pronouns had a written accent mark. This is no longer necessary.
éste y aquél *or*
este y aquel

¿Cómo lo digo?

22 **¿Qué precio tienen?** Sigan el modelo.

el abrigo ⟶
¿Qué precio tiene el abrigo?
¿Cuál? ¿Este abrigo aquí?
No, aquel abrigo en el escaparate.

1. los guantes
2. la falda
3. el suéter
4. las corbatas
5. el cinturón
6. los pantalones
7. la blusa
8. los calcetines

Buenos Aires, Argentina

23 **El plano que tú tienes** Completen con **este, ese** o **aquel**.

1. ____ plano de la ciudad que tú estás mirando es bueno pero ____ que tiene Felipe es malo. No sirve para nada.
2. ____ calle aquí es una calle peatonal pero ____ allá no es sólo para peatones. Y tiene mucho tráfico.
3. ____ estación de metro aquí en el centro de la ciudad es mucho más grande que ____ estación en las afueras.
4. ____ edificios aquí en el centro mismo de la ciudad son muy altos. ____ que están más lejos en las afueras no son tan altos.
5. ____ novela que yo estoy leyendo tiene lugar aquí en ____ ciudad. Pero ____ novela que tiene Pedro, no la conozco. No sé dónde tiene lugar.

24 **Preferencias** Trabaja con un(a) compañero(a). Miren esta foto de un escaparate de una tienda de ropa en Caracas. Discutan lo que a cada uno(a) de ustedes le gusta y no le gusta. Luego comparen sus preferencias.

Caracas, Venezuela

25 **Juego ¿Cuál?** Trabaja con un(a) compañero(a). Haz una frase usando **este, ese** o **aquel**. Tu compañero(a) te dirá si hablas de algo **aquí, allí** o **allá.** Luego cambien de rol.

Andas bien. ¡Adelante!

Conversación

El campo y la ciudad

Lupe ¿Te gusta vivir en el campo? ¿Qué haces? ¿No es aburrido?

Mónica De ninguna manera. El otro día estaba hablando con mi amigo Miguel. Estaba diciéndole todo lo que podemos hacer aquí en este pueblo.

Lupe Pero en la ciudad tenemos cines, museos. Tenemos de todo. Y puedes tomar el bus o el metro para ir de un lugar a otro. Todo es tan conveniente.

Mónica Sí, pero aquí no tienes que esperar el semáforo para cruzar la calle. ¿Y sabes lo que es el automóvil? Tenemos uno y podemos usarlo sin pasar horas en el tráfico.

Lupe Sí, lo sé. Pero yo nunca viviría en el campo.

Mónica Y yo nunca viviría en la ciudad. No me gustaría vivir sin aire puro y mucho espacio. Voy a pasear a caballo. ¿Quieres acompañarme?

Lupe ¿A caballo?

¿Comprendes?

Contesten.

1. ¿Qué le pregunta Lupe a Mónica?
2. ¿Con quién estaba hablando Mónica el otro día?
3. ¿Cree Mónica que el campo es aburrido?
4. ¿Por qué prefiere Lupe la ciudad?
5. ¿Por qué dice ella que todo es tan conveniente?
6. Según Mónica, ¿hay mucho tráfico en el campo?
7. ¿Quién no viviría nunca en el campo? ¿Por qué no?
8. ¿Qué va a hacer Mónica?
9. ¿Qué crees? ¿La va a acompañar Lupe?

Vamos a hablar más

A **Donde quiere vivir** Trabaja con un(a) compañero(a). Discutan si preferirían vivir en la ciudad o en el campo. Den sus razones.

El Alcázar, Segovia, España

Palacio de Bellas Artes, Ciudad de México

B **Explica por qué.** Trabaja con un(a) compañero(a). Él o ella te preguntará por qué no hiciste algo ayer. Explica que no lo hiciste ayer porque estabas haciendo otra cosa. Dile lo que estabas haciendo. Luego cambien de rol. Pueden usar el modelo como guía.

—¿Por qué no me llamaste ayer?
—No te llamé porque estaba leyendo un libro interesante.

Lecturas culturales

Buenos Aires, Argentina

Reading Strategy

Taking notes to remember what has been read If you are reading material that you do not know much about, it is often a good idea to take notes to help you remember and organize what you read. One way to take notes is to summarize the content of a selection. Another way is to jot down key words and ideas about the topic. These notes will come in handy later when you need to study for a test.

Buenos Aires, la capital de Argentina, es una ciudad muy bonita. Se dice que esta ciudad es la más europea de todas las ciudades de Latinoamérica.

Recientemente Sandra Connors, una americana, estaba visitando a Buenos Aires. Un día, mientras estaba caminando por el centro de la ciudad, les dijo a algunos conocidos porteños[1] que no sabía si estaba en Buenos Aires, Londres o Madrid.

La calle Florida es una calle peatonal en la zona comercial de la ciudad. En esta calle no permiten carros. Si te gusta ir de compras tienes que caminar por esta calle con sus cientos de tiendas.

La avenida más ancha del mundo es la Avenida 9 de Julio. Aquí puedes sentarte en una confitería[2] y mirar a la gente que pasa. Si tienes hambre, puedes ir a uno de los carritos de la Costanera norte. Los verdaderos carritos del pasado se han transformado en una fila de restaurantes al borde del río de la Plata. Aquí sirven el delicioso bife argentino.

[1]porteños *inhabitants of Buenos Aires*
[2]confitería *café, tea room*

Calle Florida y Avenida Córdoba

Avenida 9 de Julio, Buenos Aires

El bife argentino viene del ganado que cuidan los gauchos en las pampas argentinas. Muchos porteños ricos tienen estancias en las pampas. Una estancia es una finca grande donde crían ganado. Los ricos van a su estancia para divertirse en sus lujosas[3] casas de campo.

Es imposible hablar de las ciudades de Latinoamérica sin mencionar el problema de los pobres que vienen a las ciudades desde el campo en busca de trabajo. Estos pobres viven en chabolas que se encuentran principalmente en las afueras. En Buenos Aires se llaman «villas miseria».

[3]lujosas *luxurious*

Un gaucho en las pampas argentinas

Use your StudentWorks**Plus** CD for more practice.

Una estancia, Argentina

Una villa miseria, Buenos Aires

¿Comprendes?

Buenos Aires Identifiquen y describan.
1. la calle Florida
2. la Avenida 9 de Julio
3. los carritos de la Costanera norte
4. las pampas
5. una estancia
6. una «villa miseria»

Lima, Perú

Lima, Perú

Lima, la capital de Perú, es una ciudad muy hermosa. En el centro mismo de la ciudad hay un gran barrio histórico. Muchos de los edificios de este barrio datan de la época colonial.

Hay dos plazas importantes en el centro de Lima—la Plaza de Armas y la Plaza San Martín. El famoso Jirón de la Unión enlaza[1] estas dos plazas. El Jirón de la Unión es una calle peatonal con muchas tiendas y centros o galerías comerciales. Hoy día hay también muchos vendedores ambulantes. Estos vendedores ambulantes han venido a la capital de los pueblos pequeños del altiplano.

En los alrededores de Lima cerca de las playas del Pacífico hay muchas zonas residenciales muy bonitas. En las calles bordeadas de palmas hay edificios altos con apartamentos y condominios. Hay también casas lujosas[2].

Una vez más, es imposible hablar de las ciudades de Latinoamérica sin mencionar el problema de los pobres que vienen a las ciudades desde el campo en busca de trabajo. Como hemos aprendido, los barrios pobres donde viven se llaman «villas miseria» en Buenos Aires. En Perú se llaman «pueblos jóvenes».

[1]enlaza *joins*   [2]lujosas *luxurious*

Jirón de la Unión, Lima

¿Comprendes?

Lima Contesten.
1. ¿Cuál es la capital de Perú?
2. ¿Cómo es el centro de Lima?
3. ¿De qué época datan muchos de los edificios?
4. ¿Cuáles son dos plazas importantes en el centro de Lima?
5. ¿Qué calle enlaza estas dos plazas?
6. ¿Qué es el Jirón de la Unión?
7. ¿Quiénes son los vendedores ambulantes?
8. ¿Qué hay en los alrededores de Lima?
9. ¿Por qué van los campesinos a la ciudad?
10. ¿Qué es un «pueblo joven»?

Lectura opcional ②

Plaza Central, Santa Fe

Una ciudad norteamericana con profundas raíces hispanas

Santa Fe, la capital de Nuevo México, está al pie de las montañas Sangre de Cristo. Esta ciudad fue fundada[1] por los españoles en 1609 sobre unas ruinas indígenas prehistóricas. Durante doscientos años Santa Fe fue un centro para el comercio entre los españoles y varios grupos indígenas. En 1680 los indios pueblo se levantaron contra los españoles. Querían echarlos[2] de Santa Fe y así hicieron. Pero doce años después, los españoles, bajo Diego de Vargas, volvieron a Santa Fe y restablecieron su dominio.

Si abres la guía telefónica o simplemente miras los nombres en las casas, verás que la influencia hispana todavía vive en Santa Fe. Sigue existiendo no solamente en los museos sino en carne y hueso. Las familias hispanas predominan en esta ciudad que es la capital más antigua de Estados Unidos.

[1]fundada *founded*
[2]echarlos *throw them out*

Calle comercial, Santa Fe

¿Comprendes?

A La geografía Busquen en un mapa dónde está la ciudad de Santa Fe y dónde están las montañas Sangre de Cristo.

B Santa Fe Contesten.
1. ¿Qué edad tiene Santa Fe?
2. Antes de la fundación de Santa Fe, ¿qué había en el mismo sitio?
3. ¿Para qué servía la ciudad durante dos siglos?
4. ¿Qué hicieron los indios pueblo en 1680?
5. ¿Qué hicieron los españoles en 1692?

C El significado En tus propias palabras, explica lo que dice el último párrafo de la lectura.

Conexiones

Las ciencias sociales

La demografía

Demography is the study of human populations, of their distribution, density, and vital statistics. Demographics explain where people choose to live and why. They also explain population shifts—why people move around.

The demography of Latin America is particularly interesting. You will see some marked contrasts between the demographics of the two Americas.

Bogotá, Colombia

La demografía de Latinoamérica

La demografía es el estudio de las poblaciones humanas. El demógrafo nos explica dónde decide vivir la gente y por qué decide vivir allí. Nos explica también cuándo y por qué la gente decide mudarse para establecerse en otro lugar. Es decir que el demógrafo explica las razones por la migración.

Lima, Perú

Algunas estadísticas

Si contrastamos las poblaciones de Latinoamérica y Estados Unidos, lo primero que notamos es que Latinoamérica tiene una población mucho más numerosa. Durante muchos años Nueva York y Los Ángeles fueron las dos ciudades más grandes de las Américas. Ya no.

| Nueva York | 8.050.000 | México D.F. | 8.681.000 |
| Los Ángeles | 3.903.000 | São Paulo, Brasil | 17.900.000 |

Patrones migratorios

En las últimas décadas los centros urbanos de Latinoamérica han crecido dramáticamente. Los campesinos se han ido del campo a la ciudad en busca de trabajo y mejores condiciones de vida. En muchos casos ellos no han encontrado mejor vida, sino miseria. Las ciudades no pueden acomodar a todos los que allí buscan mejor vida. No hay bastante trabajo. Y no hay viviendas adecuadas. Los pobres tienen que vivir en barrios sin agua corriente ni electricidad.

La edad

Otra estadística significativa es la de la edad de las poblaciones de las Américas. Latinoamérica es una región de jóvenes, mientras que Estados Unidos es un país de envejecientes. Como ejemplo, vamos a comparar a México con Estados Unidos.

	% menos de 5 años	% 5 a 14 años	% más de 65 años
EE.UU.	7.5	14.1	12.4
México	13.8	25.1	4.1

¿Comprendes?

A ¿Cuál es la palabra? Busquen la palabra cuya definición sigue.

1. el acto de trasladarse para establecerse en otro lugar
2. personas que se están poniendo viejos
3. el estudio de las poblaciones humanas
4. casas, residencias donde la gente vive
5. una zona o parte de una ciudad

B La demografía Digan que sí o que no.

1. El demógrafo nos enseña dónde vive la gente y por qué decide vivir allí.
2. Las ciudades de Estados Unidos son más grandes que las ciudades de Latinoamérica.
3. Las ciudades latinoamericanas siempre han sido más grandes que las ciudades de Estados Unidos.
4. Los campesinos que se establecen en las ciudades de Latinoamérica siempre encuentran mejor vida.
5. No hay bastante trabajo para todos en el campo y no hay bastante trabajo en las ciudades.
6. Hay más viejos o ancianos en Latinoamérica que en Estados Unidos.
7. La población latinoamericana es más vieja (mayor) que la población estadounidense.

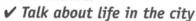

¡Te toca a ti!

Use what you have learned

1 **La ciudad**

✔ *Talk about life in the city*

Con un(a) compañero(a), miren
esta foto de la ciudad de Barcelona.
Hablen juntos y describan todo lo
que ven en la foto. Luego decidan
si es una ciudad que les
gustaría visitar.

Barcelona, España

2 **Transporte público**

✔ *Talk about public transportation*

Tu compañero(a) es un(a) joven ecuatoriano(a) que está visitando
tu pueblo o ciudad. Quiere saber algo sobre los medios de
transporte público. Si no hay transporte público donde vives,
describe los medios de transporte en una ciudad cercana.

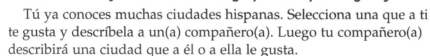

3 **Una ciudad hispana**

✔ *Talk about life in an interesting Spanish-speaking city*

Tú ya conoces muchas ciudades hispanas. Selecciona una que a ti
te gusta y descríbela a un(a) compañero(a). Luego tu compañero(a)
describirá una ciudad que a él o a ella le gusta.

4 **¿Hablas de la ciudad o del campo?**

✔ *Talk about city or country life*

Trabaja con un(a) compañero(a). Haz una frase que describe
algún aspecto de la ciudad o del campo. Tu compañero(a) te dirá de
qué hablas—la ciudad o el campo. Luego cambien de rol.

Spanish Online
To compare the tourist activities of Buenos
Aires with those of the ranches in rural
Argentina, go to the Chapter 9 **WebQuest**
on the Glencoe Spanish Web site at
glencoe.com.

ESCRIBIR

5 Yo nunca viviría en...

✔ *Give your opinion about city life versus country life*

Vas a escribir una composición titulada «Yo nunca viviría en... ».
Tienes que completar el título con **la ciudad** o **el campo.**

Writing Strategy

Comparing and contrasting
Comparing and contrasting involves writing about similarities and differences between two or more related things. A Venn diagram will help you do this. First draw two intersecting circles; title the circles with the subject to be compared. List unique features of each subject. Then list the similarities of the two subjects in the area where the circles intersect. This tool, or any other similar one you can think of, will help you organize your thoughts so you can clearly and effectively write your comparison.

ESCRIBIR

6 Dos ciudades

Think of two cities you have visited. Write a paper, comparing the two places. If you are not familiar with two different cities, compare the town where you live with a nearby city or other town. Be sure to organize your thoughts with a list or a graphic, showing the similarities and differences.

Viña del Mar, Chile

Santiago, Chile

Assessment

Vocabulario

1 Contesten.

1. ¿Qué hay en una zona comercial de una ciudad?
2. ¿Qué hay en las esquinas de muchas ciudades que ayudan a controlar el tráfico?

To review **Palabras 1**, turn to pages 262–263.

2 Completen.

3. Los obreros trabajan en una ____ en una zona industrial en las afueras de la ciudad.
4. Muchas calles y avenidas ____ en la plaza.
5. Los ____ andan (a pie) por la acera.
6. La gente espera el bus en la ____.

3 Identifiquen.

7.

8.

9.

10.

To review **Palabras 2**, turn to pages 266–267.

4 Completen.

11. El ____ es el árbol que da manzanas.
12. Los agricultores ____ animales domésticos.
13. Los campesinos ____ los campos.

Estructura

5 **Escriban según el modelo.**

> Ellos cosechan el arroz. →
> Estaban cosechando el arroz.

14. Ellos construyen una fábrica.
15. Yo repito las direcciones.
16. La gallina duerme.
17. Yo no leo nada.
18. ¿Quién lo dice?

To review the imperfect progressive, turn to page 270.

6 **Escriban de otra manera.**

19. ¿El plano de la ciudad? Yo quería dárselo.
20. ¿Los campos? Estaban cultivándolos.
21. ¿El tique? Él estaba metiéndolo en la ranura del torniquete.

To review the placement of object pronouns, turn to page 272.

7 **Contesten con adjetivos o pronombres demostrativos.**

22. ¿Qué casa prefieres? (la casa que veo allá lejos)
23. ¿Qué periódicos te interesan más? (los periódicos que tengo aquí)

To review demonstrative adjectives and pronouns, turn to page 274.

Cultura

8 **Identifiquen.**

24. la capital de Argentina
25. la avenida que tiene fama de ser la más ancha del mundo

To review this cultural information, turn to pages 278-279.

Spanish Online
For more Chapter 9 test preparation go to the Chapter 9 **Self-Check Quiz** on the Glencoe Spanish Web site at glencoe.com.

¡Hablo como un pro!

Tell as much as you can about this illustration.

Vocabulario

Talking about the city

la ciudad	la zona industrial	el apartamento
la zona comercial	las afueras	(departamento)
el rascacielos	la fábrica	el condominio
el edificio	el/la obrero(a)	la casa privada
la oficina	la zona residencial	

Talking about the layout of a city

el plano	el semáforo
la plaza	el cruce de peatones
la avenida, el bulevar	caminar
la calle	cruzar
el barrio viejo	desembocar
la esquina	pintoresco(a)
la acera	ancho(a)
los peatones	angosto(a)

Talking about public transportation

la estación del metro	el torniquete
la boca del metro	la ranura
la escalera mecánica	la parada del bus
el tique	el autobús, la guagua, el camión

Talking about the country

el campo	la casa de campo
el pueblo	el campesino
la finca	

How well do you know your vocabulary?

- Choose a word from the list.
- Have a classmate tell whether it relates more to the city, the country, or both.
- Take turns.

Talking about farming

la siembra	el huerto
la cosecha	el manzano
el maíz	el peral
el trigo	cultivar
los cereales	sembrar
la huerta	cosechar
los vegetales	criar los animales

VIDEOTUR

Episodio 9

In this video episode, you will join Claudia and Julián as they do a school assignment. See page 488 for more information. As you watch, look for gestures the speakers use to help convey their message.

Identifying some farm animals

el ganado	el cerdo
la vaca	la gallina

Capítulo 10

La cocina hispana

Objetivos

In this chapter you will learn to:

❖ talk about foods and food preparation

❖ give commands

❖ refer to people and things previously mentioned

❖ prepare some regional specialties

❖ talk about the origin of several foods

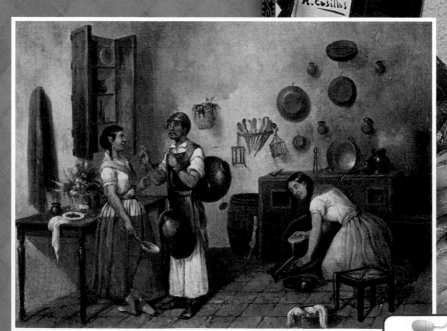

Manuel Serrano *A Mexican Kitchen in 1885*

Spanish Online
To interact with your online edition of
¡Buen viaje! go to: glencoe.com.

La cocina

Use your **StudentWorks** Plus CD for more practice.

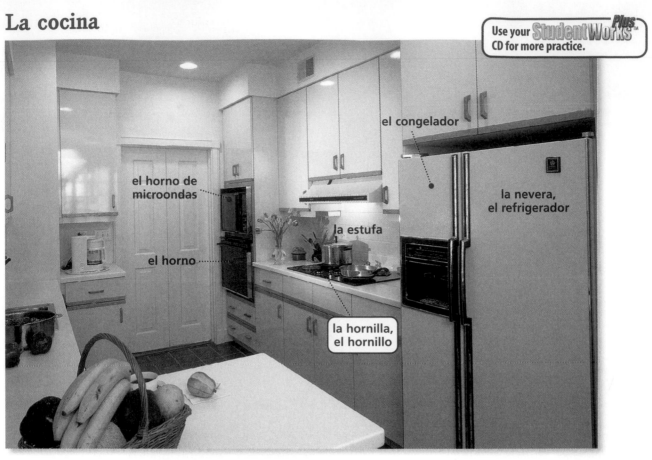

el horno de microondas

el horno

la estufa

el congelador

la nevera, el refrigerador

la hornilla, el hornillo

¡A cocinar!

freír

el/la sartén

hervir

la olla

la cazuela

revolver

la parrilla

asar

Algunos comestibles

la coliflor

la lechuga

la lima

la toronja

el limón

las uvas

las zanahorias

las cebollas

el pepino

las papas, las patatas

la pimienta

la sal

el azúcar

la carne de res

el pollo

la costilla

la salchicha, el chorizo

la chuleta de cerdo

el cordero

la ternera

Señorita, coma Ud. más.

Señor, ase Ud. el pollo en el horno.

Señora, fría Ud. las patatas.

Vocabulario

¿Qué palabra necesito?

1 Historieta En la cocina Contesten.

1. ¿Está la señora en la cocina?
2. ¿Es una cocina moderna o anticuada?
3. ¿Cuántas hornillas tiene la estufa?
4. ¿Es una estufa eléctrica o de gas?
5. ¿Hay un refrigerador moderno en la cocina?
6. ¿Cuántas puertas tiene el refrigerador?
7. ¿Tiene congelador un refrigerador moderno?
8. ¿Qué haces tú en la cocina?

Restaurante El Sur, Estepona, España

2 ¿Qué necesita el cocinero? Completen.

1. El cocinero necesita una _____ porque va a freír algo.
2. El cocinero necesita una parrilla porque va a _____ algo.
3. El cocinero necesita una _____ porque va a hervir algo.
4. El cocinero va a _____ el agua.
5. El cocinero va a _____ las chuletas de cerdo.
6. El cocinero va a _____ los huevos.

3 Lo que me gusta y lo que no me gusta
Contesten.

1. ¿Te gustan las uvas?
2. ¿Te gusta la ensalada de lechuga y tomates?
3. ¿Te gustan las papas asadas?
4. ¿Te gustan más las toronjas o las naranjas?
5. ¿Te gustan más las legumbres o las frutas?
6. ¿Te gusta el limón?
7. ¿Te gusta más el pollo frito o el pollo asado?
8. ¿Te gusta más la carne o el pescado?

4 ¿A qué grupo pertenece?

Digan la categoría a la cual pertenece cada comestible.

1. la cebolla
2. la toronja
3. la zanahoria
4. el cerdo
5. la papa
6. el cordero
7. el limón
8. las uvas
9. la pimienta

Mercado de San Miguel, Madrid, España

5 Nuestras comidas favoritas

Con un(a) compañero(a) hagan una lista de sus comidas favoritas. Luego decidan a cuál de los dos le gustan más las comidas que son buenas para la salud.

6 Una cocina

Trabaja con un(a) compañero(a). Miren esta foto de una cocina. Juntos describan la cocina. Indiquen si es una cocina moderna o anticuada.

¡A preparar la comida!

limpiar

pelar

rallar

las rebanadas

rebanar

cortar

agregar, añadir

picar

los pedacitos, los trocitos

tapar

Anita pone la cacerola al fuego.

Anita quita (retira) la cacerola del fuego.
Apaga el fuego.

Más comestibles

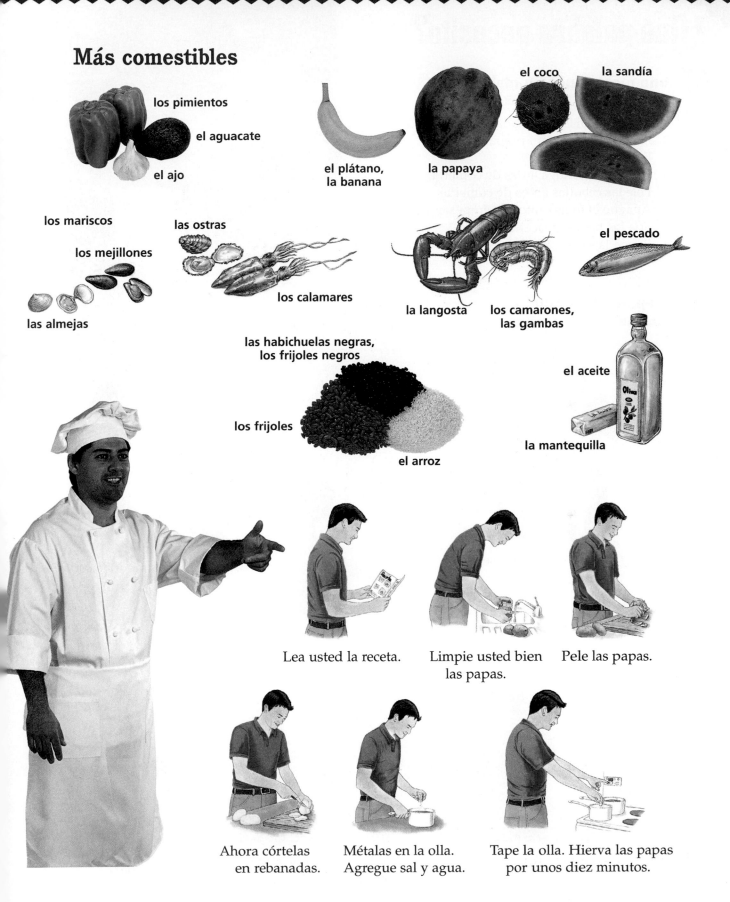

los pimientos

el aguacate

el ajo

el plátano,
la banana

la papaya

el coco

la sandía

los mariscos

los mejillones

las almejas

las ostras

los calamares

la langosta

los camarones,
las gambas

el pescado

las habichuelas negras,
los frijoles negros

los frijoles

el arroz

el aceite

la mantequilla

Lea usted la receta.

Limpie usted bien
las papas.

Pele las papas.

Ahora córtelas
en rebanadas.

Métalas en la olla.
Agregue sal y agua.

Tape la olla. Hierva las papas
por unos diez minutos.

LA COCINA HISPANA

doscientos noventa y siete 297

Vocabulario

¿Qué palabra necesito?

7 **Una receta buena o mala**

¿Es algo que se hace o no?

1. Corte el pan en rebanadas para tostarlo.
2. Hierva el agua para preparar el té.
3. Fría bien la sandía.
4. Limpie la lechuga antes de comerla.
5. Pele las cebollas antes de comerlas.
6. Apague el fuego antes de empezar a cocinar.
7. Fría las papas en aceite.
8. Ponga la sartén al fuego para hervir el agua.

Lima, Perú

8 **Preparando la comida**

Contesten según las fotos.

1. ¿Qué está picando la señora?

2. ¿Qué está rebanando el señor?

3. ¿Qué está cortando la señorita?

4. ¿Qué está pelando el joven?

5. ¿Qué está limpiando la muchacha?

9 **¿Qué opinas?** Digan si se puede o no.

1. ¿Se puede hervir o freír el arroz?
2. ¿Se puede rallar la lechuga?
3. ¿Se puede rallar el queso o el coco?
4. ¿Se puede rebanar la sandía?
5. ¿Se puede picar la carne de res?
6. ¿Se puede freír la chuleta?
7. ¿Se puede asar el arroz?
8. ¿Se puede tapar la olla?

10  **Historieta** Cocinando algo
Contesten según se indica.

1. ¿Qué estás preparando? (un pollo)
2. ¿Lo vas a asar o freír? (asar)
3. ¿Qué tienes que hacer con el pollo antes de asarlo? (lavarlo)
4. ¿Lo vas a asar entero? (no)
5. ¿Qué vas a hacer? (cortarlo en pedazos)
6. ¿Vas a sazonar el pollo? (sí, con ajo, sal y pimienta)
7. ¿Dónde lo vas a asar? (en el horno)
8. ¿Lo vas a asar a fuego lento? (sí)
9. ¿Qué vas a servir con el pollo? (una ensalada)
10. Y de postre, ¿qué hay? (frutas)

Le invitamos a conocer el mundo del arroz

11 **Una comida norteamericana** Estás en Lima, Perú, con la familia Sandoval. Ellos quieren comer una comida típica norteamericana. La señora Sandoval (tu compañero[a]) te pide describir una comida típica norteamericana. Describe la comida y dile a la señora cómo prepararla. Después cambien de rol.

Spanish Online
For a fun way to review this vocabulary, go to the Chapter 10 **eGame** on the Glencoe Spanish Web site at glencoe.com.

12 **Juego** **¿Qué categoría es?** Trabaja con un(a) compañero(a). Miren las siguientes categorías. Tienen tres minutos. Trabajando independientemente, completen cada lista en español, dando los nombres de los comestibles que conocen que pertenecen a cada grupo. La persona que ha escrito el mayor número de comestibles en cada categoría gana.

marisco   fruta   pescado   vegetal   carne

*For more practice using words from **Palabras 1** and **2**, do Activity 10 on page H11 at the end of this book.*

Estructura

Imperativo formal: formas regulares
Telling people what to do

Use your StudentWorks Plus CD for more practice.

1. You use the command form of the verb—the imperative—to tell someone what to do. To form the **usted** and **ustedes** commands, you drop the **o** from the present tense **yo** form and add the following endings.

INFINITIVE	YO—PRESENT	UD. COMMAND	UDS. COMMAND
preparar	preparø	prepare Ud.	preparen Uds.
leer	leø	lea Ud.	lean Uds.
abrir	abrø	abra Ud.	abran Uds.

You form the imperative of stem-changing verbs in the same way. The **yo** form of the present tense serves as the stem.

pensar	piensø	piense Ud.	piensen Uds.
volver	vuelvø	vuelva Ud.	vuelvan Uds.
hervir	hiervø	hierva Ud.	hiervan Uds.
pedir	pidø	pida Ud.	pidan Uds.

Note that the endings used for the formal commands have the vowel opposite to the vowel usually associated with the conjugation. The **-ar** verbs have **e** and the **-er** and **-ir** verbs have **a.**

¿Te acuerdas?
Remember the following spelling patterns.
busca — busque
agrega — agregue
empieza — empiece

2. To make these commands negative, simply place **no** before the verb.

prepare Ud.	no prepare Ud.	preparen Uds.	no preparen Uds.
pida Ud.	no pida Ud.	pidan Uds.	no pidan Uds.
abra Ud.	no abra Ud.	abran Uds.	no abran Uds.

¿Cómo lo digo?

13 **La ensalada** Contesten según el modelo.

¿Preparo la comida?

Sí, prepare Ud. la comida.

1. ¿Preparo la comida?
2. ¿Limpio la lechuga?
3. ¿Pelo los tomates?
4. ¿Pico el ajo?
5. ¿Hiervo el agua?
6. ¿Frío el pollo?
7. ¿Tapo la sartén?
8. ¿Retiro la sartén del fuego?

Gazpacho

Caracas, Venezuela

14 **¿Preparamos la comida?**
Contesten según el modelo.

¿Preparamos la comida? ⟶
No, no preparen ustedes la comida.
   Yo la voy a preparar.

1. ¿Preparamos la comida?
2. ¿Limpiamos la lechuga?
3. ¿Pelamos los tomates?
4. ¿Picamos el ajo?
5. ¿Hervimos el agua?
6. ¿Freímos el pollo?
7. ¿Tapamos la sartén?
8. ¿Retiramos la sartén del fuego?

Estructura

15 **¿Qué debo hacer con la carta?** Contesten con el imperativo.

1. ¿Debo aceptar la carta?
2. ¿Debo abrir la carta?
3. ¿Debo leer la carta?
4. ¿Debo contestar la carta?
5. ¿Debo escribir la carta en inglés?

16 **Debe hacer lo que quiere hacer.** Sigan el modelo.

> Quiero viajar a España.

> Entonces, ¡viaje Ud. a España!

San Martín y el pordiosero de El Greco

1. Quiero viajar a España.
2. Quiero pasar un mes en Madrid.
3. Quiero tomar el tren a Toledo.
4. Quiero visitar la capital.
5. Quiero ver los cuadros de El Greco.
6. Quiero aprender el español.
7. Quiero comer una paella.
8. Quiero beber horchata.
9. Quiero vivir con una familia española.

17 **Soy yo el/la profesor(a).** Trabajen en grupos de tres. Uno(a) de ustedes va a ser el/la profesor(a). Los otros serán los alumnos. El/La profesor(a) les va a dar una orden. Los alumnos van a decir si quieren hacerlo o no. El/La profesor(a) puede usar las siguientes palabras.

hablar   escribir   abrir   cerrar

estudiar   leer

volver   trabajar   escuchar   jugar

Imperativo formal: formas irregulares
Telling people what to do

1. A verb that has an irregularity in the **yo** form of the present tense will keep the same irregularity in the command form, since the **yo** form of the present tense serves as the root for the command. Study the following.

INFINITIVE	YO—PRESENT	UD. COMMAND	UDS. COMMAND
hacer	hagø	haga Ud.	hagan Uds.
poner	pongø	ponga Ud.	pongan Uds.
salir	salgø	salga Ud.	salgan Uds.
venir	vengø	venga Ud.	vengan Uds.
decir	digø	diga Ud.	digan Uds.
introducir	introduzcø	introduzca Ud.	introduzcan Uds.

2. The following verbs are the only ones in Spanish that have irregular command forms.

INFINITIVE	UD. COMMAND	UDS. COMMAND
ir	vaya Ud.	vayan Uds.
ser	sea Ud.	sean Uds.
saber	sepa Ud.	sepan Uds.
estar	esté Ud.	estén Uds.
dar	dé Ud.	den Uds.

Málaga, España

¿Cómo lo digo?

18 **Voy de compras.** Sigan el modelo.

Quiero hacer las compras.

Pues, haga Ud. las compras.

1. Quiero hacer las compras.
2. Quiero salir ahora.
3. Quiero ir al mercado de Santa Tecla.
4. Quiero poner mis compras en esta bolsa.
5. Quiero ir a pie.

19 **¿Podemos salir?** Sigan el modelo.

¿Podemos
salir ahora?

¡Cómo no! ¡Salgan
Uds. ahora!

1. ¿Podemos salir mañana?
2. ¿Podemos usar el carro?
3. ¿Podemos llevar a Anita?
4. ¿Podemos volver?
5. ¿Podemos poner las
   maletas en la maletera?

20 **Una llamada telefónica**
Completen con el imperativo.

1. ____ (llamar) usted por teléfono.
2. ____ (hacer) usted la llamada esta noche.
3. ____ (ir) usted a una cabina telefónica.
4. ____ (descolgar) usted el auricular.
5. ____ (introducir) usted la tarjeta telefónica
   en la ranura.
6. ____ (esperar) usted el tono.
7. ____ (marcar) usted el número.
8. ____ (esperar) usted la contestación.
9. ____ (decir) usted quien es.
10. ____ (preguntar) usted por Antonio.
11. ____ (hablar) usted con él.

Estepona, España

21 **Dos recetas** Trabaja con un(a) compañero(a). Selecciona
(Escoge) uno de tus platos favoritos—un plato no muy complicado.

Luego dile a tu compañero(a) cómo se prepara el plato—es decir,
le vas a dar la receta. Luego tu compañero(a) te dará la receta para
su plato favorito.

22 **Juego** **¡Hágalo!** Have some fun. Get together in
small groups and make up commands telling your teacher
what to do. Now it's your turn because a teacher always
tells you what to do. **¿Verdad?**

Spanish Online
For more information about typical dishes
and recipes from the Spanish-speaking
world, go to the Chapter 10 **WebQuest**
on the Glencoe Spanish Web site at
glencoe.com.

Colocación de los pronombres de complemento
Referring to things already stated

The object pronouns are attached to the affirmative command. They come before, or precede, the negative command.

Lave los platos.	Lávelos.	No los lave Ud.
Coma la ensalada.	Cómala.	No la coma Ud.
Sirva el postre.	Sírvalo.	No lo sirva Ud.
Déme la receta.	Démela.	No me la dé Ud.

¿Lo sabes?

To maintain the same stress, use a written accent with either one or two pronouns.

Diga. Dígame. Dígamelo.

¿Cómo lo digo?

23 **¿Qué debo hacer?** Contesten según el modelo.

> ¿Debo limpiar la lechuga? ⟶
> Sí, límpiela.
> No, no la limpie usted.

1. ¿Debo lavar los cuchillos?
2. ¿Debo pelar las naranjas?
3. ¿Debo abrir la lata?
4. ¿Debo leer la receta?

5. ¿Debo picar el ajo?
6. ¿Debo rallar el queso?
7. ¿Debo revolver los huevos?
8. ¿Debo poner el pollo en la nevera?

24 **Ellos no lo hicieron.**
Sigan el modelo.

> Ellos no cortaron la carne. ⟶
> Pues, córtenla ustedes.

1. Ellos no rebanaron el pan.
2. Ellos no hirvieron la sopa.
3. Ellos no frieron los huevos.
4. Ellos no taparon las ollas.
5. Ellos no añadieron azúcar.
6. Ellos no pusieron el pollo en el horno.

Una merienda, España

Andas bien. ¡Adelante!

¿Yo? ¿En la cocina?

Jaime David, ¿te gusta cocinar?

David A mí, ¿cocinar? ¿Hablas en serio? En la cocina soy un desastre. ¿A ti te gusta cocinar?

Jaime Sí, bastante.

David ¿Qué sabes preparar?

Jaime Muchas cosas, pero mi plato favorito es la paella.

David La paella, dices. ¿Qué es?

Jaime Pues, es una especialidad española, de Valencia. Lleva muchos ingredientes— mariscos, arroz.

David Se comen muchos mariscos en España, ¿no?

Jaime Sí, hombre. Y algún día te voy a preparar una buena paella.

¿Comprendes?

Contesten.

1. ¿A quién le gusta cocinar?
2. ¿Quién es un desastre en la cocina?
3. ¿Cuál es el plato que a Jaime le gusta mucho preparar?
4. ¿Dónde se come la paella?
5. ¿De qué región de España es la paella una especialidad?
6. ¿Qué opinas? ¿Te gustaría la paella o no?

Vamos a hablar más

A **La cafetería de la escuela**

Tu compañero(a) es la persona responsable de la cafetería de tu escuela. Dile cuáles son los platos que sirven en la cafetería que te gustan y cuáles son los platos que no te gustan. Dale algunas sugerencias *(suggestions).* Dile lo que debe preparar y servir en la cafetería. Luego cambien de rol.

Colegio Santa Teresita, Santurce, Puerto Rico

Un restaurante, Ronda, España

B **En un restaurante** Trabaja con un(a) compañero(a). Miren la foto de unas personas que están comiendo en un restaurante. Trabajando juntos, describan todo lo que ven en el restaurante. Decidan si a ustedes les gustaría comer en este restaurante.

C **Una comida española** Aquí ves una foto de un plato típico español. Trabaja con un(a) compañero(a). Identifiquen todos los ingredientes que ven. Luego expliquen cómo creen que se prepara este plato.

Lecturas culturales

Una receta española 🔄 🎧

Como le dijo Jaime a David, la paella es un plato delicioso que es una especialidad de la cocina española. Quien no ha comido una paella no sabe lo que se ha perdido. La paella valenciana lleva muchos ingredientes. Aquí tiene usted una receta bastante sencilla para preparar una paella. Decida si a usted le gustaría comer este plato delicioso.

Reading Strategy

Reading for detailed information Some readings require a reader to focus in on details. When you need to do so, you will need to read a selection more than once and pay close attention. Sometimes when you need to be aware of details, it is helpful to take notes on what you read or make a list of the important details. Reading for detail is especially necessary with recipes. You must understand each step and follow the procedure carefully to ensure that the final product is as good as it can be.

LA PAELLA

INGREDIENTES

3 tomates
2 cebollas grandes
2 pimientos (uno verde y uno rojo)
4 dientes[1] de ajo
1/2 kilo de camarones

4 calamares
12 almejas
12 mejillones
langosta (opcional)
1 pollo en partes
3 chorizos

1 paquete de guisantes congelados
1 bote de pimientos morrones
1 1/2 tazas de arroz
3 tazas de consomé de pollo
4 pizcas[2] de azafrán[3]
1/4 taza de aceite de oliva

PREPARACIÓN

1. Pique los tomates, los pimientos, las cebollas y el ajo.
2. Lave las almejas y los mejillones en agua fría.
3. Limpie y pele los camarones.
4. Limpie y corte en rebanadas los calamares.
5. Corte en rebanadas los chorizos.
6. Fría o ase el pollo aparte.

COCCIÓN

Se usa una paellera o una olla.
1. Fría ligeramente[4] en el aceite los pimientos y las cebollas picadas.
2. Agregue el ajo y los tomates y fría ligeramente a fuego lento unos dos o tres minutos.
3. Agregue el arroz.
4. Revuelva el arroz con los tomates, las cebollas, los pimientos y el ajo.
5. Agregue el consomé de pollo y llévelo a la ebullición[5].
6. Baje el fuego y agregue los camarones, los calamares, el chorizo, el pollo, las almejas y los mejillones.
7. Agregue el azafrán.
8. Ponga sal y pimienta a su gusto.
   Si se prepara la paella en una olla, tape la olla y cocine a fuego lento encima de la estufa unos 40 minutos. En una paellera, ase la paella en el horno sin tapa o cocine a fuego lento encima de la estufa. Al final agregue los guisantes y los pimientos y sirva. Usted notará que el arroz tiene un bonito color amarillo. Es del azafrán.

[1]dientes *cloves*
[2]pizcas *pinches*

[3]azafrán *saffron*
[4]ligeramente *lightly*

[5]a la ebullición *to a boil*

¿Comprendes?

A ¿Cuál es la palabra? Completen según la receta.
1. una ____ para hacer la paella
2. medio ____ de camarones
3. un ____ de guisantes congelados
4. cuatro ____ de ajo
5. una ____ de sal
6. tres ____ de consomé de pollo

B La paella Preparen una lista de los ingredientes que lleva una paella.

C La cocción Digan que sí o que no.
1. Se puede asar la paella en el horno.
2. La paella lleva muchas papas.
3. Hay muchas especias en una paella.
4. El arroz de una paella se pone amarillo.
5. El chorizo es un tipo de salchicha española.

D Para pensar Miren el mapa de España en la página xxx y expliquen por qué se comen muchos mariscos en España.

Use your **StudentWorks** Plus
CD for more practice.

Valencia, España

LA COCINA HISPANA

trescientos nueve 309

Lectura opcional 1

Ica, Perú

El tomate, ¿comida o veneno?

¿Sabías que durante muchos años los ingleses y los norteamericanos no comían el tomate? Ellos creían que el tomate era venenoso[1]. Creían que al comer un tomate, uno se moriría[2]. Comer un tomate era fatal.

Cuando los españoles llevaron los primeros tomates de América a Europa, los usaban solamente como adorno, y no como comida. Pero en poco tiempo los españoles y los italianos descubrieron que el tomate era delicioso y no venenoso. Pero los ingleses, no. Hasta el siglo XIX, los ingleses y los norteamericanos seguían creyendo que el tomate era veneno.

[1]venenoso *poisonous*   [2]se moriría *would die*

¿Comprendes?

A **El tomate** Contesten según la lectura.
1. El tomate, ¿es de origen europeo o americano?
2. ¿Qué creían los ingleses que pasaría a la persona al comer un tomate?
3. ¿Para qué se usaban los tomates en Europa originalmente?
4. ¿Quiénes, en Europa, fueron los primeros en comer el tomate?
5. ¿Hasta cuándo creían los norteamericanos que el tomate era venenoso?

B **La superstición** ¿Conoces tú alguna superstición acerca de alguna comida? ¿Cuál es? ¿Podrías decirnos?

El maíz y la papa, regalos de las Américas

Los españoles llegaron a las Américas en el siglo XV. En Europa no había maíz ni papas. Los europeos no cultivaban estos vegetales. Los europeos no los conocían. La papa y el maíz tienen su origen en las Américas.

Los indios cultivaban el maíz en toda la América. El maíz era la base de la dieta de muchos indios. La tortilla de maíz sigue siendo muy importante en la cocina mexicana y centroamericana.

La papa tiene su origen en el altiplano sudamericano. Los incas cultivaban la papa en la región que hoy es Perú y Bolivia. Los españoles llevaron la papa a Europa donde, en poco tiempo, llegó a ser la base de la dieta de varios países, como Irlanda y Polonia.

Santiago Atitlán, Guatemala

¿Comprendes?

A ¿Sí o no? Contesten.

1. En el siglo XVIII los primeros españoles llegaron a las Américas.
2. Los europeos cultivaban la papa y el maíz antes del siglo XV.
3. La tortilla se hace de papa.
4. Los incas cultivaban la papa en el altiplano.
5. La tortilla es muy importante en la dieta de Perú y Bolivia.
6. La tortilla de maíz se come mucho en México.
7. La papa era muy importante en Irlanda y Polonia.

B ¿Qué país es? Identifiquen.

1. Irlanda está en Europa. Está cerca de Inglaterra. Su capital es Dublín. ¿Cómo se llama Irlanda en inglés?
2. Polonia está en el noreste de Europa. Está cerca de Rusia. Su capital es Varsovia. Los polacos son de Polonia. ¿Cómo se llama Polonia en inglés?

Urubamba, Perú

Conexiones
Las ciencias

La nutrición

Everyone is aware of the importance of a healthy diet. What constitutes a healthy diet? What effect does diet have on our lives? How does the diet of Hispanic countries differ from ours?

Madrid, España

La dieta

Vamos a comparar la dieta típica de un español y un norteamericano.

Carnes y legumbres: El norteamericano come bastante carne, especialmente carne roja, como el biftec. También consume legumbres como los guisantes, las zanahorias y las papas, pero casi siempre en pequeñas cantidades con la carne. El español come poca carne, y muy poca carne roja. Las carnes que consume, en pequeñas cantidades, son el pollo, la ternera y el cordero. Las legumbres que come son, muchas veces, el plato principal, basado en frijoles, garbanzos[1], lentejas[2] y similares. Una de las mayores diferencias es en el consumo de pescado y mariscos. El español come pescado y mariscos tres o cuatro veces a la semana. Muchos españoles consumen más pescado que carne. El norteamericano come poco pescado.

Frutas y verduras: El norteamericano come frutas con el cereal por la mañana y cuando tiene hambre entre comidas. Para el español las frutas son postre, y las come todos los días. Los norteamericanos y los españoles comen mucha ensalada. La ensalada de lechuga y tomate es tradicional en España. En Latinoamérica se añade el aguacate (la palta) a la ensalada. Muchos platos de los países sudamericanos llevan vegetales, tales como las papas y el maíz.

[1]garbanzos *chick peas*   [2]lentejas *lentils*

Otavalo, Ecuador

Productos lácteos (de la leche):
El norteamericano consume mucha mantequilla. El español come poquísima mantequilla y nunca cocina con mantequilla. El español consume menos mantequilla que cualquier otro europeo. El norteamericano toma leche. En España y en Latinoamérica solamente los bebés y los niños pequeños toman leche. Pero el español consume bastante queso. El queso con frutas es un postre popular. Los españoles también toman yogur como postre. Al norteamericano le gusta mucho el helado. También les gusta a los españoles, pero ellos consumen mucho menos.

Pan y cereales: Los norteamericanos y los españoles comen mucho pan, pero el español casi nunca come pan con mantequilla. El norteamericano come cereales para el desayuno. El español come pan con su café con leche. Los espaguetis y otras pastas son más y más populares en EE.UU. Pero el norteamericano, a diferencia del español, come poco arroz. El español consume grandes cantidades de arroz.

Es importante notar que muchos jóvenes, españoles y norteamericanos, tienen una dieta muy diferente a la dieta de la gente mayor. Muchos jóvenes son vegetarianos. Consumen poca grasa y muchas verduras, cereales y legumbres.

¿Comprendes?

A **¿Es español o norteamericano?**
Escojan.
1. Pide un plato de garbanzos.
2. Está comiendo un biftec grande.
3. No quiere mantequilla con su pan.
4. Come pescado tres veces a la semana.
5. Pide un vaso de leche.
6. Quiere camarones con arroz.
7. Para el desayuno toma cereal con fruta, pan con mantequilla y un vaso de leche.
8. Para el postre pide queso y fruta.
9. Usa aceite de oliva para freír, no mantequilla.

B **¿Qué opinas?** Contesten.
1. Para ti, ¿en qué consiste una dieta buena?
2. ¿Qué opinas? ¿Tienen los norteamericanos una dieta buena? ¿Por qué o por qué no?

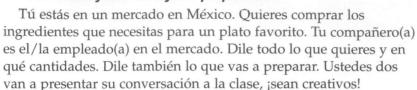

Use what you have learned

1 En el mercado

✔ *Talk about foods and food preparation*

Tú estás en un mercado en México. Quieres comprar los ingredientes que necesitas para un plato favorito. Tu compañero(a) es el/la empleado(a) en el mercado. Dile todo lo que quieres y en qué cantidades. Dile también lo que vas a preparar. Ustedes dos van a presentar su conversación a la clase, ¡sean creativos!

Guanajuato, México

2 Comidas étnicas

✔ *Describe an ethnic dish that you like*

¿Hay restaurantes étnicos, restaurantes que sirven comida de otras partes del mundo, en tu comunidad? Si los hay, con un(a) compañero(a) preparen una lista de estos restaurantes y el tipo de comida que sirven. Luego describan un plato típico de uno de los restaurantes que les gusta.

3 Simón dice...

✔ *Use commands*

Trabajen en grupos de cinco. Van a jugar **Simón dice.** Cada líder dará cinco órdenes y luego escogerán a otro líder.

ESCRIBIR
¡Qué comida más deliciosa!
✔ *Describe a dish you really liked*

Estás viajando por México. Anoche fuiste a cenar en un restaurante y pediste algo que salió delicioso, muy rico. Te gustó mucho. Escribe una tarjeta postal a tus padres. Descríbeles el restaurante y el plato que te gustó tanto. Si puedes, explícales cómo crees que el cocinero preparó el plato.

San Miguel de Allende, México

Writing Strategy

Writing about a process
When you write about a process or how to do something, you must remember to tell all the little details involved. Describe the process accurately and thoroughly. In this type of expository writing, be sure to define any terms you think your readers will not be familiar with and also to put the various steps of the process in logical order.

ESCRIBIR
Un(a) americano(a) en Aranjuez

You are living with a Spanish family in Aranjuez, near Madrid. One day last week you prepared your favorite American dish for them. They loved it! They want you to write out the recipe for them before you leave to return to the United States. Since they don't speak much English, you will have to write the recipe in Spanish. Be sure to explain all the steps as clearly as possible so that they prepare something delicious rather than a disaster!

Vocabulario

1 **Identifiquen.**

1.

2.

3.

4.

To review **Palabras 1**, turn to pages 292–293.

2 **Pareen.**

5. freír   a. la parrilla
6. hervir   b. la olla
7. asar   c. el/la sartén

3 **Identifiquen.**

8.

9.

To review **Palabras 2**, turn to pages 296–297.

10.

11.

12.

13.

14.

Estructura

4 **Completen con el imperativo.**

15. ____ usted la comida. (preparar)
16. ____ usted la receta. (leer)
17. ____ usted otra vez. (volver)
18. ____ ustedes el menú. (pedir)
19. ____ usted el aceite en la sartén. (poner)
20. ____ ustedes con nosotros. (salir)

To review the imperatives, turn to pages 300 and 303.

5 **Escriban con el pronombre.**

21. Sirva usted el postre.
22. No sirva usted las papas.
23. Déme la receta.

To review object pronouns with commands, turn to page 305.

Cultura

6 **Contesten.** (*Answer.*)

24–25. ¿Cuáles son algunos ingredientes que lleva una paella?

To review this cultural information, turn to page 308.

Tell all you can about this illustration.

Vocabulario

Talking about some kitchen appliances and utensils

la cocina
el congelador
la nevera, el refrigerador
la estufa
el horno
el horno de microondas

la hornilla, el hornillo
la cazuela, la cacerola
el/la sartén
la parrilla
la olla

Talking about food preparation

limpiar
pelar
rallar
picar
cortar

rebanar
agregar, añadir
tapar
los pedacitos, los trocitos
las rebanadas

> ### How well do you know your vocabulary?
> • Choose words from the list and describe a meal you would like to serve.
> • Describe as many steps as you can in the preparation of the meal.

Talking about some cooking procedures

cocinar
revolver
freír
asar

hervir
poner al fuego
quitar del fuego
apagar el fuego

Identifying more foods

la coliflor
las cebollas
el pepino
las zanahorias
la lechuga
las papas, las patatas
los pimientos
el aguacate
el ajo
el arroz
las habichuelas negras,
   los frijoles negros
la lima
el limón

la toronja
las uvas
la papaya
el coco
la sandía
el plátano, la banana
la carne de res
el cerdo
el cordero
la salchicha, el chorizo
la ternera
el pollo
la costilla
la chuleta

el pescado
los mariscos
la langosta
los camarones, las gambas
las almejas
los calamares
los mejillones
las ostras
la sal
la pimienta
el azúcar
el aceite
la mantequilla

 VIDEOTUR

Episodio 10

In this video episode, you will join Alejandra and Vicky as they show off their culinary talents. See page 489 for more information. As you watch, look for gestures the speakers use to help convey their message.

El coche y la carretera

Objetivos

In this chapter you will learn to:

❖ talk about cars and driving
❖ give directions on the road
❖ tell family and friends what to do and what not to do
❖ talk about highways in the Hispanic world

Norberto Russo *De mi Buenos Aires*

Vocabulario

El coche

el descapotable, el convertible

Use your StudentWorks Plus
CD for more practice.

el conductor

El conductor maneja
(conduce) con cuidado.

el sedán

el cupé

el coche (carro) deportivo

el permiso de conducir,
la licencia

el cinturón de seguridad

la maletera,
el baúl

el parabrisas

el capó

las luces

la puerta

las direccionales

la goma, la llanta,
el neumático

la bocina,
el claxon

la llanta de repuesto
(de recambio)

los frenos

La estación de servicio, La gasolinera

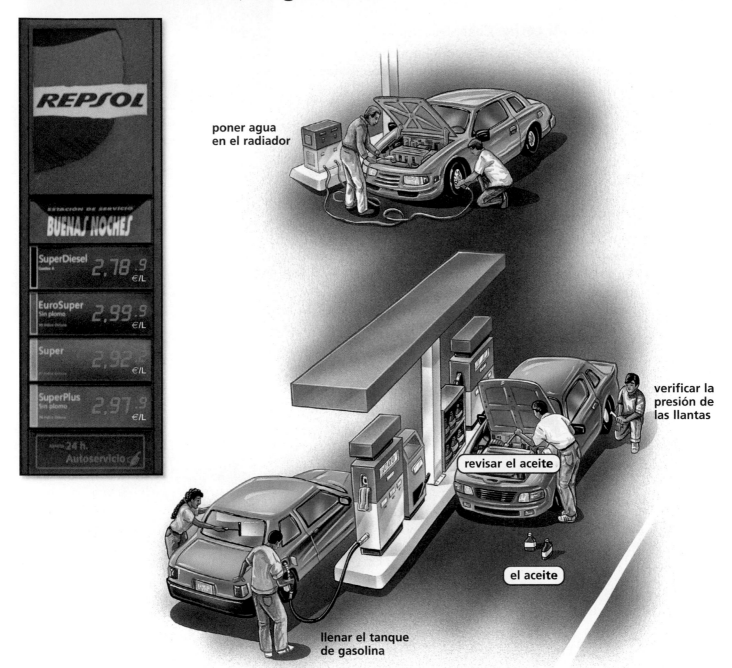

poner agua
en el radiador

verificar la
presión de
las llantas

revisar el aceite

el aceite

llenar el tanque
de gasolina

El muchacho llenó el tanque de gasolina.
La muchacha limpió el parabrisas.
El otro muchacho puso aire en las llantas.

Vocabulario

¿Qué palabra necesito?

 1 **Historieta** **Mi coche** Contesten.

1. ¿Tienes un coche o quieres tener un coche algún día?
2. En el estado donde vives, ¿cuántos años tienes que cumplir para tener el permiso de conducir?
3. ¿Qué tipo de coche quieres?
4. ¿Tienes un modelo favorito? ¿Cuál es?
5. ¿Vas a manejar con cuidado?
6. ¿Vas a llevar tu coche a la estación de servicio con frecuencia?

Un coche clásico, La Habana, Cuba

2 **Coches** Digan que sí o que no.

1. El motor de un coche está en la maletera.
2. El motor del coche está debajo del capó.
3. Es una buena idea tener una llanta de repuesto en la maletera del carro.
4. Es necesario tocar la bocina cada vez que pasas por un hospital.
5. Es necesario tener el cinturón abrochado cuando estás en un asiento delantero del carro.
6. Es necesario poner los frenos para parar el coche.
7. Los coches tienen tres neumáticos.
8. Se limpia el parabrisas con gasolina.

3 **Historieta** **En la gasolinera**
Describan cada dibujo.

2.

1.

3.

4 **En la gasolinera** Escojan.

1. En la gasolinera el señor llena el tanque de ____.
   a. agua   **b.** aceite   **c.** gasolina
2. El muchacho revisa ____.
   a. el agua en los neumáticos   **b.** el tanque   **c.** el nivel del aceite
3. El señor pone agua en ____.
   a. los neumáticos   **b.** el radiador   **c.** el tanque
4. La señora podría verificar ____.
   a. la presión de los neumáticos   **b.** el aire del radiador
   c. el parabrisas
5. El parabrisas está muy sucio. No puedo ver nada. ¿Me lo ____ usted, por favor?
   a. llenaría   **b.** revisaría   **c.** limpiaría

5 **Mi carro** ¿Tienes un carro (coche) o no? Si no tienes carro, ¿te comprarás uno algún día? Trabaja con un(a) compañero(a). Cada uno de ustedes describirá el carro de sus sueños.

6 **Un carro nuevo** Estás pasando un año estudiando en Puerto Rico. Decides comprarte un carro. Como tienes muy poco dinero, tienes que comprar un carro usado (de ocasión). Visitas una agencia. Estás hablando con el/la vendedor(a) (tu compañero[a]). Él o ella te quiere vender un carro—cualquier carro, no importa la calidad ni la condición. Discutan juntos.

7 **Trabajo a tiempo parcial** Imagínate que trabajas en una gasolinera. Tu compañero(a) cree que a él o a ella le gustaría trabajar a tiempo parcial en una gasolinera para ganar unos dólares extra. Te va a hacer preguntas sobre el trabajo que haces. Contesta a sus preguntas.

Una gasolinera,
Miraflores, Perú

En la carretera

el rótulo

la salida

la autopista, la autovía

la velocidad máxima

120 km

la garita de peaje

el peaje

el carril

la entrada

Alejandro, quédate en el carril derecho. Paga el peaje. Y luego, sal de la autopista en la próxima salida.

Donde está el rótulo, dobla a la derecha. Y luego sigue derecho.

¡Cuidado! Está prohibido adelantar. Hay solamente un carril en cada sentido.

En la ciudad

el semáforo

la luz roja

una cuadra

un cruce,
una bocacalle

Es necesario parar cuando hay una luz roja.

No podemos entrar. Es una calle de sentido único. Tenemos que ir en el sentido contrario.

de sentido único

el parquímetro

estacionar el coche, aparcar

Vocabulario

¿Qué palabra necesito?

8 Historieta En la carretera
Contesten según se indica.

1. ¿Qué vamos a tomar? (la autopista)
2. ¿Qué tendremos que pagar? (el peaje)
3. ¿Dónde lo tenemos que pagar? (en la garita)
4. ¿Cuántos carriles tiene la autopista en cada sentido? (tres)
5. ¿Cuál es la velocidad máxima? (ciento veinte kilómetros por hora)
6. ¿Está prohibido adelantar? (no)
7. ¿Está prohibido exceder la velocidad máxima? (sí)

9 Buenos o malos consejos Digan que sí o que no.

1. Maneja con cuidado.
2. Estaciona el coche donde está prohibido el estacionamiento.
3. Excede la velocidad indicada en el rótulo.
4. Quédate en el carril derecho para adelantar un carro.
5. Mete una moneda en la ranura del parquímetro.
6. Paga el peaje en la garita.
7. Al llegar a un cruce, para y mira a la derecha y a la izquierda antes de seguir.
8. Cuando vas a parar, pon las direccionales.
9. Pon las direccionales porque vas a doblar a la izquierda.

Motril, España

10 Historieta Donde vivo yo Contesten.

1. ¿Cuál es una autopista cerca de donde tú vives?
2. ¿Es una autopista de peaje?
3. ¿Cuánto es el peaje?
4. ¿Dónde tienes que pagar peaje? ¿En la salida de la autopista? Si no, ¿a cada cuántos kilómetros hay garitas de peaje?
5. ¿Cuál es el número de la salida más cerca de tu casa?
6. ¿Cuál es la velocidad máxima en la autopista?
7. ¿Cuántos carriles tiene?
8. A la salida, ¿hay un rótulo que indica los pueblos cercanos?

Spanish Online
For more information about Ecuador, go to the Glencoe Spanish Web site at glencoe.com.

11 Las autopistas Estás viajando por Ecuador. Un(a) amigo(a) ecuatoriano(a) (tu compañero[a]) te hace preguntas sobre las autopistas donde tú vives. Contesta a todas sus preguntas y descríbele las autopistas de tu estado.

12 Ventajas En las autopistas es casi siempre necesario pagar peaje. En las carreteras secundarias no hay peaje. Con un(a) compañero(a), discutan por qué es mejor tomar la autopista y pagar el peaje. ¿Cuáles son las ventajas *(advantages)*?

La carretera panamericana, Perú

Zafra, España

 For more practice using words from **Palabras 1** *and* **2**, *do Activity 11 on page H12 at the end of this book.*

Estructura

Imperativo familiar: formas regulares
Telling friends what to do

Use your StudentWorks *Plus* CD for more practice.

You use the **tú** command when speaking with friends, family, people you know well, and children. The regular **tú** form of the command is the same form as the **usted** form in the present tense.

PRESENT (UD.)	IMPERATIVE (TÚ)
Ud. maneja.	¡Maneja!
Ud. aprende.	¡Aprende!
Ud. escribe.	¡Escribe!
Ud. comienza.	¡Comienza!
Ud. vuelve.	¡Vuelve!
Ud. sigue.	¡Sigue!

Estepona, España

¿Cómo lo digo?

13 **¿Qué debo hacer?**
Sigan el modelo.

¿Debo hablar?

Sí, Pepe, habla.

1. ¿Debo parar?
2. ¿Debo doblar?
3. ¿Debo dar la vuelta?
4. ¿Debo doblar a la derecha?
5. ¿Debo leer el rótulo?
6. ¿Debo seguir derecho?
7. ¿Debo volver?
8. ¿Debo pedir direcciones?

14 Historieta El instructor Completen con el imperativo.

Estepona, España

Luis, primero __1__ (prender) el motor. __2__ (Prestar) atención a la carretera. Ahora __3__ (entrar) en la carretera. Bien. __4__ (Adelantar) en el carril izquierdo. Ahora __5__ (volver) al carril derecho. __6__ (Seguir) derecho hasta la salida. __7__ (Manejar) siempre con calma. __8__ (Parar) aquí. __9__ (Apagar) el motor. __10__ (Tomar) este manual y __11__ (leer). Es todo para hoy.

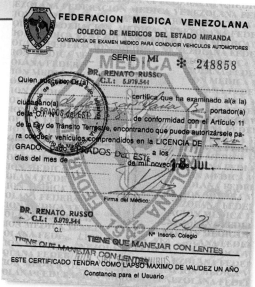

15 Una visita a Argentina Sigan el modelo.

Quiero visitar a Argentina.

Pues, visita a Argentina.

1. Quiero viajar a Argentina.
2. Quiero tomar un avión.
3. Quiero pasar un mes allí.
4. Quiero visitar a Buenos Aires.
5. Quiero subir a la cordillera.
6. Quiero esquiar en Bariloche.
7. Quiero comer un biftec allí.
8. Quiero nadar en los lagos.

Imperativo familiar: formas irregulares
Telling friends what to do

The following verbs have irregular forms for the **tú** commands.

INFINITIVE	IMPERATIVE (TÚ)
decir	di
ir	ve
ser	sé
salir	sal
hacer	haz
tener	ten
venir	ven
poner	pon

¿Cómo lo digo?

16 **A casa del abuelo**
Contesten con **sí** y el imperativo.

1. ¿Debo venir mañana?
2. ¿Debo salir temprano?
3. ¿Debo hacer el viaje en carro?
4. ¿Debo poner aire en las llantas?
5. ¿Debo decir adiós a mi hermano?
6. ¿Debo ir por la carretera vieja?
7. ¿Debo tener cuidado?

La carretera panamericana, cerca de Riobamba, Ecuador

17 **Historieta** **El mecánico experto y el mecánico nuevo**
Completen con el imperativo.

___1___ (Oír), Paco. ___2___ (Venir) aquí. Hay aceite en el piso, así es
que ___3___ (tener) cuidado. Bien, ___4___ (mirar) lo que yo hago, y tú,
___5___ (hacer) lo mismo. ___6___ (Poner) la luz aquí y ___7___ (ser) atento.
Ahora, ___8___ (decir) todo lo que aprendiste hoy.

 18 **Historieta** **Tito el tímido**

Sigan el modelo.

> **No sé si debo manejar.** ⟶
> **¡Maneja, hombre!**

1. No sé si debo hacer el viaje.
2. No sé si debo salir de la ciudad.
3. No sé si debo manejar.
4. No sé si debo ir por la autopista.
5. No sé si debo pedir un día de vacación.
6. No sé si debo volver tarde.

 19 **Las direcciones** Habla con un(a)
compañero(a). Dale direcciones para ir
de la escuela a tu casa. Luego tu
compañero(a) te dirá cómo ir a su casa.

 20 **Una llamada telefónica** Estás hablando con un(a) estudiante de
intercambio de Buenos Aires, Argentina. Él o ella quiere hacer una
llamada desde un teléfono público. Dile lo que tiene que hacer. Si él o
ella no entiende, te hará preguntas.

Buenos Aires,
Argentina

 21 **A la capital** Alicia acaba de recibir su permiso de conducir. Mañana
sus padres le van a permitir usar el carro. Alicia tiene que ir a la capital
y no conoce la ruta. Explícale cómo puede ir de tu pueblo a la capital de
tu estado. Si él o ella no entiende, te hará preguntas. Contesta a todas
sus preguntas.

Estructura

Imperativo negativo
Telling friends what not to do

1. The negative **tú** commands are formed the same way as the formal **(usted, ustedes)** commands. You drop the **o** of the **yo** form of the present tense and add **es** to **-ar** verbs and **as** to **-er** and **-ir** verbs.

INFINITIVE	PRESENT (YO)	NEGATIVE COMMAND (TÚ)
hablar	hablø	no hables
comer	comø	no comas
abrir	abrø	no abras
volver	vuelvø	no vuelvas
pedir	pidø	no pidas
hacer	hagø	no hagas
salir	salgø	no salgas

2. The same verbs that are irregular in the formal command are irregular in the negative **tú** command.

ir	no vayas
ser	no seas
saber	no sepas
estar	no estés
dar	no des

¿Te acuerdas?

Object pronouns are attached to affirmative formal commands and precede negative commands. The same is true of familiar commands.

¡Levántate!
¡No te levantes!
¡Dámelo!
¡No me lo des!
¡Cómpramelo!
¡No me lo compres!
¡Mírame!
¡No me mires!
¡Díselo!
¡No se lo digas!

¿Cómo lo digo?

Spanish Online
For a fun way to practice this grammar point, go to the Chapter 11 **eGame** on the Glencoe Spanish Web site at glencoe.com.

22  **Historieta ¿Hago el viaje o no?** Contesten según el modelo.

¿Voy temprano o no?

No, no vayas temprano.

1. ¿Voy temprano o no?
2. ¿Salgo a las nueve o no?
3. ¿Tomo la carretera vieja o no?
4. ¿Manejo el convertible o no?
5. ¿Excedo la velocidad máxima o no?
6. ¿Le digo la verdad a Pepe o no?
7. ¿Vuelvo tarde o no?
8. ¿Hago el viaje o no?

23 **En la gasolinera** Contesten con **no** y el imperativo.

1. ¿Lleno el tanque?
2. ¿Abro el capó?
3. ¿Reviso el aceite?
4. ¿Pongo agua en el radiador?
5. ¿Limpio el parabrisas?
6. ¿Pongo aire en las llantas?

24 **¡Qué dormilona es Marisa!**
Practiquen la conversación.

MAMÁ   Marisa, levántate. Ya es hora.
MARISA   ¡Ay, mamá! Que no. ¡Déjame, por favor!
MAMÁ   Bien. No te levantes. Y no te laves ni te vistas. Quédate en cama.
MARISA   Perdóname, mami, pero estoy muy cansada.

Ciudad de México

Un coche eléctrico, Puerto Banús, España

25 **¿Lo compro o no?** Sigan el modelo.

—¿Compro el carro o no?
—Sí, cómpralo. / No, no lo compres.

1. ¿Compro las baterías o no?
2. ¿Compro el aceite o no?
3. ¿Compro la gasolina o no?
4. ¿Compro el convertible o no?
5. ¿Compro los neumáticos o no?

26 **Sí, dámelas.** Contesten según el modelo.

—¿Te doy las direcciones?
—Sí, dámelas.

1. ¿Te doy el mapa?
2. ¿Te doy las instrucciones?
3. ¿Te doy el dinero para el parquímetro?
4. ¿Te doy los tiques?
5. ¿Te doy la licencia?

Andas bien. ¡Adelante!

Conversación

Un sitio para estacionar

María	Anita, ¿puedo estacionar aquí?
Anita	Aquí, no. ¿No ves que es un cruce de peatones? Hay un estacionamiento municipal en la plaza.
María	¿Cómo voy a la plaza?
Anita	Toma la avenida Cisneros. Quédate en el carril derecho porque a dos cuadras de aquí vas a doblar a la derecha.
María	¿En la esquina donde está la estación de servicio?
Anita	Precisamente. Repito—dobla a la derecha y sigue derecho hasta el primer semáforo. Al primer semáforo, dobla a la izquierda y verás la plaza.
María	¿Y puedo estacionar en la plaza?
Anita	En la plaza misma, no. Pero hay un estacionamiento subterráneo. Hay un rótulo para indicar la entrada.

¿Comprendes?

Contesten.

1. ¿Qué quiere saber María?
2. Según Anita, ¿por qué no se puede estacionar allí?
3. ¿Dónde se puede estacionar?
4. ¿Sabe María ir allí?
5. ¿Por qué debe María quedarse en el carril derecho?
6. ¿Qué hay en la esquina donde debe doblar?
7. Después de doblar a la derecha, ¿qué debe hacer María?
8. ¿Cuándo debe doblar a la izquierda?
9. ¿Dónde se encuentra el estacionamiento?
10. ¿Qué hay para indicar la entrada?

Vamos a hablar más

A **Las señales de tránsito** Trabaja con un(a) compañero(a). Tú escogerás una señal y explicarás a tu compañero(a) lo que significa. Tu compañero(a) tiene que adivinar cuál de las señales estás describiendo. Luego cambien de rol.

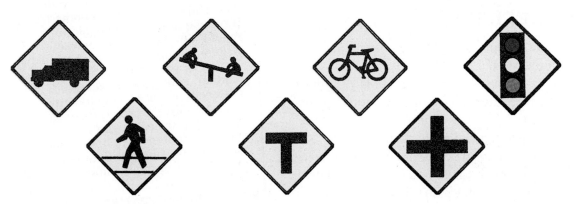

B *Juego* **¿No lo hago?** Have some fun. Your parents and teachers are always telling you what not to do. Get together in small groups and in a nice way imitate your parents and teachers. State all those things they do indeed tell each of you not to do.

Santo Domingo, República Dominicana

Lecturas culturales

La carretera panamericana 🔁 🎧

La carretera panamericana es la carretera más larga del mundo—47.516 kilómetros. La panamericana es un sistema de carreteras y caminos que se extiende desde la frontera de Estados Unidos y México hasta la ciudad de Puerto Montt en Chile. Además de extenderse del norte al sur de los continentes americanos, la carretera enlaza[1] la costa oriental con la costa occidental de la América del Sur. Enlaza también las capitales de diecisiete países latinoamericanos. Esta carretera es una ruta importante para el transporte de materias primas y productos agrícolas.

Reading Strategy

Summarizing When you read informative passages, you must develop ways to try to remember what you read. This is most important if you are reading about a topic you know nothing about. Summarizing is a good way to do this. The easiest way to summarize is to take notes as you begin to read. From your notes, you can write a sentence about each section or paragraph of the reading. From your paragraph sentences, it will be easy to write one sentence describing the main idea of the selection. Use all your summary sentences to help trigger your memory about the contents of each part of the reading.

La carretera panamericana
cerca de Buenos Aires

En algunas partes la carretera panamericana es una carretera moderna con dos o más carriles en cada sentido. En su mayor parte la carretera está pavimentada—en algunos casos en buenas condiciones y en otros casos en malas condiciones. En muchos trayectos de la carretera la tierra es muy inhóspita. Se puede decir que la carretera también es inhóspita. Hay que manejar con mucho cuidado porque nunca sabes cuándo encontrarás un bache[2] muy profundo. A veces el pavimento desaparece repentinamente y te encuentras en un camino de rocas, piedras y lodo[3].

[1]enlaza *connects*
[2]bache *pothole*
[3]lodo *mud*

Use your **StudentWorks Plus** CD for more practice.

Una estación de servicio en la carretera panamericana, cerca de Icá, Perú

¡Ten cuidado! Hay otro peligro. La mayor parte de la carretera no tiene borde. Por consiguiente cuando un carro o un camión tiene una avería[4], el conductor pone unas ramas[5] de árboles o plantas a unos metros detrás del carro. Estas ramas advierten[6] a los conductores que se están acercando que hay un carro averiado. Pero al reparar el carro o cambiar la llanta pinchada[7], el conductor sale y allí se quedan las ramas. Y de noche es difícil verlas.

Como ya hemos dicho, en muchas áreas la carretera panamericana es una carretera moderna y conveniente. Pero en las zonas remotas que recorre, tomar la panamericana es una verdadera aventura.

[4]avería *breakdown*   [6]advierten *warn*
[5]ramas *branches*   [7]pinchada *flat*

La carretera panamericana, Guatemala

¿Comprendes?

A La panamericana Contesten.
1. ¿Cuál es la carretera más larga del mundo?
2. ¿Qué es la panamericana?
3. ¿Dónde empieza la panamericana y dónde termina?
4. ¿Enlaza a cuántas capitales?
5. ¿Cómo es la carretera en algunas partes?
6. ¿Cómo es en otras partes?

B Palabras Empleen las siguientes palabras en una oración.
1. carril
2. enlaza (hace enlace con)
3. bache
4. avería
5. llanta pinchada

Lectura opcional ①

El estacionamiento

Buenos Aires, Argentina

En todas las grandes ciudades de España y Latinoamérica es difícil estacionar. En algunas calles donde no está prohibido el estacionamiento hay parquímetros donde uno puede meter una moneda. Entonces el parquímetro indicará el tiempo que puedes estacionar.

Hay también aparcamientos públicos y garajes privados donde es necesario pagar. En muchas ciudades hay aparcamientos municipales donde no hay parquímetros pero tienes que pagar.

—Dime lo que tengo que hacer si voy a uno de estos estacionamientos.

—Busca la (máquina) distribuidora de tiques. Introduce una o varias monedas en la distribuidora. Pon suficiente dinero para el tiempo deseado. Oprime el botón y saldrá un papelito o tique. Indicará el tiempo que puedes estacionar.

Pon el papelito o el tique en el interior del parabrisas del coche donde lo pueden ver los guardias o policías. Si no lo ven, te darán una multa[1].

[1]multa *fine*

¿Comprendes?

¿Qué hago para estacionar?

Explica a un(a) amigo(a) todo lo que tiene que hacer para estacionar el coche (aparcar el carro) en un aparcamiento público con una distribuidora de tiques.

Las señales de tránsito

Desde hace muchos años, en España, Latinoamérica y en otras partes del mundo, se han usado las señales de tránsito internacionales. En Estados Unidos la introducción de estas señales fue más reciente, pero ahora se ven en todas partes. Lo bueno de las señales internacionales es que no es necesario saber el idioma del país, porque muchas de las señales no usan palabras.

Estas son las señales más comunes.

¿Comprendes?

¿Qué quiere decir... ?
Identifiquen las señales de tránsito.

Conexiones
Las ciencias

Ciudad de México

La ecología

Ecology is a subject of great interest to people around the world. People are becoming more aware of the damage being done to our environment. Many of the ecological problems that exist in one area of the world are common in many other areas. People in Mexico City are as concerned about their polluted air as are the residents of Los Angeles.

Quito, Ecuador

La ecología

El problema de la contaminación del medio ambiente[1] ha dado lugar al movimiento ecologista. El término «ecología» significa el equilibrio entre los seres vivientes y la naturaleza.

La contaminación del aire

La contaminación del aire es un problema serio en muchas partes del mundo. España y Latinoamérica no son ninguna excepción. El aire de muchas ciudades de España y Latinoamérica está contaminado. Los gases que salen de los tubos de escape de los automóviles, camiones y buses son una causa principal de la contaminación.

[1]medio ambiente *environment*

Campañas ecológicas

Muchas ciudades están experimentando con programas para controlar o eliminar la contaminación. La Ciudad de México, que tiene uno de los problemas más serios en cuanto a la contaminación del aire, no permite a los autobuses de largo recorrido entrar en el centro de la ciudad.

En algunas ciudades los carros con placa de número par[2] circulan un día y los carros con placa de número impar circulan el otro. Es una manera de tratar de eliminar el número de vehículos y así reducir la emisión de gases que contaminan el aire.

Ciudad de México

[2]placa de número par *license plate with an even number*

¿Comprendes?

Sea buen ciudadano: recicle las latas de aluminio.

Autoridad de Desperdicios Sólidos
Reciclando hoy para un mejor mañana
Tel. (809) 765-7575/1-800-981-RECI

A **¿Cuál es la palabra?**
Busquen la palabra equivalente en la lectura.
1. pollution
2. environment
3. human beings
4. campaign

B **Donde vivimos** Contesten.
1. ¿Está muy contaminado el aire donde ustedes viven?
2. ¿Hay otros tipos de contaminación?
3. ¿Hay mucho o poco tráfico donde ustedes viven?
4. ¿Tiene su pueblo o ciudad un programa para controlar la contaminación?
5. En su ciudad o pueblo, ¿pueden circular todos los vehículos el mismo día?
6. ¿Sabes el número de la placa del carro de tu familia?
7. ¿Tiene un número par o impar?

Use what you have learned

1   Cerca de donde vives

✔ *Talk about cars and driving*

Con un(a) compañero(a) de clase, selecciona (escoge) una ciudad que está cerca de donde ustedes viven. Indiquen las carreteras que pueden tomar para ir a esa ciudad.

2   Leyendo el mapa

✔ *Give directions*

Con un(a) compañero(a), miren el mapa de España. Han alquilado un coche y quieren ir de Madrid a otra ciudad que los dos escogen. Discutan cómo van a ir y las carreteras que van a tomar. ¡A ver si pueden adivinar cuánto tiempo durará *(will take)* el viaje!

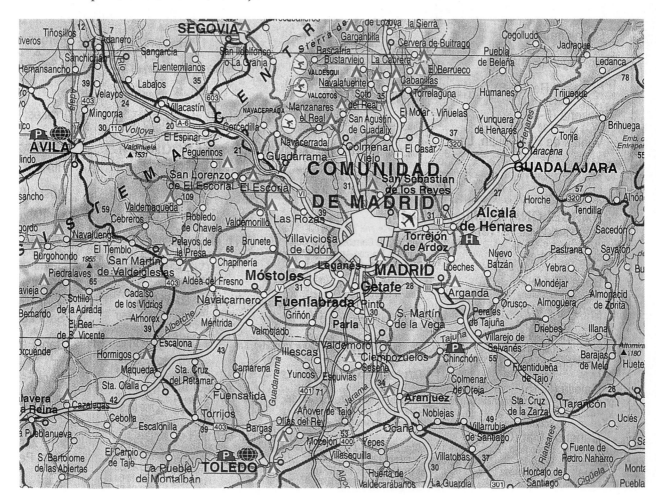

3 Del aeropuerto a nuestra casa
✔ *Write directions*

Tú tienes un buen amigo que vive en Venezuela. Te va a visitar dentro de poco. Viene con su familia y al llegar al aeropuerto van a alquilar un carro. Escríbele a tu amigo(a) dándole direcciones para ir del aeropuerto a tu casa.

4 Instrucciones
✔ *Write orders or commands*

Tus padres van a salir este fin de semana. Ellos te han escrito una lista de cosas que debes hacer y otra lista de cosas que no debes hacer. Escribe lo que dice la lista. Luego compara tu lista con la de un(a) compañero(a).

5 Tú y Antonio llegaron muy tarde

You were driving to school with Antonio, the high school exchange student living with you. You missed your first period class, which happens to be your driver education class. And to make matters worse, you had a test that day. You tried to explain to your teacher what happened but he asked you to write it down for him because it seemed so complicated. Write an imaginative story to tell why you and Antonio were late. It might be fun to use the road signs below to help you make up excuses. Be as humorous and creative as you can. Remember, you have to be convincing enough so your teacher will let you make up the exam rather than take a zero.

Assessment

Vocabulario

1 Identifiquen.

1.

2.

3.

4.

To review **Palabras 1**, turn to pages 322–323.

2 Completen.

5. El ____ tiene sólo dos puertas. Un sedán tiene cuatro.
6. El buen conductor ____ con cuidado.
7. El señor va a la gasolinera para ____ el tanque.

To review **Palabras 2**, turn to pages 326–327.

3 Completen.

8. Un ____ o una bocacalle es donde se encuentran dos calles.
9. En muchas autopistas, es necesario pagar el ____.
10. Una autopista tiene varios ____ en cada sentido.
11. Hay un ____ que indica la salida de la autopista.

Estructura

4 **Completen con el imperativo (tú).**

12. Francisco, ¡____ con cuidado! (manejar)
13. ____ la autopista. (tomar)
14. ____ derecho. (seguir)
15. ____ cuidado. (tener)
16. ____ de la autopista en la salida. (salir)

To review the familiar imperative, turn to pages 330 and 332.

5 **Escriban en la forma negativa.**

17. Entra en la carretera.
18. Escribe las direcciones.
19. Toma la carretera.
20. Vuelve por la misma carretera.
21–22. Sal de la carretera y toma las calles locales.

To review negative imperatives, turn to page 334.

Cultura

To review this cultural information, turn to pages 338-339.

6 **Completen.**

23. La ____ es la carretera más larga del mundo.
24. Esta carretera empieza en ____ y termina en ____.
25. Esta carretera enlaza ____.

For more Chapter 11 test preparation go to the Chapter 11 **Self-Check Quiz** on the Glencoe Spanish Web site at <u>glencoe.com</u>.

La carretera panamericana, Guatemala

Tell all you can about this illustration.

Vocabulario

Talking about cars

el descapotable, el convertible
el coche (carro) deportivo
el permiso de conducir,
   la licencia

el sedán
el cupé
el conductor

Identifying parts of a car

el cinturón de seguridad
el capó
la puerta
la maletera, el baúl
el parabrisas

las luces
los frenos
las direccionales
la bocina, el claxon

la goma, la llanta,
   el neumático
la llanta de repuesto
   (de recambio)

Talking about services at a gas station

la estación de servicio,
   la gasolinera
el aceite
la gasolina
   súper
   diesel

limpiar el parabrisas
llenar el tanque
poner agua en el radiador
revisar el aceite
verificar la presión

How well do you know your vocabulary?

- Choose words to describe getting around a city by car.
- Write three or four sentences about what a good driver should and should not do.

Talking about driving on the highway

la carretera
la autopista, la autovía
el carril
el peaje
la garita de peaje

la entrada
la salida
el rótulo
la velocidad máxima

Giving directions

seguir derecho
quedarse en el carril
doblar
estar prohibido

adelantar
entrar
parar

VIDEOTUR

Episodio 11

In this video episode, you will join Alejandra and Claudia on an evening out. See page 490 for more information. As you watch, look for gestures the speakers use to help convey their message.

Talking about the city

la cuadra
el cruce, la bocacalle
el semáforo, la luz roja

estacionar el coche, aparcar
el parquímetro
una calle de sentido único

Lectura

Accidente entre un camión y un coche

Ha habido un accidente entre un camión y un coche privado en el pueblo de Mirasierra en el kilómetro 55 de la carretera nacional 3A. La policía local ha cerrado dos carriles de la carretera en dirección norte. Los socorristas han llegado al escenario y en este momento están administrando los primeros auxilios a los lesionados (heridos). Parece que la conductora del coche ha sufrido heridas más graves. Ha sido transportado en ambulancia al Hospital del Sagrado Corazón en la ciudad de San Cristóbal.

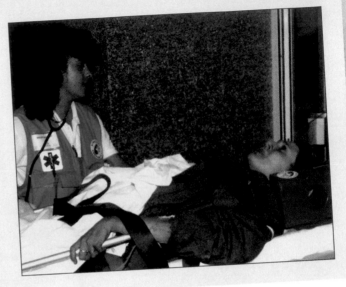

¿Comprendes?

En la carretera Contesten.

1. ¿Dónde ha habido un accidente?
2. ¿Qué ha cerrado la policía?
3. ¿Quiénes han llegado al escenario?
4. ¿Qué están haciendo los socorristas?
5. ¿Quién ha sufrido lesiones o heridas más graves?
6. ¿Adónde la han transportado?
7. ¿Cómo la han transportado?

Bogotá, Colombia

Estructura

El presente perfecto

1. The present perfect is used to express an action completed recently. The present perfect is formed by using the present tense of the verb **haber** and the past participle. Review the forms of regular verbs.

HABLAR	COMER	VIVIR
he hablado	he comido	he vivido
has hablado	has comido	has vivido
ha hablado	ha comido	ha vivido
hemos hablado	hemos comido	hemos vivido
habéis hablado	*habéis comido*	*habéis vivido*
han hablado	han comido	han vivido

2. The following verbs have irregular past participles.

DECIR	**dicho**	VOLVER	**vuelto**
HACER	**hecho**	MORIR	**muerto**
VER	**visto**	CUBRIR	**cubierto**
ESCRIBIR	**escrito**	ABRIR	**abierto**
PONER	**puesto**		

Historieta Una comida deliciosa

Contesten.

1. ¿Ha preparado una comida buena Lucinda?
2. ¿La has ayudado?
3. ¿Han hecho ustedes una paella?
4. ¿La han cocinado en el horno?
5. ¿Han llegado los invitados?
6. ¿Ya han comido?

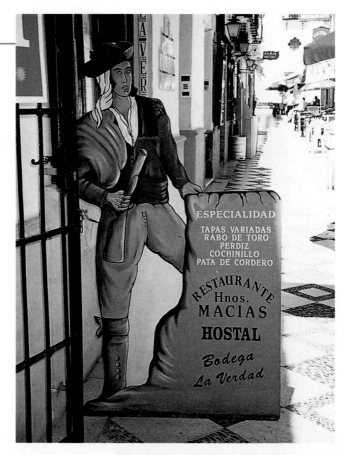

Un restaurante,
Ronda, España

Pronombres con el participio y el infinitivo

When a sentence has an infinitive **(hablar)** or a present participle **(hablando),** the object pronouns can either be added to the infinitive or participle or they can precede the helping verb.

> El médico quiere examinar**lo.**
> El médico **lo** quiere examinar.
>
> El técnico está tomándo**le** los rayos equis.
> Está tomándo**selos** en el hospital.
> Él **se** los está tomando.

San Juan, Puerto Rico

2 En la sala de emergencia
Sigan el modelo.

> ¿Quiere el médico examinarle la garganta? ⟶
> Sí, se la quiere examinar.
> Sí, quiere examinársela.

1. ¿Quiere el médico tomarle una radiografía?
2. ¿Está dándole una inyección contra el tétano la enfermera?
3. ¿Están ayudando al paciente los socorristas?
4. ¿Quiere el cirujano reducirle la fractura?
5. ¿Le está poniendo el vendaje el enfermero?
6. ¿Tiene que ponerle puntos el médico?

3 Historieta Una visita a la ciudad
Sigan el modelo.

> Él quiere ver el plano de la ciudad. ⟶
> Él lo quiere ver.
> Él quiere verlo.

1. Él está mirando el plano de la ciudad.
2. Quiere visitar la ciudad.
3. Tiene que cruzar la calle en el cruce para peatones.
4. Va a tomar el metro.
5. Está esperando el metro en la estación Plaza de España.
6. Muchos pasajeros están bajando la escalera mecánica.

Plaza de España, Madrid, España

Comparación de igualdad

The comparative of equality means that two items being compared have equal characteristics. Remember that **tan… como** is used with adjectives and adverbs and **tanto… como** is used with nouns. **Tanto** must agree with the noun it modifies.

> **Él es tan rico como su hermano.**
> **Él tiene tanto dinero y tanta fortuna como su hermano.**

4 **Comparaciones** Contesten según el modelo.

> **¿Hay más tráfico en Lima que en Caracas?** ⟶
> **No, hay tanto tráfico en Lima como en Caracas.**

1. ¿Es más alto el edificio Latar que el edificio Lamar?
2. ¿Tiene el edificio Latar más pisos que el edificio Lamar?
3. ¿Es la Plaza Simón Bolívar más bonita que la Plaza San Martín?
4. ¿Tiene la Plaza Simón Bolívar más estatuas que la Plaza San Martín?
5. ¿Es más larga la calle Luna que la calle Londres?
6. ¿Hay más tiendas en la calle Luna que en la calle Londres?
7. ¿Hay más gente en la boca del metro que en la parada del autobús?

Caracas, Venezuela

5 **La ciudad o el campo** Trabaja con un(a) compañero(a). Van a hacer un viaje juntos. Discutan si prefieren ir a un lugar en el campo o a una ciudad. Den sus preferencias y expliquen por qué.

6 **De aquí a mi casa** Habla con un(a) compañero(a). Dale direcciones para ir de la escuela a tu casa. Entonces tu compañero(a) te dirá cómo ir a su casa.

7 **Un accidente** Has visto un accidente. Un(a) compañero(a) te va a hacer preguntas sobre el accidente. Contesta sus preguntas. Recuerda que es un accidente ficticio.

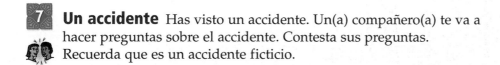

Literary Companion

You may wish to read the adaptation of *El cohítre: Una leyenda puertorriqueña* by Ester M. Feliciano Mendoza, on pages 468–471. The activities for this reading will help you continue to practice your reading comprehension skills.

Entérate Centroamérica

Piedras que hablan

Entérate de lo que cuentan dos grandes ciudades: Copán, de Honduras, y Tikal, de Guatemala. Por su "mensaje", son hoy Patrimonio de la Humanidad.

Estela maya

Copán

■ Ciudad fundada en el siglo V a.C.

■ Sus ruinas revelan que fue un importante centro cultural y observatorio astronómico. Por ello, se la conoce como "la Atenas[1] del Nuevo Mundo".

■ Aún hoy causan admiración sus plazas y templos: Su acrópolis —sitio alto y fortificado, como en las ciudades griegas—, cuenta con el Templo del Sol y la impresionante Escalera de los jaguares. La Escalera de los jeroglíficos contiene el texto más importante de la civilización maya. La cancha para el juego de pelota era el centro social de la ciudad.

■ Los pobladores de Copán comerciaban con lugares tan distantes como las regiones centrales de lo que hoy es México.

■ Copán fue el centro principal de la cultura maya durante tres siglos y medio.

■ De pronto[2] y en todo el esplendor de su grandeza cultural, artística y científica, sus habitantes se marcharon[3]. Existen varias conjeturas, pero hasta hoy se desconocen las razones por las que Copán fue abandonada. Todo ello forma parte del "misterio maya".

Tikal

■ Ochenta y seis estelas[4] cuentan la historia de esta urbe[5] del imperio maya. Su mensaje aún no ha sido descifrado, pero es innegable[6] que estas piedras tienen mucho que contar. Calladamente nos hablan de una alta civilización cuyos logros[7] aún nos asombran.

■ Su símbolo es el Templo I, impresionante pirámide de 44 metros de altura. Otro de sus templos mide 70 metros de altura.

■ El Templo del gran jaguar, el Templo de la serpiente de dos cabezas, el Palacio de las siete ventanas y tres canchas de juegos de pelota son muestras del esplendor de Tikal.

■ Consta[8] además de numerosos palacios, residencias, calzadas[9], estelas y tumbas, que se extienden por 16 kilómetros.

■ Se sabe que Tikal fue un gran centro comercial.

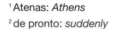
Templo I, Tikal

---

[1] Atenas: *Athens*
[2] de pronto: *suddenly*
[3] se marcharon: *left*
[4] estelas: *stelae*
[5] urbe: *major city*

[6] innegable: *undeniable*
[7] logros: *accomplishments*
[8] consta: *It has*
[9] calzadas: *wide streets*

Los asombrosos[1] mayas

Escultura, Copán

■ En Occidente[2], el concepto del número cero proviene de[3] la India. Los avances matemáticos de los mayas los llevaron al mismo concepto del cero, independientemente de la India.

■ Inventaron un calendario de 260 días con el que controlaban las tareas agrícolas y la vida diaria. Otro calendario se basaba en la rotación de la Tierra alrededor del Sol. Tenía 365 días y era tan exacto como el nuestro.

■ Los mayas eran excelentes "dentistas". Desarrollaron un empaste[4] muy duradero[5]. Los dentistas actuales[6] se alegrarían mucho al descubrir la composición química de esa mezcla.

■ El *Popol Vuh* es el libro sagrado[7] de los quiché. Estos descendientes de los mayas cuentan sus mitos[8] en ese libro.

---

[1] asombrosos: *amazing*
[2] Occidente: *Western world*
[3] proviene de: *comes from*
[4] empaste: *amalgam*

[5] duradero: *lasting*
[6] actuales: *present-day*
[7] sagrado: *sacred*
[8] mitos: *myths*

el mundo salvaje

■ Si te gusta surfear, pensarás que las playas de Costa Rica son el paraíso de los surfeadores, o sea, "¡pura vida!", como dicen los costarricenses. Lugares como Playa Hermosa o Playa Guines tienen olas[1] ideales. Además, la temperatura del agua es tan agradable que no hay necesidad de llevar traje de surfear[2].

Playa de Costa Rica

■ El Cocibolca, también llamado lago de Nicaragua, es el segundo lago más grande de América latina. Tiene olas, una isla con dos volcanes ¡y hasta tiburones[3]! Sí, en este lago se encuentran los únicos tiburones de agua dulce[4] del planeta.

■ Una cadena[5] volcánica recorre la costa oeste de Centroamérica. El volcán Arenal de Costa Rica es uno de los más impresionantes. Noche a noche, es todo un espectáculo cuando la lava incandescente desciende por sus laderas[6]. Incluso, con un poco de suerte, ¡lo oirás rugir[7]!

Volcán Arenal

■ El territorio de Costa Rica mide 51,000 kilómetros cuadrados y el 25% de estos ¡está reservado para parques nacionales y áreas protegidas! El ecoturismo es tradición en este país centroamericano.

■ ¿Te gustaría ver delfines nadar libremente en las aguas transparentes del Caribe? En Roatán, Honduras, un instituto de ciencias marinas ofrece la oportunidad de nadar con estos bellos e inteligentes seres marinos.

[1] olas: *waves*	[4] agua dulce: *freshwater*	[6] laderas: *slopes*
[2] traje de surfear: *wet suit*	[5] cadena: *chain*	[7] rugir: *roar*
[3] tiburones: *sharks*		

SUCESOS

La paz se estudia en una universidad que queda en Costa Rica; se trata de la Universidad de la Paz. Costa Rica es una de las democracias más antiguas de América. ¡Es el único país del mundo que no tiene ejército[1]!

Centroamérica cuenta con dos ganadores del premio Nóbel de la Paz: la guatemalteca **Rigoberta Menchú** y el expresidente de Costa Rica, **Óscar Arias Sánchez.**

Sandoval

Neida Sandoval es presentadora de "Despierta América" (Univisión). Con la sonrisa y el profesionalismo de esta hondureña, los latinos de Estados Unidos reciben las noticias todas las mañanas. Neida obtuvo dos premios Emmy por su participación en este programa, el matutino[2] número uno de la televisión en español.

[1] ejército: *army*   [2] matutino: *morning [news]*

Atolillo de mamá Elsa

micocina

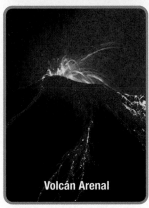

Luis Enrique

La dulzura de Luis Enrique
El cantante nicaragüense **Luis Enrique** admite no ser buen cocinero. Sin embargo, es conocedor de la cocina de su país y no pierde ocasión de compartir recetas de su abuela, quien prepara — según él — el mejor atolillo. Hay muchas versiones de este reconfortante postre[1] en toda Latinoamérica. Anímate a preparar el atolillo de mamá Elsa y, ¡a ver qué opinas tú!

Ingredientes
1 litro de leche
2 yemas de huevo
1 taza de azúcar blanco
2 onzas de maizena (fécula de maíz)
1/8 cucharadita de sal
1/2 taza de pasas
astillas de canela[2] al gusto

Preparación
En una taza y media de leche, mezclar bien la maizena y las yemas de huevo. Aparte, combinar el azúcar, la canela, las pasas y la sal con el resto de la leche. La segunda mezcla se pone a fuego lento, removiéndola[3] constantemente para evitar grumos. Cuando está hirviendo, incorporar la primera mezcla, pasándola por un colador[4], sin dejar de remover. Continuar la cocción[5] hasta lograr una consistencia espesa[6]. Servir caliente y, ¡buen provecho!

[1] postre: *dessert*
[2] astillas de canela: *cinnamon sticks*
[3] removiéndola: *stirring it*
[4] colador: *strainer*
[5] cocción: *cooking*
[6] espesa: *thick*

Rubén Darío

El español antes y después...

Ya conoces a Cervantes, el creador de *El Quijote*. Ahora tienes que conocer a **Rubén Darío**. Como todas las cosas vivas, los idiomas nacen, envejecen[1] y mueren. A finales del siglo XIX, el español era un idioma gastado[2], poco expresivo, débil[3]. Era necesario darle nueva vida.

Quien hace esa revolución y convierte al español en una lengua apta para expresar las cosas del siglo XX es Rubén Darío. El escritor nicaragüense logró que el español sonara como una orquesta capaz[4] de interpretar todos los tonos y melodías. Para ello empleó la mayor variedad de metros[5] que hasta ahora ha utilizado un solo poeta. ¡Sus estudiosos[6] han contado nada menos que 134 tipos distintos de versos!

[1] envejecen: *grow old*
[2] gastado: *worn-out*
[3] débil: *weak*
[4] capaz: *able*
[5] metros: *meters*
[6] estudiosos: *scholars*

¿Tú o vos?

¿Querés que te cuente algo? ¿Sabías vos que en todos los países centroamericanos, excepto Panamá, se dice casi siempre *vos* en vez de *tú?* Lo mismo ocurre en Argentina, Uruguay y en partes de Venezuela y Colombia. Los centroamericanos creen que es más "sabroso"[1] hablar de *vos*, o vosearse. ¿Qué creés vos?

Gentilicios[2] chistosísimos[3]

Si conoces a alguien de Nicaragua, no lo llames nicaragüense, llámalo *nica*. Alguien de Costa Rica no es costarricense; mejor dile *tico*. A un hondureño, lo llamarás *catracho*. Si es de El Salvador, dile *guanaco*. Y nada de decir guatemalteco, se dice *chapín*. Sorprendentemente, los panameños se quedaron sin gentilicio chistoso. ¿Cómo los llamarías tú?

[1] sabroso: *fun*
[2] gentilicios: *name given to the people from a particular region or country*
[3] chistosísimos: *very funny*

Centroamérica y su literatura

Belli

Gioconda Belli es escritora y poeta nicaragüense. Ha ganado varios premios internacionales. Sus obras se han traducido a varios idiomas.

Monterroso

Augusto Monterroso, escritor guatemalteco nacido en Honduras, ganó el Premio Príncipe de Asturias en 2001. Suyo es el cuento más corto que se conoce. ¿Quieres que te lo cuente?: "Cuando se despertó, el dinosaurio todavía estaba ahí".

Alegría

Cuando era jovencita, **Claribel Alegría** mostró sus escritos[1] al famoso escritor español Juan Ramón Jiménez. Actualmente, la obra de esta salvadoreña es conocida en todo el mundo.

Miguel Ángel Asturias tradujo al lenguaje moderno todo el rico pasado cultural de su país, Guatemala. Esta hazaña[2] lo llevó a ganar el Premio Nóbel de Literatura.

[1] escritos: *writings*
[2] hazaña: *achievement*

música

Cardenal

Katia Cardenal nació en Nicaragua, pero ahora vive muy lejos de allí. Ha llevado la dulzura de su canto a Noruega[1], donde la adoran.

Ricardo Arjona, de Guatemala, escribe poesía y la canta con toda el alma.

Al cantante, músico y compositor **Luis Enrique,** de Nicaragua, se lo conoce como el príncipe de la salsa. También ha sido percusionista de Ricky Martin y Gloria Estefan.

Rubén Blades es el salsero consentido[2]. Este cantante, actor de cine y compositor panameño es embajador de la salsa en todo el mundo.

Álvaro Torres es compositor y cantante salvadoreño. Cantó su canción "Buenos amigos" a dúo con Selena, hecho que lanzó a la fama a la cantante tejana.

Los roqueros[3] no podían faltar[4] en Centroamérica. La prueba[5] es **¡Rabanes!,** el grupo de rock panameño.

[1] Noruega: *Norway*
[2] consentido: *overly adored*
[3] roqueros: *rock musicians*
[4] faltar: *be absent*
[5] prueba: *proof*

Álvaro Torres

Mujer kuna

Escuela primitivista de Solentiname

Numerosos pintores nicaragüenses pintan en el estilo[1] primitivista. El pintor primitivista a veces carece de[2] conocimiento técnico, pero representa libremente el paisaje y la vida diaria de su país.

El pueblo kuna

Los indios kunas viven en el archipiélago de San Blas, en Panamá. Han logrado mantener su identidad cultural desde tiempos ancestrales. Su manera de vestirse y adornar el cuerpo es toda una obra de arte. Las molas, vistosas blusas que llevan las mujeres, son artesanías[3] que cuentan tradiciones de la cultura kuna.

Arte moderno

El arte moderno latinoamericano tiene un importante representante en la obra internacionalmente reconocida del pintor nicaragüense **Armando Morales.**

[1] estilo: *style*
[2] carece de: *lacks*
[3] artesanías: *crafts*

Chang Díaz

Fanático de alto vuelo

El costarricense Franklin R. Chang Díaz es físico[1] y astronauta de la NASA. Uno de sus viajes a bordo del transbordador espacial[2], para la misión *Endeavor,* ocurrió durante el Campeonato Mundial de Fútbol que se llevó a cabo en Japón y Corea. Desde el espacio, el astronauta siguió atentamente los juegos donde participó el equipo de su país. ¡Hasta llevó una camiseta[3] del conjunto costarricense para honrarlo[4] desde las alturas!

[1] físico: *physicist*
[2] transbordador espacial: *space shuttle*
[3] camiseta: *t-shirt*
[4] honrarlo: *honor it*

Capítulo

12

Los servicios al público

In this chapter you will learn to:

❖ **talk about going to the hairdresser/barbershop**

❖ **talk about having your clothes cleaned**

❖ **talk about using the services of the post office and bank**

❖ **talk about things that may or may not happen**

❖ **express what you would like, wish, or hope others would do**

Hernán Miranda *Metro*

Vocabulario

En la peluquería

Use your StudentWorks Plus
CD for more practice.

Más corto por los lados, por favor.

el peluquero, el barbero

el peine
la raya

el pelo,
el cabello

una navaja

Paco quiere un corte de pelo.

Quiere que el barbero le corte el pelo con navaja.

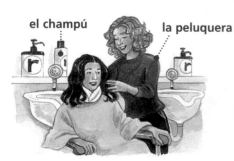

el champú

la peluquera

Teresa quiere que la peluquera
le lave el pelo.
Quiere un champú.

las tijeras

Quiere que le corte el pelo
con tijeras.

el secador

Quiere que le seque el pelo
con el secador.

En la tintorería

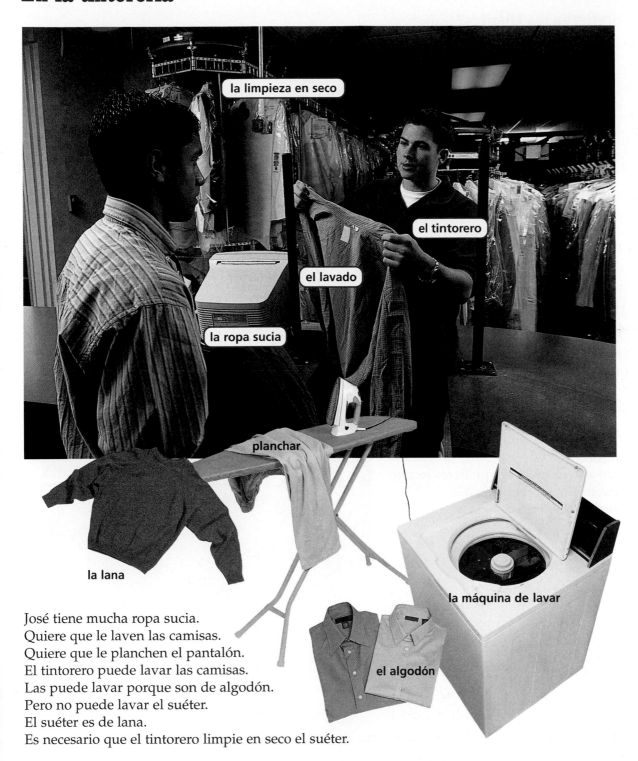

la limpieza en seco

el tintorero

el lavado

la ropa sucia

planchar

la lana

la máquina de lavar

el algodón

José tiene mucha ropa sucia.
Quiere que le laven las camisas.
Quiere que le planchen el pantalón.
El tintorero puede lavar las camisas.
Las puede lavar porque son de algodón.
Pero no puede lavar el suéter.
El suéter es de lana.
Es necesario que el tintorero limpie en seco el suéter.

¿Qué palabra necesito?

1 **¿Qué prefieren los clientes?** Pareen.

 a.

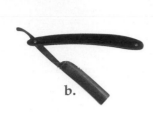 b.

c.

 d.

1. La señora quiere que le corten el pelo con tijeras.
2. Ella quiere que le laven el pelo.
3. Y después quiere que lo sequen.
4. El señor quiere que el barbero use la navaja.

2 **Historieta** **A la peluquería**

Contesten personalmente.

1. ¿Prefieres llevar el pelo largo o corto?
2. ¿A qué peluquería vas?
3. ¿Con qué frecuencia te cortas el pelo?
4. ¿Prefieres lavarte el pelo o que te lo laven en la peluquería?
5. ¿Prefieres que te corten el pelo con tijeras o con navaja?
6. Cuando te lavas el pelo, ¿prefieres secarlo con una toalla o con un secador?
7. ¿Cuántas veces al día te peinas?

San Miguel de Allende, México

Ciudad de México

3 Historieta En la tintorería Contesten.

1. ¿Tiene el joven mucha ropa sucia?
2. ¿La lleva a la tintorería?
3. ¿Quiere que la tintorera le lave las camisas?
4. ¿De qué material son las camisas?
5. ¿Puede lavarlas la tintorera?
6. ¿De qué material es el saco?
7. ¿Puede lavar el saco la tintorera?
8. ¿Es necesario que lo limpie en seco?
9. ¿Quiere el joven que la tintorera le planche el pantalón?
10. ¿Quiere que le planche las camisas también?

Lima, Perú

4 Preguntas personales Contesten.

1. ¿Qué ropa llevas a la tintorería?
2. ¿Qué ropa lavas en casa?
3. ¿Prefieres que te planchen o que no te planchen las camisas?
4. ¿Planchas los blue jeans o no?
5. ¿Tienes mucho lavado cada semana?

5 La peluquería Trabaja con un(a) compañero(a). Dile con qué frecuencia vas a la peluquería. Descríbele todo lo que hace el/la peluquero(a). Luego cambien de rol.

6 En la tintorería Estás en la tintorería. Tienes mucha ropa sucia. Ten una conversación con el/la tintorero(a) (tu compañero[a]). Dile todo lo que necesitas. Luego cambien de rol.

7 En una lavandería Estás trabajando a tiempo parcial *(part time)* en una lavandería *(laundromat)* en tu comunidad donde hay muchos clientes hispanohablantes. Explícale a un(a) cliente (tu compañero[a]) cómo usar la máquina de lavar. Puedes usar las siguientes expresiones.

Lima, Perú

prender la máquina

escoger la temperatura

sacar el lavado

poner blanqueador

esperar media hora

introducir monedas

añadir detergente

poner la ropa sucia

Vocabulario

PALABRAS **2**

Use your **StudentWorks** Plus
CD for more practice.

El correo

la carta

el sobre

el sello,
la estampilla

la tarjeta postal,
la postal

El correo aéreo cuesta más que el correo ordinario.

La señora echa la carta en el buzón.

el buzón

la ventanilla

La empleada pesa el paquete.

El banco

la cuenta corriente

las monedas

los billetes

el dinero en efectivo

el cajero

la cajera

endosar

el cheque de viajero

La señorita quiere cobrar un cheque de viajero.
Ella endosa el cheque.
Ella firma el cheque.

La casa de cambio

¿Cuál es el tipo de cambio?

El cambio está a 130 pesos el dólar.

el cambista

El joven quiere que le cambien dólares en pesos.

el tipo de cambio, la tasa de cambio

CAMBIO

el suelto

El cajero le da muchos billetes grandes.
El joven quiere cambio de un billete de cinco mil. Quiere suelto también.

Vocabulario

¿Qué palabra necesito?

Ciudad de México

8 Tu experiencia personal Contesten.

1. ¿Tú escribes muchas cartas o prefieres hablar por teléfono?
2. Cuando viajas, ¿mandas tarjetas postales? ¿A quién?
3. ¿Quién te escribe a ti con frecuencia?
4. ¿Dónde está el buzón más cerca de tu casa?
5. ¿Cuánto cuesta un sello para una carta por correo ordinario?
6. ¿Cuándo fue la última vez que recibiste un paquete por correo?
7. ¿Qué había en el paquete?

9 La correspondencia Escojan.

1. Acabo de escribir esta carta, pero no tengo un ____ en que meterla.
   a. sello   **b.** sobre   **c.** buzón
2. Y ahora tengo que ponerle un ____ para correo aéreo.
   a. sello   **b.** sobre   **c.** buzón
3. Quiero echar la carta al correo. ¿Hay un ____ en esta calle?
   a. sello   **b.** sobre   **c.** buzón
4. El correo aéreo es caro. Es posible que sea mejor que yo la mande por correo ____.
   a. postal   **b.** ordinario   **c.** pesado

10 Historieta Cosas bancarias Contesten.

1. ¿Tiene tu familia una cuenta en el banco?
2. ¿Quién en tu familia escribe cheques?
3. ¿Tú has recibido un cheque alguna vez?
4. ¿De quién o para qué?
5. ¿Dónde cobraste el cheque?
6. ¿Tuviste que endosar el cheque?
7. ¿Te dio billetes grandes el cajero?
8. ¿Le pediste cambio?

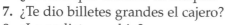
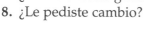

11 **La palabra, por favor.** Identifiquen.

1. Es necesario ponerlo en un sobre antes de enviar una carta.
2. Debes saberlo antes de cambiar una moneda por otra.
3. Lo necesitas cuando tienes solamente billetes grandes.
4. Lo necesitas cuando tienes solamente billetes.
5. Tienes que tener uno para escribir cheques.

12 **En el correo** Estás en el correo en Chosica, no muy lejos de Lima. Tienes unas tarjetas postales que quieres mandar a casa. No sabes cuántos sellos necesitas ni cuánto te costará mandarlas. Y quieres tener una idea de cuándo van a llegar tus tarjetas. Ten una conversación con el/la empleado(a) en el correo (tu compañero[a]). Luego cambien de rol.

13 **Cambio** Estás viajando por Guatemala y te quedan muy pocos quetzales. Ve al banco para cambiar dinero. Tu compañero(a) será el/la cajero(a) en el banco.

Una lavandería pública, Antigua, Guatemala

*For more practice using words from **Palabras 1** and **2**, do Activity 12 on page H13 at the end of this book.*

El subjuntivo
Telling what may or may not happen

1. All verb forms you have learned so far are in the indicative. All tenses of the indicative mood are used to express actions that actually do, did, or will take place. They are used to express real events.

> **José tiene el pelo muy largo.**
> **No fue a la peluquería ayer.**
> **Irá mañana.**

All these statements express factual, real information.

> *José has long hair. He didn't go to the barber's yesterday,*
>   *but he will go tomorrow.*

2. Now you will learn the subjunctive mood. The subjunctive is used to express that which is not necessarily true or real. It expresses things that might happen, that you hope or want to happen. Let's compare the following two sentences.

> **José tiene el pelo muy largo y va a la peluquería.**
> **Los padres de José no quieren que él tenga**
>   **el pelo tan largo y esperan que él vaya a**
>   **la peluquería.**

The first sentence tells you that José has long hair and that he goes to the barber's. The information is factual. For this reason you use the indicative. The second sentence tells you that José's parents don't want him to have long hair, but that doesn't mean that his hair will necessarily be short. The sentence also tells us that they hope he goes to the barber, but this doesn't mean that he will. The second sentence tells you things that may happen. It does not present facts and, for this reason, you use the subjunctive.

Spanish Online
For more information about paintings and art museums in the Spanish-speaking world, go to **Web Explore** on the Glencoe Spanish Web site at glencoe.com.

El peinado de Pablo Picasso

3. To form the present tense of the subjunctive of regular verbs, you drop the **o** of the **yo** form of the present indicative. This is true of verbs that also have an irregular form in the present tense of the indicative. Add **e** endings to all **-ar** verbs and **a** endings to all **-er** and **-ir** verbs.

INFINITIVE	PRESENT (YO)	STEM	PRESENT SUBJUNCTIVE (YO)
mirar	miro	mir-	mire
comer	como	com-	coma
vivir	vivo	viv-	viva
salir	salgo	salg-	salga
hacer	hago	hag-	haga
decir	digo	dig-	diga
conducir	conduzco	conduzc-	conduzca

4. Study the forms for the present tense of the subjunctive.

MIRAR	COMER	VIVIR	SALIR
mire	coma	viva	salga
mires	comas	vivas	salgas
mire	coma	viva	salga
miremos	comamos	vivamos	salgamos
miréis	comáis	viváis	salgáis
miren	coman	vivan	salgan

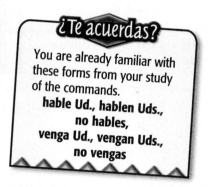

¿Te acuerdas?

You are already familiar with these forms from your study of the commands.

hable Ud., hablen Uds., no hables, venga Ud., vengan Uds., no vengas

5. The following are the only verbs that do not follow the normal pattern for the formation of the present subjunctive.

DAR	ESTAR	IR	SABER	SER
dé	esté	vaya	sepa	sea
des	estés	vayas	sepas	seas
dé	esté	vaya	sepa	sea
demos	estemos	vayamos	sepamos	seamos
deis	estéis	vayáis	sepáis	seáis
den	estén	vayan	sepan	sean

¿Cómo lo digo?

14 **¿Qué quieren los padres de Adela?**
Quieren que ella haga muchas cosas.
Sigan el modelo.

> estudiar ⟶
> **Los padres de Adela quieren que ella estudie.**

1. estudiar mucho
2. trabajar duro
3. tomar cursos avanzados
4. leer mucho
5. comer bien
6. escribir a sus abuelos
7. recibir buenas notas
8. asistir a la universidad
9. salir bien en sus exámenes
10. decir la verdad
11. ser generosa
12. ir a una universidad buena
13. conducir con cuidado

Ciudad de Guatemala

15 **Los profesores insisten.**
Sigan el modelo.

> estudiar ⟶
> **Los profesores insisten en
> que estudiemos.**

1. trabajar
2. prestar atención
3. tomar apuntes
4. aprender
5. recibir buenas notas
6. hacer nuestras tareas
7. estar presentes
8. ser puntuales

Colegio Santa Teresita,
Santurce, Puerto Rico

El subjuntivo en cláusulas nominales
Expressing wishes and orders

As you have seen, the subjunctive is used with the verbs **querer** and **insistir**. Even though someone wants or insists that something be done, it will not necessarily happen. The information in the clause introduced by either **querer** or **insistir** is not factual. It may or may not happen. Other verbs like **querer** and **insistir** that take the subjunctive are:

desear *to wish*	**mandar** *to order*
esperar *to hope*	**temer** *to fear*
preferir *to prefer*	**tener miedo de** *to be afraid*

Quiero que mis amigos vayan a la fiesta.
Y espero que no lleguen tarde.
Tengo miedo de que no sepan las direcciones.

¿Cómo lo digo?

16 **Historieta** **En la peluquería** Contesten.

1. ¿Quiere Antonio que el peluquero le corte el pelo?
2. ¿Quiere que le dé un champú?
3. ¿Quiere que use las tijeras?
4. ¿Quiere que le ponga la raya a la derecha o a la izquierda?
5. ¿Quiere que le seque el pelo con el secador?

17 **Historieta** **Una carta** Sigan el modelo.

Tú le escribes. ⟶
Yo prefiero que tú le escribas.

1. Le escribes en español.
2. Le mandas una tarjeta.
3. Pones un sello para correo aéreo.
4. Vas al correo.
5. Pones la tarjeta en el buzón delante del correo.

Estructura

18 Historieta ¿Qué temen ellos?
Sigan el modelo.

> Yo no tengo bastante dinero. ⟶
> Temen que yo no tenga bastante dinero.

1. Yo no voy al banco.
2. Yo no tengo bastante dinero en efectivo.
3. No compro cheques de viajero.
4. Cambio demasiados dólares en pesos.
5. No sé dónde firmar el cheque.

Valladolid, España

19 Historieta ¡Vamos todos! Contesten.

1. ¿Quieres que vayamos a Sevilla?
2. ¿Prefieres que yo conduzca?
3. ¿Insistes en que yo no exceda el límite de velocidad?
4. ¿Prefieres que yo tome la autopista?
5. ¿Temes que yo no pague el peaje?
6. ¿Esperas que lleguemos a Sevilla antes de la hora de cenar?

20 Historieta Cada uno quiere otra cosa.
Completen.

Yo no sé lo que vamos a hacer esta noche. Pablo quiere que nosotros __1__ (ir) al cine. Él insiste en que nosotros __2__ (ver) la película en el cine Apolo. Carlota teme que mañana __3__ (ser) el último día. Tiene miedo de que ellos __4__ (cambiar) las películas los sábados. Y tú, ¿quieres que nosotros __5__ (ir) al cine o que __6__ (hacer) otra cosa? ¿Qué me dices? Que Felipe quiere que ustedes __7__ (quedarse) en casa. ¿Por qué? Ah, él quiere que todo el grupo __8__ (ir) a su casa. Él prefiere que nosotros __9__ (escuchar) música y que __10__ (bailar). ¡Buena idea!

21 **Lo que quieren mis padres** Dile a un(a) compañero(a) de clase lo que tus padres siempre quieren que hagas. Tu compañero(a) te dirá lo que sus padres quieren que él o ella haga. Luego pongan sus dos listas juntas y decidan cuáles son los mismos consejos *(advice)* que ustedes reciben de sus padres. ¿Están ustedes de acuerdo con los deseos de sus padres? Den sus opiniones sobre sus consejos o deseos.

22 **Mi mejor amigo(a)** Trabaja con un(a) compañero(a). Cada uno(a) de ustedes va a preparar una lista de características que ustedes quieren que tenga su mejor amigo(a). Luego comparen sus listas y determinen las características que ustedes dos buscan en su mejor amigo(a).

 # El subjuntivo con expresiones impersonales
Expressing opinions

1. The subjunctive is also used after the following impersonal expressions.

es imposible	**es probable**
es posible	**es necesario**
es bueno	**es fácil**
es mejor	**es difícil**
es importante	

2. These expressions are followed by the subjunctive because it is uncertain whether the action of the verb will take place or not.

> **Es necesario que cambiemos el dinero mañana.**
> **Es importante que sepas el tipo de cambio.**
> **Es posible que el banco esté cerrado.**

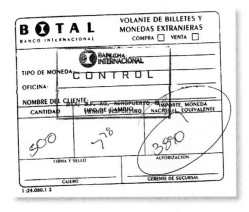

Estructura

¿Cómo lo digo?

23 **¿Sí o no? ¿Cuál es tu opinión?** Contesten.

1. ¿Es importante que los jóvenes estudien lenguas?
2. ¿Es fácil que reciban buenas notas?
3. ¿Es bueno que hablen mucho?
4. ¿Es posible que visiten otros países?
5. ¿Es mejor que aprendan el español?

Benidorm, España

24 **Voy a la ciudad. Pues, es importante que...**
Sigan el modelo.

> **tener cuidado** ⟶
> **Pues, es importante que tengas cuidado.**

1. desayunar antes
2. tener cuidado
3. tomar el tren
4. llevar bastante dinero
5. llamar a los abuelos

Spanish Online

For a fun way to review this grammar
point, go to the Chapter 12 **eGame** on
the Glencoe Spanish Web site at
glencoe.com.

25 **Historieta** **Finanzas** Contesten.

1. ¿Es importante que tú tengas dinero en el banco?
2. ¿Es posible que tengas una cuenta corriente?
3. ¿Es importante que todos pongamos dinero en el banco?
4. ¿Es necesario que endosemos un cheque antes de cobrarlo?
5. ¿Es mejor que paguemos con una tarjeta de crédito?

26 Historieta ¿Dónde están los nietos? Completen.

Abuelito está un poco nervioso. Es posible que sus nietos __1__ (llegar) mañana por la mañana. Es importante que abuelito __2__ (saber) cuándo van a llegar. Pero es difícil que abuelita le __3__ (decir) la hora precisa de la llegada de los nietos. Es posible que mañana __4__ (hacer) mal tiempo. Como los nietos vienen en carro será necesario que __5__ (manejar) despacio y con mucho cuidado si hay mucha nieve. Es mejor que ellos __6__ (llegar) un poco tarde. Abuelito no quiere que ellos __7__ (tener) un accidente. Es mejor que __8__ (llegar) tarde pero sanos y salvos.

Tolima, Colombia

27 Cosas fáciles y difíciles Prepara una lista de cosas que es probable que tú hagas con frecuencia porque es fácil hacerlas. Prepara otra lista que indica lo que es difícil que tú hagas. Luego compara tus listas con las listas que ha preparado tu compañero(a).

28 Juego No, no. Es imposible. Work in a small group. Talk together and tell one another what you think is important, necessary, or a good idea that some other member of the group do. Whoever is told to do it will answer with a good excuse as to why it's impossible.

Andas bien. ¡Adelante!

En la casa de cambio

Empleada	Sí, señor. ¿En qué puedo servirle?
Felipe	Quiero cambiar dólares en pesos.
Empleada	¿Tiene usted dólares en efectivo o en cheque de viajero?
Felipe	Cheque de viajero. ¿Cuál es el tipo de cambio hoy, por favor?
Empleada	Para cheques de viajero 223 pesos por dólar. ¿Para cuánto es el cheque?
Felipe	Cien dólares. ¿Quiere usted que yo lo endose?
Empleada	Sí, claro. Y necesito su pasaporte también.
Felipe	Aquí lo tiene.
Empleada	Gracias.

¿Comprendes?

Contesten.

1. ¿Qué va a hacer Felipe?
2. ¿Quiere cambiar dinero en efectivo o un cheque de viajero?
3. ¿Cuántos pesos recibirá Felipe por un dólar?
4. ¿Cuántos dólares quiere cambiar?
5. ¿Qué tiene que hacer Felipe con el cheque?
6. ¿Qué más tiene que darle a la empleada?

Vamos a hablar más

Spanish nline
To learn more about public services offered in the Spanish-speaking world, go to the Chapter 12 **WebQuest** on the Glencoe Spanish Web site at glencoe.com.

A **En la peluquería** Estás en una peluquería en un país hispano. Habla con el/la peluquero(a) (tu compañero[a]). Dile cómo quieres el pelo. Dile todo lo que quieres que él o ella haga. Luego cambien de rol.

B **Sí, sí, pero…** Habla con un(a) compañero(a). Dile algunas cosas que quieres que él o ella haga. Tu compañero(a) te contestará que sabe que es bueno que él o ella haga lo que quieres pero en este momento es imposible que lo haga porque es importante que haga otra cosa. Luego cambien de rol.

Sevilla, España

Baños, Ecuador

Ávila, España

Lecturas culturales

Muchos quehaceres

José Luis y un grupo de amigos de su colegio en Madrid han decidido que van a hacer una gira por el sur de España—por Andalucía. Van a ir a Córdoba, Granada y Sevilla donde quieren visitar los famosos monumentos de los árabes. Los árabes o los moros estuvieron en España por casi ocho siglos—desde 711 hasta 1492.

En Córdoba van a visitar la Mezquita.
En Granada, la Alhambra.
Y en Sevilla, el Alcázar.
Saben que en agosto va a hacer mucho calor en estas ciudades. Por consiguiente van a pasar unos días en una playa de la Costa del Sol antes de volver a casa.

Reading Strategy

Recognizing text organization Before you begin to read a passage, take a look at it quickly to figure out how it is organized. Doing so will help you guess the meanings of words you do not know, because it will help you figure out the overall meaning of the material. In addition, knowing how a selection is organized will help you identify where in the reading you can find a certain piece of information.

La Alhambra, Granada

La Mezquita, Córdoba

El Alcázar, Sevilla

Como les quedan sólo dos días antes de salir para Andalucía, todos tienen muchos quehaceres[1]. José Luis tiene que ir a la peluquería. Quiere que el peluquero le corte el pelo. Tiene el pelo bastante largo y es mejor que tenga el pelo corto para la playa. Piensa nadar mucho en el Mediterráneo.

Teresa tiene mucho lavado. Tiene que llevar su ropa sucia a la lavandería. No es necesario que ella vaya a la tintorería. No es necesario limpiar en seco la ropa que va a llevar durante el viaje. Sólo tiene algunas camisetas, blusas y pantalones. Y Teresa no va a planchar la ropa tampoco[2]. Va a poner todo en su mochila y sabe que se va a arrugar[3].

Elena quiere ir al correo para comprar sellos. Querrá enviar unas postales a sus amigos y parientes y no quiere perder tiempo haciendo cola en el correo de Córdoba o Sevilla.

Y, ¿adónde tienen que ir todos? ¡Al banco! Sí, todos tienen que ir al banco porque necesitan dinero. En el banco no tienen que cambiar dinero porque estarán viajando dentro de España. Pero tienen que cobrar un cheque porque es necesario que tengan algún dinero en efectivo. Es probable que no compren cheques de viajero porque si no pagan sus cuentas en efectivo, pueden usar una tarjeta de crédito.

Pues, ¡buen viaje a todos! Y esperamos que lo pasen bien en Andalucía—¡que se diviertan!

[1]quehaceres *chores*
[2]tampoco *either*
[3]arrugar *to wrinkle*

Use your StudentWorks Plus CD for more practice.

¿Comprendes?

A Preparativos para un viaje Contesten.

1. ¿Quiénes han decidido hacer una gira por el sur de España?
2. ¿Por qué van a pasar unos días en la Costa del Sol?
3. ¿Qué tienen que hacer todos?
4. ¿Adónde tiene que ir José Luis?
5. ¿Qué quiere él?
6. ¿Cómo quiere el pelo para la playa?
7. ¿Adónde tiene que ir Teresa?
8. ¿Por qué no es necesario que ella vaya a la tintorería?
9. ¿Qué quiere hacer Elena en el correo?
10. ¿Qué van a hacer todos en el banco?

B Una gira Identifiquen.

1. una región del sur de España
2. tres ciudades de esta región
3. un monumento de Córdoba
4. un monumento de Granada
5. un monumento de Sevilla
6. el año 711

Lectura opcional ①

La Moneda: un edificio con mucha historia

Palacio de la Moneda, Santiago de Chile

En pleno centro de Santiago, la capital de Chile, está el edificio de la Moneda. El edificio se construyó entre 1788 y 1805. Es un bello ejemplo de arquitectura colonial.

Desde 1846 hasta 1958 la Moneda sirvió de residencia a los presidentes de la República de Chile. Pero el edificio no se construyó para residencia presidencial. Era donde se acuñaba[1] la moneda en tiempos coloniales. Hasta 1929, los presidentes vivían en el edificio mientras se continuaba acuñando las monedas allí.

En 1973 el edificio de la Moneda apareció en los periódicos de todo el mundo. El 11 de septiembre durante un golpe[2] militar, unos aviones atacaron la Moneda y en las ruinas murió el presidente Salvador Allende.

La Moneda fue restaurada y hoy sirve de sede[3] al gobierno chileno.

[1]se acuñaba *they minted*
[2]golpe *a coup (the overthrow of a government)*
[3]sede *seat (of government)*

¿Comprendes?

A La Moneda Completen según la lectura.
1. La Moneda es un ____.
2. Está en el ____ de la ciudad.
3. Los presidentes del país vivían en el edificio desde ____ hasta ____.
4. El año 1929 fue el último año en que ____ dinero en el edificio.
5. La construcción del edificio tomó ____ años.

B Las noticias de 1973 Expliquen lo que ocurrió de importancia en 1973.

Guatemala

Lectura opcional 2

El pelo y el peinado

En muchas culturas del mundo el pelo y el peinado siempre han tenido un gran significado. Aún hoy los jueces[1] en Gran Bretaña siguen llevando peluca[2] en la corte.

En las Américas, entre los indígenas, el peinado, igual que el vestido, frecuentemente identifica al grupo o a la tribu. Y el pelo largo no tiene nada que ver con el sexo de la persona. En algunos grupos las mujeres tienen el pelo largo y llevan trenzas[3] que adornan con cintas[4] de colores vivos. En otros grupos, como los indios otavaleños de Ecuador, son los hombres quienes llevan trenzas.

Y, ¿quién se encarga[5] del cuidado del pelo y de la barba[6]? Los barberos o peluqueros, por supuesto. En la literatura hispana, el barbero es un personaje especial. Ha tenido fama de ser muy independiente—casi anarquista. Trabaja por si mismo. No tiene jefe y conoce todos los secretos del pueblo. Y el hombre que pone el cuello bajo la navaja del barbero pone allí su vida. Este ha sido el tema o argumento de varios cuentos españoles y latinoamericanos.

[1]jueces *judges* [3]trenzas *braids* [5]se encarga *takes charge*
[2]peluca *wig* [4]cintas *ribbons* [6]barba *beard*

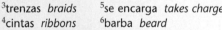
Ecuador

Barbados

¿Comprendes?

Costumbres interesantes Digan que sí o que no.
1. Los jueces en Gran Bretaña no tienen pelo.
2. Entre los indígenas de las Américas, el peinado identifica el grupo al que pertenecen.
3. Sólo las mujeres llevan el pelo largo.
4. En algunos grupos indígenas los señores llevan trenzas.
5. El barbero es un personaje especial en la literatura hispana.

Conexiones

Las finanzas

La banca

At one time or another we must all get involved in matters of money and finances. A bank is a good provider of financial services. We may want to pay some bills by check or put some money aside and open a savings account. These are two of the many services offered by a bank. Today many of our banking needs can be taken care of without even entering the bank. We can do our transactions at the ATM, or Automated Teller Machine.

Let's learn a few very commonly used banking terms in Spanish.

la cuenta corriente

la cuenta de ahorros

el saldo

el cajero automático

el estado de cuenta

la chequera, el talonario

El banco

Una cuenta corriente

El servicio que te da el banco es muy importante. Es muy conveniente pagar tus facturas de gas, electricidad, etc., con un cheque. Para escribir cheques es necesario tener una cuenta corriente en el banco. Pero hay que tener mucho cuidado. Es necesario que tengas suficientes fondos o dinero en tu cuenta para cubrir los cheques.

Cada mes el banco te envía un estado de cuenta. Es necesario conciliar el saldo—es decir, verificar que el saldo que tiene el banco es el mismo saldo que tú tienes.

Guanajuato, México

Una cuenta de ahorros

¿Te gusta ahorrar[1] dinero? Entonces puedes abrir una cuenta de ahorros. Ingresas dinero (haces un depósito) en la cuenta de ahorros y el banco te paga interés. Así va subiendo el saldo de tu cuenta y vas haciéndote más rico.

Préstamos

A veces es necesario pedir prestado[2] dinero. Es posible que quieras comprar un carro o una casa. Es posible que no tengas bastante dinero. El banco te hará un préstamo[3].

Una hipoteca es un préstamo para comprar una casa. Es un ejemplo de un préstamo a largo plazo[4]. Durante unos veinte o veinticinco años tendrás que hacer pagos. Cada pago incluye el interés que el banco te cobra[5]. La tasa de interés varía. Por ejemplo, la tasa de interés para un préstamo a corto plazo es generalmente más alta que la tasa de interés para un préstamo a largo plazo.

Hoy día puedes efectuar casi todas las funciones bancarias sin entrar en el banco. El banco te dará una tarjeta para el cajero automático. Introduces la tarjeta en el cajero automático y aparecen en la pantalla las instrucciones para cualquier función bancaria.

[1]ahorrar *to save*
[2]pedir prestado *to borrow*
[3]préstamo *loan*
[4]a largo plazo *long-term*
[5]cobra *charges*

Un cajero automático, España

¿Comprendes?

Ahorros para el futuro Escojan.

1. Roberto quiere tener dinero para el futuro. Debe abrir ____.
   a. una cuenta corriente   b. una cuenta de ahorros
   c. un banco
2. Si Roberto quiere ahorrar mucho dinero, tendrá que ____.
   a. retirar mucho dinero   b. ingresar muchos fondos
   c. cobrar muchos cheques
3. Roberto no paga siempre con dinero en efectivo o con tarjeta de crédito. Él paga con ____.
   a. billetes   b. libretas   c. cheques
4. Roberto no tiene más cheques. Necesita ____.
   a. otra cuenta   b. otro talonario   c. otro estado
5. No se puede escribir otro cheque si no hay ____ en la cuenta corriente.
   a. fondos   b. cheques   c. depósitos
6. Una hipoteca es un préstamo ____.
   a. para un carro   b. a largo plazo   c. a corto plazo

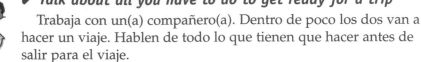

¡Te toca a ti!

Use what you have learned

HABLAR

1

Planes para un viaje
✔ *Talk about all you have to do to get ready for a trip*

Trabaja con un(a) compañero(a). Dentro de poco los dos van a hacer un viaje. Hablen de todo lo que tienen que hacer antes de salir para el viaje.

HABLAR
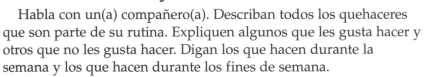
2

Quehaceres
✔ *Discuss those chores you like or don't like to do*

Habla con un(a) compañero(a). Describan todos los quehaceres que son parte de su rutina. Expliquen algunos que les gusta hacer y otros que no les gusta hacer. Digan los que hacen durante la semana y los que hacen durante los fines de semana.

HABLAR

3

En la peluquería
✔ *Go to the hairdresser in a Spanish-speaking country*

Estás en una peluquería en México. Habla con el/la peluquero(a). Dile lo que necesitas y lo que quieres que él o ella haga.

Málaga, España

4 En la casa de correos
✔ *Use words and expressions related to postal services*

Estás viajando por España y quieres enviar unas tarjetas postales a tus amigos y parientes. Vas a la casa de correos donde hablas con el/la empleado(a) en la ventanilla (tu compañero[a]).

5 Todo es fabuloso
✔ *Write to a friend telling what country you would like him or her to visit*

Estás viajando por un país hispano. Te encanta. Te gusta mucho. Quieres que un(a) amigo(a) venga a visitar el mismo país. Escríbele una carta diciéndole por qué te gusta tanto y por qué quieres que él o ella lo visite también. Luego dile todas las cosas que es posible o importante que él o ella haga durante su estadía *(stay)* en el país.

Writing Strategy

Writing dialogue Dialogue is the conversational element of a story—the written composition representing two or more people talking. Dialogue within a story can help bring characters and events to life. Good dialogue within a story can do several things. It can reveal things about characters, create a sense of time and place, and move the plot along. You can use dialogue for these purposes and for many more.

6 Un viaje con un(a) amigo(a)

You and a friend are going to Chile for a semester to study. Part of your credit for this coursework is writing about your entire trip, from beginning to end. This includes, of course, the planning stage as well. You are going to leave soon and your Spanish teacher would like you to submit a story about what it was like to prepare for this exciting upcoming adventure. Write about the meeting you and your friend had when you discussed everything you had to do to get ready. Use dialogue in your story to make it more lively. Be imaginative and creative.

Universidad de Chile

Assessment

Vocabulario

1 **Completen.**

1. Cuando Juan necesita un corte de pelo, va a la ____.
2. El barbero le corta el pelo con una navaja o con ____.
3. Teresa quiere que la peluquera le lave el pelo. Quiere un ____.
4. Paco lava su ____ en la máquina de lavar.
5. Es necesario ____ el suéter porque es de lana.

To review **Palabras 1**, turn to pages 360-361.

2 **Identifiquen.**

6.

7.

To review **Palabras 2**, turn to pages 364-365.

8.

9.

3 **¿Sí o no?**

10. El dinero en efectivo es un cheque de viajero.
11. Es necesario tener una cuenta corriente en el banco para poder escribir un cheque.
12. El joven quiere cambio porque el cajero le da muchos billetes pequeños.

Spanish Online

For more Chapter 12 test preparation go to the Chapter 12 **Self-Check Quiz** on the Glencoe Spanish Web site at glencoe.com.

386 ✿ *trescientos ochenta y seis*

CAPÍTULO 12

Estructura

4 Completen.

13–14. Los padres de Lucio quieren que él ____ mucho y que ____ mucha suerte. (escribir, tener)

15–16. El profesor insiste en que sus alumnos ____ puntuales y que ____ todas sus tareas. (ser, hacer)

17. Quiero que tú me lo ____. (decir)

18. Él prefiere que nosotros lo ____. (escribir)

19. Él tiene miedo de que yo no le ____. (hablar)

To review the subjunctive, turn to pages 368–369 and 371.

5 Completen.

20. Ustedes van. Es bueno que ____.

21. Cambiamos dinero. Es necesario que ____.

22. No tienes bastante dinero. Es posible que ____.

To review the subjunctive with impersonal expressions, turn to page 373.

Cultura

6 Identifiquen.

23. dos ciudades famosas de Andalucía

24. un monumento famoso de los moros

25. las fechas de la ocupación mora en España

To review this cultural information, turn to pages 378–379.

Tell all you can about this illustration.

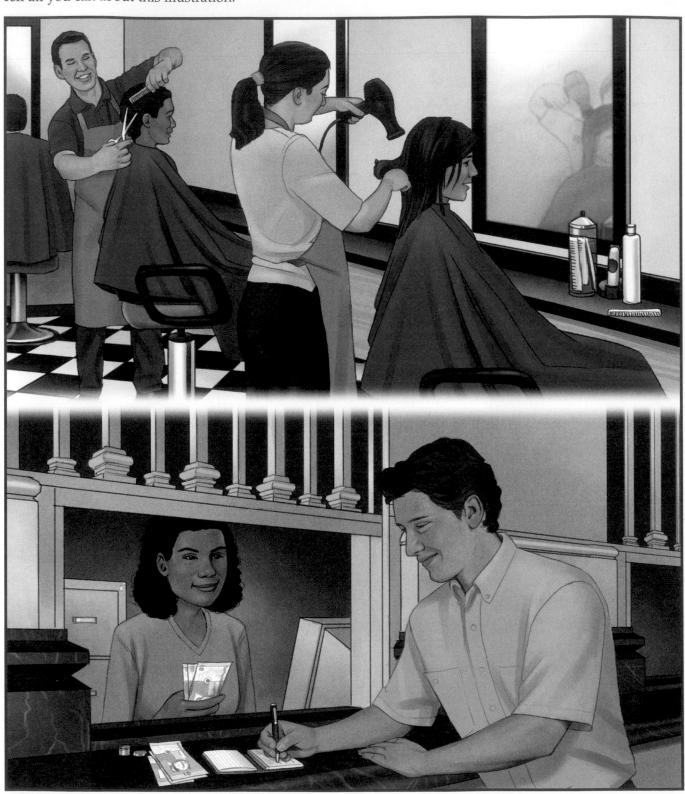

Vocabulario

Talking about the hairdresser

la peluquería
el/la peluquero(a),
   el barbero
el pelo, el cabello
un corte de pelo
el lado
la raya

la navaja
las tijeras
el secador
el champú
cortar
lavar
secar

Talking about the dry cleaners

la tintorería
el/la tintorero(a)
la ropa sucia
el lavado
la máquina de lavar

de algodón
de lana
planchar
limpiar en seco

How well do you know your vocabulary?

- Pick words from the list that relate to a chore you need to do.
- Write several sentences describing what chore you did.

Talking about the post office

el correo
el buzón
la ventanilla
la carta
el sobre
el sello, la estampilla

la tarjeta postal,
   la postal
el correo aéreo
el correo ordinario
pesar el paquete
echar la carta

Talking about the bank

el/la cajero(a)
el dinero en efectivo
las monedas
los billetes
la cuenta corriente

el cheque de viajero
el suelto
endosar
firmar
cobrar

VIDEOTUR

Talking about changing currency

la casa de cambio
el/la cambista
el tipo (la tasa) de cambio
cambiar
estar a

Episodio 12

In this video episode, Claudia talks Francisco into getting his hair cut at a salon. See page 491 for more information. As you watch, notice gestures the speakers use to help convey their message.

Capítulo 13

¡Fiestas!

Objetivos

In this chapter you will learn to:

❖ **describe and talk about parties and weddings**

❖ **talk about some holidays**

❖ **give advice and make recommendations**

❖ **express doubt, uncertainty, or disbelief**

❖ **express emotional reactions to what others do**

❖ **talk about New Year's Eve in the Hispanic world**

Alfredo Ramos Martínez *Casamiento indio*

Spanish Online
To interact with your online edition of
¡Buen viaje! go to: glencoe.com.

El cumpleaños

Use your StudentWorks Plus CD for more practice.

abril

L M M J V S D

				1	2	3	4	5
6	7	8	9	10	11	12
13	14	15	16	17	18	19
20	21	22	23	24	25	26
27	28	29	30

¡Feliz cumpleaños!

las velas

el pastel, la torta, el bizcocho

Anita nació el ocho de abril.
Su familia y sus amigos celebran su cumpleaños con una fiesta.
No hay duda que todos se divierten.
Anita se alegra de que todos sus parientes vengan a la fiesta.

La boda

Los novios acaban de casarse.
La recepción es en un salón elegante.
Los novios reciben muchos regalos.

¿Qué palabra necesito?

1 Historieta Una fiesta

Contesten personalmente.

1. ¿Cuándo es tu cumpleaños?
2. ¿Cuándo naciste?
3. ¿Te preparan una torta para tu cumpleaños?
4. ¿Qué clase de torta te gusta?
5. ¿Cuántas velas tendrás en tu próxima torta?
6. ¿Te dan una fiesta para tu cumpleaños?
7. ¿Quiénes asisten a la fiesta?
8. ¿Recibes muchos regalos?
9. ¿Qué hacen ustedes en la fiesta?
10. ¿Qué regalo te gustaría recibir para tu próximo cumpleaños?

En Tu Cumpleaños, Querida Hija

Que el día de tu cumpleaños
Celebres con alegría
Y que tu vida esté siempre
Llena de dicha, Hija mía.

Que Seas Muy
Feliz Siempre

Madrid, España

2 Historieta La boda

Contesten. Inventen una historia.

1. ¿Acaba de casarse la pareja?
2. ¿La mujer vestida de blanco es la dama de honor o la novia?
3. ¿Los novios dan o reciben regalos?
4. ¿Van a dar una recepción?
5. ¿La música será de CDs o de una orquesta?
6. ¿Dónde van a pasar los novios su luna de miel?

3 **Preguntas personales** Contesten.

1. ¿Has asistido a una boda alguna vez? ¿Quiénes se casaron?
2. ¿Cómo era la ropa de la novia?
3. ¿La ceremonia fue religiosa o civil?
4. ¿Quiénes fueron el padrino y la dama de honor?
5. ¿Fuiste a la recepción?
6. ¿Dónde tuvieron la recepción?
7. ¿Qué hiciste en la recepción?

Una boda, España

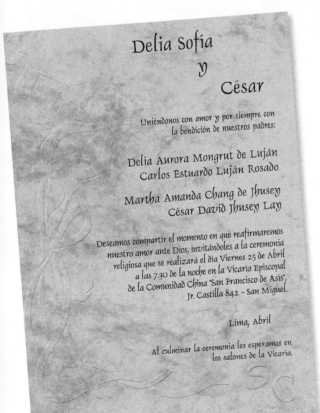

Delia Sofía
y
César

Uniéndonos con amor y por siempre con
la bendición de nuestros padres:

Delia Aurora Mongrut de Luján
Carlos Estuardo Luján Rosado

Martha Amanda Chang de Jhusey
César David Jhusey Lay

Deseamos compartir el momento en que reafirmaremos
nuestro amor ante Dios, invitándoles a la ceremonia
religiosa que se realizará el día Viernes 25 de Abril
a las 7.30 de la noche en la Vicaría Episcopal
de la Comunidad China "San Francisco de Asís"
Jr. Castilla 842 - San Miguel.

Lima, Abril

Al culminar la ceremonia les esperamos en
los salones de la Vicaría.

4 **Una boda** Trabaja con un(a) compañero(a). Cada uno(a) de ustedes va a describir una boda a la que ha asistido. Luego comparen las dos bodas. ¿Había algunas diferencias entre las dos? ¿Cuáles eran las diferencias?

5 **Fiestas de cumpleaños** A muchas personas les gusta mucho tener fiestas en su honor. A otras no les gusta. Trabaja con un(a) compañero(a). Dile si a ti te gustan las fiestas en tu honor o no. Explica por qué. Luego tu compañero(a) te dará sus opiniones. ¿Están de acuerdo o no?

Navidad

el árbol de Navidad

¡Feliz Navidad!

Diciembre

L	M	M	J	V	S	D
	1	2	3	4	5	6
7	8	9	10	11	12	13
14	15	16	17	18	19	20
21	22	23	24	(25)	26	27
28	29	30	31			

La Navidad es el veinticinco de diciembre.

Nochebuena es el veinticuatro de diciembre.

Año Nuevo

¡Próspero Año Nuevo!

La víspera de Año Nuevo (Nochevieja) es el treinta y uno de diciembre.
La gente celebra cuando el reloj da las doce.

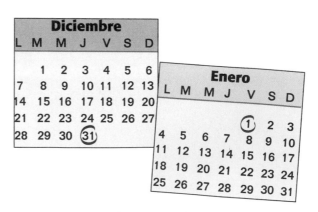

Diciembre

L	M	M	J	V	S	D
	1	2	3	4	5	6
7	8	9	10	11	12	13
14	15	16	17	18	19	20
21	22	23	24	25	26	27
28	29	30	(31)			

Enero

L	M	M	J	V	S	D
				(1)	2	3
4	5	6	7	8	9	10
11	12	13	14	15	16	17
18	19	20	21	22	23	24
25	26	27	28	29	30	31

Año Nuevo es el primero de enero, el primer día del año.

Los Reyes Magos

el camello

los Reyes Magos

la paja

El seis de enero es el Día de los Reyes.
Los padres les dicen a los niños que pongan paja
    para los camellos en sus zapatos.
Los niños esperan que los Reyes les traigan regalos.

Hanuka

¡Feliz Hanuka!

la menora

Hanuka es la fiesta de las luces.
Es una fiesta hebrea. La fiesta dura ocho días.
Durante la fiesta le piden al hijo mayor que encienda las velas de la menora.
La menora tiene nueve brazos.

Vocabulario

¿Qué palabra necesito?

 6 **¿Qué celebran?** Identifiquen según se indica.

1.

2.

3.

4.

5.

 7 **Historieta** **Los regalos** Contesten.

1. En Estados Unidos, ¿quién les trae regalos a los niños, San Nicolás o los Reyes?
2. ¿Quiénes les traen regalos a los niños hispanos?
3. ¿Qué decoran para Navidad las familias norteamericanas?
4. ¿Cuándo reciben sus regalos los niños norteamericanos?
5. ¿Cuándo reciben sus regalos los niños hispanos?
6. ¿Para quiénes es la paja en los zapatos?
7. ¿Quiénes les dicen a los niños que pongan la paja en sus zapatos?
8. ¿Están contentos los niños que los Reyes les traigan regalos?

Paja para los camellos

UN POCO MÁS *For more practice using words from **Palabras 1** and **2**, do Activity 13 on page H14 at the end of this book.*

8 **Algunas tradiciones** Completen.

1. La «fiesta de las luces» se llama ____.
2. La menora lleva ____ brazos.
3. En cada brazo hay una ____.

4. La persona que enciende las velas
   es el ____.
5. Esta fiesta dura ____ días.

Girona, España

9 **Una fiesta de invierno** El/La alumno(a) de intercambio
(tu compañero[a]) quiere saber qué fiesta celebra tu familia en el
invierno y cómo la celebran. Descríbele las costumbres y tradiciones
de tu familia para Navidad, Hanuka, Kwanza o cualquier otra fiesta
de invierno. Después cambien de rol.

10 **Entrevista** Si es posible, busca en tu comunidad a una
persona mayor hispana. Prepara una entrevista con esta
persona sobre las costumbres de Navidad o Reyes en su
país. Luego prepara un reportaje y preséntalo a la clase.

Spanish Online

For a fun way to review this vocabulary, go
to the Chapter 13 **eGame** on the Glencoe
Spanish Web site at glencoe.com.

Estructura

El subjuntivo de los verbos de cambio radical
Telling what may or may not take place

1. Verbs that have a stem change in the present indicative also have a stem change in the present subjunctive.

Use your StudentWorks *Plus* CD for more practice.

INFINITIVE	E → IE		O → UE	
	cerrar	perder	encontrar	poder
yo	cierre	pierda	encuentre	pueda
tú	cierres	pierdas	encuentres	puedas
él, ella, Ud.	cierre	pierda	encuentre	pueda
nosotros(as)	cerremos	perdamos	encontremos	podamos
vosotros(as)	*cerréis*	*perdáis*	*encontréis*	*podáis*
ellos, ellas, Uds.	cierren	pierdan	encuentren	puedan

Other verbs with the **e → ie** stem change like **cerrar** are:

> **sentarse, comenzar, empezar, pensar**

Other **o → ue** verbs like **encontrar** are:

> **acostarse, recordar, volver**

2. The verbs **sentir (e → ie), dormir (o → ue),** and **pedir (e → i)** have a stem change in every person of the present subjunctive.

INFINITIVE	E → IE	O → UE	E → I
	sentir	dormir	pedir
yo	sienta	duerma	pida
tú	sientas	duermas	pidas
él, ella, Ud.	sienta	duerma	pida
nosotros(as)	sintamos	durmamos	pidamos
vosotros(as)	*sintáis*	*durmáis*	*pidáis*
ellos, ellas, Uds.	sientan	duerman	pidan

Other verbs with the **e → i** stem change like **pedir** are:

> **repetir, freír, seguir, servir**

Ultima Hora

Levante las solapas y compruebe su suerte

el juego de los

Tres Reyes Magos

MOSA PEUGEOT — El Corte Inglés

Si no ha ganado, rellene la parte posterior de este cupón, puede ganar magníficos regalos con los Reyes Magos de **Ultima Hora**

¿Cómo lo digo?

 11 **Historieta** **Yo quiero.** Sigan el modelo.

Él vuelve pronto. ⟶
Yo quiero que él vuelva pronto.

1. Él vuelve mañana.
2. Él nos encuentra en el restaurante.
3. Él se sienta a nuestra mesa.
4. Él pide algo bueno.
5. Él me recomienda un plato.
6. El mesero nos sirve atentamente.

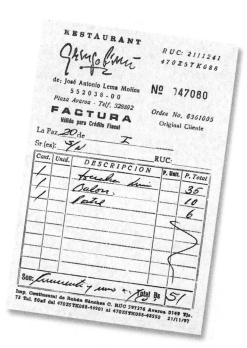

Ronda, España

12 **Historieta** **Necesitamos a Luis.** Completen.

Espero que Luis __1__ (volver) mañana. Quiero que él __2__ (encontrar)
un vuelo temprano. Esperamos que él __3__ (poder) llegar por la mañana.
Es posible que el partido __4__ (comenzar) a las dos de la tarde. Para
nosotros, es mejor que el partido __5__ (empezar) más tarde. Temo que
Luis no __6__ (poder) jugar si llega tarde. Y sin Luis, es probable que
nosotros __7__ (perder) el partido.

Estructura

 El subjuntivo con verbos como pedir y aconsejar
Giving advice and making suggestions

1. The subjunctive is used with the following verbs because even though you may advise, recommend, suggest, ask, or order someone to do something, he or she may not do it.

pedir *to ask*   **rogar** *to beg, to plead*
aconsejar *to advise*   **exigir** *to demand*
sugerir *to suggest*

Él pide que yo vaya.
Y yo le aconsejo que se quede aquí.
Mamá nos sugiere que salgamos ahora.

2. An indirect object pronoun often goes with these verbs. The pronoun serves as the subject of the dependent clause.

Él me pide que (yo) sirva de padrino.
Les ruego que (ustedes) no se casen en junio porque no voy a estar.

3. The verbs **decir** and **escribir** call for the subjunctive only when they imply a command or request, such as: "He writes me to come right away."

Ellos me dicen que no me case.
Yo le escribo que venga pronto.

¿Cómo lo digo?

13 **Mamá te pide que...**
 Completen según el modelo.

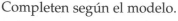

> **limpiar tu cuarto** ⟶
> **Mamá te pide que limpies tu cuarto.**

1. levantarte temprano
2. limpiar tu cuarto
3. bañarte
4. tomar el desayuno
5. no jugar hoy
6. dormir bastante
7. volver a casa en el bus

Coyoacán, México

14 ¿Qué te escribe tu primo? Sigan el modelo.

ir a la fiesta ⟶
Mi primo me escribe que vaya a la fiesta.

1. ir al cine
2. tomar el tren
3. llegar un día antes de la fiesta
4. no ir a un hotel
5. quedarse en casa de mis tíos

 15 El profesor exige que... Sigan el modelo.

Estudiamos mucho. ⟶
El profesor nos exige que estudiemos mucho.

1. Llegamos temprano a clase.
2. Hacemos preguntas.
3. Estudiamos.
4. No perdemos el tiempo.
5. Pensamos antes de hablar.

16 Consejos de mis padres Contesten.

1. ¿Tus padres te aconsejan que seas bueno?
2. ¿Tus padres te piden que ayudes un poco con las tareas domésticas?
3. ¿Te piden que les digas adónde vas y con quiénes?
4. ¿Tus padres te sugieren que hagas tus tareas antes de poner la televisión?
5. ¿Te dicen que te acuestes antes de las once?

Santurce, Puerto Rico

 17 Los consejos de don o doña Sabelotodo
Tú vas a ser don o doña Sabelotodo—y no hay duda que tú lo sabes todo. Además sabes lo que todo el mundo debe hacer. Trabaja con un(a) compañero(a). Dale muchos consejos, sugerencias y recomendaciones. Tu compañero(a) te dirá si va a seguir tus consejos o no. Luego cambien de rol.

El subjuntivo con expresiones de duda
Expressing doubt or uncertainty

1. The subjunctive is always used after expressions that imply doubt or uncertainty.

> **Dudo que ellos se casen.**
> **No creo que ellos tengan una recepción.**

2. If the statement implies certainty, however, the indicative rather than the subjunctive is used. The verb is frequently in the future tense.

> **No dudo que ellos se casarán.**
> **Creo que tendrán una gran recepción.**

3. Study the following expressions of doubt and certainty.

SUBJUNCTIVE	INDICATIVE
dudar	no dudar
es dudoso	no es dudoso
no estar seguro(a)	estar seguro(a)
no creer	creer
no es cierto	es cierto

Parque del Amor, Lima, Perú

¿Cómo lo digo?

18 **¿Lo crees o no lo crees?**

Introduzcan la oración con **creo** o **no creo**.

1. Los aviones vuelan a un millón de millas por hora.
2. Las bicicletas contaminan el aire.
3. Hace mucho calor en Siberia.
4. Todos los españoles hablan inglés.
5. Todos los compañeros de clase bailan muy bien.
6. Sirven comida excelente en la cafetería.
7. Las muchachas son más inteligentes que los muchachos.

ESTE MOTOR...
NO CONTAMINA

19 Martín nunca dice la verdad.
Sigan el modelo.

> Yo soy el más inteligente de la clase. ⟶
> No, Martín. Dudo que seas el más
> inteligente de la clase.

1. Yo tengo mucho talento.
2. También soy muy guapo.
3. Recibo las mejores notas de la clase.
4. Yo bailo como un profesional.
5. Mis padres son millonarios.
6. Las muchachas me adoran.
7. Voy a Madrid mañana.
8. Me quieren en Hollywood.

20 Historieta La boda de mi mejor amigo(a)
Contesten con **creo** o **dudo.**

1. Tu mejor amigo(a) se casa pronto.
2. Te invita a la recepción.
3. La recepción es en un gran hotel.
4. La orquesta toca música clásica.
5. Tú le regalas un coche.
6. Los novios viajan a Buenos Aires.

21 ¿Pasará o no pasará? Con un(a) compañero(a), determinen
las cosas o los eventos que ustedes creen que van a pasar u ocurrir en
su vida y cosas que no creen que pasen ni ocurran. Luego comparen
sus dos listas para determinar lo que ustedes creen que tienen en
común.

Estructura

El subjuntivo con expresiones de emoción
Expressing emotional reactions

1. The subjunctive is used in a dependent clause that is introduced by a verb or expression of emotion.

> **Me alegro de que tú celebres tu cumpleaños.**
> **Siento que tu hermano no pueda asistir.**
> **Es una lástima que él tenga que trabajar.**

2. The following are verbs and expressions that convey emotion.

> **alegrarse de**
> **estar contento**
> **sorprender**
> **gustar**
> **sentir**
> **ser una lástima**

Santiago de Chile

¿Cómo lo digo?

22 **Sara, sí, y Nora, no.** Sigan el modelo.

> **Tenemos un examen mañana.** ⟶
> **Sara se alegra de que tengamos un examen mañana.**
> **Nora siente que tengamos un examen mañana.**

Sara   Nora

1. Tenemos clase mañana.
2. El profesor nos da un examen.
3. El examen es difícil.
4. No podemos usar los libros.

5. Escribimos una composición.
6. Hacemos una presentación oral.
7. El profesor lee las composiciones.

23 **¿Se alegra o no se alegra Andrés?** Contesten. Empiecen las frases con **Andrés se alegra** o **Andrés no se alegra**.

1. La escuela cierra temprano.
2. Los chicos pueden jugar.
3. Va a llover.
4. Acaba de llover.
5. Su equipo pierde.
6. Los padres les compran pizza.
7. Juegan otra vez mañana.

24 **Historieta** **El Día de los Reyes y Hanuka** Contesten.

1. ¿Están contentos los niños que llegue el seis de enero?
2. ¿Se alegran de que vengan los Reyes?
3. ¿Están alegres que los Reyes les traigan regalos?
4. ¿Les sorprende que los camellos coman la paja en los zapatos?
5. ¿Te sorprende que la fiesta de Hanuka dure ocho días?
6. ¿Los niños se alegran de que los padres les den un regalo cada uno de los ocho días?
7. ¿Se alegran los padres de que su hijo mayor encienda las velas de la menora?

25 **Emociones** Trabaja con un(a) compañero(a). Van a hablar de su escuela y de su vida escolar. Es cierto que en la escuela hay cosas que les ponen contentos y hay otras cosas que les ponen tristes. Al hablar de su vida escolar usen las expresiones **Me alegro de que, Siento que, Estoy contento(a) que, Estoy triste que** y den sus opiniones.

Santurce, Puerto Rico

Andas bien. ¡Adelante!

Conversación

Año Nuevo

Ramón ¿Qué vas a hacer para Año Nuevo?

Yolanda ¿Año Nuevo? Estaré durmiendo.
Pero Nochevieja voy a una fiesta.

Ramón Me alegro de que vayas a una fiesta.
Yo me quedaré en casa.

Yolanda ¿Por qué? ¿Qué pasa?

Ramón Pues, invité a Cristina a ir a la fiesta de
Luis Miguel y ella me dijo que no podía.

Yolanda Claro que no podía. Ella no puede ir
contigo porque va con Antonio.

Ramón ¡Pero Antonio es tu novio! Es imposible
que Cristina vaya con él.

Yolanda Pues, imposible o no, es verdad. Créeme.
¡Oye, tengo una idea!

Ramón No es necesario que me digas. Ya lo sé.
Y es excelente idea. ¡Vamos tú y yo a
la fiesta!

Yolanda Muchas gracias por la invitación. Acepto.

¿Comprendes?

Contesten.

1. ¿Qué va a hacer Yolanda durante
Año Nuevo?
2. ¿Cuándo va ella a una fiesta?
3. ¿Quién da la fiesta?
4. ¿Qué piensa hacer Ramón?
5. ¿A quién pensaba Ramón invitar a
la fiesta?
6. ¿Qué le dijo ella?
7. ¿Por qué no puede Cristina ir a
la fiesta con Ramón?
8. ¿Quién es Antonio?
9. ¿Cuál es la idea que tiene Yolanda?
10. ¿Qué van a hacer Yolanda y Ramón?

408 *cuatrocientos ocho*

CAPÍTULO 13

Vamos a hablar más

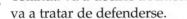

A **¡Qué horror!** Trabaja con un(a) compañero(a). Uno(a) de ustedes va a ser (tomar el papel de) Yolanda en la conversación en la página 408. El/La otro(a) tomará el papel de Antonio que va a salir con otra. Yolanda va a decirle a Antonio todo lo que ella piensa de él. Antonio va a tratar de defenderse.

Ciudad de México

B **La víspera de Año Nuevo** Trabaja con un(a) compañero(a). Discutan todo lo que ustedes hacen o no hacen para celebrar el Año Nuevo.

Lecturas culturales

Las doce uvas de la felicidad 🔄 🎧

Reading Strategy

Visualizing while reading When you are reading a passage, making a mental picture of what you are reading about will help you remember. This is called "visualizing," that is, allowing yourself to imagine the setting and events and picture them in your mind. This is especially helpful when reading about a topic that is new to you or one about which you have no background information.

Madrid, la capital de España, está en el centro del país. Y en el mismo centro de Madrid está la Puerta del Sol. La Puerta del Sol es una plaza donde desembocan muchas calles. La Puerta del Sol tiene gran importancia histórica. Es allí donde los madrileños se reúnen cuando algo importante ha ocurrido o va a ocurrir.

Cada Nochevieja miles y miles de madrileños llenan la Puerta del Sol para esperar la llegada del Año Nuevo. Todos miran el reloj que está en la torre de la antigua Casa de Correos. Están contentos que llegue otro año. En los momentos antes de las doce de la noche, una bola dorada[1] comienza a bajar, segundo por segundo. Cuando baja completamente, el año ha terminado, y un año nuevo comienza. Mientras el reloj da las doce los madrileños tienen la costumbre de comerse doce uvas, una por una. Estas uvas se llaman las uvas de la felicidad. Comerlas es garantía de un año nuevo próspero y feliz.

[1]dorada *golden*

Puerta del Sol, Madrid

Use your **StudentWorks Plus** CD for more practice.

¿Comprendes?

A **Nochevieja en Madrid** Contesten según la lectura.

1. ¿Qué tienen en común Madrid y la Puerta del Sol?
2. ¿Por qué es importante históricamente la Puerta del Sol?
3. ¿Qué día del año llenan los madrileños la Puerta del Sol?
4. ¿Qué hacen ellos allí?
5. ¿Qué hay en la antigua Casa de Correos?

B **¿Cómo es Nochevieja?** Expliquen en sus propias palabras las tradiciones de Nochevieja en España.

Puerta del Sol, Madrid

Lectura opcional ①

La boda

    Ángel y Mónica seguían saliendo juntos y cada mes se querían más. Sabían que querían casarse. Ángel fue a la casa de Mónica y le pidió al padre la mano de su hija. Poco después los padres anunciaron el compromiso[1] de sus hijos. Hubo un cóctel elegante en el que fijaron la fecha para su boda y todos los parientes de las dos familias y los amigos íntimos festejaron a los nuevos comprometidos. Estas fiestas y reuniones familiares son muy importantes porque el matrimonio es el enlace de las dos familias y durante las fiestas antenupciales las dos familias van conociéndose.

    Se casaron un año después. El día de la boda hay generalmente dos ceremonias—la civil y la religiosa. Los novios van a la iglesia acompañados del padrino y de la madrina, de sus pajes de honor y de sus damas de honor. La madre de Mónica le sirvió de madrina y el padre de Ángel le sirvió de padrino. Después de la ceremonia Ángel y Mónica salieron de la iglesia como esposo y esposa y fueron a una recepción en donde sus familiares y sus amigos íntimos les dieron la enhorabuena.

    Al terminar la recepción, Ángel y Mónica salieron para su viaje de novios. Fueron a Europa a pasar su luna de miel[2].

[1]compromiso *engagement*
[2]luna de miel *honeymoon*

¿Comprendes?

Los novios Contesten.

1. ¿Quiénes son Ángel y Mónica?
2. ¿Qué hizo Ángel cuando supo que él y Mónica iban a comprometerse?
3. ¿Qué hubo para anunciar su compromiso?
4. ¿Para qué sirven las fiestas antenupciales?
5. ¿Cuántas ceremonias hay para la boda?
6. ¿A quiénes escogieron Ángel y Mónica para su padrino y madrina?
7. ¿Adónde fueron los recién casados para su luna de miel?

Lectura opcional 2

Freyssiner–Parada

El reverendo Manuel Belman Robles, S.J., impartió la bendición nupcial a Sandra Freyssiner y César Parada, durante una ceremonia que tuvo lugar el pasado sábado por la tarde en la iglesia de Nuestra Señora del Socorro.

A la hora señalada llegaron los novios con su comitiva y en la puerta fueron recibidos por el sacerdote[1], quien les acompañó hasta el altar mayor, donde participaron del calvario de Cristo.

La iglesia fue profusamente iluminada y decorada con arreglos de flores naturales mientras el coro interpretó trozos de música sacra, lo que dio mayor lucimiento a la ceremonia.

El sacerdote oficiante pronunció un emotivo fervorín en donde dio consejos a los novios para su vida espiritual.

Estuvieron los padres de los contrayentes Jaime Freyssiner de la Barrera, Gloria Márquez Marrón, Francisco Javier Parra Jiménez y Amelia López de Parada.

Asimismo fueron madrinas Gloria Freyssiner Márquez, Karu Noval de Freyssiner, Amelia Parada de Hernández, Leticia Parada de Alba y Beatriz Alvarez.

Como pajes actuaron los niños Elvira Parada Dommarco y Cristina Hernández Parada.

Al finalizar el acto religioso, los nuevos esposos desfilaron[2] por el pasillo central y en el atrio[3] recibieron felicitaciones de amigos y parientes.

Más tarde se ofreció una recepción en su honor en donde se brindó[4] por la felicidad de la pareja, la que más tarde salió de viaje de bodas.

[1]sacerdote *priest*
[2]desfilaron *paraded*
[3]atrio *vestibule, entrance*
[4]se brindó *everyone toasted*

¿Comprendes?

La boda Contesten.
1. ¿Cómo se llama el sacerdote que le dio la bendición nupcial a la pareja?
2. ¿Dónde tuvo lugar la ceremonia?
3. ¿Cuándo tuvo lugar?
4. ¿Dónde recibió a la pareja el sacerdote?
5. ¿Adónde los acompañó?
6. ¿Con qué fue decorada la iglesia?
7. Después de la ceremonia, ¿dónde recibieron felicitaciones los nuevos esposos?
8. ¿Qué se ofreció después de la ceremonia en la iglesia?
9. ¿Para dónde salió la pareja después de la recepción?

Conexiones
Las bellas artes

Las artes plásticas

From earliest times, religion has had a profound influence on art. The temples of the Far East, the Gothic cathedrals of Europe, the pyramids of the Mayas, and the great mosques of Cordoba and Cairo are artistic expressions of profound religious feeling. Throughout the centuries, the painters of Europe, especially the Spaniards, often employed religious themes in their work. *The Adoration of the Magi* by Velázquez and *The Return of the Prodigal Son* by Murillo are two notable examples.

Diego Velázquez

Bartolomé Murillo

La escuela española

Como ya saben ustedes, hay diferentes épocas y «escuelas» de arte y, en particular, de pintura. Velázquez y Murillo son representantes de la «escuela española». Pero también se puede decir que eran clásicos. Cuando hablamos de los clásicos en el arte, nos referimos a los artistas que se notan por su claridad, elegancia y atención a las formas de los griegos y los romanos.

Los dos artistas nacieron[1] en Sevilla. Velázquez (1599–1660) era de una familia noble. Murillo (1617–1682) era de una familia pobre. Perdió a sus padres cuando tenía sólo diez años. Velázquez fue a Madrid a pintar para la corte donde su talento artístico fue reconocido enseguida. Murillo se quedó en Sevilla donde se ganó la vida pintando y vendiendo sus cuadros en el mercado. En poco tiempo ganó fama y fue reconocido como el pintor principal de la ciudad.

[1]nacieron *were born*

La adoración de los Magos
de Diego Velázquez

Los temas favoritos de la escuela española eran la mitología y la religión. Este cuadro de Velázquez, *La adoración de los Magos*, representa a los tres Reyes Magos—Melchor, Gaspar y Baltasar—ofreciendo sus regalos al Niño Jesús. Notarán ustedes los anacronismos en esta obra. Por ejemplo, la época del evento es del primer siglo. Las ropas son contemporáneas con la época del pintor del siglo XVII. Noten los colores que emplea el artista. Velázquez es maestro de colorido.

Este cuadro de Murillo, *El regreso del hijo pródigo*, describe la historia bíblica del mismo nombre. Todos los personajes y objetos que aparecen[2] en la historia bíblica están incluidos en el cuadro. Vemos al padre que recibe a su hijo que regresa y los sirvientes que le traen zapatos y ropa nueva. El cuadro no tiene líneas definidas ni un fuerte contraste de colores. El pintor quería una composición sencilla y armoniosa. No hay nada en el cuadro que nos distraiga[3] de la contemplación de la alegría del padre.

[2]aparecen *appear*   [3]distraiga *distracts*

El regreso del hijo pródigo de Bartolomé Murillo

¿Comprendes?

A La escuela española Contesten.

1. ¿Quiénes son representantes de la «escuela española»?
2. ¿Dónde nacieron?
3. ¿Quién era de una familia noble y rica?
4. ¿Quién era de una familia pobre?
5. ¿Dónde pintó Velázquez?
6. ¿Dónde pintó Murillo?
7. ¿Cuáles eran los temas favoritos de la «escuela española»?
8. ¿Cómo se llama el cuadro de Velázquez?
9. ¿Qué representa?
10. ¿Cómo se llama el cuadro de Murillo?

B Tu preferencia ¿Cuál de los dos cuadros te gusta más? ¿Por qué?

¡Te toca a ti!

Use what you have learned

1 Una situación delicada
✔ *Give someone advice*

Tu mejor amigo(a) (tu compañero[a]), iba a casarse. Pero ahora ha cambiado de idea. Él o ella no sabe qué hacer. Te pide consejos. Conversen juntos.

2 Mi fiesta favorita
✔ *Talk about your favorite holiday*

Trabaja con un(a) compañero(a). Descríbele tu fiesta favorita. Explícale por qué te gusta tanto. Luego cambien de rol.

Spanish Online
To find out more about holidays and festivals in the Spanish-speaking world, go to the Chapter 13 **WebQuest** on the Glencoe Spanish Web site at glencoe.com.

3 Resoluciones para el Año Nuevo
✔ *Tell what you believe or doubt what one another will do*

Trabaja con un(a) compañero(a) de clase. Cada uno(a) de ustedes le dirá al/a la otro(a) lo que crees que él o ella hará en el Año Nuevo y lo que dudas que él o ella haga.

4 Una invitación

✔ *Write an invitation*

Escribe una invitación para un cumpleaños, una boda o cualquier otra fiesta. Da todos los informes necesarios.

¡Alguien Cumple Años!

Writing Strategy

Classifying a subject When writing, one way to effectively organize your material is to classify your subject. For example, if you are writing about clothing, there are several categories your subject could fit into: clothing for school, clothing for weekends, clothing for doing chores, and many more. By choosing a category and classifying your subject, you will be able to organize your information more appropriately and use this classification to construct a good paragraph or paper.

5 Las fiestas

Obviously you celebrate many holidays throughout the year. This does not mean, however, that you and your classmates celebrate the same ones. Write a paper about some of the holidays you celebrate and describe what these celebrations entail. It would be impossible to write about all the holidays you celebrate; therefore, narrow your list by selecting a category for your holidays: holidays I like best, religious holidays, winter holidays, summer holidays, or any other you can think of. Include an introduction and a conclusion.

Assessment

Vocabulario

To review
Palabras 1, turn to
pages 392–393.

1 **Contesten.**

1. ¿En qué pones velas?
2. ¿Qué dices a una persona que celebra su cumpleaños?
3. ¿Quiénes van a casarse?
4. ¿Qué reciben los novios?

To review **Palabras 2**,
turn to pages 396–397.

2 **¿Sí o no?**

5. La víspera de Año Nuevo es la Nochevieja.
6. Año Nuevo es el mismo día que la Navidad.
7. Hanuka se llama también la fiesta de las luces y es una fiesta hebrea.
8. Los niños hispanos ponen paja en sus zapatos el 31 de diciembre cuando el reloj da las doce.

Estructura

To review the
subjunctive of stem-
changing verbs,
turn to page 400.

3 **Escriban cada oración de nuevo.**

9. Mis padres quieren que nos acostemos temprano.
   Mis padres quieren que yo _____.
10. Es necesario que tú duermas aquí.
    Es necesario que nosotros _____.
11. Ellos prefieren que tú lo pidas.
    Ellos prefieren que ustedes _____.
12. Es posible que volvamos temprano.
    Es posible que yo _____.

4 Completen.

13. Él se va a casar y pide que (yo) le ____ de padrino. (servir)
14. Yo les ruego a ustedes que ____ a la celebración. (asistir)
15. El profesor te ruega que ____ tus tareas con cuidado. (hacer)

To review the subjunctive for giving advice and making suggestions, turn to page 402.

5 Escriban cada oración de nuevo.

16. Dudo que ellos vengan.
    No dudo ____.
17. Es cierto que él saldrá.
    No es cierto ____.
18. Creo que él lo sabrá.
    No creo ____.

To review the subjunctive with expressions of doubt, turn to page 404.

6 Completen.

19. Estoy contento que ustedes ____ asistir. (poder)
20. Me sorprende que él no ____ nada. (saber)
21. Me alegro de que tú ____ de acuerdo. (estar)
22. Sandra siente que yo no ____ el viaje. (hacer)

To review the subjunctive with expressions of emotion, turn to page 406.

Cultura

7 Contesten.

23. ¿Dónde tiene lugar la celebración de las doce uvas de la felicidad?
24. ¿Cuándo tiene lugar?
25. ¿Dónde está la Puerta del Sol?

To review this cultural information, turn to page 410.

For more Chapter 13 test preparation go to the Chapter 13 **Self-Check Quiz** on the Glencoe Spanish Web site at glencoe.com.

Tell as much as you can about this illustration.

Talking about a birthday party

el cumpleaños
el pastel, la torta,
　el bizcocho
las velas
el regalo

los parientes
nacer
venir a la fiesta
divertirse
¡Feliz cumpleaños!

Talking about a wedding

la boda
la novia
el novio
la dama de honor
el padrino
la madrina

la recepción
el salón
la orquesta
casarse
¡Felicitaciones!
¡Enhorabuena!

Talking about Christmas

la Navidad
el árbol de Navidad
la Nochebuena
los Reyes Magos

los camellos
la paja
¡Feliz Navidad!

Talking about Chanukah

la fiesta de las luces
la menora
hebreo(a)
encender las velas
durar
¡Feliz Hanuka!

How well do you know your vocabulary?

- Choose words that describe a holiday you enjoy.
- Write a few sentences about how you and your family or friends celebrate this holiday.

Talking about New Year's

el Año Nuevo
La víspera de Año Nuevo
　(Nochevieja)
el reloj
dar las doce
celebrar
¡Feliz (Próspero) Año Nuevo!

Other useful expressions

alegrarse

VIDEOTUR

Episodio 13

In this video episode you will join Vicky in her new business adventure. See page 492 for more information. As you watch, look for gestures the speakers use to help convey their message.

Capítulo

14

Profesiones y oficios

Objetivos

In this chapter you will learn to:

❖ talk about professions and occupations
❖ interview for a job
❖ state work qualifications
❖ talk about future events
❖ talk about probable events

Antonio Gattorno *Agricultores*

Spanish Online
To interact with your online edition of
¡Buen viaje! go to: glencoe.com.

Vocabulario

PALABRAS **1**

La oficina

Use your **StudentWorks Plus** CD for more practice.

el secretario

la contable

Otras profesiones

la ingeniera

la programadora
de informática

el gerente

La tienda

El gobierno municipal

el funcionario

la cajera

el comerciante

el alcalde

la alcaldía

el arquitecto

La corte

el juez

la abogada

el tribunal

el bufete del abogado

424 *cuatrocientos veinticuatro*

Algunos oficios

el electricista

el plomero, el fontanero

la carpintera

el albañil

Los oficios son los trabajos de especialistas
como plomeros y carpinteros.
Estos especialistas tienen que tener (poseer)
un talento.

Las profesiones son los trabajos que
requieren un título universitario.
Es necesario que los profesionales tengan
un título universitario.

Los comerciantes se dedican a la compra
y venta de mercancía.
Quieren que sus clientes compren mucho.
¡Ojalá estén satisfechos!

Vocabulario

¿Qué palabra necesito?

1 **¿Qué es y quiénes trabajan aquí?** Contesten.

1.

2.

3.

4.

5.

2 **¿Quién trabaja dónde?** Escojan.

a. el mecánico

b. la funcionaria

c. el cocinero

d. la profesora

i. el campesino

e. el mesero

f. el contable

g. la juez

h. el pintor

1. ¿Quién trabaja en una fábrica?
2. ¿Quién trabaja en la sala de consulta?
3. ¿Quién cuida de los animales?
4. ¿Quién siembra los campos?
5. ¿Quién pinta cuadros?
6. ¿Quién enseña?
7. ¿Quién repara el carro?
8. ¿Quién prepara los platos en el restaurante?
9. ¿Quién les sirve a los clientes en el restaurante?
10. ¿Quién prepara cuentas y documentos financieros?
11. ¿Quién trabaja en la corte y decide quién es inocente o no?
12. ¿Quién trabaja para el gobierno municipal, estatal o federal?

j. la obrera

k. el médico

l. la veterinaria

3 **¿A quién necesitas si… ?** Contesten.

1. quieres construir un garaje para tu casa
2. tienes un problema legal
3. necesitas medicina y tienes una receta del médico
4. quieres ayuda con tus maletas en el aeropuerto
5. quieres unos audífonos en el avión
6. estás buscando ayuda en una tienda

4 **Una carrera que me interesaría** Sigan el modelo.

agente de policía ⟶
**Sí, me gustaría ser agente de policía. Me interesaría./
No, no me gustaría ser agente de policía. No me
interesaría nada.**

1. médico
2. arquitecto
3. gerente de una gran empresa o compañía
4. abogado
5. dentista
6. contable
7. electricista
8. programador
9. funcionario en una agencia del gobierno
10. veterinario

Un cocinero, Marbella

Una abogada, Ciudad de México

5 **Una profesión** Trabaja con un(a) compañero(a). Hablen de las profesiones u oficios que les interesarían. Expliquen por qué les interesaría cierta profesión.

6 *Juego* **¿Qué soy?** Piensa en un oficio o profesión. Tu compañero(a) te puede hacer un máximo de cinco preguntas para adivinar o acertar el oficio o la profesión en que estás pensando. Luego cambien de rol.

 UN POCO MÁS *For more practice using words from **Palabras 1**, do Activity 14 on page H15 at the end of this book.*

En busca de un puesto

Jorge está buscando un puesto que
    sea interesante.
Quiere que le paguen bien.
Es posible que vea un anuncio en el periódico.
¡Quizás encuentre algo que le interese!

Jorge no quiere trabajar a tiempo completo
    (cuarenta horas por semana).
Quizás le ofrezcan un trabajo a tiempo parcial.

el departamento de recursos humanos

RECURSOS HUMANOS

la solicitud de empleo

McGraw-Hill
Interamericana

SOLICITUD DE EMPLEO

FECHA

EMPLEO QUE SOLICITA

PROFESIÓN

SECUNDARIA	CARRERA COMERCIAL	LICENCIATURA	MAESTRÍA
PREPARATORIA	CARRERA TÉCNICA	OTRO	

SUELDO DESEADO

DATOS GENERALES

NOMBRE(S)   APELLIDO PATERNO   APELLIDO MATERNO

FECHA DE NACIMIENTO   EDAD   NACIONALIDAD   EDO. CIVIL

DOMICILIO ACTUAL   CALLE   NÚMERO   COLONIA   C.P.

CIUDAD   ESTADO   TELÉFONOS
CASA
OFICINA
CELULAR

Catalina busca un puesto también.
Ella llena una solicitud de empleo.

la entrevistadora

el candidato, el aspirante

El candidato tiene una entrevista.
La entrevistadora le hace preguntas.
¡Ojalá (que) conteste bien a las preguntas!
Es posible que esté un poco nervioso.
Quizás esté nervioso durante la entrevista.

Vocabulario

¿Qué palabra necesito?

7 Historieta Una entrevista

Contesten según la foto.

1. ¿Están entrevistando a la señorita?
2. ¿Estará buscando ella un puesto que sea interesante y que le pague bien?
3. ¿Tiene la candidata una carta de recomendación?
4. ¿Tiene que llenar una solicitud de empleo?
5. ¿Quiere la señorita que la entrevistadora lea su carta de recomendación?
6. ¿Es posible que la candidata esté un poco nerviosa?

Caracas, Venezuela

8 Historieta Mi trabajo Contesten.

1. ¿Trabajas?
2. ¿Dónde trabajas?
3. ¿Trabajas a tiempo completo o a tiempo parcial?
4. ¿Prefieres trabajar a tiempo completo o a tiempo parcial?
5. ¿Recibes un salario?
6. ¿Cuánto te pagan?

Empresa de primer orden de **INGENIERIA Y SISTEMAS DE CONTROL DE TRAFICO Y TRANSPORTE**, con presencia consolidada en ámbitos internacionales, ofrece puesto de

ingeniero de compras y logística

- Buscamos un profesional, con formación de **Ingeniero Superior o Técnico**, dominio del **inglés** y disponibilidad para viajar por España y el extranjero.
- **Se valorará:**
  - La experiencia adquirida en el área de compras y logística en Empresa Industrial.
  - La formación específica sobre la materia.
  - La capacidad de negociación con proveedores nacionales y extranjeros.
- La remuneración es a convenir, en función de la formación y experiencia aportada por los candidatos.

Rogamos envíen Historial Profesional detallado, con pretensiones económicas, fotografía, señas y teléfono de contacto, indicando la Ref.: 22.229 a:

GM&A Selección C/ Don Ramón de la Cruz, 33
28001 Madrid

SE SOLICITA RECEPCIONISTA
Para importante empresa. Presentarse de lunes a viernes, en Av. 20 de Octubre # 1743 (esq. Conchitas) de 9 a 10:30 con currículum y referencias.

9 **Historieta** **Él solicita trabajo.** Contesten según se indica.

1. ¿Juan busca trabajo? (sí)
2. ¿Qué ha leído? (un anuncio en el periódico)
3. ¿Qué compañía está buscando (reclutando) empleados? (Austral)
4. ¿Adónde va Juan? (al departamento de recursos humanos de Austral)
5. ¿Qué tiene que llenar? (una solicitud de empleo)
6. ¿A quién le da la solicitud? (a la recepcionista)
7. ¿Qué va a tener? (una entrevista)

10 **Una entrevista** Eres un(a) empleado(a) en una agencia de empleos. Un(a) compañero(a) es un(a) candidato(a) para un empleo. Tú vas a darle una entrevista. Pregúntale sobre sus estudios, experiencia, aptitudes personales, talentos artísticos, etc. Luego cambien de rol.

11 **En la oficina del/de la consejero(a) de orientación**

El/La consejero(a) de orientación (*guidance counselor*) de tu escuela te ha pedido ayudar a un(a) estudiante hispanohablante que acaba de llegar de un país latinoamericano. Quiere que le hagas preguntas para determinar una carrera que le interesaría. Luego quiere que le expliques todo lo que tiene que hacer para prepararse para esa carrera.

Guadalajara, México

Infinitivo o subjuntivo

Saying what you would like to do and what you would like others to do

1. With any verbs or expressions that require the subjunctive, the subjunctive is used only when there is a change of subject. In other words, the subjunctive is used when the subject of the main clause is different from the subject of the dependent clause that follows **que**.

MAIN CLAUSE		DEPENDENT CLAUSE
Tú quieres	que	yo vaya al banco.
Nosotros preferimos	que	ustedes cambien dinero.
Es necesario	que	alguien decida.

2. If there is no change of subject, the infinitive is used.

Tú quieres ir al banco.
Nosotros preferimos cambiar dinero.
Es necesario decidir.

Caracas, Venezuela

¿Cómo lo digo?

12 **Historieta** **No. Yo quiero hacerlo.**
Contesten según el modelo.

¿Quieres que yo vaya al banco?

No. Yo quiero ir al banco.

1. ¿Quieres que yo vaya al banco?
2. ¿Quieres que yo endose el cheque?
3. ¿Quieres que yo cobre el cheque?
4. ¿Quieres que yo pida la tasa de cambio?
5. ¿Quieres que yo cambie dólares?
6. ¿Quieres que yo abra una cuenta?

13 Historieta Nosotros también Sigan el modelo.

Yo espero que Uds. hagan el viaje.

Nosotros también esperamos hacer el viaje.

1. Yo espero que ustedes hagan el viaje.
2. Espero que ustedes viajen en avión.
3. Espero que tomen un vuelo directo.
4. Espero que lleguen a tiempo.
5. Espero que visiten los museos.
6. Espero que vean los monumentos.
7. Espero que coman bien.
8. Espero que tengan bastante dinero.
9. Espero que vuelvan en una semana.

Ciudad de México

Museo de Arte Contemporáneo, Ciudad de México

14 Historieta La ropa sucia Contesten.

1. ¿Quieres lavar la ropa sucia?
2. ¿O prefieres que yo la lave?
3. ¿Quieres ir a la lavandería?
4. ¿O prefieres que yo vaya?
5. ¿Quieres que yo te lave el suéter?
6. ¿O es necesario limpiarlo en seco?
7. ¿Quieres que yo lo lleve a la tintorería?

15 Este fin de semana Pregúntale a tu

compañero(a) lo que él o ella quiere hacer este fin de semana. Después, pregúntale lo que sus padres quieren que él o ella haga. Luego cambien de rol.

El subjuntivo con ojalá y quizá(s)
Stating *perhaps* or *maybe*

The expressions **ojalá** (*I wish* or *I hope*) and **quizá(s)** (*perhaps* or *maybe*) are always followed by the subjunctive.

> **¡Ojalá que tengas una entrevista!**
> **¡Ojalá que te salga bien!**
> **¡Quizá te ofrezcan el puesto!**

¿Cómo lo digo?

16 **Historieta** **¡Ojalá que sí!** Contesten con **ojalá**.

1. ¿Él va a buscar un puesto?
2. ¿Va a ir al departamento de recursos humanos?
3. ¿Va a pedir una solicitud de empleo?
4. ¿Va a llenar la solicitud?
5. ¿Le van a dar una entrevista?
6. ¿No va a estar muy nervioso?
7. ¿Le van a ofrecer el puesto?
8. ¿Le va a pagar bien el trabajo?

Ciudad de México

17 **El corte de pelo** Contesten según el modelo.

> ¿Dónde estará Marta? (la peluquería) ⟶
> Quizás esté en la peluquería.

1. ¿Dónde estará Marta? (la peluquería)
2. ¿Qué pedirá ella? (un corte de pelo)
3. ¿Qué usarán para cortarle el pelo? (tijeras)
4. ¿Qué más le darán? (un champú)
5. ¿Quién le cortará el pelo? (Nilda)
6. ¿Cuánto tiempo tomará? (media hora)
7. ¿Cuánto le cobrarán? (20 pesos)

18 **Quizá y ojalá** Habla con un(a) compañero(a). Usando **quizá**, dile algunas cosas que es posible que ocurran en el futuro. Si es algo que quieres que ocurra, sigue hablando usando **ojalá**. Por ejemplo, **¡Quizá seas rico(a)! ¡Ojalá seas rico(a)!** Luego cambien de rol.

El subjuntivo en cláusulas relativas
Describing indefinite persons or things

A grouping of words that modifies a noun is called a relative clause. A relative clause can modify or describe a noun that refers to a specific, definite person or thing or an indefinite person or thing. When the clause describes a definite person or thing, the verb in the clause is in the indicative. If, however, it modifies an indefinite person or thing, the verb is in the subjunctive. Note too that the **a personal** is omitted when the object is indefinite.

> **Conocemos a una secretaria que habla bien el español.**
> **Buscamos una secretaria que hable bien el español.**

¿Cómo lo digo?

19 **Un conocido** Contesten según el modelo.

> una persona que habla español ⟶
> **No necesito una persona que hable español.**
> **Conozco a una persona que habla español.**

1. una persona que es bilingüe
2. una persona que tiene experiencia
3. una persona que conoce el mercado
4. una persona que puede viajar

20 **Historieta** **Están buscando empleados.** Contesten.

1. ¿Está ofreciendo la compañía Vensa un puesto que paga bien?
2. ¿Buscan alguien que tenga experiencia en ventas?
3. ¿Quieren alguien que pueda viajar?
4. ¿Necesitan una persona que conozca más de un idioma?

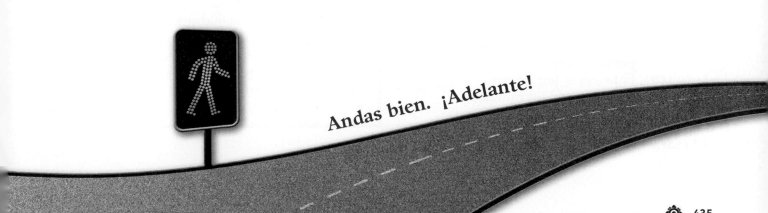

Andas bien. ¡Adelante!

Conversación

Planes para el futuro

Interactive Conversations

Lorenzo ¿Piensas asistir a la universidad, Alejandra?

Alejandra Sí. Tengo muy buenas notas y me gustan los estudios académicos.

Lorenzo ¿Tienes una idea de lo que quieres hacer?

Alejandra No sé exactamente. Quizás me especialice en comercio o marketing.

Lorenzo Son dos campos interesantes.

Alejandra Creo que me gustaría trabajar con una empresa multinacional. Quiero un puesto que me permita viajar.

Lorenzo Entonces es importante que continúes con tus estudios del español. ¡Ojalá tengas mucha suerte en tu carrera!

Alejandra Gracias.

¿Comprendes?

Contesten.

1. ¿Qué piensa hacer en el futuro Alejandra?
2. ¿Por qué quiere asistir a la universidad?
3. ¿Sabe Alejandra lo que quiere hacer después?
4. ¿En qué campos piensa especializarse?
5. ¿Por qué dice que le gustaría trabajar con una empresa multinacional?
6. ¿Qué le aconseja Lorenzo?

Vamos a hablar más

A **Un trabajo ideal** Piensa en lo que tú considerarías un trabajo ideal, algo que a ti te gustaría mucho hacer. Describe tu trabajo ideal a un(a) compañero(a). Luego cambien de rol.

B **Posibles carreras** Trabaja con un(a) compañero(a). Cada uno(a) de ustedes va a preparar una lista de las cosas que le interesan y de las materias o asignaturas que le gustan. Luego miren sus listas. Determinen los intereses que tienen en común. Luego discutan las profesiones o los oficios que les interesarían a los dos.

Spanish Online
For a fun activity on looking for a job in the Spanish-speaking world, go to the Chapter 14 **Web Quest** on the Glencoe Spanish Web site at glencoe.com.

C **Buscando un puesto** Trabaja con un(a) compañero(a). Miren las fotos y describan lo que pasa en cada una.

a.

b.

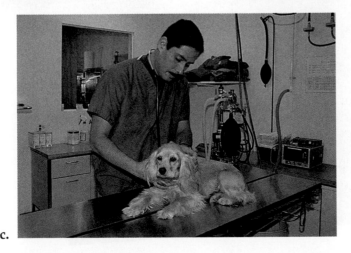
c.

Lecturas culturales

Reading Strategy

Scanning for specific information An important strategy is using titles and pictures to preview a reading selection and to help you know what it is about. Previewing a passage will help give an idea as to its purpose, organization, and content.

Un muchacho que se llama Bobby

Esta historia no es ficción. Bobby, a quien hoy le llaman don Roberto, es norteamericano. Asistió a una escuela pública donde estudió el español por cuatro años. Siguió con sus estudios del español en la universidad, aunque el español no era su campo de especialización. Se especializó en ciencias políticas.

Después de graduarse de la universidad Bobby entró al Cuerpo de Paz[1] como voluntario. Pasó unos meses de entrenamiento[2] en Puerto Rico. Después fue a Centroamérica donde trabajaba con campesinos en proyectos de irrigación y reforestación. Cuando terminó su período de voluntario, Bobby tomó el examen para el Departamento de Estado.

Bobby fue a trabajar con el Departamento de Estado y ascendió rápidamente. Fue cónsul en Costa Rica y agregado cultural en España. Él ha representado a Estados Unidos en Centroamérica, Sudamérica y España. Y hoy Bobby es embajador.

[1]Cuerpo de Paz *Peace Corps*
[2]entrenamiento *training*

Bolivia

Ecuador

¿Dónde y cómo comenzó esta ilustre carrera diplomática? Según don Roberto, «en el noveno grado, en mi clase de español uno».

¡Ojalá que tú también tengas una carrera tan interesante como la de Bobby! ¡Quizás seas nuestro embajador o embajadora en España o en México! ¿Qué opinas? ¿Te interesa la posibilidad de un puesto que te pague bien y que te permita ver el mundo al mismo tiempo?

Perú

Embajada norteamericana, Santiago, Chile

¿Comprendes?

Una carrera interesante Contesten.

1. ¿Cómo le llaman a Bobby hoy?
2. ¿De qué nacionalidad es?
3. ¿Cuántos años estudió el español en la escuela secundaria?
4. ¿Dónde siguió con sus estudios del español?
5. ¿En qué se especializó?
6. ¿Qué hizo en el Cuerpo de Paz?
7. Al terminar su período con el Cuerpo de Paz, ¿adónde fue a trabajar Bobby?
8. ¿Qué ha sido él?

Lectura opcional ①

La importancia de las lenguas extranjeras

No hay duda que el conocimiento de un idioma extranjero como el español puede ser un beneficio en muchas carreras. Hoy en día el comercio internacional tiene más y más importancia. No es suficiente sólo exportar nuestros productos al extranjero. Hay que tener una presencia real en muchos países. Por consiguiente muchas grandes empresas norteamericanas han llegado a ser multinacionales. Quiere decir que tienen instalaciones o sucursales[1] y filiales[2] en el extranjero. ¡Imagínate! Es posible que algún día tú trabajes con una compañía americana y que tu oficina esté en Caracas, Lima o Madrid.

Quizás el español en sí[3] no sea una carrera. Pero el español con otra especialización le da a uno una ventaja incalculable. Si tú conoces la contabilidad, el marketing o la informática, por ejemplo, y además dominas bien el español, podrás trabajar con una empresa multinacional. El español y tu otra especialización te permitirán encontrar un trabajo que te pague bien, que te sea interesante y que te dé la oportunidad de viajar y ver el mundo. ¡Ojalá! ¿No?

[1]sucursales *branches*   [2]filiales *subsidiaries*   [3]en sí *in itself*

Ceuta

Caracas, Venezuela

¿Comprendes?

La importancia de una lengua extranjera
Discutan.
¿Por qué es importante estudiar una lengua extranjera?
¿Cómo te puede ayudar en tu vida?

Lectura opcional ②

Málaga, España

AHORA EN MADRID   LA LUNA
ABRE SUS PUERTAS

y para integrar su equipo profesional
te necesitamos en los puestos de

GERENTES DE RESTAURANTE, GERENTE DE TIENDA, GERENTE DE VENTAS Y UN CHEF

Requisitos para chef:
- Inglés (nivel medio).
- Edad no mayor de 40 años.
- Escolaridad mínima de BUP o Secundaria, con estudios de especialización en alimentos y bebidas.
- Experiencia mínima comprobable de 4 años como chef en restaurantes de medio o alto volumen, con conocimientos de control de costos, gastos y manejo de personal.
- Buena presencia.

Requisitos para gerentes de tienda, gerente de ventas y gerente de restauración:
- Inglés (dominio).
- Edad entre 28 y 35 años.
- Estudios en administración, turismo, mercadotecnia o comercio (requisito sustituible únicamente con experiencia comprobable).
- Experiencia mínima comprobable de dos años como responsable del área.
- Con excelente actitud de servicio y ventas.
- Excelente presentación.

Ofrecemos para todos los puestos:
- Sueldo a convenir.
- Bonificación semestral y otras ventajas sociales.

Los interesados deberán enviar *currículum vitae*, con fotografía, por correo, a: C/ Antonio Maura, 12, 4.º derecha, 28014 MADRID, a la atención de La Luna   Madrid. Fax 91 522 08 53.

La confirmación de los expedientes seleccionados se realizará telefónicamente para un proceso de entrevistas que se efectuará en Madrid.

LA FECHA LÍMITE PARA RECEPCIÓN DE DATOS ES EL 14 DE OCTUBRE

¿Comprendes?

El restaurante «La Luna» Contesten.

1. ¿Qué abre sus puertas en Madrid?
2. ¿Quién necesita saber más inglés, el chef o el gerente de ventas?
3. ¿Cuál es la edad máxima para el chef? ¿Y para los otros puestos?
4. ¿Cuántos años de experiencia tiene que tener el chef? ¿Y los otros?
5. ¿Dónde tendrán lugar las entrevistas?
6. ¿Qué deben enviar los interesados con su currículum vitae?
7. ¿Cómo van a informar a las personas que seleccionan para presentarse para una entrevista?

Conexiones

Las ciencias sociales

La economía

Economics is the science that deals with the production, distribution, and consumption of goods and services for the welfare of humankind. It is an interesting and complex science. People need or desire all kinds of goods and services. However, we do not have at our disposal all the resources we would need to produce all that society would like to have. For this reason, economists provide the information necessary to those who must make crucial decisions as to what will and will not be produced.

La economía

¿Qué es la economía?

Hay varias definiciones de economía. La economía es el estudio de las decisiones que tomamos en la producción, distribución y consumo de bienes y servicios[1]. Es el estudio de las maneras en que las sociedades deciden lo que van a producir y para quién. También es el estudio del uso y control de recursos[2] para satisfacer las necesidades y los deseos humanos. Este es un aspecto muy importante de la economía porque los deseos humanos no tienen límite. Las necesidades humanas pueden ser de primera necesidad como la comida y la ropa. Hay también bienes y servicios que no son de primera necesidad pero que son importantes para algunas personas—los diamantes y un chófer, por ejemplo. Si las necesidades y los deseos humanos no tienen límite, no es el caso con los recursos. Los recursos son limitados. La verdad es que hay una escasez[3] de recursos.

Barcelona, España

[1]bienes y servicios *goods and services*
[2]recursos *resources*
[3]escasez *shortage*

Recursos económicos

Los recursos económicos son el total de los recursos naturales, fabricados[4] y humanos que se emplean en la producción de bienes y la provisión de servicios. Los recursos naturales son la materia prima[5], lo que viene de la Tierra. Los recursos fabricados incluyen las fábricas, los edificios comerciales y todo tipo de equipo mecánico y técnico. Los recursos humanos incluyen la mano de obra[6] de toda clase—profesional, técnica, gerencial y obrera.

Una fábrica, Barcelona, España

Costo de oportunidad

Como todos los recursos son limitados, es imposible dar a la sociedad todos los bienes y servicios que desea. La escasez de materiales y recursos nos obliga a escoger lo que vamos a producir porque no podemos producir todo. Si usamos los recursos disponibles[7] para producir una cosa, perdemos la oportunidad de usar estos mismos recursos para producir otra cosa. Este sacrificio se llama «el costo de oportunidad». Si todos los trabajadores en una fábrica van a producir televisores, la fábrica no puede producir otro producto. Es el costo de oportunidad. Todo lo que hacemos tiene su costo de oportunidad. Si decides ir al cine en vez de estudiar para un examen, estás sacrificando la oportunidad de estudiar. Es el costo de oportunidad de ir al cine.

[4]fabricados *manufactured*
[5]materia prima *raw material*
[6]mano de obra *workforce*
[7]disponibles *available*

¿Comprendes?

A Términos económicos Contesten.
1. ¿Cuál es un ejemplo de una necesidad esencial?
2. ¿Cuál es un ejemplo de una necesidad que no es esencial?
3. ¿Cuáles son algunos recursos económicos?
4. ¿Cuál es un ejemplo de una materia prima?

B Costo de oportunidad Expliquen.
Explica lo que significa «el costo de oportunidad».

¡Te toca a ti!

Use what you have learned

1 La importancia del español
✔ *Talk about the advantages of learning Spanish for your future employment*

Tú y un(a) compañero(a) van a hablarles a los alumnos en una clase del primer año de español. Les van a decir por qué deben continuar con sus estudios del español. Les van a explicar por qué es muy importante el estudio del español. Traten de ser creativos y usen su sentido del humor.

2 Ventajas y desventajas
✔ *Talk about professions*

Trabaja con un(a) compañero(a) de clase. Piensen en varias carreras. Hablen de lo que consideran las ventajas y desventajas de cada una. Decidan cuáles son algunas carreras que les interesarían.

Se necesita en Estepona
DEPENDIENTA TIENDA
2 días en semana
— Sueldo fijo y alta en S. S.
— Inglés
Telf. 952 80 80 77

Empresa Constructora en pleno proceso de expansión
precisa incorporar para su delegación en CATALUÑA

Ingeniero de Caminos

Con el objetivo de dirigir un grupo de Obras Edificación y Obra Civil

SI TIENES:
• Entre 25 y 35 años.
• Experiencia en obras.
• Ganas de crecer con nosotros.

Envía tu Currículum Vitae al Apdo. de Correos 48061, 28080 Madrid.

CENTRO HOSPITALARIO
UNIDAD CORONARIA
DE MANRESA
FUNDACIÓN PRIVADA

MÉDICO INTENSIVISTA

CON TÍTULO ESPECIALISTA
VÍA M. I. R.

Ofrecemos:
• Contrato a tiempo completo más guardias.
• Se valorará experiencia en intensi-vos-cardiológicos.

Presentar solicitud a: **Departa-mento de Relaciones Laborales.** Avenida de Manresa, 6-8, 08240 Manresa (Barcelona). Recepción de solicitudes y CV hasta el 29-11-2001.

3 ESCRIBIR

Mi currículum vitae
✔ *Write your personal resumé*

Vas a preparar tu currículum vitae o resumen personal en español. En tu resumen incluye los siguientes detalles: nombre, dirección, preparación académica, título, talentos, intereses y hobbys.

CURRICULUM VITAE

1. DATOS PERSONALES

Nombre: Yolanda
Apellidos: Amer Dengra
Dirección: C/Fco. Martin Mora, n°1-7°-2ª ESC.B
C.P.:07011
Fecha de nacimiento: 21-04-73
N.I.F.: 43.090.440-D
Estado Civil: Soltera
Tlf. de Contacto: (971) 73.60.54

2. DATOS ACADEMICOS

2.A. Enseñanza oficial
Graduado Escolar: C.P. Jaime 1, en la localidad de Palma de Mca. provincia de Baleares.

2.B. Formación complementaria
Curso de Informática de gestión. Centro de estudios "Didact 1", C/Naranjas 3, en la localidad de Jerez de la Fra., Provincia de Cádiz.

3. EXPERIENCIA LABORAL

Aux. Administrativo en la empresa "Rucoplasti Andalucía", Plz. Madre de Dios S/N. (Duración: 1 año)
Localidad: Jerez de la Fra. (CADIZ)

Aux. De Clínica en la residencia geriátrica "Los Angeles", C/Granados, 7 Urb. El Almendral. (Duración 6 meses).
Localidad: Mairena de Aljarafe (SEVILLA).

Depependienta en cafetería-pub "Sin comentarios", Urb. San Joaquín. (Duración 7 meses)
Localidad: Jerez de la Fra. (CÁDIZ)

Dependienta en tienda de moda "Detalles". Vía Sindicato, 4. (Duración 1 mes)
Localidad: Palma de Mca. (BALEARES)

4. OTROS DATOS

Incorporación inmediata
Don de gentes

Writing Strategy

Using visuals Well-organized writing that is clearly expressed is the key to good communication. However, visuals can help organize, clarify, and expand many different kinds of data. A visual can help you illustrate an important concept. Good visuals can portray at a glance an idea that might take several paragraphs to express in words.

4 ESCRIBIR

¿Cuáles son los intereses de la clase?

It is likely that many of your classmates have varied plans for the future. Prepare a survey to administer to your classmates, asking what they would like to do. After you have gathered the data, prepare a visual that gives an overview of the possible careers and job interests your class has. You may wish to use a computer to help you create your visual to convey your information to your readers.

Assessment

Vocabulario

1 Identifiquen.

1.

2.

3.

4.

5.

To review **Palabras 1**, turn to pages 424–425.

Spanish Online
For more Chapter 14 test preparation go to the Chapter 14 **Self-Check Quiz** on the Glencoe Spanish Web site at glencoe.com.

2 Completen.

6. Los ____ son los trabajos de especialistas como albañiles y electricistas.

7. Las ____ son los trabajos que requieren un título universitario.

8. Los comerciantes se dedican a la ____ de mercancía.

To review **Palabras 2**, turn to pages 428–429.

3 ¿Sí o no?

9. Hay anuncios para puestos vacantes en los periódicos.

10. Trabajar a tiempo parcial es trabajar cuarenta horas por semana.

11. Cuando uno busca un puesto es casi siempre necesario llenar una solicitud de empleo.

12. El candidato o aspirante es el que busca trabajo.

Estructura

4 **Completen.**

13–14. Él quiere ____ dinero. (cambiar)
Él quiere que nosotros ____ dinero.

15–16. Nosotros preferimos que tú lo ____. (hacer)
Nosotros lo preferimos ____.

To review the infinitive versus the subjunctive, turn to page 432.

5 **Escojan.**

17. Están buscando una persona ____.
   a. que hable tres idiomas
   b. que habla tres idiomas

18. ¿Sí? Yo tengo un amigo ____.
   a. que hable tres idiomas
   b. que habla tres idiomas

19. Todos queremos un trabajo ____.
   a. que nos pague bien
   b. que nos paga bien

20. Yo sé que hay un puesto con nuestra compañía ____.
   a. que pague muy bien
   b. que paga muy bien

To review the subjunctive in relative clauses, turn to page 435.

Tell all you can about this illustration.

Vocabulario

Identifying some office personnel

el/la programador(a)
  de informática
el/la secretario(a)

la oficina
el/la gerente
el/la contable

Talking about merchandising

el/la comerciante
el/la cliente
el/la cajero(a)
la venta

la compra
la mercancía
satisfecho(a)

Discussing some legal professions

el tribunal
el/la juez

el/la abogado(a)
el bufete del abogado

Identifying some municipal government workers

la alcaldía
el alcalde

el/la funcionario(a)

How well do you know your vocabulary?

• Choose an occupation from the list.
• Write a few sentences about the job and how you would apply for the position.

Talking about some professions

la profesión
el título universitario

el/la ingeniero(a)
el/la arquitecto(a)

Identifying some trades

el oficio
el/la especialista
el/la electricista
el/la albañil

el/la plomero(a),
  el/la fontanero(a)
el/la carpintero(a)

Talking about job opportunities

un puesto
el anuncio
el departamento de
  recursos humanos

el/la candidato(a),
  el/la aspirante
el/la entrevistador(a)
la entrevista

la solicitud de empleo
ofrecer un trabajo
  a tiempo completo
  a tiempo parcial

Other useful expressions

ojalá
quizá(s)

VIDEOTUR

Episodio 14

In this video episode, you will join our friends as they peek into the future. See page 493 for more information. As you watch, look for gestures the speakers use to help convey their message.

Conversación

La futura jefa de banquetes

Antonia ¿Adónde vas, Isabel?

Isabel Voy a la peluquería. Tengo el pelo un poco largo. Necesito un corte. Y después voy al correo.

Antonia ¿Por qué es necesario que vayas al correo?

Isabel Tengo que enviar las invitaciones. Quiero que lleguen a tiempo.

Antonia ¿Qué invitaciones?

Isabel Pues, el día 13 voy a dar una gran fiesta.

Antonia ¿Qué estás celebrando?

Isabel No te voy a decir. ¡Ya verás!

Antonia Ay, pero siempre estás dando fiestas.

Isabel Pues, me gustan las fiestas y me gusta darlas.

Antonia Algún día, ¡quizás seas una jefa de banquetes que planee fiestas y recepciones para bodas y bautizos.

Isabel ¡Tal vez! ¿Quién sabe?

¿Comprendes?

Un trabajo para Isabel Contesten.

1. ¿Adónde va Isabel?
2. ¿Por qué va allí?
3. Y después, ¿adónde va?
4. ¿Por qué es necesario que ella vaya allí?
5. ¿Cuándo será la fiesta?
6. ¿Para qué es?
7. ¿Por qué da muchas fiestas Isabel?
8. Un día, ¿es posible que ella haga qué tipo de trabajo?

Estructura

Usos del subjuntivo

The indicative mood of the verb is used to express events and actions that actually have taken, are taking, or will take place. The subjunctive, on the other hand, is used to express events that may or may not take place. Some introductory statement makes the actual event uncertain. The following are some expressions that are followed by the subjunctive.

querer	es posible	alegrarse de
esperar	es imposible	sentir
temer	es probable	estar contento
preferir	es necesario	estar triste
pedir	es importante	
sugerir	es bueno, es mejor	
aconsejar	es fácil	
exigir	es difícil	
mandar		
insistir		

Quiero que él vaya. Espero que él vaya. Le pido que vaya. La verdad es que insisto en que él vaya porque es importante que él vaya. Más que importante, es necesario que él vaya. Pero la verdad es que yo no sé si va a ir o no.

1 Historieta En la peluquería

Contesten.

1. ¿Quiere José que el peluquero le corte el pelo?
2. ¿Prefiere que el peluquero use la navaja o las tijeras para cortarle el pelo?
3. ¿Le pide que le dé un champú también?
4. ¿Quiere el peluquero que José le diga cómo quiere el pelo?
5. ¿Insiste José en que el peluquero le ponga una raya?

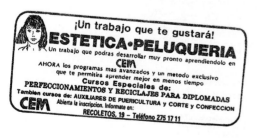

¡Un trabajo que te gustará!
ESTETICA·PELUQUERIA
CEM
Un trabajo que podrás desarrollar muy pronto aprendiéndolo en
AHORA los programas más avanzados y un método exclusivo que te permitirá aprender mejor en menos tiempo
Cursos Especiales de:
PERFECCIONAMIENTOS Y RECICLAJES PARA DIPLOMADAS
También cursos de: AUXILIARES DE PUERICULTURA y CORTE y CONFECCION
CEM Abierta la inscripción. Infórmate en:
RECOLETOS, 19 – Teléfono 275 17 11

2 Consejos Contesten.

1. ¿Quieren tus padres que escojas una buena carrera?
2. ¿Te aconseja tu profesor que sigas con tus estudios del español?
3. ¿Te sugiere que tomes un curso de informática?
4. ¿Están contentos tus padres que estudies mucho y que saques buenas notas?
5. ¿Es probable que tú vayas a la universidad?
6. ¿Es importante que tú sepas la carrera que vas a escoger antes de ir a la universidad?

3 Historieta En la estación de servicio
Sigan el modelo.

> Yo quiero / él / llenar el tanque ⟶
> Yo quiero que él llene el tanque.

1. Yo quiero / él / poner gasolina sin plomo
2. Le pido / revisar el aceite
3. Me alegro de que / él / limpiar el parabrisas
4. Es necesario / él / poner aire en las llantas
5. Es importante / nosotros / manejar con cuidado
6. El empleado prefiere / yo / pagar con cheque

Universidad Nacional Autónoma de México, Ciudad de México

Más usos del subjuntivo

1. The subjunctive is also used when introduced by a statement that conveys doubt. When the statement implies certainty, however, the indicative is used.

Dudo que él asista a la boda.
Pero creo que los novios van a recibir muchos regalos.

2. The subjunctive is also used in a clause that modifies an indefinite antecedent. If the antecedent refers to a specific person or thing, the indicative is used.

La compañía está buscando un candidato que hable inglés.
La compañía tiene un candidato que habla inglés.

4 **Historieta** **Una carta** Contesten con **sí.**

1. ¿Crees que José te ha escrito?
2. ¿Piensas que él ha puesto la carta en un buzón?
3. ¿Dudas que él vaya al correo para mandar la carta?
4. ¿Es dudoso que la carta llegue hoy?
5. ¿Es cierto que la carta tiene bastantes sellos?

5 **Hay que tener ciertas calificaciones.** Completen.

1. La compañía Vensa está buscando alguien que ____ (tener) experiencia, que ____ (conocer) bien el español y el inglés y que ____ (poder) viajar.
2. El director de recursos humanos me dijo que necesitan alguien que ____ (estar) libre inmediatamente.
3. Han entrevistado a dos candidatos. Hay un candidato que ____ (tener) experiencia, que ____ (querer) y ____ (poder) trabajar enseguida.
4. Desgraciadamente él no habla inglés y la compañía sigue buscando alguien que ____ (hablar) inglés y que ____ (conocer) el mercado norteamericano.

6 **Carreras** Trabaja con un(a) compañero(a). Identifiquen las carreras que creen que les interesarían. Identifiquen también las carreras que no les interesarían. Digan por qué. Decidan si tienen muchos intereses en común. ¿Es posible que sigan o escojan la misma carrera?

7 **Fiestas** Trabaja con un(a) compañero(a). Planeen una gran fiesta. Discutan por qué van a dar la fiesta y todo lo que van a hacer durante la fiesta. Entonces decidan todo lo que tienen que hacer antes de la fiesta.

8 **En la peluquería** Con un(a) compañero(a), entablen una conversación que tiene lugar en una peluquería. Uno(a) de ustedes será el/la peluquero(a) y el/la otro(a) será el/la cliente.

Literary Companion

Reading Focus

You may wish to read the adaptation of *Tierra* by Gregorio López y Fuentes, on pages 472–477. The activities for this reading will help you continue to practice your reading comprehension skills.

People EN ESPAÑOL Entérate Colombia y Venezuela

Salto Ángel

De la mano de la naturaleza

La UNESCO declaró estos sitios Patrimonio de la Humanidad.

Parque Nacional Los Katíos Existe un paso natural entre Centro y Suramérica. Es la puerta de entrada a América del Sur. Para pasar, los viajeros tienen que tomar un barco de Panamá a Colombia. ¿Sabes por qué es imposible cruzar en automóvil por la región? Este "puente" es uno de los terrenos más inhóspitos[1] y lluviosos del planeta. Llueve tanto que las aguas alimentan uno de los ríos más caudalosos[2] del mundo: el Atrato. El Atrato vierte[3] al Caribe casi 5,000 metros cúbicos de agua por segundo. El parque tiene una gran riqueza de flora y fauna que debe protegerse.

Parque Nacional Canaima El piloto norteamericano Jimmy Ángel va en su avión. De pronto, las nubes lo envuelven y pierde el rumbo. Al despejarse[4] el día, Ángel descubre la séptima maravilla[5] natural del planeta, que hoy lleva su nombre. Imagínate un río que cae, con una caída libre[6] de casi 1,000 metros. ¿Te lo imaginas? ¡Es el salto más alto del mundo: el Salto Ángel! Es el tesoro que guarda celosamente[7] este parque, donde además viven especies animales y vegetales únicas en el planeta. También viven allí en armonía con la naturaleza, los pueblos nativos de la región.

De la mano del ser humano

Cartagena de Indias Visitar esta bellísima ciudad colonial, sus plazas, fuertes y castillos, es pasear por 500 años de historia.

Coro Esta ciudad, la más antigua de Venezuela, fue fundada en 1527. Su arquitectura demuestra muchas de las posibilidades de la construcción en barro[8].

Cartagena de Indias

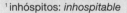

[1] inhóspitos: *inhospitable*
[2] caudalosos: *with large volume of water*
[3] vierte: *pours*
[4] despejarse: *clear up*
[5] maravilla: *marvel*
[6] caída libre: *free fall*
[7] guarda celosamente: *keeps zealously*
[8] barro: *mud, adobe*

Coro

Representantes del pueblo kogi

Los "hermanos mayores" hablan de ecología

En las altas montañas de la Sierra Nevada de Colombia vive un pueblo precolombino muy pacífico: los kogis. Su aislamiento[1] es total y voluntario. ¿Por qué? Quieren vivir en total armonía con la naturaleza. Desde hace tiempo, los kogis observan los cambios climáticos que ocurren en nuestro planeta. Hace unos años, los sabios[2] del pueblo, que se consideran nuestros hermanos mayores, decidieron enviar un mensaje al resto de los habitantes del planeta, sus hermanos menores. Es necesario que oigamos su mensaje, dicen ellos. De eso depende nuestro futuro. En el documental de Alan Ereira *Desde el corazón de la Tierra: Nuestros hermanos mayores,* los kogis piden que cuidemos de nuestro planeta. Dicen que la solución está en nuestras manos.

[1] aislamiento: *isolation*   [2] sabios: *wise ones*

Calendario de fiestas

Carnaval de Barranquilla

¡Cumbia…! Al grito de la desbordante[1] música caribeña se celebra el famoso Carnaval de Barranquilla, uno de los más importantes del mundo. La fiesta dura cuatro días, en los que la gente de esta ciudad festeja su herencia[2] africana y europea. Como dicen los colombianos, el Carnaval de Barranquilla se celebra sana y alegremente "hasta que el cuerpo aguante[3]".

Carnaval de Barranquilla

Feria del Orinoco

Esta fiesta gira alrededor de un pez. La sapoara es un pez que sólo se encuentra en el río Orinoco. Las aguas del gran río bajan de caudal[4] en el mes de agosto. Entonces los habitantes de Ciudad Bolívar, en Venezuela, pescan sapoaras. La persona que pesque la sapoara más grande gana un premio. Alegres bailes, competencias de otros deportes acuáticos y exposiciones industriales y ganaderas[5] son también parte de la diversión. ¡A pescar se ha dicho!

Tambores de San Juan

Así se llama una fiesta popular de la zona central de Venezuela, donde se mezclan bailes afroantillanos y costumbres españolas. Los tambores resuenan[6] y los pobladores y miles de visitantes no dejan de bailar por las calles.

---

[1] desbordante: *bursting*

[2] herencia: *heritage*

[3] hasta que el cuerpo aguante: *as long as the body can take it*

[4] caudal: *volume of water*

[5] ganaderas: *cattle*

[6] resuenan: *resound*

Museos

El Museo del Oro Al entrar al museo, las luces están apagadas. Se encienden las luces y se escucha: "¡Ah!". El brillo de una barca en miniatura hecha de oro puro y otras extraordinarias reliquias[1] indígenas asombran[2] al mundo entero en Bogotá.

Fernando Botero

Museo de Arte Contemporáneo de Caracas

Los maestros de las artes plásticas modernas, tanto extranjeros como venezolanos, han encontrado su casa en este museo de importancia internacional.

Fernando Botero y sus gorditos Botero cuida muy bien su figura pero envía a sus "gorditos" a recorrer el mundo. Hace unos años, sus gatos, figuras humanas y otras esculturas gigantescas impresionaron a los neoyorquinos desde la avenida Park. En 2003, el mismo asombro se apoderó[3] de italianos y turistas que paseaban por Venecia[4].

---

[1] reliquias: *relics*   [3] apoderó: *took hold*

[2] asombran: *amaze*   [4] Venecia: *Venice*

Arepas

micocina

Una reina pepeada, por favor

La arepa es la "hamburguesa" venezolana. Realmente, la arepa es un pan. Los venezolanos acompañan sus comidas con este pan de maíz. También es un plato principal. Todo depende del relleno. Se acompaña con mantequilla, frijoles, queso, pescado, huevo y todo tipo de carnes. Una de las más famosas es la reina pepeada. Disfruta de una y tú también dirás: "¡Déme una reina pepeada, por favor!"

Ingredientes

    2 tazas de harina de maíz
      blanco precocida
    1 cucharadita de sal
    1 taza y ½ de agua
    1 cucharada de aceite

Preparación

En un recipiente hondo, poner el agua, la sal y el aceite. Agregar poco a poco la harina, evitando[1] que se formen grumos[2]. Amasar con las manos hasta obtener una masa suave que no se pegue[3] a las manos. Hacer bolas medianas y aplanarlas[4] formando las arepas. Ponerlas en una plancha[5] caliente y engrasada y cocinarlas por ambos lados. Luego ponerlas al horno precalentado a 350°. Dejarlas hasta que, al golpearlas suavemente, suenen a huecas[6] y estén doradas.

Relleno

Hacer una mezcla de pollo hervido y desmenuzado[7], aguacate en trozos y mayonesa.

Servir las arepas en el momento, acompañadas del relleno, ¡y a disfrutar del banquete!

---

[1] evitando: *avoiding*   [5] plancha: *skillet*

[2] grumos: *lumps*   [6] huecas: *hollow*

[3] pegue: *stick*   [7] desmenuzado: *shredded*

[4] aplanarlas: *flatten*

455

Gabriel García Márquez

Nóbel para una "canción"

Gabriel García Márquez es autor de una novela considerada
entre las mejores del siglo XX. Gabo, como le dicen sus
amigos, es una persona muy particular. Por ejemplo:

■ Recibe el Premio Nóbel vestido de liqui-liqui, traje típico de
los llanos¹ venezolanos.

■ Siempre escribe con una flor amarilla en su escritorio.

■ Es fanático de Shakira. ¡Hasta ha escrito sobre ella!

■ Tanto le gusta la música, que dice que *Cien años de soledad*
es un vallenato —música de acordeón típica de la región de
Valledupar— de 400 páginas, y *El amor en los tiempos del cólera*
—otra novela famosa— es un bolero de 380 páginas. Confiesa leer
en voz alta todos sus escritos, aún el más pequeño párrafo que
escribe: "…un relato literario es un instrumento hipnótico, como
lo es la música…" dice, y agrega: "…cualquier tropiezo² del ritmo
puede malograr³ el hechizo⁴. De esto me cuido hasta el punto de
que no mando un texto a la imprenta mientras no lo lea en voz
alta para estar seguro de su fluidez⁵".

■ El cine es otra de sus pasiones. Gabo ha escrito guiones⁶ de cine.
Su novela *El coronel no tiene quien le escriba* es también película;
Salma Hayek aparece en esa versión cinematográfica.

¹ llanos: *plains*

² tropiezo: *slip, mistake*

³ malograr: *spoil*

⁴ hechizo: *spell*

⁵ fluidez: *smooth flow*

⁶ guiones: *scripts*

Gabriel García Márquez

Velázquez

Patricia Velázquez Actúa en
las películas *La momia* y *El
regreso de la momia*. Sí, el
personaje que interpreta esta
artista venezolana ¡es quien
hace despertar¹ la venganza
de la momia!

Alonso

María Conchita Alonso
Tiene gran trayectoria en
Hollywood y en la televisión
estadounidense. Figura al lado
de grandes estrellas como
Arnold Schwarzenegger y
Robin Williams.

Vergara

Sofía Vergara Si buscas a una
artista de cine y televisión que
sea talentosa y altruista², te
presentamos a Sofía Vergara.
La famosa colombiana es la
portavoz³ de una campaña
nacional contra el SIDA.
¡Bravo, Sofía!

Leguizamo

John Leguizamo Su nombre
brilla tanto en Hollywood
como en Broadway. Es el
Toulouse Lautrec de *Moulin
Rouge*, al lado de Nicole
Kidman; actuó como Tibaldo,
acompañando a Leonardo
di Caprio en la más reciente
versión llevada al cine de
Romeo y Julieta. Además,
Leguizamo anima con su voz
a *Sid the Sloth*, en la película
de dibujos animados *Ice Age*.
Recientemente, debutó como
director de cine en una película
en la que también actúa. ¿Hay
algo más que se pueda decir de
este triunfador? Sí, ¡nació en
Colombia!

¹ hace despertar: *awakens*

² altruista: *altruistic*

³ portavoz: *spokeswoman*

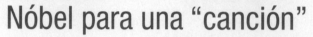

música

Súbele el volumen

Juanes

Juanes Aunque su nombre indique que se trata de más de una persona, Juanes es sólo uno, pero vale por[1] cinco… Fíjate bien en este cantante colombiano. En la más reciente entrega de los Grammys latinos, ¡cinco premios fueron para Juanes! Entre estos, ganó el del Mejor álbum y el de la Mejor canción.

Shakira ¿Dudas que alguien no sepa que esta joven colombiana es la diva indiscutible[2] de la actualidad?

Aterciopelados La música de este grupo de rock colombiano no es nada aterciopelada[3], pero los jóvenes la escuchan a todo volumen.

Oscar de León La mejor música de salsa y el venezolano Oscar de León son una sola cosa.

[1] vale por: *he's worth* [2] indiscutible: *undeniably* [3] aterciopelada: *velvety*

Shakira

Atletas que destacan

Baena

Cecilia Baena "La Chechi Baena", como la llaman cariñosamente los colombianos, es campeona mundial de patinaje sobre ruedas[1] del maratón juvenil.

Juan Carlos Montoya El corredor colombiano de autos de Fórmula Uno, en 2003, ocupó el tercer puesto en el campeonato mundial de automovilismo.

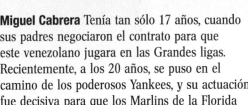
Cabrera

Miguel Cabrera Tenía tan sólo 17 años, cuando sus padres negociaron el contrato para que este venezolano jugara en las Grandes ligas. Recientemente, a los 20 años, se puso en el camino de los poderosos Yankees, y su actuación fue decisiva para que los Marlins de la Florida ganaran la Serie Mundial de 2003.

Daniela Larreal La ciclista venezolana sabe que el cielo es el límite. Después de ganar dos medallas de plata en los pasados Juegos Panamericanos, se prepara para conquistar medallas en las Olimpíadas de Atenas.

Larreal

[1] patinaje sobre ruedas: *roller blading*

SUCESOS

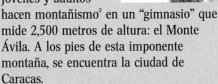
Herrera

Carolina Herrera El traje de novia, sobrio[1] y elegante, que Carolina Kennedy vistió el día de su boda fue creación de la diseñadora venezolana.

Gimnasio de altura Jóvenes y adultos hacen montañismo[2] en un "gimnasio" que mide 2,500 metros de altura: el Monte Ávila. A los pies de esta imponente montaña, se encuentra la ciudad de Caracas.

Rodrigo García El hijo de García Márquez es talentoso como su padre. Es camarógrafo, escritor y director de cine. Trabajó en películas tan exitosas como *Danzón* y *Frida*.

[1] sobrio: *unassuming*
[2] montañismo: *mountain climbing*

457

Literary Companion

These literary selections develop reading and cultural skills and introduce students to Hispanic literature.

Barranco,
Lima, Perú ▶

Platero y yo (fragmento) de Juan Ramón Jiménez

Vocabulario

el burro

el prado

la piedra

el hocico

los cascabeles

las flores

celeste

gualda

rosa

El burro anda por el prado.
Acaricia las florecitas con su hocico.

los higos

el escarabajo

la miel

---

el cascabeleo el sonido de los cascabeles
la pena algo triste
los gemelos dos cosas iguales o dos
   hermanos nacidos al mismo tiempo
el acero un metal muy duro
la plata un metal blanco, valioso; se usa
   para monedas

blando(a) lo contrario de «duro(a)»
suelto(a) libre
peludo(a) con mucho pelo
tibiamente suavemente
acariciar tocar suavemente
la abeja un insecto que produce la
    miel del néctar de las flores

Actividades

A **¿Sí o no?** Digan que sí o que no.

1. Los higos son una flor.
2. A veces un gato lleva un collar de cascabeles.
3. Las abejas son insectos.
4. Los escarabajos producen la miel del néctar de las flores.
5. Otro nombre para «celeste» es blanco.
6. Otro nombre para «gualda» es amarillo.
7. Se hacen monedas de la plata.

B **La palabra, por favor.** Completen.

1. Yo tengo un dólar, pero no es de papel; es de ____.
2. Los dos hermanos nacieron el mismo día; ellos son ____.
3. No es blando; es muy ____.
4. Pero el otro es duro, muy duro, duro como el ____.
5. El animal puede ir adonde quiera; siempre anda ____.
6. Está muy triste; tiene muchas ____.
7. El hombre pasa la mano sobre el burrito; lo ____.

Andalucía, España

INTRODUCCIÓN   Esta obra no es prosa, ni es poesía. Se puede decir que es prosa poética. Muchos creen que don Juan Ramón escribió la obra para niños, pero en su prólogo el autor dice: «Ese breve libro, en donde la alegría y la pena son gemelos, cual las orejas de Platero, estaba escrito para… qué sé yo para quien… para quien escribimos los poetas líricos». Juan Ramón Jiménez recibió el Premio Nóbel de Literatura en 1956.

    El fragmento que sigue se titula «Platero», y es uno de 139 capítulos. Es una descripción del burrito, amigo y compañero constante de don Juan Ramón en el pequeño pueblo de Moguer en Andalucía, España.

Platero y yo

Platero es pequeño, peludo, suave; tan blando por fuera que se diría todo de algodón, que no lleva huesos. Sólo los espejos de azabache° de sus ojos son duros cual dos escarabajos de cristal negro.

Lo dejo suelto, y se va al prado, y acaricia tibiamente con su hocico, rozándolas° apenas, las florecillas rosas, celestes y gualdas. Lo llamo dulcemente: —¿Platero?— y viene a mí con un trotecillo alegre que parece que se ríe, en no sé qué cascabeleo ideal… Come cuanto le doy. Le gustan las naranjas mandarinas, las uvas moscateles°, todas de ámbar, los higos morados, con su cristalina gotita de miel…

Es tierno° y mimoso° igual que un niño, que una niña…; pero fuerte y seco por dentro, como de piedra. Cuando paso sobre él, los domingos, por las últimas callejas del pueblo, los hombres del campo, vestidos de limpio y despaciosos°, se quedan mirándolo: —Tien´ asero—… Tiene acero. Acero y plata de luna, al mismo tiempo.

espejos de
   azabache
   black mirrors

rozándolas
   *brushing against
   them*

uvas moscateles
   *tipo de uva muy
   dulce*
tierno *tender*
mimoso *pampered*

despaciosos *con
   calma*

Moguer, Andalucía

¿Comprendes?

A **Looking for information** Completen.

1. Platero no es grande; es ____.
2. Y no es duro; es ____.
3. Las uvas moscateles son del color de ____.
4. Platero acaricia las florecillas con su ____.
5. El día de la semana que el autor pasa sobre su burro es el ____.

B **Recalling information** Contesten.

1. Cuando el autor suelta al burro, ¿adónde va el animalito?
2. ¿Con quiénes compara el autor a Platero?
3. ¿Qué le gusta comer a Platero?
4. ¿Quiénes miran a Platero cuando pasa por el pueblo?

C **Guessing meaning from context** Adivinen.

Los campesinos dicen que el burrito «Tien´ asero… » ¿Qué quiere decir esa frase, y por qué lo escribe de esa forma el autor?

D **Interpreting** Expliquen.

1. El autor describe a Platero en formas contradictorias, especialmente cuando habla de lo exterior y de lo interior del animalito. Explica.
2. Al final del capítulo don Juan Ramón dice: «Acero y plata de luna, al mismo tiempo». Interpreta esa frase.

E **Identifying literary devices** Contesten.

A metaphor is a figure of speech in which a word that means one thing is substituted for another to indicate a similarity or likeness, for example, "In the springtime of life." A simile is a figure of speech in which two very different things are compared to each other, usually using the word *like* **(como),** for example, "eyes like stars, hands like hams," etc. What metaphors and similes can you identify in this selection?

Un campesino con su burro, Andalucía, España

La muralla de Nicolás Guillén

Vocabulario

el monte

la paloma

el laurel

el ruiseñor

el ciempiés

el horizonte

la muralla

el alacrán

la serpiente

la rosa

el clavel

Las dos niñas están cerca de la muralla.
Ellas juntaban las manos.

el veneno una sustancia que puede matar, como el arsénico
el puñal un tipo de cuchillo
alzar levantar

Actividades

A Estudio de palabras Pareen.

1. el horizonte
2. la serpiente
3. la rosa
4. el veneno
5. el monte

a. poison, venom
b. horizon
c. mountain
d. rose
e. serpent

B ¿Sabes? Identifiquen.

1. dos flores
2. dos pájaros
3. un reptil
4. dos insectos

C ¿Cuál es? Escojan.

1. Entre las flores había unos preciosos ____.
   a. claveles b. puñales c. venenos
2. La serpiente podría matar con su ____.
   a. flor b. veneno c. cuchillo
3. Sí, sí, el criminal tenía un cuchillo; era un ____.
   a. alacrán b. clavel c. puñal
4. No, no lo va a bajar; al contrario, lo va a ____.
   a. alzar b. matar c. abrir

Cañaverales, Cuba

INTRODUCCIÓN   El poeta cubano Nicolás Guillén presenta, en sus versos, elementos de folklore negro. Él es uno de los cultivadores de la poesía «afrocubana». En el poema que sigue, el poeta nos presenta un lindo mensaje de comprensión y tolerancia.

La muralla

Para hacer esta muralla,
tráiganme todas las manos:
los negros sus manos negras,
los blancos sus blancas manos.
Ay,
una muralla que vaya
desde la playa hasta el monte,
desde el monte hasta la playa, bien,
allá sobre el horizonte.
—¡Tun, tun!
—¿Quién es?
—Una rosa y un clavel…

¡Abre la muralla!
—¡Tun, tun!
—¿Quién es?
—El sable° del coronel°…
—¡Cierra la muralla!
—¡Tun, tun!
—¿Quién es?
—La paloma y el laurel…
—¡Abre la muralla!
—¡Tun, tun!
—¿Quién es?
—El alacrán y el ciempiés…
—¡Cierra la muralla!

sable *sword, saber*
coronel *colonel*

Al corazón del amigo,
abre la muralla;
al veneno y al puñal,
cierra la muralla;
al mirto° y la yerbabuena°,
abre la muralla;
al diente de la serpiente,
cierra la muralla;
al ruiseñor en la flor,
abre la muralla…
Alcemos una muralla
juntando todas las manos;
los negros, sus manos negras,
los blancos sus blancas manos.
Una muralla que vaya
desde la playa hasta el monte,
desde el monte hasta la playa, bien,
allá sobre el horizonte…

mirto *myrtle*
yerbabuena *mint*

¿Comprendes?

A Recalling information Contesten.
1. ¿Dónde van a construir la muralla?
2. ¿Quiénes la van a construir?

B Making inferences Contesten.
1. ¿Qué palabras usa el poeta para describir cosas buenas o agradables?
2. ¿Qué palabras usa el poeta para describir cosas malas o desagradables?

C Interpreting Contesten.
1. Según el poeta, ¿cuándo se debe abrir la muralla?
2. ¿Cuándo se debe cerrar la muralla?
3. ¿Cuál es el significado del título del poema?

D Identifying main ideas Contesten.
¿Cuál es el mensaje o la moraleja de este poema?

Literatura ◆3◆

El cohítre
Una leyenda puertorriqueña
de Ester M. Feliciano Mendoza

Vocabulario

neblinoso · el cerro · el cielo · el castillo

La niña hacía un castillo.   A lo lejos había un cerro.
Era muy feliz.   No lo podía ver bien porque era muy neblinoso.

el reflejo · los caracoles

La niña veía su reflejo en el agua.

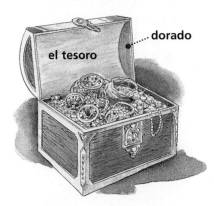

el tesoro — dorado

las lágrimas

arrodillarse — la tumba

El padre lloraba. Lloraba porque su hija murió.

liláceo(a) del color de las lilas
el alma el espíritu, no el cuerpo
el barro la combinación de tierra y agua
reidor(a) que se ríe
enjugar secar, lavar

la súplica la petición, el ruego
rogar, rezar decir u ofrecer una oración a Dios
ofrendar ofrecer
brotar salir

Actividades

A **Otra manera de decirlo** Expresen la parte indicada de otra manera.

1. Los ojos de la niña eran *del color de las lilas*.
2. El padre y la hija subieron *el pequeño monte*.
3. Allí encontraron *muchas riquezas*.
4. En ese monte los indios *ofrecían* regalos a sus dioses.
5. Con los regalos también hacían *peticiones* a los dioses.

B **La palabra, por favor.** Escojan.

1. El niño lloraba y su madre le ____ las lágrimas.
   a. enjugó   **b.** ofrendó   **c.** modeló
2. Donde cayeron las lágrimas pronto ____ unas flores de la tierra.
   a. ofrecieron   **b.** ofrendaron   **c.** brotaron
3. Era difícil ver el cerro claramente porque era muy ____.
   a. neblinoso   **b.** reidor   **c.** liláceo
4. Los religiosos creen que ____ es más importante que el cuerpo.
   a. el alma   **b.** la ofrenda   **c.** el reflejo
5. La niña vio ____ de su cara en el agua.
   a. el barro   **b.** el reflejo   **c.** la figurita
6. La familia puso flores en ____ del abuelo.
   a. la tumba   **b.** el alma   **c.** el caracol

Los indios taínos

INTRODUCCIÓN Ester Feliciano Mendoza (1918–1988) escribió en varios géneros, pero se destacó más como poeta. Esta selección viene de una de sus colecciones de leyendas. Esta leyenda nos habla de una flor típica de Puerto Rico y cómo llegó a ser. Los indios de Puerto Rico eran los taínos. La niña de la leyenda es hija de un español y una india. El padre de la niña quiere marcharse a Perú en busca de tesoro. La niña quiere quedarse en su isla amada.

Un cerro neblinoso

El cohítre°

Tenía los ojos azules y la piel dorada. Cuando nació, su padre creyó ver en sus pupilas los mismos reflejos liláceos de las tardes de Castilla. La amó por él y por la india que se murió rogando por su niña que no era ni india ni española.

La niña criolla fue tímida y amorosa. Amiga de los cerros neblinosos y las playas reidoras, conoció los secretos de las flores y de los caracoles. Aprendió a modelar cemíes° con la carne dócil del barro y a hacer castillos con las arenas escurridizas°. Amó al indio tanto como al español y a unos y otros enjugó las heridas del cuerpo y del alma. La niña criolla era feliz.

Un día el padre oyó hablar de las riquezas de Perú. Por primera vez la niña sintió el temor de la ausencia. Lloró los días que vendrían lejos de la isla querida. Se arrodilló ante la Virgen blanca y ofrendó flores y frutas a Yocahu, en una misma súplica: «No me dejen marchar». A los pies del altar cristiano rogaba también el padre español: «Dios nos lleve a Perú». Mirando a lo lejos el neblinoso monte Yukiyú, pensaba sin embargo: ¿Valdrá la pena marcharme?

Enfermó de angustia la niña criolla. Veía los cielos de Castilla en las pupilas azules, pero el padre no vio cómo la muerte lentamente las cubría de nubes… Y la niña, un día claro, se murió de pena.

Desde los brazos del padre voló a las regiones de Yocahu y de la virgencita blanca. Y pasaron los días… Sobre la tumba amada vio el padre español brotar, apretadita a la tierra, con sus florecitas azules reflejando el cielo de la isla, la yerba del cohítre… Y así fue para siempre en la tierra de Puerto Rico.

cohítre *wild herb*

cemíes *clay figures made by Taíno Indians of Puerto Rico*
escurridizas *slippery*

Un cementerio, Viejo San Juan, Puerto Rico

¿Comprendes?

A Confirming information Confirmen si la
información es correcta o no. Si no es correcta, corríjanla.

1. La niña tenía los ojos azules.
2. La piel de la niña era del color del oro.
3. El padre de la niña era indio.
4. La madre de la niña murió.
5. La madre rogaba por su marido.

B Recalling information Escojan.

1. La niña hacía figuritas de ____.
   a. arena   **b.** agua   **c.** barro
2. Para construir castillos usaba ____.
   a. arena   **b.** agua   **c.** barro
3. El padre de la niña se interesó en Perú por
   sus ____.
   a. castillos   **b.** cerros   **c.** riquezas
4. La niña le ofreció a Yocahu ____.
   a. flores y frutas   **b.** riquezas   **c.** caracoles
5. La niña murió de ____.
   a. una herida   **b.** pena   **c.** temor

C Interpreting Expliquen.

1. La niña «no era ni india ni española».
2. La niña «modelaba cemíes y hacía castillos».
3. La niña «rogaba a la Virgen blanca y a Yocahu».

D Making inferences Expliquen.

¿Qué infiere el autor al relatar a sus lectores lo que veía el padre cada vez que
miraba los ojos de su hija?

EL COHÍTRE

cuatrocientos setenta y uno 471

Tierra de Gregorio López y Fuentes

Vocabulario

la cuadra

el bigote

el soldado

- **el portal** puerta principal
- **el tianguis** un mercado indio
- **el corneta** soldado que toca la corneta
- **el cabo** rango inferior al de sargento

- **voltear** dar la vuelta
- **alargarse** hacer más largo
- **la esperanza** hope

Actividades

A **La hacienda** Completen.

1. En ese espacio grande los indios hacían el ____; compraban y vendían sus productos.
2. Cuando abrieron el ____ todos entraron al patio.
3. Cerca del patio estaba la ____ donde estaban los caballos y los coches.
4. Había seis soldados, un ____ y un sargento.
5. El sargento no tenía barba, pero sí tenía un gran ____.

B **¿Cuál es?** Expliquen.

1. ¿Cuáles son dos suboficiales militares?
2. ¿Cuál será la diferencia entre «el corneta» y «la corneta»?

Una hacienda, México

Estatua de Emiliano Zapata,
Chinameca, México

INTRODUCCIÓN Gregorio López y Fuentes
(1895–1966) escribió la novela *Tierra* inspirada en la
lucha de Emiliano Zapata por los indígenas del sur de
México. Zapata fue traicionado y asesinado por tropas
bajo el mando del Coronel Jesús María Guajardo.
Guajardo le invitó a Zapata a cenar con él en la
hacienda de Chinameca. Le dijo que quería unirse a
su movimiento. El fragmento que sigue nos dice lo
que pasó.

Tierra

La casa de la hacienda, en Chinameca, es enorme, con un portal inmenso.
Tiene habitaciones para las visitas y una gran cuadra para coches y caballos.
Frente a la casa, un espacio cuadrangular, tan grande, que en él se hace el
tianguis. El rectángulo está encerrado por una muralla. A derecha e
izquierda, la muralla tiene anchas puertas. En Chinameca esperaba Guajardo
al general Zapata. Dentro de la casa estaban los soldados, situados en los
mejores y más ocultos lugares. La persona que llegara no vería más que seis
hombres armados en cada una de las puertas de la muralla. Allí también
había un corneta.

El general Zapata tardaba en llegar. Pronto llegó un emisario. No se le
permitió entrar. Pocos momentos después comenzó a llegar la escolta
del general. También a estos hombres se les negó entrar al patio. Los
soldados tenían órdenes de no dejarlos pasar porque tenían que hacer los
honores al jefe. El general entraría por la puerta derecha. Los seis soldados
estaban formados impecablemente, en actitud de firmes.

Apareció el jefe. Se le conocía por la bravura de su caballo, por sus
grandes bigotes y por algo que siempre se nota en los acompañantes de

un jefe. Cuando estaban a veinte metros de la puerta
el corneta comenzó a tocar «marcha de honor». En
cuanto sonó la corneta el cabo ordenó con voz enérgica:
—Presenten… ¡armas!

El caballo se adelantó, todo nervioso, todo electrizado
con el toque de la corneta. Los soldados seguían
presentando armas. El general había avanzado cinco
metros y estaba dentro del patio. Entonces, los seis
hombres que presentaban armas hicieron un pequeño
movimiento,… y se escuchó una descarga.

El general Zapata, violentamente, intentó voltear el caballo, quizás con la idea de salir de allí. Pero él se quedó a la mitad del movimiento. Se cayó al suelo. Pero el animal salió y se escapó. El cabo se acercó al general. Con la carabina le dio el tiro de gracia. Pusieron el cadáver en una mula. Los pies por un lado y los brazos por el otro lado. Tomaron el camino a Cuautla. Al trotar de la mula, las piernas hacían un movimiento como el de andar, como si Zapata seguía corriendo por el Estado de Morelos. Los brazos parecían alargarse, quizás queriendo tocar la tierra para sus muchachos, por la que tanto luchó, tan cerca y al mismo tiempo tan distante.

En Cuautla fue exhibido el cadáver y en voz baja comenzó la leyenda:

No es el general.

¡No va a ser! Está así, deformado, por haber venido como vino. La sangre se le fue a la cabeza.

No, compadre, el general tenía una seña muy particular, allí en la cara, y éste no la tiene.

¡Claro! Allí mismo le entró el tiro de gracia.

¡Quién sabe!

Y el «quién sabe» lleno de esperanzas, era como un lamento. Pero otros decían, muy contentos: —¡Vaya, por fin cayó este bandido!

Hacienda de San Juan Bautista, Taxco, México

¿Comprendes?

A Confirming information Confirmen si la información es correcta o no. Si no es correcta, corríjanla.

1. La casa de la hacienda en Chinameca es pequeña.
2. El portal de la casa es grande.
3. El tianguis se hace en un espacio enfrente de la casa.
4. El espacio donde se hace el tianguis es triangular.
5. Guajardo era general.
6. La casa donde Guajardo esperaba estaba en Chinameca.

B Recalling information Escojan.

1. Alrededor del espacio donde hacían el tianguis había ____.
   a. una cuadra **b.** una muralla **c.** un portal
2. La muralla tiene dos ____, una a la derecha y la otra a la izquierda.
   a. puertas **b.** habitaciones **c.** cornetas
3. Los soldados dentro de la casa estaban en lugares muy ____.
   a. anchos **b.** firmes **c.** ocultos
4. Antes de llegar el general, llegó un ____.
   a. cabo **b.** emisario **c.** soldado
5. En la cara del general se le veía unos grandes ____.
   a. ojos **b.** bigotes **c.** tiros

Emiliano Zapata

C **Sequencing** Pongan en orden las acciones que ocurrieron en la casa en Chinameca.

D **Analyzing** Discutan.
1. Expliquen por qué el cabo tomó la carabina y le dio el tiro de gracia al general.
2. Expliquen la reacción de la gente en Cuautla al ver el cadáver.

E **Interpreting** Interpreten el significado de las últimas frases de este capítulo de la novela.
Y el «quién sabe», lleno de esperanzas, era como un lamento. Pero otros decían, muy contentos:—¡Vaya, por fin cayó este bandido!

Las tropas de Emiliano Zapata

Video Companion
Using video in the classroom

The use of video in the classroom can be a wonderful asset to the World Languages teacher and a most beneficial learning tool for the language student. Video enables students to experience whatever it is they are learning in their textbook in a real-life setting. With each lesson, they are able to take a vicarious field trip. They see people interacting at home, at school, at the market, etc., in an authentic milieu. Students sitting in a classroom can see real people going about their real life in real places. They may experience the target culture in many countries. The cultural benefits are limitless.

Developing listening and viewing skills

In addition to its tremendous cultural value, video, when properly used, gives students much needed practice in developing good listening and viewing skills. Video allows students to look for numerous clues that are evident in a tone of voice, facial expressions, and gestures. Through video students can see and hear the diversity of the target culture and, as discerning viewers and listeners, compare and contrast the Spanish-speaking cultures to each other and to their own culture. Video introduces a dimension into classroom instruction that no other medium—teachers, overhead, text, audio CDs—can provide.

Reinforcing learned language

Video that is properly developed for classroom use has speakers reincorporate the language students have learned in a given lesson. In keeping with reality, however, speakers introduce some new words, expressions, and structures because students functioning in a real-life situation would not know every word native speakers use with them in a live conversation. The lively and interactive nature of video allows students to use their listening and viewing skills to comprehend new language in addition to seeing and hearing the language they have learned come to life.

Getting the most out of video

The intrinsic benefit of video is often lost when students are allowed to read the scripted material before viewing. In many cases, students will have come to understand language used by the speakers in the video by means of reading comprehension, thus negating the inherent benefits of video as a tool to develop listening and viewing skills. Because today's students are so accustomed to the medium of video as a tool for entertainment and learning, a well-written and well-produced video program will help them develop real-life language skills and confidence in those skills in an enjoyable way.

¡Viva el mundo hispano!

Episodio 1

Francisco y Claudia leen un libro.

«Una mujer misteriosa» en la estación de ferrocarril

Antes de mirar

¿Qué piensan ustedes? Inventen algo.

1. ¿Dónde están Francisco y Claudia?

2. ¿Qué tipo de libro leen?

3. ¿Hacen un viaje?

4. ¿Adónde van?

5. ¿Quién es el otro señor con «la mujer misteriosa»?

Después de mirar

Expansión   As you can see from the video, train travel is very popular in some Spanish-speaking countries. Do you think it is as popular where you live? What is your favorite means of transportation for long trips? Why? Survey your friends to find out their preferred means of travel. Share your results with the class.

VIDEOTUR

¡Viva el mundo hispano!

Episodio 2

Alberto en el restaurante de su tío

Vicky y Alberto con cara de sorpresa

Antes de mirar

¿Qué ven ustedes?

1. un camarero
2. un cliente
3. las papas
4. una propina
5. un vaso de agua

Después de mirar

Expansión Are there many Hispanic restaurants in your community? Are they representative of a variety of different Spanish-speaking countries? Which ones are they? Do you have a favorite? Look at the menus of the different restaurants in your community or do research on the Internet to find some menus of Hispanic restaurants in this country. Are the foods very different? If any of the Hispanic restaurants in your community are run by a family, speak with one of the family members about the history of their business. Try to do this in Spanish if possible.

UIDEOTUR

¡Viva el mundo hispano!

Episodio 3

Alejandra y Julián están en el café Internet.

Julián trata de ayudar a Alejandra.

Antes de mirar

¡Adivinen!

1. ¿Qué hacen Alejandra y Julián en el café Internet?
2. ¿De qué hablan Alejandra y Julián?
3. ¿Qué hace la otra gente en el café Internet?

Después de mirar

Expansión You are going to participate in a contest to appear in *People en español* with your favorite latino actor or musician. You have to send a photograph of yourself and a letter explaining why you admire the artist of your choice. Write the letter. Then explain how you are going to send the letter and the photograph. Think about ways you can do this with modern technology.

Videotur

¡Viva el mundo hispano!

Episodio 4

Julián y Francisco van de compras.

Francisco y Julián están muy guapos.

Antes de mirar

¿Qué ven ustedes?

1. flores
2. unos carritos
3. una caja
4. el pasillo
5. dos amigos muy bien vestidos

Después de mirar

Expansión   You see in the video that a fifteenth birthday is an important occasion for a young Hispanic girl. What is considered one of the most important birthdays for a young female in the United States? Do some research on the Internet to find out more information about a **quinceañera** and tell how it compares to a Sweet Sixteen celebration. Give similarities and differences.

¡Viva el mundo hispano!

Episodio 5

Francisco y Alejandra andan en bicicleta.

Una aventura nueva para Francisco

Antes de mirar

¿Sí o no?

1. Alejandra y Francisco están en el parque.
2. Hay un payaso en el parque.
3. Francisco está contento porque va a subir la pared de escala.
4. Alejandra va a subir también.

Después de mirar

Expansión   What are some leisure activities that you saw in the video? Are any of them leisure activities that you might enjoy? Do you and your friends go often to the beach or to the park? How do you spend your free time? Do you think Alejandra y Francisco would enjoy doing some of the things you enjoy doing in your free time?

¡Viva el mundo hispano!

Episodio 6

Francisco habla con el recepcionista en el hotel.

Francisco está en el cuarto del hotel.

Antes de mirar

¡Usen su imaginación!

The name of the hotel that Francisco is going to stay in is **El Sportsman.** Try to think of what kind of a night he is going to have. In groups, act out what you think might happen if you were to stay in a hotel with that name. Then watch the video to find out what really happens.

Después de mirar

Expansión In the video you visited **La Recoleta,** a cemetery in Buenos Aires. Do some research to find out more about this famous cemetery and some of the people who are buried there. Write a report about one of these people.

Videotur

¡Viva el mundo hispano!

Episodio 7

Los amigos discuten algo importante.

¿Qué hacen los amigos?

Antes de mirar

¡Usen su imaginación!

1. ¿Qué hacen los amigos?
2. ¿De qué hablan?
3. ¿Qué hace Julián?
4. ¿Qué ropa lleva Alberto? ¿Qué es?

Después de mirar

Expansión In the Major Leagues in the United States, there are many Hispanic baseball players that have come from a number of Spanish-speaking countries, especially those in the Caribbean. Do some research on the Internet to find out some information about them. Have you ever seen any of them play either at a stadium or on television? Choose one whom you admire and give some information about his life.

VIDEOTUR

¡Viva el mundo hispano!

Episodio 8

Alberto y Vicky hablan con un chico.

El doctor Ernesto ayuda a Vicky.

Antes de mirar

¡Usen su imaginación!

Completen el diálogo.

Vicky: Hola, chico.

Chico: ¿Qué tal?

Después de mirar

Expansión   Good health is associated with physical activity. Describe an exercise routine or participation in a sport that could keep you fit. Describe how the sport you play or the exercise you do helps different parts of your body. Describe a weekly schedule that you follow to keep physically fit. If you do not exercise regularly, discuss what type of schedule you would maintain if you were to begin.

UIDEOTUR

¡Viva el mundo hispano!

Episodio 9

Julián está en la ciudad.

Claudia está en el campo.

Antes de mirar

Contesten.

1. ¿Dónde están Julián y Claudia?
2. Describe el lugar donde está Julián.
3. Describe el lugar donde está Claudia.
4. ¿Son muy distintos los dos lugares?

Después de mirar

Expansión ¿Prefieres la ciudad o el campo? ¿Por qué? ¿Qué te gusta hacer allí?

Videotur

¡Viva el mundo hispano!

Episodio 10

Vicky y Alejandra preparan una comida.

Julián y Alberto llegan con una sorpresa.

Antes de mirar

Contesten.

1. ¿Dónde están Vicky y Alejandra?
2. Escribe una lista de los ingredientes que hay en la mesa.
3. ¿Qué preparan ellas?
4. ¿Quiénes llegan a la puerta?
5. ¿Qué lleva Julián?

Después de mirar

Expansión Encuentra en el Internet una receta para una comida hispana que te gusta. Prepara una lista de compras y si es posible prepara la comida para tu familia.

Videotur

¡Viva el mundo hispano!

Episodio 11

Alejandra y Claudia viajan por el campo.

Las dos amigas hablan con un policía.

Antes de mirar

¡Usen su imaginación!

1. ¿Adónde van Claudia y Alejandra?
2. ¿Por qué hablan con un policía?

Después de mirar

Expansión   In the video you see some interesting things about transportation in Peru. Have you ever seen a llama? Is there a farm near you with llamas? Do some research on the Internet to find out more about how useful these animals were and still are in many parts of the Spanish-speaking world. Compare their use there with the way they might be used where you live. Are there many similarities?

¡Viva el mundo hispano!

Episodio 12

Francisco y Claudia están en una peluquería.

Chiquitín hace su «magia».

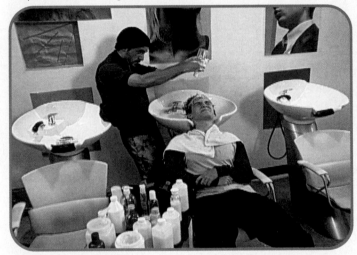

Antes de mirar

Contesten.

1. ¿Qué miran Francisco y Claudia?
2. Describe la peluquería que ves en la foto.
3. ¿Está muy contento Francisco?

Después de mirar

Expansión   Find in a magazine a hairstyle that you like. Describe to the hairdresser the new haircut or hairstyle that you would like.

VIDEOTUR

¡Viva el mundo hispano!

Episodio 13

Vicky trabaja con dos clientes.

Vicky escucha atentamenta a sus clientes.

Antes de mirar

Contesten.

1. Mira bien la foto. ¿Dónde trabaja Vicky?
2. ¿Qué hace Vicky en su trabajo?
3. Describe a los clientes.
4. Describe la oficina.

Después de mirar

Expansión Look for a photograph of a fiesta—a wedding, a birthday, or any other celebration. The photograph can be of your family or from a magazine. Make up a story about the fiesta.

x

Videotur

¡Viva el mundo hispano!

Episodio 14

Los amigos están en el parque.

Alejandra acepta un premio.

Antes de mirar

¡Usen su imaginación!

1. ¿Qué hacen los amigos en el parque?
2. ¿De qué hablan?
3. ¿Qué premio acepta Alejandra?

Después de mirar

Expansión Do you ever think about what you would like to do when you have finished with your education? How are you preparing yourself for this work? Where is it that you would like to work? Will you be famous? Do you know anyone who does the kind of work you are interested in? If so, interview him or her about the work.

Handbook

Susana y Pedro

Alberto

Señora Rivas

Alumno A Answer your partner's questions based on the pictures below.

Alumno A Ask your partner the following questions. Correct answers are in parentheses.

1. ¿Quién es el revisor?
   (*El señor Martínez es el revisor.*)

2. ¿El revisor está en el coche-cama o en el pasillo?
   (*El revisor está en el pasillo.*)

3. ¿Están Pablo y Ramona en el coche-comedor o en sus asientos?
   (*Están en sus asientos.*)

4. ¿Luis y Antonia van a bajar o van a subir? (*Luis y Antonia van a bajar.*)

Alumno B Answer your partner's questions based on the pictures below.

Ramona   Pablo   Señor Martínez

Luis y Antonia

Alumno B Ask your partner the following questions. Correct answers are in parentheses.

1. ¿Dónde comen Susana y Pedro?
   (*Susana y Pedro comen en el coche-comedor/ coche-cafetería.*)

2. ¿Alberto sube al tren o baja del tren? (*Alberto baja del tren.*)

3. ¿La señora Rivas compra un billete o transborda?
   (*La señora Rivas transborda.*)

4. ¿La señora Rivas va a subir al tren o va a la sala de espera?
   (*La señora Rivas va a subir al tren.*)

Activity 2

Alumno A Ask your partner the following questions. Correct answers are in parentheses.

1. ¿Quién pide el pescado?
   (*Juanita pide el pescado.*)

2. ¿Qué piden Marta y Teresa?
   (*Marta y Teresa piden la langosta.*)

3. ¿Quién pide una ensalada?
   (*José pide una ensalada.*)

4. ¿Qué piden los muchachos?
   (*Los muchachos piden pollo.*)

Alumno A Answer your partner's questions based on the pictures below.

Antonio

Paco y Mercedes

Norma

Los turistas

Alumno B Answer your partner's questions based on the pictures below.

Marta y Teresa

José

Juanita

Los muchachos

Alumno B Ask your partner the following questions. Correct answers are in parentheses.

1. ¿Quién pide las almejas?
   (*Antonio pide las almejas.*)

2. ¿Qué piden Paco y Mercedes?
   (*Paco y Mercedes piden la carne.*)

3. ¿Qué piden los turistas?
   (*Los turistas piden el maíz.*)

4. ¿Quién pide los camarones?
   (*Norma pide los camarones.*)

4.

3.

1–2.

Alumno A Answer your partner's questions based on the pictures below.

Alumno A Ask your partner the following questions. Correct answers are in parentheses.

1. ¿El joven hace una llamada telefónica o manda un documento por fax?
(El joven hace una llamada telefónica.)

2. ¿Introduce una moneda o una tarjeta telefónica?
(Introduce una tarjeta telefónica.)

3. ¿Cuál es el prefijo de país del número de teléfono?
(El prefijo de país es cincuenta y seis.)

4. ¿Cuál es la clave de área?
(La clave de área es treinta y dos.)

Alumno B Answer your partner's questions based on the pictures below.

1.

2.

(056) 32 678-1945

3–4.

Alumno B Ask your partner the following questions. Correct answers are in parentheses.

1. ¿La joven hace una llamada telefónica o usa la computadora?
(La joven usa la computadora.)

2. ¿Entra los datos con el teclado o el ratón? (Entra los datos con el teclado.)

3. ¿Qué mete en la ranura?
(Mete un CD en la ranura.)

4. ¿Qué transmite por fax?
(Transmite un documento por fax.)

Activity 4

Alumno A Ask your partner the following questions. Correct answers are in parentheses.

1. ¿Qué es, una carnicería o una verdulería? (Es una carnicería.)

2. ¿Qué se vende allí? (Se vende carne.)

3. ¿Qué es, una pastelería o una frutería? (Es una frutería.)

4. ¿Qué se vende allí? (Se venden frutas.)

5. ¿Qué es, una panadería o una pescadería? (Es una pescadería.)

6. ¿Qué se vende allí? (Se vende pescado./Se venden mariscos.)

Alumno A Answer your partner's questions based on the pictures below.

5–6.

3–4.

1–2.

Alumno B Answer your partner's questions based on the pictures below.

1–2.

3–4.

5–6.

Alumno B Ask your partner the following questions. Correct answers are in parentheses.

1. ¿Qué es, una pescadería o una panadería? (Es una panadería.)

2. ¿Qué se vende allí? (Se vende pan.)

3. ¿Qué es, una frutería o una pastelería? (Es una pastelería.)

4. ¿Qué se vende allí? (Se venden pasteles.)

5. ¿Qué es, una verdulería o una carnicería? (Es una verdulería.)

6. ¿Qué se vende allí? (Se venden legumbres/vegetales.)

3–4.

1–2.

(Los jóvenes reman en el bote.)

4. ¿En qué reman los jóvenes?

(Los jóvenes reman por el lago.)

3. ¿Qué hacen los jóvenes en el lago?

(Sí, la gente camina por la senda.)

2. ¿Camina la gente por la senda?

zoológico? (La gente camina por el parque.)

1. ¿Camina la gente por el parque o por el

questions. Correct answers are in parentheses.

Alumno A Ask your partner the following

Alumno A Answer your partner's questions based on the pictures below.

Alumno B Answer your partner's questions based on the pictures below.

1–2.

3–4.

Alumno B Ask your partner the following questions. Correct answers are in parentheses.

1. ¿Quién toma una piragua, un muchacho o una muchacha?
(Un muchacho toma una piragua.)

2. ¿Quién come un helado, un muchacho o una muchacha?
(Una muchacha come un helado.)

3. ¿Dónde hacen cola en el parque de atracciones?
(Hacen cola en la boletería.)

4. ¿Qué está detrás del tiovivo, la noria o la montaña rusa?
(La montaña rusa está detrás del tiovivo.)

Activity 6

Alumno A Answer your partner's questions based on the picture below.

Alumno A Ask your partner the following questions. Correct answers are in parentheses.

1. ¿Es el recepcionista o el mozo? *(Es el mozo.)*

2. ¿Va a subir el equipaje o limpiar el cuarto? *(Va a subir el equipaje.)*

3. ¿El huésped paga la cuenta o llena la ficha? *(El huésped paga la cuenta.)*

4. ¿Cómo paga su factura? *(Paga con tarjeta de crédito.)*

Alumno B Answer your partner's questions based on the pictures below.

1–2. 3–4.

Alumno B Ask your partner the following questions. Correct answers are in parentheses.

1. ¿Es la camarera o la recepcionista? *(Es la camarera.)*

2. ¿Cambia las toallas o hace la cama? *(Hace la cama.)*

3. ¿Es un cuarto sencillo o doble? *(Es un cuarto sencillo.)*

4. ¿Tiene el cuarto un sofá o un sillón? *(El cuarto tiene un sillón.)*

3-4.

1-2.

(*Sí, la asistente de vuelo lleva un chaleco salvavidas.*)
4. La asistente de vuelo lleva un chaleco salvavidas.

(*No, el señor está en su asiento.*)
3. El señor está en el pasillo.

(*Sí, una señora usa audífonos.*)
2. Una señora usa audífonos.

1. La asistente de vuelo está en su asiento. (*No, la asistente de vuelo está en el pasillo.*)

in parentheses.
true/false statements. Correct responses are

Alumno A Read your partner the following

information based on the pictures below.

Alumno A Give your partner the correct

Alumno B Give your partner the correct information based on the picture below.

Alumno B Read your partner the following *true/false* statements. Correct responses are in parentheses.

1. Es el despegue. (*No, es el aterrizaje.*)

2. Es un helicóptero. (*No, es un avión.*)

3. El muchacho está en la terminal de pasajeros. (*No, el muchacho está en el avión/en su asiento.*)

4. El muchacho se abrocha el cinturón de seguridad. (*Sí, el muchacho se abrocha el cinturón de seguridad.*)

Alumno A Answer your partner's questions based on the pictures below.

Carlos
1–2.

Juanita
3–5.

Alumno A Ask your partner the following questions. Correct answers are in parentheses.

1. ¿Marta tiene una herida en la pierna o en el dedo? *(Marta tiene una herida en el dedo.)*

2. ¿La médica ha puesto un vendaje o un yeso? *(La médica ha puesto un vendaje.)*

3. ¿Alberto se lastimó la pierna o la cabeza? *(Alberto se lastimó la pierna.)*

4. ¿Cómo anda Alberto, en muletas o en una silla de ruedas? *(Alberto anda en una silla de ruedas.)*

5. ¿Quién llenó el formulario, Alberto o su amigo? *(Su amigo llenó el formulario.)*

Alumno B Answer your partner's questions based on the pictures below.

Marta
1–2.

Alberto
3–5.

Alumno B Ask your partner the following questions. Correct answers are in parentheses.

1. ¿Carlos se rompió el brazo o la pierna? *(Carlos se rompió el brazo.)*

2. ¿La médica toma una radiografía o el pulso? *(La médica toma el pulso.)*

3. ¿Juanita se rompió el hombro o la pierna? *(Juanita se rompió la pierna.)*

4. ¿Tiene Juanita un yeso o un vendaje? *(Juanita tiene un yeso.)*

5. ¿Cómo anda Juanita, en muletas o en una silla de ruedas? *(Juanita anda en muletas.)*

InfoGap

Activity 9

CAPÍTULO 9, Palabras 1, 2, pages 262–263, 266–267

Alumno A Ask your partner the following questions. Correct answers are in parentheses.

1. ¿Qué animal es? *(Es un cerdo.)*

2. ¿Los obreros trabajan en una oficina o en una fábrica? *(Los obreros trabajan en una fábrica.)*

3. ¿La joven está en el campo o en la ciudad? *(La joven está en el campo.)*

4. ¿Es una zona industrial o residencial? *(Es una zona residencial.)*

5. ¿Hay muchos apartamentos? *(Sí, hay muchos apartamentos.)*

Alumno A Answer your partner's questions based on the pictures below.

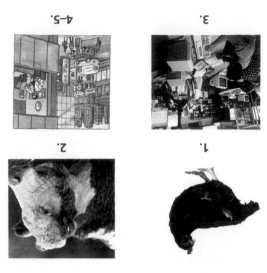

1. 2. 3. 4–5.

Alumno B Answer your partner's questions based on the pictures below.

1. 2.

3. 4–5.

Alumno B Ask your partner the following questions. Correct answers are in parentheses.

1. ¿Qué animal es? *(Es una gallina.)*

2. ¿Qué animal es? *(Es una vaca.)*

3. ¿La gente trabaja en una oficina o en una fábrica? *(La gente trabaja en una oficina.)*

4. ¿Es una zona residencial o comercial? *(Es una zona comercial.)*

5. ¿Hay rascacielos en la zona? *(Sí, hay rascacielos en la zona.)*

Alumno A Answer your partner's questions based on the picture below.

Alumno A Ask your partner the following questions. Correct answers are in parentheses.

1. ¿La muchacha limpia o pela las papas?
(La muchacha pela las papas.)

2. ¿Qué agrega a la olla el muchacho?
(El muchacho agrega sal.)

3. ¿Qué lee el joven? (El joven lee la receta.)

4. ¿Qué es? (Es langosta.)

Alumno B Answer your partner's questions based on the pictures below.

1. 2.

3. 4.

Alumno B Ask your partner the following questions. Correct answers are in parentheses.

1. ¿Cuántas puertas tiene la nevera?
(La nevera tiene dos puertas.)

2. ¿El refrigerador tiene un congelador?
(Sí, el refrigerador tiene un congelador.)

3. ¿Hay plátanos en la cocina?
(Sí, hay plátanos en la cocina.)

4. ¿Hay ollas en la estufa?
(Sí, hay ollas en la estufa.)

3–5.

1–2.

Alumno A Answer your partner's questions based on the pictures below.

Alumno A Ask your partner the following questions. Correct answers are in parentheses.

1. ¿Dónde están las personas? (*Las personas están en la estación de servicio/la gasolinera.*)

2. ¿Qué llena Carlos? (*Carlos llena el tanque de gasolina.*)

3. ¿Luis limpia el parabrisas? (*No, Luis no limpia el parabrisas.*)

4. ¿Qué revisa Ricardo? (*Ricardo revisa el aceite.*)

5. ¿Antonio verifica la presión de las llantas? (*Sí, Antonio verifica la presión de las llantas.*)

Alumno B Answer your partner's questions based on the picture below.

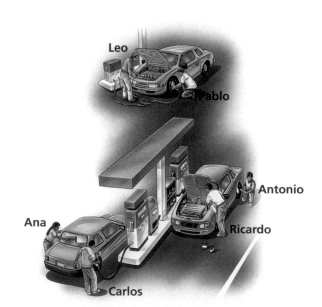

Alumno B Ask your partner the following questions. Correct answers are in parentheses.

1. ¿El conductor tiene que doblar a la izquierda o a la derecha? (*El conductor tiene que doblar a la derecha.*)

2. ¿El rótulo indica una calle de sentido único o la velocidad máxima? (*El rótulo indica una calle de sentido único.*)

3. ¿Está el coche en la autopista o en una bocacalle? (*El coche está en la autopista.*)

4. ¿El rótulo indica una entrada a la autopista o un carril en cada sentido? (*El rótulo indica un carril en cada sentido.*)

5. ¿El conductor puede adelantar? (*No, el conductor no puede adelantar.*)

InfoGap

Activity 12   **CAPÍTULO 12, Palabras 1, 2, pages 360–361, 364–365**

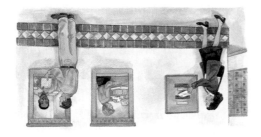

Alumno A   Answer your partner's questions based on the picture below.

Alumno A   Ask your partner the following questions. Correct answers are in parentheses.

1. ¿La peluquera lava o corta el pelo de la joven? (*La peluquera corta el pelo de la joven.*)

2. ¿La peluquera usa tijeras o una navaja? (*La peluquera usa tijeras.*)

3. ¿La peluquera seca o lava el pelo? (*La peluquera seca el pelo.*)

4. ¿Qué usa la peluquera para secar el pelo? (*La peluquera usa un secador.*)

Alumno B   Answer your partner's questions based on the pictures below.

1–2.

3–4.

Alumno B   Ask your partner the following questions. Correct answers are in parentheses.

1. ¿Qué compra el señor, sellos o una tarjeta postal? (*El señor compra sellos.*)

2. ¿Qué echa la señora en el buzón? (*La señora echa una carta en el buzón.*)

3. ¿Cuántas ventanillas hay? (*Hay dos ventanillas.*)

4. ¿Qué hace la empleada? (*La empleada pesa el paquete.*)

3-4.

1-2.

Alumno A Answer your partner's questions based on the pictures below.

Alumno A Ask your partner the following questions. Correct answers are in parentheses.

1. ¿Es una recepción de boda o una fiesta de cumpleaños? (*Es una recepción de boda.*)

2. ¿Los novios cantan o bailan? (*Los novios bailan.*)

3. ¿La familia celebra Hanuka o la Navidad? (*La familia celebra Hanuka.*)

4. ¿Qué tiene nueve brazos? (*La menora tiene nueve brazos.*)

Alumno B Answer your partner's questions based on the pictures below.

1-2.

3-4.

Alumno B Ask your partner the following questions. Correct answers are in parentheses.

1. ¿La familia celebra Hanuka o la Navidad? (*La familia celebra la Navidad.*)

2. ¿Es Nochebuena o Nochevieja? (*Es Nochebuena.*)

3. ¿Celebran un cumpleaños o una boda? (*Celebran un cumpleaños.*)

4. ¿Qué llevan los amigos a la fiesta? (*Los amigos llevan regalos a la fiesta.*)

InfoGap

Alumno A　Ask your partner the following questions. Correct answers are in parentheses.

1. ¿Qué hace la mecánica?
   (La mecánica repara el coche.)

2. ¿Qué hace el arquitecto?
   (El arquitecto hace planes de construcción.)

3. ¿Qué hace el plomero? *(El plomero repara el lavabo y el inodoro.)*

4. ¿Qué hace la contable? *(La contable calcula un plan financiero.)*

Alumno A　Choose the correct information from the chart below to answer your partner's questions.

| ...repara las lámparas. |
| ...escribe programas en la computadora. |
| ...compra y vende mercancía. |
| ...defiende a los criminales en el tribunal. |

Alumno B　Choose the correct information from the chart below to answer your partner's questions.

| ...repara el lavabo y el inodoro. |
| ...hace planes de construcción. |
| ...repara el coche. |
| ...calcula un plan financiero. |

Alumno B　Ask your partner the following questions. Correct answers are in parentheses.

1. ¿Qué hace el comerciante?
   (El comerciante compra y vende mercancía.)

2. ¿Qué hace la abogada? *(La abogada defiende a los criminales en el tribunal.)*

3. ¿Qué hace el electricista?
   (El electricista repara las lámparas.)

4. ¿Qué hace la programadora?
   (La programadora escribe programas en la computadora.)

For students and parents/guardians

This guide is designed to help you as students achieve success as you embark on the adventure of learning another language and to enable your parents or guardians to help you on this exciting journey. There are many ways to learn new information. You may find some of these suggestions more useful than others, depending upon which style of learning works best for you. Before you begin, it is important to understand how we acquire language.

Receptive Skills

Each day of your life you receive a great deal of information through the use of language. In order to get this information it is necessary to understand the language being used. It is necessary to understand the language in two different ways. First you must be able to understand what people are saying when they speak to you. This is referred to as oral or listening comprehension. Oral comprehension or listening comprehension is the ability to understand the spoken language.

You must also be able to understand what you read. This is referred to as reading comprehension. Reading comprehension is the ability to understand the written language.

Listening comprehension and reading comprehension are called *receptive skills*. They are receptive skills because as you listen to what someone else says or read what someone else has written you receive information without having to produce any language yourself.

It is usually very easy to understand your native language. It is a bit more problematic to understand a second language that is new to you. As a beginner you are still learning the sounds of the new language, and you recognize only a few words. Throughout **¡Buen viaje!** we will give you hints or suggestions to help you understand when people are speaking to you in Spanish or when you are reading in Spanish.

Hints for Listening Comprehension

When you are listening to a person speaking Spanish, don't try to understand every word. It is not necessary to understand everything to get the idea of what someone is saying. Listen for the general message. If some details escape you, it doesn't matter. Also, never try to translate what people are saying in Spanish into English. It takes a great deal of experience and expertise to be a translator. Trying to translate will hinder your ability to understand.

Hints for Reading Comprehension

Just as you will not always understand every word you hear in a conversation, you will not necessarily understand every word you encounter in a reading selection, either. In **¡Buen viaje!,** we have used only words you know or can easily figure out in the reading selections. This will make reading comprehension much easier for you. However, if at some time you wish to read a newspaper or magazine article in Spanish, you will most certainly come across some unfamiliar words. Do not stop reading. Continue to read to get the "gist" of the selection. Try to guess the meanings of words you do not know.

Productive Skills

There are two productive skills in language. These two skills are speaking and writing. They are called *productive skills* because it is you who has to produce the language when you say or write something. When you speak or write, you have control over the language and which words you use. If you don't know how to say something, you don't have to say it. With the receptive skills, on the other hand, someone else produces the language that you listen to or read, and you have no control over the words they use.

There's no doubt that you can easily speak your native language. You can write, too, even though you may sometimes make errors in spelling and punctuation. In Spanish, there's not a lot you can say or write as a beginner. You can only talk or write about those topics you have learned in Spanish class.

Hints for Speaking

Try to be as accurate as possible when speaking. Try not to make mistakes. However, if you do, it's not the end of the world. Spanish speakers will understand you. You're not expected to speak a language perfectly after a limited time. You have probably spoken with people from other countries who do not speak English perfectly, but you can understand them. Remember:

❖ Keep talking! Don't become inhibited for fear of making a mistake.

❖ Say what you know how to say. Don't try to branch out in the early stages and attempt to talk about topics or situations you have not yet learned in Spanish.

Hints for Writing

There are many activities throughout each chapter of **¡Buen viaje!** that will help you to speak and write in Spanish. When you have to write something on your own, however, without the guidance or assistance of an activity in your book, be sure to choose a topic for which you know the vocabulary in Spanish. Never attempt to write about a topic you have not yet studied in Spanish. Write down the topic you are going to write about. Then think of the words you know that are related to the topic. Be sure to include some action words (verbs) that you will need.

From your list of words, write as many sentences as you can. Read them and organize them into a logical order. Fill in any gaps. Then proof your paragraph(s) to see if you made any errors. Correct any that you find.

When writing on your own, be careful not to rely heavily, if at all, on a bilingual dictionary. It's not that bilingual dictionaries are bad, but when you look up a word you will very often find that there are several translations for the same word. As a beginning language student, you do not know which translation to choose; the chances are great that you will pick the wrong one.

As a final hint, never prepare your paragraph(s) in English and attempt to translate word for word. Always write from scratch in Spanish.

Study Tips

Capítulo 1

Vocabulario
PALABRAS 1 y 2 *(pages 2–9)*

1. Listen to the new words in **Palabras 1** and repeat them orally before reading them.

2. After learning the new words, match the following opposites.

la llegada	bajar de
de ida y vuelta	ocupado
subir a	la salida
libre	tarde
a tiempo	sencillo

3. Read the answers aloud to all the **Historieta** activities.

Estructura
El pretérito de los verbos irregulares
(pages 12–13)

Note that these irregular verbs have the same endings in the preterite as regular verbs except in the **yo** and **él, ella, usted** forms.

	Regular	Irregular
yo	-í	-e
él, ella, Ud.	-ió	-o

Lectura cultural
En el AVE *(pages 18–19)*

1. Before reading this selection, look at the photo of the bird—**el ave, el pájaro**. What's the association of the bird with the train?

2. Scan the reading selection to get just the general idea.

3. Read the selection again and look for some more precise details about a trip on the **AVE**.

Capítulo 2

Vocabulario
PALABRAS 1 y 2 *(pages 32–39)*

1. Do some review as you learn this new vocabulary. Think of all the foods you have learned in Spanish. You may wish to refer back to Chapter 5 in **¡Buen viaje!, Level 1.**

Hint If you´re the type of learner who has to write something before you can remember it, write the new words several times.

2. Activity 8 on page 39 reviews the use of **gustar**. You may review **interesar** and **gustar** on page 215 of **¡Buen viaje!, Level 1.**

Estructura
Verbos con el cambio e → i *(pages 40–41)*

1. You have already come across this type of stem change in the irregular verb **decir.**
   digo, dices, dice, decimos, *decís,* dicen

2. As with other stem-changing verbs you have learned so far (**e → ie, o → ue**), these verbs take the same endings as any other verb that belongs to that conjugation.

Hint If you pronounce these verbs correctly, you will never have trouble spelling them. Remember **i** is pronounced like *ee* in English *see* and **e** is pronounced like the *a* in *ate*.

Lectura cultural
La comida mexicana *(pages 46–47)*
If you have ever been to a Mexican restaurant, think about what you ate there. It will help you visualize what you are reading about.

Capítulo 3

Vocabulario
PALABRAS 1 *(pages 60–63)*

1. When studying the vocabulary on your own, be sure to pronounce the words orally. Then read them silently, always concentrating on the illustration to ascertain meaning.

2. When you think you are quite familiar with the new words, cover up the Spanish and see what you can say about each illustration on your own.

3. If you are the type of learner who has to write something before you can retain it, copy each word two or three times on a piece of paper.

Práctica

1. The first time you do these activities you may want to go back to pages 60–61 to look for the answers.

2. If you are a diligent student, however, you should get to know the material well enough that you can do these activities without having to look up the answers or at least the vast majority of them.

3. If you are studying at home with a classmate or person who knows Spanish, you can do Activities 4–6 on page 63 together.

PALABRAS 2 *(pages 64–67)*
1. Once again remember to go over the vocabulary orally as well as reading it.

Hint Think about the order of things you have to do to make a phone call from a public phone. After studying the vocabulary, determine if you can describe each step in Spanish without reading it.

Study Tips

Estructura
Imperfecto de los verbos en –ar *(pages 68–70)*

1. Repeat the verb forms *aloud*.

2. Take the verb **tomar** and write out the complete conjugation at least once.

3. Read the "model" sentences aloud.

Hint   As you do, concentrate on the fact that it is not important when each action began nor when it ended, if it ever did.

4. To test your ability to use these new endings, try to do Activity 14 without having to look up any of the endings, that is to say without having to refer to the verb charts on page 68.

Imperfecto de los verbos en –er e –ir *(pages 70–71)*

1. Pronounce the endings aloud in isolation.

2. Write the endings at least once.

3. Read aloud all the forms in the verb chart.

Hint   Read the verb forms down the first different endings. Then read them across to help you associate the ending with the subject.

    Ex:

tú   leías   comías   escribías   vivías

Imperfecto de los verbos *ser* y *ir* *(pages 72–73)*

1. Follow the same suggestions given for the previous verb sections in the chapter.

Usos del imperfecto *(pages 74–75)*

Hint   Concentrate on the fact that this tense, the imperfect, is used to describe or reminisce about the past. It is not used to describe what happened in the past.

Conversación *(page 76)*

1. Listen carefully to the conversation. You can listen to your teacher or use the CD-ROM. Listen more than once. Each time you'll pick up some more information

2. Read the conversation aloud several times.

3. Try to answer the questions that follow without looking up the answers in the conversation.

Lectura cultural *(pages 78–79)*
Futura ingeniera

1. You should have no problem reading this selection since it only includes Spanish you have already learned.

2. Read the selection quickly to get the general idea.

3. Read it a second time to get more details.

4. Read all the questions on page 79.

5. Read the selection again. As you find the answer to each question, write it down.

6. As a final check, read each question again. See how many questions you can answer without looking up the information. You should be able to answer at least eight of them.

Capítulo 4

Vocabulario
PALABRAS 1 y 2 *(pages 92–99)*

1. Look at each photo or illustration carefully.

2. Read the labels. What does each word refer to?

3. The words are then used in a meaningful context in a complete sentence. Repeat the sentence aloud as you look at the illustration.

4. To help you learn vocabulary, work with a friend or classmate. Have a contest. See who can say the most about each illustration or photo.

5. To review the vocabulary and see how much of it you know, cover the words and sentences and say as much as you can about each photo or illustration.

6. Do the activities that follow both orally and in writing.

Hint When you have finished studying the vocabulary, write a list of all the articles of clothing and a list of all the foods you can remember.

Estructura
El pretérito y el imperfecto *(pages 100–102)*
Hint Always remember—if you know exactly when something happened, you use the preterite. If the precise time at which it happened is not important, you use the imperfect.

1. Read the model sentences on page 100, keeping in mind the above **Hint.** Relate the **Hint** to each of the sentences.

2. Exercises 14 and 15 on page 101 help you zero in on the time concept.

Dos acciones en una oración *(pages 103–104)*
Hint When trying to determine whether to use the imperfect or the preterite, pretend you are at the theater watching a play or that you are watching a movie. All the scenery or activity that is going on in the background is expressed by the imperfect. What the actors or actresses did is in the preterite. Just remember, background— imperfect; actio[...]

1. As you do Activity 19 on page 103, keep in mind the above **Hint.** This will help you understand what you are doing.

La voz pasiva con se. *(pages 106–107)*
Hint Remember the **se** construction is used with only two verb forms— one singular, the other plural.

Aquí:	se habla español	se vende pescado	se escribe poesía
Aquí:	se hablan idiomas	se venden legumbres	se escriben novelas

Conversación *(page 108)*

1. Intonation is the melody of a language. Intonation is produced by the rise and fall of the voice. Each language has its own intonation patterns. English intonation is very different from Spanish intonation. Pay special attention to the rise and fall of the speaker's voice as you listen to the conversations on the CDs or CD-ROM.

2. Try to imitate the speakers' intonation as accurately as possible. If you do, you'll sound much more like a heritage Spanish speaker. Don't be inhibited. Pretend you are acting while you imitate the intonation.

Study Tips

Lectura cultural
De compras *(pages 110–111)*

1. Go over the Reading Strategy. Once you follow the suggestions in the Reading Strategy you will certainly know what this reading is about.

Hint Then think about what you already know about the topic. What's it like to shop in a supermarket? What's it like to shop in a small market, either a small vegetable stand or farmer's market? What's it like to shop in a gigantic outlet store?

2. Visualizing the answers to the above will help you understand rather easily the content of this reading selection.

3. When you think you know the information in the reading selection quite well, go over the questions on page 111 and see how many you can answer without having to look up information.

Lectura opcional *(page 112–113)*
Even if your teacher does not assign this optional reading you may wish to read it quickly. It gives you some interesting cultural information and once again reinforces language you have already learned. Remember, the more you are reintroduced to language you have already learned the easier Spanish will be.

Vocabulario *(page 120)*
Look at each word. Determine how many you know. If there are some you don't remember, go back to pages 92–93 and 96–97 to look for them.

Capítulo 5

Vocabulario
PALABRAS 1 y 2 (*pages 132–139*)

1. In **Palabras 1,** remember to listen to the words and repeat them orally before reading them.

2. After you have learned the new words in **Palabras 2,** look at each illustration, use sentences, and say as much as you can about the illustration. If you can describe the illustration,

you know your vocabulary. If you cannot describe it, you have to study some more.

3. Look at each sentence again. Find each verb. Verbs you will encounter are:

irá	jugará	será
comprará	ganará	llenará

Since several sentences are introduced by **mañana,** what tense of the verb do you think this is?

a) present   b) future   c) past

If you chose future, you are correct.

Estructura
Futuro de los verbos regulares *(pages 140–143)*

1. Remember that the entire infinitive serves as the root for the formation of the future tense. This is the first tense you have learned in which you add the ending to the infinitive.

2. In the verb charts, read the verb across to help you associate the ending with its corresponding subject:

yo   estudiaré   leeré   escribiré

Hint Read or say aloud all the answers to the **Historieta** activities to give you some practice telling coherent stories in Spanish.

Comparativo y superlativo *(pages 144–145)*
In this section you are going to learn how to compare persons or things. Think of as many adjectives as you can. You have already learned quite a few. See how many you can come up with on your own before referring to the following list.

alto	serio	grande	fácil
bajo	ambicioso	inteligente	difícil
guapo	perezoso	interesante	popular
bonita	fantástico	joven	moderno
lindo	tímido	feo	sincero
moreno	honesto	rubio	generoso
flaco	simpático	gordo	aburrido
gracioso	pequeño	cómico	viejo

1. If you want to be a diligent student, after doing Activities 19 and 20 on page 145, you can make up many additional sentences in the comparative and superlative using the above adjectives.

Lectura cultural

El domingo en el parque *(pages 148–149)*

1. To reinforce the grammar point you learned in this chapter, skim the reading selection and find all the verbs in the future tense.
2. Be sure to write the answers to the Activities on page 149.
3. If you feel you are sufficiently familiar with the context of the reading selection, go over the questions on page 149 and see how many you can answer without having to look up information.

2. When doing the activities that follow each **Palabras** section, read aloud all the answers to each **Historieta** activity. By doing this you will be telling a story in Spanish. Always remember, the more you practice speaking Spanish, the better you'll be able to communicate.

3. In class, pay attention to the responses of the other students in class. Don't turn them off. The more you hear the new words used, the easier it will be for you to remember them.

Capítulo 6

Vocabulario
PALABRAS 1 y 2 *(pages 162–169)*

1. It can be fun to study with a classmate. You can do the following.
   ❖ Ask one another questions in Spanish about the illustrations.
   ❖ Have a contest. See who can give more Spanish words describing the illustrations in a three-minute period.
   ❖ Tell your friend which of the items you would order if you were at a café.

Estructura
Futuro de los verbos irregulares *(pages 170–173)*

1. This point should be easy for you since the endings are the same as those you already learned for the future of regular verbs in Chapter 5.

2. When going over the activities at home, be sure to do them aloud. Then write down the answers.

3. Retell the information in the **Historieta** activities in your own words.

4. See if you can give all of the future endings without having to look them up.

Me lo, te lo, nos lo *(pages 173–175)*

Hint When learning another language it is often necessary to repeat the same thing many times before you can use it quickly and easily. The object pronouns you are learning in this lesson are a case in point. When you are carrying on a normal conversation it is impossible to ask yourself the gender of the object, the pronoun that replaces it and its place in the sentence—before or after the other pronoun. So, what's the solution? It's simple, practice makes perfect. Go over the activities as often as you can. Read the question aloud and then answer it. The more you hear **me lo, te lo,** etc. the easier it will be to use it.

Hint Be diligent in doing your Spanish homework. Work for at least a brief period of time each day. This enables you to learn everything in small doses. Do not let things pile up.

Lectura cultural
Los paradores de España *(pages 178–179)*

1. As you read this selection find examples of the future tense to review the structure point of the lesson.

2. When you have finished studying the **Lectura,** just sit back and think about all the sentences you can make up to summarize the content of the reading selection.

Capítulo 7

Vocabulario
PALABRAS 1 y 2 *(pages 192–199)*

1. You already know some vocabulary related to airports and air travel from **¡Buen viaje!,** Level 1. Before going over the vocabulary, think of the words that you already know about this topic.

Hint If you're the type of learner who has to write something before you can remember it, copy the words in the **Palabras** section once or twice. Use the following learning sequence: listen, repeat, read, write.

2. Go over exercises 7, 8, 9, and 10 on pages 198–199 orally before writing them.

3. As you are about to finish studying the vocabulary at home, consult the vocabulary list on page 220. See how many words you understand without having to use the illustrations on pages 192, 193, 196, and 197.

Estructura

Modo potencial o condicional de verbos regulares *(pages 200–202)*

1. See if you remember the endings for the imperfect of **–er** and **–ir** verbs. You will use these endings again with the conditional.

2. This grammatical point should be quite easy for you:
   ❖ The conditional is used in Spanish in exactly the same way as it is in English.
   ❖ You are already familiar with the root for the conditional—the entire infinitive. You have already used the root for the future tense.
   ❖ You are also already familiar with the endings from your study of the imperfect.

3. Write the answers to the activities after doing them aloud.

Modo potencial de verbos irregulares *(pages 203–205)*

1. Remember, the root of irregular verbs is the same for the future and the conditional tenses.

Dos complementos con se *(pages 205–207)*

1. Re-read the **Hint** for **me lo, te lo, nos lo** on page H24. If you want to give yourself more practice, you can do the following substitution exercises. Follow the model:

   Yo le di el boleto.
   Yo se lo di a él.

   (los boletos, la tarjeta de embarque, el maletín, las maletas, el periódico, las revistas, las fotografías, el carro, las llaves, la carta, el sello, el bolígrafo, el cuaderno, los lápices, la carpeta, la goma de borrar)

·················· Capítulo 8 ··················

Vocabulario

PALABRAS 1 y 2 *(pages 232–239)*

1. Think of all the parts of the body you have already learned.

2. Look at each photo or illustration carefully.

3. Read the labels. What does each word refer to?

4. The words are then used in a meaningful context in a complete sentence. Repeat the sentence aloud as you look at the illustration.

5. To help you learn vocabulary, work with a friend or classmate. Have a contest. See who can say the most about each illustration or photo.

6. To review the vocabulary and see how much of it you know, cover the words and sentences and say as much as you can about each photo or illustration.

7. Do the activities that follow both orally and in writing.

Estructura

El presente perfecto *(pages 240–242)*

1. Give the past participle of the following verbs:

hablar	aprender	vivir
estudiar	leer	salir
buscar	vender	servir
comprar	poder	reducir

2. After reading the explanation on page 240, go over Activities 13–16 on pages 241–242 first aloud and then write them out. It is suggested that you do one activity at a time.

Los participios irregulares *(pages 242–243)*

1. Repeat the irregular past participles aloud several times.

2. After you have gone over the activities, see if you can write all the verbs that have an irregular past participle without referring to the list on page 242.

Comparación de igualdad *(pages 244–245)*

1. Just remember:
   tan... como with an adjective.
   tanto... como with a noun
   (tanto... como, tanta... como, tantos... como, tantas... como)

2. Be sure to go over activities 22 and 23 orally.

Study Tips

Hint If you're the type of learner who has to write something in order to remember it, copy the words in the **Estructura** section once or twice. Use the following learning sequence: listen, repeat, read, write.

Conversación *(page 246)*
When listening to people speak Spanish, the tone of voice can very often help you understand what the person is saying. When listening to this conversation, pay particular attention to the speaker's tone.

Intonation is the rising and dropping of the voice. As you know the intonation for a question is quite different than for a declarative sentence. This conversation includes quite a few questions and question words. Pay particular attention to the rising intonation.

··········· *Capítulo* **9** ···········

Vocabulario
PALABRAS 1 y 2 *(pages 262–269)*
1. The **Palabras 1** section on pages 262 and 263 has many sentences. Only a small part of each sentence contains new words. An excellent study technique is to ask yourself questions about each sentence as you study.
   Example:
   ¿Qué hay en la zona comercial?
   ¿Dónde hay muchas oficinas y tiendas?
   ¿Qué hora es?
   ¿Quién estaba saliendo?
   ¿De dónde estaba saliendo la gente?

You can answer these questions with a complete sentence or with just the necessary words.
   Example:
   La gente estaba saliendo de sus oficinas.
   De sus oficinas.

This gives you the opportunity to use the words several times. The more you use them the easier it will be to remember them.

Hint Remember to go over the vocabulary activities at least once orally before writing them.

Estructura
El imperfecto progresivo (pages 270–271)

Hint Remember that if you pronounce correctly, you will not misspell words. The vowel **i** is pronounced *ee* as in *see*. If you pronounce the following words correctly, you will never try to spell them with an **e**.

> **pidiendo**
> **sirviendo**
> **repitiendo**
> **diciendo**

1. This grammar point is quite easy. Pronounce the irregular past participles several times aloud. You may also want to copy them once in written form before doing the activities.

Colocación de los pronombres de complemento (pages 272–273)

1. As you have already read in previous Study Tips sections, the more you hear and use the object pronouns, the more comfortable you will be with them. For this reason it is suggested that you go over each activity twice.

Adjetivos y pronombres demonstrativos (pages 274–275)

1. Remember
   ❖ something near you— a form of **este**
   ❖ something near the person you're speaking to— a form of **ese**
   ❖ something distant from the two of you— a form of **aquel**

2. You will often see the pronoun written with an accent to differentiate it from the adjective but current usage no longer requires this distinction.

Lectura cultural
Buenos Aires, Argentina (pages 278–279)
After you read each paragraph, stop reading and think about the most important information you learned in the paragraph.

Lecturas opcionales (pages 280–281)
Even if your teacher does not assign either of these reading selections, you may want to read them very quickly not only to familiarize yourself with two other interesting cities but to give yourself the opportunity to be exposed once again to Spanish you have already learned. It cannot be emphasized enough that the more you are reintroduced to Spanish you have already learned, the easier the language will be.

Capítulo 10

Vocabulario
PALABRAS 1 y 2 (pages 292–299)

1. Make a mental list of all the foods you have already learned in Spanish.

2. After studying the new words, cover each printed word and see if you can give the correct word by looking only at the illustration.

Study Tips

Estructura
Imperativo formal: formas regulares
(pages 301–302)

Review Since you will use the **yo** form of the present indicative to form the command for most verbs, review the following:

hablo	hago
como	pongo
escribo	traigo
vuelvo	salgo
empiezo	tengo
pido	vengo
sirvo	

1. Be sure to pronounce the command forms correctly. If you pronounce the **–e** and **–a** sounds clearly, you will never have a problem spelling the commands.

Imperativo formal: formas irregulares
(pages 303–304)

Hint Once again, say these forms aloud quite a few times. The more you hear them, the more automatic they will become and you will have no trouble using them. When speaking you do not have time to resort to the rule "take the **yo** form of the present, drop the **–o** ending, and add the vowel opposite to the typical vowel of that conjugation." The rule enables you to understand how the command is formed, but it is the practice that will enable you to use it.

Colocación de los pronombres de complemento
(page 305)

1. Go over the activities at least twice orally. Then write them out. Check your answers. Then read them at least once aloud.

Lectura cultural
Una receta española *(pages 308–309)*
Pay particular attention to the command forms as you read this selection.

·················· **Capítulo 11** ··················

Vocabulario
PALABRAS 1 y 2 *(pages 322–329)*

1. After studying the vocabulary, make three lists to determine how well you know the new vocabulary.
   - ❖ list 1—car parts and models
   - ❖ list 2—at a gas station
   - ❖ list 3—on the road

2. Go over each activity at least once orally before writing it.

Estructura
Imperativo familiar: formas regulares
(pages 330–331)

1. There is no doubt that the command forms of the verbs in Spanish are tricky even though they involve only two sounds: **–e** and **–a**. For starters, be sure to pronounce these sounds as carefully and clearly as you can. There is no substitute for good, old practice but the following may help you a bit:

   Verbs that take **–a** in the formal command (**usted**) take **–e** in the informal command.

2. Go over each activity several times.

Imperativo familiar: formas irregulares
(pages 332–333)
These verbs follow no set pattern and the only way to learn them is to use them.

1. Say them orally several times.

2. Go over each activity at least twice.

Classroom Suggestion   Listen to your classmates as they respond to the structure activities. The more you hear the form, the more readily you will be able to use it.

Conversación *(page 336)*
When listening to the conversation, pay particular attention to the intonation for the command.

Lectura cultural
La carretera panamericana *(pages 338–339)*
When you have finished studying this selection, make a list of some of the interesting facts about the Panamerican Highway.

········· Capítulo 12 ·········

Vocabulario
PALABRAS 1 y 2 *(pages 360–367)*

1. These vocabulary sections contain words that will be of great help to you when trying to get around in a Spanish-speaking area. After going over the vocabulary, make yourself a few "survival" lists.
   ❖ Words I need to get my hair cut.
   ❖ Words I need to get my clothes cleaned.
   ❖ Words I need to mail something.
   ❖ Words I need to get money.

2. Go over the activities both orally and in writing as you do your homework.

Estructura
El subjuntivo *(pages 368–375)*

1. Many students learning Spanish consider the subjunctive to be very difficult. The subjunctive is traditionally presented as the verb form that is used following many different types of expressions such as: desire, volition, necessity, possibility, doubt, etc. It is difficult to keep all these categories in mind when speaking or using the subjunctive and it is not necessary.

    The subjunctive is almost always introduced by **que.** If what follows **que** may or may not take place, if it is not a reality, you will then use the subjunctive. Always ask yourself, "really or maybe?" If the answer is maybe, you will almost always have to use the subjunctive.

2. To contrast the indicative, which you have already learned, and the subjunctive, which you are about to learn, take into account the following regarding the meaning of these words:

   Indicative   Indicates something – points something out – is objective – can stand alone – is independent.

   Subjunctive   Subjective – does not indicate anything concrete – is not objective; it is the opposite of objective – cannot stand alone – is dependent upon something else.

Indicative	**Subjunctive**
He gets good marks.	I hope he *gets good marks.* I want him to *get good marks.* His parents insist that he *get good marks.* It's necessary for him to *get good marks.* He'll get a present when he *gets good marks.*

3. You are already familiar with the subjunctive forms of the verb from your study of the command. The **usted, ustedes** and negative **tú** commands are actually subjunctive forms.

4. Once again, practice makes "perfect" in acquiring the subjunctive. Do each activity orally, then write it and after writing it, read your answers aloud.

Lectura cultural
Muchos quehaceres *(pages 378–379)*

1. Before reading the **Lectura** at home, read the questions in Activity A on page 379. As you read, focus on looking for the answers to these questions. When you finish reading, write down the answers to the questions.

Capítulo 13

Vocabulario
PALABRAS 1 y 2 *(pages 392–399)*

1. Many of the activities in this vocabulary section are **Historieta** activities. As you complete each one, take a few minutes to retell the story in your own words.

Estructura
El subjuntivo de los verbos de cambio radical *(pages 400–401)*

Hint   Remember once again that if you pronounce your vowels carefully, you will have no problems with either the oral or written forms of these verbs.

El subjuntivo con verbos como pedir y aconsejar *(pages 402–407)*

1. If you refer to the explanation of the subjunctive given in the previous chapter you will note that the same explanation holds. You may, however, question why after a verb such as **creer** (to believe) the indicative, rather than the subjunctive, is used since there is still a bit of the "may or may not" involved. The only explanation is placed on the belief that what follows **creer** will indeed take place.

2. The expressions of emotion on pages 406–407 are somewhat different. They take the subjunctive because they are introduced by and thus dependent upon a subjective emotion.
   For example:
   Estoy contento(a) que Juan asista.
   You could be happy that John is attending but someone else could say:
   Yo no estoy contento que Juan asista.
   Francamente, yo prefiero que no asista.

Capítulo 14

Vocabulario

PALABRAS 1 y 2 *(pages 424–431)*

Hint If you are the type of learner who has to write something before you remember it, write each new word two or three times.

1. Go over the vocabulary activities orally before you write them.

2. Retell the **Historieta** activities on pages 430–431 in your own words.

Estructura

Infinitivo o subjuntivo *(pages 432–433)*

1. Make up additional sentences with:
   Yo quiero....
   Yo quiero que tú...
   Ellos prefieren que yo...
   Nosotros preferimos...

Verb Charts

REGULAR VERBS			
INFINITIVO	**hablar** *to speak*	**comer** *to eat*	**vivir** *to live*
PRESENTE	hablo hablas habla hablamos *habláis* hablan	como comes come comemos *coméis* comen	vivo vives vive vivimos *vivís* viven
PRETÉRITO	hablé hablaste habló hablamos *hablasteis* hablaron	comí comiste comió comimos *comisteis* comieron	viví viviste vivió vivimos *vivisteis* vivieron
IMPERFECTO	hablaba hablabas hablaba hablábamos *hablabais* hablaban	comía comías comía comíamos *comíais* comían	vivía vivías vivía vivíamos *vivíais* vivían
FUTURO	hablaré hablarás hablará hablaremos *hablaréis* hablarán	comeré comerás comerá comeremos *comeréis* comerán	viviré vivirás vivirá viviremos *viviréis* vivirán
CONDICIONAL	hablaría hablarías hablaría hablaríamos *hablaríais* hablarían	comería comerías comería comeríamos *comeríais* comerían	viviría vivirías viviría viviríamos *viviríais* vivirían
SUBJUNTIVO **[PRESENTE]**	hable hables hable hablemos *habléis* hablen	coma comas coma comamos *comáis* coman	viva vivas viva vivamos *viváis* vivan

Verb Charts

REGULAR VERBS			
INFINITIVO	**hablar** *to speak*	**comer** *to eat*	**vivir** *to live*
PARTICIPIO PRESENTE	hablando	comiendo	viviendo
PARTICIPIO PASADO	hablado	comido	vivido
PRESENTE PERFECTO	he hablado has hablado ha hablado hemos hablado *habéis hablado* han hablado	he comido has comido ha comido hemos comido *habéis comido* han comido	he vivido has vivido ha vivido hemos vivido *habéis vivido* han vivido
IMPERATIVO FORMAL	hable (Ud.) no hable (Ud.) hablen (Uds.) no hablen (Uds.)	coma (Ud.) no coma (Ud.) coman (Uds.) no coman (Uds.)	viva (Ud.) no viva (Ud.) vivan (Uds.) no vivan (Uds.)
IMPERATIVO FAMILIAR	habla (tú) no hables (tú)	come (tú) no comas (tú)	vive (tú) no vivas (tú)

Verb Charts

STEM-CHANGING VERBS (-ar and -er verbs)				
INFINITIVO	empezar (e → ie)[1] *to begin*	almorzar (o → ue)[2] *to eat lunch*	perder (e → ie)[3] *to lose*	volver (o → ue) *to return*
PRESENTE	empiezo empiezas empieza empezamos *empezáis* empiezan	almuerzo almuerzas almuerza almorzamos *almorzáis* almuerzan	pierdo pierdes pierde perdemos *perdéis* pierden	vuelvo vuelves vuelve volvemos *volvéis* vuelven

[1] **Comenzar, sentar,** and **pensar** are similar.
[2] **Acostar, costar,** and **jugar (u → ue)** are similar.
[3] **Defender** and **entender** are similar.

STEM-CHANGING VERBS (-ir verbs)			
INFINITIVO	preferir (e → ie, i) *to prefer*	dormir (o → ue, u)[4] *to sleep*	pedir (e → i, i)[5] *to ask for*
PRESENTE	prefiero prefieres prefiere preferimos *preferís* prefieren	duermo duermes duerme dormimos *dormís* duermen	pido pides pide pedimos *pedís* piden
PRETÉRITO	preferí preferiste prefirió preferimos *preferisteis* prefirieron	dormí dormiste durmió dormimos *dormisteis* durmieron	pedí pediste pidió pedimos *pedisteis* pidieron

[4] **Morir** is similar.
[5] **Repetir, freír,** and **servir** are similar.

Verb Charts

IRREGULAR VERBS[1]

abrir *to open*

PARTICIPIO PASADO	abierto

andar *to walk*

PRETÉRITO	anduve	anduviste	anduvo	anduvimos	*anduvisteis*	anduvieron

caer *to fall, to drop*

PARTICIPIO PRESENTE	cayendo

conocer *to know, to be familiar with*

PRESENTE	conozco	conoces	conoce	conocemos	*conocéis*	conocen

cubrir *to cover*

PARTICIPIO PASADO	cubierto

dar *to give*

PRESENTE	doy	das	da	damos	*dais*	dan
PRETÉRITO	di	diste	dio	dimos	*disteis*	dieron
SUBJUNTIVO [PRESENTE]	dé	des	dé	demos	*deis*	den

IMPERATIVO FORMAL	dé (Ud.)	den (Uds.)
	no dé (Ud.)	no den (Uds.)

decir *to say*

PRESENTE	digo	dices	dice	decimos	*decís*	dicen
PRETÉRITO	dije	dijiste	dijo	dijimos	*dijisteis*	dijeron
FUTURO	diré	dirás	dirá	diremos	*diréis*	dirán
CONDICIONAL	diría	dirías	diría	diríamos	*diríais*	dirían

(continued on H36)

[1]Note that only irregular forms are shown.

Verb Charts

IRREGULAR VERBS

decir *to say* *(continued from H35)*

PARTICIPIO PRESENTE	diciendo
PARTICIPIO PASADO	dicho
IMPERATIVO FAMILIAR	di (tú)

escribir *to write*

PARTICIPIO PASADO	escrito

estar *to be*

PRESENTE	estoy estás está estamos *estáis* están
PRETÉRITO	estuve estuviste estuvo estuvimos *estuvisteis* estuvieron
SUBJUNTIVO [PRESENTE]	esté estés esté estemos *estéis* estén
IMPERATIVO FORMAL	esté (Ud.) estén (Uds.) no esté (Ud.) no estén (Uds.)

hacer *to do, to make*

PRESENTE	hago haces hace hacemos *hacéis* hacen
PRETÉRITO	hice hiciste hizo hicimos *hicisteis* hicieron
FUTURO	haré harás hará haremos *haréis* harán
CONDICIONAL	haría harías haría haríamos *haríais* harían
PARTICIPIO PASADO	hecho
IMPERATIVO FAMILIAR	haz (tú)

Verb Charts

IRREGULAR VERBS		
incluir *to include*		
PARTICIPIO PRESENTE	incluyendo	
ir *to go*		
PRESENTE	voy vas va vamos *vais* van	
PRETÉRITO	fui fuiste fue fuimos *fuisteis* fueron	
IMPERFECTO	iba ibas iba íbamos *ibais* iban	
SUBJUNTIVO [PRESENTE]	vaya vayas vaya vayamos *vayáis* vayan	
PARTICIPIO PRESENTE	yendo	
PARTICIPIO PASADO	ido	
IMPERATIVO FORMAL	vaya (Ud.) vayan (Uds.) no vaya (Ud.) no vayan (Uds.)	
IMPERATIVO FAMILIAR	ve (tú) no vayas (tú)	
leer *to read*		
PARTICIPIO PRESENTE	leyendo	
morir *to die*		
PARTICIPIO PRESENTE	muriendo	

Verb Charts

IRREGULAR VERBS	
oír *to hear*	
PRESENTE	oigo oyes oye oímos *oís* oyen
PRETÉRITO	oí oíste oyó oímos *oísteis* oyeron
PARTICIPIO PRESENTE	oyendo

poder *to be able*	
PRESENTE	puedo puedes puede podemos *podéis* pueden
PRETÉRITO	pude pudiste pudo pudimos *pudisteis* pudieron
FUTURO	podré podrás podrá podremos *podréis* podrán
CONDICIONAL	podría podrías podría podríamos *podríais* podrían
PARTICIPIO PRESENTE	pudiendo

poner *to put*	
PRESENTE	pongo pones pone ponemos *ponéis* ponen
PRETÉRITO	puse pusiste puso pusimos *pusisteis* pusieron
FUTURO	pondré pondrás pondrá pondremos *pondréis* pondrán
CONDICIONAL	pondría pondrías pondría pondríamos *pondríais* pondrían
PARTICIPIO PASADO	puesto
IMPERATIVO FAMILIAR	pon (tú)

Verb Charts

IRREGULAR VERBS	
querer *to want, to wish*	
PRESENTE	quiero quieres quiere queremos *queréis* quieren
PRETÉRITO	quise quisiste quiso quisimos *quisisteis* quisieron
FUTURO	querré querrás querrá querremos *querréis* querrán
CONDICIONAL	querría querrías querría querríamos *querríais* querrían
romper *to break*	
PARTICIPIO PASADO	roto
saber *to know*	
PRESENTE	sé sabes sabe sabemos *sabéis* saben
PRETÉRITO	supe supiste supo supimos *supisteis* supieron
FUTURO	sabré sabrás sabrá sabremos *sabréis* sabrán
CONDICIONAL	sabría sabrías sabría sabríamos *sabríais* sabrían
SUBJUNTIVO [PRESENTE]	sepa sepas sepa sepamos *sepáis* sepan
IMPERATIVO FORMAL	sepa (Ud.) sepan (Uds.) no sepa (Ud.) no sepan (Uds.)
salir *to leave*	
PRESENTE	salgo sales sale salimos *salís* salen
FUTURO	saldré saldrás saldrá saldremos *saldréis* saldrán
CONDICIONAL	saldría saldrías saldría saldríamos *saldríais* saldrían
IMPERATIVO FAMILIAR	sal (tú)

Verb Charts

IRREGULAR VERBS	
ser *to be*	
PRESENTE	soy eres es somos *sois* son
PRETÉRITO	fui fuiste fue fuimos *fuisteis* fueron
IMPERFECTO	era eras era éramos *erais* eran
SUBJUNTIVO [PRESENTE]	sea seas sea seamos *seáis* sean
IMPERATIVO FORMAL	sea (Ud.) sean (Uds.) no sea (Ud.) no sean (Uds.)
IMPERATIVO FAMILIAR	sé (tú) no seas (tú)
tener *to have*	
PRESENTE	tengo tienes tiene tenemos *tenéis* tienen
PRETÉRITO	tuve tuviste tuvo tuvimos *tuvisteis* tuvieron
FUTURO	tendré tendrás tendrá tendremos *tendréis* tendrán
CONDICIONAL	tendría tendrías tendría tendríamos *tendríais* tendrían
IMPERATIVO FAMILIAR	ten (tú)
traer *to bring*	
PRESENTE	traigo traes trae traemos *traéis* traen
PRETÉRITO	traje trajiste trajo trajimos *trajisteis* trajeron
PARTICIPIO PRESENTE	trayendo

IRREGULAR VERBS

venir *to come*

PRESENTE	vengo vienes viene venimos *venís* vienen
PRETÉRITO	vine viniste vino vinimos *vinisteis* vinieron
FUTURO	vendré vendrás vendrá vendremos *vendréis* vendrán
CONDICIONAL	vendría vendrías vendría vendríamos *vendríais* vendrían
PARTICIPIO PRESENTE	viniendo
IMPERATIVO FAMILIAR	ven (tú)

ver *to see*

PRESENTE	veo ves ve vemos *veis* ven
PRETÉRITO	vi viste vio vimos *visteis* vieron
IMPERFECTO	veía veías veía veíamos *veíais* veían
PARTICIPIO PASADO	visto

volver *to return*

PARTICIPIO PASADO	vuelto

VERBS WITH A SPELLING CHANGE IN THE PRETERITE
(-car, -gar, -zar)

INFINITIVO	**practicar**[1] *to practice*	**llegar**[2] *to arrive*	**comenzar**[3] *to begin*
PRETÉRITO	practiqué	llegué	comencé
	practicaste	llegaste	comenzaste
	practicó	llegó	comenzó
	practicamos	llegamos	comenzamos
	practicasteis	*llegasteis*	*comenzasteis*
	practicaron	llegaron	comenzaron

[1] **Buscar** and **sacar** are similar.
[2] **Jugar** and **pagar** are similar.
[3] **Empezar** and **almorzar** are similar.

Spanish-English Dictionary

The Spanish-English Dictionary contains all productive and receptive vocabulary from Levels 1 and 2. The numbers following each productive entry indicate the chapter and vocabulary section in which the word is introduced. For example, **3.2** in dark print means that the word was taught in this textbook **Capítulo 3, Palabras 2.** A light print number means that the word was introduced in *¡Buen viaje!*, Level 1. BV refers to the introductory *Bienvenidos* lessons in Level 1. If there is no number following an entry, this means that the word or expression is there for receptive purposes only.

A

a at; to
> **a bordo de** aboard, on board, **7.1**
> **a eso de** at about (time), 4.1
> **a fines de** at the end of
> **a la española** Spanish style
> **a lo menos**
> **a menudo** often, **3.2**
> **a pie** on foot, 4.1
> **a plazos** in installments
> **a propósito** by the way
> **a solas** alone
> **a tiempo** on time, 11.1
> **a veces** sometimes, 7.1
> **a ver** let's see

abandonar el cuarto to check out, **6.1**
abarrotes: la tienda de abarrotes grocery store, **4.2**
la **abeja** bee, **8.1**
el/la **abogado(a)** lawyer, **14.1**
abordar to get on, board
el **abrigo** overcoat, **4.1**
abril April, BV
abrir to open, 8.2
abrocharse to fasten, **7.1**
> **abrocharse el cinturón de seguridad** to fasten one's seatbelt, **7.1**

la **abuela** grandmother, 6.1
el **abuelo** grandfather, 6.1
los **abuelos** grandparents, 6.1
abundante plentiful

aburrido(a) boring, 2.1
aburrir to bore
el **abuso** abuse
acabar de to have just (done something), **8.1**
la **academia** academy, school
acariciar to caress
el **acceso** access
el **accidente** accident, **8.1**
la **acción** action
el **aceite** oil, 14.2; **2.2**
aceptar to accept
la **acera** sidewalk, **9.1**
acerca de about, concerning
acercarse(a) to approach
acertar (ie) to guess right
acomodar to accommodate
el **acompañamiento** accompaniment
acompañar to accompany
aconsejar to advise
acostarse (ue) to go to bed, 12.1
el **acrílico** acrylic
la **actividad** activity
activo(a) active
el **actor** actor, 10.2
la **actriz** actress, 10.2
la **actuación** behavior
actualmente at the present time
la **acuarela** watercolor
acuático(a): el esquí acuático water-skiing, 9.1
acuerdo: de acuerdo OK, all right; in agreement
acuñar to coin, mint
adaptar to adapt
adecuado(a) adequate

adelantar to overtake, pass (car), **11.2**
adelante ahead
además moreover; besides
además de in addition to
la **adicción** addiction
adiós good-bye, BV
adivinar to guess
admirar to admire
admitir to admit, 8.2
la **adolescencia** adolescence
el/la **adolescente** adolescent, teenager
¿adónde? where?, 1.1
la **adoración** adoration
adorar to adore
adornar to adorn
el **adorno** ornament
la **aduana** customs, 11.2
advertir to warn
aérea: la línea aérea airline
aeróbico(a) aerobic
el **aerodeslizador** hydrofoil
el **aeropuerto** airport, 11.1
afeitarse to shave, 12.1
> **la crema de afeitar** shaving cream, 12.1

aficionado(a) fond of, 10.1
el/la **aficionado(a)** fan (sports)
afortunado(a) fortunate
africano(a) African
afroamericano(a) African American
las **afueras** outskirts, **9.1**
la **agencia** agency
> **la agencia de empleos** employment agency

el/la **agente** agent, 11.1

    el/la agente de aduana customs agent, 11.2

    el/la agente de policía police officer

agosto August, BV

agradable pleasant

agregar to add, **10.2**

agrícola agricultural

el/la **agricultor(a)** farmer, **9.2**

el **agua** (f.) water, 9.1

    el agua corriente running water

    el agua mineral mineral water, 12.2

    esquiar en el agua to water-ski, 9.1

el **aguacate** avocado, **10.2**

el **águila** (f.) eagle

el **agujero** hole

ahora now, 4.2

ahorrar to save

el **aire** air, **11.1**

    al aire libre outdoor (adj.)

el **aire acondicionado** air conditioning, 6.2

el **ajedrez** chess, **5.1**

el **ají** chili pepper

el **ajo** garlic, 14.2; **2.2**

el **ajuar de novia** trousseau

ajustar to adjust

al to the

    al aire libre outdoor (adj.)

    al bordo de alongside, on the banks of (river)

    al contrario on the contrary

    al lado de beside, **5.2**

    al máximo at the most

    al principio at the beginning

alarmarse to be alarmed

el/la **albañil** bricklayer, **14.1**

la **alberca** swimming pool, 9.1

el **albergue para jóvenes (juvenil)** youth hostel, 12.2

el **álbum** album

la **alcachofa** artichoke, 14.2; **2.2**

el **alcalde** mayor, **14.1**

la **alcaldesa** female mayor

la **alcaldía** city hall, **14.1**

alcanzar to reach, attain

el **alcohol** alcohol

el **alcoholismo** alcoholism

alegrarse de to be glad about, **13.1**

alegre happy

la **alegría** happiness

el **alemán** German (language), 2.2

la **alergia** allergy, 8.2

el **álgebra** algebra, 2.2

algo something, 5.2

    ¿Algo más? Anything else?, 5.2

el **algodón** cotton, **12.1**

alguien someone

algunos(as) some, 4.1

el **alimento** food, 14.2; **2.2**

allá there

allí there

almacenar to store

la **almeja** clam, 14.2; **2.2**

la **almohada** pillow, **6.2**

almorzar (ue) to eat lunch

el **almuerzo** lunch, 5.2

    tomar el almuerzo to have, eat lunch

alojarse to stay, lodge

la **alpargata** sandal

alquilar to rent, **5.2**

alrededor de around, 6.2

los **alrededores** outskirts

alternar to alternate

el **altiplano** high plateau, **7.2**

la **altitud** altitude, **7.2**

altivo arrogant, haughty

alto(a) tall, 1.1; high, 4.2

    en voz alta aloud

    la nota alta high grade, 4.2

la **altura** height; altitude, **7.2**

el/la **alumno(a)** student, 1.1

amar to love

amarillo(a) yellow, 3.2

amazónico(a) Amazonian

ambicioso(a) hardworking, 1.1

el **ambiente** environment; atmosphere

la **ambulancia** ambulance, **8.1**

ambulante itinerant

la **América Central** Central America

la **América del Norte** North America

la **América del Sur** South America

americano(a) American, 1.1

el/la **amigo(a)** friend, 1.1

el **amor** love

el **análisis** analysis

analítico(a) analytical

analizar to analyze

anaranjado(a) orange, 3.2

el/la **anarquista** anarchist

ancho(a) wide, **4.1**

anciano(a) old, 6.1

el/la **anciano(a)** old person

andaluz(a) Andalusian

andante: el caballero andante knight errant

el **andén** railway platform, 13.1; **1.1**

andino(a) Andean

la **anécdota** anecdote

angosto(a) narrow, **9.1**

el **anillo** ring, **4.1**

el **animal** animal

    el animal doméstico farm animal, **9.2**

el **aniversario** anniversary

anoche last night, 9.2

el **anorak** parka, 9.2

la **Antártida** Antarctic

anteayer the day before yesterday

antenupcial prenuptial

los **anteojos de sol** sunglasses, 9.1

antes de before, 5.1

el **antibiótico** antibiotic, 8.2

anticipación: de anticipación ahead of time

anticuado(a) antiquated

la **antigüedad** antiquity

antiguo(a) old, ancient, **5.1**

anunciar to announce

el **anuncio** announcement; **7.1**; advertisement, **14.2**

   dar anuncios to make announcements, **7.1**

añadir to add, **10.2**

el **año** year, BV

   cumplir... años to be . . . years old

   el año pasado last year, 9.2

   este año this year, 9.2

   tener... años to be . . . years old, 6.1

el **Año Nuevo** New Year, **13.2**

   ¡Próspero Año Nuevo! Happy New Year!, **13.2**

apagar to turn off, **3.1**

el **aparato** appliance, device, **3.2**

el **aparcamiento** parking lot

aparcar to park, **11.2**

aparecer to appear

la **apariencia** appearance

el **apartamento** apartment, 6.2

   la casa de apartamentos apartment house, 6.2

apasionado(a) passionate

el **apellido** last name

la **apendicitis** appendicitis

la **apertura** opening

   la apertura de clases beginning of the school year

aplaudir to applaud, **10.2**

el **aplauso** applause, 10.2

   dar aplausos to applaud, **10.2**

   recibir aplausos to receive applause, 10.2

aplicar to apply

el **apóstol** apostle

aprender to learn, 5.1

apropiado(a) appropriate

la **aptitud** aptitude

el **apunte: tomar apuntes** to take notes, 4.2

aquel, aquella that

   en aquel entonces at that time

aquí here

   Aquí tiene (tienes, tienen)... Here is (are) . . .

   por aquí right this way

el/la **árabe** Arab

   aragonés(esa) from Aragon (Spain)

el **árbol** tree

   el árbol de Navidad Christmas tree, **13.2**

el **arco** arc

el **área** (f.) area

la **arena** sand, 9.1

el **arete** earring, **4.1**

   argentino(a) Argentinian, 2.1

el **argumento** plot

   árido(a) arid

la **aritmética** arithmetic, 2.2

el **arma** (f.) weapon

el **armario** closet, **6.2**

la **arqueología** archeology

   arqueológico(a) archaeological

el/la **arqueólogo(a)** archaeologist

el/la **arquitecto(a)** architect, **14.1**

   arrancar to pull out

   arrogante arrogant

el **arroyo** stream, brook

el **arroz** rice, 5.2

   arrugar to wrinkle

el **arsenal** arsenal

el **arte** (f.) art, 2.2

   las bellas artes fine arts

el **artefacto** artifact

el/la **artista** artist, 10.2

   artístico(a) artistic

   asado(a) roasted

   asar to roast, **10.1**

la **ascendencia** background

   de ascendencia mexicana (peruana, etc.) of Mexican (Peruvian, etc.) ancestry

   ascender to rise

el **ascensor** elevator, 6.2

   asegurar to assure

el **aseo** restroom, **7.1**

   así so; thus

el **asiento** seat, 11.1

   el número del asiento seat number, 11.1

la **asignatura** subject, discipline, 2.2

el/la **asistente de vuelo** flight attendant, 11.2

   asistir to attend

el **asno** donkey

el **aspa** arm (of a windmill)

el **aspecto** aspect

el/la **aspirante** candidate, **14.2**

la **aspirina** aspirin, 8.2

   astuto(a) astute

   asustarse to be frightened

   atacar to attack

el **ataque** attack

la **atención: prestar atención** to pay attention, 4.2

   atender (ie) to assist, wait on (customer), **4.1**

   atento(a) polite, courteous

el **aterrizaje** landing, **7.2**

   aterrizar to land, 11.2

el/la **atleta** athlete

   atlético(a) athletic

la **atmósfera** atmosphere

las **atracciones** amusement park rides, 5.2

   el parque de atracciones amusement park, **5.2**

   atractivo(a) attractive

   atrapar to catch, **7.2**

   atrás behind, in the rear

   atravesar (ie) to cross

el **atún** tuna, 5.2

los **audífonos** earphones, **7.1**

   aumentar to increase

el **aumento** increase

   aun even

   aún yet

   aunque although

el **auricular** telephone receiver, **3.2**; headphone, **7.1**

   austral former Argentine unit of currency

   auténtico(a) authentic

el **autobús** bus, 10.1

> **perder el autobús (la guagua, el camión)** to miss the bus, 10.1

automáticamente automatically, **7.1**

el **automóvil** automobile

la **autopista** highway, **11.2**

el/la **autor(a)** author, 10.2

autorizado(a) authorized

el **autorretrato** self-portrait

la **autovía** highway, **11.2**

los **auxilios: los primeros auxilios** first aid

el **avance** advance

el **ave** *(f.)* bird

la **avenida** avenue, 9.1

la **aventura** adventure

la **avería** breakdown

averiado(a) broken down

la **aviación** aviation

el **avión** airplane, 11.1

el **avión de reacción** jet, **7.2**

la **avioneta** small airplane, **7.2**

ayer yesterday, 9.2

> **ayer por la mañana** yesterday morning, 9.2

> **ayer por la tarde** yesterday afternoon, 9.2

la **ayuda** assistance, help

ayudar to help, 13.1; **1.1**

el **azafrán** saffron

el **azúcar** sugar, **10.1**

azul blue, 3.2

azul oscuro dark blue

B

el **bache** pothole

el **bachillerato** bachelor's degree

la **bacteria** bacteria

la **bahía** bay

bailar to dance, 4.2

el **baile** dance

bajar to lower; to go down, 9.2; to get off, 13.2; **1.2**

bajar(se) del tren to get off the train, 13.2; **1.2**

bajar las maletas to take the luggage down, **6.1**

bajo: bajo cero below zero, 9.2

bajo(a) short, 1.1; low, 4.2

> **la planta baja** ground floor, 6.2

> **la nota baja** low grade, 4.2

el **balneario** beach resort, 9.1

el **balón** ball, 7.1

> **tirar el balón** to throw (kick) the ball, 7.2

el **baloncesto** basketball, 7.2

la **banana** banana, 10.2

la **banca** banking

bancario(a) banking

el **banco** bank, **12.2**

la **banda** music band

la **banda elástica** elastic band

la **bandeja** tray, **7.1**

el **bando** team

el **bañador** bathing suit 9.1

> **bañarse** to take a bath, 12.1

la **bañera** bathtub, **6.2**

el **baño** bathroom, 6.2; bath

> **el cuarto de baño** bathroom, 6.2

> **el traje de baño** bathing suit, 9.1

barato(a) cheap, inexpensive, 3.2

la **barba** beard

el/la **barbero(a)** barber, **12.1**

la **barra** bar

> **la barra de jabón** bar of soap, 12.2

el **barrio** neighborhood, 9.1

basado(a) based (on)

basar to base

basarse to be based

la **báscula** scale, 11.1

la **base** base, 7.2; basis

básico(a) basic

el **básquetbol** basketball, 7.2

> **la cancha de básquetbol** basketball court, 7.2

bastante enough, rather, quite, 1.1

el **bastón** ski pole, 9.2

la **batalla** battle

el **bate** bat, 7.2

el/la **bateador(a)** batter, 7.2

batear to hit (baseball), 7.2

la **batería** battery

el **batú** Taíno Indian game

el **baúl** trunk, **11.1**

el **bautizo** baptism

el/la **bebé** baby

> **beber** to drink, 5.1

la **bebida** beverage, drink, **7.1**

la **beca** scholarship

el **béisbol** baseball, 7.2

> **el campo de béisbol** baseball field, 7.2

> **el juego de béisbol** baseball game, 7.2

> **el/la jugador(a) de béisbol** baseball player, 7.2

el/la **beisbolista** baseball player

la **belleza** beauty

> **bello(a)** beautiful, pretty, 1.1

> **las bellas artes** fine arts

la **bendición** blessing

el **beneficio** benefit

la **berenjena** eggplant, 14.2; **2.2**

bíblico(a) biblical

la **bicicleta** bicycle

> **ir en bicicleta** to go by bike, 12.2

bien fine, well, BV

> **muy bien** very well, BV

los **bienes y servicios** goods and services

la **bienvenida: dar la bienvenida** to welcome, 11.2

el **bife** beef

el **biftec** steak, 14.2; **2.2**

bilingüe bilingual

el **billete** ticket, 11.1; bill (currency), **12.2**

> **el billete de ida y vuelta** round-trip ticket, 13.1; **1.1**

> **el billete sencillo** one way ticket, 13.1; **1.1**

la **biografía** biography

la **biología** biology, 2.2

biológico(a) biological

el/la **biólogo(a)** biologist

el **bizcocho** cake, **13.1**

blanco(a) white, 3.2

el **blanqueador** bleach

el **bloc** notebook, writing pad, 3.1

bloquear to stop, block, 7.1

el **blue jean** jeans, 3.2

la **blusa** blouse, 3.2

la **boca** mouth, 8.2

boca abajo face down, **3.1**

boca arriba face up, **3.1**

la **boca del metro** subway entrance, **9.1**

la **bocacalle** intersection, **11.2**

el **bocadillo** sandwich, 5.1

la **bocina** horn, **11.1**

tocar la bocina to honk the horn

la **boda** wedding, **13.1**

la **bola** ball

la **boletería** ticket window, 9.2

el **boleto** ticket, 9.2

el **bolígrafo** ballpoint pen, 3.1

la **bolsa** bag, 5.2

la **bolsa de plástico** plastic bag, **4.2**

el **bolsillo** pocket, **4.1**

bonito(a) pretty, 1.1

el **borde** border, side, shoulder (road)

bordear to border

la **bota** boot, 9.2

el **bote** can, 5.2; boat, **5.2**

la **botella: la botella de agua mineral** bottle of mineral water, 12.2

el **botón** button (on a machine), **3.1**; (on clothing), **4.1**

el **botones** bellhop, **6.1**

el **brazo** arm, 7.1; branch (of candelabra, menorah, etc.), **13.2**

breve brief

brillante bright

brillar to shine, 9.1

el **bronce** bronze, 10.2

bronceado(a) tan

bronceador(a): la loción bronceadora suntan lotion, 9.1

bucear to dive; to swim underwater, 9.1

el **buceo** diving, underwater swimming, 9.1

buen good

estar de buen humor to be in a good mood, 8.1

Hace buen tiempo. The weather is nice., 9.1

la **buenaventura** fortune

bueno(a) good, 1.2

Buenas noches. Good evening., BV

Buenas tardes. Good afternoon., BV

Buenos días. Hello, Good morning., BV

sacar una nota buena to get a good grade, 4.2

tener buena pinta to look good (food), 4.2

la **bufanda** scarf, **4.1**

el **bufete del abogado** lawyer's office, **14.1**

el **bulevar** boulevard, **9.1**

el **bus** bus, 4.1

el bus escolar school bus, 4.1

busca: en busca de in search of

buscar to look for, 3.1

la **butaca** seat (theater), 10.1

el **buzón** mailbox, **12.2**

C

el **caballero** knight; gentleman, man, **4.1**

el caballero andante knight errant

la tienda de ropa para caballeros men's clothing shop, **4.1**

el **caballete** easel

el **caballito** carousel horse, **5.2**

el **caballo** horse

pasear a caballo to go horsebook riding

el **cabello** hair, **12.1**

caber to fit, **7.1**

la **cabeza** head, 7.1

la **cabina** cabin, **7.1**

la cabina de mando (vuelo) cockpit, **7.1**

el **cacahuete (cacahuate)** peanut

la **cacerola** saucepan, **10.2**

cada each, every, 1.2

la **cadena** chain (necklace), **4.1**

la cadena de oro gold chain, **4.1**

caerse to fall, drop, **7.1**

el **café** coffee, BV; café, 5.1

el café al aire libre outdoor café

el café con leche coffee with milk, 5.1

el café solo black coffee, 5.1

la **cafetería** cafeteria

la **caja** cash register, 3.1; box, **4.2**

el/la **cajero(a)** teller, **12.2**; cashier, **14.1**

el **cajero automático** automatic teller

los **calamares** squid, **10.2**

los **calcetines** socks, 3.2

la **calculadora** calculator, 3.1

calcular to calculate

el **cálculo** calculus, 2.2

calentarse (ie) to heat

la **calidad** quality

la **calificación** qualification

la **calle** street, 6.2

la calle de sentido único one-way street, **11.2**

la calle peatonal pedestrian street

la **callecita** narrow street, alley, **9.1**

el **calor: Hace calor.** It's hot., 9.1

la **caloría** calorie

calzar to take, wear (shoe size), 3.2

la **cama** bed, 8.1

guardar cama to stay in bed, 8.1

hacer la cama to make the bed, 6.2

la **camarera** maid, 6.2

el/la **camarero(a)** waiter, waitress, 5.1

los **camarones** shrimp, 14.2; **2.2**

cambiar to change; exchange, **12.2**

cambiar de tren to change trains (transfer), 13.2; **1.2**

cambiar las toallas to change the towels, **6.2**

el **cambio** change, exchange, **12.2**

la casa de cambio foreign exchange office, **12.2**

el tipo (la tasa) de cambio exchange rate, **12.2**

el/la **cambista** money changer, **12.2**

el **camello** camel, **13.2**

la **camilla** stretcher, 8.1

caminar to walk, 5.1

caminar por la senda to walk along the path, **5.2**

la **caminata: dar una caminata** to take a hike, 12.2

el **camino** trail, path

el **camión** bus (Mexico), 10.1, truck

la **camisa** shirt, 3.2

la camisa de mangas cortas short-sleeved shirt, **4.1**

la camisa de mangas largas long-sleeved shirt, **4.1**

la **camiseta** T-shirt, undershirt, 3.2

la **campaña** campaign

el/la **campeón(ona)** champion, 5.1

el **campeonato** championship

el/la **campesino(a)** farmer, peasant, **9.2**

el **campo** country; field, **9.2**

el campo de béisbol baseball field, 7.2

el campo de fútbol soccer field, 7.1

la casa de campo country home

canadiense Canadian

el **canal** channel (TV)

la **canasta** basket, 7.2

la **cancha** court, 7.2

la cancha cubierta enclosed court, 9.1

la cancha de básquetbol basketball court, 7.2

la cancha de tenis tennis court, 9.1

la **canción** song

el/la **candidato(a)** candidate, **14.2**

cansado(a) tired, 8.1

cantar to sing, 4.2

el **cante jondo** traditional flamenco singing

la **cantidad** amount

el **canto** singing

el **cañón** canyon

el **capacho** cloth shopping bag

la **capital** capital

el/la **capitán** captain

el **capítulo** chapter

el **capó** hood (automobile), **11.1**

la **cara** face, 12.1

el **carácter** character

la **característica** characteristic

el **carbohidrato** carbohydrate

cardinal: los puntos cardinales cardinal points

la **cardiología** cardiology

el/la **cardiólogo(a)** cardiologist

el **cardo** thistle

los **cargos** charges

el **Caribe** Caribbean

el mar Caribe Caribbean Sea

el/la **caricaturista** caricaturist

la **carne** meat, 5.2

la carne de res beef, 14.2; **2.2**

la **carnicería** butcher shop, meat market, 4.2

caro(a) expensive, 3.2

la **carpeta** folder, 3.1

el/la **carpintero(a)** carpenter, 14.1

la **carrera** race, career

la **carretera** highway, 11.2

el **carril** lane (of highway), **11.2**

el **carrito** cart (shopping), **4.2**; (airplane), **7.1**

empujar el carrito to push the cart, **4.2**

el **carro** car, 4.1

el carro deportivo sports car, **11.1**

en carro by car, 4.1

la **carta** letter, **12.2**

la carta de recomendación letter of recommendation

la **casa** home, house, 6.2

en casa at home

la casa de apartamentos (departamentos) apartment house, 6.2

la casa de campo country home, **9.2**

la casa privada (particular) private house, 6.2

la **casa de cambio** foreign exchange office, **12.2**

casado(a): estar casado(a) to be married

casarse to get married, **13.1**

casi almost, practically

el **caso** case, **7.1**

castellano(a) Castillian

el **castigo** punishment

el **castillo** castle

el **catarro** cold (illness), 8.1

tener catarro to have a cold, 8.1

el/la **cátcher** catcher, 7.2

la **catedral** cathedral

la **categoría** category

católico(a) Catholic

catorce fourteen, BV

la **causa** cause

causar to cause

la **cazuela** pot, 10.1

el **CD** compact disc, 4.2

Spanish-English Dictionary

el **CD-ROM** CD-ROM, **3.1**

la **cebolla** onion, **10.1**

la **celebración** celebration

celebrar to celebrate, **13.1**

célebre famous

la **célula** cell

celular: el teléfono celular
cell phone, **3.2**

la **cena** dinner, 5.2

cenar to have dinner

el **centavo** penny

central central

el **centro** downtown, **5.1**; center

cepillarse to brush one's
hair, 12.1

cepillarse los dientes to
brush one's teeth, 12.1

el **cepillo** brush, 12.2

el cepillo de dientes
toothbrush, 12.2

cerca de near, 6.2

cercano(a) nearby

el **cerdo** pig (pork), 14.2; **2.2**

el **cereal** cereal, 5.2; grain, **9.2**

la **ceremonia** ceremony, 13

cero zero, BV

cerrar (ie) to close, **8.2**

cerrar la herida to close
the wound, **8.2**

la **cesta** basket (jai alai)

el **cesto** basket, 7.2

la **chabola** shack

el **chaleco** vest

el **chaleco salvavidas** life
jacket, **7.1**

el **chalet** chalet

el **champú** shampoo, 12.2

¡Chao! Good-bye!, BV

la **chaqueta** jacket, 3.2

charlar to chat

la **chaucha** string bean

el **cheque de viajero**
traveler's check, **12.2**

la **chequera** checkbook

el/la **chico(a)** boy (girl)

chileno(a) Chilean

la **chimenea** chimney

la **china** orange (fruit)

el **chisme** piece of gossip

¡chist! shh!

el **choclo** corn

el **chocolate: de chocolate**
chocolate (adj.), 5.1

el **chófer** chauffeur

el **chorizo** pork and garlic
sausage, **10.1**

la **chuleta** chop, **10.1**

la chuleta de cerdo pork
chop, **10.1**

el **churro** (type of) doughnut

el **ciclismo** cycling

el **cielo** sky, 9.1

la **ciencia-ficción** science
fiction

las **ciencias** science, 2.2

las ciencias naturales
natural sciences

las ciencias políticas
political science

las ciencias sociales
social sciences, 2.2

el/la **científico(a)** scientist

científico(a) scientific

cien(to) one hundred, 3.2

cierto: Es cierto que... It is
certain that . . .

cierto(a) certain

cinco five, BV

cincuenta fifty, 2.2

el **cine** movie theater,
10.1

la **cinta** ribbon

el **cinturón** belt, **4.1**

el cinturón de seguridad
seat belt, **7.1**

circular to circulate, travel,
drive

el **círculo** circle

el/la **cirujano(a)** surgeon, **8.2**

**el/la cirujano(a)
ortopédico(a)** orthopedic
surgeon, **8.2**

cítrico(a) citric

la **ciudad** city, 9.1

la **claridad** clarity

el **clarinete** clarinet

claro(a) clear

¡Claro! Certainly!, Of
course!

¡Claro que no! Of course
not!

la **clase** class (school), 2.1; class
(ticket), 13.1; **1.1**; kind, type

la apertura de clases
beginning of the school
year

la sala de clase
classroom, 4.1

el salón de clase
classroom, 4.1

primera clase first class,
13.1; **1.1**

segunda clase second
class, 13.1; **1.1**

clásico(a) classic

clasificar to classify

la **clave de área** area code, **3.2**

el **claxon** horn, **11.1**

el **clic** click

el/la **cliente** customer, 5.1; hotel
guest, **6.1**

el **clima** climate

climático(a) climatic

la **clínica** clinic

el **club** club, 4.2

el Club de español
Spanish Club, 4.2

cobrar to charge

cobrar un cheque to cash
a check, **12.2**

la **cocción** cooking

el **coche** car, 4.1; train car,
13.2; **1.2**

el coche deportivo sports
car, **11.1**

en coche by car, 4.1

el **coche-cafetería** cafeteria
(dining) car, 13.2; **1.2**

el **coche-cama** sleeping car,
13.2; **1.2**

el **coche-comedor** dining car,
13.2; **1.2**

el **coche deportivo** sports
car, **11.1**

el **cocido** stew

la **cocina** kitchen, 6.2

cocinar to cook, **10.1**

el/la **cocinero(a)** cook, 14.1; **2.1**

el **coco** coconut, **10.2**

el **cóctel** cocktail party

el **codo** elbow, **8.1**

la **coincidencia** coincidence

cojo(a) lame

el **cola** soda, soft drink

la **cola** line (queue), 10.1

　hacer cola to line up, to stand in line, 10.1

la **colección** collection

coleccionar to collect, **5.1**

el/la **coleccionista** collector, **5.1**

la **colecta: hacer una colecta** to take up a collection

el **colector** collector

el **colegio** school, 1.1

el **colesterol** cholesterol

el **colgador** clothes hanger, **6.2**

colgar (ue) to hang, hang up

la **coliflor** cauliflower, **10.1**

el **colmado** grocery store, **4.2**

la **colocación** placement

colocar to put, place

colombiano(a) Colombian, 1.1

la **colonia** suburb, colony

el **color** color, 3.2

　de color colored

　de color marrón brown, 3.2

　¿De qué color es? What color is it?, 3.2

el/la **comandante** pilot, captain, 11.2

la **comedia** comedy

el **comedor** dining room, 6.2

comenzar (ie) to begin

comer to eat, 5.1

comercial: la zona comercial business district, **9.1**

el/la **comerciante** businessman (woman), **14.1**

el **comercio** business

el **comestible** food, 14.2; **2.2**

cómico(a) funny, 1.1

la **comida** food, meal, 5.2

la **comisión** commission

el **comité** committee

como like; as; since, 1.2

　¿cómo? how?, what?, 1.1

　¿Cómo está…? How is…?, 8.1

　¡Cómo no! Of course!

la **comodidad** comfort

compacto(a): el disco compacto compact disk, CD, 4.2

el/la **compañero(a)** friend, 1.2

la **compañía** company

la **comparación** comparison

comparar to compare

el **compartimiento** compartment, 13.2; **1.2**

　el compartimiento sobre la cabeza overhead compartment, **7.1**

　el compartimiento superior overhead compartment, **7.1**

la **competencia** competition

la **competición** competition, contest

competir (i, i) to compete

completar to complete

completo(a) full (train), 13.2; **1.2**

　a tiempo completo full time (adj.), **14.2**

componer to compose

comportarse to behave

la **composición** composition

la **compra** buying, **4.1**

comprar to buy, 3.1

las **compras** shopping; purchases, **4.2**

　hacer las compras to go shopping, **4.2**

　ir de compras to go shopping, to shop, 5.2

comprender to understand, 5.1

comprometerse to get engaged

el **compromiso** engagement

la **computadora** computer, **3.1**

común common

la **comunicación** communication

comunicarse to communicate with each other, **3.1**

la **comunidad** community

con with

　con cuidado carefully, cautiously, **11.1**

con frecuencia often, 3.2

con mucha plata rich

¿con quién? with whom?

con retraso with a delay, 13.2; **1.2**

con una demora with a delay, late, 11.1

el **concierto** concert

conciliar to reconcile

el/la **conde(sa)** count(ess)

la **condición** condition

el **condimento** seasoning

el **condominio** condominium, **9.1**

conducir to drive, 11.1

el/la **conductor(a)** driver, 11.1

conectar to connect

la **conexión** connection

la **conferencia** lecture

confirmar to confirm

la **confitería** café, tearoom

Conforme. Agreed., Fine., 14.2; **2.2**

confrontar to confront

congelado(a): los productos congelados frozen food, 5.2

el **congelador** freezer, **10.1**

el **conjunto** set, collection

conocer to know, to be familiar with, 11.1

el/la **conocido(a)** acquaintance

el **conocimiento** knowledge

la **conquista** conquest

el **conquistador** conquerer

conquistar to conquer

el/la **consejero(a) de orientación** guidance counselor

el **consejo** advice

consentir (ie, i) to allow, tolerate

conservar to save

considerar to consider

consiguiente: por consiguiente consequently

consistir (en) to consist of

construir to construct

la **consulta del médico** doctor's office, 8.2

consultar to consult, 13.1; **1.1**

el **consultorio** medical office, 8.2

el/la **consumidor(a)** consumer

consumir to consume

el **consumo** consumption

la **contabilidad** accounting

el/la **contable** accountant, **14.1**

el **contacto** touch

contagioso(a) contagious

la **contaminación** pollution

contaminado(a) polluted

contaminar to pollute

contemporáneo(a) contemporary

contener (ie) to contain

contento(a) happy, 8.1

la **contestación** answer, response

el **contestador automático** answering machine, **3.2**

contestar to answer, **3.2**

el **continente** continent

continuar to continue, 7.2

contra against, 7.1

contrario(a) opposite

lo contrario the opposite

contrastar to contrast

contribuir to contribute

el **control** inspection, 11.1

el **control de pasaportes** passport inspection, 11.1

el **control de seguridad** security check, 11.1

el/la **controlador(a)** air traffic controller

controlar to control

convencer to convince

conveniente convenient

el **convento** convent

la **conversación** conversation

conversar to talk, speak

el **convertible** convertible, **11.1**

convertir (ie, i) to convert, transform

la **coordinación** coordination

la **copa: la Copa mundial** World Cup

la **copia** copy

copiar to copy

el/la **copiloto** copilot, 11.2

el **corazón** heart

la **corbata** tie, 3.2

el **cordero** lamb, 14.2; **2.2**

la **cordillera** mountain range, **7.2**

el **cordoncillo** piping (embroidery)

la **coreografía** choreography

coreográfico(a) choreographic

la **córnea** cornea

el **coro** choir, chorus

el **correo** mail; post office, **12.2**

el **correo aéreo** airmail, **12.2**

el **correo electrónico** e-mail, electronic mail, **3.1**

el **correo ordinario** regular mail, **12.2**

correr to run, 7.2

la **correspondencia** correspondence

corriente: el agua corriente running water

cortar to cut, **8.1**

cortarse el pelo to get one's hair cut

la **corte** court, 14.1

el **corte de pelo** haircut, **12.1**

cortés courteous

la **cortesía** courtesy, BV

corto(a) short, 3.2

el **pantalón corto** shorts, 3.2

las **mangas cortas (largas)** short (long) sleeves, **4.1**

la **cosa** thing

la **cosecha** crop, harvest, **9.2**

cosechar to harvest, **9.2**

coser to sew

la **costa** coast

costar (ue) to cost, 3.1

costarricense Costa Rican

la **costilla** rib, 10.1

la **costumbre** custom

la **costura** sewing

el **cráter** crater

la **creación** creation

crear to create

crecer to grow, increase

el **crecimiento** growth

crédito: la tarjeta de crédito credit card, 14.1; **2.1**

creer to believe, 8.2; to think so

la **crema: la crema de afeitar** shaving cream, 12.1

la **crema dentífrica** toothpaste, 12.2

la **crema protectora** sunblock, 9.1

criar to raise, 9.2

criollo(a) Creole

cristiano(a) Christian

el **cruce** crossing, intersection, 11.2

el **cruce de peatones** crosswalk, 9.1

el **crucigrama** crossword puzzle, **5.1**

llenar un crucigrama to do a crossword puzzle, **5.1**

cruel cruel

cruzar to cross, 9.1

el **cuaderno** notebook, 3.1

la **cuadra** (city) block, **11.2**

el **cuadro** painting, 10.2

cuadros: a cuadros check, plaid

¿cuál? which?, what?, BV

¿Cuál es la fecha de hoy? What is today's date?, BV

¿cuáles? which ones?, what?

cualquier any

cuando when, 4.2

¿cuándo? when?, 4.1

cuanto: en cuanto a in regard to

¿cuánto? how much?, 3.1

¿A cuánto está(n)... ? How much is (are) . . . ?, 5.2

¿Cuánto cuesta(n)... ? How much do(es) . . . cost?, 3.1

¿Cuánto es? How much does it cost?, 3.1

¿cuántos(as)? how many?, 2.1

¿Cuántos años tienes? How old are you?

cuarenta forty, 2.2

el **cuarto** room, bedroom 6.2; quarter, 2.2

el cuarto de baño bathroom, 6.2

el cuarto de dormir bedroom

el cuarto doble double room, **6.1**

el cuarto sencillo single room, **6.1**

menos cuarto a quarter to (the hour), 2.2

y cuarto a quarter past (the hour), 2.2

cuarto(a) fourth, 6.2

cuatro four, BV

cuatrocientos(as) four hundred, 3.2

cubano(a) Cuban

cubanoamericano(a) Cuban American

cubrir to cover

la **cuchara** tablespoon, 14.1; **2.1**

la **cucharita** teaspoon, 14.1; **2.1**

el **cuchillo** knife, 14.1; **2.1**

el **cuello** neck, **4.1**

la **cuenca** basin

la **cuenta** bill, check, 5.1

la **cuenta corriente** checking account, **12.2**

la **cuenta de ahorros** savings account

el/la **cuentista** short-story writer

el **cuento** story

la **cuerda** string (instrument)

el **cuerpo** body, **8.1**

el **Cuerpo de Paz** Peace Corps

el **cuestionario** questionnaire

¡cuidado! careful!

con cuidado carefully

el cuidado intensivo intensive care

tener cuidado to be careful

cuidar to raise, look after, care for

cultivar to cultivate, to grow, **9.2**

el **cultivo** cultivation, growing, **9.2**

culto(a) cultured

cultural cultural

el **cumpleaños** birthday, 6.1

¡Feliz cumpleaños! Happy birthday!, **13.1**

cumplir: cumplir... años to be . . . years old, 6.1

el **cupé** coupe, **11.1**

la **cura** cure, treatment

el/la **curandero(a)** folk healer

curar to heal, get well

el **curso** course, class, 2.1

el curso obligatorio required course

el curso opcional elective course

D

la **dama** lady-in-waiting, woman

la dama de honor maid of honor, **13.1**

las **damas** checkers, 5.1

la **danza** dance

dañar to hurt

daño: hacerse daño to hurt oneself, **8.1**

dar to give, 4.2

dar a to open onto, look out on

dar a entender to imply that

dar auxilio to help

dar énfasis to emphasize

dar la mano to shake hands

dar la vuelta to turn around

dar las doce to strike twelve, **13.2**

dar un examen to give a test, 4.2

dar un paseo to take a walk, 5.2

dar una fiesta to give (throw) a party, 4.2

dar una representación to put on a performance, 10.2

datar to date

los **datos** data, information, **3.1**

entrar los datos to enter, keyboard information, **3.1**

de of, from, for, BV

de... a... from (time) to (time), 2.2

de joven as a young person

De nada. You're welcome., BV

de ninguna manera by no means, 1.1

¿De parte de quién? Who's calling?, **3.2**

de vez en cuando sometimes

debajo (de) under, below, **7.1**

deber must; should; to owe

la **década** decade

decidir to decide

décimo(a) tenth, 6.2

decir to say, 13

¡Diga! Hello! (answering the telephone–Spain), 14.2; **2.2**

declarar to declare

la **decoración** decoration

decorado(a) decorated

decorar to decorate

dedicarse to devote oneself, **14.1**

el **dedo** finger, **4.1**

el **defecto** fault, flaw

defender (ie) to defend

la **definición** definition

definir to define

definitivamente once and for all

dejar to leave (something), 14.1; **2.1**; to let, allow

dejar un mensaje to leave a message, **3.2**

Spanish-English Dictionary

del of the, from the

delante de in front of, 10.1

delantero(a) front (adj.)

delgado(a) thin

delicado(a) delicate

delicioso(a) delicious

demás other, rest

demasiado too (much)

la **demografía** demography

el/la **demógrafo(a)** demographer

la **demora: con una demora** with a delay, 11.1

demostrar (ue) to demonstrate

la **densidad** density

dentífrico(a): la pasta (crema) dentífrica toothpaste, 12.2

el/la **dentista** dentist

dentro de within

dentro de poco soon

el **departamento** apartment, 6.2; department, **14.2**

la casa de departamentos apartment house, 6.2

el departamento de recursos humanos human resources department, **14.2**

depender (ie) (de) to depend (on)

el/la **dependiente(a)** salesperson, 3.1

el **deporte** sport, 7.1

el deporte de equipo team sport

el deporte individual individual sport

deportivo(a) (related to) sports, 6.2

la emisión deportiva sports program (TV), 6.2

el **depósito** deposit

derecho(a) right, 7.1

a la derecha to the right, **5.2**

derecho straight (ahead), **11.2**

seguir derecho to go straight, **11.2**

la **dermatología** dermatology

el/la **dermatólogo(a)** dermatologist

derrotar to defeat

desagradable unpleasant

desamparado(a): los niños desamparados homeless children

desaparecer to disappear

el **desarrollo** development

el **desastre** disaster

desastroso(a) disastrous

desayunarse to eat breakfast, 12.1

el **desayuno** breakfast, 5.2

tomar el desayuno to eat breakfast, 12.1

descansar to rest

el **descapotable** convertible, **11.1**

el/la **descendiente** descendant

descolgar (ue) to pick up (the telephone), **3.2**

describir to describe

descubrir to discover

el **descuento** discount

desde since, from

desear to want, wish, 3.2

¿Qué desea usted? May I help you? (in a store), 3.2

los **desechos** waste

desembarcar to disembark, 11.2

desembocar to lead, go (one street into another), **9.1**; to empty

el **desenlace** conclusion

el **deseo** desire

el **desierto** desert

despachar to sell, 8.2

despacio slowly

despegar to take off (airplane), 11.2

el **despegue** take-off (airplane), **7.2**

despertarse (ie) to wake up, 12.1

después (de) after, 5.1; later

el **destino** destination, 11.1

con destino a to

la **desventaja** disadvantage

el **detalle** detail

el **detergente** detergent, **4.2**

determinar to determine

detrás de behind, **5.2**

devolver (ue) to return (something), 7.2

el **día** day, BV

Buenos días. Good morning., BV

el Día de los Reyes Epiphany (January 6), **13.2**

hoy (en) día nowadays, these days

¿Qué día es (hoy)? What day is it (today)?, BV

la **diagnosis** diagnosis, 8.2

el **diálogo** dialogue

el **diamante** diamond

diario(a) daily

dibujar to draw

el **dibujo** drawing

diciembre December, BV

diecinueve nineteen, BV

dieciocho eighteen, BV

dieciséis sixteen, BV

diecisiete seventeen, BV

el **diente** tooth

cepillarse los dientes to brush one's teeth, 12.1

el cepillo de dientes toothbrush, 12.2

diesel diesel (gas), **11.1**

la **dieta** diet

diez ten

la **diferencia** difference

diferente different

difícil difficult, 2.1

la **dificultad** difficulty

¡Diga! Hello! (telephone), 14.2; **2.2**

diminuto(a) tiny, minute

la **dinamita** dynamite

el **dinero** money, 14.1; **2.1**

el dinero en efectivo cash, **12.2**

¡Dios mío! Gosh!

el/la **diplomado(a)** graduate

diplomático(a) diplomatic

la **dirección** direction; address

en dirección a toward

las **direccionales** turn signals, **11.1**

directo(a) direct

el/la **director(a)** director, principal

dirigir to direct

la **disciplina** subject area (school), 2.2

el **disco compacto** compact disk, CD, 4.2; **3.1**

discutir to discuss

el/la **diseñador(a)** designer

el **diseño** design

disfrutar to enjoy

disponible available

la **disputa** quarrel, argument

el **disquete** disk, diskette, 3.1

la **distancia** distance

distinto(a) different, distinct

distraer to distract

la **distribución** distribution

la **distribuidora** parking meter that dispenses tickets

distribuir to pass out, distribute, **7.1**

la **diversión** amusement

divertido(a) fun, amusing

divertirse (ie, i) to enjoy oneself, 12.2

dividir to divide

la **división** division

divorciarse to get divorced

doblado(a) dubbed, 10.1

doblar to turn, **11.2**

doble: el cuarto doble double room, **6.1**

dobles doubles, 9.1

doce twelve, BV

la **docena** dozen, **4.2**

el/la **doctor(a)** doctor

la **documentación** documentation

el **documento** document, **3.1**

el **dólar** dollar, **12.2**

doler (ue) to hurt, 8.2

Me duele(n)... My . . . hurt(s) me, 8.2

el **dolor** pain, ache, 8.1

el dolor de cabeza headache, 8.1

el dolor de estómago stomachache, 8.1

el dolor de garganta sore throat, 8.1

Tengo dolor de... I have a pain in my . . . , 8.2

doméstico(a): los animales domésticos farm animals, **9.2**

la economía doméstica home economics, 2.2

el **domingo** Sunday, BV

dominicano(a) Dominican, 2.1

la República Dominicana Dominican Republic

el **dominio** control, authority

el **dominó** dominos, **5.1**

don courteous way of addressing a man

donde where, 1.2

¿dónde? where?, 1.2

doña courteous way of addressing a woman

dorado(a) golden

dormido(a) asleep

el/la **dormilón(ona)** sleepy head

dormir (ue, u) to sleep

el saco de dormir sleeping bag, 12.2

dormirse (ue, u) to fall asleep, 12.1

el **dormitorio** bedroom, 6.2

dos two, BV

doscientos(as) two hundred, 3.2

la **dosis** dose, 8.2

el/la **dramaturgo(a)** playwright

driblar to dribble, 7.2

la **droga** drug

la **drogadicción** drug addiction

la **ducha** shower, 12.1

tomar una ducha to take a shower, 12.1

la **duda** doubt

dudar to doubt

dudoso(a) doubtful

duele(n): Me duele(n) mucho. It (They) hurt(s) me a lot., **8.2**

dulce sweet

el pan dulce sweet roll, 5.1

la **duración** duration

durante during

durar to last, **13.2**

duro(a) hard, difficult, 2.1

el **DVD** digital video disc (DVD)

E

la **ebullición** boiling

echar to throw

echar la carta (en el buzón) to mail the letter, **12.2**

echar (tomar) una siesta to take a nap

echarle flores to pay someone a compliment

la **ecología** ecology

ecológico(a) ecological

la **economía** economics; economy

la economía doméstica home economics, 2.2

económico(a) economical, 12.2

la **ecuación** equation

ecuatoriano(a) Ecuadorean, 2.1

la **edad** age

el **edificio** building, 9.1

la **educación** education

la educación física physical education, 2.2

educar to educate

efectivo: el dinero en efectivo cash

efectuar to carry out

ejemplo: por ejemplo for example

ejercicio: hacer los ejercicios to exercise

el **ejote** string bean

el the (m. sing.), 1.1

él he, 1.1

la **electricidad** electricity

el/la **electricista** electrician, **14.1**

eléctrico(a) electric

electrónico(a): el correo electrónico e-mail, electronic mail, **3.1**

la **elegancia** elegance

elegante elegant, **13.1**

el **elemento** element

la **elevación** elevation

elevado(a) elevated, high

el **elevador** elevator, **6.1**

elevar to elevate

eliminar to eliminate

ella she, 1.1

ellos(as) they, 2.1

el **elote** corn (Mex.)

el/la **embajador(a)** ambassador

embarcar to board, 11.2

embarque: la tarjeta de embarque boarding pass, 11.1

la puerta de embarque departure gate

la **emergencia** emergency, **7.1**

la sala de emergencia emergency room, **8.1**

la **emisión** program (TV), 6.2; emission

la emisión deportiva sports program, 6.2

emitir to emit

la **emoción** emotion

emocional emotional

empalmar to connect

empatado(a) tied (score), 7.1

El tanto queda empatado. The score is tied., 7.1

empezar (ie) to begin, 7.1

el/la **empleado(a)** employee, clerk, 3.1

emplear to employ

el **empleo** employment, job

una solicitud de empleo a job application, **14.2**

la **empresa** business

el/la **empresario(a)** entrepreneur, businessperson

empujar to push, **4.2**

empujar el carrito to push the cart, **4.2**

en in; on

en aquel entonces at that time

en caso de in case of

en punto on the dot, sharp, 4.1

en sí in itself

el/la **enamorado(a)** sweetheart, lover

encantador(a) charming

encantar to delight

encargarse to take charge

encender (ie) to light, **13.2**

encestar to put in (make) a basket, 7.2

la **enchilada** enchilada, BV

encima (de) above

por encima de above, 9.1

encontrar (ue) to find

encontrarse (ue) to meet

la **encuesta** survey

endosar to endorse, **12.2**

el/la **enemigo(a)** enemy

la **energía** energy

enero January, BV

enfadado(a) angry

el **énfasis: dar énfasis** to emphasize

enfatizar to emphasize

la **enfermedad** illness

la **enfermería** nursing

el/la **enfermero(a)** nurse, **8.2**

enfermo(a) sick, 8.1

el/la **enfermo(a)** sick person, 8.1

enfrente de in front of

el **enganche** down payment

¡Enhorabuena! Congratulations!, **13.1**

el **enlace** union

enlatado(a) canned

enlazar to join, connect

enorme enormous

la **ensalada** salad, 5.1

enseguida right away, immediately, 5.1

enseñar to teach, 4.1; to show, **4.1**

entablar to start, begin

entero(a) entire, whole

enterrar (ie) to bury

el **entierro** burial

entonces then

en aquel entonces at that time

la **entrada** inning, 7.2; admission ticket, 10.1; entrance, **5.2**

entrar to enter, 4.1

entrar en escena to come (go) on stage, 10.2

entre between, 7.1

entregar to deliver

el **entrenamiento** training

entretenido(a) entertaining

la **entrevista** interview, **14.2**

el/la **entrevistador(a)** interviewer, **14.2**

entrevistar to interview

entusiasmado(a) enthusiastic

el/la **envejeciente** aging person

enviar to send

envuelto(a) wrapped

el **episodio** episode

la **época** period of time, epoch

el **equilibrio** equilibrium

el **equipaje** baggage, luggage, 11.1

el equipaje de mano carry-on luggage, 11.1

el **equipo** team, 7.1; equipment

el deporte de equipo team sport, 7.2

el **equivalente** equivalent

erróneo(a) wrong, erroneous

la **escala** stopover, **7.2**

hacer escala to stop over, make a stop, **7.2**

la **escalera** stairway, 6.2

la **escalera mecánica** escalator, **9.1**

los **escalofríos** chills, 8.1

escamotear to secretly take

escapar to escape

el **escaparate** shop window, **4.1**

la **escasez** shortage

la **escena** stage

entrar en escena to come (go) on stage, 10.2

el **escenario** scenery, set (theater), 10.2

escoger to choose

escolar (related to) school, 2.1

el bus escolar school bus, 4.1

el horario escolar school schedule

la vida escolar school life

los materiales escolares school supplies, 3.1

esconder to hide

escribir to write, 5.1

escuchar to listen (to), 4.2

el **escudero** squire, knight's attendant

la **escuela** school, 1.1

la escuela intermedia middle school

la escuela primaria elementary school

la escuela secundaria high school, 1.1

la escuela superior high school

el/la **escultor(a)** sculptor, 10.2

la **escultura** sculpture

ese(a) that

esencial essential

eso that (one)

a eso de at about (time), 4.1

esos(as) those

el **espacio** space

el **espagueti** spaghetti

espantoso(a) frightful

España Spain

el **español** Spanish (language), 2.2

español(a) Spanish (adj.)

la **espátula** palette knife, spatula

la **especia** spice

especial special

la **especialidad** specialty, specialization

el/la **especialista** specialist, **14.1**

especializar to specialize

especialmente especially

el **espectáculo** show, 10.2

ver un espectáculo to see a show, 10.2

el/la **espectador(a)** spectator, 7.1

el **espejo** mirror, 12.1

espera: la sala de espera waiting room, 13.1; **1.1**

esperar to wait (for), 11.1; to hope

espontáneo(a) spontaneous

la **esposa** wife, spouse, 6.1

el **esposo** husband, spouse, 6.1

el **esquí** skiing, 9.2; ski

el esquí acuático water skiing, 9.1

el/la **esquiador(a)** skier, 9.2

esquiar to ski, 9.2

esquiar en el agua to water-ski, 9.1

la **esquina** corner, **9.1**

establecerse to settle

el **establecimiento** establishment

la **estación** season, BV; station, 10.1

la estación de esquí ski resort, 9.2

la estación de ferrocarril train station, 13.1; **1.1**

la estación del metro subway station, 10.1

la estación de servicio service station, **11.1**

el **estacionamiento** parking

estacionar to park

la **estadía** stay

el **estadio** stadium, 7.1

la **estadística** statistic

el **estado** state

el **estado del banco** bank statement

Estados Unidos United States

estadounidense from the United States

la **estancia** ranch (Argentina)

estar to be, 4.1

¿Está... ? Is . . . there?, **3.2**

estar cansado(a) to be tired, **8.1**

estar contento(a) (triste, etc.) to be happy (sad, etc.), **8.1**

estar de buen (mal) humor to be in a good (bad) mood, **8.1**

estar enfermo(a) to be sick

estar nervioso(a) (tranquilo[a]) to be nervous (calm), **8.1**

estar resfriado(a) to have a cold, 8.1

estatal pertaining to state (adj.)

la **estatua** statue, 10.2

este(a) this

el **este** east

estereofónico(a) stereo

el **estilo** style

estimado(a) esteemed

esto this (one)

el **estómago** stomach, 8.1

estornudar to sneeze, 8.1

estos(as) these

la **estrategia** strategy

estrecho(a) narrow, **4.1**

la **estrella** star

la **estructura** structure

el/la **estudiante** student

el/la estudiante de intercambio exchange student

la residencia para estudiantes student housing, dormitory, **3.2**

estudiantil (relating to) student

estudiar to study, 4.1

Spanish-English Dictionary

el **estudio** study, 14

la **estufa** stove, **10.1**

estupendo(a) stupendous

eterno(a) eternal

étnico(a) ethnic

el **euro** euro (currency)

Europa Europe

europeo(a) European

exactamente exactly

exacto(a) exact

exagerado(a) exaggerated

exagerar to exaggerate

el **examen** test, exam, 4.2

examinar to examine, 8.2

la **excavación** excavation

excavar to dig, excavate

exceder to exceed

excelente excellent

la **excepción** exception

exclamar to exclaim

exclusivamente exclusively

la **exhibición** exhibition

exigir to demand

la **existencia** existence

existir to exist

el **éxito** success

la **expedición** expedition

la **experiencia** experience

experimentar to experiment

el/la **experto(a)** expert, 9.2

explicar to explain, 4.2

el/la **explorador(a)** explorer

la **explosión** explosion

exportar to export

la **exposición (de arte)** (art) exhibition, 10.2

la **expresión** expression

el modo de expresión means of expression

la **extensión** extension

extranjero(a) foreign

el país extranjero foreign country, 11.2

el/la **extranjero(a)** foreigner

en el extranjero abroad

extraordinario(a) extraordinary

extravagante strange

extremo(a) extreme

F

la **fábrica** factory, 9.1

fabricado(a) manufactured

fabuloso(a) fabulous

fácil easy, 2.1

facilitar to facilitate

el **facsímil** fax, 3.1

la **factura** bill, 6.1; invoice

facturar el equipaje to check luggage, 11.1

la **Facultad** school (of a university)

la **faja** sash

la **falda** skirt, 3.2

falso(a) false

la **fama: tener fama de** to have the reputation of

la **familia** family, 6.1

familiar (related to the) family

famoso(a) famous, 1.2

fantástico(a) fantastic, 1.2

el/la **farmacéutico(a)** druggist, pharmacist, 8.2

la **farmacia** drugstore, 8.2

fascinar to fascinate

Favor de (+ infinitive) Please (+ verb)

favorito(a) favorite, 11

el **fax** fax, 3.1

mandar (transmitir) un fax to send a fax, to fax, 3.1

febrero February, BV

la **fecha** date, BV

¿Cuál es la fecha de hoy? What is today's date?, BV

la **felicidad** happiness

¡Felicitaciones! Congratulations!, **13.1**

feliz happy

¡Feliz cumpleaños! Happy birthday!, **13.1**

¡Feliz Hanuka! Happy Chanukah!, **13.2**

¡Feliz Navidad! Merry Christmas!, **13.2**

feo(a) ugly, 1.1

el **ferrocarril** railroad, 13.1, **1.1**

la estación de ferrocarril train station, 13.1, **1.1**

festejar to celebrate

la **ficción** fiction

la **ficha** piece (game), **5.1**; registration card, **6.1**

ficticio(a) fictitious

la **fiebre** fever, 8.1

tener fiebre to have a fever, 8.1

fiel faithful

la **fiesta** party, **13.1**

dar una fiesta to give (throw) a party, 4.2

la **fiesta de las luces** The Festival of Lights, **13.2**

la **figura** figure

figurativo(a) figurative

fijar to fix

fijo(a) fixed

la **fila** row (of seats); line (queue), 10.1

el **filete** fillet

el **film** film, 10.1

el **fin** end

a fines de at the end of

el fin de semana weekend, BV

el **final: al final (de)** at the end (of)

financiero(a) financial

las **finanzas** finances

la **finca** farm, **9.2**

fino(a) fine

firmar to sign, 12.2

la **física** physics, 2.1

físico(a): la educación física physical education, 2.2

flaco(a) thin, 1.2

flamenco(a) flamenco

la **flauta** flute

flechar to become enamored of (to fall for)

la **flor** flower

el **folleto** pamphlet

el **fondo** fund

el/la **fontanero(a)** plumber, **14.1**

la **forma** shape

formar to make up, to form

el **formulario** form, **8.2**

llenar un formulario to fill out a form, **8.2**

la **fortaleza** strength

la **fortificación** fortification

la **foto** photo

la **fotografía** photograph

el/la **fotógrafo(a)** photographer

la **fractura** fracture, **8.1**

el **fragmento** fragment

el **francés** French, 2.2

franco(a) frank, candid, sincere

el **frasco** jar, **4.2**

la **frase** phrase, sentence

la **frazada** blanket, **6.2**

frecuentemente frequently

freír (i, i) to fry, 14.1; **2.1**

los **frenos** brakes, **11.1**

la **frente** forehead, **8.1**

fresco(a) fresh, **4.2**

el **frijol** bean, 5.2

los **frijoles negros** black beans, **10.2**

el **frío: Hace frío.** It's cold., 9.2

frito(a) fried, 5.1

las **papas fritas** French fries, 5.1

el **frontón** wall (of a jai alai court)

la **fruta** fruit, 5.2

la **frutería** fruit store, **4.2**

el **fuego** fire, **10.2**

a fuego lento on a low flame, heat

quitar (retirar) del fuego to take (something) off the heat, **10.2**

la **fuente** source

fuerte strong

la **fuerza** strength; force

fumar: la sección de (no) fumar (no) smoking area, 11.1

la **señal de no fumar** no smoking sign, **7.1**

la **función** performance, 10.2; function

el **funcionamiento** functioning

el/la **funcionario(a)** city hall employee, **14.1**

la **fundación** foundation

fundado(a) founded, established

fundar to found, establish

la **furia** fury

furioso(a) furious

el **fútbol** soccer, 7.1

el campo de fútbol soccer field, 7.1

el **futbolín** table soccer, **5.1**

el **futuro** future

G

la **gabardina** raincoat, **4.1**

las **gafas de sol** sunglasses, 9.1

el **galán** beau, heartthrob

la **galaxia** galaxy

la **galería comercial** shopping mall

el **galón** gallon

gallardo(a) gallant, fine-looking

la **gallina** hen, **9.2**

las **gambas** shrimp, **10.2**

el **ganado** cattle, **9.2**

ganar to win, 7.1; to earn

ganar la vida to earn one's living

la **ganga** bargain

el **garaje** garage, 6.2

la **garantía** guarantee

la **garganta** throat, 8.1

la **garita de peaje** toll booth, **11.2**

la **gaseosa** soda, 5.1

la **gasolina** gasoline, **11.1**

la **gasolinera** service station, **11.1**

gastar to spend

el/la **gato(a)** cat, 6.1

el/la **gemelo(a)** twin

general: en general generally

por lo general in general, usually

generalmente usually, generally

el **género** genre

generoso(a) generous, 1.2

la **gente** people

la **geografía** geography, 2.2

la **geometría** geometry, 2.2

geométrico(a) geometric

gerencial managerial

el/la **gerente** manager, **14.1**

el **gesto** gesture

el **gigante** giant

el **gimnasio** gymnasium

la **ginecología** gynecology

el/la **ginecólogo(a)** gynecologist

la **gira** tour, 12.2

el **globo** balloon, **5.2**

el **gobierno** government, **14.1**

el gobierno estatal state government

el gobierno federal federal government

el gobierno municipal municipal government

el **gol: meter un gol** to score a goal, 7.1

el **golfo** gulf

el **golpe** coup (overthrow of a government)

golpear to hit, 9.2

la **goma** tire, **11.1**

la **goma de borrar** eraser, 3.1

gordo(a) fat, 1.2

la **gorra** cap, hat, 3.2

gozar to enjoy

Gracias. Thank you., BV

gracioso(a) funny, 1.1

el **grado** degree (temperature), 9.2; grade

graduarse to graduate

la **gramática** grammar

el **gramo** gram

gran, grande big, large, great

las **Grandes Ligas** Major Leagues

el **grano** grain

la **grasa** fat

grave serious, grave

el/la **griego(a)** Greek

la **gripe** flu, 8.1

gris gray, 3.2

el **grupo** group

la **guagua** bus (Puerto Rico, Cuba), 10.1

el **guante** glove, 7.2

guapo(a) handsome, 1.1

guardar to guard, 7.1; to keep, save, 3.1

guardar cama to stay in bed, 8.1

el/la **guardia** police officer

guatemalteco(a) Guatemalan

la **guerra** war

la **guerrilla** band of guerrillas

el/la **guía** tour guide; guide

la **guía telefónica** telephone book, 3.2

el **guisante** pea, 5.2

la **guitarra** guitar

gustar to like, to be pleasing

el **gusto** pleasure; taste

Mucho gusto. Nice to meet you.

haber to have (in compound tenses)

la **habichuela** bean, 5.2

la habichuela tierna string bean

las habichuelas negras black beans, 10.2

la **habitación** bedroom, room, 6.1

el/la **habitante** inhabitant

habla: los países de habla española Spanish-speaking countries

hablar to speak, talk, 3.1

hace: Hace... años . . . years ago

Hace buen tiempo. The weather is nice., 9.1

Hace calor. It's hot., 9.1

Hace frío. It's cold., 9.2

Hace mal tiempo. The weather is bad., 9.1

Hace sol. It's sunny., 9.1

hacer to do, to make

hacer caso to pay attention

hacer cola to line up, 10.1

hacer la cama to make the bed, 6.2

hacer la maleta to pack one's suitcase

hacer las compras to shop, 4.2

hacer las tareas to do homework, 3.1

hacer preguntas to ask questions, 14.2

hacer un viaje to take a trip, 11.1

hacer una llamada telefónica to make a telephone call, 3.2

hacerse daño to hurt oneself, 8.1

hacia toward

la **hacienda** ranch

hallar to find

hambre: tener hambre to be hungry, 14.1; 2.1

la **hamburguesa** hamburger, 5.1

Hanuka Chanukah, 13.2

¡Feliz Hanuka! Happy Chanukah!, 13.2

harmonioso(a) harmonious

hasta until, BV

¡Hasta luego! See you later!, BV

¡Hasta mañana! See you tomorrow!, BV

¡Hasta pronto! See you soon!, BV

hay there is, there are, BV

hay que one must

Hay sol. It's sunny., 9.1

No hay de qué. You're welcome., BV

hebreo(a) Jewish, 13.2

hecho(a) made

helado(a): el té helado iced tea, 5.1

el **helado** ice cream, 5.1

el helado de chocolate chocolate ice cream, 5.1

el helado de vainilla vanilla ice cream, 5.1

el **helicóptero** helicopter, 7.2

el **hemisferio norte** northern hemisphere

el **hemisferio sur** southern hemisphere

la **herencia** inheritance

la **herida** wound, 8.1

el/la **herido(a)** injured person

la **hermana** sister, 6.1

el **hermano** brother, 6.1

hermoso(a) beautiful, pretty, 1.1

el/la **héroe** hero

hervir (ie) to boil, 10.1

el **hidrofoil** hydrofoil

la **higiene** hygiene

higiénico(a): el papel higiénico toilet paper, 12.2

la **hija** daughter, 6.1

el **hijo** son, 6.1

los hijos children, 6.1

hinchado(a) swollen, 8.1

el **hipermercado** hypermarket, 4.2

la **hipoteca** mortgage

hispano(a) Hispanic

hispanoamericano(a) Spanish-American

hispanohablante Spanish-speaking

el/la **hispanohablante** Spanish speaker

la **historia** history, 2.2; story

el/la **historiador(a)** historian

histórico(a) historical

la **historieta** short story

el **hobby** hobby, 5.1

la **hoja: la hoja de papel** sheet of paper, 3.1

¡Hola! Hello!, BV

el **hombre** man

    ¡hombre! good heavens!, you bet!

el **hombro** shoulder, **8.1**

honesto(a) honest, 1.2

el **honor** honor

la **hora** hour; time

    ¿A qué hora? At what time?, 2.2

    la hora de salida departure hour

    la hora de la cena dinner hour

el **horario** schedule, 13.1; **1.1**

    el horario escolar school schedule

la **horchata** cold drink made from almonds, milk, and sugar

la **hornilla** stove burner, **10.1**

el **hornillo** stove burner, **10.1**

el **horno** oven, **10.1**

el **horno de microondas** microwave oven, **10.1**

horrible horrible

hospedarse to lodge, stay

el **hospital** hospital, **8.1**

el **hostal** inexpensive hotel, 12.2

la **Hostia** Host (religious)

el **hotel** hotel, **6.1**

hoy today, BV

    hoy (en) día nowadays, these days

el **huarache** sandal

el/la **huerto(a)** vegetable garden, orchard, **9.2**

el **hueso** bone, **8.2**

el/la **huésped** guest, **6.1**

el **huevo** egg, 5.2

    humano(a): el ser humano human being

    húmedo(a) humid

    humilde humble

el **humor** mood, 8.1

    estar de buen humor to be in a good mood, 8.1

    estar de mal humor to be in a bad mood, 8.1

el **huso horario** time zone

I

el **icono** icon

    ida: de ida y vuelta round-trip (ticket), 13.1; **1.1**

la **idea** idea

    ideal ideal, 1.2

el/la **idealista** idealist

    identificar to identify

    idílico(a) idyllic

el **idioma** language

la **iglesia** church

    igual equal, alike

        igual que like, as

la **ilusión** illusion

    ilustre distinguished

la **imagen** image

la **imaginación** imagination

    imaginado(a) imagined, dreamed of

    imaginar to imagine

    imaginario(a) imaginary

    impar: el número impar odd number

el **imperativo** imperative

el **impermeable** raincoat, **4.1**

    importante important

    importar to be important

    imposible impossible

    impresionar to affect, influence

la **impresora** printer, **3.1**

    inaugurar to inaugurate

el/la **inca** Inca

    incluido(a): ¿Está incluido el servicio? Is the tip included?, 5.1

    incluir to include, 5.1

    increíble incredible

la **independencia** independence

el **indicador: el tablero indicador** scoreboard, 7.1

    indicar to indicate, 11.1

    indígena native, indigenous

el/la **indígena** native person

    indio(a) Indian

    indispensable indispensable

    individual individual

    el deporte individual individual sport

el **individuo** individual

    industrial: la zona industrial industrial area, **9.1**

la **inferencia** inference

la **influencia** influence

la **información** information

    informar to inform, 13.2; **1.2**

la **informática** computer science, 2.2

el **informe** report

la **ingeniería** engineering

el/la **ingeniero(a)** engineer, **14.1**

el **inglés** English, 2.2

el **ingrediente** ingredient

    ingresar to make a deposit (bank)

    inhospital inhospitable

    inhóspito(a) desolate, inhospitable

    inmediatamente immediately

    inmediato(a) immediate

    inmenso(a) immense

la **innovación** innovation

    inocente innocent

el **inodoro** toilet, **6.2**

    insistir to insist

    inspeccionar to inspect, 11.1

la **instalación** installation

    instantáneo(a) instantaneous

el **instante** instant

la **instrucción** instruction

el **instrumento** instrument

    el instrumento musical musical instrument

    íntegro(a) integral

    inteligente intelligent, 2.1

el **intercambio** exchange

    el/la estudiante (alumno[a]) de intercambio exchange student

el **interés** interest

    interesante interesting, 2.1

    interesar to interest

intergaláctico(a)
intergalactic
**intermedio(a): la escuela
intermedia** middle school
internacional international
Internet Internet, **3.1**
la **interpretación**
interpretation
el/la **intérprete** interpreter
interrumpir to interrupt
la **interrupción** interruption
intervenir to intervene
íntimo(a) intimate, close
la **introducción** introduction
introducir to insert,
3.2
**introducir la tarjeta
telefónica** to insert the
phone card, **3.2**
el **invento** invention
inverso(a) reverse
la **investigación** investigation
el/la **investigador(a)** researcher
el **invierno** winter, BV
la **invitación** invitation
el/la **invitado(a)** guest
invitar to invite, 6.1
la **inyección** injection, shot,
8.2
poner una inyección to
give a shot
ir to go, 4.1
ir a (+ infinitive) to be
going to (do something)
ir a pie to go on foot, to
walk, 4.1
ir de compras to go
shopping, 5.2
ir en bicicleta to go by
bicycle, 12.2
ir en carro (coche) to go
by car, 4.1
ir en tren to go by train
la **irrigación** irrigation
la **isla** island
italiano(a) Italian
izquierdo(a) left, 7.1
a la izquierda to the left,
5.2

el **jabón** soap, 12.2
**la barra (pastilla) de
jabón** bar of soap, 12.2
jamás never
el **jamón** ham, 5.1
el **jardín** garden, 6.2
el/la **jardinero(a)** outfielder, 7.2
la **jaula** cage, **5.2**
el/la **jefe(a)** boss
el **jet** jet
el **jonrón** home run, 7.2
joven young, 6.1
de joven as a young
person
el/la **joven** youth, young
person, 10.1
la **joya** jewel, **4.1**
la **joyería** jewelry store, **4.1**
la **judía verde** green bean,
5.2
el **juego** game
el juego de béisbol
baseball game, 7.2
el juego de tenis tennis
game, 9.1
el juego de video video
game, 5.1
los Juegos Olímpicos
Olympic Games
la sala de juegos game
arcade, **5.1**
el **jueves** Thursday, BV
el/la **juez** judge, **14.1**
el/la **jugador(a)** player, 7.1
el/la jugador(a) de béisbol
baseball player, 7.2
jugar (ue) to play, 7.1
**jugar (al) béisbol (fútbol,
baloncesto, etc.)** to play
baseball (soccer,
basketball, etc.), 7.1
el **jugo** juice
el jugo de naranja orange
juice, 12.1
el **juguete** toy
julio July, BV

la **jungla** jungle
junio June, BV
juntos(as) together
juvenil: el albergue juvenil
youth hostel, 12.2
la **juventud** youth

el **kilo** kilogram, 5.2
el **kilómetro** kilometer

la the (f. sing.), 1.1; it, her
(pron.)
el **labio** lip, **8.1**
el **laboratorio** laboratory
el **lado** side
al lado de beside, next
to, **5.2**
el **lago** lake, 5.2
el **lamento** lament
la **lana** wool, **12.1**
la **langosta** lobster, 14.2; **2.2**
la **lanza** lance
el/la **lanzador(a)** pitcher, 7.2
lanzar to throw, 7.1; to
launch
el **lápiz** pencil, 3.1
largo(a) long, 3.2
de largo recorrido long
distance (trip)
las them (f. pl. pron.)
la **lástima: ser una lástima**
to be a pity (a shame)
lastimarse to get hurt, **8.1**
la **lata** can, 5.2
lateral side (adj.), 13.2; **1.2**
el **latín** Latin, 2.2
latino(a) Latin (adj.)
Latinoamérica Latin
America, 1.1
latinoamericano(a) Latin
American

el **lavabo** washbasin, **6.2**; restroom, **7.1**

el **lavado** laundry, **12.1**

la **lavandería** laundromat

lavar: la máquina de lavar washing machine, **12.1**

lavarse to wash oneself, 12.1

lavarse los dientes to brush one's teeth, 12.1

le to him, to her; to you *(formal) (pron.)*

la **lección** lesson, 4.2

la **leche** milk

el café con leche coffee with milk, 5.1

el **lechón** suckling pig

la **lechuga** lettuce, 5.2

la **lectura** reading

leer to read, 5.1

la **legumbre** vegetable

lejos far, **12.2**

la **lengua** language, 2.2

el **lenguaje** language

la **lenteja** lentil

lento(a) slow, **10.2**

el **león** lion

les to them; to you *(formal pl.) (pron.)*

el/la **lesionado(a)** injured person

la **letra** letter (of alphabet)

levantar to lift, to raise

levantarse to get up, 12.1; to rise up (against)

levantarse el sol the sun rises

el/la **libertador(a)** liberator

la **libra** pound

libre free, 5.1

al aire libre outdoor *(adj.)*

el **libro** book, 3.1

la **licencia** driver's license, **11.1**

el **liceo** high school

el **lienzo** canvas (painting)

la **liga** league

las Grandes Ligas Major Leagues

ligero(a) light (cheerful)

la **lima** lime, 10.1

limeño(a) from Lima (Peru)

el **límite de velocidad** speed limit

el **limón** lemon, 10.1

la **limonada** lemonade, BV

limpiar to clean, 6.2

limpiar el cuarto to clean the room, 6.2

limpiar en seco to dry clean, 12.1

limpio(a) clean

la **limusina** limousine

lindo(a) pretty, 1.1

la **línea** line

la línea aérea airline

la línea ecuatorial equator

la línea paralela parallel line

la línea telefónica telephone line

el **lípido** lipid, fat

líquido(a) liquid

lírico(a) lyric

la **lista** list

listo(a) ready; clever, **5.1**

la **litera** berth, 13.2; **1.2**

literal literal

literario(a) literary

la **literatura** literature, 2.1

el **litro** liter

la **llamada larga** long distance call, **3.2**

la **llamada telefónica** telephone call, **3.2**

hacer una llamada telefónica to make a (telephone) call, 3.2

poner la llamada to put the call through

llamado(a) called

llamar to call; to telephone, 3.2

llamarse to be named, to call oneself, 12.1

la **llanta** tire, **11.1**

la llanta de recambio (repuesto) spare tire, 11.1

la **llanura** plain, **7.2**

la **llave** key, **6.1**

la **llegada** arrival, arriving, 11.1

llegar to arrive, 4.1

llenar to fill, fill out

llenar un crucigrama to do a crossword puzzle, 5.1

llenar el formulario to fill out the form, 8.2

lleno(a) full

llevar to carry, 3.1; to wear, 3.2; to bring, 6.1; to bear; to have (subtitles, ingredients, etc.); to take, 8.1

llover (ue) to rain

Llueve. It's raining., 9.1

la **lluvia** rain

lo it; him *(m. sing.) (pron.)*

lo que what, that which

local local, 13.2; **1.2**

la **loción: la loción bronceadora** suntan lotion, 9.1

loco(a) insane

el **lodo** mud

lógico(a) logical

los them *(m. pl.) (pron.)*

el **loto** lotto

las **luces** headlights, **11.1**

luchar to fight

luego later; then, BV

¡Hasta luego! See you later!, BV

el **lugar** place

tener lugar to take place, **8.1**

lujo: de lujo deluxe

lujoso(a) luxurious

la **luna** moon

la **luna de miel** honeymoon

lunares: con lunares with polka dots

el **lunes** Monday, BV

la **luz** light

la luz roja red light, **11.2**

M

la **madera** wood

la **madre** mother, 6.1

madrileño(a) native of Madrid

la **madrina** godmother

el/la **maestro(a)** teacher

magnífico(a) magnificent

el **maíz** corn, 14.2; **2.2**

mal bad, 14.2; **2.2**

estar de mal humor to be in a bad mood, 8.1

Hace mal tiempo. The weather's bad., 9.1

la **maleta** suitcase, 11.1

el/la **maletero(a)** trunk (of a car), 11.1; porter, 13.1; **1.1**

malhumorado(a) bad-tempered

malo(a) bad, 2.1

sacar una nota mala to get a bad grade, 4.2

la **mamá** mom

el **mambo** mambo

mandar to send, **3.1**; to order

manejar to drive, **11.1**

la **manera** way, manner, 1.1

de ninguna manera by no means, 1.1

la **manga** sleeve, **4.1**

de manga corta (larga) short- (long-) sleeved, **4.1**

el **maní** peanut

la **mano** hand, 7.1

dar la mano to shake hands

la **mano de obra** workforce

la **manta** blanket, **6.2**

el **mantel** tablecloth, 14.1; **2.1**

mantener to maintain

mantenerse en forma to keep in shape

la **mantequilla** butter, **10.2**

la **manzana** apple, 5.2

el **manzano** apple tree, 9.2

mañana tomorrow, BV

¡Hasta mañana! See you tomorrow!, BV

la **mañana** morning

de la mañana A.M. (time), 2.2

por la mañana in the morning

el **mapa** map

el **maquillaje** makeup, 12.1

ponerse el maquillaje to put one's makeup on, 12.1

maquillarse to put one's makeup on, 12.1

la **máquina** machine, device

la máquina de lavar washing machine, **12.1**

prender la máquina to turn (a device) on, **3.1**

el **mar** sea, 9.1

el mar Caribe Caribbean Sea

maravilloso(a) marvelous

el **marcador** marker, 3.1

marcar to dial, **3.2**

marcar el número to dial the number, **3.2**

marcar un tanto to score a point, 7.1

marchar to march

el **marfil** ivory

el **marido** husband, 6.1

el/la **marino(a)** sailor

los **mariscos** shellfish, 5.2; **10.2**

marrón: de color marrón brown, 3.2

el **martes** Tuesday, BV

marzo March, BV

más more, 2.2

más tarde later

más o menos more or less

la **masa** mass

la **máscara de oxígeno** oxygen mask, **7.1**

matar to kill

las **matemáticas** mathematics, 2.1

la **materia** matter, subject; material

la materia prima raw material

el **material** supply, 3.1; material

los materiales escolares school supplies, 3.1

el **matrimonio** marriage

máximo(a) maximum, **11.2**

la velocidad máxima speed limit, **11.2**

el/la **maya** Maya

mayo May, BV

la **mayonesa** mayonnaise, **4.2**

mayor greater, greatest; elderly, older

la mayor parte the greater part, the most

la **mayoría** majority

me me (pron.)

el/la **mecánico(a)** mechanic

la **medalla** medal

media average

y media half-past (time)

mediano(a) medium, **4.1**

la **medianoche** midnight

las **medias** stockings, pantyhose

el **medicamento** medicine (drugs), 8.2

la **medicina** medicine (discipline), 8.2; medicine

el/la **médico(a)** doctor, 8.2

la **medida** measurement

el **medio** medium, means

el medio de transporte means of transportation

medio(a) half, 5.2; average

media hora half an hour

el **medio ambiente** environment

el **mediodía** noon

medir (i, i) to measure

la **mejilla** cheek, 8.1

los **mejillones** mussels, 10.2

mejor better

el/la mejor the best

melancólico(a) melancholic

el **melocotón** peach

la **memoria** memory

mencionar to mention

menor lesser, least

la **menora** menorah, **13.2**

menos less, fewer

a menos que unless

menos cuarto a quarter to (the hour)

el **mensaje** message, **3.2**

dejar un mensaje to leave a message, **3.2**

la **mensualidad** monthly installment

mentiroso(a) lying

el **menú** menu, 5.1

el **mercadeo** marketing

el **mercado** market, 5.2

la **mercancía** merchandise, **14.1**

el **merengue** merengue

la **merienda** snack, 4.2

tomar una merienda to have a snack, 4.2

la **mermelada** jam, marmalade

el **mes** month, BV

la **mesa** table, 5.1; plateau

la **mesera** waitress, 5.1

el **mesero** waiter, 5.1

la **meseta** plateau, **7.2**

la **mesita** tray table, **7.1**

el/la **mestizo(a)** mestizo

el **metabolismo** metabolism

el **metal: instrumentos de metal** brass (instruments in orchestra)

meter to put, place, 7.1; to put in, insert, **3.1**

meter un gol to score a goal, 7.1

el **método** method

la **métrica** metrics

el **metro** subway, 10.1; meter, **7.2**

mexicano(a) Mexican, 1.1

mexicanoamericano(a) Mexican American

la **mezcla** mixture

mi my

mí me

el **microbio** microbe

microscópico(a) microscopic

el **microscopio** microscope

el **miedo** fear

tener miedo to be afraid

el **miembro** member, 4.2

mientras while

el **miércoles** Wednesday, BV

la **migración** migration

mil (one) thousand, 3.2

el **militar** soldier

la **milla** mile

el **millón** million

el/la **millonario(a)** millionaire

el/la **mimo** mime, **5.2**

la **miniatura** miniature

la **miniaturización** miniaturization

el **ministerio** ministry

el **minuto** minute

mirar to look at, watch, 3.1

mirarse to look at oneself, 12.1

¡Mira! Look!

el/la **mirón(ona)** spectator

la **miseria** poverty

mismo(a) same, 2.1; myself, yourself, him/her/itself, ourselves, yourselves, themselves

el **misterio** mystery

misterioso(a) mysterious

la **mitad** half

la **mitología** mythology

mixto(a) co-ed (school)

la **mochila** backpack, 3.1; knapsack, 12.2

la **moción** motion

la **moda** style

de moda in style

la **modalidad** mode, type

el/la **modelo** model

el **módem** modem

la **moderación** moderation

moderno(a) modern

el **modo** manner, way

el modo de expresión means of expression

el **molino de viento** windmill

el **momento** moment

el **monasterio** monastery

la **moneda** coin, currency, **3.2**

el **monitor** monitor, computer screen, **3.1**

el **mono** monkey, **5.2**

monocelular single-celled

el **monstruo** monster

la **montaña** mountain, 9.2

la **montaña rusa** roller coaster, **5.2**

montañoso(a) mountainous

montar (caballo) horseback ride

el **monumento** monument

moreno(a) dark, brunette, 1.1

morir (ue, u) to die

el/la **moro(a)** Moor

morrón: el pimiento morrón sweet pepper

la **mortalidad** mortality

el **mostrador** counter, 11.1

mostrar (ue) to show

el **motivo** reason, motive; theme

el **motor** motor

mover (ue) to move

el **movimiento** movement

el/la **mozo(a)** porter (train station) 13.1; **1.1**; bellman (hotel), **6.1**

la **muchacha** girl, 1.1

el **muchacho** boy, 1.1

mucho(a) a lot; many, 2.1

Mucho gusto. Nice to meet you.

mudarse to move

los **muebles** furniture

la **muerte** death

la **mujer** wife, 6.1

la **muleta** crutch, 8.2

la **multa** fine

multinacional multinational

la **multiplicación** multiplication

multiplicar to multiply

mundial worldwide, (related to the) world

la Copa mundial World Cup

la Serie mundial World Series

el **mundo** world

todo el mundo everyone

la **muñeca** wrist, **4.1**

el **mural** mural, 10.2

el/la **muralista** muralist

la **muralla** wall

muscular muscular

el **museo** museum, 10.2

la **música** music, 2.2

el/la **músico(a)** musician

muy very, BV

muy bien very well, BV

nacer to be born, **13.1**

nacido(a) born

nacional national

la **nacionalidad** nationality, 1.2

¿de qué nacionalidad? what nationality?

nada nothing, 5.2

De nada. You're welcome., BV

Nada más. Nothing else., 5.2

Por nada. You're welcome., BV

nadar to swim, 9.1

nadie no one

la **naranja** orange, 5.2

el **narcótico** narcotic

la **nariz** nose, **8.1**

la **narración** narration

narrar to narrate

la **natación** swimming, 9.1

natural: los recursos naturales natural resources, 2.1

las ciencias naturales natural sciences

la **naturaleza** nature

la **navaja** razor, 12.1

navegar to navigate

navegar por la red to surf the Net

la **Navidad** Christmas, 13.2

el árbol de Navidad Christmas tree, 13.2

¡Feliz Navidad! Merry Christmas!, 13.2

necesario(a) necessary

la **necesidad** necessity

necesitar to need, 3.1

negativo(a) negative

negro(a) black, 3.2

nervioso(a) nervous, 8.1

el **neumático** tire, **11.1**

nevar (ie) to snow, 9.2

la **nevera** refrigerator, **10.1**

la **nieta** granddaughter, 6.1

el **nieto** grandson, 6.1

la **nieve** snow, 9.2

ninguno(a) not any, none

de ninguna manera by no means, 1.1

el/la **niño(a)** child

los niños desamparados homeless children

el **nivel** level

el nivel del mar sea level

no no, BV

No hay de qué. You're welcome., BV

no hay más remedio there's no other alternative

noble noble

la **noche** night, evening

Buenas noches. Good night., BV

de la noche P.M. (time), 2.2

esta noche tonight, 9.2

por la noche in the evening, at night

la **Nochebuena** Christmas Eve, **13.2**

la **Nochevieja** New Year's Eve, **13.2**

nombrar to mention

el **nombre** name

¿a nombre de quién? in whose name?, 14.2; **2.2**

la **noria** Ferris wheel, **5.2**

el **noroeste** northwest

el **norte** north

norteamericano(a) North American

nos (to) us (pl. pron.)

nosotros(as) we, 2.2

la **nota** grade, 4.2

la nota buena (alta) good (high) grade, 4.2

la nota mala (baja) bad (low) grade, 4.2

sacar una nota buena (mala) to get a good (bad) grade, 4.2

notable notable

notar to note

las **noticias** news, 6.2

novecientos(as) nine hundred, 3.2

la **novela** novel

el/la **novelista** novelist

noveno(a) ninth, 6.2

noventa ninety, 2.2

la **novia** bride, **13.1**; fiancée, girlfriend

noviembre November, BV

el **novio** groom, **13.1**; fiancé, boyfriend

los **novios** bride and groom, newlyweds, **13.1**

la **nube** cloud, 9.1

Hay nubes. It's cloudy., 9.1

nublado(a) cloudy, 9.1

nuestro(a) our

nueve nine, BV

nuevo(a) new

de nuevo again

el **número** number, 1.2; size (shoes), 3.2

el número de teléfono telephone number, **3.2**

el número del asiento seat number, 11.1

el **número del vuelo**
flight number, 11.1
el **número equivocado**
wrong number
numeroso(a) numerous
nunca never
nupcial nuptial, wedding
la **nutrición** nutrition

O

o or
o sea in other words
el **objetivo** objective
el **objeto** object
la **obligación** obligation
obligatorio(a): el curso obligatorio required course
la **obra** work
la **obra de arte** work of art
la **obra dramática** play
la **obra teatral** play, 10.2
el/la **obrero(a)** worker, **9.1**
la **observación** observation
el/la **observador(a)** observer
observar to observe
el **obstáculo** obstacle
obtener to obtain
obvio(a) obvious
la **ocasión** occasion
occidental western
el **océano** ocean
ochenta eighty, 2.2
ocho eight, BV
ochocientos(as) eight hundred, 3.2
octavo(a) eighth, 6.2
octubre October, BV
ocupado(a) taken, 5.1; busy (phone); occupied, **7.1**
ocurrir to happen
el **oeste** west
oficial official
la **oficina** office, **9.1**
el **oficio** trade, **14.1**
ofrecer to offer, **14.2**

la **oftalmología** ophthalmology
el/la **oftalmólogo(a)** ophthalmologist
el **oído** ear, **4.1**
oír to hear
oír el tono to hear the dial tone, **3.2**
ojalá I hope, **14.1**
el **ojo** eye, 8.2
la **ola** wave, 9.1
el **óleo** oil (religious)
la **oliva: el aceite de oliva** olive oil
la **olla** pot, **10.1**
once eleven, BV
la **oncología** oncology
el/la **oncólogo(a)** oncologist
la **onza** ounce
opcional: el curso opcional elective course
la **ópera** opera
el/la **operador(a)** operator
operar to operate
la **opereta** operetta
opinar to think, to express an opinion, **10.2**
la **opinión** opinion
la **oportunidad** opportunity
oprimir to push
opuesto(a) opposite
oralmente orally
la **orden** order (restaurant), 5.1
el **ordenador** computer, **3.1**
la **oreja** ear, **4.1**
el **orfanato** orphanage
el **organillo** organ
el **organismo** organism
organizar to organize
el **órgano** organ
oriental eastern
el **origen** origin
original: en versión original in its original (language) version, 10.1
la **orilla** bank (of a river, lake, etc.)
a orillas de on the shores of

el **oro** gold
de oro (made of) gold, **4.1**
la **orquesta** orchestra, **13.1**
la **orquesta sinfónica** symphony orchestra
la **ortiga** nettle
la **ortopedia** orthopedics
oscuro(a) dark
la **ostra** oyster, **10.2**
otavaleño(a) of or from Otavalo (Ecuador)
el **otoño** autumn, BV
otro(a) other, another
el **oxígeno** oxygen
¡oye! listen!

P

la **paciencia** patience
el/la **paciente** patient
el **padre** father, 6.1
el **padre (religioso)** father (religious)
los **padres** parents, 6.1
el **padrino** godfather; best man, **13.1**
los **padrinos** godparents
pagar to pay, 3.1
pagar en la caja to pay at the cashier, 3.1
pagar la factura to pay the bill, **6.1**
la **página** page
la **página Web** Web page
el **pago** payment
el **pago mensual** monthly payment
el **país** country, 11.2
el **país extranjero** foreign country
el **paisaje** landscape
la **paja** straw, **13.2**
el **pájaro** bird
el **paje** page (wedding)
la **palabra** word
el **palacio** palace
la **palma** palm tree

el **pan** bread, **4.2**

  el pan dulce sweet roll, 5.1

  el pan tostado toast, 5.2

la **panadería** bakery, **4.2**

panameño(a) Panamanian, 2.1

panamericano(a) Panamerican

el **panqueque** pancake

la **pantalla** screen (movies), 10.1; computer monitor, **3.1**

  la pantalla de salidas y llegadas arrival and departure screen, 11.1

el **pantalón** pants, trousers, 3.2

  el pantalón corto shorts, 3.2

el **pañuelo** handkerchief, **4.1**

la **papa** potato, 5.1

  las papas fritas French fries, 5.1

el **papá** dad

la **papaya** papaya, **10.2**

el **papel** paper, 3.1; role, part

  el papel higiénico toilet paper, 12.2

  la hoja de papel sheet of paper, 3.1

la **papelería** stationery store, 3.1

el **paquete** package, 5.2

par: número par even number

el **par** pair, **4.1**

  el par de tenis pair of tennis shoes, 3.2

para for

  ¿para cuándo? for when?, 14.2; **2.2**

el **parabrisas** windshield, **11.1**

la **parada** stop, 13.2; **1.2**

  la parada de bus bus stop, **9.1**

el **parador** inn

el **paraíso** paradise

parar to stop, to block, 7.1

parcial: a tiempo parcial part-time *(adj.)*, **14.2**

pardo(a) brown

parear to pair, match

parecer to look like; to seem, **8.1**

parecido(a) similar

la **pared** wall

la **pareja** couple

el/la **pariente** relative, 6.1

el **parque** park, 5.2

  el parque de atracciones amusement park, 5.2

el **parquímetro** parking meter, **11.2**

el **párrafo** paragraph

la **parrilla** grill, 10.1

la **parte** part, 8.1

  ¿De parte de quién? Who's calling?, 3.2

  la mayor parte the greatest part, the most

  la parte superior upper part

  por todas partes everywhere

particular private, 6.2

  la casa particular private house, 6.2

particularmente especially

la **partida** departure

el **partido** game, match, 7.1

el **pasado** the past

pasado(a) past; last

  el (año) pasado last (year)

el/la **pasajero(a)** passenger, 11.1

el **pasaporte** passport, 11.1

pasar to pass, 7.2; to spend; to happen

  Lo están pasando muy bien. They're having a good time., 12.2

  pasar por to go through, 11.1

  pasar el tiempo to spend time, 5.1

  ¿Qué te pasa? What's the matter (with you)?, 8.1

el **pasatiempo** hobby, **5.1**

el **pase** pass (permission)

  pasear a caballo to go horseback riding

el **pasillo** aisle, 13.2; **1.2**

el **paso** step

la **pasta (crema) dentífrica** toothpaste, 12.2

el **pastel** pastry, 4.2; cake, **13.1**

la **pastelería** bakery, **4.2**

la **pastilla** pill, 8.2

  la pastilla de jabón bar of soap, 12.2

la **patata** potato, 10.1

el **patinaje lineal** roller blading

el **patrón** pattern

pavimentado(a) paved

el **pavimento** pavement

el **payaso** clown, 5.2

el **peaje** toll, 11.2

  la garita de peaje tollbooth, **11.2**

el **peatón** pedestrian, 9.1

el **pecho** chest, **8.1**

el **pedacito** little piece, **10.2**

el **pedazo** piece

el/la **pediatra** pediatrician

la **pediatría** pediatrics

  pedir (i, i) to ask for, 14.1; **2.1**

  pedir la cuenta to ask for the bill, **6.1**

  pedir prestado to borrow

el **peinado** hairdo

  peinarse to comb one's hair, 12.1

el **peine** comb, 12.1

  pelar to peel, **10.2**

la **película** film, movie, 6.2

  ver una película to see a film, 10.1

el **peligro** danger

  peligroso(a) dangerous

  pelirrojo(a) redheaded

el **pelo** hair, 12.1

la **pelota** ball (tennis, baseball, etc.), 7.2

  la pelota vasca jai alai

el/la **pelotari** jai alai player

la **peluca** wig

la **peluquería** hair salon, **12.1**

el/la **peluquero(a)** hair stylist, **12.1**

el **pendiente** earring, **4.1**

la **península** peninsula

el **pensamiento** thought

pensar (ie) to think

la **pensión** boarding house, 12.2

peor worse, worst

el/la peor the worst

el **pepino** cucumber, **10.1**

pequeño(a) small, 2.1

la **pera** pear, **9.2**

el **peral** pear tree, **9.2**

la **percha** clothes hanger, **6.2**

la **percusión** percussion

perder (ie) to lose, 7.1; to miss, 10.2

perder el autobús (la guagua, el camión) to miss the bus, 10.2

perdón excuse me

el/la **peregrino(a)** pilgrim

perezoso(a) lazy, 1.1

perfeccionar to perfect

el **periódico** newspaper, 6.2

el **período** period

el **permiso de conducir** driver's license, **11.1**

permitir to permit, 11.1

pero but

el **perrito** puppy

el **perro** dog, 6.1

la **persona** person, 1.2

el **personaje** character

el **personal** personnel, **14.2**

la **personalidad** personality

personalmente personally

pertenecer to belong

peruano(a) Peruvian

la **pesa** weight

pesado(a) heavy

pesar to weigh, **12.2**

la **pescadería** fish market, **4.2**

el **pescado** fish, 5.2

la **peseta** former monetary unit of Spain

el **peso** peso (monetary unit of several Latin American countries), BV; weight

la **petición** petition

el **petróleo** petroleum, oil

petrolero(a) oil (relating to)

el **piano** piano

la **picadura** sting, **8.1**

picar to sting, **8.1**; to dice, **10.2**

el/la **pícher** pitcher, 7.2

el **pico** peak, **7.2**

y pico just after (time)

el **pie** foot, 7.1; down payment

a pie on foot, 4.1

al pie de at the foot of

de pie standing

la **piedra** stone

la **pierna** leg, 7.1

la **pieza** room; piece

la **píldora** pill, 8.2

el/la **piloto** pilot, 11.2

la **pimienta** pepper, 14.1; **2.1**

el **pimiento** bell pepper, **10.2**

el **pimiento morrón** sweet pepper

pinchado(a) flat

el **pincel** brush, paintbrush

la **pinta** pint

pinta: tener buena pinta to look good (food), **4.2**

pintar to paint, **14.1**

el/la **pintor(a)** painter

pintoresco(a) picturesque, **9.1**

la **pintura** painting

la **piragua** crushed ice with syrup over it, **5.2**

los **pirineos** Pyrenees

la **pirueta** pirouette

la **piscina** swimming pool, 9.1

el **piso** floor, 6.2, apartment

la **pista** (ski) slope, 9.2; runway, **7.2**

la **pizarra** chalkboard, 4.2

el **pizarrón** chalkboard, 4.2

la **pizca** pinch

la **pizza** pizza, BV

la **placa** license plate

la **plaga** plague, menace

la **plancha de vela** sailboard, 9.1

practicar la plancha de vela to go windsurfing, 9.1

planchar to iron, **12.1**

planear to plan

el **plano** plan, map, **9.1**

la **planta** floor, 6.2; plant

la planta baja ground floor, 6.2

plástico(a) plastic, **4.2**

la bolsa de plástico plastic bag, **4.2**

la **plata** money (income)

el **plátano** banana, plantain, 5.2

el **platillo** home plate, 7.2; saucer, 14.1; **2.1**

el **plato** plate, dish, 14.1; **2.1**

la **playa** beach, 9.1

playera: la toalla playera beach towel, 9.1

la **plaza** seat, 13.2; **1.2**; town square, **9.1**

plazo: a corto (largo) plazo short- (long-)term

pleno: en pleno + (noun) in the middle of (noun)

el/la **plomero(a)** plumber, 14.1

plomo: sin plomo unleaded, **11.1**

la **pluma** pen, 3.1

la **población** population, people

pobre poor

el/la **pobre** the poor boy (girl)

el/la **pobretón(ona)** poor man (woman)

poco(a) little, few, 2.1

un poco (de) a little

poder (ue) to be able, 7.1

el **poema** poem

la **poesía** poetry

el/la **poeta** poet

el/la **policía** police officer

policíaco(a): novela policíaca detective fiction, mystery

político(a) political

Spanish-English Dictionary

el **pollo** chicken, 5.2

el **poncho** poncho, shawl, wrap

poner to put, 11.1

   poner en un yeso to put a cast on, **8.2**

   poner la mesa to set the table, 14.1; **2.1**

ponerse to put on, 12.1

   ponerse el maquillaje to put one's makeup on, 12.1

   ponerse la ropa to dress oneself, to put on clothes, 12.1

popular popular, 2.1

la **popularidad** popularity

por for

   por aquí over here

   por ciento percent

   por ejemplo for example

   por eso therefore, for this reason, that's why

   por favor please, BV

   por fin finally

   por hora per hour

   por la noche in the evening

   por lo general in general

   Por nada. You're welcome., BV

   por tierra overland

¿por qué? why?

el **porche** porch

el **pordiosero** beggar

el **poroto** string bean

porque because

portátil portable

el/la **porteño(a)** inhabitant of Buenos Aires

la **portería** goal line, 7.1

el/la **portero(a)** goalkeeper, goalie, 7.1

poseer to possess

la **posibilidad** possibility

posible possible

la **posición** position

la **postal** postcard, **12.2**

el **postre** dessert, 5.1

el/la **practicante** nurse practitioner

practicar to practice

   practicar el surfing (la plancha de vela, etc.) to go surfing (windsurfing, etc.), 9.1

el **precio** price

precioso(a) precious, beautiful

preciso(a) precise

precolombino(a) pre-Columbian

la **predicción** prediction

predominar to predominate

el **predominio** predominance

preferir (ie, i) to prefer

el **prefijo de país** country code, **3.2**

la **pregunta** question

preguntar to ask (a question)

el **premio: el Premio Nóbel** Nobel Prize

prender to turn on, **3.1**

   prender la máquina to turn (a device) on, **3.1**

la **preparación** preparation

preparar to prepare

la **presencia** presence

la **presentación** presentation

presentar to show (movie); to present

presente present (adj.)

el/la **presidente** president

la **presión** pressure, **11.1**

   la presión arterial blood pressure, **8.2**

   prestado: pedir prestado to borrow

el **préstamo** loan

prestar: prestar atención to pay attention, 4.2

el **prestigio** prestige

prevalecer to prevail

primario(a): la escuela primaria elementary school

la **primavera** spring, BV

primero(a) first, BV

en primera (clase) first-class, 13.1; **1.1**

los **primeros auxilios** first aid

el/la **primo(a)** cousin, 6.1

primordial fundamental

la **princesa** princess

principal main, principal

principalmente mainly

el/la **principiante** beginner, 9.2

prisa: a toda prisa as fast as possible

privado(a) private

   la casa privada private house, 6.2

probable probable

probarse (ue) to try on, **4.1**

el **problema** problem

procesar to process

la **procesión** procession

el **proceso** process

proclamar to proclaim

pródigo prodigal

la **producción** production

producido(a) produced

producir to produce

el **producto** product, 5.2

   los productos congelados frozen food, 5.2

la **profesión** profession, **14.1**

el/la **profesor(a)** teacher, professor, 2.1

profundo(a) deep

el **programa** program

el/la **programador(a) de informática** computer programmer, **14.1**

el **progreso** progress

prohibido(a) forbidden, **11.2**

la **promesa** promise

la **promoción** promotion

promover (ue) to promote

el **pronombre** pronoun

el **pronóstico** forecast

pronto: ¡Hasta pronto! See you soon!, BV

la **propaganda** publicity, advertising

la **propina** tip, 14.1; **2.1**

propio(a) (one's) own

la **prosa** prose

próspero(a): ¡Próspero Año Nuevo! Happy New Year, **13.2**

el/la **protagonista** protagonist

la **protección** protection

protector(a): la crema protectora sunblock, 9.1

la **proteína** protein

protestar to protest

el **protoplasma** protoplasm

el/la **proveedor(a)** provider

proveer to provide

la **provisión** provision

próximo(a) next, 13.2; **1.2**

en la próxima parada at the next stop, 13.2; **1.2**

proyectar to project, 10.1

el **proyecto** project

el/la **psiquiatra** psychiatrist

la **psiquiatría** psychiatry

publicar to publish

el **público** audience, 10.2

el **pueblo** town, 9.2

los pueblos jóvenes shantytowns (Peru)

el **puerco** pork

la **puerta** gate, 11.1; door, **6.1**

la puerta de salida departure gate, 11.1

puertorriqueño(a) Puerto Rican

pues well

el **puesto** market stall, **4.2**; position, **14.2**

la **pulgada** inch

pulsar: pulsar el botón to push the button, **3.1**

la **pulsera** bracelet, **4.1**

el **pulso: tomar el pulso** to take one's pulse, **8.2**

el **punto** stitch, **8.1**; dot, point

en punto on the dot, sharp, 4.1

los puntos cardinales cardinal points

poner puntos to give (someone) stitches

puntual punctual

el **puré de papas** mashed potatoes

puro(a) pure

Q

que who, that

¿qué? what? how?

qué what; how, BV

¡Qué absurdo! How absurd!

¡Qué enfermo(a) estoy! I'm so sick!

¿Qué tal? How are you?, BV

¿Qué te pasa? What's the matter (with you)?, 8.2

quechua Quechuan

quedar to remain, 7.1

quedar: No me queda(n) bien. It (They) doesn't (don't) look good on (fit) me., **4.1**

los **quehaceres** chores

querer (ie) to want, wish; to love

el **queso** cheese, 5.1

el **quetzal** quetzal (currency of Guatemala)

¿quién? who?, 1.1

¿De parte de quién? Who is calling?, **3.2**

¿quiénes? who? *(pl.)*, 2.1

la **química** chemistry, 2.2

químico(a) chemical

quince fifteen, BV

la **quinceañera** fifteen-year-old (girl)

quinientos(as) five hundred, 3.2

quinto(a) fifth, 6.2

el **quiosco** newsstand, 13.1; **1.1**

el **quirófano** operating room

Quisiera... I would like . . . , 14.2; **2.2**

quitar to take off, remove, **10.2**

quizás perhaps, 14.2

R

el **radiador** radiator, **11.1**

la **radiografía** X-ray, 8.2

la **raíz** root

rallar to grate, 10.2

la **rama** branch

la **ranura** disk drive, **3.1**; slot, **3.2**

rápidamente quickly

rápido quickly

la **raqueta** racket (sports), 9.1

raro(a) rare

el **rascacielos** skyscraper, **9.1**

el **rato** while

el **ratón** mouse (computer), **3.1**

la **raya** part (in hair), **12.1**

rayas: a rayas striped

los **rayos equis** X-rays

la **razón** reason

razonable reasonable

la **reacción** reaction

real royal

realista realistic

el/la **realista** realist

realmente really

la **rebanada** slice, **4.2**

rebanar to slice, **10.2**

rebotar to rebound

la **recámara** bedroom, 6.2

la **recepción** front desk (hotel), 6.1; admissions (hospital), 8.2; reception (party)

el/la **recepcionista** hotel clerk, **6.1**

el/la **receptor(a)** catcher, 7.2

la **receta** prescription, 8.2; recipe, **10.2**

recetar to prescribe, 8.2

recibir to receive, 5.1

el **reciclaje** recycling

recién recently

reciente recent

Spanish-English Dictionary

recitar to recite

reclamar to claim (luggage), 11.2

el **reclamo de equipaje** baggage claim, 11.2

reclutar to recruit

recoger to pick up

recoger el equipaje to claim one's luggage, 11.2

la **recomendación** recommendation

recomendar (ie) to recommend

reconocer to recognize

recordar (ue) to remember

recorrer to travel through

el **recorrido** trip, distance traveled

de largo recorrido long distance

el **recreo** recreation

el **rectángulo** rectangle

el **recuerdo** memory, recollection

la **recuperación: la sala de recuperación** recovery room

el **recurso: los recursos naturales** natural resources

el **departamento de recursos humanos** human resources department, 14.2

la **red** net, 9.1

navegar por la red to surf the Net

reducido(a) reduced (price)

reducir to set (bone), 8.2

reemplazar to replace

referir (ie, i) to refer

reflejar to reflect

el **reflejo** reflection

reflexionar to reflect

la **reforestación** reforestation

el **refresco** drink, beverage, 5.1

el **refrigerador** refrigerator, 10.1

el **refugio** refuge

regalar to give

el **regalo** gift, 6.1

la **región** region

regional regional

el **regionalismo** regionalism

registrar to register

la **regla** rule

regresar to return

el **regreso** return

el viaje de regreso return trip, trip back

regular regular, average, 2.2

la **reina** queen

reír to laugh

la **relación** relation

relacionado(a) related

relativamente relatively

religioso(a) religious

rellenar to fill

el **reloj** watch, **4.1**; clock, **13.2**

remar to row, 5.2

el **remedio** solution

renombrado(a) well-known

rentar to rent

renunciar to renounce, give up

reparar to repair

repentinamente suddenly

repetir (i, i) to repeat; to take seconds (meal)

el **reportaje** report

la **representación** performance (theater), 10.2

dar una representación to put on a performance, 10.2

el/la **representante** representative

representar to represent

representativo(a) representative

la **república** republic

la **República Dominicana** Dominican Republic

requerir (ie, i) to require, **14.1**

el **requisito** requirement

la **reservación** reservation, **6.1**

reservado(a) reserved, 13.2; **1.2**

reservar to reserve, 14.2; **2.2**

resfriado(a): estar resfriado(a) to have a cold, 8.1

la **residencia: la residencia para estudiantes** student housing, dormitory, **3.2**

el/la **residente** resident

resolver (ue) to solve

el **respaldo** back (of seat), **7.1**

la **respiración** breathing

respirar to breathe

responder to respond

la **responsabilidad** responsibility

responsabilizarse to make oneself responsible

la **respuesta** answer

restar to subtract

el **restaurante** restaurant, 14.1; **2.1**

restaurar to restore

el **resto** rest, remainder

los **restos** remains

el **resultado** result

la **retina** retina

el **retintín** jingle

retirar del fuego to remove from the heat (stove), **10.1**

el **retraso: con retraso** with a delay, late, 13.2; **1.2**

el **retrato** portrait

la **reunión** gathering

reunirse to get together

revisar to inspect, 11.1; to check

revisar el boleto to check the ticket, 11.1

revisar el aceite to check the oil (car), **11.1**

el/la **revisor(a)** (train) conductor, 13.2; **1.2**

la **revista** magazine, 6.2

la **revolución** revolution

revolver (ue) to turn around; to stir, **10.1**

el **rey** king

los **Reyes Magos** Three Wise Men, **13.2**

el Día de los Reyes Epiphany (January 6), **13.2**

rico(a) rich; delicious, 14.2; **2.2**

el/la **rico(a)** rich person

riguroso(a) rigorous

el **río** river, **7.2**

el **ritmo** rhythm

el **rito** ritual

el/la **rival** rival

la **roca** rock

rodar (ue) to roll

la **rodilla** knee, 7.1

rogar (ue) to beg, to plead

rojo(a) red, 3.2

el **rol** role

el **rollo de papel higiénico** roll of toilet paper, 12.2

el/la **romano(a)** Roman

romántico(a) romantic

romperse to break, **8.1**

la **ropa** clothing, 3.2

la ropa interior underwear, **4.1**

la ropa para caballeros (señoras) men's (women's) clothing, **4.1**

la ropa sucia dirty laundry, **12.1**

la tienda de ropa clothing store, 3.2

la **rosa** rose

rosado(a) pink, 3.2

el **rótulo** sign, **11.2**

rubio(a) blond(e), 1.1

las **ruedas: la silla de ruedas** wheelchair, **8.2**

la **ruina** ruin

el **rumor** rumor

la **ruta** route

la **rutina** routine, 12.1

rutinario(a) routine (adj.)

S

el **sábado** Saturday, BV

la **sábana** sheet, **6.2**

el/la **sabelotodo** know-it-all

saber to know (how), 11.2

sabio(a) wise

sabroso(a) delicious

sacar to get, 4.2; to take out, **3.1**

sacar un billete to buy a ticket

sacar una nota buena (mala) to get a good (bad) grade, 4.2

el **sacerdote** priest

el **saco** jacket, **4.1**

el saco de dormir sleeping bag, 12.2

sacrificar to sacrifice

el **sacrificio** sacrifice

la **sal** salt, 14.1; **2.1**

la **sala** room; living room, 6.2

la sala de clase classroom, 4.1

la sala de consulta doctor's office

la sala de emergencia emergency room, **8.1**

la sala de espera waiting room, 13.1; **1.1**

la sala de juegos game arcade, **5.1**

la sala de recuperación recovery room

la sala de salida departure area, 11.1

la sala de urgencias emergency room

el **salario** salary

la **salchicha** sausage, **10.1**

el **saldo** balance (bank)

la **salida** departure, leaving, 11.1; exit, **11.2**

la hora de salida departure hour, 13.1; **1.1**

la pantalla de llegadas y salidas arrival and departure screen, 11.1

la sala de salida departure area, 11.1

la salida de emergencia emergency exit, **7.1**

salir to leave, 10.1; to go out; to turn out

salir a tiempo to leave on time, 11.1

salir bien (en un examen) to do well (on an exam), 10.1

salir tarde to leave late, 11.1

el **salón** hall, **13.1**; room

el salón de clase classroom, 4.1

saltar to jump

la **salud** health

saludar to greet

el **saludo** greeting, BV

salvaje wild

salvar to save

salvo(a) safe

la **sandalia** sandal, **4.1**

la **sandía** watermelon, **10.2**

el **sándwich** sandwich, BV

la **sangre** blood

sano(a) healthy

el **santo** saint

el/la **sartén** frying pan, **10.1**

satisfacer to satisfy

satisfecho(a) satisfied, **14.1**

el **saxofono** saxophone

sazonar to season

el **secador** hair dryer, **12.1**

secar to dry, **12.2**

la **sección de (no) fumar** (no) smoking section, 11.1

seco(a) dry

el/la **secretario(a)** secretary, **14.1**

el **secreto** secret

secundario(a) secondary

la escuela secundaria high school, 1.1

Spanish-English Dictionary

sed: tener sed to be thirsty, 14.1; **2.1**

el **sedán** sedan, **11.1**

la **sede** seat (of government)

seguir (i, i) to follow, to continue, **11.2**

  Sigue derecho. Go straight.

según according to

segundo(a) second, 6.2

  el segundo tiempo second half (soccer), 7.1

  en segunda (clase) second-class, 13.1; **1.1**

la **seguridad** security, **7.1**

  el control de seguridad security (airport), 11.1

el **seguro** insurance

seguro(a): estar seguro(a) to be sure

seis six, BV

seiscientos(as) six hundred, 3.2

la **selección** selection

seleccionar to select

el **sello** stamp, **5.1**

la **selva** jungle

el **semáforo** traffic light, **9.1**

la **semana** week, BV

  el fin de semana weekend, BV

  el fin de semana pasado last weekend

  la semana pasada last week, 9.2

sembrar to sow, plant, **9.2**

el **semestre** semester

el/la **senador(a)** senator

sencillo(a) easy, simple

  el billete sencillo one-way ticket, 13.1; **1.1**

  el cuarto sencillo single room, **6.1**

la **senda** path, **5.2**

  caminar por la senda to walk along the path, **5.2**

  sentarse (ie) to sit down, 12.1

el **sentido** meaning, significance; direction, **11.2**

el sentido contrario opposite way, **11.2**

en cada sentido in either direction, **11.2**

una calle de sentido único one-way street, **11.2**

sentir (ie, i) to be sorry

sentirse (ie, i) bien (mal) to feel well (ill), **8.1**

la **señal de no fumar** no smoking sign, **7.1**

la **señal de tránsito** traffic sign

el **señor** sir, Mr., gentleman, BV

la **señora** Ms., Mrs., madam, BV

la **señorita** Miss, Ms., BV

separado(a) separated

septiembre September, BV

séptimo(a) seventh, 6.2

ser to be

  ser una lástima to be a pity

el **ser: el ser humano** human being

  el ser viviente living creature, being

la **serie** series

  la Serie mundial World Series

serio(a) serious, 1.1

  en serio seriously

el **servicio** service, tip, 5.1

  ¿Está incluido el servicio? Is the tip included?, 5.1

el **servicio de primeros auxilios** first aid service, paramedics, **8.1**

la **servilleta** napkin, 14.1; **2.1**

servir (i, i) to serve, 14.1; **2.1**

  ¿En qué puedo servirle? How may I help you?, **4.1**

sesenta sixty, 2.2

la **sesión** show (movies), 10.1

setecientos(as) seven hundred, 3.2

setenta seventy, 2.2

el **sexo** sex

sexto(a) sixth, 6.2

el **show** show

si if

sí yes

el **sida** AIDS

la **siembra** sowing

siempre always, 7.1

  de siempre y para siempre eternally, forever

la **sierra** sierra, mountain range

siete seven, BV

el **siglo** century

el **significado** meaning

significante meaningful

significar to mean

significativo(a) significant

siguiente following

la **silla** chair

la **silla de ruedas** wheelchair, **8.2**

el **sillón** armchair, **6.2**

similar similar

simpático(a) nice, 1.2

simple simple

sin without

  sin escala nonstop

sincero(a) sincere, 1.2

singles singles, 9.1

el **síntoma** symptom, 8.2

el **sirope** syrup

el/la **sirviente(a)** servant

el **sistema** system

  el sistema métrico metric system

el **sitio** place

la **situación** situation

situar to situate

sobre on top of; over; on, about

  sobre todo especially

el **sobre** envelope, **12.2**

sobresaltar to jump up

sobrevolar to fly over, **7.2**

la **sobrina** niece, 6.1

el **sobrino** nephew, 6.1

social: las ciencias sociales social sciences

la **sociedad** society

la **sociología** sociology

socorrer to help

el/la **socorrista** paramedic, **8.1**

el **socorro** help

el **sofá** sofa, **6.2**

el **sol** Peruvian coin; sun, 9.1

    Hace (Hay) sol. It's sunny., 9.1

    tomar el sol to sunbathe, 9.1

solamente only

el/la **soldado** soldier

soler (ue) to be accustomed to, tend to

la **solicitud de empleo** job application, **14.2**

solitario(a) solitary, lone

sólo only

solo(a) alone

    a solas alone

    el café solo black coffee, 5.1

soltero(a) single, bachelor

la **solución** solution

el **sombrero** hat

sonar (ue) to ring, **3.2**

el **sonido** sound

la **sonrisita** little smile

la **sopa** soup, 5.1

el **sorbete** sherbet, sorbet

el/la **sordo(a)** deaf person

sorprender to surprise

sostener to support

su his, her, their, your

subir to go up, 6.2; to board, to get on; to take up

    subir al tren to get on, to board the train, 13.1; **1.1**

subterráneo(a) underground

el **subtítulo** subtitle, 10.1

    con subtítulos with subtitles, 10.1

el **suburbio** suburb

suceder to happen

suceso: el buen suceso great event

sucio(a) dirty

    la ropa sucia dirty laundry, **12.1**

la **sucursal** branch (office)

sudamericano(a) South American

el **sudoeste** southwest

el **suegro** father-in-law

el **suelo** ground

el **suelto** change, **12.2**

el **sueño** dream

la **suerte** luck

    ¡Buena suerte! Good luck!

el **suéter** sweater, **4.1**

suficiente enough

sufrir to suffer

la **sugerencia** suggestion

sugerir (ie, i) to suggest

la **Suiza** Switzerland

sumar to add

súper super (gas), **11.1**

la **superficie** surface

superior: la escuela superior high school

el **supermercado** supermarket, 5.2

la **superstición** superstition

supuesto: por supuesto of course

el **sur** south

    sureste southeast

el **surf de nieve** snowboarding

el **surfing** surfing, 9.1

    practicar el surfing to surf, 9.1

el **suroeste** southwest

el **surtido** assortment

sus their, your *(pl.)*, 6.1

suspirar to sigh

la **sustancia: la sustancia controlada** controlled substance

la **sutura** stitch

T

el **T-shirt** T-shirt, 3.2

la **tabla: la tabla hawaiana** surfboard, 9.1

el **tablero** board, 7.1; gameboard, **5.1**

    el tablero de llegadas arrival board, 13.1; **1.1**

    el tablero de salidas departure board, 13.1; **1.1**

    el tablero indicador scoreboard, 7.1

la **tableta** pill, 8.2

el **taco** taco, BV

el **tacón** heel, **4.1**

taíno(a) Taino

la **tajada** slice, **4.2**

    tal: ¿Qué tal? How are you?, BV

el **talento** talent, 14.1

la **talla** size (clothing), 3.2

el **talón** luggage claim ticket, 11.1

el **talonario** checkbook

el **tamal** tamale, BV

el **tamaño** size, 3.2

también also

tampoco either

tan so

tan... como as . . . as, 8.2

el **tango** tango

el **tanque** gas tank, **11.1**

    llenar el tanque de gasolina to fill the tank with gas, **11.1**

el **tanto** point, 7.1

    marcar un tanto to score a point

    tanto(a) so much

    tanto(a)... como as much . . . as

    tantos(as)... como as many . . . as, **8.2**

tapar to cover, **10.2**

la **taquilla** box office, 10.1

tardar to take time

    tarda el viaje the trip takes (+ time)

tarde late

la **tarde** afternoon

    Buenas tardes. Good afternoon., BV

    esta tarde this afternoon, 9.2

por la tarde in the afternoon

la **tarea** task

hacer las tareas to do one's homework, **3.1**

la **tarifa** fare, rate

la **tarjeta** card, 11.1; registration card (hotel), **6.1**

la tarjeta de crédito credit card, 14.1; **2.1**

la tarjeta de embarque boarding pass, 11.1

la tarjeta de identidad estudiantil student I.D. card

la tarjeta postal postcard, **12.2**

la tarjeta telefónica telephone card, **3.2**

la **tasa** rate

la tasa de cambio exchange rate, **12.2**

la tasa de desempleo unemployment rate

el **taxi** taxi, 11.1

la **taza** cup, 14.1; **2.1**

te you (fam. pron.)

el **té** tea, 5.1

el té helado iced tea, 5.1

teatral theatrical, 10.2

el **teatro** theater, 10.2

salir del teatro to leave the theater, 10.2

la **tecla** key (on keyboard), **3.2**

el **teclado** keyboard, **3.1**; telephone keypad, **3.2**

el/la **técnico(a)** technician, **8.2**

la **tecnología** technology

la **telecomunicación** telecommunication, **3.1**

telefonear to telephone

telefónico(a) (related to the) telephone

la línea telefónica telephone line

la llamada telefónica telephone call, **3.2**

el **teléfono** telephone

el teléfono celular cellular telephone, **3.2**

el teléfono de botones push-button telephone, **3.2**

el teléfono público public (pay) telephone, **3.2**

hablar por teléfono to talk on the phone

el **telesilla** chairlift, 9.2

el **telesquí** ski lift, 9.2

la **televisión** television, 6.2

el **televisor** television set, **6.2**

el **telón** curtain (stage), 10.2

el **tema** theme, subject

temer to fear

la **temperatura** temperature, 9.2

templado(a) temperate

temprano early, 12.1

el **tenedor** fork, 14.1; **2.1**

tener (ie) to have, 6.1

tener un accidente to have an accident, **8.1**

tener... años to be ... years old, 6.1

tener buena pinta to look good, **4.2**

tener cuidado to be careful

tener hambre to be hungry, 14.1; **2.1**

tener lugar to take place, occur, **8.1**

tener miedo to be afraid

tener que to have to

tener sed to be thirsty, 14.1; **2.1**

el **tenis** tennis, 9.1

los **tenis** tennis shoes, 3.2

el par de tenis pair of tennis shoes, 3.2

el/la **tenista** tennis player

la **tensión arterial** blood pressure, **8.2**

tercer(o)(a) third, 6.2

la **terminal: la terminal de pasajeros** passenger terminal, **7.2**

terminar to end, finish, **3.1**

el **término** term

la **ternera** veal, 14.2; **2.2**

la **terraza** terrace (sidewalk café)

terrible terrible

el **terror** terror, fear

el **tétano** tetanus

la **tía** aunt, 6.1

el **ticket** ticket, 9.2

el **tiempo** time; weather, 9.1; half (game)

a tiempo on time, 11.1

a tiempo completo (parcial) full- (part-) time (adj.), **14.2**

el segundo tiempo second half (game), 7.1

pasar el tiempo to spend (pass) time, **5.1**

la **tienda** store, 3.2

la tienda de abarrotes grocery store, **4.2**

la tienda de departamentos department store

la tienda de ropa clothing store, 3.2

la tienda de ropa para caballeros men's clothing store, **4.1**

la tienda de ropa para señoras women's clothing store, **4.1**

la tienda de ultramarinos grocery store, **4.2**

la tienda de videos video store

tierno(a) tender

la **tierra** land

por tierra by land, overland

el **tigre** tiger

las **tijeras** scissors, **12.1**

el **tilde** accent

tímido(a) timid, shy, 1.2

la **tintorería** dry cleaner, **12.1**

el/la **tintorero(a)** dry cleaner, **12.1**

el **tío** uncle, 6.1

los tíos aunt and uncle, 6.1

el **tiovivo** merry-go-round, **5.2**

típicamente typically

típico(a) typical

el **tipo** type

el **tipo de cambio** exchange rate, **12.2**

el **tique** ticket, **9.1**

tirar to kick, 7.1; to throw

  tirar el balón to kick (throw) the ball, 7.2

el **título universitario** university degree, **14.1**

la **toalla** towel, **6.2**

  la toalla playera beach towel, 9.1

el **tobillo** ankle, **8.1**

tocar to touch; to play (music)

  tocar la bocina to honk the horn

todavía yet, still

todo: todo el mundo everyone

todos(as) everybody, 2.2; everything, all

  por todas partes everywhere

tomar to take, 4.1

  tomar agua (leche, café) to drink water (milk, coffee)

  tomar apuntes to take notes, 4.2

  tomar el bus (escolar) to take the (school) bus, 4.1

  tomar el desayuno to eat breakfast, 12.1

  tomar el pulso to take someone's pulse, 8.2

  tomar el sol to sunbathe, 9.1

  tomar fotos to take photos

  tomar la tensión (presión) arterial to take someone's blood pressure, 8.2

  tomar un refresco to have (drink) a beverage

  tomar un vuelo to take a flight, 11.1

  tomar una ducha to take a shower, 12.1

  tomar una merienda to have a snack, 4.2

  tomar una radiografía to take an X-ray, **8.2**

el **tomate** tomato

el **tomo** volume

la **tonelada** ton

el **tono** dial tone, **3.2**; hue

  tonto(a) foolish

  torcerse (ue) to twist, **8.1**

el **torniquete** turnstile, **9.1**

la **toronja** grapefruit, **10.1**

  torpe stupid

la **torre: la torre de control** control tower, **7.2**

la **torta** cake, **13.1**

la **tortilla** tortilla, 5.1

la **tos: tener tos** to have a cough, 8.1

  toser to cough, 8.1

la **tostada** toast

  tostadito(a) sunburned, tanned

  tostado(a): el pan tostado toast, 5.2

  tostar to toast

el **tostón** fried plantain slice

  totalmente totally, completely

  tóxico(a) toxic

el/la **trabajador(a)** worker

  trabajar to work, 3.2

    trabajar a tiempo completo to work full-time, 14.2

    trabajar a tiempo parcial to work part-time, 14.2

el **trabajo** work; job, **14.2**

  el trabajo a tiempo completo (parcial) full-time (part-time) job, 14.2

la **tradición** tradition

  tradicional traditional

  traer to bring, 14.1; **2.1**

el **tráfico** traffic

la **tragedia** tragedy

el **traje** suit, 3.2

  el traje de baño bathing suit, 9.1

  el traje de gala evening gown, dress

el **tramo** stretch

  tranquilo(a) peaceful; calm; quiet

  transbordar to transfer, 13.2; **1.2**

  transformar to transform

  transmitir to send, to transmit, 3.1

el **transporte** transportation

  tras after

  trasladar to transfer, move

el **tratamiento** treatment

  tratar to treat; to try

el **trayecto** stretch (of road)

  trece thirteen, BV

  treinta thirty, BV

  treinta y uno thirty-one, 2.2

el **tren** train, 13.2; **1.2**

  el tren directo non-stop train, 13.2; **1.2**

  el tren local local train, 13.2; **1.2**

la **trenza** braid

  tres three, BV

  trescientos(as) three hundred, 3.2

la **tribu** tribe

el **tribunal** court, **14.1**

el **trigo** wheat, **9.2**

la **tripulación** crew, 11.2

  triste sad, 8.1

  triunfante triumphant

el **trocito** piece, **10.2**

el **trombón** trombone

la **trompeta** trumpet

  tropical tropical

  tu your (sing. fam.)

  tú you (sing. fam.)

el **tubo de escape** exhaust pipe

el **tubo de pasta (crema) dentífrica** tube of toothpaste, 12.2

la **turbulencia** turbulence, **7.2**

el/la **turista** tourist, 10.2

Spanish-English Dictionary

U

u or (used instead of **o** before words beginning with **o** or **ho**)

Ud., usted you *(sing. form.)* 3.2

Uds., ustedes you *(pl. form.)*, 2.2

último(a) last

ultramarinos: la tienda de ultramarinos grocery store, **4.2**

un(a) a, an, 1.1

la **una** one o'clock, 2.2

único(a) only; unique

la **unidad: la unidad de cuidado intensivo** intensive care unit

el **uniforme** uniform

la **universidad** university

universitario(a) (related to) university

uno one, BV

unos(as) some

urbano(a) urban

urgencias: la sala de urgencias emergency room

la **urología** urology

el/la **urólogo(a)** urologist

usado(a) used

usar to wear (size), 3.2; to use

utilizar to use

las **uvas** grapes, 10.1

V

la **vaca** cow, 9.2

la **vacación** vacation, 6.2

el/la **vago(a)** loafer, idler

el **vagón** train car, 13.1; **1.1**

la **vainilla: de vainilla** vanilla *(adj.)*, 5.1

la **vainita** string bean

¡vale! OK!

valer to be worth

valeroso(a) brave

valiente brave

el **valle** valley, 7.2

el **valor** value, worth

    el valor real true value

vamos let's go

la **variación** variation

variado(a) varied

variar to vary, change

la **variedad** variety

vario(a) various

el **varón** male

vasco(a) Basque

    la pelota vasca jai alai

el **vaso** (drinking) glass, 12.1

el **váter** toilet, **6.2**

el/la **vecino(a)** neighbor

el **vegetal** vegetable, 5.2

el/la **vegetariano(a)** vegetarian

veinte twenty, BV

veinticinco twenty-five, BV

veinticuatro twenty-four, BV

veintidós twenty-two, BV

veintinueve twenty-nine, BV

veintiocho twenty-eight, BV

veintiséis twenty-six, BV

veintisiete twenty-seven, BV

veintitrés twenty-three, BV

veintiuno twenty-one, BV

la **vela** candle, **13.1**

la **velocidad** speed, **11.2**

    la velocidad máxima speed limit, **11.2**

vencer to conquer

el **vendaje** bandage, **8.2**

    poner un vendaje to put a bandage on, **8.2**

el/la **vendedor(a)** salesperson, **11.1**

vender to sell, 5.2

el **veneno** poison

venenoso(a) poisonous

venezolano(a) Venezuelan

venir to come, 11.1

el **viernes (sábado, etc.) que viene** next Friday (Saturday, etc.)

la **venta** sale, **14.1**

la **ventaja** advantage

la **ventanilla** ticket window, 9.2; window (airplane), **7.1**; teller's window, **12.2**

ver to see; to watch, 5.1

el **verano** summer, BV

el **verbo** verb

la **verdad** truth

    ¡verdad! that's right (true)!

verdadero(a) true, real

verde green, 3.2

    la judía verde green bean, 5.2

la **verdulería** greengrocer store, **4.2**

la **verdura** vegetable

verificar to check, 13.1; **1.1**

la **versión: en versión original** in (its) original version, 10.1

el **verso** verse

vertical vertical

vestido(a) dressed

el **vestido** dress, 4.1

    los vestidos clothes *(pl.)*

vestirse (i, i) to get dressed

el/la **veterinario(a)** veterinarian

la **vez** time

    a veces at times, sometimes, 7.1

    de vez en cuando now and then

    en vez de instead of

    una vez más one more time, again

la **vía** track, 13.1; **1.1**

viajar to travel

    viajar en avión to travel by plane, 11.1

el **viaje** trip

    el viaje de novios honeymoon

    el viaje de regreso return trip

hacer un viaje to take a
trip, 11.1
el/la **viajero(a)** traveler
viceversa vice versa
víctima victim, **8.1**
victorioso(a) victorious
la **vida** life
la vida escolar school life
el **video** video
viejo(a) old, 6.1
el/la **viejo(a)** old person
el **viento** wind
el **viernes** Friday, BV
villa: villa miseria
shantytown (Arg.)
el **vinagre** vinegar
la **viola** viola
el **violín** violin
visible visible
visitar to visit
la **víspera de Año Nuevo**
New Year's Eve, **13.2**
la **vista** view
vital vital
la **vitamina** vitamin
la **vitrina** shop window, **4.1**
la **vivienda** housing
viviente: el ser viviente
living creature, being

vivir to live, 5.2
vivo(a) living, alive
la **vocal** vowel
volar (ue) to fly, **7.2**
el **voleibol** volleyball
el/la **voluntario(a)** volunteer
volver (ue) to return, 7.1
volver a casa to return
home, 10.2
la **voz** voice
en voz alta aloud
el **vuelo** flight, 11.1
el número del vuelo
flight number, 11.1
el vuelo directo direct
flight, **7.2**
el vuelo nacional
domestic flight
tomar un vuelo to take a
flight, 11.1
la **vuelta: dar la vuelta** to
turn around

y and, BV
y cuarto a quarter past
(the hour)

y media half past
(the hour)
y pico just after (the hour)
ya now; already
la **yarda** yard
el **yeso** cast, **8.2**
yo I, 1.1
el **yogur** yogurt

la **zanahoria** carrot,
5.2
la **zapatería** shoe store,
4.1
el **zapato** shoe, 3.2
la **zona** zone, area,
district
la zona comercial
business district, **9.1**
la zona industrial
industrial area, **9.1**
la zona residencial
residential area, **9.1**
el **zoológico** zoo, **5.2**
el **zumo de naranja** orange
juice (Spain)

English-Spanish Dictionary

This English-Spanish Dictionary contains all productive and receptive vocabulary from Levels 1 and 2. The numbers following each productive entry indicate the chapter and vocabulary section in which the word is introduced. For example, **3.2** in dark print means that the word was first taught in **Capítulo 3, Palabras 2.** A light print number means that the word was introduced in **¡Buen viaje!,** Level 1. BV refers to the introductory **Bienvenidos** lessons in Level 1. If there is no number following an entry, this means that the word or expression is there for receptive purposes only.

a, an un(a), 1.1
aboard, on board a bordo de
about sobre; acerca de; **(time)** a eso de, **4.1**
above encima; por encima de, 9.1
abroad en el extranjero
abstract abstracto(a)
abuse el abuso
academic académico(a)
academy la academia
accent el tilde
to **accept** aceptar
access el acceso
accident el accidente, **8.1**
to **accommodate** acomodar
accompaniment el acompañamiento
to **accompany** acompañar
according to según
account (bank) la cuenta
  checking account la cuenta corriente, **12.2**
  savings account la cuenta de ahorros
accountant el/la contable, **14.1**
ache el dolor, 8.1
to **ache: My . . . ache(s).** Me duele(n)… , **8.2**
acrylic el acrílico
action la acción
active activo(a)
activity la actividad
actor el actor, 10.2

actress la actriz, 10.2
to **adapt** adaptar
to **add** sumar; agregar, añadir, **10.2**
addiction la adicción
addition: in addition to además de
address la dirección
adequate adecuado(a)
to **adjust** ajustar
to **admire** admirar
admission ticket la entrada, 10.1
to **admit** admitir, **8.2**
adolescence la adolescencia
adolescent el/la adolescente
adorable adorable
adoration la adoración
to **adore** adorar
to **adorn** adornar
advance el avance
advantage la ventaja
adventure la aventura
advertisement el anuncio, **14.2**
advertising la propaganda
advice el consejo
to **advise** aconsejar
aerobic aeróbico(a)
to **affect** impresionar
African africano(a)
African American afroamericano(a)
after después (de), 5.1; tras
afternoon la tarde
  Good afternoon. Buenas tardes., BV

  in the afternoon por la tarde
  this afternoon esta tarde, 9.2
again de nuevo
against contra, 7.1
age la edad
  how old are you? ¿Cuántos años tienes?
agency la agencia
  employment agency la agencia de empleos
agent el/la agente, 11.1
  customs agent el/la agente de aduana, 11.2
aging person el/la envejeciente
agreed, Fine. Conforme. 14.2
agricultural agrícola
ahead adelante
AIDS el sida
air el aire, **11.1**
air conditioning el aire acondicionado, **6.2**
air traffic controller el/la controlador(a), **7.2**
airline la línea aérea
airmail el correo aéreo, **12.2**
airplane el avión, 11.1
  small airplane la avioneta, **7.2**
airport el aeropuerto, 11.1
aisle el pasillo, 13.2; **1.2**
album el álbum
alcohol el alcohol
alcoholism el alcoholismo
algebra el álgebra, 2.2

alive vivo(a)

all todos(as)

allergy la alergia, 8.2

to **allow** consentir (ie, i); dejar

almost casi

alone solo(a); a solas

aloud en voz alta

already ya

also también

to **alternate** alternar

although aunque

altitude la altitud, la altura, **7.2**

always siempre, 7.1

ambassador el/la embajador(a)

ambulance la ambulancia, **8.1**

American americano(a), 1.1

amount la cantidad

amusement la diversión

amusement park el parque de atracciones, **5.2**

amusement park ride la atracción, **5.2**

amusing divertido(a)

analysis el análisis

analytical analítico(a)

to **analyze** analizar

ancient antiguo(a), **5.1**

and y, BV

Andalusian andaluz(a)

Andean andino(a)

anecdote la anécdota

angry enfadado(a)

animal el animal

farm animal el animal doméstico, **9.2**

ankle el tobillo, **8.1**

anniversary el aniversario

to **announce** anunciar

announcement el anuncio, **7.1**

another otro(a)

to **answer** contestar, 3.2

answer la respuesta

answering machine el contestador automático, **3.2**

Antarctic la Antártida

antibiotic el antibiótico, 8.2

antiquated anticuado(a)

antiquity la antigüedad

any cualquier

apartment el apartamento, el departamento, 6.2; el piso

apartment house la casa de apartamentos (departamentos), 6.2

apostle el apóstol

to **appear** aparecer

appearance la apariencia

appendicitis la apendicitis

to **applaud** aplaudir, 10.2

applause el aplauso, 10.2

to receive applause recibir aplausos, 10.2

apple la manzana, 5.2

apple tree el manzano, **9.2**

application (job) la solicitud (de empleo)

to **apply (for a job)** solicitar trabajo

to **approach** acercarse (de)

appropriate apropiado(a)

April abril, BV

aptitude la aptitud

Arab el/la árabe

archaeological arqueológico(a)

archaeologist el/la arqueólogo(a)

archeology la arqueología

architect el/la arquitecto(a), **14.1**

area el área (f.); la zona

area code la clave de área, **3.2**

Argentinian argentino(a), 2.1

argument la disputa

arid árido(a)

arithmetic la aritmética, 2.2

arm el brazo, 7.1

armchair el sillón, **6.2**

around alrededor de, 6.2

arrival la llegada, 11.1

arrival and departure screen la pantalla de llegadas y salidas, 11.1

to **arrive** llegar, 4.1

arrogant altivo(a), arrogante

art el arte (f.), 2.2

fine arts las bellas artes

artichoke la alcachofa, 14.2; **2.2**

artifact el artefacto

artist el/la artista, 10.2

artistic artístico(a)

as como, 1.2

as . . . as tan... como, **8.2**

as many . . . as tantos(as)... como, **8.2**

as much . . . as tanto(a)... como

to **ask (a question)** preguntar; (questions) hacer preguntas, **14.2**

to **ask for** pedir (i, i), 14.1

to ask for the bill pedir la cuenta, **6.1**

to **ask questions** hacer preguntas, **14.2**

asleep dormido(a)

aspect el aspecto

aspirin la aspirina, 8.2

to **assist** atender (ie), **4.1**

assortment el surtido

to **assure** asegurar

astute astuto(a)

at a

at that time en aquel entonces

athlete el/la atleta

athletic atlético(a)

atmosphere el ambiente; la atmósfera

to **attack** atacar

attack el ataque

to **attend** asistir

attention: to pay attention prestar atención, 4.2

attractive atractivo(a)

audience el público, 10.2

August agosto, BV

aunt la tía, 6.1

aunt and uncle los tíos, 6.1

authentic auténtico(a)

author el/la autor(a), 10.2

automatic teller el cajero automático

English-Spanish Dictionary

automatically
automáticamente

automobile el automóvil

autumn el otoño, BV

available disponible

avenue la avenida, **9.1**

average medio(a); regular,
2.2

aviation la aviación

avocado el aguacate, **10.2**

B

baby el/la bebé

bachelor's degree el
bachillerato

back (of seat) el respaldo, **7.1**

background (ancestry)
la ascendencia

backpack la mochila, 3.1

bacteria la bacteria

bad malo(a), 2.1; mal, 14.2;
2.2

   **to be in a good (bad)
mood** estar de buen
(mal) humor, **8.1**

   bad-tempered
malhumorado(a)

bag la bolsa, 5.2

   cloth shopping bag el
capacho

   plastic bag la bolsa de
plástico, **4.2**

baggage el equipaje, 11.1

baggage claim el reclamo
de equipaje, 11.2

   carry-on baggage el
equipaje de mano

bakery la panadería, la
pastelería, **4.2**

balance (bank) el saldo

ball (soccer, basketball) el
balón 7.1; **(baseball,
tennis)** la pelota , 7.2

balloon el globo, **5.2**

ballpoint pen el bolígrafo,
3.1

banana el plátano, 5.2; la
banana, **10.2**

band (music) la banda

bandage el vendaje, **8.2**

   to put a bandage on
poner un vendaje, **8.2**

bank (of a river) la orilla

bank el banco, **12.2**

bank statement el estado
del banco

banking bancario(a)

baptism el bautizo

bar: bar of soap la barra de
jabón, la pastilla de jabón,
12.2

barber el barbero, **12.1**

bargain la ganga

to **base** basar

base la base, 7.2

baseball el béisbol, 7.2

baseball field el campo de
béisbol, 7.2

baseball game el juego de
béisbol, 7.2

baseball player el/la
beisbolista; el/la
jugador(a) de béisbol, 7.2

based (on) basado(a)

basic básico(a)

basket (basketball) el
canasto, la canasta, el
cesto, 7.2; **(jai alai)** la cesta

basketball el baloncesto, el
básquetbol, 7.2

basketball court la cancha
de básquetbol, 7.2

   to put in (make) a basket
encestar, 7.2

Basque vasco(a)

bat el bate, 7.2

bath el baño

   to take a bath bañarse,
12.1

bathing suit el bañador, el
traje de baño, 9.1

bathroom el baño, el cuarto
de baño, 6.2

bathtub la bañera, **6.2**

batter el/la bateador(a), 7.2

battery la batería

battle la batalla

bay la bahía

to **be** ser, 1.1; estar, 4.1

   to be afraid tener miedo

   **to be in a good (bad)
mood** estar de buen
(mal) humor

   to be happy (sad) estar
contento(a) (triste)

   to be hungry tener
hambre, 14.1; **2.1**

   to be married estar
casado(a)

   to be sick estar enfermo(a)

   to be thirsty tener sed,
14.1; **2.1**

   to be tired esta cansado(a)

   to be . . . years old tener...
años, 6.1

   to be able poder (ue), 7.1

to **be accustomed to, tend
to** soler (ue)

to **be alarmed** alarmarse

to **be based** basarse

to **be born** nacer, **13.1**

to **be called** llamarse, 12.1

to **be familiar with** conocer,
11.1

to **be frightened** asustarse

to **be glad about** alegrarse
de, **13.1**

to **be going to (do something)**
ir a + *infinitive*

to **be important** importar

to **be named** llamarse, 12.1

to **be sorry** sentir (i, i)

to **be worth** valer

   beach la playa, 9.1

   beach resort el balneario, 9.1

   beach towel la toalla
playera, 9.1

   bean el frijol, la habichuela,
5.2

      black bean la habichuela
negra, el frijol negro, **10.2**

      string (green) bean la
habichuela tierna

to **bear** llevar

   beard la barba

   beau, heartthrob el galán

   beautiful bello(a),
hermoso(a), 1.1; precioso(a)

   beauty la belleza

   because porque

to **become enamored of (to
fall for)** flechar

bed la cama, 8.1

  to go to bed acostarse (ue), 12.1

  to make the bed hacer la cama, **6.2**

  to stay in bed guardar cama, 8.1

bedroom el cuarto de dormir; el cuarto, el dormitorio, la recámara, 6.2; la habitación, **6.1**

bee la abeja, **8.1**

beef la carne de res, 14.2; **2.2**

before antes de, 5.1

to **beg** rogar (ue)

to **begin** comenzar (ie); empezar (ie), 7.1

beginner el/la principiante, 9.2

beginning: at the beginning al principio

  beginning of the school year la apertura de clases

to **behave** comportarse

behavior la actuación

behind atrás; detrás de, **5.2**

to **believe** creer, 8.2

bell pepper el pimiento, **10.2**

bellhop el botones, **6.1**

to **belong** pertenecer

below debajo (de), **7.1**

below zero bajo cero, 9.2

belt el cinturón, **4.1**

  seat belt el cinturón de seguridad, **7.1**

benefit el beneficio

berth la litera, 13.2; **1.2**

beside al lado de, **5.2**

besides además

best man el padrino, **13.1**

better, best mejor

between entre, 7.1

beverage el refresco, 5.1; la bebida, **7.1**

biblical bíblico(a)

to **bicycle** ir en bicicleta, 12.2

bicycle la bicicleta

big gran, grande

bilingual bilingüe

bill la factura, **6.1**; (money) el billete, **12.2**; (check) la cuenta, 5.1

biography la biografía

biological biológico(a)

biologist el/la biólogo(a)

biology la biología, 2.2

bird el ave (f.); el pájaro

birthday el cumpleaños, 6.1

black negro(a), 3.2

blanket la frazada, la manta, **6.2**

bleach el blanqueador

blessing la bendición

block (city) la cuadra, **11.2**

to **block** bloquear, parar, 7.1

blond(e) rubio(a), 1.1

blood la sangre

blood pressure la presión arterial, la tensión arterial, **8.2**

blouse la blusa, 3.2

blue azul , 3.2

  dark blue azul oscuro

blue jeans el blue jean, 3.2

to **board** embarcar, 11.2; subir, 13.1; **1.1**; abordar

to **board the train** subir al tren, 13.1; **1.1**

board el tablero, 7.1

  arrival board el tablero de llegadas, 13.1; **1.1**

  departure board el tablero de salidas, 13.1; **1.1**

  scoreboard el tablero indicador, 7.1

boarding house la pensión, 12.2

boarding pass la tarjeta de embarque, 11.1

boat el bote, **5.2**

body el cuerpo, **8.1**

to **boil** hervir (ie, i), **10.1**

boiling la ebullición

bone el hueso, **8.2**

  to set the bone reducir el hueso, **8.2**

book el libro, 3.1

boot la bota, 9.2

to **border** bordear

border el borde

to **bore** aburrir

boring aburrido(a), 2.1

born nacido(a)

to **borrow** pedir prestado

boss el/la jefe(a)

bottle la botella, 4.2

  bottle of mineral water la botella de agua mineral, 12.2

boulevard el bulevar, **9.1**

box office la taquilla, 10.1

boy el muchacho, 1.1; el chico

boyfriend el novio

bracelet la pulsera, **4.1**

braid la trenza

to **brake** poner los frenos

brakes los frenos, **11.1**

branch (office) la sucursal; la filial

branch (of menora) el brazo, **13.2**

branch (tree) la rama

brass (instruments in orchestra) instrumentos de metal

brave valeroso(a); valiente

bread el pan, **4.2**

to **break** romperse, **8.1**

breakdown la avería

breakfast el desayuno, 5.2

to **breathe** respirar

breathing la respiración

bricklayer el/la albañil, **14.1**

bride la novia, **13.1**

brief breve

bright brillante

to **bring** llevar, 6.1; traer, 14.1; **2.1**

broken down averiado(a)

bronze el bronce, 10.2

brook el arroyo

brother el hermano, 6.1

brown de color marrón, 3.2; pardo(a)

brunette moreno(a), 1.1

brush el cepillo, 12.2; (paint) el pincel

to **brush one's hair** cepillarse, 12.1

to **brush one's teeth** cepillarse los dientes, lavarse los dientes, 12.1

building el edificio, **9.1**

burial el entierro

burner (stove) la hornilla, **10.1**

to **bury** enterrar (ie)

bus el bus, 4.1; el autobús, 10.1; **(Mexico)** el camión, 10.1; **(Puerto Rico, Cuba)** la guagua, 10.1

　　school bus el bus escolar, 4.1

　　bus stop la parada de bus, **9.1**

business el comercio; la empresa, **14.1**

business district la zona comercial, **9.1**

businessman (woman) el/la comerciante, **14.1**; el/la empresario(a)

busy (phone) ocupado

but pero

butcher shop la carnicería, **4.2**

butter la mantequilla, **10.2**

button el botón, **3.1**

to **buy** comprar, 3.1

buying la compra, **14.1**

by no means de ninguna manera, 1.1

by the way a propósito

cabin la cabina, **7.1**

café el café, 5.1; la confitería

　　outdoor café el café al aire libre

cafeteria la cafetería

cage la jaula, **5.2**

cake el bizcocho, la torta, el pastel, **13.1**

to **calculate** calcular

calculator la calculadora, 3.1

calculus el cálculo, 2.2

to **call oneself, be named** llamarse, 12.1

to **call; to telephone** llamar, **3.2**

　　Who is calling? ¿De parte de quién?, **3.2**

call la llamada (telefónica), **3.2**

　　long distance call la llamada larga, **3.2**

called llamado(a)

calm tranquilo(a)

calorie la caloría

camel el camello, **13.2**

campaign la campaña

can el bote, la lata, 5.2

Canadian canadiense

candid franco(a)

candidate el/la aspirante, el/la candidato(a), **14.2**

candle la vela, **13.1**

canned enlatado(a)

canvas (painting) el lienzo

canyon el cañón

cap la gorra, 3.2

capital la capital

captain (airplane) el/la comandante, 11.2

car el carro, el coche, 4.1

　　by car en carro, 4.1

　　dining car el coche-comedor, el coche-cafetería, 13.2

　　sleeping car el coche cama, 13.2

　　sports car el carro deportivo, **11.1**

　　train car el coche, 13.2

carbohydrate el carbohidrato

card la tarjeta, 11.1

　　credit card la tarjeta de crédito, 14.1; **2.1**

　　registration card (hotel) la tarjeta, la ficha, **6.1**

　　student I.D. card la tarjeta de identidad estudiantil

　　telephone card la tarjeta telefónica, **3.2**

cardinal points los punto cardinales

cardiologist el/la cardiólogo(a)

cardiology la cardiología

care: intensive care el cuidado intensivo

career la carrera

careful! ¡cuidado!

　　to be careful tener cuidado

carefully con cuidado

to **caress** acariciar

Caribbean el Caribe

Caribbean Sea el mar Caribe

caricaturist el/la caricaturista

carousel horse el caballito, 5.2

carpenter el/la carpintero(a), **14.1**

carrot la zanahoria, 5.2

to **carry** llevar, 3.1

to **carry out** efectuar

cart el carrito, **4.2**

case el caso, **7.1**

cash el dinero en efectivo, **12.2**

cash register la caja, 3.1

to **cash a check** cobrar un cheque, **12.2**

cashier el/la cajero(a), **14.1**

cast el yeso, **8.2**

castillian castellano(a)

castle el castillo

cat el/la gato(a), 6.1

to **catch** atrapar, 7.2

　　catcher el/la cátcher, el/la receptor(a), 7.2

category la categoría

cathedral la catedral

catholic católico(a)

cattle el ganado, 9.2

cauliflower la coliflor, **10.1**

to **cause** causar

cause la causa

CD-ROM el CD-ROM, **3.1**

to **celebrate** celebrar, **13.1**

celebration la celebración

cell phone el teléfono celular, **3.2**

cellular celular

center el centro

central central

Central America la América Central

century el siglo

cereal el cereal, 5.2

ceremony la ceremonia

certain cierto(a)

Certainly!, Of course! ¡Claro!

chain (necklace) la cadena, **4.1**

 gold chain la cadena de oro, **4.1**

chair la silla

 armchair el sillón, **6.2**

chairlift el telesilla, 9.2

chalkboard la pizarra, el pizarrón, 4.2

champion el/la campeón(ona), **5.1**

championship el campeonato

change el cambio, **12.2**

to **change** variar; cambiar, **12.2**

 to change the towels cambiar las toallas, **6.2**

 to change trains (transfer) transbordar, 13.2; **1.2**

channel (TV) el canal

Chanukah Hanuka, **13.2**

 Happy Chanukah! ¡Feliz Hanuka!, **13.2**

chapter el capítulo

character el carácter; el personaje

characteristic la característica

to **charge** cobrar

charges los cargos

charming encantador(a)

to **chat** charlar

chauffeur el chófer

cheap barato(a), 3.2

check (plaid) a cuadros

to **check luggage** facturar el equipaje, 11.1

to **check out** abandonar el cuarto, **6.1**

to **check the oil** revisar el aceite, **11.2**

to **check the ticket** revisar el boleto, 11.1

checkbook la chequera; el talonario

checkers las damas, **5.1**

checking account la cuenta corriente, **12.2**

cheek la mejilla, **8.1**

cheese el queso, 5.1

chemical químico(a)

chemistry la química, 2.2

chess el ajedrez, **5.1**

chest el pecho, **8.1**

chicken el pollo, 5.2

child el/la niño(a)

children los hijos, 6.1

chilean chileno(a)

chili pepper el ají

chills los escalofríos, 8.1

chimney la chimenea

chocolate (adj.) de chocolate, 5.1

choir el coro

cholesterol el colesterol

to **choose** escoger

chop la chuleta, 10.1

chores los quehaceres

chorus el coro

Christian cristiano(a)

Christmas la Navidad, **13.2**

 Merry Christmas! ¡Feliz Navidad!, **13.2**

Christmas Eve la Nochebuena, **13.2**

Christmas tree el árbol de Navidad, **13.2**

church la iglesia

circle el círculo

to **circulate** circular

citric cítrico(a)

city la ciudad, 9.1

city hall la alcaldía, **14.1**

city hall employee el/la funcionario(a), **14.1**

to **claim (luggage)** reclamar, 11.2

 to claim one's luggage recoger el equipaje, 11.2

clam la almeja, 14.2; **2.2**

clarinet el clarinete

clarity la claridad

class la clase, el curso, 2.1

 first class primera clase, 13.1; **1.1**

 second class segunda clase, 13.1

classic clásico(a)

to **classify** clasificar

classroom la sala de clase, el salón de clase, 4.1

clean limpio(a)

to **clean** limpiar, 6.2

 to clean the room limpiar el cuarto, 6.2

clear claro(a)

clerk el/la dependiente(a); el/la empleado(a), 3.1

clever listo(a), **5.1**

click el clic

climate el clima

clinic la clínica

close cercano(a)

to **close** cerrar (ie)

 to close the wound cerrar la herida, **8.2**

closet el armario, 6.2

clothes (pl.) la ropa, los vestidos

 to put on (one's) clothes ponerse la ropa, 12.1; vestirse (i, i)

clothes hanger el colgador, la percha, **6.2**

clothing la ropa, 3.2

clothing store la tienda de ropa, 3.2

 men's clothing store la tienda de ropa para caballeros, **4.1**

 women's clothing store la tienda de ropa para señoras, **4.1**

cloud la nube, 9.1

cloudy nublado(a), 9.1
 It's cloudy. Hay nubes., 9.1

clove (of garlic) el diente (de ajo)

clown el payaso, 5.2

club el club, 4.2

 Spanish Club el Club de español, 4.2

co-ed (school) mixto(a)

coast la costa

coat el abrigo, **4.1**

cockpit la cabina de mando (vuelo), **7.1**

coconut el coco, **10.2**

code: country code el prefijo de país, **3.2**

   area code la clave de área, **3.2**

coffee el café, BV

   black coffee el café solo, 5.1

   coffee with milk el café con leche, 5.1

coin, currency la moneda, **3.2**

coincidence la coincidencia

cold (illness) el catarro, 8.1

   It's cold. Hace frío., 9.2

   to have a cold tener catarro, estar resfriado(a), 8.1

to **collect** coleccionar, **5.1**

collection el conjunto; la colección; la colecta

collector el/la coleccionista, **5.1**

Colombian colombiano(a), 1.1

colonial colonial

colony la colonia

color el color, 3.2

   What color is it? ¿De qué color es?, 3.2

colored de color

comb el peine, 12.1

to **comb one's hair** peinarse, 12.1

to **come** venir, 11.1

   to come (go) on stage entrar en escena, 10.2

comedy la comedia

comfort la comodidad

commission la comisión

committee el comité

common común

to **communicate with each other** comunicarse, **3.1**

communication la comunicación

community la comunidad

compact disk CD, el disco compacto, 4.2

company la compañía

to **compare** comparar

comparison la comparación

compartment el compartimento, 13.2; **1.2**

   overhead compartment el compartimiento superior, el compartimiento sobre la cabeza, **7.1**

to **compete** competir (i, i)

competition la competencia; la competición

to **complete** completar

completely totalmente

compliment: to pay someone a compliment echarle flores

to **compose** componer

composition la composición

computer el ordenador, la computadora, **3.1**

computer programmer el/la programador(a) de informática, **14.1**

computer science la informática, 2.2

concert el concierto, 2.1

conclusion el desenlace

condition la condición

condominium el condominio, **9.1**

conductor (train) el/la revisor(a), 13.2; **1.2**

to **confirm** confirmar

to **confront** confrontar

Congratulations! ¡Enhorabuena!, ¡Felicitaciones!, **13.1**

to **connect** conectar; enlazar

connection la conexión

to **conquer** conquistar; vencer

conqueror el conquistador

conquest la conquista

consequently por consiguiente

to **consider** considerar

to **consist of** consistir (en)

to **construct** construir

to **consult** consultar, 13.1; **1.1**

to **consume** consumir

consumer el/la consumidor(a)

consumption el consumo

contagious contagioso(a)

to **contain** contener (ie)

contemporary contemporáneo(a)

contest la competición

continent el continente

to **continue** continuar, 7.2; seguir (i, i), **11.2**

   contrary: on the contrary al contrario

to **contrast** contrastar

to **control** controlar

   control tower la torre de control, **7.2**

convenient conveniente

convent el convento

conversation la conversación

to **convert** convertir (ie, i)

   convertible el convertible, el descapotable, **11.1**

to **convince** convencer

to **cook** cocinar, **10.1**

   cook el/la cocinero(a), 14.1; **2.1**

   cooking la cocción

coordination la coordinación

copilot el/la copiloto, 11.2

to **copy** copiar

   copy la copia

   corn (Mex.) el elote; el choclo; el maíz, 14.2; **2.2**

cornea la córnea

corner la esquina, **9.1**

correspondence la correspondencia

corridor el pasillo, 13.2; **1.2**

to **cost** costar (ue), 3.1

   How much do(es) it (they) cost? ¿Cuánto cuesta(n)?

Costa Rican costarricense

cotton el algodón, **12.1**

cough la tos, 8.1

   to have a cough tener tos, 8.1

English-Spanish Dictionary

to **cough** toser, 8.1
counter el mostrador, 11.1
country el país, 11.2; el campo, **9.2**
  foreign country el país extranjero
coup (overthrow of a government) el golpe
coupe el cupé, **11.1**
couple la pareja
course el curso, 2.1
  elective course el curso opcional
  required course el curso obligatorio
court la corte, el tribunal, **14.1**
court la cancha, 7.2
  basketball court la cancha de básquetbol, 7.2
  enclosed court la cancha cubierta, 9.1
  outdoor court la cancha al aire libre, 9.1
  tennis court la cancha de tenis, 9.1
courteous atento(a); cortés
courtesy la cortesía, BV
cousin el/la primo(a), 6.1
to **cover** cubrir; tapar, **10.2**
cow la vaca, **9.2**
to **create** crear
credit card la tarjeta de crédito, 14.1; **2.1**
creole criollo(a)
crew la tripulación, 11.2
crop la cosecha, **9.2**
to **cross** atravesar (ie); cruzar, **9.1**
crossing el cruce, **11.2**
crosswalk el cruce de peatones, **9.1**
crossword puzzle el crucigrama, **5.1**
  to do a crossword puzzle llenar un crucigrama, **5.1**
crutch la muleta, 8.2
Cuban cubano(a)
Cuban American cubanoamericano(a)

cucumber el pepino, **10.1**
to **cultivate** cultivar, **9.2**
cultivation el cultivo
cultural cultural
cultured culto(a)
cup la taza, 14.1; **2.1**
cure la cura
curtain (stage) el telón, 10.2
custom la costumbre
customer el/la cliente, 5.1
customs la aduana, 11.2
customs agent el/la agente de aduana, **11.2**
to **cut** cortar, **8.1**
cycling el ciclismo

D

dad el papá
daily diario(a)
to **dance** bailar, 4.2
dance el baile
dance la danza
danger el peligro
dangerous peligroso(a)
dark oscuro(a)
dark-haired moreno(a), 1.1
data los datos, **3.1**
to **date** datar
date la fecha, BV
  What is today's date? ¿Cuál es la fecha de hoy?, BV
daughter la hija, 6.1
day el día, BV
  What day is it (today)? ¿Qué día es (hoy)?, BV
death la muerte
decade la década
December diciembre, BV
to **decide** decidir
to **declare** declarar
to **decorate** decorar
decorated decorado(a)
decoration la decoración
to **dedicate** dedicar, **14.1**

deep profundo(a)
to **defeat** derrotar
to **defend** defender (ie)
to **define** definir
definition la definición
degree (temperature) el grado, 9.2
delay: with a delay con una demora, 11.1; con retraso, 13.2; **1.2**
delicate delicado(a)
delicious rico(a), 14.2; **2.2**; delicioso(a), sabroso(a)
to **delight** encantar
to **deliver** entregar
deluxe de lujo
to **demand** exigir
demography la demografía
to **demonstrate** demostrar (ue)
density la densidad
dentist el/la dentista
department el departamento, 14.2
  department of human resources el departamento de recursos humanos, 14.2
  department store la tienda de departamentos
departure la salida, 11.1; la partida
  departure area la sala de salida, 11.1
  departure gate la puerta de salida, 11.1; la puerta de embarque
  departure hour la hora de salida, 13.1; **1.1**
to **depend (on)** depender (ie) (de)
deposit el depósito
  to make a deposit ingresar
dermatologist el/la dermatólogo(a)
dermatology la dermatología
descendant el/la descendiente
to **describe** describir
desert el desierto
design el diseño

designer el/la diseñador(a)

dessert el postre, 5.1

destination el destino, 11.1

detail el detalle

detective policíaco(a)

detergent el detergente, **4.2**

to **determine** determinar

development el desarrollo

device el aparato, **3.1**

to **devote oneself to** dedicarse, **14.1**

diagnosis la diagnosis, 8.2

to **dial** marcar (el número), **3.2**

dial tone el tono, **3.2**

dialogue el diálogo

diamond el diamante

to **dice** picar, **10.2**

to **die** morir (ue, u)

diesel gasoline diesel, 11.1

diet la dieta

difference la diferencia

different diferente

difficult difícil, duro(a), 2.1

difficulty la dificultad

to **dig** excavar

to **dine, have dinner** cenar

dining car el coche comedor, el coche cafetería, 13.2

dining room el comedor, 6.2

dinner la cena, 5.2

diplomatic diplomático(a)

direct directo(a)

to **direct** dirigir

direction la dirección; el sentido, 11.2

in each direction en cada sentido, **11.2**

in the opposite direction en el sentido contrario, **11.2**

director el/la director(a)

dirty sucio(a), **11.1**

dirty laundry la ropa sucia, **12.1**

disadvantage la desventaja

to **disappear** desaparecer

disaster el desastre

disastrous desastroso(a)

discount el descuento

to **discover** descubrir

to **discuss** discutir

to **disembark** desembarcar, 11.2

dish el plato, 14.1; **2.1**

disk, diskette el disquete, 3.1

disk drive la ranura, **3.1**

distance la distancia

distinct distinto(a)

distinguished ilustre

to **distract** distraer

to **distribute** distribuir, **7.1**

distribution la distribución

to **dive** bucear, 9.1

to **divide** dividir

diving el buceo, 9.1

division la división

divorce: to get divorced divorciarse

to **do** hacer

to do homework hacer las tareas, **3.1**

to do well (on an exam) salir bien (en un examen)

doctor el/la doctor(a); el/la médico(a), 8.2

doctor's office la consulta (el consultorio) del médico, 8.2; la sala de consulta

document el documento, **3.1**

documentation la documentación

dog el perro, 6.1

dollar el dólar, 12.2

Dominican dominicano(a), 2.1

Dominican Republic la República Dominicana

dominos el dominó, **5.1**

donkey el asno

door la puerta, 6.1

dose la dosis, 8.2

dot el punto

on the dot, sharp en punto, 4.1

doubles dobles, 9.1

to **doubt** dudar

doubt la duda

doubtful dudoso(a)

down payment el enganche

downtown el centro; en el centro (de la ciudad)

dozen la docena, 4.2

to **draw** dibujar

drawing el dibujo

dream el sueño

dress el vestido, **4.1**

to **dress oneself, to put on clothes** ponerse la ropa, 12.1

to get dressed vestirse (i, i)

dressed (in) vestido(a) (de)

to **dribble** driblar, 7.2

to **drink** beber, 5.1

to drink a beverage tomar un refresco

to drink water (milk, coffee) tomar agua (leche, café)

drink el refresco, 5.1; la bebida, **7.1**

to **drive** conducir, manejar, **11.1**

driver el/la conductor(a), **11.1**

driver's license la licencia, el permiso de conducir, **11.1**

to **drop** caer, **7.1**

drug la droga

drug addiction la drogadicción

druggist el/la farmacéutico(a), 8.2

drugstore la farmacia, 8.2

to **dry** secar, **12.2**

dry seco(a)

to **dry clean** limpiar en seco, **12.1**

dry cleaner el/la tintorero(a), **12.1**

dry cleaners la tintorería, **12.1**

dubbed doblado(a), 10.1

during durante

E

e-mail, electronic mail el correo electrónico, **3.1**

English-Spanish Dictionary

each cada, 1.2

in each direction en cada sentido, **11.2**

eagle el águila *(f.)*

ear la oreja, **4.1**; el oído, **8.1**

early temprano, 12.1

to **earn** ganar

to earn one's living ganar la vida

earphones los audífonos, los auriculares, **7.1**

earring el arete, el pendiente, **4.1**

easel el caballete

east el este

eastern oriental

easy fácil, 2.1; sencillo(a)

to **eat** comer, 5.1

to eat breakfast desayunarse, tomar el desayuno, 12.1

to eat dinner cenar

ecological ecológico(a)

ecology la ecología

economical económico(a), 12.2

economics la economía

home economics la economía doméstica, 2.2

economy la economía

Ecuadorean ecuatoriano(a), 2.1

to **educate** educar

education la educación

physical education la educación física, 2.2

egg el huevo, 5.2

eggplant la berenjena, 14.2; **2.2**

eight ocho, BV

eight hundred ochocientos(as), 3.2

eighteen dieciocho, BV

eighth octavo(a), 6.2

eighty ochenta, 2.2

either tampoco

elbow el codo, 8.1

elective course el curso opcional

electric eléctrico(a)

electrician el/la electricista, **14.1**

electricity la electricidad

electronic electrónico(a)

electronic mail el correo electrónico, **3.1**

elegance la elegancia

elegant elegante, **13.1**

element el elemento

elementary school la escuela primaria

to **elevate** elevar

elevated elevado(a)

elevation la elevación

elevator el ascensor, 6.2; el elevador, **6.1**

eleven once, BV

to **eliminate** eliminar

emergency la emergencia, **7.1**

emergency exit la salida de emergencia, **7.1**

emergency room la sala de emergencia, la sala de urgencias, **8.1**

emission la emisión

to **emit** emitir

emotion la emoción

emotional emocional

to **emphasize** dar énfasis; enfatizar

to **employ** emplear

employee el/la dependiente(a), el/la empleado(a), 3.1

enchilada la enchilada, BV

end el fin

at the end (of) al final (de); a fines de

to **end** terminar, 3.1

to **endorse** endosar, **12.2**

enemy el/la enemigo(a)

energy la energía

engagement el compromiso

engine el motor

engineer el/la ingeniero(a), **14.1**

engineering la ingeniería

English el inglés, 2.2

to **enjoy** disfrutar; gozar

to **enjoy oneself** divertirse (ie, i), 12.2

enormous enorme

enough bastante, 1.1; suficiente

to **enter** entrar, 4.1

entertaining entretenido(a)

enthusiastic entusiasmado(a)

entire entero(a)

entrance la entrada, **5.2**

entrepreneur el/la empresario(a)

envelope el sobre, **12.2**

environment el ambiente; el medio ambiente

episode el episodio

epoch la época

equal igual; par

equation la ecuación

equator la línea ecuatorial

equilibrium el equilibrio

equipment el equipo

equivalent el equivalente

eraser la goma de borrar, 3.1

erroneous erróneo(a)

escalator la escalera mecánica, **9.1**

to **escape** escapar

especially especialmente; particularmente; sobre todo

essential esencial

to **establish** establecer, fundar

establishment el establecimiento

eternal eterno(a)

eternally de siempre y para siempre

ethnic étnico(a)

euro euro (currency)

Europe la Europa

European europeo(a)

even aun

evening la noche

in the evening por la noche

evening gown el traje de gala

event: great event el buen suceso

every cada, 1.2

everybody todos(as), 2.2

everyone todo el mundo

everything todos(as)

everywhere por todas partes

exact exacto(a)

exactly exactamente

to exaggerate exagerar

exaggerated exagerado(a)

exam el examen, 4.2

to examine examinar, 8.2

example: for example por ejemplo

to excavate excavar

excavation la excavación

to exceed exceder

excellent excelente

exception la excepción

to exchange cambiar, 12.2

exchange: exchange rate el tipo (la tasa) de cambio, 12.2

exchange student el/la estudiante de intercambio

to exclaim exclamar

exclusively exclusivamente

excuse me perdón

to exercise hacer los ejercicios

exhaust pipe el tubo de escape

exhibition (art) la exposición (de arte), 10.2; la exhibición

to exist existir

existence la existencia

exit la salida, 11.2

expedition la expedición

expensive caro(a), 3.2

experience la experiencia

to experiment experimentar

expert el/la experto(a), 9.2

to explain explicar, 4.2

explorer el/la explorador(a)

explosion la explosión

to export exportar

to express an opinion opinar, 10.2

expression la expresión

means of expression el modo de expresión

expressway la autopista, 11.2

extension la extensión

extraordinary extraordinario(a)

extreme extremo(a)

eye el ojo, 8.2

F

fabulous fabuloso(a)

face la cara, 12.1

face down boca abajo, 3.1

face up boca arriba, 3.1

to facilitate facilitar

factory la fábrica, 9.1

factory worker el/la obrero(a), 9.1

faithful fiel

to fall caerse

to fall asleep dormirse, 12.1

false falso(a)

fame la fama

family la familia, 6.1

family (related to the) familiar

famous famoso(a), 1.2; célebre

fan (sports) el/la aficionado(a)

fantastic fantástico(a), 1.2

far lejos, 12.2

fare la tarifa

farm la finca, 9.2

farm animals los animales domésticos, 9.2

farmer el/la agricultor(a)

to fascinate fascinar

fast: as fast as possible a toda prisa

to fasten abrocharse, 7.1

fat gordo(a), 1.2

fat la grasa

father el padre, 6.1

father-in-law el suegro

fault el defecto

favorite favorito(a)

fax el facsímil, el fax, 3.1

fear el miedo; el terror

to fear temer

February febrero, BV

to feel sentirse (ie, i), 8.1

Ferris wheel la noria, 5.2

to fete festejar

fever la fiebre, 8.1

to have a fever tener fiebre, 8.1

few poco(a), 2.1

fewer menos

fiancé(e) el/la novio(a)

fiction la ficción

fictitious ficticio(a)

field el campo, 9.2

baseball field el campo de béisbol, 7.2

soccer field el campo de fútbol, 7.1

fifteen quince, BV

fifteen-year-old (girl) la quinceañera

fifth quinto(a), 6.2

fifty cincuenta, 2.2

to fight luchar

figurative figurativo(a)

figure la figura

to fill rellenar

to fill out llenar, 5.1

to fill out the form llenar el formulario, 8.2

fillet el filete

film la película, 6.2; el film, 10.1

to see a film ver una película, 10.1

finally por fin

finances las finanzas

financial financiero(a)

to find encontrar (ue); hallar

fine bien, BV

fine la multa

finger el dedo, 4.1

to finish terminar, 3.1

fire el fuego, 10.2

first primero(a), BV

first aid service el servicio de primeros auxilios, 8.1

first class en primera (clase), 13.1

fish (food) el pescado, 5.2
fish market la pescadería, **4.2**
to **fit** caber
It (They) do(es)n't fit me. No me queda(n) bien., **4.1**
five cinco, BV
five hundred quinientos(as), 3.2
to **fix** fijar
fixed fijo(a)
flamenco flamenco(a)
traditional flamenco singing el cante jondo
flat (tire) pinchado(a)
flaw el defecto
flight el vuelo, 11.1
direct flight el vuelo directo
domestic flight el vuelo nacional
flight number el número del vuelo, 11.1
to take a flight tomar un vuelo, 11.1
flight attendant el/la asistente de vuelo, 11.2
floor el piso, la planta, 6.2
ground floor la planta baja, 6.2
flower la flor
flu la gripe, 8.1
flute la flauta
to **fly** volar (ue), **7.2**
to **fly over** sobrevolar, **7.2**
folder la carpeta, 3.1
folk healer el/la curandero(a)
to **follow** seguir (i, i)
following siguiente
fond of aficionado(a) a, 10.1
food la comida, 5.2; el alimento, el comestible, 14.2; **2.2**
foolish tonto(a)
foot el pie, 7.1
on foot a pie, 4.1
for de, BV; para; por
for example por ejemplo
for when? ¿para cuándo?, 14.2; **2.2**
forbidden prohibido(a), **11.2**
forecast el pronóstico
forehead la frente, **8.1**
foreign extranjero(a)
foreign country el país extranjero, 11.2
foreign exchange office la casa de cambio, **12.2**
foreigner el/la extranjero(a)
forever de siempre y para siempre
fork el tenedor, 14.1; **2.1**
form el formulario, **8.2**
to **form** formar
fortification la fortificación
fortunate afortunado(a)
fortune la buenaventura
forty cuarenta, 2.2
to **found** fundar
foundation la fundación
four cuatro, BV
four hundred cuatrocientos(as), 3.2
fourteen catorce, BV
fourth cuarto(a), 6.2
fracture la fractura, **8.1**
fragment el fragmento
frank franco(a)
free libre, 5.1
freezer el congelador, **10.1**
French el francés, 2.2
French fries las papas fritas, 5.1
frequently frecuentemente, con frecuencia, **3.2**
fresh fresco(a), **4.2**
Friday el viernes, BV
fried frito(a), 5.1
friend el/la amigo(a), 1.1; el/la compañero(a), 1.2
frightful espantoso(a)
from de, BV; desde
from (time) to (time) de… a…, 2.2
front desk la recepción, **6.1**
in front of delante de, 10.1
frozen congelado(a), **4.2**
frozen food los productos congelados, 5.2
fruit la fruta, 5.2
fruit store la frutería, **4.2**
to **fry** freír (i, i), 14.1; **2.1**
frying pan el/la sartén, **10.1**
full lleno(a)
full (train) completo(a), 13.2
full-time job un trabajo a tiempo completo, **14.2**
fun divertido(a)
function la función, 10.2
functioning el funcionamiento
fund el fondo
fundamental primordial
funny cómico(a), gracioso(a), 1.1
furious furioso(a)
furniture los muebles
fury la furia
future el futuro

G

galaxy la galaxia
gallant gallardo(a)
gallon el galón
game el juego; **(match)** el partido, 7.1; **(of dominos, etc.)** la partida
baseball game el juego de béisbol, 7.2
Olympic Games los Juegos Olímpicos
tennis game el juego de tenis, 9.1
video game el juego de video, **5.1**
game arcade la sala de juegos, **5.1**
game board el tablero, **5.1**
game piece la ficha, **5.1**
garage el garaje, 6.2
garantee la garantía
garden el jardín, 6.2
garlic el ajo, 14.2; **2.2**
gas station la gasolinera, **11.1**
gas tank el tanque, **11.1**
gasoline la gasolina, **11.1**
regular (super) gasoline súper, **11.2**
unleaded sin plomo, **11.1**

gate la puerta, 11.1

gathering la reunión

generally en general; generalmente

  in general, usually por lo general

generous generoso(a), 1.2

genre el género

gentleman el caballero, **4.1**

geography la geografía, 2.2

geometric geométrico(a)

geometry la geometría, 2.2

German (language) el alemán, 2.2

gesture el gesto

to **get** sacar, 4.2

to **get a good (bad) grade** sacar una nota buena (mala), 4.2

to **get, buy a ticket** sacar un billete

to **get engaged** comprometerse

to **get off** bajar, 13.2; **1.2**

to **get off the train** bajar(se) del tren, 13.2; **1.2**

to **get on** subir, 13.2; abordar

to **get on the train** subir al tren, 13.1; **1.1**

to **get together** reunirse

to **get up** levantarse, 12.1

  giant el gigante

  gift el regalo, 6.1

  girl la muchacha, 1.1; la chica

  girlfriend la novia

to **give** dar, 4.2

  to give back devolver (ue)

  to give (throw) a party dar una fiesta, 4.2

  to give (someone) a present regalar

  to give (someone) a shot (an injection) poner una inyección

  to give a test dar un examen, 4.2

to **give up** renunciar

  glass (drinking) el vaso, 12.1

  glove el guante, 7.2

to **go** ir, 4.1

  let's go vamos

  to go back volver (ue), 7.1

  to go back home volver (ue) a casa, 10.2

  to go by bicycle ir en bicicleta, 12.2

  to go by car ir en carro (coche), 4.1

  to go by train ir en tren

  to go on a trip viajar, 11.1

  to go on foot ir a pie, 4.1

  to go shopping ir de compras, 5.2

  to go through pasar por, 11.1

to **go down** bajar, 9.2

to **go surfing (windsurfing, etc.)** practicar el surfing (la plancha de vela, etc.), 9.1

to **go swimming** nadar, 9.1

to **go to bed** acostarse (ue), 12.1

to **go up** subir, 6.2

  goal line la portería, 7.1

  goalkeeper, goalie el/la portero(a), 7.1

  godfather el padrino, **13.1**

  godmother la madrina

  godparents los padrinos

  gold el oro

  gold chain una cadena de oro, **4.1**

  golden dorado(a)

  good buen; bueno(a), 1.2

  Good afternoon. Buenas tardes., BV

  Good evening. Buenas noches., BV

  Good heavens!, You bet! ¡hombre!

  Good morning. Hello. Buenos días., BV

  to be in a good mood estar de buen humor, 8.1

  good-bye adiós, ¡Chao!, BV

  goods and services los bienes y servicios

  Gosh! ¡Dios mío!

  gossip item el chisme

  government el gobierno, **14.1**

federal government el gobierno federal

municipal government el gobierno municipal, **14.1**

state government el gobierno estatal

grade el grado; la nota, 4.2

  high grade la nota alta, 4.2

  low grade la nota baja, 4.2

  to get a good (bad) grade sacar una nota buena (mala), 4.2

graduate el/la diplomado(a)

to **graduate** graduarse

grain el cereal, **9.2**

grain el grano

gram el gramo

grammar la gramática

granddaughter la nieta, 6.1

grandfather el abuelo, 6.1

grandmother la abuela, 6.1

grandparents los abuelos, 6.1

grandson el nieto, 6.1

grapefruit la toronja, **10.1**

grapes las uvas, **10.1**

to **grate** rallar, **10.2**

grave (serious) grave

gray gris, 3.2

great gran, grande

greater, greatest mayor

  greater part, the most la mayor parte

Greek el/la griego(a)

green verde, 3.2

green bean la judía verde, 5.2

greengrocer store la verdulería, **4.2**

to **greet** saludar

greeting el saludo, BV

grill la parrilla, **10.1**

grocery store el colmado, la tienda de abarrotes, la tienda de ultramarinos, **4.2**

groom el novio, **13.1**

ground el suelo

group el grupo

to **grow** cultivar, **9.2**

growth el crecimiento

to **guard** guardar, 7.1

Guatemalan guatemalteco(a)

guerrilla band la guerrilla

to **guess** adivinar

to **guess right** acertar (ie)

guest el/la invitado(a); el/la huésped, **6.1**

guidance counselor el/la consejero(a) de orientación

guide el/la guía

guitar la guitarra

gulf el golfo

gymnasium el gimnasio

gynecologist el/la ginecólogo(a)

gynecology la ginecología

hair el pelo, **12.1**; el cabello, **12.1**

hair dryer el secador, **12.1**

hair salon la peluquería, **12.1**

hair stylist el/la peluquero(a), **12.1**

haircut el corte de pelo, **12.1**

hairdo el peinado

half la mitad

half medio(a), 5.2

half an hour media hora

half-past (time) y media

half (game) el tiempo

second half (game) el segundo tiempo, 7.1

hall el salón, **13.1**

ham el jamón, 5.1

hamburger la hamburguesa, 5.1

hand la mano, 7.1

to hand out distribuir, **7.1**

to shake hands dar la mano

handkerchief el pañuelo, **4.1**

handsome guapo(a), 1.1

to **hang, hang up** colgar (ue)

to **happen** ocurrir, suceder; pasar

happiness la alegría; la felicidad

happy contento(a), 8.1; alegre

Happy birthday! ¡Feliz cumpleaños!, **13.1**

hard duro(a), 2.1

hardworking ambicioso(a), 1.1

harmonious harmonioso(a)

to **harvest** cosechar, **9.2**

harvest la cosecha, **9.2**

hat el sombrero; la gorra, 3.2

to **have** tener (ie), 6.1

to have (subtitles, ingredients, etc.) llevar

to have a cold tener catarro, estar resfriado(a), 8.1

to have a cough tener tos, 8.1

to have a headache tener dolor de cabeza, 8.1

to have a snack tomar una merienda, 4.2

to have a sore throat tener dolor de garganta, 8.1

to have to tener que

to **have just (done something)** acabar de, **8.1**

he él, 1.1

head la cabeza, 7.1

headache el dolor de cabeza, 8.1

health la salud

healthy sano(a)

to **hear** oír

to hear the dial tone oír el tono, **3.2**

heart el corazón

heat: on low heat a fuego lento

heavy pesado(a)

heel el tacón, **4.1**

height la altura, **7.2**

helicopter el helicóptero, **7.2**

Hello! ¡Hola!, BV

Hello! (answering the telephone–Spain) ¡Diga!, 14.2; **2.2**

to **help** ayudar, 13.1; dar auxilio; socorrer

help el socorro, la ayuda

hemisphere: northern hemisphere el hemisferio norte

southern hemisphere el hemisferio sur

hen la gallina, **9.2**

her (f. sing.) (pron.) la

her su

here aquí

Here is (are) . . . Aquí tiene (tienes, tienen)...

hero el/la héroe

to **hide** esconder

high alto(a), 4.2; elevado

high school el liceo; la escuela secundaria, 1.1; la escuela superior

highway la carretera, la autovía, la autopista, **11.2**

hike: to take a hike dar una caminata, 12.2

him (m. sing.) (pron.) lo

to him, to her; to you (pron.) le

his su

Hispanic hispano(a), hispánico(a)

historian el/la historiador(a)

historical histórico(a)

history la historia, 2.2

to **hit** golpear, 9.2

to **hit (baseball)** batear, 7.2

hobby el pasatiempo, el hobby, **5.1**

hole el agujero

home la casa, 6.2

at home en casa

country home la casa de campo, **9.2**

home economics la economía doméstica, 2.2

home plate el platillo, 7.2

home run el jonrón, 7.2

honest honesto(a), 1.2

English-Spanish Dictionary

honeymoon la luna de miel

to **honk the horn** tocar la bocina

honor el honor

maid of honor la dama de honor, **13.1**

hood (automobile) el capó, **11.1**

to **hope** esperar

I hope ojalá, **14.1**

horn el claxon, la bocina, **11.1**

horrible horrible

horse el caballo

horseback: to go horseback riding pasear a caballo; montar a caballo

hospital el hospital, **8.1**

hot: It's hot. Hace calor., **9.1**

hotel el hotel, **6.1**

inexpensive hotel el hostal, 12.2

hour la hora

departure hour la hora de salida

house la casa, 6.2

apartment house la casa de apartamentos (departamentos), 6.2

private house la casa privada (particular), 6.2

housing la vivienda

how? ¿qué?, BV; ¿cómo?, 1.1

How absurd! ¡Qué absurdo!

How are you? ¿Qué tal?, BV

How is ...? ¿Cómo está...?, 8.1

How may I help you? ¿En qué puedo servirle?, **4.1**

How much do(es) . . . cost? ¿Cuánto cuesta(n)... ?, 3.1

How much is (are) . . . ? ¿A cuánto está(n)... ?, 5.2

how many? ¿cuántos(as)?, 2.1

how much? ¿cuánto?, 3.1

human being el ser humano

humble humilde

humid húmedo(a)

hungry: to be hungry tener hambre, 14.1; **2.1**

to **hurt** doler (ue), 8.2

My . . . hurt(s) me. Me duele(n)..., 8.2

to **hurt oneself** hacerse daño, lastimarse, **8.1**

husband el marido, el esposo, 6.1

hydrofoil el aerodeslizador; el hidrofoil

hygiene la higiene

hypermarket el hipermercado, **4.2**

I

I yo, 1.1

ice cream el helado, 5.1

chocolate ice cream el helado de chocolate, 5.1

vanilla ice cream el helado de vainilla, 5.1

icon el icono

idea la idea

ideal ideal, 1.2

idealist el/la idealista

to **identify** identificar

if si

illness la enfermedad

illusion la ilusión

image la imagen

imaginary imaginario(a)

imagination la imaginación

to **imagine** imaginar

imagined, dreamed of imaginado(a)

immediate inmediato(a)

immediately enseguida, 5.1; inmediatamente

immense inmenso(a)

imperative el imperativo

to **imply that** dar a entender

important importante

impossible imposible

in en

in case of en caso de, **7.1**

in general por lo general

in itself en sí

in regard to en cuanto a

to **inaugurate** inaugurar

Inca el/la inca

inch la pulgada

to **include** incluir, 5.1

to **increase** aumentar

incredible increíble

independence la independencia

Indian indio(a)

to **indicate** indicar, 11.1

indigenous indígena

indispensable indispensable

individual el individuo

individual: individual sport el deporte individual

industrial industrial

inexpensive barato(a), 3.2

to **influence** impresionar

influence la influencia

to **inform** informar, 13.2; **1.2**

information la información; los datos, **3.1**

ingredient el ingrediente

inhabitant el/la habitante

inheritance la herencia

inhospitable inhospitable

injection la inyección, 8.2

to give (someone) an injection poner una inyección

inn el parador; el albergue

inning la entrada, 7.2

innocent inocente

innovation la innovación

insane loco(a)

to **insert** meter, **3.1**; introducir, **3.2**

to **inspect** inspeccionar, 11.1

inspection el control, 11.1

installation la instalación

installments: in installments a plazos

instant el instante

instantaneous instantáneo(a)

instead of en vez de

instruction la instrucción

instrument el instrumento

insurance el seguro

integral íntegro(a)

intelligent inteligente, 2.1
interest el interés
to **interest** interesar
interesting interesante, 2.1
international internacional
Internet Internet, 3.1
interpretation la interpretación
interpreter el/la intérprete
to **interrupt** interrumpir
interruption la interrupción
intersection el cruce, la bocacalle, **11.2**
to **intervene** intervenir
to **interview** entrevistar
interview la entrevista, **14.2**
interviewer el/la entrevistador(a), **14.2**
introduction la introducción
invention el invento
investigation la investigación
invitation la invitación
to **invite** invitar, 6.1
invoice la factura, **6.1**
to **iron** planchar, **12.1**
irrigation la irrigación
island la isla
it la, lo
Italian italiano(a)
itinerant ambulante
ivory el marfil

jacket la chaqueta, 3.2; el saco, **4.1**
jai alai la pelota vasca
jai alai player el/la pelotari
jam la mermelada
January enero, BV
jar el frasco, **4.2**
jeans el blue jean, 3.2
jet el avión de reacción, el jet, **7.2**
jewel la joya, **4.1**
jewelry store la joyería, **4.1**
Jewish hebreo(a), **13.2**

job el trabajo
job application la solicitud de empleo, **14.2**
  full- (part-) time job el trabajo a tiempo completo (parcial), **14.2**
to **join** enlazar
judge el/la juez, **14.1**
juice el jugo
  orange juice el jugo de naranja, 12.1
July julio, BV
to **jump** saltar
June junio, BV
jungle la jungla; la selva
just: just after (time) y pico
  to have just (done something) acabar de (+ *infinitive*), **8.1**

to **keep** guardar, **3.1**
to **keep in shape** mantenerse en forma
key la tecla, **3.2**; la llave, **6.1**
keyboard el teclado, **3.1**
to **keyboard** entrar los datos, **3.1**
to **kick** tirar, 7.1
  to kick (throw) the ball tirar el balón, 7.2
to **kill** matar
kilogram el kilo, 5.2
kilometer el kilómetro
kind la clase
king el rey
  The Three Kings (Wise Men) Los Reyes Magos, **13.2**
kitchen la cocina, 6.2
knapsack la mochila, 12.2
knee la rodilla, 7.1
knife el cuchillo, 14.1; **2.1**
knight el caballero
knight errant el caballero andante
to **know** conocer, 11.1
to **know (how)** saber, 11.2
  knowledge el conocimiento

L

laboratory el laboratorio
lady-in-waiting la dama
lake el lago, **5.2**
lamb el cordero, 14.2; **2.2**
lame cojo(a)
lament el lamento
lance la lanza
to **land** aterrizar, 11.2
land la tierra
  by land por tierra
landing el aterrizaje, **7.2**
landscape el paisaje
lane (of highway) el carril, **11.2**
language la lengua, 2.2; el lenguaje; el idioma
large gran, grande
to **last** durar, **13.2**
last pasado(a); último(a)
last (year) el (año) pasado
late tarde; con una demora, 11.1; con retraso, 13.2; **1.2**
later luego, BV; después; más tarde
  See you later! ¡Hasta luego! , BV
Latin el latín, 2.2
Latin (*adj.*) latino(a)
Latin America Latinoamérica, 1.1
Latin American Latinoamericano(a)
to **laugh** reír
to **launch** lanzar
laundromat la lavandería
laundry el lavado, **12.1**
  dirty laundry la ropa sucia, **12.1**
lavatory el aseo, el lavabo, **7.1**
lawyer el/la abogado(a), **14.1**
lawyer's office el bufete del abogado, **14.1**
lazy perezoso(a), 1.1
to **lead, go (one street into another)** desembocar, 9.1

league la liga
  Major Leagues las Grandes Ligas
to **learn** aprender, 5.1
to **leave (something)** dejar, 14.1; **2.1**
  to leave a tip dejar una propina, 14.1; **2.1**
to **leave** salir, 10.1
  to leave late salir tarde, 11.1
  to leave on time salir a tiempo, 11.1
  to leave the theater salir del teatro, 10.2
lecture la conferencia
left izquicrdo(a), 7.1
  to the left a la izquierda, **5.2**
leg la pierna, 7.1
lemon el limón, **10.1**
lemonade la limonada, BV
lentil la lenteja
less menos
lesser, least menor
lesson la lección, 4.2
to **let** dejar
letter (of alphabet) la letra
letter la carta, **12.2**
letter of recommendation la carta de recomendación
lettuce la lechuga, 5.2
level el nivel
liberator el/la libertador(a)
license plate la placa
life la vida
  school life la vida escolar
life jacket el chaleco salvavidas, **7.1**
to **lift** levantar
light (cheerful) ligero(a)
to **light** encender (ie), **13.2**
light la luz, **11.1**
  red light la luz roja, **11.2**
like como, 1.2
to **like, to be pleasing** gustar
lime la lima, **10.1**
limousine la limusina
line (queue) la cola, 10.1; la fila, **5.2**
  to stand (wait) in line hacer cola, **10.1**

line la línea
  parallel line la línea paralela
  telephone line la línea telefónica
to **line up** hacer cola, 10.1
lion el león
lip el labio, **8.1**
liquid líquido(a)
list la lista
to **listen (to)** escuchar, 4.2
  Listen! ¡Oye!
liter el litro
literal literal
literary literario(a)
literature la literatura, 2.1
little poco(a), 2.1
  a little un poco (de)
to **live** vivir, 5.2
  living: to earn one's living ganar la vida
  living room la sala, 6.2
loan el préstamo
lobster la langosta, 14.2; **2.2**
local local, 13.2; **1.2**
to **lodge** alojarse; hospedarse
logical lógico(a)
long largo(a), 3.2
to **look at** mirar, 3.1
  Look! ¡Mira!
to **look at oneself** mirarse, 12.1
to **look for** buscar, 3.1
to **look good (food)** tener buena pinta, 4.2
to **look like** parecer, 8.1
to **lose** perder (ie), 7.1
  lotto el loto
  love el amor
to **love** querer; amar; encantar
low bajo(a), 4.2
to **lower** bajar, 9.2
  luck la suerte
  Good luck! ¡Buena suerte!
luggage el equipaje, 11.1
  carry-on luggage el equipaje de mano, 11.1
  to check luggage facturar el equipaje, 11.1
  to claim luggage reclamar

lunch el almuerzo, 5.2
  to have, eat lunch tomar el almuerzo, almorzar (ue)
luxurious lujoso(a)
lying mentiroso(a)
lyric lírico(a)

made hecho(a)
magazine la revista, 6.2
magnificent magnífico(a)
maid la camarera, **6.2**
maid of honor la dama de honor, **13.1**
mail el correo, **12.2**
  air mail el correo aéreo, **12.2**
  e-mail el correo electrónico, **3.1**
  regular mail el correo ordinario, **12.2**
to **mail the letter** echar la carta (en el buzón), **12.2**
mailbox el buzón, **12.2**
main principal
mainly principalmente
to **maintain** mantener
majority la mayoría
to **make** hacer
  to make a telephone call hacer una llamada telefónica, **3.2**
  to make the bed hacer la cama, **6.2**
to **make up** formar
makeup el maquillaje, 12.1
  to put one's makeup on maquillarse, poner el maquillaje, 12.1
male el varón
man el hombre; el caballero, **4.1**
manager el/la gerente, **14.1**
manner el modo; la manera, 1.1
manufactured fabricado(a)

English-Spanish Dictionary

many; a lot muchos(as), 2.1

map el mapa; el plano, **9.1**

March marzo, BV

to **march** marchar

marker el marcador, 3.1

market el mercado, 5.2

meat market la carnicería, **4.2**

marketing el mercadeo

marmalade la mermelada

marriage el matrimonio

to get married casarse, **13.1**

marvelous maravilloso(a)

mass la masa

to **match** parear

material el material

raw material la material prima

mathematics las matemáticas, 2.1

matter la materia

maximum máximo(a), **11.2**

May mayo, BV

Maya el/la maya

mayonnaise la mayonesa

mayor el alcalde, **14.1**; la alcaldesa

me (*pron.*) me

to me a mí

meal la comida, 5.2

to prepare the meal preparar la comida

to **mean** significar

meaning el significado; el sentido

meaningful significante

means el medio

means of expression el modo de expresión

means of transportation el medio de transporte

to **measure** medir (i, i)

measurement la medida

meat la carne, 5.2

mechanic el/la mecánico(a)

medal la medalla

medical office el consultorio, 8.2

medicine (discipline) la medicina, 8.2

medicine (drugs) el medicamento, 8.2

medium mediano(a), **4.1**

medium el medio

to **meet** encontrarse (ue)

melancholic melancólico(a)

member el miembro, 4.2

memory la memoria; el recuerdo

men: men's clothing store la tienda de ropa para caballeros, **4.1**

menace la plaga

menorah la menora, **13.2**

to **mention** mencionar

menu el menú, 5.1

merchandise la mercancía, **14.1**

merengue el merengue

merry-go-round el tiovivo, **5.2**

message el mensaje, 3.2

mestizo el/la mestizo(a)

metabolism el metabolismo

meter el metro

method el método

metrics la métrica

metro entrance la boca del metro, **9.1**

Mexican mexicano(a), 1.1

Mexican American mexicanoamericano(a)

microbe el microbio

microscope el microscopio

microscopic microscópico(a)

microwave oven el horno de microondas, **10.1**

middle: in the middle of (noun) en pleno + *noun*

middle school la escuela intermedia

midnight la medianoche

migration la migración

mile la milla

milk la leche

million el millón

millionaire el/la millonario(a)

mime el/la mimo, **5.2**

miniature la miniatura

miniaturization la miniaturización

ministry el ministerio

to **mint** acuñar

minute el minuto

mirror el espejo, 12.1

to **miss** perder (ie), 10.2

to miss the bus perder el autobús (la guagua, el camión), 10.1

Miss, Ms. la señorita, BV

mixture la mezcla

mode la modalidad

model el/la modelo

modem el módem

moderation la moderación

modern moderno(a)

mom la mamá

moment el momento

monastery el monasterio

Monday el lunes, BV

money el dinero, 14.1; **2.1**

money (income) la plata

money changer el/la cambista, **12.2**

monitor el monitor, 3.1

monkey el mono, 5.2

monster el monstruo

month el mes, BV

monthly installment la mensualidad

monument el monumento

mood el humor, 8.1

to be in a bad (good) mood estar de mal (buen) humor, 8.1

moon la luna

Moor el/la moro(a)

more más, 2.2

more or less más o menos

moreover además

morning la mañana

A.M. (time) de la mañana

in the morning por la mañana

mortality la mortalidad

mortgage la hipoteca

mother la madre, 6.1

motion la moción

motive el motivo

English-Spanish Dictionary

motor el motor
mountain la montaña, 9.2
mountain range la sierra; la cordillera, **7.2**
mountainous montañoso(a)
mouse el ratón, **3.1**
mouth la boca, 8.2
to move mover (ue), mudarse
movement el movimiento
movie la película, 6.2
movie theater el cine, 10.1
Ms., Mrs., madam la señora, BV
much; a lot mucho(a), 2.1
mud el lodo
multinational multinacional
multiplication la multiplicación
to multiply multiplicar
mural el mural, 10.2
muralist el/la muralista
muscular muscular
museum el museo, 10.2
music la música, 2.2
musical instrument el instrumento musical
musician el/la músico(a)
mussels los mejillones, **10.2**
must deber
mute mudo(a)
my mi
mysterious misterioso(a)
mystery el misterio
mythology la mitología

name el nombre
  in whose name? ¿a nombre de quién?, 14.2; **2.2**
  last name el apellido
nap: to take a nap echar (tomar) una siesta
napkin la servilleta, 14.1; **2.1**
narcotic el narcótico
to narrate narrar
narration la narración
narrow estrecho(a), **4.1**; angosto(a), **9.1**

narrow street la callecita, **9.1**
national nacional
nationality la nacionalidad, 1.2
  what nationality? ¿de qué nacionalidad?
native indígena
native person el/la indígena
natural resources los recursos naturales, 2.1
natural sciences las ciencias naturales
nature la naturaleza
navegable navegable
to navigate navegar
near cerca de, 6.2
nearby cercano(a)
necessary necesario(a)
necessity la necesidad
neck el cuello, **4.1**
to need necesitar, 3.1
negative negativo(a)
neighbor el/la vecino(a)
neighborhood el barrio, **9.1**; la zona
nephew el sobrino, 6.1
nervous nervioso(a), 8.1
net la red, 9.1
  Net (Internet) net
nettle la ortiga
never jamás; nunca
new nuevo(a)
newlyweds los novios, **13.1**
New Year el Año Nuevo, **13.2**
  Happy New Year! ¡Próspero Año Nuevo!, **13.2**
New Year's Eve la Nochevieja, la víspera de Año Nuevo, **13.2**
news las noticias, 6.2
newspaper el periódico, 6.2
newsstand el quiosco, 13.1; **1.1**
next próximo(a),13.2; 1.2
  at the next stop en la próxima parada, 13.2; 1.2
nice simpático(a), 1.2
niece la sobrina, 6.1
night la noche
  Good night. Buenas noches., BV

  in the evening, at night por la noche
  last night anoche, 9.2
  P.M. (time) de la noche
nine nueve, BV
nine hundred novecientos(as), 3.2
nineteen diecinueve, BV
ninety noventa, 2.2
ninth noveno(a), 6.2
no no, BV
no one nadie
no smoking sign la señal de no fumar, **7.1**
Nobel Prize el Premio Nóbel
noble noble
none, not any ninguno(a)
  by no means de ninguna manera, 1.1
nonstop sin escala
noon el mediodía
north el norte
North America la América del Norte
North American norteamericano(a)
northwest el noroeste
nose la nariz, **8.1**
notable notable
to note notar
notebook el cuaderno, 3.1
notes: to take notes tomar apuntes, 4.2
nothing nada, 5.2
  Nothing else. Nada más., 5.2
novel la novela
novelist el/la novelista
November noviembre, BV
now ahora, 4.2; ya
  now and then de vez en cuando
  nowadays, these days hoy (en) día
number el número, 1.2
  flight number el número del vuelo, 11.1
  local number el número local
  seat number el número del asiento, 11.1

telephone number el número de teléfono

wrong number el número equivocado

numerous numeroso(a)

nuptial, wedding nupcial

nurse el/la enfermero(a), **8.2**; el/la practicante

nutrition la nutrición

O

object el objeto

objective el objetivo

obligation la obligación

observation la observación

to **observe** observar

observer el/la observador(a)

obstacle el obstáculo

to **obtain** obtener

obvious obvio(a)

occasion la ocasión

occupied, taken ocupado(a), 5.1

ocean el océano

October octubre, BV

odd: odd number el número impar

of de, BV

Of course! ¡Cómo no!; por supuesto

of the, from the del

to **offer** ofrecer, **14.2**

office la oficina, **9.1**

official oficial

often con frecuencia, a menudo, **3.2**

oil el aceite, **14.2**; el óleo

oil (relating to) petrolero(a)

OK, all right; in agreement de acuerdo; ¡vale!

old viejo(a), anciano(a), 6.1; antiguo(a), **5.1**

old person el/la anciano(a); el/la viejo(a)

olive oil el aceite de oliva

on en; sobre

on foot a pie, **4.1**

on the dot, sharp en punto, **4.1**

once and for all definitivamente

oncologist el/la oncólogo(a)

oncology la oncología

one uno, BV

one o'clock la una

one-way street la calle de sentido único, **11.2**

one-way ticket el billete sencillo, **13.1**; **1.1**

one hundred cien(to), **3.2**

onion la cebolla, **10.1**

only único(a); sólo; solamente

to **open** abrir, **8.2**

opening la apertura

opera la ópera

to **operate** operar

operating room el quirófano

operator el/la operador(a)

operetta la opereta

ophthalmologist el/la oftalmólogo(a)

ophthalmology la oftalmología

opinion la opinión

opportunity la oportunidad

opposite opuesto(a); contrario(a)

the opposite lo contrario

the opposite direction el sentido contrario, **11.2**

or o; u (used instead of **o** before words beginning with **o** or **ho**)

orally oralmente

orange (fruit) la china; la naranja, **5.2**

orange anaranjado(a), **3.2**

orange juice el jugo de naranja, **12.1**; el zumo de naranja

orchard el/la huerto(a), **9.2**

orchestra la orquesta

symphony orchestra la orquesta sinfónica

order (restaurant) la orden, **5.1**

to **order** mandar; **(restaurant)** pedir (i, i)

organ el órgano

organism el organismo

to **organize** organizar

origin el origen

ornament el adorno

orthopedic surgeon el/la cirujano(a) ortopédico(a), **8.2**

orthopedics la ortopedia

other otro(a)

ounce la onza

our nuestro(a)

outdoor *(adj.)* al aire libre

outdoor café (market, etc.) el café (mercado, etc.) al aire libre

outfielder el/la jardinero(a), **7.2**

outskirts los alrededores; las afueras, **9.1**

oven el horno, **10.1**

over sobre

overcoat el abrigo, **4.1**

overland por tierra

to **overtake** adelantar, **11.2**

to **owe** deber

own: one's own propio(a)

oxygen el oxígeno

oxygen mask la máscara de oxígeno, **7.1**

oyster la ostra, **10.2**

P

to **pack one's suitcase** hacer la maleta

package el paquete, **5.2**

page la página

pain el dolor, **8.1**

I have a pain in my . . . Tengo dolor de..., **8.2**

to **paint** pintar, **14.1**

paintbrush el pincel

painter el/la pintor(a)

painting el cuadro, **10.2**; la pintura

pair el par, **4.1**

pair of tennis shoes el par de tenis, **3.2**

palace el palacio

palette knife la espátula

palm tree la palma

English-Spanish Dictionary

pamphlet el folleto
Panamanian panameño(a), 2.1
Panamerican panamericano(a)
pancake el panqueque
pants el pantalón, 3.2
papaya la papaya, 10.2
paper el papel, 3.1
  sheet of paper la hoja de papel, 3.1
  toilet paper el papel higiénico, 12.2
paradise el paraíso
paragraph el párrafo
paramedics el servicio de primeros auxilios, los socorristas, **8.1**
parents los padres, 6.1
to **park** aparcar, estacionar, **11.2**
park el parque, **5.2**
parka el anorak, 9.2
parking el estacionamiento
parking lot el aparcamiento
parking meter el parquímetro, **11.2**
part (in hair) la raya, 12.1
part la parte
  the greatest part, the most la mayor parte
  upper part la parte superior
party la fiesta, **13.1**
  to give (throw) a party dar una fiesta, 4.2
pass (permission) el pase
to **pass** pasar, 7.2; **(car)** adelantar, **11.2**
passenger el/la pasajero(a), 11.1
passionate apasionado(a)
passport el pasaporte, 11.1
passport inspection el control de pasaportes, 11.1
past pasado(a)
pastry el pastel, 4.2
path el camino; la senda, **5.2**
  to walk along the path caminar por la senda, **5.2**
patience la paciencia

patient el/la paciente
pattern el patrón
paved pavimentado(a)
pavement el pavimento
to **pay** pagar, 3.1
  to pay at the cashier pagar en la caja, 3.1
  to pay attention hacer caso; prestar atención, 4.2
  to pay the bill pagar la factura, **6.1**
payment el pago
  monthly payment el pago mensual
pea el guisante, 5.2
Peace Corps el Cuerpo de Paz
peaceful tranquilo(a)
peak el pico, **7.2**
peanut el cacahuete (cacahuate); el maní
pear la pera, **9.2**
pear tree el peral, **9.2**
pedestrian el peatón, **9.1**
pedestrian street la calle peatonal, **9.1**
pediatrician el/la pediatra
pediatrics la pediatría
to **peel** pelar, 10.2
pen la pluma, 3.1
pencil el lápiz, 3.1
peninsula la península
penny el centavo
people la gente
pepper la pimienta, 14.1; **2.1**
  bell pepper el pimiento, **10.2**
percent por ciento
percussion la percusión
to **perfect** perfeccionar
performance la función, **(theater)** la representación, 10.2
perhaps quizás, **14.2**
period el período
period of time la época
to **permit** permitir, 11.1
person la persona, 1.2
personality la personalidad
personally personalmente

Peruvian peruano(a)
petition la petición
petroleum el petróleo
pharmacist el/la farmacéutico(a), 8.2
phone el teléfono
  cell phone el teléfono celular, **3.2**
  pay phone el teléfono público, **3.2**
  phone book la guía telefónica, **3.2**
  phone call la llamada telefónica, **3.2**
  push-button phone el teléfono de botones, **3.2**
photo la foto
photograph la fotografía
photographer el/la fotógrafo(a)
phrase la frase
physics la física, 2.2
piano el piano
to **pick up** recoger
to **pick up (the telephone)** descolgar (ue), 3.2
picturesque pintoresco(a), **9.1**
piece el pedazo, 12.1; el trocito, **10.2**
  little piece el pedacito, **10.2**
pig (pork) el cerdo, 14.2; **2.2**
pilgrim el/la peregrino(a)
pill la pastilla, la píldora, la tableta, 8.2
pillow la almohada, **6.2**
pilot el/la piloto, 11.2
pinch la pizca
pink rosado(a), 3.2
pint la pinta
piping (embroidery) el cordoncillo
pirouette la pirueta
pitcher el/la lanzador(a), el/la pícher, 7.2
pity la lástima
pizza la pizza, BV
to **place** colocar; meter, 7.1
place el lugar; el sitio
placement la colocación
plague la plaga

plaid a cuadros
plain la llanura, **7.2**
plan el plano, **9.1**
to **plan** planear
plant la planta
to **plant** sembrar, **9.2**
plantain el plátano, 5.2
  fried plantain slice el tostón
plastic plástico(a), **4.2**
plate el plato, 14.1; **2.1**
plateau la mesa; la meseta, **7.2**
  high plateau el altiplano, **7.2**
to **play (music)** tocar
play la obra teatral, 10.2; la obra dramática
to **play** jugar (ue), **7.1**
  to play baseball (soccer, basketball, etc.) jugar (al) béisbol (fútbol, baloncesto, etc.), 7.1
player el/la jugador(a), 7.1
playwright el/la dramaturgo(a)
to **plead** rogar (ue)
pleasant agradable
please por favor, BV; favor de, **11.2**
pleasure el gusto
plentiful abundante
plot el argumento
plumber el/la fontanero(a), el/la plomero(a), **14.1**
pocket el bolsillo, **4.1**
poem el poema
poet el poeta
poetry la poesía
point el tanto, 7.1; el punto
poisonous venenoso(a)
police officer el/la guardia; el/la agente de policía; el/la policía
polite atento(a)
political político(a)
political science las ciencias políticas
polka dots: with polka dots con lunares
to **pollute** contaminar

polluted contaminado(a)
pollution la contaminación
poncho el poncho
poor pobre
poor boy (girl) el/la pobre
poor man (woman) el/la pobretón(ona)
popular popular, 2.1
popularity la popularidad
population, people la población
porch el porche
pork el puerco
portable portátil
porter el/la maletero(a), el/la mozo(a), 13.1; **1.1**
portrait el retrato
position la posición; el puesto, **14.2**
to **possess** poseer
possibility la posibilidad
possible posible
post office el correo, **12.2**
postcard la postal, la tarjeta postal, **12.2**
pot la cazuela, la olla, **10.1**
potato la papa, 5.1; la patata
  mashed potatoes el puré de papas
pothole el bache
pound la libra
practically casi
to **practice** practicar
pre-Columbian precolombino(a)
precious precioso(a)
precise preciso(a)
prediction la predicción
predominance el predominio
to **predominate** predominar
to **prefer** preferir (ie, i)
prenuptial antenupcial
preparation la preparación
to **prepare** preparar
to **prescribe** recetar, 8.2
prescription la receta, 8.2
presence la presencia
to **present** presentar
present *(adj.)* presente

  at the present time actualmente
presentation la presentación
president el/la presidente
pressure la presión, **11.1**
prestige el prestigio
pretty bello(a), bonito(a), hermoso(a), lindo(a), 1.1
to **prevail** prevalecer
price el precio
to **prick** picar, **8.1**
priest el sacerdote
princess la princesa
principal el/la director(a)
principal principal
printer la impresora, **3.1**
private: private house la casa particular, la casa privada, 6.2
probable probable
problem el problema
process el proceso
to **process** procesar
procession la procesión
to **proclaim** proclamar
produced producido(a)
product el producto, 5.2
production la producción
profession la profesión, **14.1**
professor el/la profesor(a), 2.1
program (TV) la emisión, 6.2; el programa
  sports program la emisión deportiva, 6.2
progress el progreso
project el proyecto
to **project** proyectar, 10.1
promiscuity la promiscuidad
promise la promesa
to **promote** promover (ue)
promotion la promoción
pronoun el pronombre
prose la prosa
prosperous próspero(a)
protagonist el/la protagonista

protection la protección

protein la proteína

to **protest** protestar

protoplasm el protoplasma

to **provide** proveer

provider el/la proveedor(a)

provision la provisión

psychiatrist el/la psiquiatra

psychiatry la psiquiatría

public público(a)

publicity la propaganda

to **publish** publicar

Puerto Rican puertorriqueño(a)

to **pull out** arrancar

pulse el pulso, **8.2**

punctual puntual

punishment el castigo

puppy el perrito

pure puro(a)

to **push** oprimir; pulsar, **3.1**; empujar, **4.2**

to **put** poner, 11.1; colocar

to **put a cast on** poner en un yeso, **8.2**

to **put in** meter, **3.1**

to **put on** ponerse, 12.1

  to put on a performance dar una representación, 10.2

  to put on makeup ponerse el maquillaje, 12.1

Pyrenees los pirineos

Q

qualification la calificación

quality la calidad

quarrel la disputa

quarter el cuarto, 2.2

  quarter after (the hour) y cuarto

  quarter to (the hour) menos cuarto

queen la reina

question la pregunta

questionnaire el cuestionario

quickly rápidamente; rápido

quiet tranquilo(a)

quite bastante, 1.1

R

race la carrera

racket (sports) la raqueta, 9.1

radiator el radiador, **11.1**

railroad el ferrocarril, 13.1, **1.1**

railway platform el andén, 13.1; **1.1**

rain la lluvia

to **rain** llover (ue)

  It's raining. Llueve., 9.1

raincoat el impermeable, la gabardina, **4.1**

to **raise** criar, **9.2**

ranch la hacienda; **(Argentina)** la estancia

rare raro(a)

rate la tarifa; la tasa

  exchange rate el tipo de cambio, la tasa de cambio, **12.2**

  unemployment rate la tasa de desempleo

rather bastante, 1.1

razor la navaja, 12.1

reaction la reacción

to **read** leer, 5.1

reading la lectura

ready listo(a)

realist el/la realista

realistic realista

really realmente

reason el motivo; la razón

reasonable razonable

to **rebound** rebotar

to **receive** recibir, 5.1

receiver (telephone) el auricular, **3.2**

recent reciente

recently recién

reception la recepción, **13.1**

receptionist el/la recepcionista, **6.1**

recipe la receta, **10.2**

to **recite** recitar

to **recognize** reconocer

recollection el recuerdo

to **recommend** recomendar (ie)

recommendation la recomendación

to **reconcile** conciliar

recreation el recreo

to **recruit** reclutar

rectangle el rectángulo

recycling el reciclaje

red rojo(a), 3.2

redheaded pelirrojo(a)

reduced (price) reducido(a)

to **refer** referir (ie, i)

to **reflect** reflejar; reflexionar

reflection; reflex el reflejo

reforestation la reforestación

refrigerator el refrigerador, la nevera, **10.1**

refuge el refugio

region la región

regional regional

regionalism el regionalismo

to **register** registrar

registration card la ficha, **6.1**

regular (gasoline) normal, **11.1**

related relacionado(a)

relation la relación

relative el/la pariente, 6.1

relatively relativamente

religious religioso(a)

to **remain** quedar, 7.1

remainder el resto

remains los restos

to **remember** recordar (ue)

to **renounce** renunciar

to **rent** alquilar, **5.2**; rentar

to **repair** reparar

to **repeat; to take seconds (meal)** repetir (i, i)

to **replace** reemplazar

report el informe; el reportaje

to **represent** representar

representative el/la representante

representative representativo(a)

republic la república

to **require** requerir (ie, i)

requirement el requisito

researcher el/la investigador(a)

reservation la reservación, **6.1**

to **reserve** reservar, 14.2; **2.2**

reserved reservado(a), 13.2; **1.2**

residence la residencia

resident el/la residente

resort la estación, 10.1

to **respond** responder

responsibility la responsabilidad

   to make oneself responsible responsabilizarse

rest demás; el resto

to **rest** descansar

restaurant el restaurante, 14.1; **2.1**

to **restore** restaurar

result el resultado

retina la retina

return el regreso

return trip, trip back el viaje de regreso

to **return** regresar; volver (ue), 7.1

   to return home volver a casa, 10.2

to **return (something)** devolver (ue), 7.2

reverse inverso(a)

revolution la revolución

rhythm el ritmo

rib la costilla, **10.1**

ribbon la cinta

rice el arroz, 5.2

rich rico(a), 14.2; **2.2**; con mucha plata

rich person el/la rico(a)

ride la atracción, **5.2**

right derecho(a), 7.1

   to the right a la derecha, **5.2**

right: that's right (true)! ¡verdad!

right away enseguida, 5.1

rigorous riguroso(a)

ring el anillo, **4.1**

to **ring** sonar (ue), **3.2**

to **rise** ascender

ritual el rito

rival el/la rival

river el río, **7.2**

to **roast** asar, **10.1**

roasted asado(a)

rock la roca

role el rol; el papel

roll of toilet paper el rollo de papel higiénico, 12.2

to **roll** rodar (ue)

roller blading el patinaje lineal

roller coaster la montaña rusa, **5.2**

Roman el/la romano(a)

romantic romántico(a)

room el cuarto, la sala, 6.2; la pieza

   double room el cuarto doble, **6.1**

   recovery room la sala de recuperación

   single room el cuarto sencillo, **6.1**

   waiting room la sala de espera, 13.1; **1.1**

root la raíz

rose la rosa

round-trip (ticket) de ida y vuelta, 13.1; **1.1**

route la ruta

routine la rutina, 12.1

routine (*adj.*) rutinario(a)

row (of seats) la fila, 10.1

to **row** remar, **5.2**

royal real

ruin la ruina

rule la regla

rumor el rumor

to **run** correr, 7.2

runway la pista, **7.2**

rural rural

sacrifice el sacrificio

to **sacrifice** sacrificar

sad triste, 8.1

safe salvo(a)

saffron el azafrán

sailboard la plancha de vela, 9.1

sailor el/la marino(a)

saint el santo

salad la ensalada, 5.1

salary el salario

sale la venta, **14.1**

salesperson el/la dependiente(a), **4.1**; el/la vendedor(a), **11.1**

salt la sal, 14.1; **2.1**

same mismo(a), 2.1

sand la arena, 9.1

sandal el huarache; la alpargata; la sandalia, **4.1**

sandwich el sándwich, BV; el bocadillo, 5.1

sash la faja

satisfied satisfecho(a), **14.1**

to **satisfy** satisfacer

Saturday el sábado, BV

saucepan la cacerola, **10.2**

saucer el platillo, 14.1; **2.1**

sausage (pork and garlic) el chorizo, la salchicha, **10.1**

to **save** ahorrar; conservar; salvar; guardar, **3.1**

savings account la cuenta de ahorros

saxophone el saxofono

to **say** decir

scale la báscula, 11.1

scarf la bufanda, **4.1**

scene la escena

scenery, set (theater) el escenario, 10.2

schedule el horario, 13.1; **1.1**

   school schedule el horario escolar

scholarship la beca

school el colegio, la escuela, 1.1; la academia

   elementary school la escuela primaria

   high school la escuela secundaria, 1.1; la escuela superior

English-Spanish Dictionary

middle school la escuela intermedia

school (of a university) la Facultad

school (related to) escolar, 2.1

school bus el bus escolar, 4.1

school life la vida escolar

school schedule el horario escolar

school supplies los materiales escolares, 3.1

science las ciencias, 2.2

science fiction la ciencia ficción

scientific científico(a)

scientist el/la científico(a)

scissors las tijeras, **12.1**

score el tanto, 7.1

to **score a goal** meter un gol, 7.1

to **score a point** marcar un tanto, 7.1

scoreboard el tablero indicador, 7.1

screen la pantalla, 10.1

arrival and departure screen la pantalla de salidas y llegadas, 11.1

sculptor el/la escultor(a), 10.2

sculpture la escultura

sea el mar, 9.1

sea level el nivel del mar

search: in search of en busca de

season la estación, BV

to **season** sazonar

seasoning el condimento

seat el asiento, 11.1; la plaza, 13.2; **1.2**

seat (of government) la sede

seat (theater) la butaca, 10.1

seat belt el cinturón de seguridad, **7.1**

seat number el número del asiento, 11.1

second segundo(a), 6.2

second class en segunda (clase), 13.1; **1.1**

second half (soccer) el segundo tiempo, 7.1

secondary secundario(a)

secret el secreto

secretary el/la secretario(a), **14.1**

to **secretly take** escamotear

security la seguridad, **7.1**

security check el control de seguridad, 11.1

sedan el sedán, **11.1**

see: See you later! ¡Hasta luego!, BV

See you soon! ¡Hasta pronto!, BV

See you tomorrow! ¡Hasta mañana!, BV

to **see** ver, 5.1

to see a show ver un espectáculo, 10.2

to **seem** parecer, **8.1**

to **select** seleccionar

selection la selección

self-portrait el autorretrato

to **sell** vender, 5.2; despachar, 8.2

semester el semestre

senator el/la senador(a)

to **send** enviar; mandar, transmitir, **3.1**

sentence la frase

separated separado(a)

September septiembre, BV

series la serie

World Series la Serie mundial

serious serio(a), 1.1; grave

servant el/la sirviente

to **serve** servir (i, i), 14.1; **2.1**

service el servicio, 5.1

service station la estación de servicio, la gasolinera, **11.1**

set el conjunto

to **set the bone** reducir el hueso, **8.2**

to **set the table** poner la mesa, 14.1; **2.1**

seven siete, BV

seven hundred setecientos(as), 3.2

seventeen diecisiete, BV

seventh séptimo(a), 6.2

seventy setenta, 2.2

to **sew** coser

sewing la costura

sex el sexo

shack la chabola

to **shake hands** dar la mano

shampoo el champú, 12.2

shantytown la villa miseria (Arg.); el pueblo jóven (Peru)

shape la forma

to **shave** afeitarse, 12.1

shaving cream la crema de afeitar, 12.1

shawl el poncho

she ella, 1.1

sheet la sábana, **6.2**

sheet of paper la hoja de papel, 3.1

shellfish los mariscos, 5.2

sherbet, sorbet el sorbete

shh! ¡chist!

to **shine** brillar, 9.1

shirt la camisa, 3.2

long-sleeved shirt la camisa de mangas largas, **4.1**

short-sleeved shirt la camisa de mangas cortas, **4.1**

shoe el zapato, 3.2

shoe store la zapatería, **4.1**

to **shop** ir de compras, 5.2; hacer las compras, **4.2**

shop window el escaparate, la vitrina, **4.1**

shopping: to go shopping hacer las compras, **4.2**; ir de compras, **5.2**

shopping mall la galería comercial

short bajo(a), 1.1; corto(a), 3.2

short- (long-) term a corto (largo) plazo

shortage la escasez

shorts el pantalón corto, 3.2

shot: to give (someone) a shot poner una inyección

should deber

shoulder el hombro, **8.1**

to **show (movie)** presentar; mostrar

show (movies) la sesión, 10.1

show el espectáculo, 10.2; el show

shower la ducha, 12.1

to take a shower tomar una ducha, 12.1

shrimp los camarones, 14.2; **2.2**; las gambas, **10.2**

shy tímido(a), 1.2

sick enfermo(a), 8.1

sick person el/la enfermo(a), 8.1

side el borde; el lado, 12.1

sidewalk la acera, **9.1**

to **sigh** suspirar

sign el rótulo, 11.2

traffic sign la señal de tránsito

to **sign** firmar, **12.2**

significance el sentido, **11.2**

significant significativo(a)

similar parecido(a); similar

simple sencillo(a); simple

since como; desde

sincere franco(a); sincero(a), 1.2

to **sing** cantar, 4.2

singing el canto

single soltero(a)

singles singles, 9.1

sir, Mr., gentleman el señor, BV

sister la hermana, 6.1

to **sit down** sentarse (ie), 12.1

to **situate** situar

situation la situación

six seis, BV

six hundred seiscientos(as), 3.2

sixteen dieciséis, BV

sixth sexto(a), 6.2

sixty sesenta, 2.2

size (shoes) número, 3.2

size el tamaño, la talla, 3.2

What size (shoe) do you wear (take)? ¿Qué número calza usted?, 3.2

What size (clothing) do you wear (take)? ¿Qué tamaño (talla) usa usted?, **3.2**

ski el esquí

to **ski** esquiar, 9.2

ski lift el telesquí, 9.2

ski pole el bastón, 9.2

ski resort la estación de esquí, 9.2

ski slope la pista, 9.2

skier el/la esquiador(a), 9.2

skiing el esquí, 9.2

skirt la falda, 3.2

sky el cielo, 9.1

skyscraper el rascacielos, **9.1**

to **sleep** dormir (ue, u)

to fall asleep dormirse (ue, u), 12.1

sleeping bag el saco de dormir, 12.2

sleeve la manga, **4.1**

long- (short-) sleeved de mangas largas (cortas), **4.1**

slice la rebanada, la tajada, **4.2**

to **slice** rebanar, **10.2**

slot la ranura, **3.1**

slow lento(a), **10.2**

slowly despacio

small pequeño(a), 2.1

smile: little smile la sonrisita

smoking: (no) smoking area la sección de (no) fumar, 11.1

snack la merienda, 4.2

to have a snack tomar una merienda, 4.2

to **sneeze** estornudar, 8.1

snow la nieve, 9.2

to **snow** nevar (ie), 9.2

snowboarding el surf de nieve

so así

so, so much tan, tanto(a)

soap el jabón, 12.2

bar of soap la barra (pastilla) de jabón, 12.2

soccer el fútbol, 7.1

soccer field el campo de fútbol, 7.1

social sciences las ciencias sociales, 2.2

society la sociedad

sociology la sociología

socks los calcetines, 3.2

soda la soda, la gaseosa, 5.1

sofa el sofá, **6.2**

soldier el militar; el/la soldado

solitary, lone solitario(a)

solution el remedio; la solución

to **solve** resolver (ue)

some algunos(as), 4.1; unos(as)

someone alguien

something algo, 5.2

sometimes de vez en cuando; a veces, 7.1

son el hijo, 6.1

song la canción

soon dentro de poco

sore throat el dolor de garganta, 8.1

sorry: to be sorry sentir (ie, i)

sound el sonido

soup la sopa, 5.1

source la fuente

south el sur

South America la América del Sur

South American sudamericano(a)

southeast el sureste

southwest el sudoeste; el suroeste

to **sow** sembrar, **9.2**

sowing la siembra

space el espacio

spaghetti el espagueti

Spain la España, 1.2

Spanish (*adj.*) español(a)

Spanish (language) el español, 2.2

Spanish American hispanoamericano(a)

Spanish speaker el/la hispanohablante

Spanish-speaking hispanohablante

Spanish-speaking countries los países de habla española

Spanish-style a la española

spare tire la llanta de recambia (repuesto), **11.1**

to **speak** hablar, 3.1; conversar

special especial

specialist el/la especialista, **14.1**

to **specialize** especializar

specialty la especialidad

spectator el/la espectador(a), 7.1; el/la mirón(ona)

speed la velocidad, **11.2**

speed limit el límite de velocidad

to **spend** pasar; gastar

to **spend time** pasar el tiempo, **5.1**

spice la especia

spontaneous espontáneo(a)

sport el deporte, 7.1

  individual sport el deporte individual

  (related to) sports deportivo(a), 6.2

  sports program (TV) la emisión deportiva, 6.2

  team sport el deporte de equipo

spring la primavera, BV

squid los calamares, **10.2**

squire, knight's attendant el escudero

stadium el estadio, 7.1

stage: to come (go) on stage entrar en escena, 10.2

stairway la escalera, 6.2

stall el puesto, **4.2**

stamp el sello, la estampilla **5.1**

to **stand on line** hacer cola

standing de pie

star la estrella

to **start** comenzar (ie), empezar (ie), 7.1

state el estado

station la estación, 10.1

  subway station la estación del metro, **10.1**

train station la estación de ferrocarril, 13.1; **1.1**

stationery store la papelería, 3.1

statistic la estadística

statue la estatua, 10.2

stay la estadía

to **stay** alojarse

to **stay in bed** guardar cama, 8.1

steak el biftec, 14.2; **2.2**

step el paso

stereo estereofónico(a)

still todavía

sting la picadura, **8.1**

to **stir** revolver (ue), **10.1**

stitch el punto, la sutura, **8.1**

stomach el estómago, 8.1

stomachache el dolor de estómago, 8.1

stone la piedra

stop la parada, 13.2; **1.2**

to **stop** bloquear, parar, 7.1

stopover la escala, **7.2**

store la tienda, 3.2

to **store** almacenar

story el cuento; la historia

  short story la historieta

stove la estufa, **10.1**

stove burner la hornilla, **10.1**

straight derecho, **11.2**

  to go straight seguir derecho, **11.2**

strange extravagante

strategy la estrategia

straw la paja, **13.2**

stream el arroyo

street la calle, 6.2

  one-way street la calle de sentido único, **11.2**

  pedestrian street la calle peatonal

strength la fortaleza

stretch (of road) el trayecto; el tramo

stretcher la camilla, **8.1**

to **strike twelve** dar las doce, **13.2**

string (instrument) la cuerda

string bean la judía verde, 5.2; el poroto; la vainita; el ejote; la chaucha

striped a rayas

strong fuerte

structure la estructura

student (relating to) estudiantil

student el/la alumno(a), 1.1; el/la estudiante

student housing la residencia para estudiantes, **3.2**

study el estudio

to **study** estudiar, 4.1

stupendous estupendo(a)

stupid torpe

style el estilo; la moda

  in style de moda

subject la asignatura, 2.1; la materia; el tema

subject area (school) la disciplina, 2.2

substance: controlled substance la sustancia controlada

subterranean subterráneo(a)

subtitle el subtítulo, 10.1

  with subtitles con subtítulos, 10.1

to **subtract** restar

suburb el suburbio; la colonia

subway el metro, 10.1

subway station la estación de metro, 10.1

success el éxito

suckling pig el lechón; el cochinillo

suddenly repentinamente

to **suffer** sufrir

sugar el azúcar, **10.1**

to **suggest** sugerir (ie, i)

suggestion la sugerencia

suit el traje, 3.2

suitcase la maleta, 11.1

summer el verano, BV

to **sunbathe** tomar el sol, 9.1

sunblock la crema protectora, 9.1

sunburned, tanned tostadito(a)

Sunday el domingo, BV

sunglasses las gafas de sol, los anteojos de sol, 9.1

sunny: It's sunny. Hace (Hay) sol., 9.1

suntan lotion la loción bronceadora, 9.1

supermarket el supermercado, 5.2

supermarket cart el carrito, **4.2**

superstition la superstición

to **support** sostener

sure seguro(a)

to **surf** practicar el surfing (la tabla hawaiana), 9.1

to surf the Net navegar por la red

surface la superficie

surfboard la tabla hawaiana, 9.1

surfing el surfing, 9.1

surgeon el/la cirujano(a), **8.2**

to **surprise** sorprender

survey la encuesta

sweater el suéter, **4.1**

sweet dulce

sweet roll el pan dulce, 5.1

sweetheart, lover el/la enamorado(a)

to **swim** nadar, 9.1

to **swim underwater** bucear, 9.1

swimming la natación, 9.1

swimming pool la alberca, la piscina, 9.1

swollen hinchado(a), **8.1**

symptom el síntoma, 8.2

syrup el sirope

system el sistema

metric system el sistema métrico

T-shirt la camiseta, el T-shirt, 3.2

table la mesa, 5.1

table soccer el futbolín, **5.1**

tablecloth el mantel, 14.1; **2.1**

tablespoon la cuchara, 14.1; **2.1**

taco el taco, BV

to **take** tomar, 4.1

to take notes tomar apuntes, 4.2

to take someone's blood pressure tomar la tensión (presión) arterial, **8.2**

to take someone's pulse tomar el pulso, 8.2

to take out sacar, 3.1

to take photos tomar fotos

to take place tener lugar, **8.1**

to take the luggage down bajar las maletas, **6.1**

to take the (school) bus tomar el bus (escolar), 4.1

to **take charge** encargarse

to **take off** quitar, **10.2**

to take off (airplane) despegar, **11.2**

to take off the fire retirar del fuego, 10.1

to **take time** tardar

takeoff (of an airplane) el despegue, 7.2

talent el talento

to **talk** hablar, 3.1; conversar

tall alto(a), 1.1

tamale el tamal, BV

tan bronceado(a)

tank el tanque, **11.1**

task la tarea

taxi el taxi, 11.1

tea el té, 5.1

iced tea el té helado, 5.1

to **teach** enseñar, 4.1

teacher el/la maestro(a); el/la profesor(a), 2.1

team el bando; el equipo, 7.1

team sport el deporte de equipo, 7.2

tearoom la confitería

teaspoon la cucharita, 14.1; **2.1**

technician el/la técnico(a), **8.2**

technology la tecnología

teenager el/la adolescente

telecommunication la telecomunicación

to **telephone** telefonear

to talk on the phone hablar por teléfono

telephone el teléfono

cell phone el teléfono celular, 3.2

public (pay) telephone el teléfono público, 3.2

push-button telephone el teléfono de botones, 3.2

(related to the) telephone telefónico(a)

telephone book la guía telefónica, 3.2

telephone call la llamada telefónica, 3.2

telephone keypad el teclado, 3.2

telephone line la línea telefónica

telephone receiver el auricular, 3.2

television la televisión, 6.2

television set el televisor, **6.2**

teller el/la cajero(a), **12.2**

teller's window la ventanilla, **12.2**

temperate templado(a)

temperature la temperatura, 9.2

ten diez

tender tierno(a)

tennis el tenis, 9.1

pair of tennis shoes el par de tenis, 3.2

tennis player el/la tenista

tennis shoes los tenis, 3.2

tenth décimo(a), 6.2

term el término

terminal el terminal

passenger terminal el terminal de pasajeros, 7.2

terrace (sidewalk café) la terraza

terrible terrible

terror el terror

test el examen, 4.2

tetanus el tétano

Thank you. Gracias., BV

that (one) eso

that aquel, aquella; ese(a)

the la, el, 1.1

theater el teatro, 10.2

theatrical teatral, 10.2

their su, sus, 6.1

them las, los

   to them; to you (*formal pl.*) (*pron.*) les

theme el motivo; el tema

then luego, BV; entonces

there allí, allá

there is, there are hay, BV

therefore, for this reason, that's why por eso

these estos(as)

they ellos(as), 2.1

thin delgado(a); flaco(a), 1.2

thing la cosa

to **think** pensar (ie); opinar, **10.2**

third tercer(o)(a), 6.2

thirsty: to be thirsty tener sed, 14.1; **2.1**

thirteen trece, BV

thirty treinta, BV

thirty-one treinta y uno, 2.2

this (one) esto

this este(a)

thistle el cardo

those aquelios(as), esos(as)

thought el pensamiento

thousand mil, 3.2

three tres, BV

three hundred trescientos(as), 3.2

Three Wise Men los Reyes Magos, **13.2**

throat la garganta, 8.1

to **throw** echar; lanzar, 7.1; tirar

   to throw (kick) the ball tirar el balón, 7.2

Thursday el jueves, BV

thus así

ticket el boleto, el ticket, 9.2; el billete, 11.1; el tique, **9.1**

luggage claim ticket el talón, 11.1

one-way ticket el billete sencillo, 13.1; **1.1**

round-trip ticket el billete de ida y vuelta, 13.1; **1.1**

ticket window la boletería, la ventanilla, 9.2

tie la corbata, 3.2

tied (score) empatado(a), 7.1

   The score is tied. El tanto queda empatado., 7.1

tiger el tigre

time la hora; el tiempo, **9.1**

   At what time? ¿A qué hora?

   on time a tiempo, 11.1

   What time is it? ¿Qué hora es?

time la vez

   at times, sometimes a veces, 7.1

   at that time en aquel entonces

   one more time, again una vez más

time zone el huso horario

timid tímido(a), 1.2

tiny diminuto(a)

tip el servicio, 5.1; la propina, 14.1; **2.1**

   Is the tip included? ¿Está incluido el servicio?, 5.1

tire el neumático, la goma, la llanta, **11.1**

   flat tire la llanta pinchada

   spare tire la llanta de recambio (repuesto), **11.1**

tired cansado(a), 8.1

to a

toast la tostada; el pan tostado, 5.2

to **toast** tostar

today hoy, BV

together juntos(as)

toilet el inodoro, el váter, **6.2**

toilet paper el papel higiénico, 12.2

to **tolerate** consentir (ie, i)

toll el peaje, 11.2

toll booth la garita de peaje, **11.2**

tomato el tomate

tomorrow mañana, BV

ton la tonelada

tonight esta noche, 9.2

too much demasiado

tooth el diente

toothbrush el cepillo de dientes, 12.2

toothpaste la pasta (crema) dentífrica, 12.2

tortilla la tortilla, 5.1

totally totalmente

touch el contacto

to **touch** tocar

tour la gira, 12.2

tour guide el/la guía

tourist el/la turista, 10.2

toward en dirección a; hacia

towel la toalla, 9.1; **6.2**

   beach towel la toalla playera, 9.1

tower la torre

   control tower la torre de control, **7.2**

town el pueblo, 9.2

town square la plaza, **9.1**

toxic tóxico(a)

toy el juguete

track la vía, 13.1; **1.1**

trade el oficio, **14.1**

tradition la tradición

traditional tradicional

traffic el tráfico

traffic light el semáforo, **9.1**

traffic sign la señal de tránsito

tragedy la tragedia

trail el camino

train el tren, 13.2; **1.2**

   local train el tren local, 13.2

   nonstop train el tren directo, 13.2; **1.2**

train car el coche, el vagón, 13.1; **1.1**

   cafeteria (dining) car el coche-cafetería, el coche-comedor, 13.2; **1.2**

   sleeping car el coche-cama, 13.2

train conductor el/la revisor(a), 13.2; **1.2**

train station la estación de ferrocarril, 13.1; **1.1**

training el entrenamiento

to **transfer** transbordar, 13.2; **1.2**; trasladar

to **transform** convertir (ie, i); transformar

to **transmit** transmitir, **3.1**

transportation el transporte

to **travel** circular; recorrer; viajar

to **travel by air** viajar en avión, 11.1

traveler el/la viajero(a)

traveler's check el cheque de viajero, **12.2**

tray la bandeja, **7.1**

tray table la mesita, **7.1**

treat tratar

treatment el tratamiento; la cura

tree el árbol

triangle el triángulo

tribe la tribu

trip el viaje

   return trip el viaje de regreso

   to take a trip hacer un viaje, 11.1

trip (distance traveled) el recorrido

triumphant triunfante

trombone el trombón

trousers el pantalón, 3.2

trousseau el ajuar de novia

true verdadero(a)

trumpet la trompeta

trunk (of a car) el/la maletero(a), 11.1; la maletera, 13.1; **1.1**; el baúl, **11.1**

to **try** tratar

to **try on** probarse (ue), **4.1**

   tube of toothpaste el tubo de pasta (crema) dentífrica, 12.2

   Tuesday el martes, BV

tuna el atún, 5.2

turbulance la turbulencia, **7.2**

to **turn** doblar, **11.2**

to **turn around** revolver (ue), **10.1**

to **turn off** apagar (gu), **3.1**

to **turn on** prender, **3.1**

turning signal la direccional, **11.1**

turnstile el torniquete, **9.1**

twelve doce, BV

twenty veinte, BV

twenty-eight veintiocho, BV

twenty-five veinticinco, BV

twenty-four veinticuatro, BV

twenty-nine veintinueve, BV

twenty-one veintiuno, BV

twenty-seven veintisiete, BV

twenty-six veintiséis, BV

twenty-three veintitrés, BV

twenty-two veintidós, BV

twin el/la gemelo(a)

twist torcer (ue), **8.1**

two dos, BV

two hundred doscientos(as), 3.2

type el tipo; la modalidad típico(a)

U

ugly feo(a), 1.1

uncle el tío, 6.1

under debajo (de)

undershirt la camiseta, 3.2

to **understand** comprender, 5.1

underwater swimming el buceo, 9.1

underwear la ropa interior, **4.1**

uniform el uniforme

union el enlace

unique único(a)

unit la unidad

United States Estados Unidos

   from the United States estadounidense

university la universidad

   related to university universitario(a)

university degree el título universitario, **14.1**

unleaded sin plomo, **11.1**

unless a menos que

unpleasant desagradable

until hasta, BV

urban urbano(a)

urologist el/la urólogo(a)

urology la urología

us *(to) (pl. pron.)* nos

to **use** utilizar

used usado(a)

usually generalmente

V

vacation la vacación, **6.2**

valley el valle, **7.2**

value el valor

vanilla *(adj.)* de vainilla, 5.1

variation la variación

varied variado(a)

variety la variedad

various varios(as)

to **vary** variar

veal la ternera, 14.2; **2.2**

vegetable el vegetal, 5.2; la legumbre

vegetable garden el/la huerto(a), **9.2**

vegetarian el/la vegetariano(a)

Venezuelan venezolano(a)

verse el verso

version: in its original (language) version en versión original, 10.1

very muy, BV

vest el chaleco

veterinarian el/la veterinario(a)

vice versa viceversa

victim la víctima, **8.1**

victorious victorioso(a)

video el video

video store la tienda de videos

view la vista

vinegar el vinagre

violin el violín, 2.1

to **visit** visitar

vitamin la vitamina

voice la voz

volleyball el voleibol

volume el tomo
volunteer el/la voluntario(a)
vowel la vocal

to **wait (for)** esperar, 11.1
 waiter, waitress el/la camarero(a), el/la mesero(a), 5.1
 waiting room la sala de espera, 13.1; **1.1**
to **wake up** despertarse (ie), 12.1
to **walk** ir a pie, 4.1; andar; caminar, **9.1**
  to take a walk dar un paseo, **5.2**
 wall la muralla; la pared
to **want** desear, 3.2; querer (ie)
  I would like ... Quisiera... , 14.2; **2.2**
 war la guerra
to **warn** advertir (ie,i)
to **wash oneself** lavarse, 12.1
 washbasin el lavabo, **6.2**
 washing machine la máquina de lavar
 waste los desechos
 watch el reloj, **4.1**
to **watch** mirar, 3.1
 water el agua (f.), 9.1
  mineral water el agua mineral, 12.2
  running water el agua corriente
to **water-ski** esquiar en el agua, 9.1
 water-skiing el esquí acuático, 9.1
 watercolor la acuarela
 watermelon la sandía, **10.2**
 wave la ola, 9.1
 way el modo; la manera, 1.1
 we nosotros(as), 2.2
 weapon el arma (f.)
to **wear** llevar, 3.2
to **wear (size)** usar, 3.2; **(shoe size)** calzar, 3.2

 weather el tiempo, 9.1
  It's cold. Hace frío., 9.2
  It's hot. Hace calor., 9.1
  It's sunny. Hace sol., 9.1
  The weather is bad. Hace mal tiempo., 9.1
  The weather is nice. Hace buen tiempo., 9.1
 Web page la página Web
 wedding la boda, 13.1
 Wednesday el miércoles, BV
 week la semana, BV
  last week la semana pasada, 9.2
  weekend el fin de semana, BV
  last weekend el fin de semana pasado
to **weigh** pesar
 weight la pesa; el peso
 welcome dar la bienvenida, 11.2
  You're welcome. De nada., Por nada., No hay de qué., BV
 well bien, BV; pues
  very well muy bien, BV
 well-known renombrado(a)
 west el oeste
 western occidental
 what, that which lo que
 what? ¿qué?, BV
  What's the matter (with you)? ¿Qué te pasa?, 8.2
 wheat el trigo, **9.2**
 wheelchair la silla de ruedas, **8.2**
 when cuando, 4.2
 when? ¿cuándo?, 4.1
 where donde, 1.2
 where? ¿adónde?, 1.1; ¿dónde?, 1.2
 which?, what? ¿cuál?, BV
 while el rato; mientras
 white blanco(a), 3.2
 who? ¿quién?, 1.1; (pl.) ¿quiénes?, 2.1
  Who is calling? ¿De parte de quién?, **3.2**
 whole entero(a)
 why? ¿por qué?

 wide ancho(a)
 wife la mujer, la esposa, 6.1
 wig la peluca
 wild salvaje
to **win** ganar, 7.1
 wind el viento
 windmill el molino de viento
 window (post office, etc.) la ventanilla; (shop) el escaparate, la vitrina, **4.1**
 windshield el parabrisas, **11.1**
 winter el invierno, BV
 wise sabio(a)
  The Three Wise Men Los Reyes Magos, 13.2
to **wish** desear, 3.2
 with con
 within dentro de
 without sin
 woman la dama
 wood la madera
 wool la lana, **12.1**
 word la palabra
 work el trabajo
to **work** trabajar, 3.2
  to work full time trabajar a tiempo completo, 14.2
  to work part time trabajar a tiempo parcial, 14.2
 work la obra
 work of art la obra de arte
 worker el/la trabajador(a); el/la obrero(a), **9.1**
 workforce la mano de obra
 world el mundo
 World Cup la Copa mundial
 World Series la Serie mundial
 worldwide, (related to the) world mundial
 worse, worst peor, el/la peor
 wound la herida, **8.1**
 wounded person el/la herido(a)
 wrapped envuelto(a)
to **wrinkle** arrugar
 wrist la muñeca, **4.1**

to **write** escribir, 5.1

writing pad el bloc, 3.1

wrong erróneo(a)

X-ray la radiografía, los rayos equis, **8.2**

yard la yarda

year el año, BV

to be . . . years old tener... años, 6.1; cumplir... años

last year el año pasado, 9.2

this year este año, 9.2

yellow amarillo(a), 3.2

yes sí

yesterday ayer, 9.2

day before yesterday anteayer

yesterday afternoon ayer por la tarde, 9.2

yesterday morning ayer por la mañana , 9.2

yet aún; todavía

yogurt el yogur

you *(sing. fam.)* tú; *(sing. form.)* Ud., usted, 3.2; *(pl. form.)* Uds., ustedes, 2.2

You're welcome. De nada., No hay de qué., BV

young joven, 6.1

as a young person de joven

your *(sing. fam.)* tu; *(form.)* su, sus, 6.1

youth la juventud

youth, young person el/la joven, 10.1

youth hostel el albergue para jóvenes (juvenil), 12.2

zero cero, BV

zone la zona

commerical zone la zona comercial, 9.1

industrial zone la zona industrial, 9.1

residential zone la zona residencial, 9.1

zoo el parque zoológico, **5.2**

Index

acabar de 233 (8)

-ar verbs imperfect tense, 68 (3); future tense, 140 (5); conditional tense, 200 (7); present perfect tense, 240 (8); imperfect progressive tense, 270 (9); formal commands, 300 (10); informal commands, affirmative, 330 (11); informal commands, negative, 334 (11); present subjunctive, 369 (12)

adjectives comparative and superlative: regular and irregular forms, 144 (5); demonstrative adjectives, 274 (9)

commands see imperative

comparative formation, 144 (5); of **bueno, malo,** 144 (5); **mayor, menor,** 144 (5)

comparing equal quantities with nouns, 244 (8)

conditional tense regular verbs, 200 (7); irregular verbs, 203 (7); see also *individual, regular, irregular,* and *stem-changing* verbs

dar formal commands, 303 (10); informal commands, affirmative, 330 (11); informal commands, negative, 334 (11); present subjunctive, 369 (12)

decir present tense, 14 (1); imperfect tense, 70 (3); future tense, 170 (6); conditional tense, 203 (7); present perfect tense, 242 (8); imperfect progressive tense, 270 (9); formal commands, 303 (10); informal commands, affirmative, 332 (11); informal commands, negative, 334 (11); present subjunctive, 369 (12)

direct object pronouns with indirect object pronouns, 173 (6); with **le** or **les,** 205 (7); placement of with present participle and infinitive, 272 (9); placement of with affirmative and negative commands, 305 (10)

-er verbs imperfect tense, 70 (3); future tense, 140 (5); conditional tense, 200 (7); present perfect tense, 240 (8); imperfect progressive tense, 270 (9); formal commands, 300 (10); informal commands, affirmative, 330 (11); informal commands, negative, 334 (11); present subjunctive, 369 (12)

estar imperfect tense, 270 (9); used to form imperfect progressive tense, 270 (9); formal commands, 303 (10); informal commands, affirmative, 330 (11); informal commands, negative, 334 (11); present subjunctive, 369 (12)

future tense regular verbs, 140 (5); irregular verbs, 170 (6); see also *individual, regular, irregular,* and *stem-changing verbs*

haber present tense, 240 (8); imperfect tense, 70 (3); used to form present perfect tense, 240 (8)

hacer future tense, 170 (6); conditional tense, 203 (7); present perfect tense, 242 (8); formal commands, 303 (10); informal commands, affirmative, 332 (11); informal commands, negative, 334 (11); present subjunctive, 369 (12)

imperative formal commands: regular verbs, 300 (10); stem-changing verbs, 300 (10); irregular verbs, 303 (10); placement of object pronouns with, 305 (10); informal commands, affirmative: regular and stem-changing verbs, 330 (11); irregular verbs, 332 (11); informal commands, negative, 334 (11); see also *individual, regular, irregular,* and *stem-changing verbs*

imperfect tense regular verbs: **-ar** verbs, 68 (3); **-er** and **-ir** verbs, 70 (3); irregular verbs: **haber,** 70 (3); **ir,** 72 (3); **ser,** 72 (3); uses, 74 (3); vs. preterite, 100 (4); in same sentence as preterite, 103 (4); with verbs of feeling, thinking, etc., 105 (4); see also *individual, regular, irregular,* and *stem-changing verbs*

imperfect progressive tense formation, 270 (9); irregular present participles, 270 9)

indirect object pronouns with direct object pronouns, 173 (6); **le** or **les** with direct object pronouns, 205 (7); placement of with present participle and infinitive, 272 (9); placement of with formal commands, 305 (10)

infinitive vs. subjunctive, 432 (14)

ir imperfect tense, 72 (3); formal comands, 303 (10); informal commands, affirmative, 332 (11); informal commands, negative, 334 (11); present subjunctive, 369 (12)

Index

Credits

90–91 Macduff Everton/CORBIS; 92 Dominic Oldershaw; 93 (l)Jeff Smith/FOTOSMITH, (r)Steve Torregrossa; 95 (t)Michelle Chaplow, (b)Ken Karp; 97 Tim Fuller; 98 (t)Don Smetzer/Tony Stone Images, (b)Tim Fuller; 99 Kelly-Mooney Photography/CORBIS; 100 Andrew Payti; 105 Steve Torregrossa; 106 (t)Robert Fried, (b)Andrew Payti; 107 Getty Images; 108 Michelle Chaplow; 109 The Stock Market; 110 (t)Francis Morgan, (b)Tim Fuller; 111 Andrew Payti; 112 Robert Frerck/Odyssey; 113 (tl)M. Philip Kahl/Bruce Coleman, Inc., (tr)Robert Frerck/Odyssey, (b)Paul Edmondson/ Tony Stone Images; 114 Aaron Haupt; 118 (tl r)Andrew Payti, (bl)Anthony Azcona; 119 Andrew Payti; 122 Dallas & John Heaton/ Westlight; 123 124 Andrew Payti; 125 Antoinette Jogen/FPG International; 126 (t)Jack Hollingsworth/Getty Images, (bl)William S. Heisel/ Getty Images, (br) Bettmann/CORBIS; 127 (t)KRT/ Newscom, (c)AP Photo/Damian Dovarganes, (b)FoodPix; 128 (t)AP Photo/Kathy Willens, (c)Jason Homa/Getty Images, (bl)AP Photo/Jim Cooper, (bcl)Zuma Press/Newscom, (bcr)Star Max Photos/Newscom, (br)Amanda Edwards/Getty Images; 129 (tl)Reuters Media, Inc./CORBIS, (tr)Tim Mosen Felder/CORBIS, (cl)AP Photo/Alden Pellett, (cr)AP Photo/Krista Niles, (b)Evan Agostini/Getty Images; 130 Private Collection/Kactus Foto/ SuperStock; 130–131 Robert Frerck/Odyssey; 132 Jeff Smith/FOTOSMITH; 133 (l)Tim Fuller, (r)Jeff Smith/FOTOSMITH; 134 Jeff Baker/FPG; 135 136 file photo 137 Chad Ehlers/International Stock; 138 (t)Beryl Goldberg, (b)Jonathan Nourok/ PhotoEdit; 140 David R. Frazier; 141 Michelle Chaplow; 142 (t)Steve Torregrossa, (c)Rob Crandall/ The Image Works, (b)Ken Karp; 143 Mark Smestad; 144 Steve Torregrossa; 145 Margot Granitsas/The Image Works; 146 Doug Bryant/DDB Stock Photo; 147 (t)Greg Johnston/International Stock, (b)Doug Bryant/DDB Stock Photo; 148 (t)Steve Vidler/ Estock, (b)Bill Bachmann/Tony Stone Images; 149 (t)Robert Frerck/Odyssey, (b)Erica Lansner/ Tony Stone Images; 150 Tim Fuller; 151 Michelle Chaplow; 152 (t)Carma Casula/Cover/The Image Works, (b)Blake Little/SYGMA; 153 Aaron Haupt; 154 Robert Frerck/Odyssey; 155 Gregory Edwards/ International Stock; 157 Chad Ehlers/International Stock; 159 (t)Jeff Baker/FPG, (b)Jeff Smith/ FOTOSMITH; 160 Christie's Images/CORBIS; 160–161 Gail Shumway/FPG; 162 (t)Tim Fuller, (bl)Bob Daemmrich, (br)Tim Fuller; 163 Doug Bryant/DDB Stock Photo; 164 (t)Robert Fried, (b)Michelle Chaplow; 165 Michelle Chaplow; 167 Geoff Butler; 169 Tim Fuller; 171 (t)Ken Karp, (b)CORBIS; 172 Tim Fuller; 173 Ken Karp; 174 (t bl)Ken Karp, (br)Tim Fuller; 175 Andrew Payti; 176 Tim Fuller; 178 (l)Tourist Office of Spain, (r)Anthony Azcona; 179 (t)Tourist Office of Spain, (b)Michelle Chaplow; 180 (l)Nick Inman, (r)Michelle Chaplow; 183 file photo 186 (t)Catherine et Bernard Desjeux, (b)Steven Ferry; 187 Michelle Chaplow; 189 Robert Fried 190 Kactus Foto, Santiago, Chile/SuperStock; 190–191 Thomas D. Mayes, Jr.; 192 (l)Larry Mangino/The Image Works, (r)Tim Fuller; 193 Doug Bryant/DDB Stock; 195 Tim Fuller; 196 (tl)David R. Frazier, (tr c)CORBIS, (b)Andrew Abshier; 197 (tl)Tim Fuller, (tr)Doug Bryant/DDB Stock, (b)Robert Frerck/Tony Stone Images; 198 (t)file photo, (b)Antonio Azcona West; 199 CORBIS; 200 Tim Fuller; 201 (l)Tim Fuller, (r)Michelle Chaplow; 202 (t)Ken Karp, (b)CORBIS; 203 Ken Karp; 204 Michelle Chaplow; 206 (t)Susan Van Etten/PhotoEdit, (b)Robert Frerck/Odyssey Productions; 207 (t)Ken Karp, (b)Robert Frerck/ Odyssey; 208 Michelle Chaplow; 209 Tim Fuller; 210 (l)Robert Frerck/Odyssey, (r)Norman Tomalin/ Bruce Coleman, Inc.; 211 Robert Frerck/Odyssey; 212 (tl b)Robert Frerck/Odyssey, (tr)Glen Allison/ Tony Stone Images, (c)Kevin Schafer/Tony Stone Images; 213 (t)Underwood & Underwood/Bettmann CORBIS, (b)UPI/Bettmann CORBIS; 214 (t)Telegraph Colour Library/FPG, (b)Anthony Azcona; 215 (t)Don & Pat Valenti/Tony Stone Images, (b)Robert Frerck/ Odyssey; 216 Phillip & Karen Smith/Tony Stone Images; 217 (b)Sven Martson/The Image Works; 218 (tl c)Andrew Abshier, (tr)David R. Frazier, (b)Robert Frerck/Tony Stone Images; 219 Robert Frerck/Odyssey; 221 Tim Fuller; 222 (t)Tim Fuller, (b)CORBIS; 223 Getty Images; 224 Robert Fried; 225 Andrew Payti; 226 (tl)Stephanie Maze/ CORBIS, (tr)Carl & Ann Parcel/CORBIS, (bl)Library of Congress, (br)Hulton Archive/Getty Images; 227 (t)AP Photo/Cristobal Herrera, (c)AP Photo/Andres Leighton, (b)Studio Bonisolli/ Stockfood; 228 (tl)Newscom, (tr)William Claxton, (tcr)KRT/Newscom, (bcr)PGI/CORBIS Sygma, (bl)Manny Hernandez, (br)Newscom; 229 (tl)Richard Bickel/CORBIS, (tr)Reuters Photo Archive/Newscom, (c)Jorge Alvarez, (bl)Giraud Philippe/CORBIS Sygma, (br)Reuters Photo Archive/Newscom; 230 Archivo Iconografico, S.A./CORBIS; 230–231 Manuel Bellver/CORBIS; 232 233 Jeff Smith/FOTOSMITH; 234 Anthony Azcona; 235 (l)Robert Frerck/Odyssey,

Credits